CÉZANNE
AND PARIS

This catalog is published to accompany the "Cezanne and Paris" exhibition
in the Musée du Luxembourg, Paris (Senate), from October 12, 2011 to February 26, 2012.

The exhibition has been organized by RMN–Grand Palais
in collaboration with the Petit Palais, Musée des Beaux-Arts de la Ville de Paris.

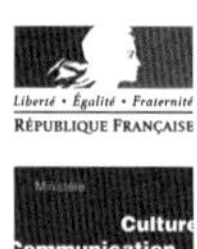

The Musée d'Orsay has kindly provided special loans for this exhibition.

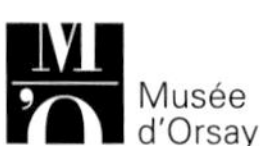

Cover:
The Rooftops of Paris (detail)
1881–82
Oil on canvas
Private collection
See cat. 2

254–256, rue de Bercy – 75577 Paris Cedex 12

ISBN: 978-2-7118-5919-1
EC 40 5919

CÉZANNE
AND PARIS

Expert supervision: Denis Coutagne

For Françoise Cachin
and Philip Conisbee

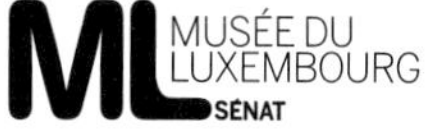

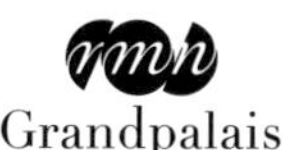

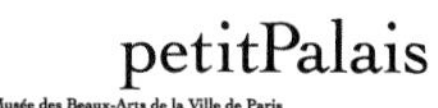

French Senate

Gérard Larcher
President of the Senate

Roland du Luart
Vice-President of the Senate

René Garrec
Senate Quaestor

Jean-Louis Schroedt-Girard
Director of the Senate President's Office

Robert Provansal
Secretary-General of the Quaestors

Xavier Canchon
Director of Architecture, Heritage and Gardens

Damien Déchelette
Principal architect

City of Paris

Bertrand Delanoë
Mayor of Paris

Danièle Pourtaud
Deputy Mayor, in charge of Heritage

Christophe Girard
Deputy Mayor, in charge of Culture

Laurence Engel
Director of Cultural Affairs

Catherine Hubault
Assistant Director of Heritage and History

Gilles Chazal
Director of the Petit Palais,
Musée des Beaux-Arts de la Ville de Paris

Gaïta Leboissetier
President of Paris Museums

Aimée Fontaine
Director of Paris Museums

RMN – Grand Palais

Jean-Paul Cluzel
President

Valérie Vesque-Jeancard
Acting Director General

Laurent Salomé
Head curator for heritage
Specialist director

Géraldine Breuil
Administrator, Musée du Luxembourg

Marion Mangon
Head of Exhibitions

Barbara Kroher
Project manager

Isabelle Mancarella
Coordinator, transportation of works

Pascale Sillard
Communications director

Expert advisory board of the Musée du Luxembourg:

Cristina Acidini, Marion Boudon-Machuel, Geneviève Bresc-Bautier, Thierry Crépin-Leblond, Jean-François Dubost, Thierry Dufrêne, Robert Fleck, David Gaimster, Bruno Gaudichon, Emmanuelle Héran, Dominique Jacquot, Brigitte Leal, Cécile Maisonneuve, Pierre Rosenberg, Xavier Salmon, Laurent Salomé, Béatrix Saule, Manfred Sellink, Marie-Paule Vial, Ian Wardropper.

Programming committee of the Musée du Luxembourg:

Pierre Arizzoli-Clémentel (President), René Garrec, Roland du Luart, Daniel Ergmann (Senate representatives),
Jean-Pierre Changeux, Michel Hochmann, Jean-Hubert Martin, Catheline Perier d'Ieteren, Jean-Louis Prat (specialist advisors),
Laurent Salomé (RMN–Grand Palais representative).

Exhibition design devised by **bGc**studio.

Organizing Committee

Director General

Gilles Chazal
Chief heritage curator
Director of the Petit Palais, Musée des Beaux-Arts de la Ville de Paris

Members

Maryline Assante di Panzillo
Heritage curator
Petit Palais, Musée des Beaux-Arts de la Ville de Paris

Denis Coutagne
Honorary heritage curator
President of the Société Paul Cézanne

Lenders

We would like to express our gratitude to all the individuals whose generous support has made this exhibition possible:

Palais Princier, Monaco

Foundation E.G. Buhrle Collection, Zurich

as well as all those who wish to remain anonymous.

Our thanks also to those responsible for the following public collections:

Germany
Hamburg, Hamburger Kunsthalle
Wuppertal, Von der Heydt-Museum

Brazil
São Paulo, MASP, Museu de Arte de São Paulo Assis Chateaubriand

United States
Boston, Museum of Fine Arts
Chicago, The Art Institute of Chicago
Cincinnati, Cincinnati Art Museum
Columbus, Columbus Museum of Art
Los Angeles, Hammer Museum
Los Angeles, The J. Paul Getty Museum
New York, The Metropolitan Museum of Art
New York, The Museum of Modern Art
Philadelphia, Philadelphia Museum of Art
Portland, Portland Art Museum
Providence, Museum of Art, Rhode Island School of Design
Washington, National Gallery of Art
West Palm Beach, Norton Museum of Art

France
Aix-en-Provence, Musée Granet, Communauté du Pays d'Aix
Aix-les-Bains, Musée Faure
Avignon, Musée Calvet
Médan, Maison Zola–Musée Dreyfus
Paris, Bibliothèque nationale de France
Paris, Musée de l'Orangerie
Paris, Musée d'Orsay
Paris, musée du Louvre, département des Arts graphiques
Paris, Petit Palais, Musée des Beaux-Arts de la Ville de Paris

United Kingdom
London, National Gallery
London, The Samuel Courtauld Trust, The Courtauld Gallery

Japan
Kanagawa, Pola Museum of Art, Pola Art Foundation
Osaka, The National Museum of Art

Netherlands
Rotterdam, Museum Boijmans Van Beuningen

Russia
St. Petersburg, The State Hermitage Museum

Sweden
Stockholm, Nationalmuseum

Switzerland
Basel, Kunstmuseum Basel, Kupferstichkabinett
(Department of Prints and Drawings)

Acknowledgements

The organizers and RMN–Grand Palais would like to thank the senior officials in the City of Paris and the Paris Museums, without whom this exhibition could not have taken place.

They are also extremely grateful to M. Guy Cogeval, President of the Musées d'Orsay et de l'Orangerie, for his generous support.

Many others have in different ways helped and given advice in the preparation of the exhibition and the catalog.

We would like to extend our sincere thanks to:
Jean Arrouye, Nina Athanassoglou-Kallmyer, Denis Belkevich, François Bourgeois, Françoise et Dominique Briquel, Rupert Burgess, Isabelle Cahn, Hubert Cavaniol, Philippe Cezanne, Nathalie Cirioux, Faya Conisbee, Marie-Jeanne Coutagne, Pauline Coutagne, Catherine, Christian, and Romain Crès, André Dombrowski, Francine Mariani-Ducray, Bruno Ely, Michel Eyriey, Walter Feilchenfeldt, Michel Fraisset, Sylvie Gache-Patin, Gloria Gloom, Pierre Gobert, Thomas Grenon, Josseline Grimoin, Raymond Hurtu, Hervé Irien, Sophie Joissains, Marie-Christine Labourdette, Jean-Claude Lebensztejn, Benedict Leca, Mary Tompkins Lewis, Pavel Machotka, Inoue Masayuki, Caroline Mathieu, Henri Mitterand, Marguerite Moquet, Joachim Pissarro, Pierre Provoyeur, Joëlle Raineau, Christine Ramilliard, Rodolphe Rapetti, Théodore Reff, Joseph Rischel, James Rubin, Xavier Salmon, Akihiro Shinkai, Bénédicte Sire, Gary Tinterow, Habiba Taïbi, Dominique Vautravers, Ludmilla Virassamynaïken, Jayne Warman, Guy Wildenstein.

Sénat de la République française and Musée du Luxembourg

Initially housed in the Palais du Luxembourg that Marie de Medici had had built between 1615 and 1630, the Musée du Luxembourg was the first museum in France to be opened to the public, in 1750.

At that time, visitors could admire twenty-four paintings by Rubens celebrating Marie de Medici and around a hundred paintings from the Royal collection *(Cabinet du Roi)* by Leonardo da Vinci, Raphael, Veronese, Titian, Poussin, Van Dyck, and Rembrandt.

These works were eventually transferred to the Louvre, and in 1818 the Musée du Luxembourg was designated a "museum for living artists," or in other words, a museum of contemporary art. David, Ingres, and Delacroix, among others, were exhibited there.

Having assumed responsibility for the Luxembourg Palace and Gardens in 1879, the Senate had the current building constructed between 1884 and 1886. There, the Impressionists were exhibited in a national museum for the first time, thanks to the Caillebotte bequest, comprising works by Pissarro, Manet, Cézanne, Sisley, Monet, and Renoir, among others. This collection is now in the Musée d'Orsay.

The Musée du Luxembourg was closed after a national museum of modern art was built in the Palais de Tokyo in 1937, and only reopened its doors to the public in 1979. The Ministry of Culture put on exhibitions there highlighting France's regional heritage and collections from provincial museums, with the Senate retaining the right to oversee the program and the use of the building.

In 2000, the Senate decided to reassume full responsibility for the Musée du Luxembourg, in order to introduce an integrated cultural policy for the Palace, Gardens, and Museum.

Although its primary objectives as a parliamentary assembly are voting on legislation, monitoring government actions, evaluating public policy and financial forecasting, the Senate also has a duty to promote the heritage site for which it is responsible.

In order to ensure wide exposure and excellence in the content and organization of exhibitions at the Musée du Luxembourg, the Senate decided to call on professionals in this sector.

The Musée du Luxembourg has since become established as one of the leading exhibition spaces in Paris, allowing its high numbers of visitors to enjoy the masterpieces of artists such as Botticelli, Raphael, Titian, Arcimboldo, Veronese, Gauguin, Matisse, Vlaminck, and Modigliani.

In 2010 the Senate delegated the museum's management to the public institution, the Réunion des Musées Nationaux and the Grand Palais des Champs-Elysées (RMN–GP), its mission being to organize ambitious exhibitions. Priority was given to three programming strands, connected to the history of the site: "*The Renaissance in Europe,*" "*Art and Power,*" and "*Palace, Gardens, and Museum: the Luxembourg in the heart of Paris, capital of the arts.*"

RMN–GP is one of the world's leading exhibition organizers. Its functions include exhibiting, publishing, disseminating, acquiring, collecting, and informing; reaching audiences of every kind, it contributes to the enrichment and better understanding of France's artistic heritage at both national and international level.

For up-to-date information about the Musée du Luxembourg, please visit the website: www.museeduluxembourg.fr.

For many, Paul Cézanne (1839–1906) is still *the* painter of Provence. His fate was however closely linked to Paris and Île-de-France, where he spent the other half of his life, traveling back and forth from north to south.

He had just turned 22 when he left the region of his birth to conquer the capital, the only possible place "to live as an artist." His first canvases reveal a passionate pictorial disposition. They were to scandalize the official institution of the Academy for nearly twenty years. But what did it matter?! In Paris Cézanne went on to shape the very essence of his art. Examining painting from the traditional to the modern, he repositioned it between the figurative and the abstract, and created his own language. In 1894 he met the art dealer Ambroise Vollard, who took his career in hand and brought him long-sought recognition.

This fall, the Musée du Luxembourg (management of which has been handed over by the Senate to RMN–Grand Palais) is devoting a brand new exhibition to this neglected side of Cézanne's career, the unique links that tied him to Paris in a love-hate relationship. Organized by RMN–Grand Palais in collaboration with the Petit Palais, Musée des Beaux-Arts de la Ville de Paris, it gives the visitor the chance to go back to the roots of the painter's work, in the very place that helped to shape the artist. When it was established, the Musée du Luxembourg was in fact dedicated to "modern art": as a young man Cézanne avidly studied the work of the artists on show, and once he was famous, he exhibited his works officially to the Paris public for the first time there.

The exhibition brings together eighty paintings from across the globe. They allow us to discover the capital and its surrounding region through the eyes of Cézanne: secret, intuitive, mysterious. They also show his unique approach to the modern age, represented in the tranquil scenes of the nearby countryside: Fontainebleau, Giverny, Auvers-sur-Oise, and Pontoise, for instance. Thus landscapes, portraits, and even still lifes tell the story of Cézanne's life in Paris.

I must start by highlighting the invaluable contribution of Gilles Chazal, the director of the Petit Palais, chief heritage curator, and the exhibition's main organizer, who was key to the smooth running of this operation. I also pay tribute to the other members of the organizing committee: Denis Coutagne, honorary heritage curator, and Maryline Assante di Panzillo, heritage curator at the Petit Palais.

I am delighted with this first collaboration on an exhibition between RMN–Grand Palais and the City of Paris Museums and would like to thank the city's councilmen and Director of Cultural Affairs for agreeing to this joint project.

I would like to convey my gratitude to all the private and public lenders in France and beyond, especially the Musée d'Orsay and its president, Guy Cogeval. Words cannot express the degree to which their generosity has been fundamental in realizing our ambitious plans.

This is also a welcome opportunity for me to pay tribute to the businesses that support the development of the Musée du Luxembourg.

Last but not least, my thanks also go to the Senate for its confidence in RMN–Grand Palais. This exhibition allows the museum to pursue its commitment to reach audiences of all kinds, by providing a range of cultural experiences that are both demanding and popular.

Jean-Paul Cluzel
President of RMN–Grand Palais

The Petit Palais, Musée des Beaux-Arts de la Ville de Paris, is on a special mission at the Musée du Luxembourg with its exhibition entitled "Cézanne and Paris." The venture is both original and highly significant, to say the least: original, because for the first time the Petit Palais is organizing an exhibition beyond its four walls but still within Paris; significant, because it is a reminder of the long-standing commitment of the Petit Palais to Cézanne. After all, it was fairly prompt in acquiring some major works by Cézanne: the portrait of the famous art dealer Ambroise Vollard, as well as one of the very first *Bathers*, the one gifted by Matisse in 1936.

In a wider sense, the Petit Palais' work contributed to Paris's development as a cultural capital at the turn of the 20th century. Without listing every exhibition organized to achieve this status, how can we forget the most recent ones devoted to De Nittis and to Forain—an artist whose reproductions were pinned on his studio walls by Cézanne.

So the theme "Cézanne and Paris" was the obvious choice for the Petit Palais after initial discussions with Denis Coutagne, who was anxious to find a location for an exhibition that would be like the second leaf of a diptych; the first had been presented in Aix in 2006 under the banner "Cézanne in Provence."

This exhibition should serve to raise awareness that Cézanne lived as a painter in Paris and the surrounding region longer than in Provence. To build up his body of work he needed, at each stage of its development, to confront the modernity of Paris. Throughout his career, from the early realist mode of expression to the global approach of his late period, Cézanne met Impressionist and Post-Impressionist painters, and was also introduced to critics and dealers; he sought recognition for his painting, which attracted plenty of attention and buyers in the last years of his life. The first collections of Cézanne were created from Paris. While Cézanne came to the capital less frequently after 1900, it was Paris that came to him on the hill of Les Lauves in Aix.

And it was Caillebotte, the Impressionist painter and collector whose bequest to the State opened the Musée du Luxembourg doors to Cézanne in 1897. At the time this was the museum in Paris dedicated to contemporary art, where Cézanne had discovered Delacroix.

Today the Musée du Luxembourg has put its entire hanging space at Cézanne's disposal, as a way of fostering appreciation of the Parisian aspects of his work. We are indebted to the French Senate, which expressed immediate interest in this exhibition and offered to host it in the Musée du Luxembourg, at a time when it was difficult for the Petit Palais programming to implement it in-house.

While some of the paintings on show here have been familiar for a long time, a number of pictures will be fresh discoveries, revealing a side of Cézanne if not completely new, at the very least "unseen." We would like to convey our warm thanks to all the lenders, especially those who have been working with the Petit Palais for many years.

As the project's initiator, the Petit Palais has taken on the organizing committee role; its academic specialists are Denis Coutagne, honorary head heritage curator, and Maryline Assante di Panzillo, curator at the Petit Palais. Overall organization is provided by RMN–Grand Palais, which manages the Musée du Luxembourg. This combination of partners—the City of Paris (which has trusteeship of the Petit Palais), the Senate, and RMN–Grand Palais—makes the exhibition unique. The Musée d'Orsay was happy to play a special role in this venture by providing a considerable number of loans.

A number of important people who were very keen to support this international event have contributed to the compilation of this catalog. I would like to extend my heartfelt thanks to them as well.

Cézanne more honoured than ever! Cézanne's roots in Paris and Ile-de-France finally revealed! These are headlines that Cézanne himself would surely have appreciated, for as the critic Geoffroy famously reported, this was the man who wanted to "astonish Paris with an apple".

Gilles Chazal
Chief heritage curator
Director of the Petit Palais, Musée des Beaux-Arts de la Ville de Paris

Contributing authors

Jean Arrouye
University professor; member of the International Association of Art Critics

Maryline Assante di Panzillo
Heritage curator, Paintings Department,
Petit Palais, Musée des Beaux-Arts de la Ville de Paris

Nina Athanassoglou-Kallmyer
Professor and Head of History of Art department
University of Delaware

Isabelle Cahn
Curator, Paintings Department
Musée d'Orsay, Paris

Philippe Cezanne
Art expert

Jean Colrat
Ph.D History of art

Denis Coutagne
Honorary heritage curator
President of the Paul Cézanne society

André Dombrowski
Assistant professor, History of Art department
University of Pennsylvania

Bruno Ely
Chief heritage curator
Director of Musée Granet, Aix-en-Provence

Walter Feilchenfeldt
Art expert

Raymond Hurtu
Painter

Benedict Leca
Curator, European Painting and Sculpture
Cincinnati Art Museum, Cincinnati

Pavel Machotka
Professor in Psychology of Art
University of California, Santa Cruz

Henri Mitterand
Emeritus Professor at the New Sorbonne, Paris and Columbia University, New York

Joachim Pissarro
Bershad Professor of Art History, Director of the Hunter College Art Galleries, Hunter College—City University of New York

Joseph J. Rischel
Senior Curator of European Painting before 1900
Senior Curator of the John G. Johnson Collection and the Rodin Museum, Philadelphia Museum of Art

James H. Rubin
Professor of Art History
Stony Brook, The State University of New York

Laure-Caroline Semmer
Art historian and part-time lecturer at the Sorbonne, Paris

Mary Tompkins Lewis
Visiting Associate Professor of Art History
Trinity College, Hartford, Connecticut

Marie-Paule Vial
Chief heritage curator
Director of the Musée de l'Orangerie, Paris

Jayne S. Warman
Art historian, New York

Translations

Translated and edited by Ann Drummond, Alayne Pullen, Rae Walter and David Price in association with First Edition Translations Ltd, Cambridge, UK.

Please note:

All the works reproduced without the artist's name being mentioned in the caption are by Paul Cézanne.

At the end of captions accompanying the reproductions of works by Cézanne, the term R followed by a number refers to the *catalogue raisonné* of the paintings by John Rewald (1996); the term RWC to the *catalogue raisonné* of watercolors (Rewald 1984); the term CH to the *catalogue raisonné* of drawings (Chappuis, 1973); the term Cherpin to the *catalogue raisonné* of engravings (Cherpin 1972).

Summary

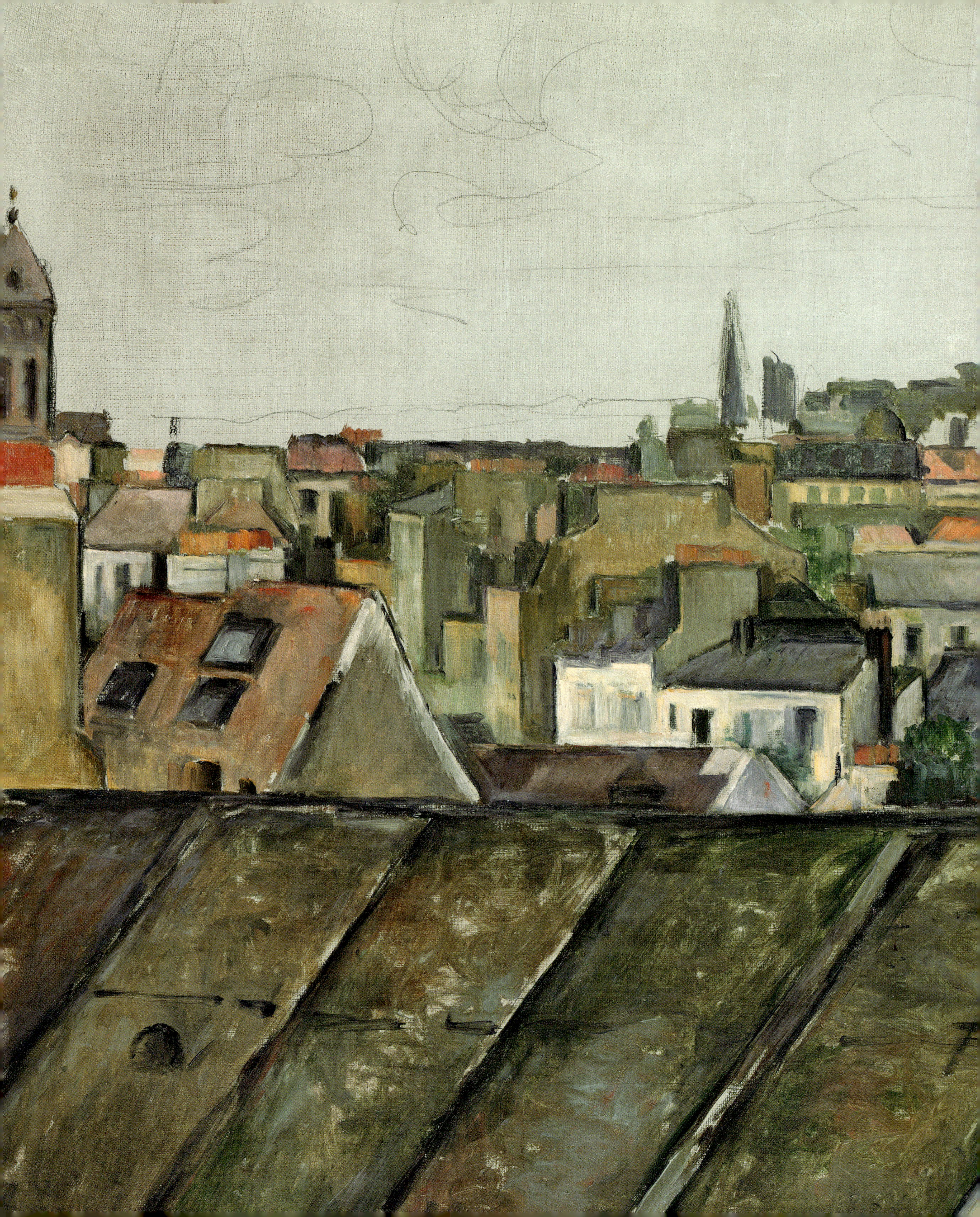

THE CHALLENGE OF PARIS FOR CÉZANNE

Denis Coutagne

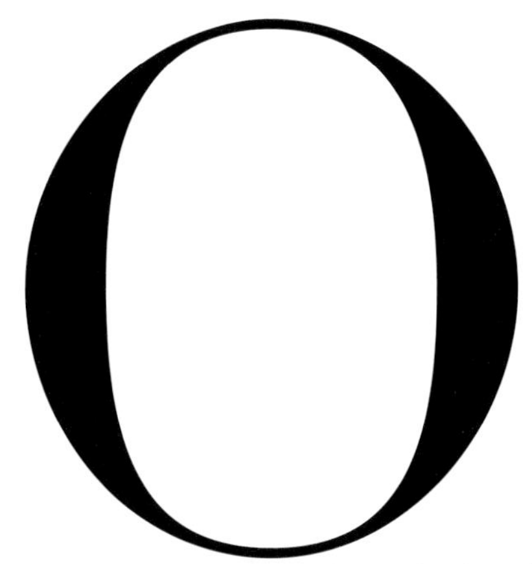

n arriving in the capital in 1861, Cézanne set himself a personal challenge: to become a painter in Paris; to make his presence felt in Paris; and to conquer Paris. The great movements of the pictorial landscape of the time were Romanticism, Realism and Naturalism. Delacroix, Ingres, Courbet, Corot, and Daubigny were still very much a presence. In 1906, when Cézanne died, Impressionism, which had been outmoded for the last twenty years, had given rise to various forms of Post-Impressionism: Pointillism, the Nabis, and indeed Symbolism. Van Gogh had been dead for fifteen years, and Gauguin for three. Fauvism had taken hold in 1905 and Cubism was in its early stages. Picasso was already working on *Les Demoiselles d'Avignon (The young women of Avignon);* Braque was moving down to L'Estaque; and Matisse had recently completed *The Joy of Life*. The Suprematism of Malevich and the Neoplasticism of Mondrian were about to emerge. Kandinsky was preparing to write *Concerning the Spiritual in Art*, and to open the way to abstractionism. Cézanne was in everyone's mind as his work had recently enjoyed great success in Paris. Rilke, about to leave for Venice in October 1907, discovered Cézanne at the autumn Salon: he canceled his trip in order to visit the exhibition every day.

So much had happened since April 1861 when Zola, impatient at his friend's failure to arrive, wrote to Baille[1]: "I interrupt this overly rapid and too unworthy analysis to exclaim: I've seen Paul!!! I've seen Paul... do you understand what that means, do you understand the melodiousness of those three words?" Cézanne's final trip to the Île-de-France, to Fontainebleau in fact, was in the summer of 1905.

The Rooftops of Paris
(detail)
See cat. 2 p. 18

A strange type of Parisian...

There had been so many obstacles, so many new beginnings from the moment that Cézanne, as a young man from Aix, had arrived at the home of his friend Émile Zola—who for more than two years had been trying to persuade him to become an artist and hence to come to Paris—to the opening of an exhibition of the artist's work devoted specifically to his relationship with Paris, the city of his ambitions, dreams, doubts, and, finally, glory. These had begun with the impasse that characterized his first stay in the city. But was this experience of failure, of incomprehension, of rejection and, indeed, of a certain poverty that only Paris could have provided, not in fact necessary to the young artist? Henri Murger had already acknowledged that it was this internal requirement of the "bohemian" that enabled artists (poets, musicians, painters and others) to fulfill their potential: "The bohemian only exists and is only possible in Paris."[2] Rilke was to revisit this theme in making his hero, Malte Laurids Brigge, a poet who could only attain his inner truth in Paris—a metropolis that lent anonymity—and, in a city that was not his own, could experience the solitude necessary to all creativity. After Rodin, Cézanne appeared to the young writer as the absolute prototype of this poet, precisely because Cézanne was in Paris but without ever being entirely there (cat. 1).

Indeed, Cézanne set the tone on his very first stay in the city when he wrote to his friend Joseph Huot: "Don't imagine that I am becoming a Parisian."[3] And given the difficulties that the young man expressed, Zola eventually recognized that "Paul may have the genius of a great painter, but he will never have the genius to become one. The slightest obstacle drives him to despair. I say again, if he wants to avoid so much worry, he should leave."[4] Zola had asked his friend to paint his portrait, arguing that "I pose like an Egyptian sphinx." But the young painter became exasper-

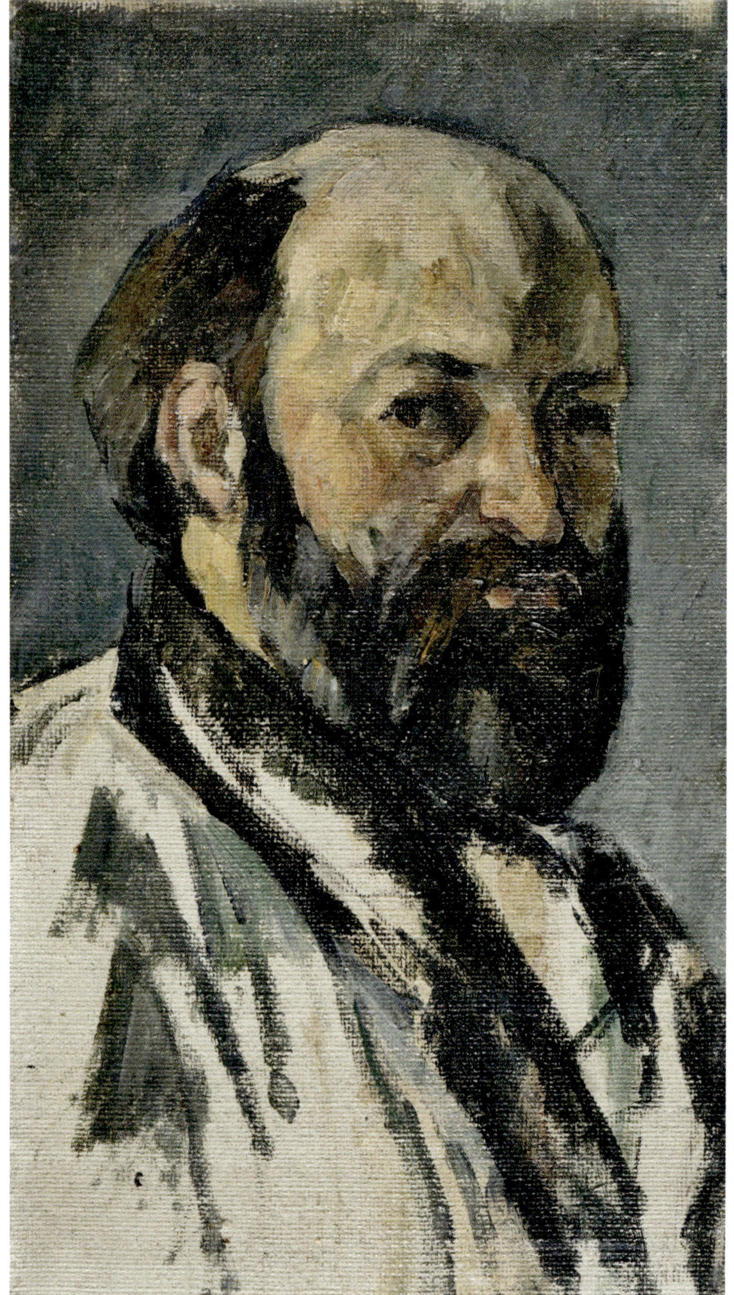

Cat. 1
Self-Portrait
c. 1877
Oil on canvas
25.5 x 14.3 cm
Musée d'Orsay, Paris,
work recovered
after the Second World War
and placed in the safekeeping
of France's national museums
R 385

ated and disheartened, as Zola recounts: "This damnable portrait that was meant to keep him in Paris yesterday came close to making him leave."[5] (fig. 9) But would Paris in fact become a place of a temptation from which he must always flee, and do so for reasons associated with painting?

To claim this would be to ignore the artist's determination. Cézanne returned to Paris in 1862 and decided to stick it out, no longer hoping for an immediate triumph, having lost his lyrical enthusiasm. If he was, one day "to amaze Paris... with an apple,"[6] he needed to work. But, right to the end of his life, Cézanne would go on wondering whether "I will ever attain the goal I have so long pursued," while humbly recognizing that "I am making slow progress." This is what he wrote to Émile Bernard in September 1906. Cézanne turned the difficulties he experienced into the very subject matter of his painting. It was no longer necessary to return to Paris: it was Paris that would come to him.

We know of some twenty different addresses at which Cézanne lived in the city, mainly on the left bank in the early years and, in the later years, on the right bank[7], as well as numerous hotels and houses in the Île-de-France region. But the fact remains that this banker's son from Aix never really settled there, in the "bourgeois" sense, with an apartment and studio[8]. Zola found a home in Médan, Monet in Giverny, Pissarro in Éragny—but in Cézanne's case there was no property in the Paris area that could be thought of as his home for any real length of time[9]. His roots remained in Provence. Was life in Paris for Cézanne simply a "nomadic" existence? Clearly such a term would be inappropriate: Cézanne alighted in each place where he painted and he made it his for as long as it took to execute a single work perhaps, though each time it seemed that he would be there for ever. In Provence, the artist's motifs could be clearly identified by reference to the places he had lived: Jas de Bouffan, L'Estaque, Gardanne, Château-Noir, Bibémus, Les Lauves—each of these names evokes iconic paintings. But the same cannot be said of Paris. One has only to list the numerous places that Cézanne stayed—Marcoussis, Auvers-sur-Oise, Pontoise, Valhermeil, Issy-les-Moulineaux, Melun, Médan, Chantilly, Maisons-Alfort, Saint-Maur-des-Fossés, Créteil and the banks of the Marne, Mennecy, Fontainebleau, Bourron-Marlotte—but none of these places (with the exception of Auvers and Melun) stands out enough to signify a lasting presence[10]. Cézanne did not transfer to Paris his way of life in Provence, where he felt truly at home, both at L'Estaque and at Gardanne; in Paris he always remained something of an outsider, even playing upon his provincial, Provençal persona to the point of earning himself something of a caricature image.

The many faces of Paris itself

What then of the work Cézanne produced in Paris and in the Île-de-France region?

One fact deserves to be pointed out: From 1861—the year in which he embarked on his career as an artist, at the age of 22—until his death in 1906, Cézanne spent as much time in the Paris region as he did in Provence—around twenty years in fact. True, the periods he spent in Île-de-France varied in length but they were dispersed throughout his life and Cézanne made more than twenty return trips between Aix and Paris. Furthermore, of the almost a thousand paintings listed in the artist's *catalogue raisonné*, more than three hundred and fifty[11] were, one may assume, executed in the north of France.

This demonstrates the importance of Cézanne's "Parisian" opus but in turn raises various questions: What does Cézanne show us of Paris that other painters have not? In what ways did he need Paris in order to become "Cézanne"? In what way did collectors, art dealers, and artists of his generation and the next recognize him as an essentially Parisian painter before Berlin, Moscow, and New York claimed him as their own?

Paris at that time had a triple identity: Firstly, the name referred to the city itself and the countryside close by; it also signified a moment and a specific form of painting in the history of art; and lastly, it meant the different aspects of Cézanne's Paris. The artist had left behind his familiar Aix and risked his art—and his art eventually won. Paris played the role of an "intangible asset": Before him, Courbet had similarly taken on the challenge of the capital of the arts, while keeping his feet firmly planted in the soil of Franche-Comté.

A painter, a place, and a time

The painter: Cézanne; the place: Paris; the time: the bare half-century between 1860 and 1905. This convergence was historic.

It is quite natural to link these three aspects: Something quite fundamental occurred between this man, this city, and this moment in time. Put simply, Cézanne portrayed Paris so often during the periods he was staying there that, through these images, this "representation," the city was given an identity that is quite unparalleled.

Granet was painting in Rome and in the surrounding area between 1820 and 1830, and he produced an account of the Eternal City in this twilight period when the power of the papacy was waning and archaeological monuments were there to be discovered. Through his artistic and religious sensibility the painter was able to describe this historical moment so well that the work he produced is perfectly reflected in the title "Granet: the painter of Rome."

This was not true of Cézanne: he was not the "painter of Paris." His relationship with the city was of a different order. But to make some sense of it, it is imperative that the work selected with reference to Paris has an internal coherence, and establishes itself as such by opening up a pictorial world that provides a before and an after in the history of painting: "I shall always be grateful to those intelligent art lovers who—through all my hesitations—had an intuitive sense of what I wished to attempt in order to renew my art. In my mind, it was not a matter of replacing the past; it was simply a matter of adding a new link..."[12] How was it then that being in Paris gave Cézanne the capacity to produce a body of work which, in terms of pictorial visibility, brought its own unique specificity? In other words, had Cézanne not existed as a painter in Paris, in what way would the very reality of painting have lacked "openness"?

In no sense did Cézanne paint Paris as Granet had painted Rome. Nor did he paint Paris in the same way as his Impressionist friends. Pissarro was keen on certain areas of the city—the Grands Boulevards, the Avenue de l'Opéra, the Tuileries Gardens; Guillaumin had a liking for the Seine and the Bercy embankments, while Monet preferred the Gare Saint-Lazare, and Renoir the Saint-Georges district, the Malaquais embankment, and the Pont-Neuf. Caillebotte made the concept of the painter looking at Paris the theme of his painting *Young Man at His Window*, as well as producing urban scenes depicting the Pont de l'Europe, the Place Saint-Augustin, Boulevard Haussmann, and the Boulevard des Capucines. Cézanne's approach was entirely different. True, there are paintings such as *The Rue des Saules in Montmartre* (cat. 27), *The Wine Market at Jussieu* (cat. 28), *The Seine at Bercy* (cat. 31) and *Fortification à la Glacière*[13] (R 494), but what district of Paris to choose? In Cézanne's work, Paris is missing as far as any vision or the urban or sophisticated is concerned. Paris is always in counter-relief, whereas Provence is always present in full relief. While, in Provence he painted chaotically formed quarries (Bibémus), on the banks of the Marne he painted pictures whose features are barely discernible, so smooth are the banks and so tranquil the water. Indeed, one painting alone stands out as truly a representation of Paris and that is *The Rooftops of Paris*.

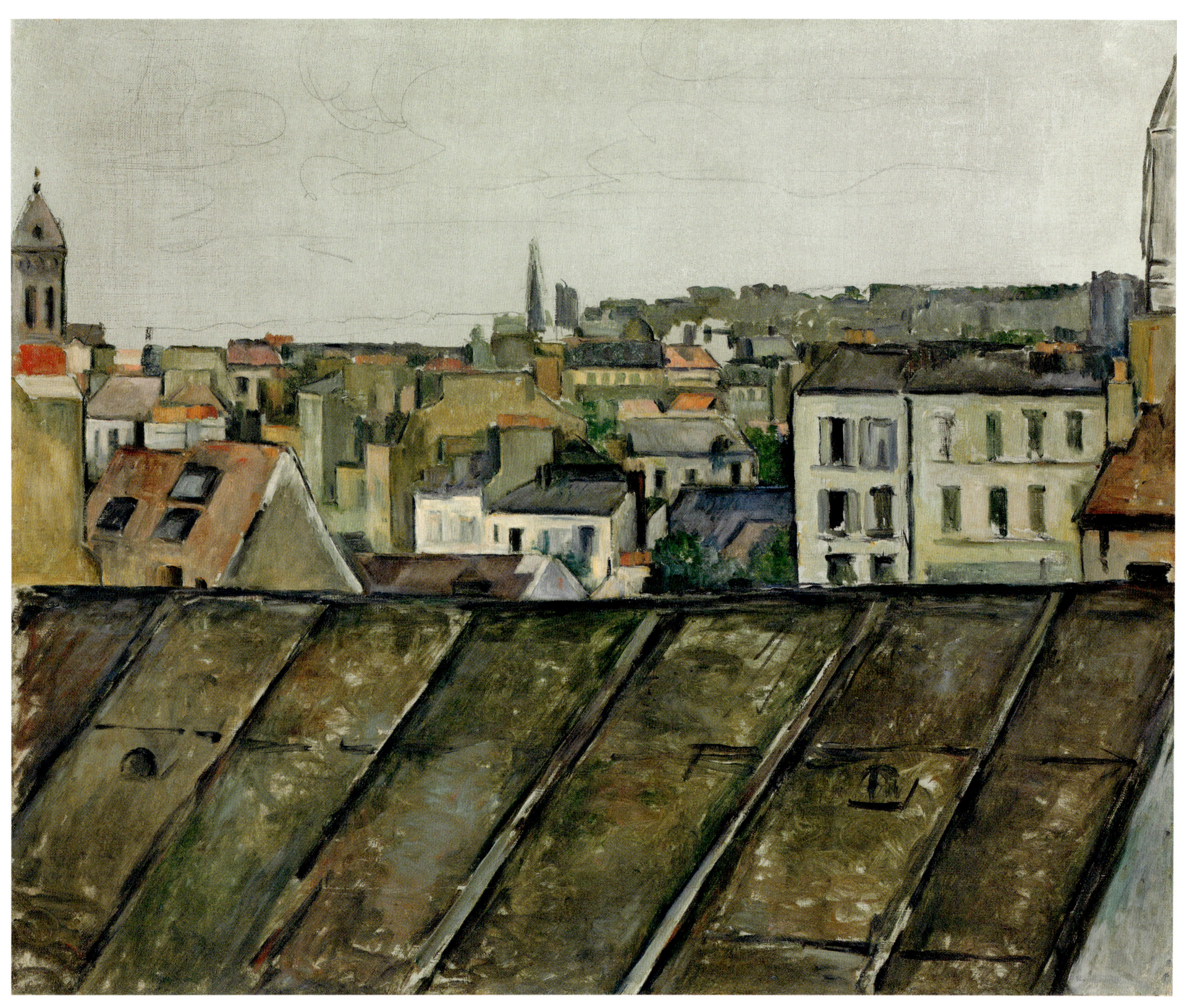

Cat. 2
The Rooftops of Paris
1881–82
Oil on canvas
59.7 x 73 cm
Private collection
R 503

The Rooftops of Paris

This canvas is divided into three sections. A dark, greenish-gray zinc roof occupies the foreground, then come the roofs and facades of buildings, whose pastel tones express a certain magic, extending up to the white sky of the third section (cat. 2).

The artist may perhaps have had only one window to open from which to compose this silent painting, far removed from the bustle of the street and the smoke and steam of the railroad station. Cézanne could however have chosen a more meaningful viewpoint; when, in his trilogy *Les Trois Villes (Three Cities)*, Zola addresses Paris after Rome, he chooses to be at the top of the hill of Montmartre in order to reveal the city to his reader (in the same way that he decided to climb the Janiculum hill to give a first panoramic view of Rome, as Stendhal had done). In *Une page d'amour*, the rooftops of Paris are seen from the heights of Passy. Of course, for the Impressionists it was no longer a matter of painting celebrated monuments in the Roman "vedutist" tradition. In 1878, Caillebotte had executed a canvas that was in fact called *The Rooftops of Paris in the Snow* (Paris, Musée d'Orsay), in which he endeavored to render the effect of snow, at nightfall, on the cornices and window ledges, playing on the effects of perspective given by the slopes and buildings. Van Gogh painted views from his apartment in rue Lepic in Montmartre[14]. With Cézanne, the painted city was composed only of rectangles and squares, the almost childlike drawing of which foreshadowed Paul Klee. The coloration makes it impossible to say whether it is morning or evening: Here daylight over Paris is indefinable, tinged at most with a vague sadness.

Cézanne never produced any other paintings on the rooftop theme. All that survives on this theme are some small drawings that reveal the complexity of the composition, involving cornices and gables, with a view over Saint-Sulpice and over the Panthéon (cat. 3).

Did Cézanne choose an area of Paris seen from above at random, making it impossible to identify the buildings? We know that between 1880 and 1882 he had an apartment on the fifth floor at 32 rue de l'Ouest. Did he feel a sudden need to escape the confines of such a small apartment, to look out over Paris? Though he may not have wished to paint a "vedutist" work, he nevertheless provides a few landmarks that help to identify the city: On the left is the church of Notre-Dame-des-Champs; in the centre the Saint-Jacques tower and the steeple of the Sainte-Chapelle; on the right, in the half-light, can be seen the towers of Notre-Dame de Paris. But the real essence of the painting lies elsewhere: With the zinc roof that occupies half the space of the canvas, the milky sky, and the abstract and apparently silent city, this painting expresses something other than an urban landscape.

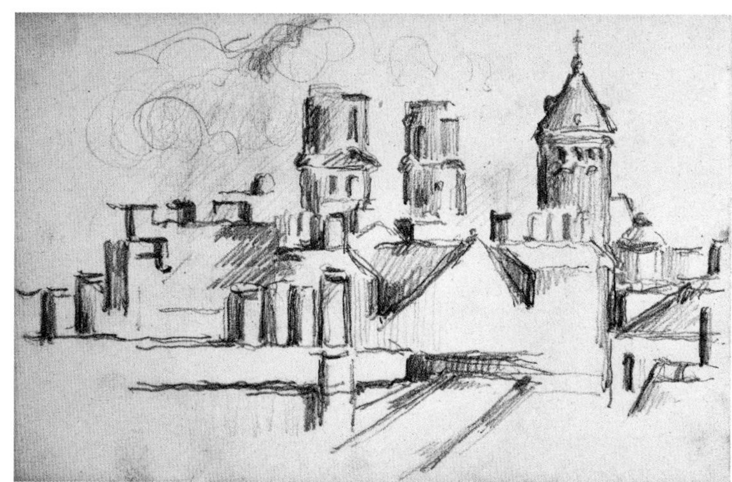

Cat. 3
St. Sulpice, view of Paris
1882
Pencil
Sketchbook I, p. 8, verso
11.6 x 18.2 cm
Philadelphia Museum of Art, Philadelphia, gift of Mr. and Mrs. Walter H. Annenberg, 1987
CH 806

A letter from Cézanne to Zola dated November 20, 1878 may shed some unexpected light on this painting: "I have finished buying the illustrated *L'Assommoir*. But the publisher would no doubt have been better served by better illustrations. When I see you face to face I shall ask you whether your opinion on painting as a means of expression of feeling is not the same as my own." What was *L'Assommoir* ? It was the story of Gervaise, Coupeau, and Lantier. And Coupeau was a zinc worker. The rooftops of Paris were his domain. He did not ponder them, did not dream of them, he worked there. In the illustrated edition that Cézanne consults, an engraving by Garnier shows Coupeau's fall: Leaning over the edge of the roof to see his daughter Nana playing in the street, the workman falls—a fall that could have been fatal. And painting as an occupation was also not without its dangers.

No doubt Cézanne had retained this description in his memory. In a sense, the painting is a tribute to Zola, to *L'Assommoir*, a novel that the painter so admired that he asked his friend for seats for the dramatization performed in 1879[15].

It is also worth recalling that Caillebotte's painting on a similar theme was described by the caricaturist Draner as "sentimental zinc work full of poetry."[16] What then might he have said of Cézanne's painting?

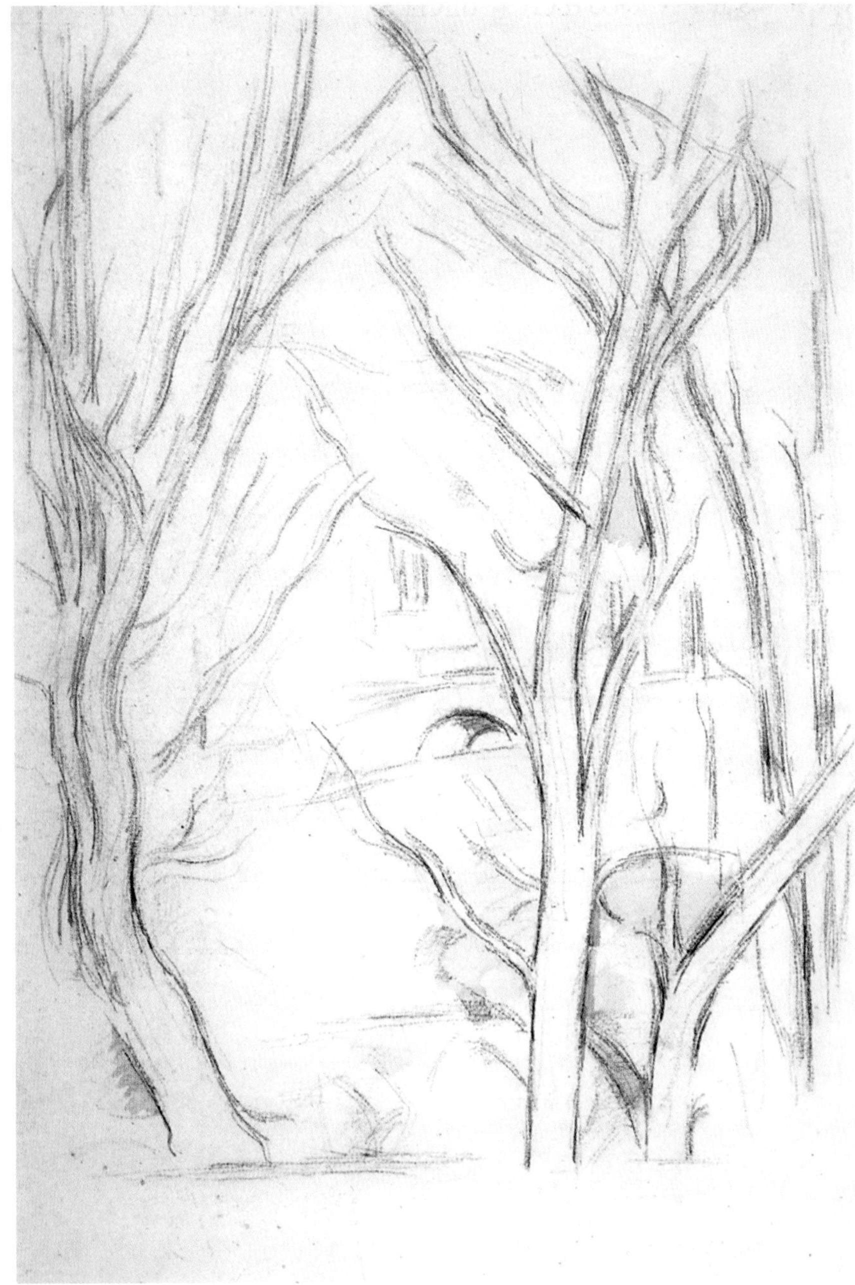

Cat. 4
Tree and bridge
1888–90
Watercolor and pencil
Private collection
RWC 325

Paris lost

For Cézanne, Paris was not a place to be recorded topographically, sociologically, or factually (cat. 4). He left this narrative record to Zola, aware that such an approach was a matter for the novel, not for painting. Cézanne learned this truth from the pen of the poet Charles Baudelaire, so critical of painters who describe and think rather than paint. Cézanne does not present the city, nor through his drawing or painting does he present a chronicle of Parisian life, as did Degas, Renoir, Toulouse-Lautrec, Fantin-Latour.

In fact, for Cézanne, Paris acted as a "temptation," one which Manet expressed so eloquently in painting *Olympia*, a work that Cézanne chose to re-create in a modern version (cat. 48, fig. 44). He never ceased expressing his desires, his fantasies, his erotic dreams, and his appreciation of fine food, to the point of repudiating them by painting—in the style of Flaubert—orgies and St. Anthonys tortured by their demons expressed in the allegorical figure of a sublime nude woman!

The interaction between the three elements mentioned obeys a logic particular to Cézanne. Indeed, the artist in Paris in the late 19th century is the artist who changes the relationship between these different aspects.

In a way, unlike Cézanne in Provence, who remained viscerally attached to his subject—even if only the Sainte-Victoire mountain, Cézanne in Paris learned to dismiss from his painting anything that would date it, define it, or confine it to a specific place.

This is perhaps why he felt the need to be constantly moving, always to be changing where he lived in this Paris, the city and its surrounding countryside, accessible by boat or train. Whatever the reason, the Second Empire, the Franco-Prussian war, the Commune and the Third Republic never feature in the artist's work. The major upheavals caused by Haussmann's renovation of the city, the development of the railroad, the buildings erected for the Great Exhibitions, including the Eiffel Tower in 1889, are almost never taken into account. Industrial modernity appears only incidentally—a barge, a distant locomotive—at most. Cézanne chose to paint apples against a background of wallpaper, figures of women on couches among abstract drapery, apparently insignificant village houses in the Paris countryside, and a burnt windmill (that can only be identified from old postcards).

The Paris that Zola took pleasure in describing did not concern Cézanne, unless one considers that Paris became the artistic space in which a transmutation of the world could take place. Proust, such a keen observer of Parisian life, achieves the literary *tour de force* of making Paris the place where the remembrance of things past (whether this was in Combray, Balbec, or Venice) is metamorphosed into things rediscovered. Cézanne does not paint "the belly of Paris" but selects certain rare objects and fruit and arranges them on a chest that he takes with him from one apartment to another, giving them the background of a wallpaper in a repeated but almost abstract diamond or lattice pattern. He discovers Chardin in the Louvre, he prefigures Cubism. He shares something in common with the character Frenhofer in Balzac's little-known masterpiece, who, according to Rilke, "had sensed that painting could suddenly lead into something immense which no one would be capable of grasping."[17]

Paris regained — the home of painting

Could it be that over the course of his career Cézanne gradually discovered that he needed Paris, not as a place in itself but as an "experience," as the "home" of painting? According to Baudelaire, whose *L'Art romantique* Cézanne read and re-read, the painter of modern life was in essence Parisian. But far from becoming the kind of painter for whom creativity meant destitution, Cézanne, despite his social marginality, appeared to be bourgeois. None of the apartments he occupied in Paris, at least those we can identify, were in any way proletarian. In Auvers he lived in a small village house, and in Melun, he overlooked the Place de la Préfecture. Of course, he experienced some difficult years (during which Zola was a generous support), but all in all, over the course of his life he was able to live comfortably as a man of independent means, with sufficient income to be able to devote himself to his one passion—painting. Could he in fact have done anything else? "I have nothing but painting; painting is what suits me best," he would acknowledge a few weeks before his death. He could therefore retire to Provence, his work having achieved firm recognition in Paris.

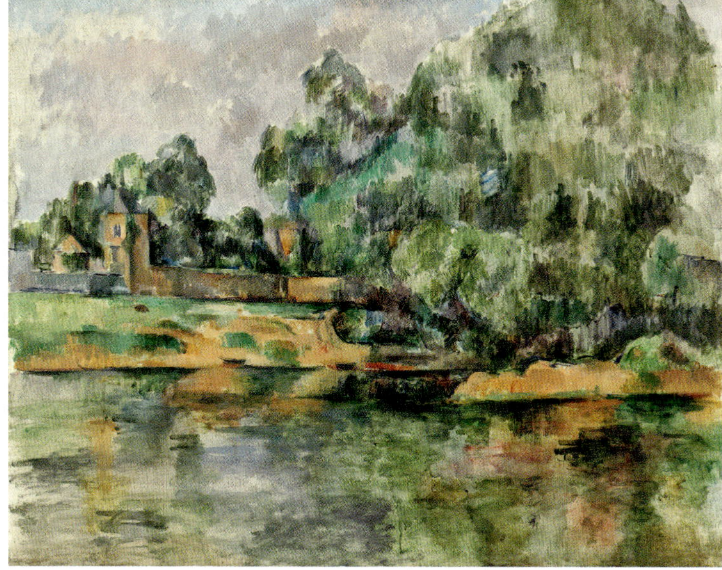

Fig. 1
At the Water's Edge
1895–98
Oil on canvas
79 × 92 cm
National Gallery of Art, Washington
R 722

The gamble of exposure

By leaving Aix for Paris, Cézanne had taken a gamble on painting because it was only in Paris that one could become an "artist." But once having acquired this status, once master of certain pictorial "formulas," the artist was bound to capitalize on what he had achieved. To do this, he had to return to Provence and submit his impressions of Paris to the sun of the south of France—the rocks of Fontainebleau became those of Bibémus, Olympia became a bather. But this process was never completed. He had to leave once again, rediscover the modernity of Paris, question once again what he had achieved in order to gamble and win. This was the challenge of this exposure: to demonstrate this creative process, so far removed from an illustration of Paris life, so far removed from any description of a city, albeit the capital of France.

Cézanne went up to Paris as an ambitious and pretentious young man. At the same time he sought to keep himself at a reasonable distance from a city that had become a temptation, that he needed to confront without succumbing. Paris became an inner city, the still lifes of which say more about quality than the social and republican epic paintings with which Zola dreamed of covering the walls of town halls and railroad stations. Paris is not Mexico and Cézanne was not Diego Rivera... nor was he Puvis de Chavannes! He remained a figure painter: his Paris women had the face of a girl from Franche-Comté, Hortense Fiquet. Some portraits of art critics, collectors and art dealers show that as an artist Cézanne had won his Paris gamble. Something "eternal" could be heard whispering along the banks of the Marne or in the forest of Fontainebleau... far removed from the harsh sunlight of Sainte-Victoire: "It seems that there is no more silence."[18]

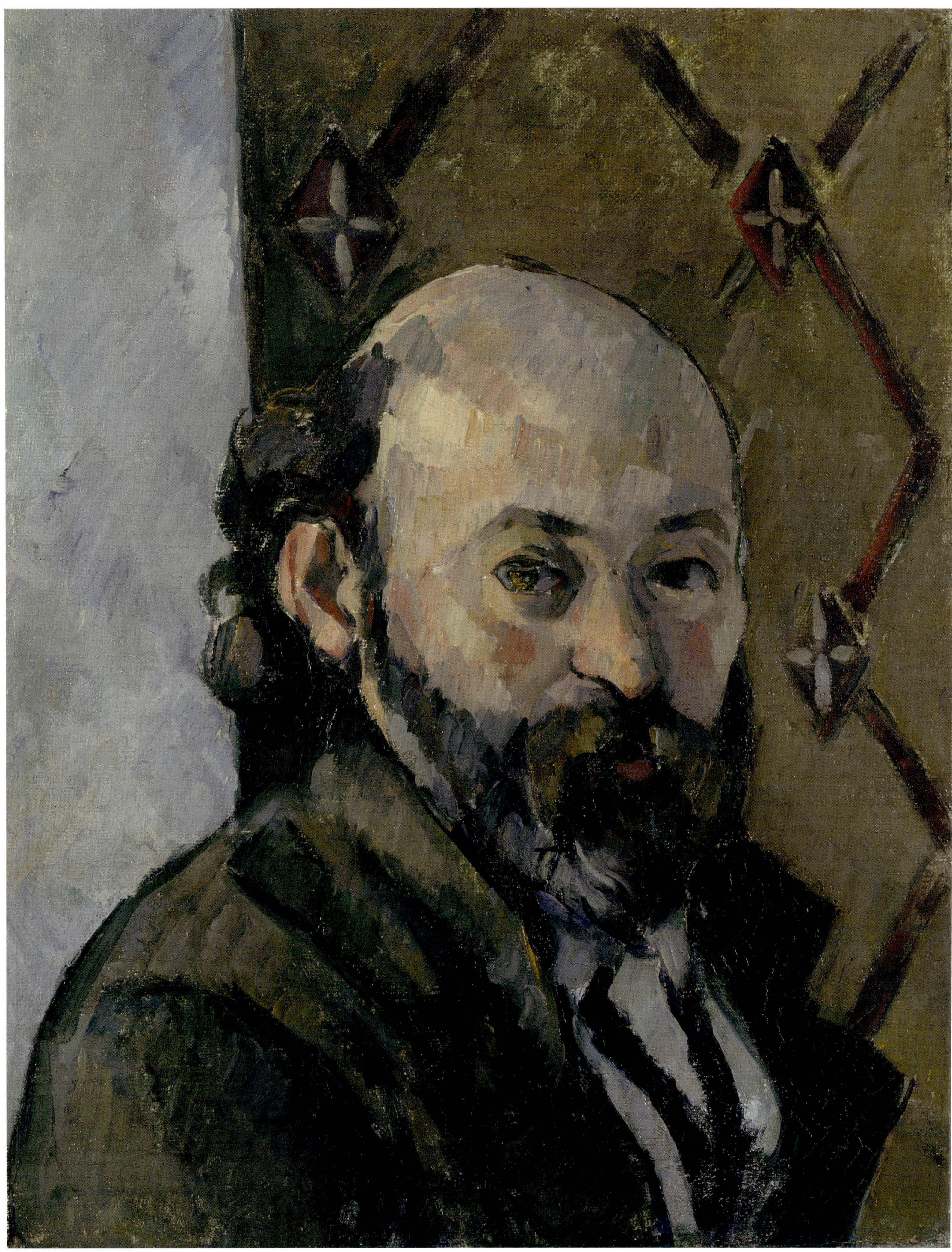

PAUL CĒZANNE — THE MAN

Philippe Cezanne

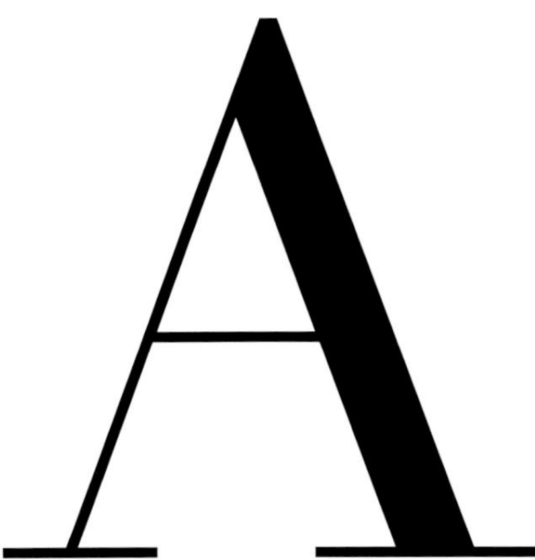

s an artist, his painting is outlandish; he is a poor colorist; he doesn't know how to draw; he is incapable of finishing a piece. In other words, he is a failed artist. As a man, he is surly, coarse, uncultivated, antisocial, quick-tempered, fickle; he has the appearance of a brigand. These were the terms in which Paul Cézanne was most often described by critics, art lovers, and official painters. Yet behind this rather unflattering exterior was a profoundly human individual who was indeed ill at ease in society, but who could be convivial enough when he wished to be.

It should be remembered that Cézanne received a classical education. He was one of the most cultivated artists of his generation and had a perfect command of Latin. Passionate about literature and poetry, he was also interested in architecture and geology.

At around the age of thirty, he realized that his life would be devoted to painting. He dedicated himself to this like a monk, adhering to regular working hours from which he only deviated occasionally to spend an evening with friends, talking about art and literature.

There are three aspects of Cézanne that can help us to understand his personality: his numerous relationships and friendships, rooted in his childhood and then developed over the course of his life; his visceral attachment to Provence; and his love-hate relationship with Paris.

Cézanne was profoundly Provençal in nature, deeply attached to the land of his birth, an area of about thirty kilometers around Aix-en-Provence. His family on both his father's and his mother's side came from a background of shopkeepers and craftsmen and had lived in the region since at least the 16th century.

What did he hope to find in Paris? Why did he return so often and unexpectedly to the south of France? The answer is complex because it includes a number of sometimes contradictory reasons but at the root of it can perhaps be found his prickly character, his fits of anger, and his persistent ill health.

In Paris, Cézanne was able to put some distance between himself and the restrictive effect of his family and was able to taste freedom, the pleasure of visits to the Louvre, and encounters at the Café Guerbois, and also to meet up with childhood friends from Aix.

However, he found the uncertainty, the bad weather, financial problems and the critics' gibes so distressing that he would return to Aix where he could once again enjoy the climate and the nature he so loved and rediscover the caring sanctuary of his family that offered protection from what he perceived to be attacks against him.

Though plagued by doubts about himself and what he was seeking to achieve, Cézanne was nevertheless certain of the path he had chosen and convinced that he was the best.

In a preface written in the 1930s, the younger Paul Cézanne—his son and my grandfather—portrays him thus: "My father had an extraordinary accent from his region that he never lost and the vibrant echo of which made him instantly recognizable from a great distance to his fellow countrymen. Physically, he appeared to be quite tall, although somewhat hampered by his careless gait. Nevertheless, his matt complexion, his brown jaw-line beard, his bare forehead, and his piercing, almost aggressive eyes, gave his face the oriental elegance of an Assyrian effigy... Temperamentally, he was prone from early on to very lively and very diverse reactions. Those close to him were left bewildered by what seemed to be his excessively sensitive, romantic, and quick-tempered responses... He continually sought out the intellectual environment of Paris, the only capital city where, as he saw it, one could truly establish one's reputation. Which

Cat. 5
Portrait de l'artiste au papier peint olivâtre [Self-Portrait]
1880–81
Oil on canvas
33.6 x 26 cm
The National Gallery, London
R 482

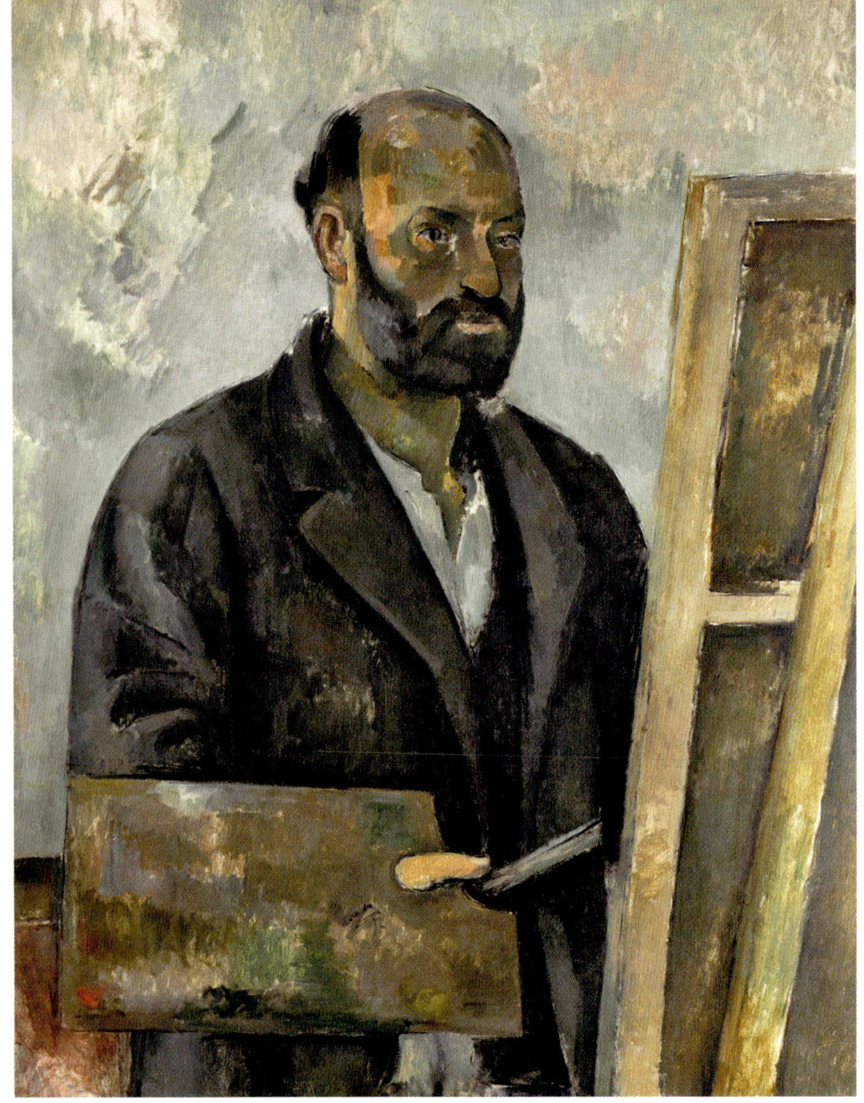

Fig. 2
Self-Portrait with Palette
c. 1890
Oil on canvas
92 x 75 cm
Fondation Collection E. G. Bührle, Zürich
R 670

is why, at regular but often quite long intervals over the course of forty years, he would repeatedly make the journey from Aix to Paris and back again."[1] (cat. 5).

A substantial correspondence, articles in the press, the writings of critics, and, above all, his many and long-lived friendships bear witness to what sort of man Cézanne really was. Through his frequent trips between Aix and Paris (we know of 22), he continued to maintain his friendships with the intellectual and artistic world of the French capital. Among the painters, writers, journalists, musicians, art dealers, and art lovers who surrounded him there, he found the vital support he needed for his art to mature and flourish.

Childhood friends

Cézanne's earliest friends dated back to his childhood and included some of his school companions. Later, many of these gravitated around him, around the writer Émile Zola, and the academic Baptistin Baille, who together became known as the "three inseparables." These companions of his youth included the painter and journalist Numa Coste, the architect Joseph Huot, the vineyard owner Aurélien Houchard, the sculptor Philippe Solari (cat. 6), the poet and journalist Antony Valabrègue, the publisher and novelist Marius Roux, the director of the Marseille Natural History Museum, Fortuné Marion, the novelist Paul Alexis, the painters Mathieu Chaillan, Auguste Truphème, François Combes, and Achille Emperaire, and the cabinetmaker and painter Justin Gabet.

Some came to visit him in Paris, several of them remained loyal friends to the very end, and some, like Valabrègue, acted as models. Valabrègue sat for him on a number of occasions in the 1860s (fig. 60), though he appeared to be unimpressed by his friend's work. In a letter to Zola, he explains that he dare not refuse and describes the portrait that Cézanne had painted: "Paul had me sit yesterday for a head study. Fiery-red flesh with scrapings of white; it's the painting of a bricklayer. I'm painted in such strong color that it reminds me of the statue of the Champfleury priest when it was coated with crushed blackberries. Fortunately, I only sat for one day."[2]

In the correspondence between Cézanne and Zola after 1858, when Zola had returned to Paris, many people from Aix, both familiar and unfamiliar, are mentioned.

Among the friends of his youth, there are some of special importance. Heinrich Morstatt was a young German musician who was living in Marseille in 1865. He met Cézanne through Marion. Morstatt had a passion for Richard Wagner and introduced his new friends to the composer's music.

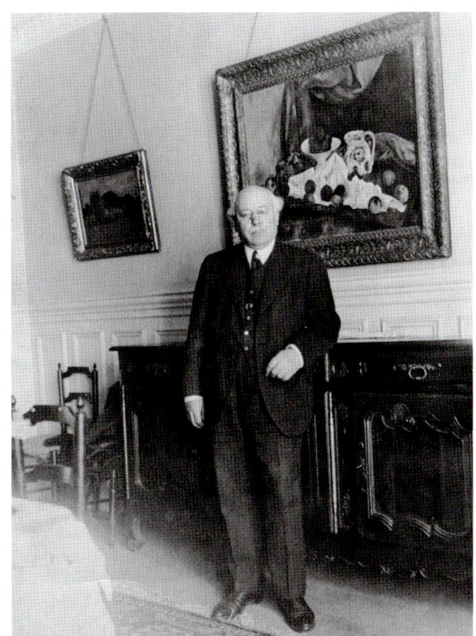

As a tribute to the musician, Cézanne painted *Young Girl at the Piano: Overture to Tannhaüser* (R 149). Fortuné Marion made Cézanne's acquaintance in 1860 and they were to remain close friends for nearly twenty years. Cézanne painted a study in which he shows him with Valabrègue setting out to paint *sur le motif* (R 99) and, in 1871, he painted a portrait of him (R 177). Marion maintained a correspondence with Morstatt from 1865 to 1869 in which he reveals a great deal about Cézanne's work, the canvases he was working on, and his technique.[3]

Another friend, Paul Alexis, studied law in Aix before turning to literature, having been influenced by Valabrègue. He moved to Paris in 1869 and became a close friend of Zola. He spent time and corresponded with Cézanne and is mentioned in the artist's correspondence up to 1886. He appears with Zola in two paintings of 1869–1870 (fig. 14, 15).

Baille, a school friend from Aix, shared in Cézanne's country outings and finally moved to Paris in 1867. For many years he visited Cézanne and wrote to him but their relationship became strained during the 1870s.

Friendship with Zola—first steps in Paris

Émile Zola occupied a unique place in Cézanne's life. He was his very close friend for over thirty years. This intense bond was punctuated by quarrels, joy, mutual admiration, and doubts about each other's artistic abilities—in other words, it was a unique relationship between two major talents. However, over the course of the years this great friendship began to wane and came to an end in 1886 because of their different life choices. However, the affection between them, founded on years of empathy, remained steadfast until death.

It was Zola who was the architect of Cézanne's move to the capital. Shortly after moving to Paris himself in 1858, he would constantly invite his friend to visit. Persuaded of Cézanne's talent, he berated him for his self-doubt and paid tribute to what he recognized as his genuine qualities as an artist. During his first stay in Paris, in 1861, Cézanne began to feel his way around. He enrolled at the Académie Suisse where he met his first artist friends: Camille Pissarro, Francisco Oller, Antoine Guillemet, Armand Guillaumin, and Frédéric Bazille. He worked closely with the painter François Villevieille, also from Aix, in both Paris and Marcoussis. Other friends he knew from art school in Aix also moved to the capital. These included Chaillan, Combes, Truphème, Emperaire, and Joseph Chautard, a friend of Villevieille. Zola grumbled to Baille: "Paul is still the same terrific and peculiar boy I knew at school. To demonstrate that he has lost nothing of his eccentricity... no sooner had he arrived here than he was already talking about traveling back to Aix... I have to say that I kept quiet and held back from stating the obvious. To convince Cézanne of something would be like persuading the towers of Notre-Dame to perform a quadrille... You won't gain an inch of ground by talking with a fellow of this caliber. You'll simply have experienced the interesting pleasure of observing such a strange individual. My plan of action is therefore very simple... To put myself at his disposal. As each of us has his particular ways, I must, if I am wise, conform to his moods if I don't want to see his friendship vanish."[4] These few lines demonstrate the admiration that Zola

Fig. 3
Paul Cézanne Jr. at home in around 1935, in front of the paintings *Copse at Jas de Bouffan* (R 234) and *Still Life* (R 845).
Photograph
Private collection

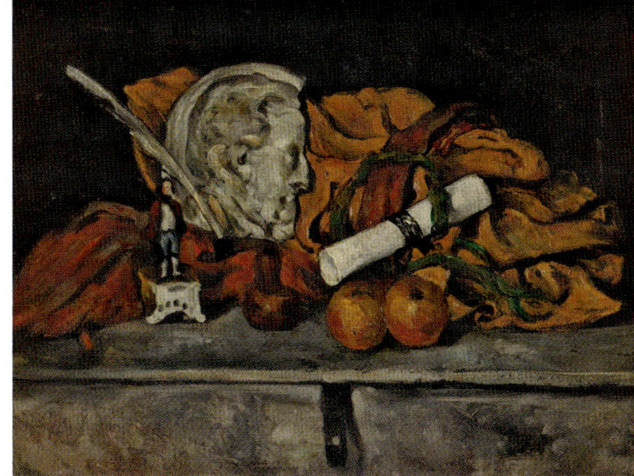

Cat. 6
Still Life with a Medallion of Solari
c. 1873
60 × 81 cm
Oil on canvas
Musée d'Orsay, Paris, gift of Paul Gachet, son of Dr. Gachet, 1951
R 211

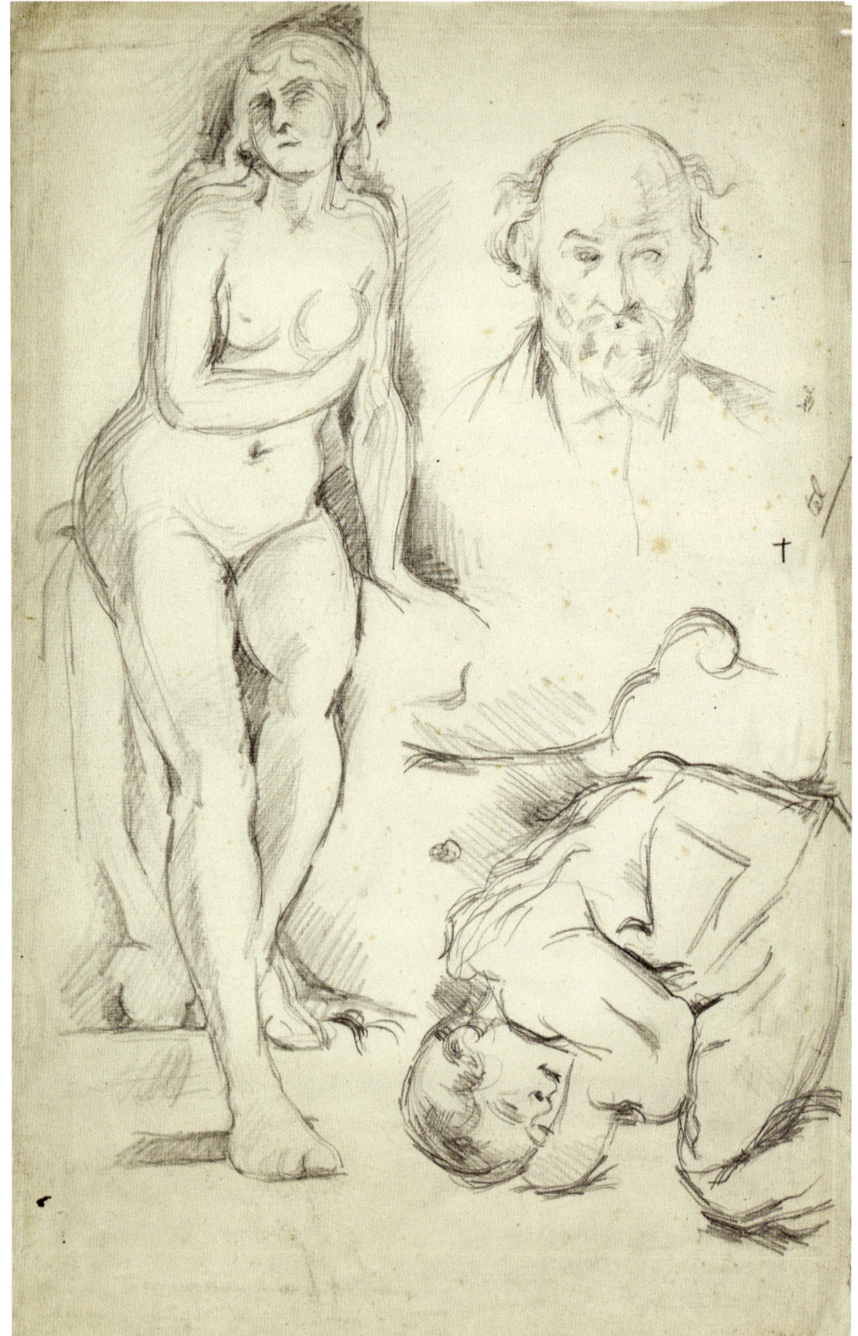

Cat. 7
Page of Studies: Psyche Abandoned, after Pajou
c. 1876, c. 1883, and c. 1885
Pencil on laid paper
48.5 × 32 cm
Museum Boijmans Van Beuningen, Rotterdam
CH 363

felt for the artist, showing that he was prepared to bow before this very strong character. However, by the autumn, disillusioned, Cézanne had returned to Aix.

Back in Paris in November 1862, Cézanne began to see a great deal of Aimable Lombard, a young artist from Draguignan, and of the painter Chautard, who corrected his work. He went back to work at the Académie Suisse and continued to make copies at the Louvre (cat. 7, 8, 9, 10, 11). Toward the end of the year, he made the acquaintance of Renoir, through Bazille. Cézanne remained in Paris until the summer of 1864. He continued to see Zola, Baille, and Lombard and stayed in touch with Numa Coste. He returned to Aix at the end of the summer of 1864 and then went back to Paris in early 1865. In March of that year he spent a few days at Saint-Germain-en-Laye. He then suggested to Pissarro that they should meet up, together with Francisco Oller, after presenting their canvases to the Salon.[5]

Cézanne was always rejected by the Salon, except on one occasion when Guillemet intervened on his behalf. But he appeared to take a certain pleasure in provoking the Salon jury he so detested by presenting works that were very likely to cause offense. In his writings, the artist delights in advance at the reaction of these official painters while, at the same time, expressing his distress at not being accepted—yet another Cézannian contradiction.

Invaders from Aix in a village on the banks of the Seine

During the spring and summer of 1866, at Guillemet's suggestion, Cézanne moved to Bennecourt, a small village on the right bank of the Seine, opposite Bonnières. An entire tribe of people from Aix, along with artist friends, invaded the village and old man Dumont's inn and outbuildings. They included Zola and Alexandrine Meley, his future wife, Baille, Roux, Chaillan, Solari, Valabrègue, Guillemet, and Pissarro.

Zola wrote twice[6] about the daily life of these animated young people and their interminable discussions about art. Two paintings survive from Cézanne's stay there: *The Ferry at Bonnières* (cat. 29) and the *Portrait of Rouvel*, the innkeeper's father-in-law (R 97). According to Zola, Cézanne was also working on other large format paintings but these have disappeared, destroyed by the artist as often happened when he failed to achieve the result he desired. All that remains is a small drawing showing Delphin, the blacksmith's son.[7]

Painter friends in Paris

After 1871, Cézanne settled periodically in Paris and forged new friendships. Three painters whom he had met at the Académie Suisse were instrumental in the development of his art: Guillemet, Guillaumin, and, of course, Pissarro.

Guillemet's convivial and relaxed nature made him easy to get on with. They worked together in Paris and in Aix-en-Provence. Guillemet was a support to Cézanne: He showed his paintings to Édouard Manet and

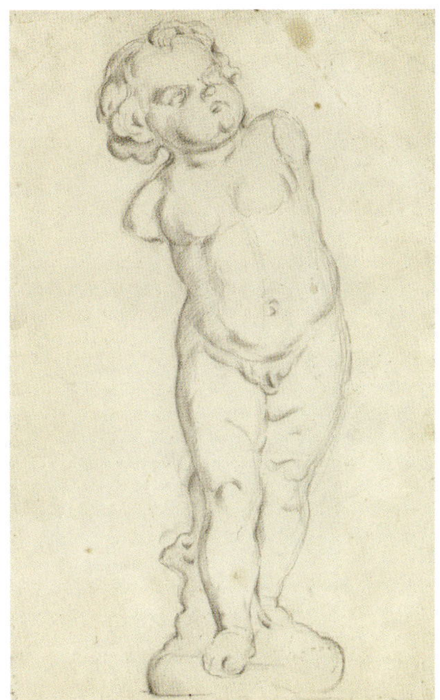

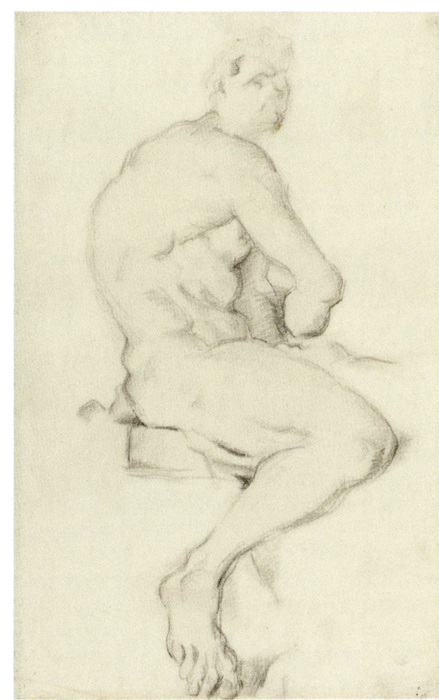

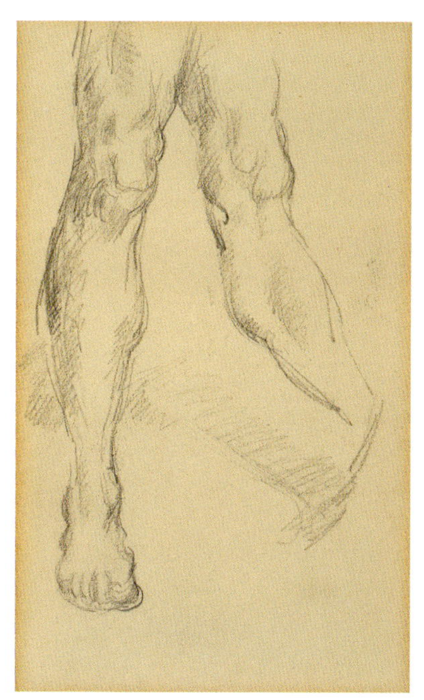

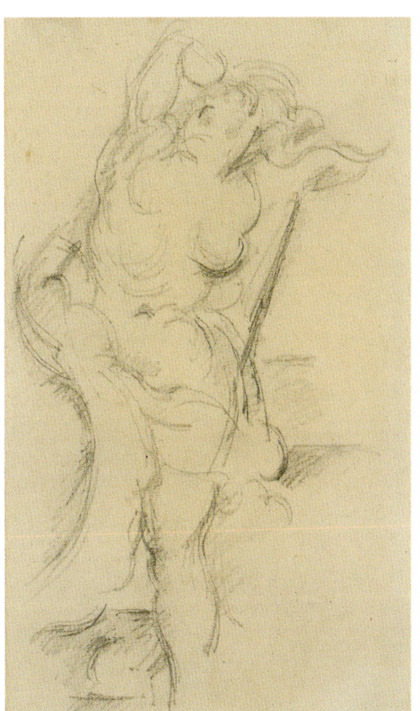

Cat. 8
Plaster Cupid
Drawing of the plaster copy of a sculpture of Cupid attributed to Puget, kept by Cézanne in his studio.
c. 1890
Pencil on paper, verso
(recto: *Sainte-Victoire with Pine Tree and Viaduct*)
48.2 × 31 cm
Museum Boijmans Van Beuningen, Rotterdam
CH 986

Cat. 9
Hercules Resting, after Puget
1884–87
Pencil on laid paper
47.3 × 31.3 cm
Museum Boijmans Van Beuningen, Rotterdam
CH 999

Cat. 10
Study of Legs, after Signorelli
1884–86
Graphite
19.4 × 11.8 cm
Musée Granet, Communauté du Pays d'Aix, Aix-en-Provence
CH 674

Cat. 11
Bellone
After Peter Paul Rubens
c. 1885–95
Pencil, recto
20.9 × 12.2 cm
Kunstmuseum Basel, Kupferstichkabinett, Basel
CH 1140

managed to get one of his works exhibited at the 1882 Salon—this appears to have been a portrait: *Louis Auguste Cézanne, the artist's father, reading* L'Événement[8] (fig. 10). He would remain a loyal friend.

Guillaumin introduced Cézanne to the area around Paris: Charenton, Issy-les-Moulineaux, Ivry-sur-Seine, and Nogent-sur-Marne. Then, in 1872, the two artists worked in Auvers and Pontoise and, in 1877, in Arcueil. They lived side by side on Quai d'Anjou in 1875 and then moved into the same building at 120 rue de Vaugirard. Around 1876, Cézanne copied a painting by Guillaumin: *The Seine at Bercy* (fig. 31). Their collaboration came to an end in the early 1880s.

Pissarro, probably the most important of Cézanne's friends, became his spiritual guide. It was Pissarro who persuaded the artist to brighten his palette and lighten his touch and who recommended that he abandon the palette knife in favor of the brush. The influence that these two artists would have on each other for almost twenty years and their mutual respect is clearly reflected in their work. Indeed, Pissarro would tell his son Lucien: "He came under my influence at Pontoise and I under his... Good Lord, we were always together! But one thing is certain, each of us held on to the only thing that matters—our feelings, something which can be clearly demonstrated."[9] In August 1872, Cézanne joined Pissarro at Pontoise and then moved, with his companion Hortense and his son Paul, born in January, to Auvers-sur-Oise for a long period in order to conceal his relationship and the birth of his child from his family. It was during this time that he borrowed from Pissarro a *View of Louveciennes* to copy (fig. 33, 34). Gustave Coquiot recounts that "The local peasants, who are less stupid than the art lovers, soon got to know the two painters and one of them said: 'I have often seen Monsieur Cézanne and Monsieur Pissarro. When working, Monsieur Pissarro stabs at the canvas whereas Monsieur Cézanne plasters it.'"[10]

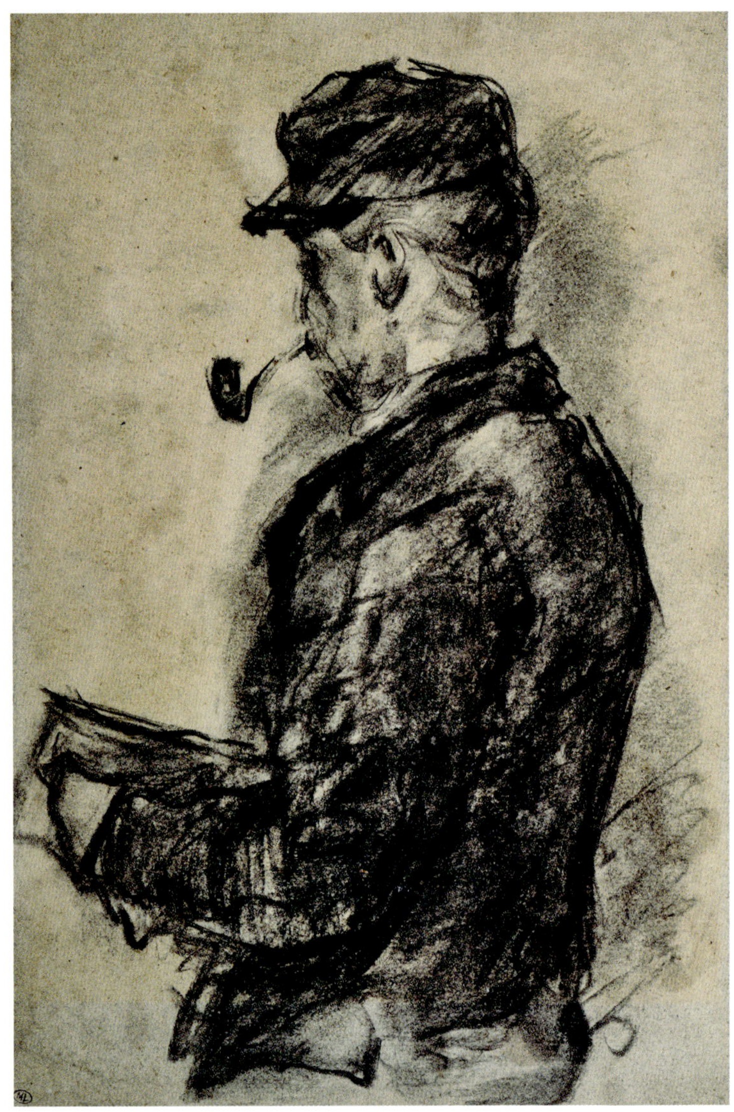

Cézanne's firm friends

Eugène Murer was an unusual and self-taught individual. A painter and writer, he was also a confectioner and restaurateur on Boulevard Voltaire. In 1872, his friend Guillaumin put him in touch with his other painter friends. A keen art lover, he bought their work, held evening events with potential buyers, and kept open house. Cézanne was regularly invited to dine at his home with his family.

Another unusual character, Julien Tanguy, known as "père Tanguy," was living in Paris in 1860 where he became a paint grinder. He moved to rue Clauzel in 1867 and formed friendships with many artists, including Cézanne, for whom he felt great admiration. The painter valued the calm and simplicity of Tanguy, who supplied his art materials, exhibited and endeavored to sell his works, allowed him to enjoy ongoing credit, and held the keys of his apartment when he was away. In 1885, Tanguy played host to young artists who came to his shop to discuss art against the backdrop of Cézanne's paintings. It was then that Paul Signac purchased *The Valley of the Oise* from him (fig. 81). It was also in Tanguy's shop window that the art dealer Ambroise Vollard first saw and admired Cézanne's work.

A civil servant, art critic, and very close friend of Renoir, Georges Rivière was also close to Cézanne and followed his career with interest. In 1877, at the time of the third Impressionist exhibition, he founded a small journal—*L'Impressioniste*—to support his artist friends. In 1933—by which time he was father-in-law to Cézanne's son Paul—he published a biography of the artist and presented us with a portrait of him: "Paul Cézanne was 35 years old at that time. He was a tall and handsome fellow with long, dark, chestnut hair and a beard of the same color, naturally curly. His slightly aquiline nose and his large, black eyes completed a certain resemblance he bore to figures in Assyrian bas-reliefs in the Louvre... Some years later, his forehead was bare, his beard and hair cut shorter and already sprinkled with gray, but his eyes had kept their sparkle... Those who knew him during this late period of his life agree that he had the appearance of an old retired officer."[11]

Dr Gachet and his Impressionist protégés

From 1872 to 1880, Cézanne lived in Auvers and Pontoise with a group of artists—Pissarro, Guillaumin, Oller, Victor Vignon, Frédéric Cordey, and in 1880, Gauguin. It was a convivial, artistic environment that seemed to agree with him. But this gathering of artists would not have been possible were it not for one particular man: Dr Gachet (cat. 12). A physician but also a painter and engraver, Gachet was a friend of Bonington, Delacroix, and Courbet. In 1872, Dr Gachet bought a house in Auvers and created a studio there. These artists came there to paint still lifes or flowers arranged by Madame Gachet. A patient patron, Gachet introduced Cézanne to engraving and gave him friendship and moral support during these years, purchasing his paintings and even intervening with his father, Louis Auguste, to obtain an increase in his allowance.

Cat. 12
Portrait of Doctor Gachet in his Studio
c. 1873
Charcoal on paper that was originally gray with traces of fixative
32.5 × 21.5 cm
Musée d'Orsay, Paris
(kept at the Musée du Louvre, Département des Arts Graphiques), gift of Paul Gachet, son of Dr. Gachet, 1951
CH 295

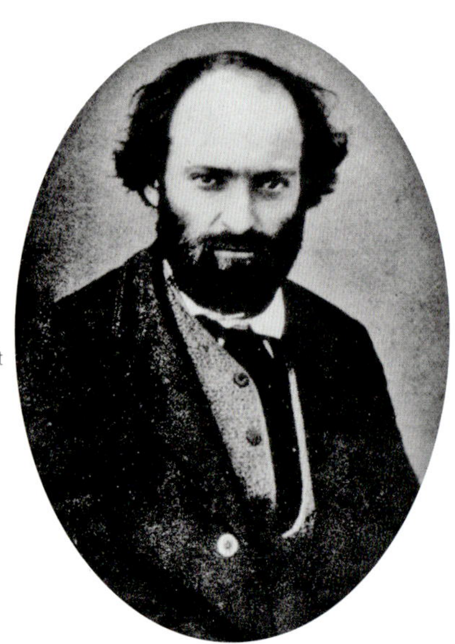

Fig. 4
Anonymous
Paul Cézanne c.1875
Photograph
Musée d'Orsay, Paris

Victor Chocquet (fig. 5), who owned one of the finest collections of drawings and watercolors by Delacroix, was one of the first collectors of Cézanne. His first purchase, a small Bather, dates from 1875, when Renoir took him to Tanguy's shop. Cézanne and Renoir often dined at Chocquet's home, the three men spending the evening discussing and admiring his works by Delacroix. Chocquet particularly liked Cézanne as a person and throughout his life ardently defended the artist's work. They enjoyed a long correspondence and, during the summers of 1882 and 1889, Cézanne stayed at the Chocquets' house in Hattenville, where he painted landscapes. It seems it was Chocquet who gave Cézanne his only commission: two decorative panels (R 643 and 644) for the collector's private residence.

Monet and Renoir

Among the Impressionists, two painters were very close to Cézanne: Renoir and Monet. They respected one another, shared a mutual appreciation of their art and, despite a few disagreements, their friendship persisted over many years. Cézanne confided to Gasquet: "I despise all living painters except Monet and Renoir."[12] Renoir, as we know, became acquainted with Cézanne in 1863. In 1882, he spent time with him at L'Estaque, "a small spot like Asnières by the sea,"[13] he wrote. During the summer of 1885, Cézanne joined the Renoir family at La Roche-Guyon with Hortense and his son. During the winter of 1887–1888, Renoir was invited to stay with the family at their Jas de Bouffan family estate but this visit came to an abrupt end following an angry outburst by Cézanne. As usual, this quarrel did not last long. In the summer of 1889, Renoir rented Montbriant, the house owned by his sister Rose Conil, in Aix.[14] He returned there again in March 1895. Renoir continued to support him with collectors and art critics. One day, he commented to his friend Georges Rivière: "Cézanne has only to apply a touch of color to a canvas for it to be interesting; it is nothing and yet it is beautiful."[15]

Monet had met Cézanne one evening at the Café Guerbois. They exhibited together at Nadar's in 1874; then, in 1876, he invited him to his house at Argenteuil with Chocquet. In 1877 at the third Impressionist exhibition, Cézanne's contribution was highly regarded by Monet. After Monet moved to Giverny, Cézanne visited him there in September 1894, where he made the acquaintance of Mary Cassatt. Then, in November, Monet introduced him to Clemenceau, Rodin, Octave Mirbeau, and Gustave Geffroy, whose portrait Cézanne would later paint. While he was sitting for this, Cézanne confided to him: "Monet is the finest of us all"[16]; and to his son, in 1902, he declared: "Monet is but an eye, but what an eye."[17] At the Chocquet sale in 1899, Monet advised Isaac de Camondo to purchase *The House of the Hanged Man* (cat. 74)

Fig. 5
Portrait of Victor Chocquet
1880–81
Oil on canvas
35.2 x 27.3 cm
Virginia Museum of Fine Arts, Richmond
R 297

Cézanne, the critics, and his first triumphs

The critics mocked Cézanne's work and it was not until 1885 that some journalists began to display an interest. Élémir Bourges wrote a short piece describing his visit to Zola in which he mentions a portrait of a woman by Cézanne "similar to a Ribera."[18] (R 75) In 1889, Roger Marx published several articles in which he spoke highly of the artist's work and, with Antonin Proust, decided to reserve a place of honor for his paintings at the 1889 and 1900 Universal Exhibitions. In 1889, J. K. Huysmans devoted a chapter rich in flavor and poetry to the artist in *Certains*. Then, in 1891, the critic Mirbeau extolled him as "the most painterly of painters"[19] and, in 1902, attempted unsuccessfully to get Henri Rougeon, the director of Fine Arts, to have Cézanne awarded the Légion d'Honneur. Rougeon responded: "...ask me to get the cross for anyone at all; but for Cézanne, this anarchist, this madman, don't even think of it!"[20] Although he claimed to be unmoved by such honors, Cézanne was in fact deeply affected by this. In 1894, Gustave Geffroy published an article in the magazine *Vie artistique* and he responded by thanking him and starting work on a portrait of Geffroy, but the painting was never completed (fig. 61).

Ambroise Vollard

At the suggestion of a number of his artist friends, Ambroise Vollard, a young art dealer, decided to hold an exhibition of Cézanne's work in his gallery in November 1895. This first retrospective of the artist's work was a revelation. Never before had such a collection of works, covering an artist's entire life, been seen. Art lovers flooded to the exhibition and his artist friends purchased works. The most celebrated critics—Thiébault-Sisson, Arsène Alexandre, Thadée Natanson, and Georges Lecomte—vied with one another in complimenting Cézanne on his talent and the originality of his paintings.

Early in 1896, Auguste Pellerin, a French industrialist, purchased his first Cézannes from Vollard. He would go on to collect almost a hundred and sixty works by the artist. Egisto Fabbri purchased 16 and expressed his admiration to the artist. Charles Loeser, another American, purchased 15 paintings. He would give eight of them to the White House. In 1901, Henri Havemayer bought his first Cézanne from Vollard on the advice of Mary Cassatt. Then, in 1906, K. E. Osthaus and his wife visited the artist in his studio and selected two paintings. During a stay at Fontainebleau in 1899, Cézanne made the acquaintance of Alfred Hauge, a Norwegian artist, and decided to paint his portrait (cat. 67).

The master and the next generation of painters

A young generation of painters, poets, and writers, including Jean Royère, Pierre Léris, and Louis Aurenche, in turn came to know the master. Cézanne would invite them for lunch or dinner at his home or at the Café Beaufort to converse over a glass of wine. They all describe him as an affable man, articulate, unstinting with his advice, and happy to discuss his ideas. Cézanne agreed to go out and paint from nature with some young artists from Aix, including Niollon, Ravaisou, and Louise Germain. A number of them recount their discussions with Cézanne: in 1912, Joachim Gasquet, son of Henri Gasquet, the artist's childhood friend, published his recollections of these encounters and Léo Larguier published *Le Dimanche avec Paul Cézanne (souvenirs)*.[21]

During his military service in Marseille in 1901, the painter Camoin visited Cézanne, who received him with great kindness. They corresponded until 1906 and the elderly artist offered him advice. He returned on a number of occasions, notably in 1904, to introduce his friend Francis Jourdain, the architect and interior designer. In 1902, Jules Borély decided to go and meet the master without any introduction. Touched by this, Cézanne received him warmly.[22] Émile Bernard, a young artist of 21, had written one of the first tributes to Cézanne. He visited the artist and corresponded with him from 1904 to 1906 and mentions him in his memoirs (1920).[23] The painter-printmakers J. F. Schnerb and R. P. Rivière also went to see Cézanne in 1905 and describe their visit in an article.[24] Maurice Denis and K. X. Roussel also made this pilgrimage in 1906. Cézanne was already familiar with the homage painted by Denis in 1900 and had thanked the artist the following year. Denis described this *sur le motif* meeting[25] and as a visual record, Roussel took photographs of the painter at work while Denis immortalized him in a painting.

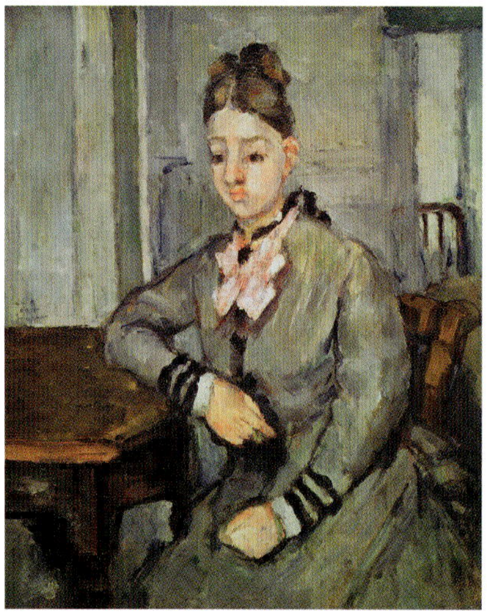

Fig. 6
Madame Cézanne Leaning on Her Elbow
1873–74
Oil on canvas
46 x 38 cm
Private collection
R 217

Cat. 13
Madame Cézanne in a Yellow Chair
1888–90
Oil on canvas
81 x 65 cm
The Art Institute of Chicago, Chicago,
Wilson L. Mead Fund
R 653

Hortense Fiquet and Paul Cézanne junior

I cannot end this piece without paying tribute to the two people who were closest to Cézanne and of whom he was fondest: my great grandmother Hortense and my grandfather Paul.

Hortense Fiquet was born in 1850 in the Jura region. In 1869 she was working as a bookbinder in Paris. She was 19 years old when she met Cézanne. She went to live with him at L'Estaque in 1870 and their son Paul was born in 1872. The earliest portraits of her date from this period. One very tender painting shows her breastfeeding her son (fig. 6), while another is more classical in its approach (cat. 13, 56, 75, fig. 89). For 17 years the artist concealed their relationship from his family: only his mother knew about it. In 1885, Hortense married Cézanne but her in-laws would not accept her. She often moved house in Paris or in the south of France at her husband's request, living on just a meager allowance. She did not understand her husband's art but for thirty years she willingly complied with his demands, posing for more than thirty paintings, four watercolors, and fifty drawings. The geographical distance between them must, in some way, have suited Cézanne. They spent time together regularly in Paris and in the south of France and their affection is obvious even though they lived in two different worlds. Cézanne always sought news of his wife and worried about her health. My grandfather, their son Paul, was one of the foundations on which the artist's life was built. Through Paul, when he was a child, Cézanne discovered feelings of affection that he had never experienced before, and once young Paul was an adult, a great intimacy developed between them. In 1895, Cézanne unburdened himself of all the problems of administration and dealings with the art market by handing these matters over to his son.

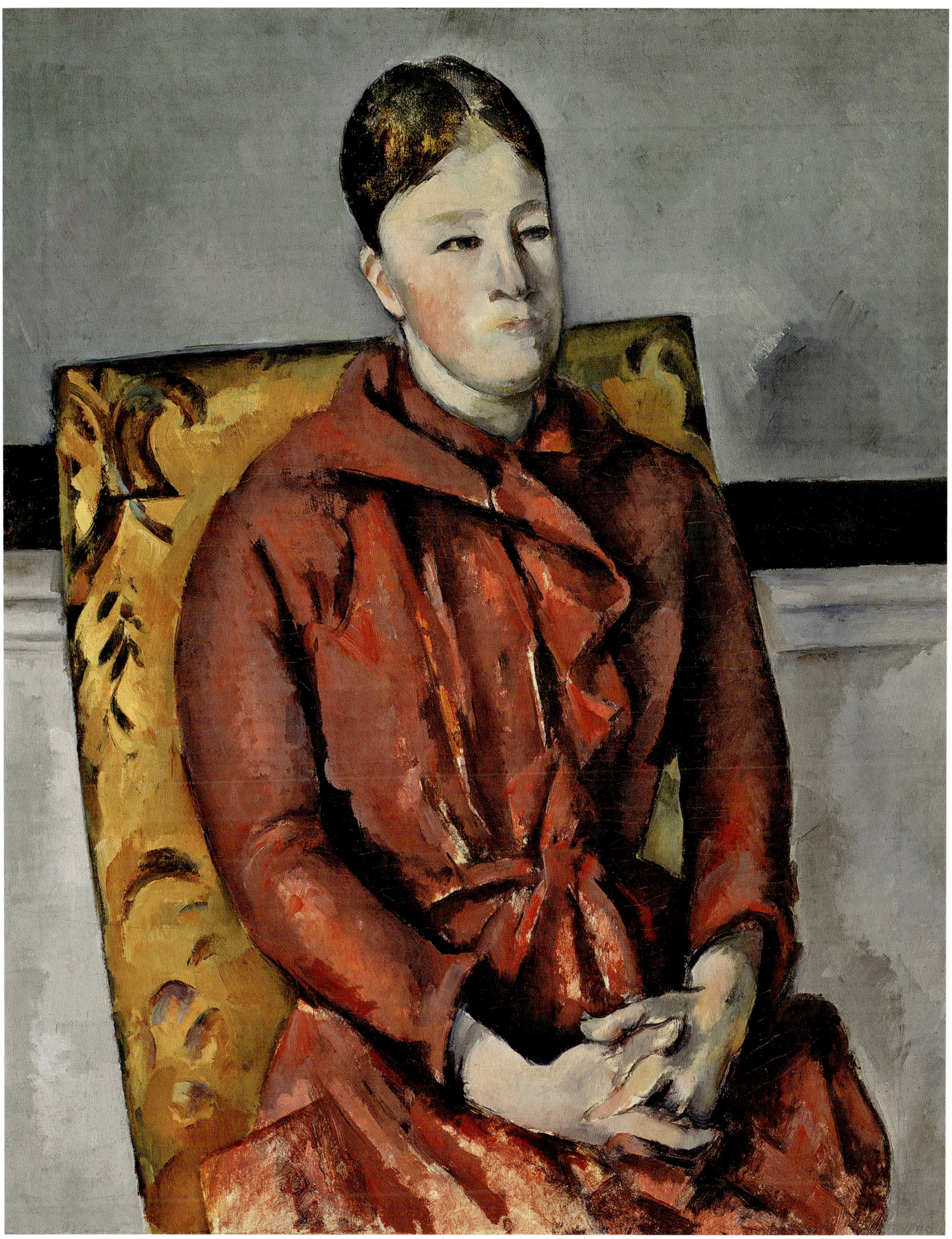

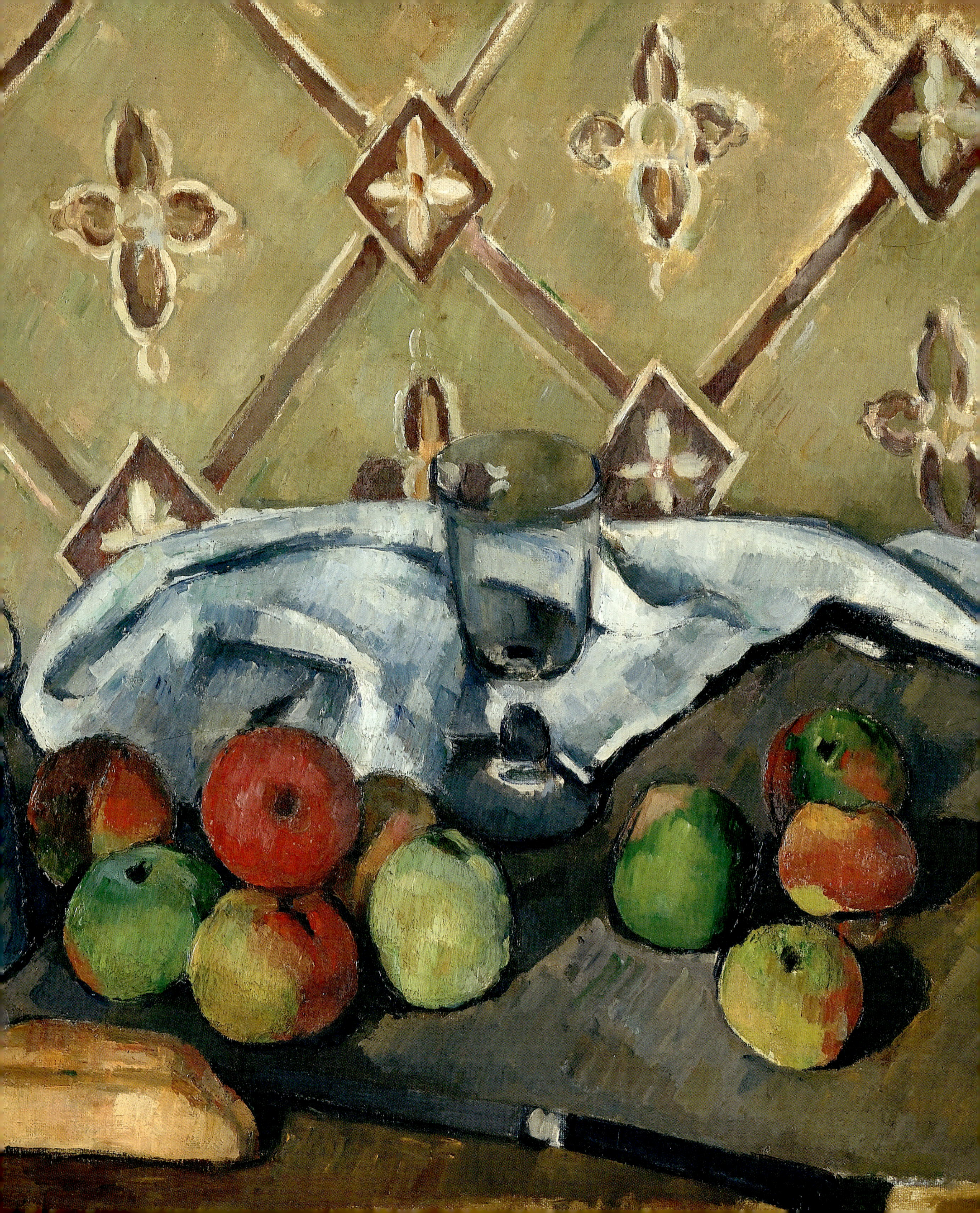

ASTONISH WITH AN PARIS APPLE

"I want to astonish Paris with an apple."[1]

When Maurice Denis painted his *Homage to Cézanne* (fig. 95) in 1901, with a number of admirers gathered around one of the artist's canvases—*Fruit Bowl, Glass, and Apples*—the apple was the center of attention. It is not surprising that, soon after arriving in Paris, Cézanne introduced the forbidden fruit into his paintings—in this instance the apple given by Paris to Aphrodite in his famous judgment, marking her out as the most beautiful of the three goddesses. Paris was not the only place in which to be an artist, but Cézanne had dreams of glory and wanted to storm the gates of the Salon. However, at first Paris was a dream that did not come true. Following Zola's orders, Cézanne came to the French capital in 1861; his father had warned against the move, but had finally given in. The young Cézanne arrived from his native Provence fired by a passion for academicism and poetry and in fact he spent more time writing verse than painting. His first letter from Paris, sent to Joseph Huot on June 4, 1861, reported on the Salon in alexandrines, finishing with the admission: "Now I have run out of rhymes." How are we to interpret this? That the Salon did not inspire the poet who was, above all, a painter and would later try in vain to be accepted there? That only ponderous versification would be fitting for this institution and that Cézanne had exhausted his poetic powers in a single letter? Might Paris have disabused him of the romantic ideas of Victor Hugo within a few weeks?

Cézanne's first stay in Paris lasted barely six months and ended in failure. He returned to Provence, where he was obliged to work in the family bank, but *Cézanne le banquier ne voit pas sans frémir / Derrière son comptoir naître un peintre à venir.* (Cézanne the banker does not see without trembling/ Behind his counter a future painter born).

Apples, Napkin, and Milk Can (detail)
See cat. 59 p. 123

The painter was now sure of his vocation. It was no longer a question of continuing to "nurture his illusions," as he put it in a note to Zola[2]. Of course the reality was hard, but he had to confront Paris again, and it became the battleground, where both tradition and modernity were discovered. Cézanne made lasting friendships and built a life there, and he met Hortense Fiquet. At that time, there was a free studio called the Académie Suisse, where you could find models and meet young painters intent on breaking the academic rules, following the example of Courbet or Delacroix. Cézanne met Pissarro, Guillemet, Guillaumin, Oller, then Renoir, Bazille, Monet, and even Manet.

Cézanne's early canvases show evidence of an unusual pictorial sense and we can understand why the dealers were not attracted to them, still less the members of the jury of an academic Salon. The adjective *couillard* (ballsy) is still appropriate to this period, which extended from around 1861 to 1871; the impasto is thick, the brush strokes violent, the subjects erotic, sometimes pornographic, and often aggressive.

Cézanne's friendship with Zola remained strong, even though the latter was forced to admit after his friend's first stay in the capital: "Paris did our friendship no good."[3] But a few years later, in 1866, at the time of the publication—in book form—of a series of articles that he had just written in defense of the new generation of painters, Zola composed a long dedication beginning with the words "To my friend Paul Cézanne."[4]

Paris? Certainly a city to be conquered, being the only city where new art was being created against all the odds and in the context of friendship and comradeship, which is fairly accurately portrayed in Zola's *L'Œuvre*. The conquest of Paris remained difficult and there would be a long road to travel.

D. C.

Henri Mitterand

BROTHERS IN ART: CĒZANNE AND ZOLA

Paul Cézanne and Émile Zola met at Collège Bourbon, a boarding school in Aix-en-Provence, in the fall of 1853: Émile was entering sixth grade and Paul going into seventh. Paul was the son of a banker and former hatter, while Émile's father was the Italian engineer, Francesco Zola, who constructed the dam and canal that would bear his name and who died in 1847 when his son was seven years old. Both, in short, sons of *parvenus*, they gravitated quite naturally to each other through a shared sense of not belonging to the "polite society" of Aix, and even more so through their intellect, their common love of nature and reading poetry, and their dreams about art and creativity.

There followed three years of friendship, sharing their desire to learn how to represent the world, and if they did not have real-life subjects they would invent imaginary ones: the one through drawing and color, and the other through writing. Occasionally Émile accompanied Cézanne to art classes; at the age of twelve he wrote a now-lost medieval novel, and a comedy (also lost) when he was fifteen or sixteen, as well as hundreds of poems. They were joined by a third schoolboy, Jean-Baptistin Baille (more oriented towards the sciences but also passionate about great literature), completing a trio who were happy to cut themselves off from the rabble of schoolkids to venture out to the surrounding countryside, reciting aloud Lamartine, Hugo and Musset, or diving into the waters of the Arc River. Paul took along his sketch book—which would later be the source for his bathers paintings. These were companionable teenage years in Provence, rooted in the southern soil, which kept on emerging on Cézanne's canvases as much as on the pages written by Zola.

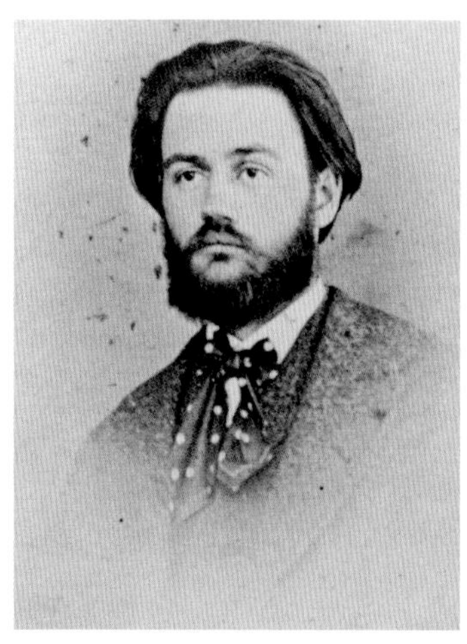

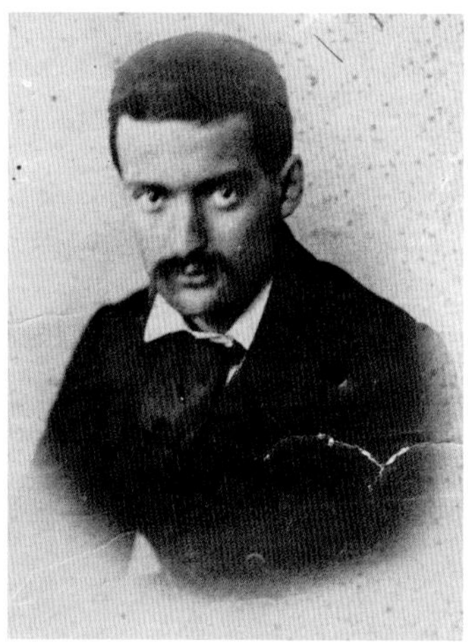

Fig. 7
A. Pinsard
Portrait of Émile Zola
c. 1865
Photograph
Bibliothèque nationale de France, Paris

Fig. 8
Anonymous
Portrait of Cézanne
c. 1861
Photograph
Musée d'Orsay, Paris

In October 1857 Zola was entering tenth grade, and Paul was heading rapidly in his final eleventh year towards the baccalaureate examinations. Did they sense that the happy, summery days in Aix were numbered? Since the death of Francesco Zola the sharks had been circling the construction company, the Société du Canal Zola. Émile's mother, Émilie Zola, was ill-equipped for the fight, and failed to win a series of law suits. In December 1857 she launched a final appeal, and left for Paris to witness the pursuit of her case. She sent for her son the following month. For Émile, the curtain suddenly fell on fifteen years of life in Aix. It was in all respects a painful ordeal for him: poverty, a journey into the unknown, and separation from his friends. Yet he realized that it was also his chance of a lifetime. Writing in Aix—what could that bring? Modernity and the real world were in Paris, as he kept telling his friends in Aix, starting with an envious Cézanne. All that remained to soften the blow of separation was to write letters. If anything, the distance was to heighten the close affinity between Paul and Émile (fig. 7 and 8). In Aix, Paul studied law and began to work in his father's office, continuing all the while to paint; in Paris, Émile attended the Lycée Saint-Louis. Uprooted, and finding little pleasure in the company of his foppish fellow pupils, he immersed himself in reading and writing poetry; after failing the baccalaureate, he took a break from his studies and moved from one temporary lodging to the next. The bohemian life... This would last for two years, during which time Cézanne was champing at the bit in the comfort of his family home, despising the "tortuous road"[1] of the law, and still cherishing an all-encompassing passion for painting.

These were not wasted years for Zola, even though he had turned his back on any career given legitimacy by qualifications, official position, and money. Just as Cézanne dreamed only of painting, his sole desire was to write. He had an aptitude for verse, so believing himself a poet he churned out hundreds of alexandrines (most of which have disappeared) and buried himself under a mountain of books that included Michelet, Sand, Hugo, and Montaigne; he also strolled endlessly through Paris, making repeat visits to museums and to studios frequented by a colony of Aix painters who were now in Paris.

This education and experience of living art combined with the Classical and Romantic tradition would have an effect on Cézanne. Without all the gossip, information, and opinions provided by Zola, who returned to Aix for two consecutive summers, would Cézanne have been able to overcome his father's reservations, extricate himself from the bank counter, and decide to "go up" to Paris in April 1861? And finally to become a full-time artist? Zola believed he had the talent to become "a great future painter."[2] He warned him against the kind of "realism" that was becoming prevalent, a combination of trivial subjects with tacky idealism: "I am telling you this for your own sake, my friend."[3] He gave him advice and encouragement, telling him that he should be wary of the latest trends, and not settle for the classes given by Gibert, the director of the drawing school in Aix; the lesson of the museums awaited him. They trained and educated each other, each getting carried away with the other's ideas, deciding that whatever pitfalls might lie ahead, together they would dedicate their lives to art. For this to happen, however, Cézanne had to flee the nest of Aix.

Finally, in early 1861, Paul reached an agreement in principle with his father. Following two more months of avoiding the issue, on March 3, Zola, who by then was well-versed in the lifestyles and rhythms needed to beg, borrow, or steal for an existence in Paris, set out a typical schedule and budget for him. One hundred francs a month; studies from a life model in a studio from six to eleven in the morning; copying masterpieces in museums from midday to 4 p.m.; evenings free, Sundays in the countryside—for *plein air* sketching. And on Sunday April 21, 1861, without any prior warning, Paul arrived at 11 rue Soufflot and called out from the bottom of the stairs... Zola expressed his surprise and happiness: "I saw Paul!! I saw Paul... Trembling, I opened my door and we embraced each other furiously."[4] Up in Zola's garret, at his friend's side, Cézanne looked out over the rooftops of Paris for the first time.

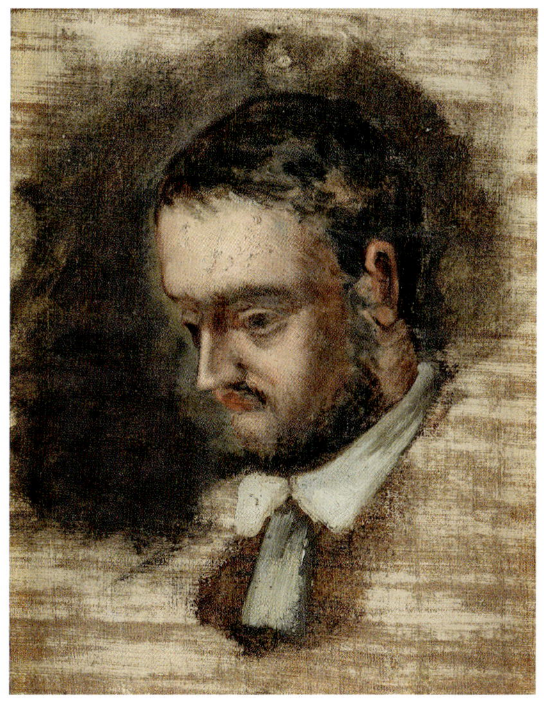

Fig. 9
Portrait of Émile Zola
1862–1864
Oil on canvas
26 x 21 cm
Musée Granet, Aix-en-Provence, Communauté du Pays d'Aix
R 78

The Batignolles group (1862–1870)

However, Paul returned to Aix in September 1861. Zola had sat for him occasionally and they had spent whole days together. In May they had paid a visit to the Salon and admired Corot, Daubigny, Courbet, and the two paintings by Manet which, exceptionally, had been accepted by the jury.[5] Paul became acquainted with Pissarro at the Académie Suisse, but he missed Provence, suffering from mood swings, and was perhaps annoyed on occasion by Zola's intellectual self-confidence. After his departure, his friend gave a description of him that was not refuted: "Still the same fine and strange fellow I knew at school... To convince Cézanne of something would be like persuading the towers of Notre-Dame to perform a quadrille... He is all one piece, stiff and hard. Nothing bends him, nothing can force him to make a concession."[6]

From then on, Émile would accept this friendship with its ups and down; a relationship that had its "eclipses." When Cézanne came back in November 1862, they were as happy as ever to see each other again. This time the young painter was to stay in Paris for almost two years. Zola was then working for the publisher Louis Hachette as the head of the advertising department. Every Thursday evening he met up with a group of friends that included Cézanne and other artists from Aix. Cézanne

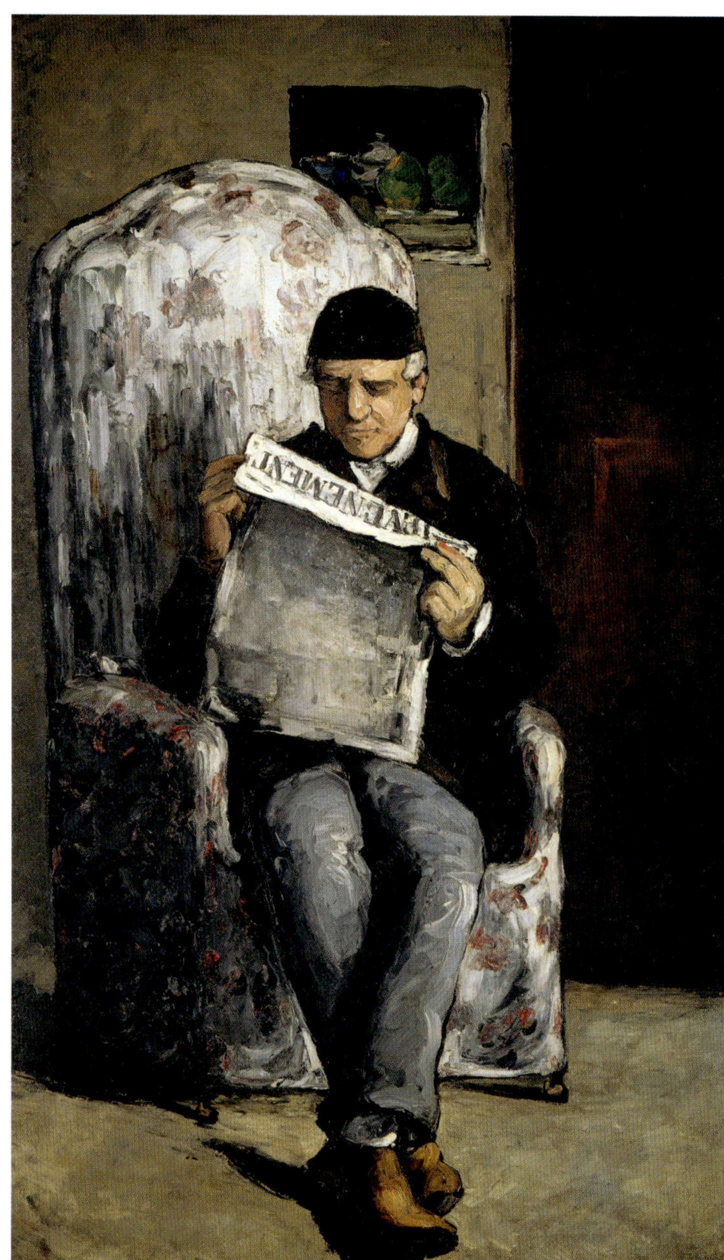

Fig. 10
Louis Auguste Cézanne, Father of the Artist, Reading L'Événement
Autumn 1866
Oil on canvas
200 x 120 cm
Washington, National Gallery of Art
R 101

struck up friendships with Pissarro, Daubigny, and Guillemet, whom he met in the Batignolles studios, and shortly after with Renoir and Bazille, and he later introduced Zola to this circle. The two painters they regarded as examples were Delacroix and Courbet. They went to see the Salon des Refusés in May 1863: Manet's *The Bath* (later known as *Luncheon on the Grass*) sent them into raptures.

In the fall of 1864 Émile met 25-year-old Alexandrine Meley, who became his mistress in December. She called herself Gabrielle, in memory of a young daughter she was forced to give up in 1859, though she re-assumed her real first name when they married. The story that she had been Cézanne's mistress before she met Zola does not hold water. Back in Paris in January 1865 after spending six months in Aix, Cézanne resumed his weekly dinners at Zola's. In May 1865, the jury of the Salon des Refusés rejected his entries. He was forced to survive in Paris on the meager allowance from his father. Until 1870 he would spend his winters in Aix where he at least had room and lodging, and where he could enjoy watching the light and colors of the sun on the mountain, Sainte-Victoire.

Once back in Paris in February 1866, he saw Zola's friendship with the young Batignolles group become firmly established. On January 31, 1866 Zola risked giving up a salaried job to make a living from writing, pinning his hopes on journalism, novels, and drama. He dedicated his first novel *La Confession de Claude (Claude's Confession)*, to his two school friends, Baille and Cézanne. Armed with his experience of studios and museums, and his friendships with painters, his intention was to make a name for himself as a critic, both art and literary. The opportunity arose, thanks to the particular hostility towards *plein air* painting of the Salon jury, the Académie des Beaux-Arts, and the established critics.

This time Cézanne joined Manet in failure. Rejected or not, all the Batignolles painters were united against the jury, and Zola acted as their spokesman in the journal *L'Événement*; he wrote a series of columns culminating in a robust defense of Manet[7], while an open letter by Cézanne to the Comte de Nieuwerkerke, the "Surintendant des Beaux-Arts," called for the reopening of the Salon des Refusés. This two-pronged and thus doubly provocative attack marked the real beginning of the "Impressionist" venture, but the Salon jury and established critics remained unperturbed. A year later in April 1867, two of Cézanne's canvases were again rejected: *Le Grog au vin* (R 115) and *Ivresse*.[8] *Le Figaro* wrote derisively about them: Zola immediately replied in the same newspaper with a defense of his friend and those painters who "are satisfied with the great realities of nature."[9] After declaring in 1866 that "Manet's place in the Louvre is reserved, like that of Courbet," he described Cézanne as the bearer of all the new painting's hopes. Who but this young 27-year-old critic could have suggested a better trio?

His painter friends were clear about the sincerity and foresight of his choices, which Zola repeated in *L'Événement illustré*[10] in 1868. In 1866 the foremost among them, Cézanne, had altered a portrait of his father, Louis Cézanne, sitting in a high-back armchair reading *Le Siècle*, replacing this newspaper with *L'Événement* (fig. 10). A whole stream of tributes followed up until 1870: In 1868 Manet showed his portrait of Zola in the Salon (fig. 11); and in 1869 and 1870 Cézanne himself, Fantin-Latour, and

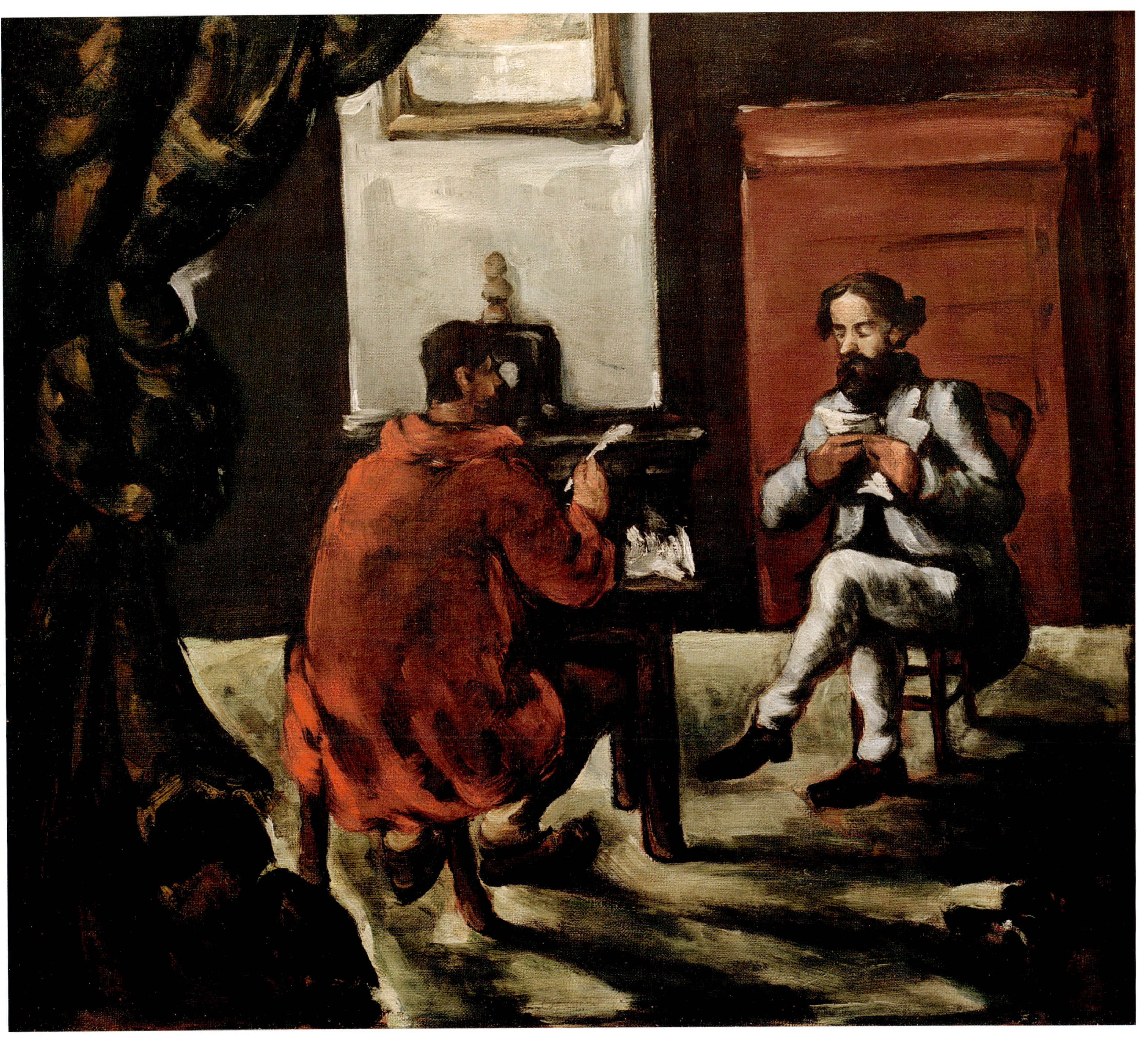

Cat. 14
Paul Alexis Reading at Zola's house
1869–70
Oil on canvas
52 × 56 cm
Private collection
R 150

Bazille would place the author of *Thérèse Raquin* and *Madeleine Férat* at the center of their canvases, as Delacroix had once done with Baudelaire.

Residents of the Batignolles quarter since late 1866, Paul and Émile frequented the Café Guerbois at 11 grande-rue des Batignolles, which later became avenue de Clichy, where other regular customers included Manet, Renoir, Bazille, Monet, Guillemet, Duret, and Duranty. In spring 1866 the two shared a holiday in the countryside by the river Seine: It was Cézanne who had discovered Bennecourt, on the banks of the Seine opposite Bonnières and above Mantes, and in May he moved into the inn there run by the Dumont family, which adjoined a smithy. One of his letters to Zola from Bennecourt has a pen and ink drawing showing the blacksmith at work. Zola and Gabrielle often went to meet him there, along with other friends from Aix: Baille, Valabrègue, Roux, Solari, and the painter Chaillan. Monet was to make the journey in 1868. Memories of these places would subsequently appear in Zola's *L'Œuvre*. Cézanne painted the church at Bonnières, and Monet the banks of an island opposite the village. These were the most festive times that were enjoyed by this group of artist friends.

Cézanne, who was mindful of the powerful symbolic importance of painting, was nevertheless won over to *plein air*. Around October 19, 1866 in Aix, he confided to Zola: "I see some superb things and I shall have to make up my mind only to work out of doors."[11] However he had doubts: "I tell you again, I am somewhat in the doldrums, though for no reason." Zola was no less delighted to hear that he was trying to do "large works, canvases measuring four to five meters." "I have great hopes for him."[12] Each winter Paul's absence weighed heavily on him, even though he received news about him from Antoine Guillemet. In December 1866: "I wait for him like a savior... Especially as he brings me all his studies to prove to me that I have to work."[13]

His wish was granted. Between 1867 and 1870 Cézanne used him as a subject on at least three occasions: in the picture of the black clock (cat. 54), the one sitting on Zola's fireplace; in *Paul Alexis reading to Émile Zola* (cat. 14); and in *Paul Alexis reading at Zola's house* (cat. 15). On May 31, 1870 he was one of the witnesses at the marriage of Zola and Alexandrine, with three others from Aix: Paul Alexis, who had arrived in Paris a year earlier, Philippe Solari, and Marius Roux, the former a sculptor and the latter a journalist, two of Zola's childhood friends.

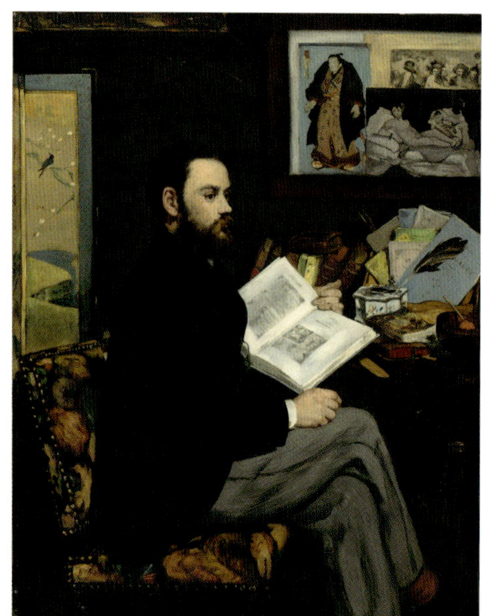

Fig. 11
Édouard Manet (1832-1883)
Émile Zola
1868
Oil on canvas
Musée d'Orsay, Paris

Cézanne's independent nature, irritable even, eventually resulted in him distancing himself from the group around Café Guerbois and Manet, whose effortless, middle-class Parisian elegance made him frown. In spite of a mutual passion for a creative process, gradually a gulf emerged between Paul and Émile too. Differences in character, work schedules, and recognition, then, might have put a strain on their artistic relationship. But the depth and strength of an ongoing bond forged in adolescence remained unshakable.

In solidarity (1871–1880)

The Franco-Prussian War did not immediately drive a wedge between the novelist of *The Fortune of the Rougons* and the painter of *A Modern Olympia* (cat. 48). On September 7, 1870, on the eve of Paris being besieged by the Prussian army, Zola took the train to Marseille. He settled in L'Estaque, a nearby village where he met up with Cézanne. But then in December he left Marseille for Bordeaux, where he became secretary to a member of the government, and then parliamentary correspondent for *La Cloche* and the *Sémaphore de Marseille*, before returning to Paris in March 1871, four days before the Commune. As for Cézanne, he withdrew from Aix with his girlfriend Hortense Fiquet, hiding her existence from his father. For four months Zola searched in vain for any trace of him, until suddenly, at the end of June 1871, he finally received a sign of life. He immediately wrote him a long letter, filled with confidence in their future work: "As I have often told you, our reign has begun... We can begin the battle again."[14]

For Zola, the battle he heralded would be vigorous, methodical, and soon victorious. Cézanne had reason to be less optimistic. The Aix group infuriated him. When he went back to Paris at the end of summer 1871, he grew impatient: He did not enjoy the café gatherings in the Guerbois

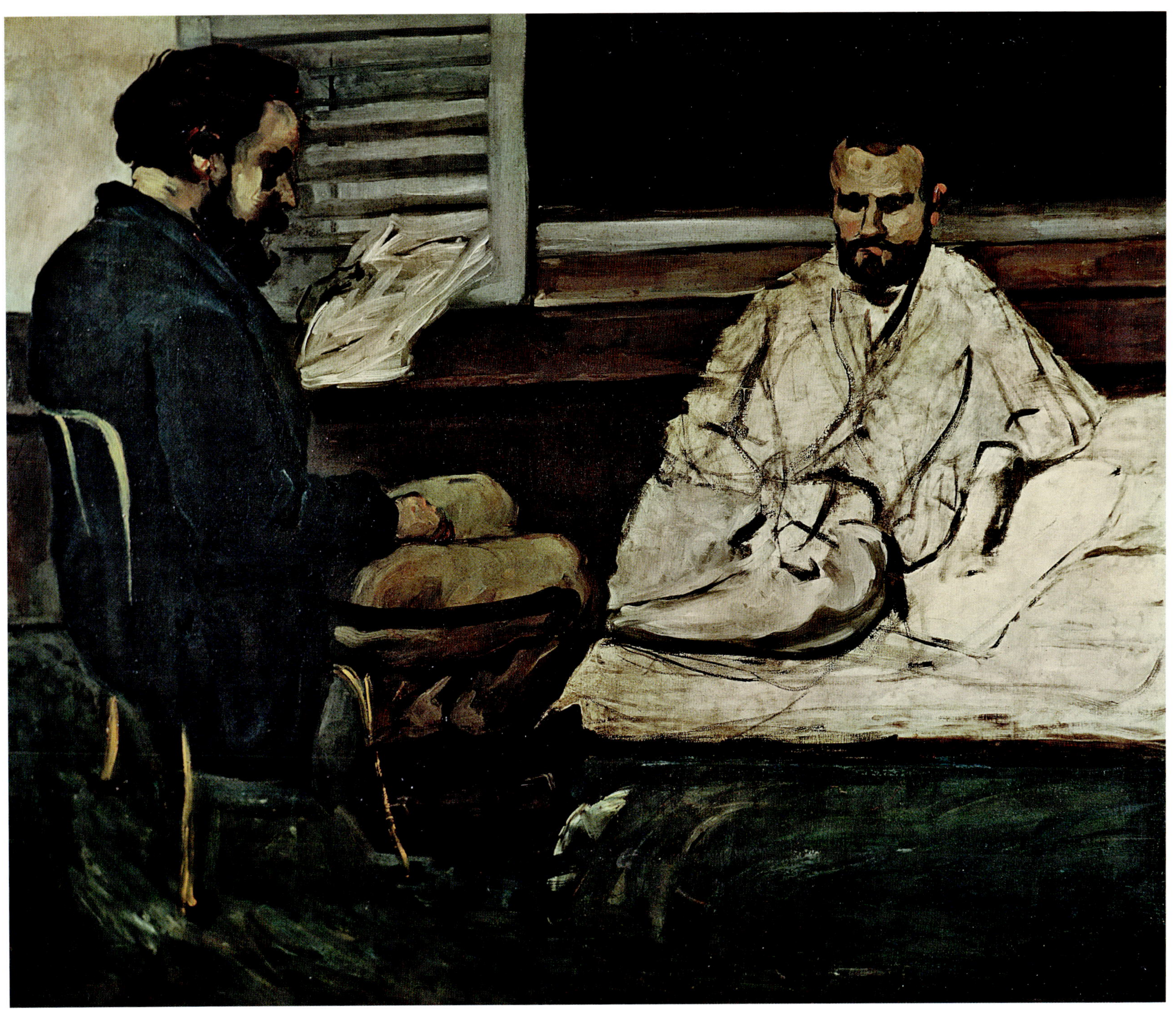

Cat. 15
Paul Alexis Reading to Émile Zola
1869–70
Oil on canvas
130 x 160 cm
MASP, Museu de Arte de São Paulo Assis
Chateaubriand, São Paulo
R 151

and then the Nouvelle-Athènes and he knew that some of his canvases with their madness of subject, form, and color ruffled the feathers of even the young future Impressionists. His confidence in Zola, whose combative energy reassured him, remained undiminished. In summer 1872, he met up with Pissarro, his closest friend among the painters, at Pontoise: he stayed there in the Hôtel du Grand Cerf, owned by Édouard Beliard, who was himself a painter and good friend of Zola, Pissarro, Guillemet, Renoir, and Sisley. Zola caught up with him there two or three times during the summer of 1872 before leaving for Auvers-sur-Oise to stay with Doctor Gachet, where he remained until 1874. Each time when Cézanne went back to Paris to take a few canvases to Tanguy, a paint merchant, he met Zola there, who was steadily producing, year after year in succession, the *Rougon-Macquart* volumes: *La Curée*, *Le Ventre de Paris*, *La Conquête de Plassans*, and very soon *La Faute de l'abbé Mouret* and *L'Assommoir*.

Zola was no longer in a position to follow his friend's work, far away from Paris as he was. At the height of the "moral order" period, his imprudent political judgments had deprived him of a regular newspaper column in Paris.[15] Notwithstanding, he was always ready to lend his support. He knew the secrets of Cézanne's private life, and kept them to himself. They were both involved in preparing for the first "Impressionist" exhibition which opened in Paris on April 15, 1874, and to which Zola made reference on April 18 in *Le Sémaphore de Marseille*. In it, Cézanne exhibited *The House of the Hanged Man* (cat. 74), *A Modern Olympia* and a *Landscape at Auvers*. In his article, Zola praised his friends from the Batignolles and Pontoise groups, especially Cézanne: "Among the canvases that struck me I would like to make particular mention of a most remarkable landscape by M. Paul Cézanne... Paul Cézanne, who has struggled for a long time, has the true temperament of a great painter."

The years passed. Cézanne alternated between stays in Paris and the Midi. The letters from Émile to Paul after 1871 have been lost,[16] but the ones from Cézanne were carefully preserved by Zola (contrary to a claim made by Ambroise Vollard).[17] The exchange of correspondence never stopped.

Cézanne's submissions to the Salon were rejected on a regular basis. He did not take part in the Second Impressionist Exhibition, though he presented 16 works at the third in 1877. Zola's review of it in the *Sémaphore de Marseille* on April 19, 1877 praises the main exhibitors perfunctorily—Monet, Renoir, Berthe Morisot, Degas, Pissarro, Sisley, Caillebotte—but to Cézanne, he devotes a whole paragraph: "...M. Paul Cézanne [who] is certainly the greatest colorist of the group. There are in the exhibition some Provençal landscapes of his that have a splendid character. The canvases of this painter, so strong and so deeply felt, may cause the bourgeois to smile, but they nevertheless contain the makings of a great artist."

Cézanne stayed in Paris from May to October 1877. His mother and Zola were the only ones who knew about his relationship with Hortense and the birth of their son Paul in 1872. In August, Zola passed on a message to Mme Cézanne: she was to look for an apartment in Marseille for Paul and Hortense. The plan was abandoned, but picked up again in spring 1878. Then, however, Louis Cézanne found out about this clandestine arrangement and threatened to withdraw his son's allowance. Cornered, Paul once again turned to Émile for help: Could he perhaps find him some kind of job or other? Louis Cézanne calmed down, and his modest support (two hundred francs a month) began to flow in again. As for Zola, he came to Hortense's aid by sending her sixty francs each month. The relations between the two men were most certainly those of two close friends—in fact they were like brothers. In April 1878, Cézanne complimented Zola on *Une page d'amour*, showing a keen understanding of the theme of passion and the composition. And when the Zolas bought their future country house in Médan in June that year, Cézanne saw it quite simply as the opportunity to relive the experiences of Bennecourt and Auvers. He invited himself casually: "With your consent, I'd like to take advantage of you to get to know the area better; and if life proves possible for me either in La Roche or in Bennecourt, or wherever, I would try to spend a year or two there, like I did in Auvers."[18] This was all from a distance, for Cézanne remained in Aix for a whole year, from March 1878 until February 1879. In February 1879 he congratulated Zola on the theatrical success of *L'Assommoir*. Once back in the Paris region, he lived in Melun and then Paris itself until the end of 1880. In February 1880 there were fresh compliments, this time for *Nana*: "A magnificent volume. This volume adds to the literary collection you have given me, and I intend to enjoy it, filling my winter evenings for a while."[19]

Their contact seems to have become as frequent as it had been during the years before the war. Cézanne continued to confide in Zola about his difficulty in earning a living and his complex relationship with his father, who was thinking of "setting him free." "There is only one good way of doing that, which is to give me 2000 or 3000 francs more each year, and not to wait until after I am dead to make me his heir, as I shall go before him for sure."[20] Every year their mutual friend Guillemet, a member of the Salon jury, recommended Paul's entries on Zola's entreaties, but he managed to get a canvas accepted only in 1882. For his part Cézanne had some of his painter friends read Zola's enraged article on "The Republic and literature,"[21] which denounced the scorn and disdain in which politicians held writers and artists. In June 1879 he spent 12 days in the house at Médan, where he worked on a few canvases. He refrained from taking part in the Impressionist exhibitions in 1879 and 1880, though he did go to see the latter. He invited himself to dine with the Zolas in the company of Paul Alexis, one of his few wholehearted admirers.

"Difficulties" and "services" (1880–1885)

On May 10, 1880 Cézanne asked Zola to write "a few words" in his column in *Le Voltaire* to support the protest by Renoir and Monet at the Salon's rules and the position that had been allocated to their paintings, as well as "demonstrating" the importance of the Impressionists. Instead of "a few words", Zola penned a long article in which he once again referred to Cézanne, who was not actually represented at the Salon: "M. Paul Cézanne has the temperament of a great painter who still struggles with problems of technique, and remains closer to Courbet than Delacroix."[22] He had heard Cézanne's views often enough to know that although he continued to use the terms "impression" and "Impressionist," he was searching for something other than the tranquil luminosity of gardens and women's faces. Cézanne thanked him, and immediately announced his intention of coming to work outdoors, *sur le motif,* at Médan.

In fact he went to stay in Médan in August 1880. Before leaving for Aix in October, he joined Zola in mourning, as he had just lost his mother. In March 1881 he received notification from Zola about a painting sale that was being organized for his musician friend Cabaner. He was once again mentioned in it, alongside Manet, Degas, and Pissarro and a few others. After moving to Pontoise in summer 1881 he contemplated a trip to Médan, but was prevented by "some minor difficulties."[23] The Zolas returned from their vacation in Granchamp on the Normandy coast on September 20; Cézanne spent the last week of October in Médan. They saw each other in Paris in spring 1882 and Cézanne ended up staying in Médan for a few more weeks in September that year. In November of the same year, he planned to entrust Zola with a copy of his will—which he did in May 1883, confirming yet again the special nature of their relationship.

He spent the years 1883 and 1884 alternating between Aix and L'Estaque. The exchange of letters continued. On November 27, 1884 Cézanne confided in Zola that he had reservations about the way painting was developing, no doubt including Impressionism: "The ignorance of harmony is being revealed more and more in the discordance of the coloring, and what is even worse, in the deadness of the tone." "But this should probably not affect you unduly."[24] He was mistaken. Zola was extremely busy with the progress of his *Rougon-Macquart* series, but he still paid attention to painting: The heirs of Manet, who died in 1883, turned to Zola to write the preface of the catalog for the posthumous exhibition of the painter's works.

1885 was the year of *Germinal*. In terms of warmth and mutual trust, it was a year just like any other. Cézanne stayed in Provence for the first five months. Then all of a sudden it became evident that his private life and moral balance were in crisis. Another woman had just come into his life. Once again it was Zola in whom he confided his love at first sight. The affair was secret, of course, but how was he to receive letters from his sweetheart? Who else to enlist but Zola, the long-term keeper of his secrets? He wrote to him hastily on May 14, showing just how much he trusted him: "You would receive some letters for me and forward them by mail to the address I shall send you later... I am either mad or very sensible! *Trahit sua quemque voluptas* [each is drawn by his own pleasure]. I am appealing to you and I implore your absolution."[25] Zola had seen other such things, and accepted this new role of postman without a fuss. Once back in Paris, Cézanne spent the evening of June 14 at the Zolas' house. He then left for La Roche-Guyon to stay with Auguste Renoir, leaving Zola a general delivery address to which he should forward his love letters. The whim was to be short-lived, but until the summer he lived through months of profound agitation under the very eyes of Zola.

He was restless in La Roche-Guyon, unable to work. It was all he could do to manage his indecision, his ever-present family, a lost love, debts to his art supplier... He could not stand it any longer, so he fled to Villennes on July 14, and then on to Vernon. He had "canvases to be painted" sent on to Médan. "Be good enough to take them in for me, and keep them in your house."[26] Still feverish, he then decided to go back to Aix as quickly as possible. "I shall go via Médan to shake your hand... I would have liked to go on with my painting, but I was in a state of very great perplexity."[27] He arrived at the Zola household on July 22. And in the last days of that month, Zola would be the silent witness to his torments. It is important not to talk of "pity" here, as some people have done, or worse, condescension or disdain, for instead Zola showed patience and discreet attention. Besides, what could he say about Cézanne's recent work, as his friend had not left Provence for over two years? Zola watched him leave toward the end of the month. Those last weeks had been the most confused and disjointed he had known in Cézanne's life. Would his old friend free himself from his demons? And more importantly, when would they see each other again?

1886: The end of the story?

There were two more letters from Paul on August 20 and 24, 1885: "As for me, the most complete isolation, the brothel in the town, or anything else, but nothing more. I pay, the word is ugly, but I need rest, and at this price I get it."[28] A letter came from Zola at the end of 1885, a miraculous survivor of the correspondence disaster post-1871, and still affectionate.[29] Then nothing again until Cézanne acknowledged receipt of *L'Œuvre* on April 4, 1886: "My dear Émile, I have just received *L'Œuvre* which you were good enough to send me. I thank the author of *Les Rougon-Macquart* for this kind token of remembrance and ask him to permit me to clasp his hand while thinking of bygone years. Ever yours, under the impulse of past times."[30]

Then followed a deafening silence, which is more difficult to explain than by the simplistic and malicious assertions (regarding Zola) that some commentaries have made about it.[31]

Was an unwelcome novel really all that it took? It has often been said that Cézanne saw himself in Claude Lantier, the dissatisfied, unrecognized, and suicidal painter in *L'Œuvre*, causing him suffering and resentment to the point of breaking off relations with Zola. Yet it requires a leap of imagination, or a skewed reading, to interpret this letter as a split. "My dear Émile", "Ever yours", and the memory of "bygone years" are not new turns of phrase for him. Cézanne had finished his letter of April 1, 1880 with an equally effusive reminder: "I am, gratefully, your old school friend from 1854." Besides, the novel went on sale on March 28, at the earliest, and so it is unlikely that Cézanne had read it in its entirety before April 4; his letter is not noticeably different from previous thank-you letters.

But the fact remains that he did not write or visit any more. There can be no one-sided explanation for this. One can concede that once he had read the whole book, he may have been hurt by the character of a cursed painter who takes a number of physical, psychological, and even biographical traits from him. But he recalled the history of the "Impressionist" group well enough to be able to identify other models, starting with Manet and Monet. Unlike Claude Lantier, whose sweeping landscapes of the Seine and female figures with the "floral sex of a mystical rose" were alien to his own art, Cézanne accumulated paintings, drawings, studies of motifs and composition, and continually progressed in spite of his personal crises; he was admired henceforth by his extremely talented colleagues and by various collectors. And he was too intelligent to confuse a fictitious career with a real one.

It is possible that some malicious voices made themselves heard around him—close friends, other painters, dealers (like Vollard somewhat later), exploiting his moral crisis and his easily-led nature, and giving him the most simplistic interpretation of *L'Œuvre*. Or it could also have been the result of his changed family and social situation—his marriage to Hortense on April 28, 1886 and his father's death on October 23, which suddenly made him a person of ample independent means—which meant he no longer needed Zola's occasional support, and thus he allowed the years to pass, isolated and withdrawn, thereby cooling his old friendships. His subsequent conversion to the Catholic faith and, even later still, his support for the anti-Dreyfusards certainly did not help matters.

Research into the genesis of *L'Œuvre* has shown that the novel is modeled on a fusion of several painters, and especially on the genealogical myth of the *Rougon-Macquart* series. In the fated Macquart branch of the tree are found the four human types carrying the most serious heredity and the most fascinating anthropological symbolism: the murderer, the whore, the priest, and *the artist*—Death and Sex, God and Art. It is this mythography that enshrouds *L'Œuvre*, more densely than is apparent, and is in any case far removed from the sophisms regarding the links between Cézanne and Lantier put forward by too many commentators.

To take it even further, in an article in *Le Figaro* on May 2 about the 1896 Salon, Zola would write one word too many, and it would cost him dearly: "I had grown up virtually in the same cradle as my friend, my brother, Paul Cézanne; one is only now beginning to discover the touches of genius in this abortive great painter." Certainly, "abortive" is a terrible word, but is it unforgivable? Does it negate the timbre of all the others, "my friend", "my brother", "genius", and "great painter"? At this point, let us plead extenuating circumstances in pointing out that Zola had not been familiar with any of Cézanne's work for ten years, and that his friend's furious growls of dissatisfaction were still ringing in his ears. According to Joachim Gasquet after a visit to Médan, it was not long before he revised his judgment,: "I am beginning to have a better understanding of his painting, which has always been to my taste, but which eluded me for a long time, for I thought it annoying, whereas it has unbelievable sincerity and truth."[32] (fig. 12).

Cézanne, for his part, expressed contradictory sentiments. In his *Memories of Paul Cézanne*,[33] Émile Bernard has him lying, attributing to him a comment that is clearly at odds with the chronology and the spirit of the meetings before 1886, and according to which there were many years in which he did not seek out Zola, well before *L'Œuvre*. Cézanne, by contrast, told Joachim Gasquet: "The pure blue smell of pines, which is bitter in the sun, has to marry the green smell of the meadows which freshen there each morning, with the smell of stones, the perfume of Sainte-Victoire's distant marble. I did not render it. It must be rendered. And in colors, without literature. As do Baudelaire and Zola, who through the simple juxtaposition of words mysteriously fill a whole poem or phrase with fragrance."[34]

And as fate would have it, it was left to him to make the final gestures. On September 29 or 30, 1902, on learning of Zola's brutal murder, he burst out sobbing and shut himself in his studio for the entire day, alone with his memories. On May 27, 1906 he went to the Méjanes library where he inaugurated a bust of Zola. When Numa Coste, a mutual friend, recalled the old dreams of the two brothers-in-arms, he burst into tears again. He in turn was to die a few months later.

In spite of the estrangement in 1886, the friendship between Zola and Cézanne is a fine story that has sadly been debased by badly informed or hostile standard texts. Some deficiencies are simply down to the approximate state of the biographical data compiled before 1960: Hence in his *Life of Cézanne*, Henri Perruchot dates the preparation for one of Cézanne's stays in Paris as February/March 1860; yet only a year later Zola would give Cézanne the benefit of his own years of experience of the artist's life. The repetition of these same false datings, long after being clarified by modern research, is less excusable.

More serious have been the untruths spread about Zola's alleged lack of visual culture. According to Cézanne's first biographers, Zola is said to have lost interest in painting after his 1866 campaign in *L'Événement*: this means either being unaware of, or concealing, the articles that Zola devoted to painting each year from 1867 to 1881, the opinions found in which have been endorsed by posterity.

High flights of fantasy have been reached in works that clearly substitute psychoanalytic fictions for any intention of biographical research—they too have little regard for exact dates and scrupulous observation of the texts. The clichés are familiar, all based on the aforementioned sleight of hand by which "Lantier is Cézanne." This makes things straightforward. Zola and Cézanne were two brothers who shared the same geography, studies, creative passion, iconoclastic battles, innovation, and public fascination. If the novelist kills Lantier, it is because metaphorically, no longer having a father to kill, he ends the life of his brother—a "hated" brother, of course. In order to conquer his own anxiety, the psychoanalyst thus compounds his garbage. After the Oedipus complex, the myth of Cain and Abel...

This kind of palimpsest is a mind game, though the shared history of Cézanne and Zola has always been cluttered with such analogies. The truth is that Zola and Cézanne were both dramatic characters, precisely because of their genius. The drama that suddenly occurred in the middle of their careers—no doubt fueled by Cézanne's circle and then conveniently distorted in subsequent commentaries—was quite simply ingrained in the difference between their respective characters, dreams about art, and brilliance. It has an even more inevitable logic when it involves two men subjected to the tremendous pressures of the creative process. At a certain point the dialog stopped, and the connection between Paris and Aix broke off, as if by a natural life process. Who can be sure that the essential part did not survive until the end, mute, tucked away, but intact

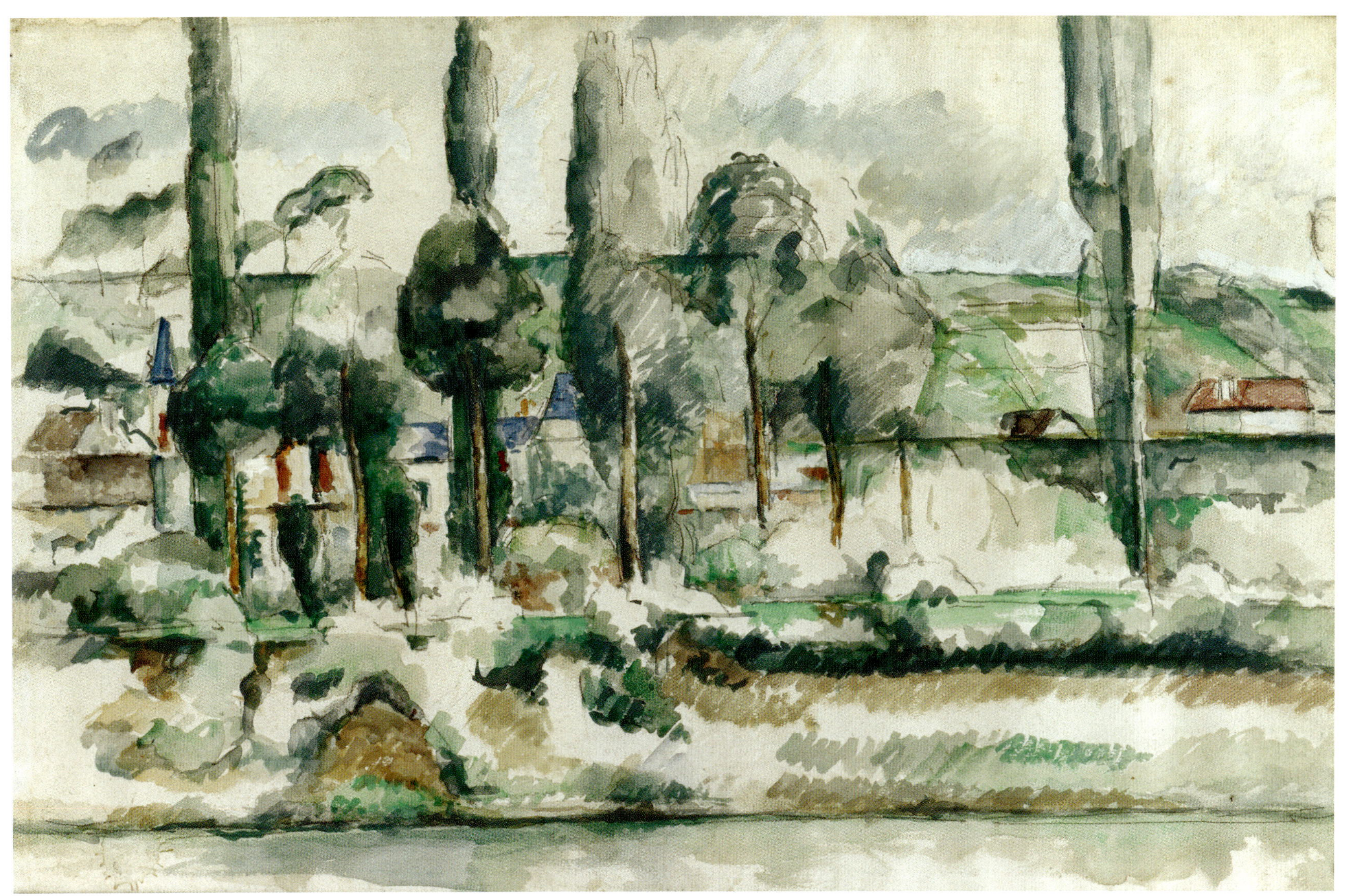

in their similar quest and shared memories?[35] The strange thing is that, while staying in Paris a few years after that (fateful) date of 1886, Cézanne set off to paint on the banks of the Marne River, above Charenton, around the place where Zola had taken him thirty years earlier, at the time of their very first jaunts into the suburbs. Denis Coutagne has clearly identified the location for the two canvases that have survived. And around the same time, the last in the *Rougon-Macquart* series, *Le Docteur Pascal*, was taking Zola back to the sunburnt landscapes of his childhood. A double, simultaneous quest of memory and nostalgia: one of André Breton's "objective chances"—the sign, surely, that the old brotherly flame had not been extinguished?

Fig. 12
Médan, Castle and Village
1887–80
Pencil, watercolor and gouache
31.3 x 47.5 cm
Private collection
RWC 89

Mary Tompkins Lewis

CĒZANNE'S EARLY YEARS IN PARIS

When Cézanne finally arrived in Paris in April 1861, he quickly discovered that the venerable capital city had been transformed by Napoléon III and his prefect, Baron Haussman, into a glistening modern metropolis. Even the florid descriptions that had peppered Émile Zola's letters urging him to move to Paris did not prepare the provincial painter for its radiant urban spectacle, which boasted broad new boulevards, splendid vistas and public gardens, magnificent monuments, and sleek, streamlined architecture. As Zola would recount in his later historical novels, however, Paris's sumptuous facade and vibrant cosmopolitan culture masked the city's fragile social and political fabric, one that would unravel and ultimately implode in 1870 with the outbreak of the Franco-Prussian War and the ensuing debacle of the Paris Commune. Many young French painters in the 1860s captured Paris's breathtaking prospects and furious pulse in expansive urban landscapes bustling with its prosperous inhabitants, while others echoed the city's ineffable aura of transience and change in strikingly modern subjects lifted from its streets, brothels, and cafes, or in more pictorial terms with increasingly fugitive, painterly effects. In contrast, and at first glance, Cézanne seems to have barely scratched the surface of all that Second Empire Paris offered a vanguard artist as both subject and formal template. And yet, the paintings and drawings that date from his first decade in Paris, which are fraught with conflict and paradox and already restive with the painter's ambition, offer a telling mirror of the city and, like it, were poised between competing visions of a monumental past and a volatile modernity. Inseparable from the whole of his art, they also set forth the major tenets of Cézanne's career.

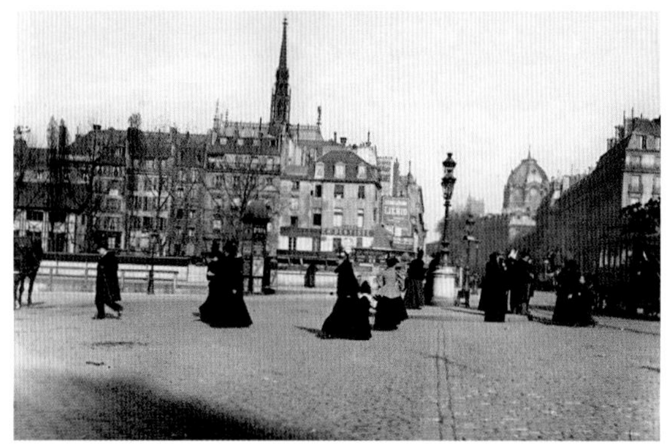

Fig. 13
Desoye
The Pont Saint-Michel and the Quai des Orfèvres
Postcard
c. 1900
The Académie Suisse is situated in the center of the photograph
Private collection

The Académie Suisse

Almost immediately and with Zola's enthusiastic encouragement, Cézanne began to study at the Académie Suisse, an informal drawing studio at 4 quai des Orfèvres (fig. 13); here, for a nominal fee, artists could draw and paint from a live model.[1] As a rule, male models were available for three weeks of each month and female models were hired for one. Though it offered no formal instruction or examinations, the academy had long provided young painters with cheap access to atelier nudes, a shared studio environment (which Cézanne may have sketched from the vantage point of his own easel, fig. 14), and much-needed camaraderie.

Founded decades before by Charles Suisse, who, allegedly, had once served as a model for the painter Jacques-Louis David, the academy attracted countless major artists in their early careers. Eugène Delacroix befriended the painter Paul Huet there in 1822[2], and years later, Delacroix's pupil, Pierre Andrieu, remembered the artist saying that Suisse had posed for several of the figures in his early painting of the *Barque of Dante*.[3] A young Honoré Daumier met the painter Philippe-Auguste Jeanron

Cat. 16
The Negro Scipio
c. 1867
Oil on canvas
107 × 83 cm
MASP, Museu de Arte de São Paulo Assis Chateaubriand, São Paulo
R 120

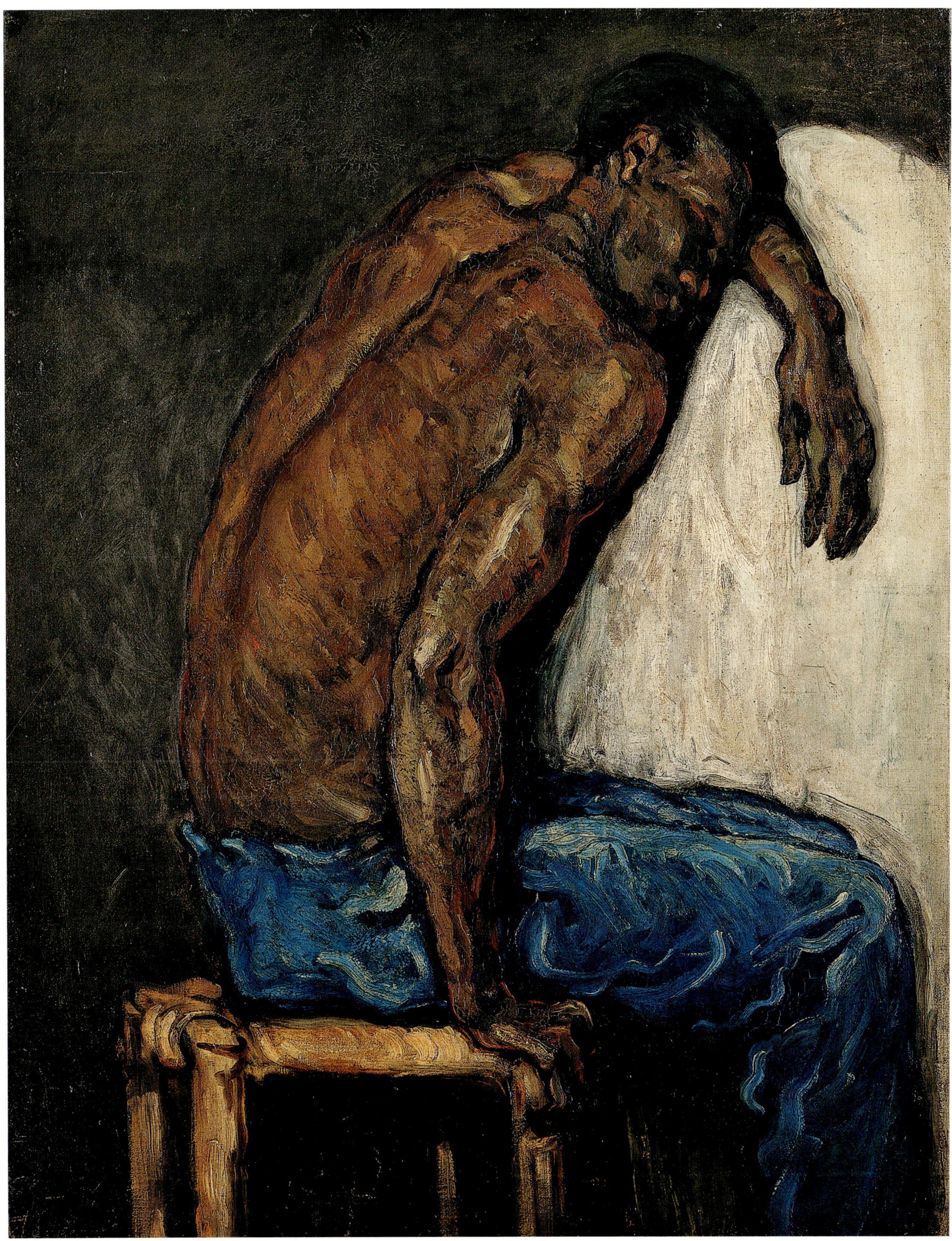

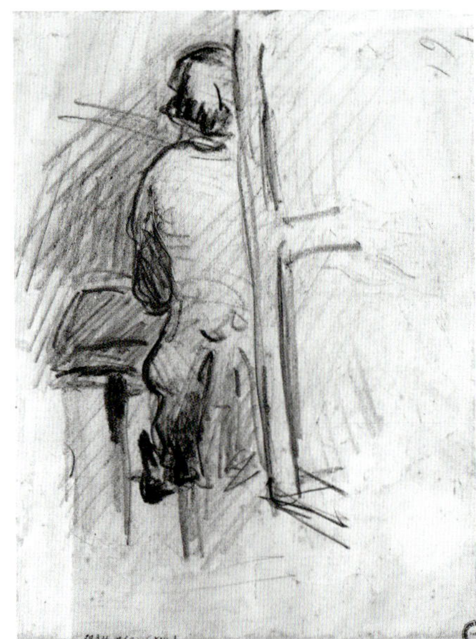

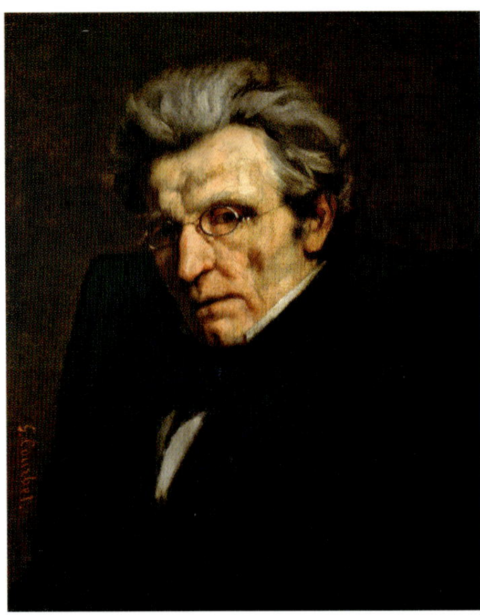

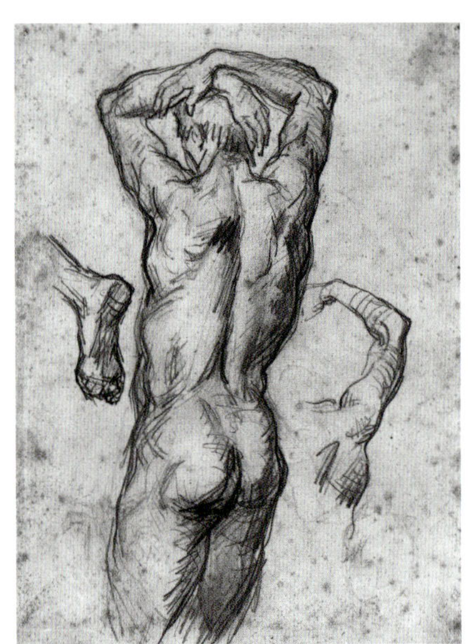

and Auguste Préault, a sculptor, at the Académie Suisse in the late 1820s.[4] Arriving in Paris from Ornans in 1839, Gustave Courbet was a regular at the academy within a year; a drawing of a nude, inscribed with a date of 1849, has led some scholars to suggest that he was still there at the end of the decade.[5] Courbet also painted its founder, the venerable *père* Suisse, as he was known, in a portrait dated to 1861 (fig. 15). Carolus-Duran met Henri de Fantin-Latour there in 1859,[6] and Edouard Manet too may have come by to draw from the nude in this period, when he was still a student of Thomas Couture.[7] In addition, in the early 1860s, the Académie Suisse was frequented by a group of young landscapists who went there to study the figure: Camille Pissarro enrolled as early as 1857,[8] Claude Monet arrived in the first few months of 1860,[9] the Puerto-Rican born Francisco Oller registered in 1861 and met Antoine Guillemet and later, Armand Guillaumin.[10] Despite its perennial focus on life drawing, by the end of the decade and almost by chance, the Académie Suisse had become a breeding ground for later Impressionism.

While at the academy, Cézanne cultivated the blustering, provincial persona that would shape so many of his early interactions in Paris. He soon met Guillaumin and also Oller, who brought Pissarro around to see his drawings. Pissarro later reminisced about those early years: "I recall that at the Académie [Suisse] there were [pupils] who were remarkably skilled and drew with astonishing sureness; later, I saw these same artists... there was still the same skill, but nothing more."[11] But he did not include Cézanne in this unfortunate lot. In a letter of 1895, the older artist memorably described how even then the artist from the south of France stood apart from his fellow students. Sensing the promise behind Cézanne's protective facade, Pissarro remembered, with a certain amount of pride: "How clear-sighted I was in 1861 when I went with Oller to see the curious Provençal at the Académie Suisse, where Cézanne's academic figures were ridiculed by all the impotents of the school."[12]

The vigorous, unconventional draftsmanship and emotional power of many of Cézanne's life studies from the Académie Suisse throw into stark relief the prim and painfully correct figure drawing championed in these years by the official art world in Paris, and also those the artist himself produced under the drawing master Joseph Gibert in Aix (CH 78). Although he hoped and no doubt assured his father that his work at the Académie Suisse would smooth his entry into the prestigious École des Beaux Arts, Cézanne's unwillingness to compromise is evident on every sheet of figures he produced at the academy. The charcoal drawing of a *Male Nude* of c. 1862–64 (CH 80), for example, marked by brilliant tonal modeling, repeated contour lines that emphasize the rhythmic curves of the figure's profile, and a background of flickering shadows rendered with

Fig. 14
The Artist, his back turned
1864–65
Black crayon
22.9 × 17.7 cm
Kunstmuseum Basel,
Kupferstichkabinett, Basel
CH 91

Fig. 15
Gustave Courbet (1819–1877)
Monsieur Suisse
1861
Oil on canvas
The Metropolitan Museum of Art, New York,
H.O. Havemeyer Collection

Fig. 16
Nude Male Seen from the Back
1863–65
Pencil
23 × 17 cm
Picker Art Gallery, Colgate University,
Hamilton, New York
CH 103

dense cross-hatching exhibits the kind of bold pictorial conception found in so many of his Académie Suisse studies, where the figures are conveyed not in terms of line but of light, shade, and rich color contrasts. Similarly, his *Nude Male Seen from the Back* of c. 1864–65 (fig. 16), in which the figure assumes a standard studio pose, is rendered with an emphatic network of lines that are scratched, rubbed, and repeated to suggest the broad, sculpted torso and implicit power of his model, in addition to its sinuous contours. And Cézanne's muscular *Male Nude* of c. 1865 (cat. 17), which is sketched on the kind of dark brown paper Courbet preferred,[13] and is marked by heavy shading, cast shadows, and luminous tonal contrasts, may well have been the product of an unorthodox studio habit Cézanne practiced at the academy. As Monet later recalled, the Provençal painter often placed a black hat and white handkerchief next to the model to establish his tonal values.[14] Yet such drawings, and there are many others (cat. 18) from his studies on the quai des Orfèvres, are marked by more than Cézanne's assertive graphic style. In the libertine

Cat. 17
Male Nude
c. 1865
Charcoal
24.9 × 29.8 cm
Kunstmuseum Basel, Kupferstichkabinett, Basel
CH 104

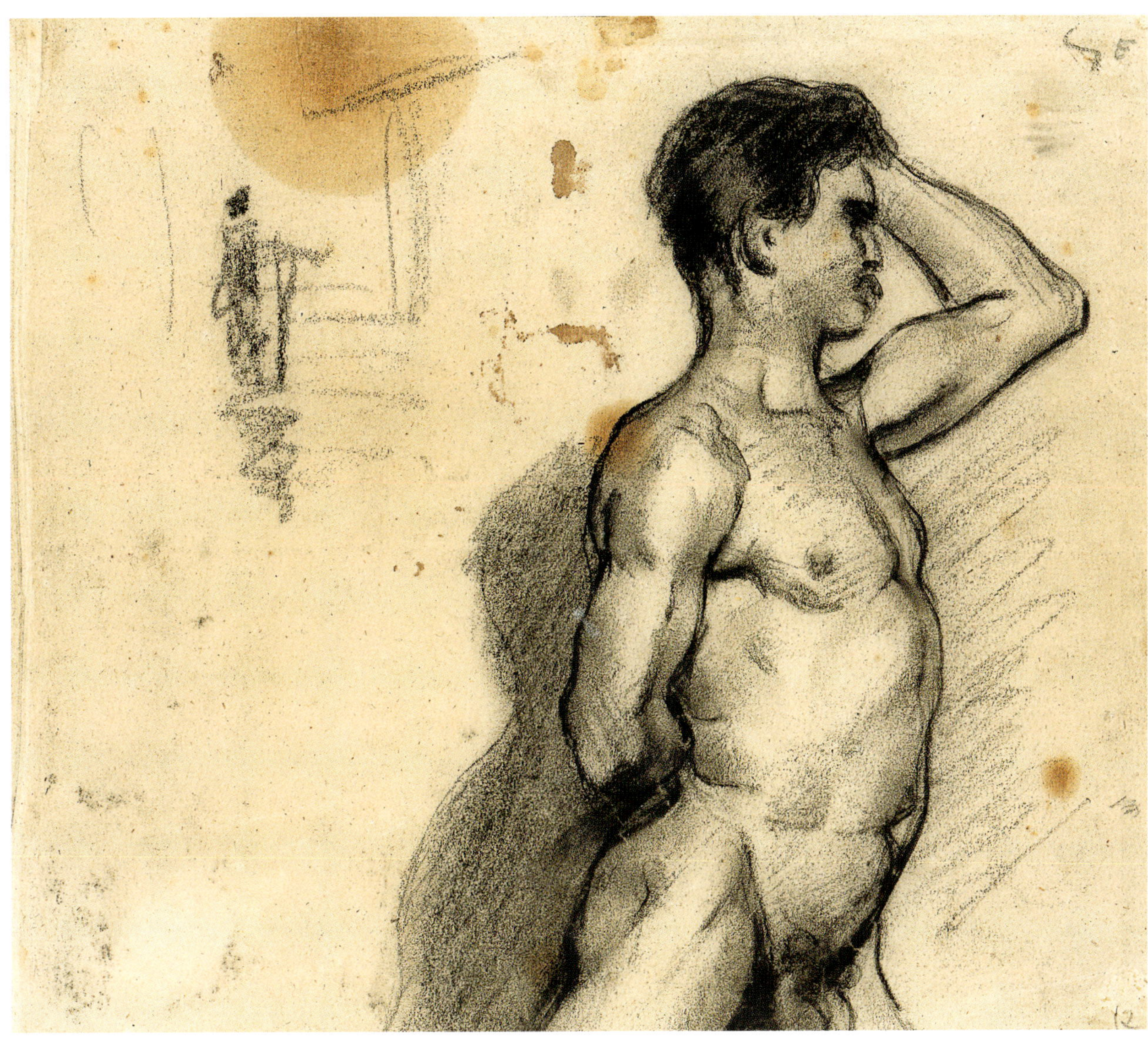

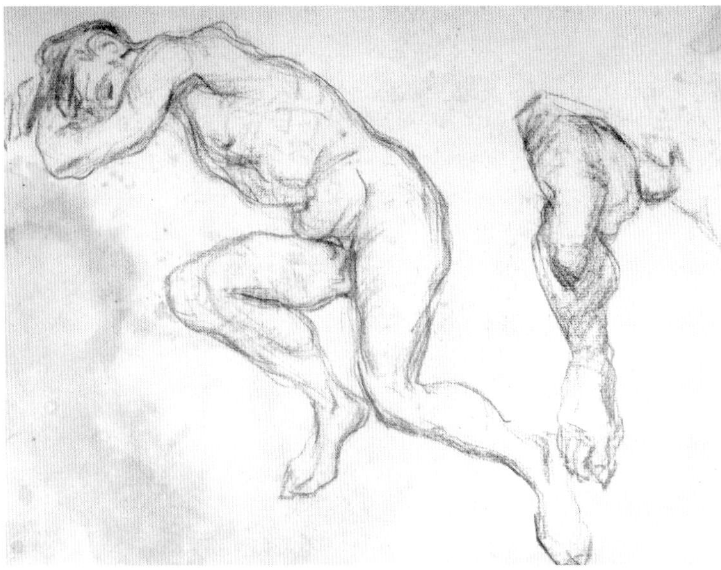

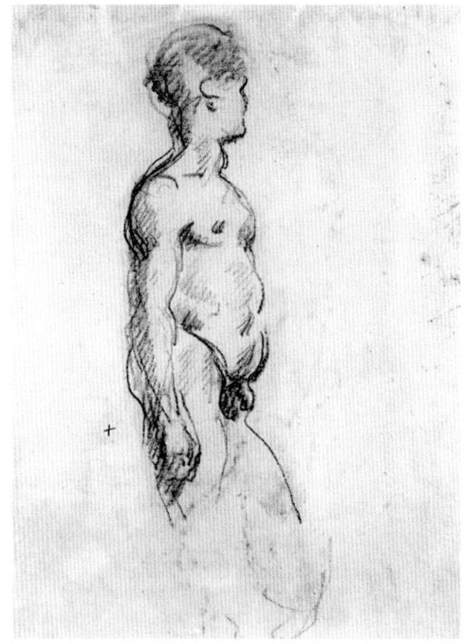

climate the Académie Suisse provided, he seemed to discover the potent emotional pull of the figure as both compelling form and impassioned subject—perhaps one reason why, as John Rewald and others have suggested, these early drawings from life seem to haunt Cézanne's later imaginary compositions and especially his paintings of bathers.

A handful of Cézanne's paintings produced in Paris in the 1860s can also be tied to his work at the *Académie Suisse*: a small painting once owned by Pissarro, *Women Dressing* (fig. 32) of c. 1867 corresponds to drawings Cézanne probably executed there and reiterates a common studio subject that captured female models in a state of partial undress.[15] Likewise, Cézanne's *The Autopsy* (fig. 17), which, as outlined below, draws on the early copies he made in the Musée du Louvre, was also informed by such academic life drawings as the charcoal and watercolor study now in Chicago of a seated male model in profile (fig. 18). The drawing includes, in the upper corner, a name and address, presumably those of the model. The acknowledged masterpiece of Cézanne's Académie Suisse oeuvre, however, is his monumental painting, *The Negro Scipio* (cat. 16), which Monet bought many years later from Ambroise Vollard and wich, according to the dealer, depicts a model who was a popular subject for Cézanne's fellow students.[16] Philippe Solari, a sculptor and friend of the painter's from Aix, depicted the same model in a plaster sculpture entitled *Negro asleep* that was accepted at the Salon of 1868 and may have originated in studio sessions the artists shared.[17] Only Cézanne's version, however, survives.

Though it was shaped in part by a series of sketches from life produced at the Académie Suisse, Cézanne's painting exhibits all of the emotional undertones of his early narrative canvases.[18] The highly finished and powerfully evocative figure of his Scipio is far more than an *étude* translated into oil—the shimmering, muscular form and arcing back which stretch almost the full height of the canvas, the sinuous curves of the subject's articulated arm and large, elegant hands, the squared profile of his legs and of the studio support below are all realized with short, swirling brushstrokes. The artist's choice of palette—shadowy bronze tones, blues and blacks softened by glints of light and thrust against a matte brown background or a cold triangle of white cloth (perhaps reflecting again the artist's unusual method of establishing tones that had so struck Monet)—as well as the painting's immense scale, add to its impressive pictorial power. Even more than in his boldly conceived life drawings, Cézanne defies here the convention of the academic male nude in a painting that derives its mute force not from props or hints of narrative but purely from the expressive potential it wrenches from the attenuated, mannered form, gleaming surface, and sable skin tones of his model. While many of his contemporaries in Paris, such as Manet, Frédéric Bazille, and Oller, employed African models in their studios and often depicted women in subservient positions (such as the background figure in Cézanne's *Women Dressing*, see fig. 32) as an exotic attendant in a staged genre setting, they rarely exploited their subjects to the same expressive effect

Cat. 18
Male Nude seen in profile and right leg of the same model
1864–67
Charcoal on laid paper
20 × 25.7 cm
Private collection
CH 208

Cat. 19
Naked Man seen in Profile
1867–70
Charcoal on laid paper
41.3 × 29.9 cm
Kunstmuseum Basel, Kupferstichkabinett, Basel
CH 112

or painted them alone and solely in terms of their corporeal demeanor. When looking at Cézanne's highly affecting *Scipio,* in fact, it is interesting to recall the overtly racist reading Zola ascribed to Solari's related *Negro asleep* in his review of the 1868 Salon, and to consider how the figure of a black model conveyed solely in formal terms could be construed in this era. After praising the sculptor's rejection of standard notions of "absolute beauty" for one that embraces "the living expression of nature [in] the individual expression of the human body," Zola interprets Solari's piece within the heated contexts of prevailing physiognomic and racial theories: "The head superb, small, flattened: the head of a human beast, stupid and mean. The body has a feline suppleness, forceful limbs, shapely, and powerful loins. There are wonderful passages in the back and arms. One feels that here is an exact rendering, for everything is logical in this figure which could be the personification of the Negro race—lazy and deceitful, obtuse and cruel—a race that we have transformed into beasts of burden."[19]

Zola's critical reading of Solari's sculpture betrays not only the prejudicial attitudes of the period but, as Hugh Honour has suggested, the typical fate of representations of black models when transferred from the context of an atelier or an artist's private studio—and, we might add, from the context of a narrative—to a public exhibition space filled with images of white figures and placed before a white viewing audience.[20] Cézanne's profoundly sympathetic painting, which Zola must have known as well, is all the more astounding in comparison.

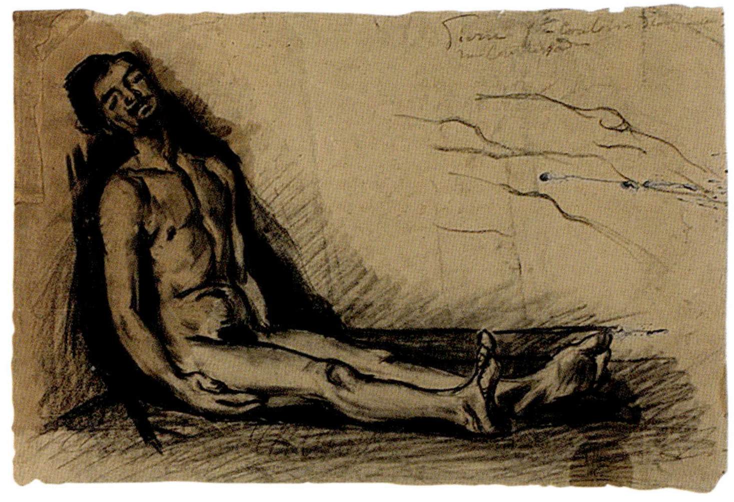

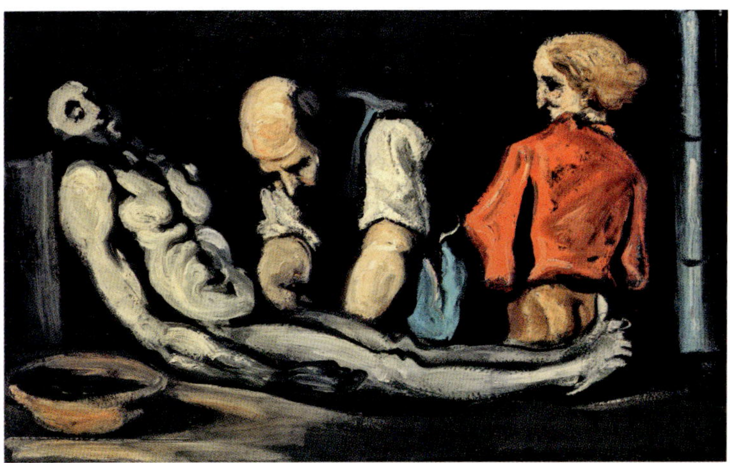

Fig. 17
The Autopsy
1869
Oil on canvas
49 × 80 cm
Private collection
R 142

Fig. 18
Male Nude
(study for ***The Autopsy***)
c. 1869
Charcoal on light-brown paper
32 × 48.7 cm
The Art Institute of Chicago, Chicago, gift of Tiffany and Margaret Blake
CH 110

Cézanne's life drawings and painting of Scipio may have found their way into other highly emotional canvases of this period: several scholars have linked the painting of Scipio to the swarthy male nude in *L'Enlèvement (The Abduction)* (fig. 35), which dates from 1867 and was also painted in Paris, and also to the female figure of *Mary Magdalene,* otherwise known as *La Douleur (Sorrow)* (R 146), which he painted later that decade on the walls of the salon at the Jas de Bouffan, his family's home in Aix. Both works share with his *Scipio* a dark, lugubrious strain, emotive figure and massive scale and, above all, announce the primacy of the figure in Cézanne's later paintings of bathers, where its compelling, expressive form would become his subject.

Cézanne's repeated efforts to gain admittance to the École des Beaux-Arts proved futile, and his stays in Paris throughout the 1860s were interrupted by frequent returns to his native Aix-en-Provence. In Paris, however, the Académie Suisse continued to serve as a source not only of models but also of the mutual support of his peers. Cézanne befriended a handful of young painters he met there, most of whom, like him, struggled for official recognition. Emboldened by the camaraderie and aura of collective defiance they shared, Cézanne joined a group of Académie Suisse students, including Pissarro and Guillaumin, who submitted paintings in 1863 to the controversial Salon des Refusés. A huge showing of works rejected that year by an usually harsh Salon jury, the exhibition was an attempt by the government, and especially Emperor Napoléon III, who was always wary of unrest, to appease the artists who had been dismissed and also to defend in a large public forum the jury's stringent selections. The canvases Cézanne presented at the Salon des Refusés can be neither numbered nor identified, and they seem to have been ignored by the countless critics who came, and even by Zola, who visited the exhibition with the artist during its brief run. But his paintings of the following few years evince a new power and conviction, and Cézanne himself assumed a bolder public posture befitting his art. In a characteristic letter to

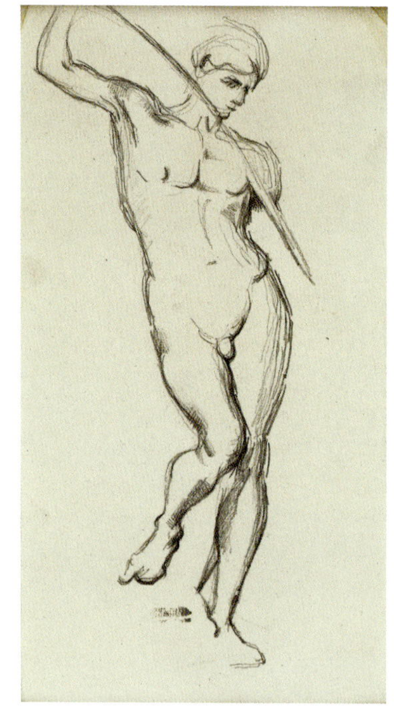

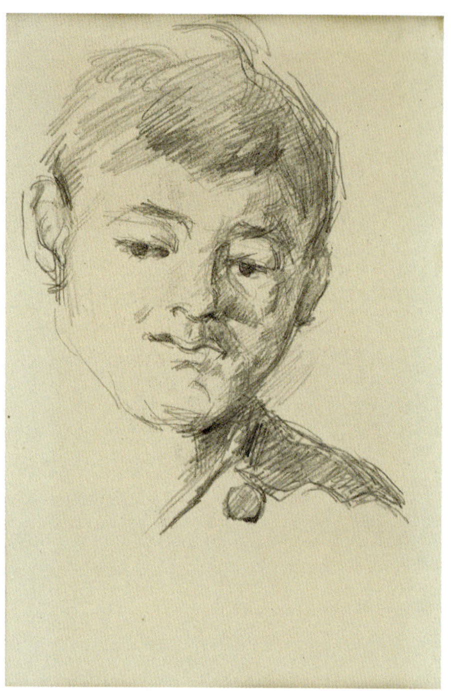

Cat. 20
David, after Mercié
1877–80
Pencil on paper, recto
21.5 × 12.4 cm
Petit Palais, Musée des Beaux-Arts de la Ville de Paris, Paris
CH 470

Cat. 20 bis
Portrait of Paul Cézanne Jr.
1877–80
Pencil on paper, verso
21.5 x 12.4 cm
Petit Palais, Musée des Beaux-Arts de la Ville de Paris, Paris
CH 851
Not on view

Pissarro of 1865, he promises that the paintings he will submit to the Salon will "make the Institute blush with rage and despair."[21]

And when Cézanne's *Portrait of a Man* (fig. 60), a painting of his friend Antony Valabrègue, was rejected the following year by the jury, he angrily exhorted the Superintendent of Fine Arts, Count Alfred-Émilien de Nieuwerkerke, to reestablish the Salon des Refusés.[22] Though Cézanne's efforts failed, his friends applauded his audacity and the brash work that so openly courted rejection. "Cézanne hopes to be refused at the exhibition [the Salon]," wrote his old Aix friend, Antoine-Fortuné Marion to his friend, the musician Heinrich Morstatt in March 1866, "and the painters of his acquaintance are preparing an ovation in his honor."[23] In 1867, when two-thirds of the three thousand artists who applied were again rejected by the Salon jury, a petition to reinstate the Refusés was circulated by a number of Cézanne's vanguard Parisian cohorts.[24] In the following decade, they would organize their own independent exhibitions and become known as the Impressionists.

Early Studies at the Musée du Luxembourg and the Louvre

For all of his outward displays of rebellion, Cézanne's motives in the 1860s were often ambivalent. In both Aix and Paris, he continued to study the figure and to discover the powerful pictorial language that would shape his later figural canvases. If his mornings and, at times, his evenings in the capital city were filled with life drawing sessions at "the Suisse," Cézanne's afternoons were often spent copying the art of the past, even the quite recent past, in museums. In November 1863 the artist registered as a copyist at the Louvre but the following month began working at the Musée du Luxembourg on a copy of Delacroix's *Barque of Dante*, the painting that had established the Romantic painter's preeminence at the outset of his own career.[25] Cézanne also made a drawing in this period after Delacroix's *Liberty Leading the People*, which, along with the painting of the *Barque of Dante*, hung in the Luxembourg until 1874.[26]

Cézanne's early studies at the Louvre, which ranged from copies of Renaissance and Baroque paintings and works on paper to drawings after 17th century sculptures by his fellow Provençal Pierre Puget (cat. 21, 22), were, however, far more numerous, and provided not only a substitute for the École des Beaux-Arts curriculum but a vast vocabulary of forms to supplement his own imaginative figures and those he borrowed from engravings or studied from life. His resultant pictorial vocabulary would be as well informed and incisive as it was, at times, defiant.

In April 1864 Cézanne again applied to copy at the Louvre and began to draw for the first time from Nicolas Poussin's *The Shepherds of Arcadia*.[27] He also sketched the figure of the water nymph (fig. 19) in Poussin's *Echo and Narcissus* and would incorporate it into his own dark fantasy of 1867, *L'Enlèvement* (fig. 35), which would assail the authority of traditional history painting even as it referenced one of its supreme masters. Likewise, several of the artist's early drawings after Veronese's massive *The Wedding Feast at Cana* in the Louvre would inform Cézanne's own more riotous banqueting scene entitled *The Orgy* (fig. 36). In one such study from the lower right corner of the massive Venetian canvas (cat. 23), Cézanne discovered in the large, tilting amphora held by an attendant the motif of the overturned vessel that would figure prominently in the foregrounds of the versions he painted on both paper and canvas. At the same time, his copies in the Louvre could share with his studies from life the hallmarks of his dynamic and increasingly authoritative graphic style. In the first of his many drawings after Peter Paul Rubens's *The Apotheosis of Henri IV and the Proclamation of the Regency of Marie de Médicis,* a large and exquisitely finished copy of c. 1864–65 (CH 102), for example, the robust tangle of curves that propel Rubens's leftmost figures upward are captured by Cézanne with the same kind of vigorous loops and dense cross-hatchings that animated some of his academic nudes (see fig. 16).

Toward the end of the decade, Cézanne painted his brooding canvas entitled *La Toilette funéraire (The Autopsy)* (see fig. 17). Although it may well reflect a morbid fascination with autopsies and morgues in contemporary Realist painting and literature,[28] it is even more a potent early synthesis of Cézanne's self-directed apprenticeship with the old masters, his studies from life, and his own figural imaginings. His somber subject may have been inspired by Titian's *Entombment* in the Louvre,[29] or an engraving of a Delacroix work showing Christ's entombment he knew and copied,[30] but Cézanne's dark painting, and especially the rigid figure of the corpse splayed across the shallow space of his canvas, was more closely informed by other versions of the subject that he studied from engravings and in the museum's collection, and then transformed into his own powerfully expressive motif. In his pencil drawing of c. 1866–69

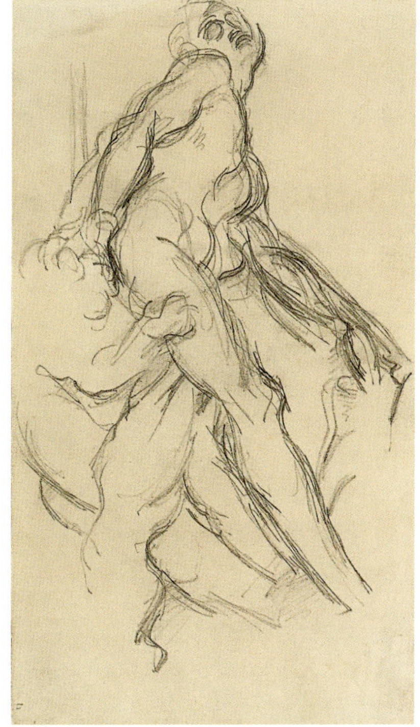

Cat. 22
Milo of Crotona
After Puget
1882–85
Pencil on paper
21.1 × 12.1 cm
Kunstmuseum Basel, Kupferstichkabinett, Basel
CH 506

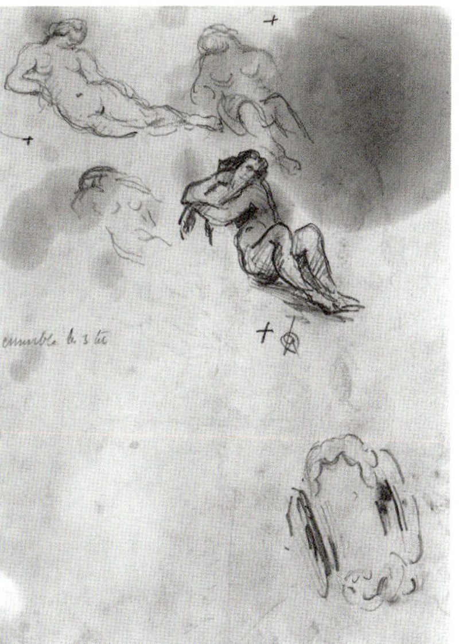

Fig. 19
Female Nudes
After Nicolas Poussin's
Echo and Narcissus
Decorated Vase
c. 1866–67
Pencil on thick paper
23.4 x 17.7 cm
Kunstmuseum Basel, Kupferstichkabinett, Basel
CH 199

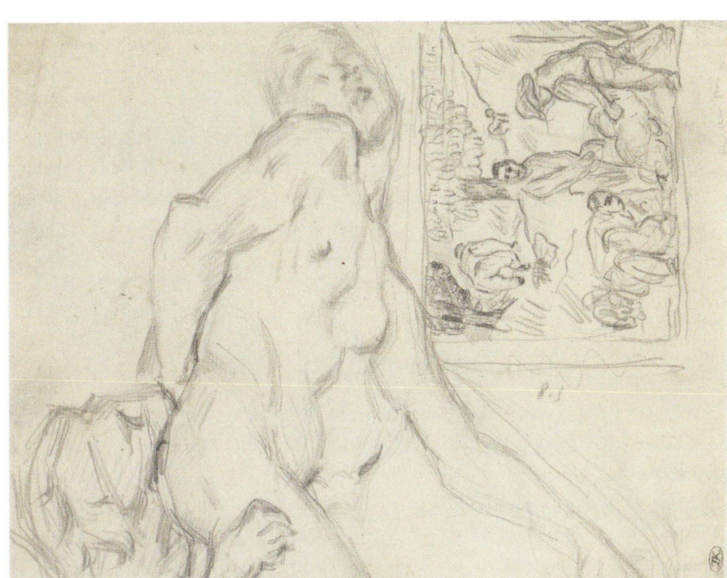

Cat. 21
Milo of Crotona
After Puget, with ***Genre scene, Three Men Lighting a Wood Fire***
1879–80
Pencil on laid paper, verso
23.8 × 31 cm
Museum Boijmans Van Beuningen, Rotterdam
CH 207

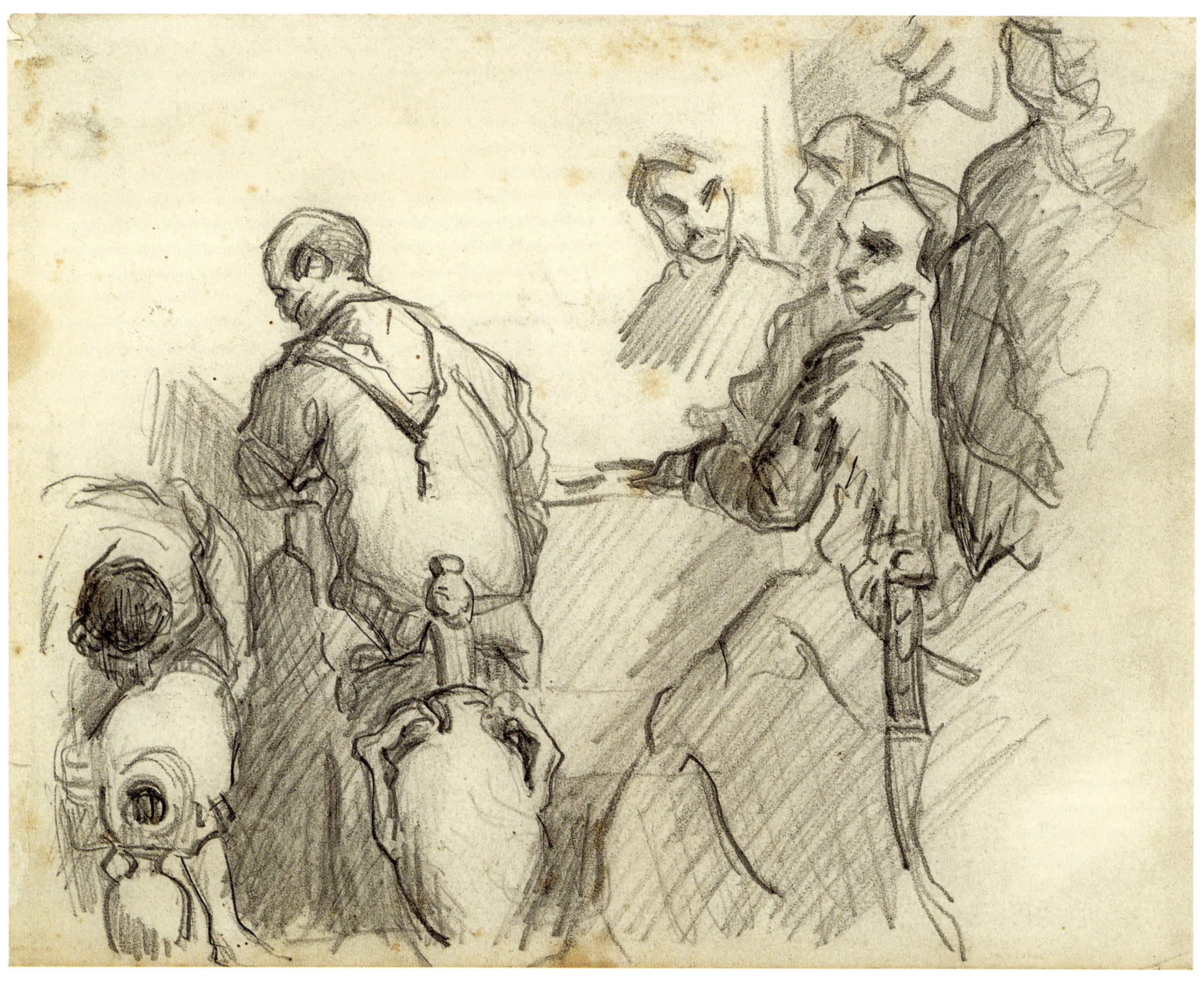

Cat. 23
The Wedding Feast at Cana
After Paul Veronese
1866–71
Black crayon
17.7 x 22.8 cm
Kunstmuseum Basel, Kupferstichkabinett, Basel
CH 168

(fig. 20) after Fra Bartolomeo della Porta's beautiful chalk rendering of *The Entombment of Christ* (fig. 21), the abruptly sketched face of Cézanne's figure, the angular arms, and the exaggerated tautness of the figure's legs transform its idealized Renaissance prototype into a brutal study of the effects of rigor mortis on the body. As numerous scholars have suggested, the Spanish master, Jusepe de Ribera, too, may have figured in Cézanne's sepulchral scene. As early as 1865 Cézanne was described by a friend as a "great admirer of Ribera and Zurbarán,"[31] and, in addition to engravings in the Spanish volume (which appeared in 1869) of Charles Blanc's *Histoire des peintres de toutes les écoles*, several *Entombment* paintings by Ribera were acquired by the Louvre in this decade and could not have failed to attract the artist. One version, installed to great acclaim at the beginning of 1869, shares with Cézanne's *La Toilette funéraire* a distinctive, patterned chiaroscuro and has been used

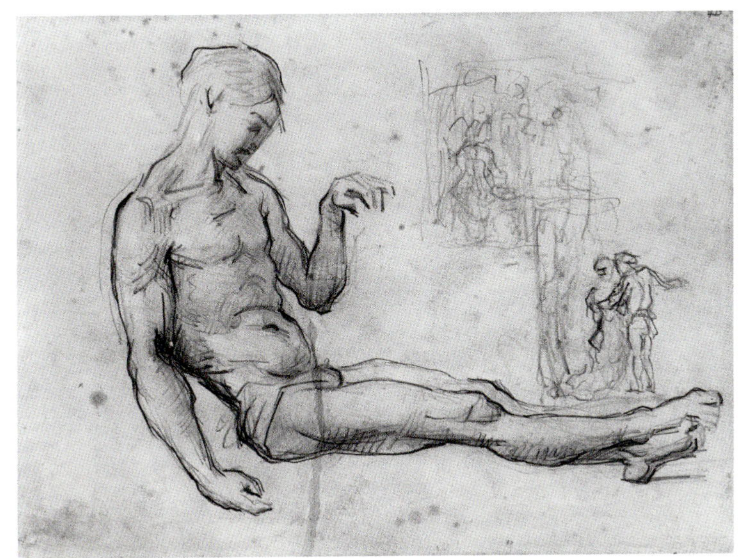

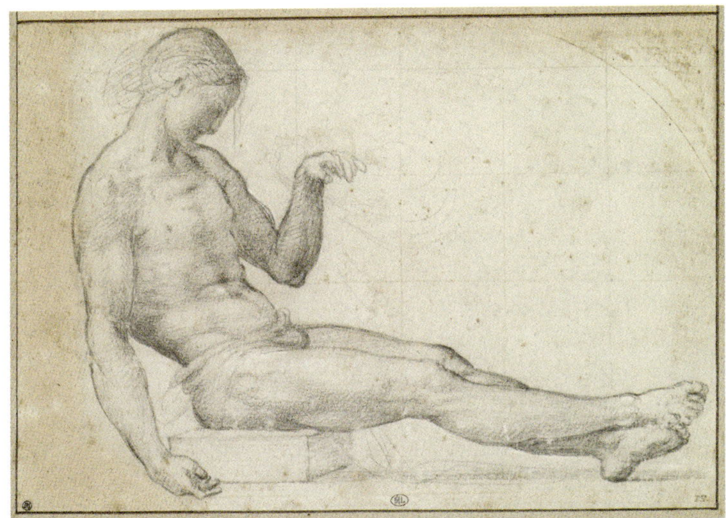

to argue the chronology of Cézanne's canvas to 1869 as well.[32] A second version of the motif, attributed in this period to Ribera but now given to Francesco di Maria (1623–1690), one of Ribera's followers in Naples, was acquired by the Louvre in 1853, and, especially in the disposition of the figure of the dead Christ, bears an even closer resemblance to Cézanne's motif. Other old master paintings in the Louvre, including Caravaggio's *Death of the Virgin*, or the flattened and starkly realist *The Dead Christ Lying on His Shroud* (fig. 22) by the 17th century French painter Philippe de Champaigne, may also have contributed to Cézanne's conception. His absorption of the past, however, rarely rendered his own work a paraphrase; it was marked, instead, and equally, as Lawrence Gowing has described, by "a sympathy with the subject" and "a resistance to the suavity of style" of his models.[33]

Though he would return to the hallowed galleries of the Louvre, after the tumultuous years of 1870–71, to copy Rembrandt's quintessential nude *Bathsheba at her Bath* (cat. 24, fig. 23), Cézanne continued to celebrate in all of his work the fiercely independent stance that, in the 1860s, was already at the core of his achievement.

Fig. 20
Study of Christ
After Fra Bartolomeo
1866–69
Pencil
17.7 x 24 cm
Kunstmuseum Basel, Kupferstichkabinett, Basel
CH 171

Fig. 21
Fra Bartolomeo (1472–1517)
Dead Christ seen in profile
Black chalk
Musée du Louvre, Paris

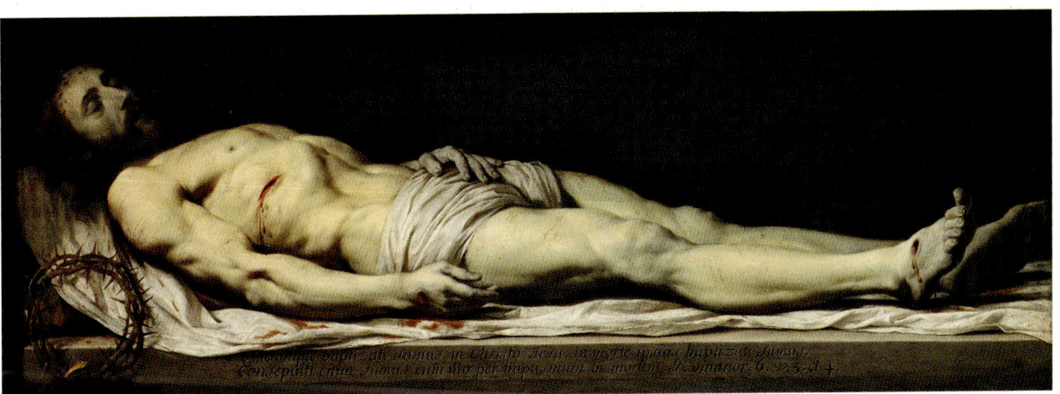

Fig. 22
Philippe de Champaigne (1602–1674)
The Dead Christ Lying on His Shroud
17th century
Oil on wood
Musée du Louvre, Paris

Bathsheba

Mary Tompkins Lewis

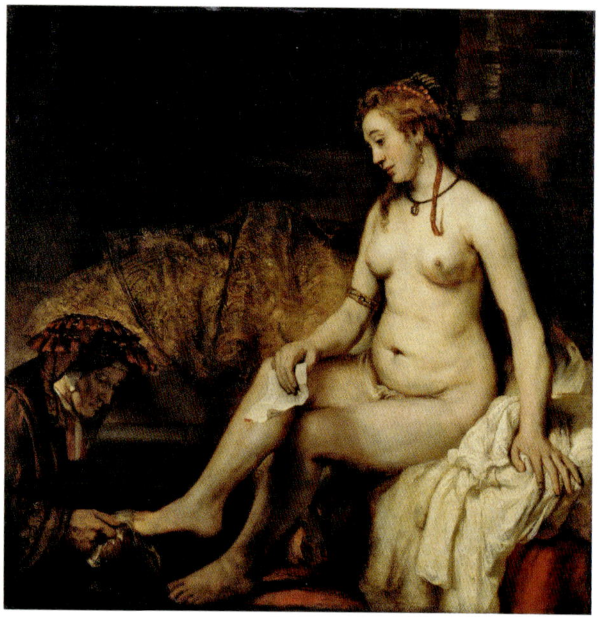

Cézanne's fascination with Rembrandt's *Bathsheba at her Bath* (fig. 23), as evidenced by his small and little known copy from the 1870s (cat. 24), puts him squarely at the center of the Dutch painter's revived critical fortunes in late 19th century France. Although his work was never out of favor or even out of view in post-revolutionary France, by the middle of the 1800s both Rembrandt and his work had achieved there a cult-like status. In her superb study of the Rembrandt revival in 19th century France, Alison McQueen has shown how the Dutch artist offered a welcome antidote to the classicizing legacy of Raphael and a model for 19th century painters who treasured his truthful rendering of observed nature and the expressive empathy of his subjects, and who, like him, sought success outside the boundaries of institutionalized artistic practice.[1] Equally, and fueled by an endless stream of popular biographies, monographs, anecdotal paintings, plays, and even a comic opera, Rembrandt became a paragon of the tormented romantic artist whose crude bluster and tragic, outsider fate were inscribed in his dark and plaintive paintings.[2] Even Rembrandt's technique was re-evaluated in this period in France in thoroughly contemporary terms. Although early 19th century exhibitions and critics encouraged appreciation of all of the painter's *oeuvre*, as the century wore on the sketch-like, unfinished, and impasto-laden technique of his late style or "rough manner", as it was called, resonant with the brash individualism and coarse mien Rembrandt's new biographers attributed to the artist, made the paintings of his final period prized above all others.[3] Thus, although it had been little known in the past, when Rembrandt's monumental late painting of *Bathsheba at her Bath* was presented to the Louvre in 1869 as part of the La Caze bequest, it embodied everything the painter had come to represent. Inscribed with the date of 1654 and exhibiting a tactile, paint-encrusted surface, a rich, dark golden tonality and soulful, contemplative figure, the canvas also became Rembrandt's most famous painting of a nude and central to the ongoing debate about the legacy of his naturalistic figures in 19th century paintings of unidealized bathers.

The cult-like stature Rembrandt enjoyed, in fact, did not insulate his work from critical reassessment, and his nudes remained particularly problematic. Several critics tried to defend the painter's revered Old Master stature by questioning the attribution of some of his more earthy erotic nudes.[4] Rembrandt's bathers in the La Caze collection—and especially his Bathsheba—came under particularly heavy fire, with one early 19th century critic complaining that they offered nothing but *une nudité grossière et informe*, a sentiment often reiterated later and captured in a series of caricatures published in *La Vie Parisienne* to mark their acquisition by the Louvre.[5]

However, for all that his Bathsheba may have riled later sensibilities, the central theme of Rembrandt's painting was the unrivalled beauty of the biblical nude. Knowing her husband was away at war, King David spied upon her as she bathed outdoors and then sent for her to join him. According to popular and visual traditions, the Old Testament patriarch made his request to Bathsheba in the form of a letter.[6] And in his painting, Rembrandt's wistful nude ponders the difficult decision required by the letter. In earlier

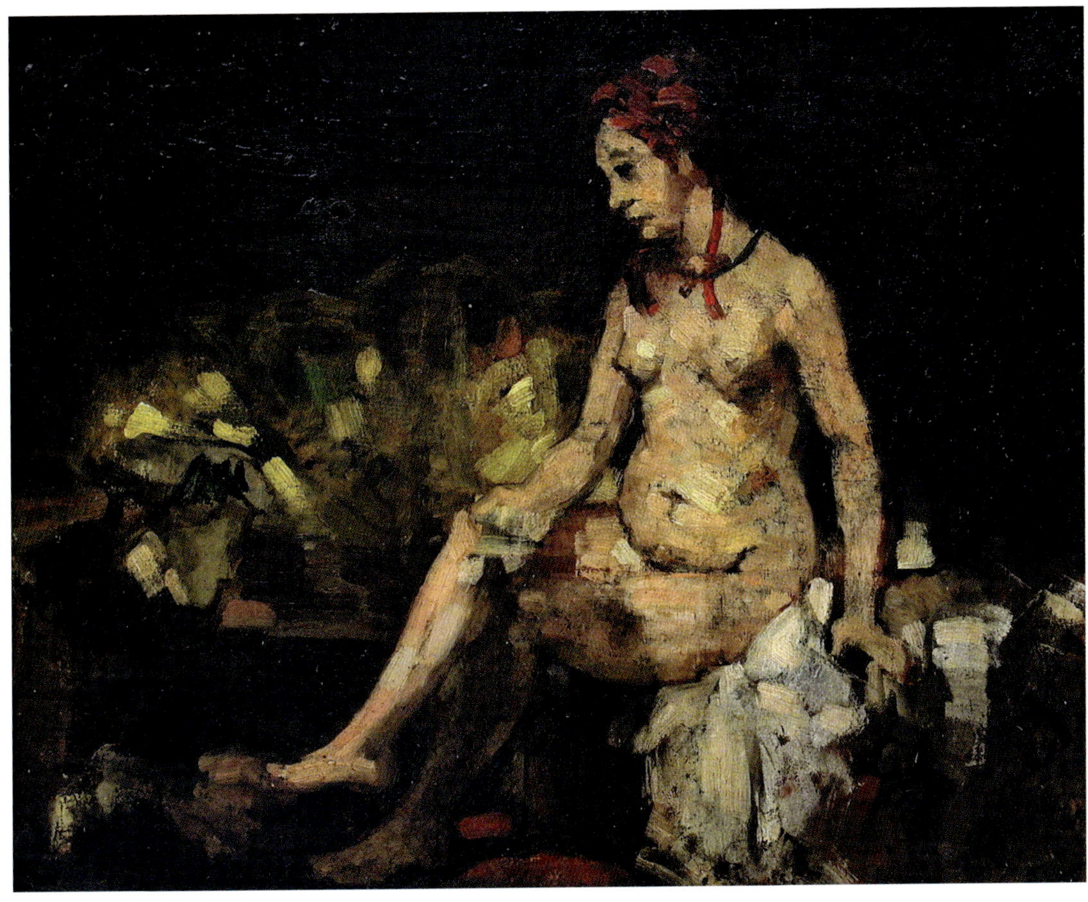

Fig. 23
Rembrandt Van Rijn (1606-1669)
Bathsheba at her Bath, Holding David's Letter
1654
Oil on canvas
142 x 142 cm
Musée du Louvre, Paris

Cat. 24
Bathsheba, after Rembrandt
1871-1874? (Rewald: c. 1870)
Oil on canvas
37 x 45.5 cm
Private collection
R 173

versions on this theme, Rembrandt had depended on standard props of the narrative that provided a pretext to depict a seductive bather in a landscape: a palace in the background, King David on the balcony, an exotic attendant, and the apparatus of the bath in front. But in his final painting of Bathsheba, Rembrandt's focus shifts away from a narrative framework to explicate the deeper significance of the story, confining it almost exclusively now to the monumental, expressive nude. Measuring almost five feet square, the life-sized scale, bold proximity and relief-like composition of the 1654 painting of Bathsheba invite the viewer's intimate contemplation.[7] The old woman attendant at lower left, traditionally an image of shriveled old age in contrast to Bathsheba's youthful allure, has faded almost into obscurity because the radiant nude on her own so powerfully projects the painting's theme of fateful beauty. Given its mood of quiet melancholy and repose, we hardly notice, in fact, the artist's unnatural manipulation of the figure to heighten its expressive force. For example, as Eric Jan Sluijter has described, her legs are painted in profile but her upper body is turned parallel to the picture plane, which renders the nude both more visible and vulnerable to our gaze.[8] The painter's brushstroke also changes dramatically across the surface of the canvas: The most palpable strokes of paint, which convey the most sexually charged areas of the body, contrast with the smooth, fragile touches of paint on her face.[9] And the two areas are linked by the red ribbon that falls from her hair and casts the most delicate of shadows just short of her breast. The only remaining facet of the narrative tradition—the letter she holds in her right hand as she looks away in despair—"focuses the viewer's attention on what cannot be visualized: Bathsheba's thoughts."[10] While this stringent narrative economy invested Rembrandt's last Bathsheba with an intensely tangible corporeality and an unprecedented emotional depth, it also freed his nude from the bonds of narrative and allowed her to function more freely as a model for 19th century realist painters. Thus, although the first known print of the La Caze Bathsheba dates to 1876, scholars have suggested that an earlier engraving may have been available to Gustave Courbet, whose painting *Sleeping Bather by a Brook* of 1845 (Detroit Institute of Arts) closely traces in reverse the contours of Rembrandt's nude.[11] Courbet and Manet as well may have had access to the painting itself when it was still in private hands: Manet's early work, *The Surprised Nymph* (Museo Nacional de Bellas Artes, Buenos Aires), which was extracted from a larger unfinished canvas laden with other motifs of biblical bathers, may also contain, as Françoise Cachin has argued, a memory of Rembrandt's late Bathsheba.[12] As Manet repeatedly modified this early work, adding and expunging figures, cutting it down, metamorphosing one allusive scene of bathers into another, his project became not so much the transcription of an established narrative, or even just an effort to paint a nude in a landscape to rival the old masters—although it was surely that—but above all an attempt to capture in modern terms the frisson of the original voyeuristic subject without depending on the tired narrative props that had sustained it in past art. Cézanne too, would take up the task.

John Rewald speculated that Cézanne's small copy of Rembrandt's Bathsheba may have depended upon an engraving, although not, he insisted, before the artist closely studied the original in the Louvre.[13] Rewald dated the copy to c. 1870, agreeing with Lionello Venturi that it bore close resemblance to the artist's copy after Delacroix's *Barque of Dante*, to which he gave the same approximate date, and quotes Venturi's observations as to its style, in which "a series of rectangular surfaces is substituted for the anatomy" of the figures. But in the case of Cézanne's copy, much of the reasoning for Rewald's chronology also depended on the availability of the La Caze collection in this period: It was put on view in the Louvre only a few months before the Franco-Prussian War broke out in the fall of 1870, and in the brief timeframe before the painting, along with much of the museum's collection, was placed in protective storage, there were no requests to copy it. However, new scholarship allows us a larger chronological window within which Cézanne could have seen and grasped all that the Dutch painting held. As Hollis Clayson has recently documented, the reinstallation of the Louvre began in January 1871, and the inventory of requests to copy its Dutch paintings in the decade immediately following the war has not survived.[14] Thus Cézanne's copy should be dated only on stylistic grounds, and they are far more elastic: The artist was back in Paris by the late summer of 1871, living with his friend Philippe Solari on the rue de Chevreuse before moving to the rue Jussieu, and may well have had access to Rembrandt's nude then, or even as late as early 1874, when he left Pontoise for a few months stay in Paris before returning to Aix for the summer. In his small copy, in fact, Cézanne follows the original painted image quite closely. Using short, thick strokes of heavily encrusted paint, a deep-toned, luminous palette and the exact same shade of crimson red, Cézanne both captures the popular 19th century conception of the Dutch painter's favored, so-called "rough manner" and transforms it with a measured touch into one of implicit order. A strong sense of Rembrandt's reductive and magnificent psychological study, which would have been far more evident in the painting than in engravings, also survives in Cézanne's small copy: We sense in it both the visual rapture and the empathy sparked by the original. However, the rich complexity of the Bathsheba theme and its traditional association of an irresistible nude with a verdant landscape, though not figuring here, were not lost on the painter. When he returned to the subject of Bathsheba in a handful of drawings and small paintings that date to the following decade, Cézanne exploited the broader visual and thematic implications that had made it such a compelling one for him in the 1870s in Paris, and also for some of his contemporaries.

In what may be the first of the later versions (R 592), Cézanne closely recalls the artistic conventions of the biblical narrative. In front of a luxuriously leafy tree, itself an allusion to Bathsheba's fecund beauty, his elegant seated nude poses at center with her legs daintily crossed, and turns just enough into the sunlight to expose her full nudity to the viewer as her maidservant kneels to wash her feet. Just beyond, we glimpse the classical colonnade of the palace, which places us again in the biblical narrative. Although it is difficult to read with certainty the sketchy center of the canvas, Cézanne's Bathsheba appears to hold the proverbial letter in which David asks her to betray her absent husband. Unlike in Rembrandt's late painting, which shows a solemn nude, lost in dark reflection, Cézanne's figure is actively reading the letter's contents. The artist seems to have prefaced his conception with a series of preparatory sketches. In the upper portion of a sheet of related drawings (CH 463, Kunstmuseum Basel), Cezanne's nude sits rather stiffly and is attended by her maidservant, but at the center of the page, Cezanne's Bathsheba figure gives way to the conventions of the iconic reclining nude. And in a second related painting (R 593), though the servant is still present, the figure sinks into a traditional pose of sensual abandon, casting aside not only the props of narrative but also the moral essence of the theme. Finally, in what may be the third painting in the series (fig. 24), the sensuality of the nude is made even more autonomous from the narrative and more expressive in solely pictorial terms. It is also explicit on the canvas's lush, painterly surface, in its rich, fluid color and especially, as Tamar Garb has described, in the way that the curvaceous contour of the figure is echoed in the corporeal outline of the landscape beyond.[15] That distant topography includes a likely vision of Mountain Sainte-Victoire, the historic mountain that hovers on the horizon of Cézanne's native Aix and in so many of his Provençal landscapes. This conflation of the landscape of Provence with an imaginary image of a nude or bathers is not without precedent in Cézanne's art. The two may be conjoined, for example, as several scholars have suggested, in his enigmatic images of *The Eternal Feminine* (cat. 44) where, amidst an admiring throng, the painter of a stark mountain reminiscent of Mountain Sainte-Victoire turns away from his easel to gaze at a fearsome recumbent nude. And it is profoundly present in Cézanne's earlier *Bathers at Rest* (fig. 84), where the broad, sculptural expanse of the mountain provides an architectonic backdrop and rigidly structured moral universe for Cézanne's heroic male figures, and frames them not in a narrative context but within the tradition of the historic landscape.[16] On a much smaller scale in his last Bathsheba canvas, though one befitting its intimate voyeuristic subject, and with a radically different technique and view of the mountain, Cézanne again transposes a familiar theme of bathing onto what was already fertile ground, one that needed no narrative explication. With each beautifully inscribed in the other, the painter celebrates the spectacle of the magnificent nude that he saw first in Paris by enshrining it within a souvenir of his native Provence. No longer voyeurs, we are privy to his rapturous equation of the two.

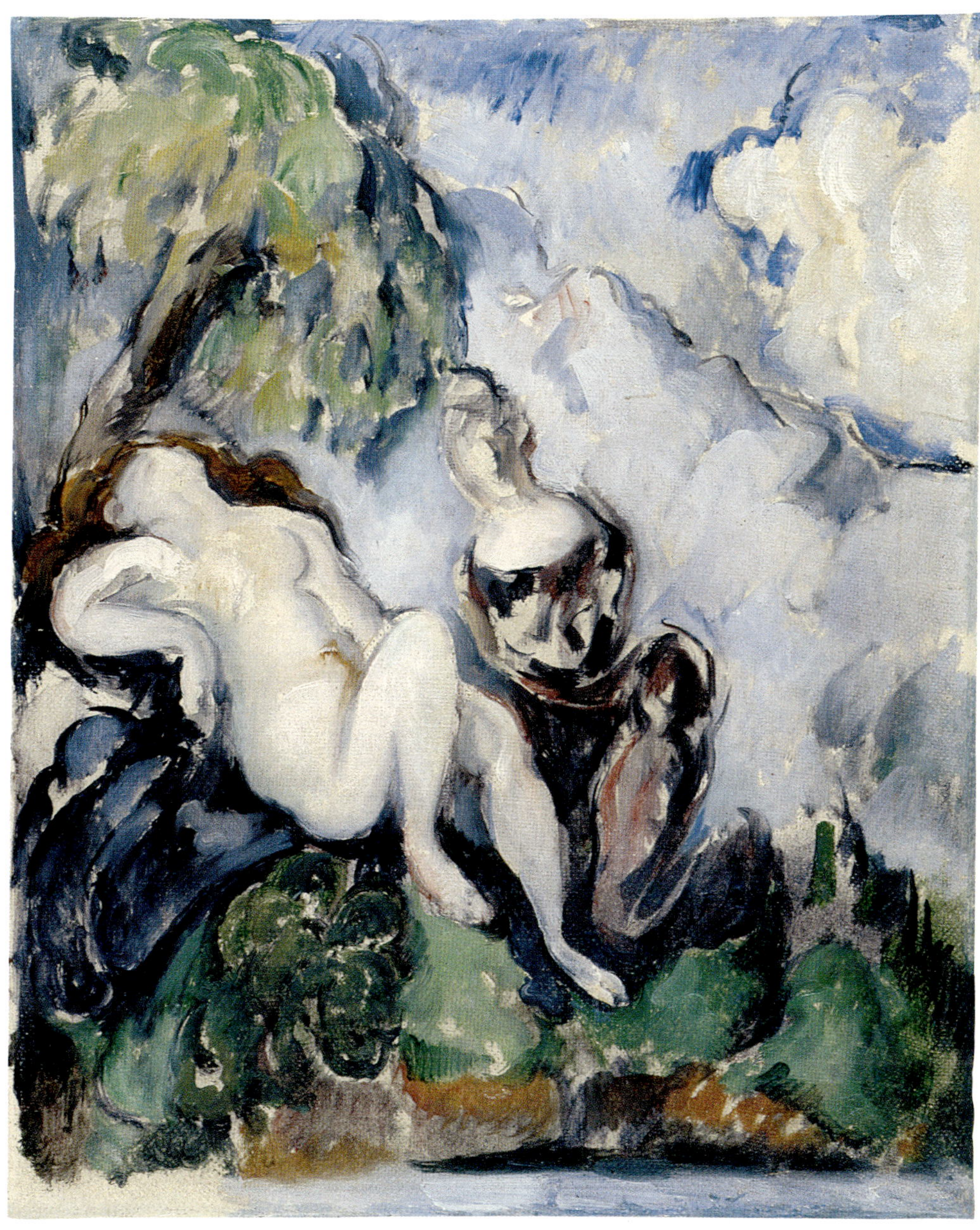

Fig. 24
Bathsheba
1885–90
Oil on canvas
29 x 25 cm
Musée d'Orsay
(in deposit at Musée Granet, Aix-en-Provence)
R 591

Nina Athanassoglou-Kallmyer

CĒZANNE AND DELACROIX — THE STORY OF A FAILED TRIBUTE

Cézanne always claimed to be an ardent admirer of Delacroix. His career bears the imprint of an ongoing dialogue with the works of this great Romantic painter. When Cézanne arrived in Paris in 1861, Delacroix had only two years left to live. His fame was emblazoned across the capital's artistic firmament and he was working on his final masterpiece: the murals in the Saints-Anges chapel at the church of Saint-Sulpice. His major canvases, exhibited at the Salons, were now in the Musée du Luxembourg. And it was at this same museum, in 1863, that the young Cézanne would execute a copy of *The Barque of Dante*, Delacroix's first success at the 1822 Salon (R 172). In the 1860s, this was followed by his drawings after Delacroix's *Entombment* for the Church of Saint-Denis-du-Sacrement (1866–1867; CH 167) and also by drawings (c. 1870; CH 325, 325) and sketches in paint (R 232) after Delacroix's *Hamlet and Horatio in the Cemetery* (1839; Louvre). It was no doubt Delacroix's death in 1863 that prompted Cézanne's black crayon drawing (fig. 25), a kind of reverent memento reproducing the late painter's features from a photograph by Eugène Durieu. In Cézanne's studio at Les Lauves there is also a framed engraving of *The Death of Sardanapalus* (1827–1828). Towards the end of his life, Cézanne received Delacroix's *Bouquet of Flowers* (1848–1850) as a gift from the art dealer Ambroise Vollard, who had purchased it from the widow of Victor Chocquet, an admirer of Delacroix and collector of his work. Cézanne hung this piece above his bed and wasted no time in copying it (1902–1904; R 894).

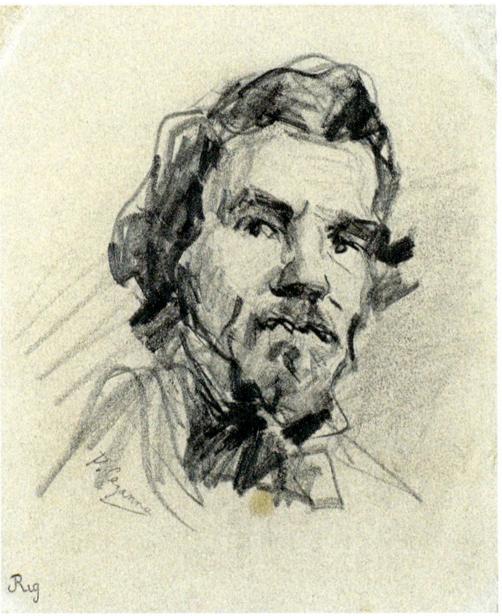

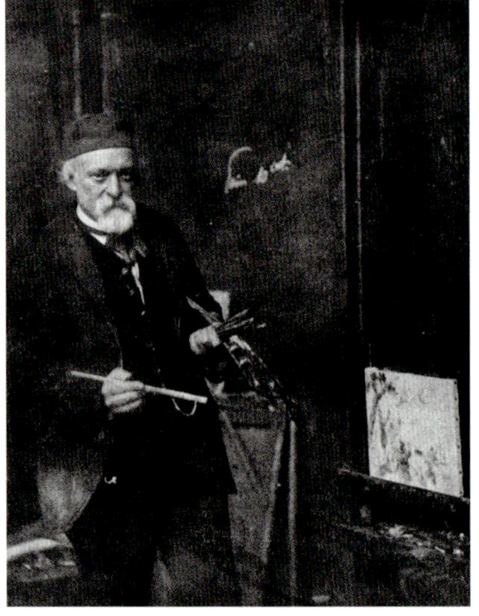

Fig. 25
Portrait of Delacroix
After a photograph by Eugène Durieu
1864–1866
Black crayon on paper
14.6 × 12 cm
Musée Calvet, Rignault collection, Avignon
CH 155

Fig. 26
Anonymous
Cézanne in his Paris studio working on his Apotheosis of Delacroix
Photograph
John Rewald collection
National Gallery of Art, Washington

Cézanne's project for a "homage painting," an "apotheosis" of Delacroix, was simply then the ultimate confirmation of this admiration that punctuated the painter's entire life. As the preliminary drawings (CH 174, 175)—a watercolor (RWC 68), and an oil sketch kept at the Musée Granet (cat. 25)—attest, this project was conceived during the 1860s. In an 1894 photo (fig. 26), the sketch is placed on the painter's easel, with Cézanne himself standing next to it, his brushes in his hand. The date of the photograph no doubt contributed to the late dating attributed to the sketch in paint (1890–1894), despite stylistic evidence that would seem to place it between 1860 and 1870[1]. Indeed, the overtly theatrical staging of the photograph would, we believe, indicate a formal declaration by the painter of his return to this earlier project, rather than a work in progress.

This homage scene takes the form of an epiphanic vision with quasi-religious elements: a Christian Assumption where reality rubs shoulders with the supernatural in the shape of a "real allegory." Against a radiant sky above a landscape that is clearly that of southern France, bathed in sunlight and planted with intensely green pines, floats the nude figure of Delacroix supported by angels, one of whom carries his palette and brushes (shown in greater detail in the preliminary watercolor). Either standing or kneeling, their eyes fixed on this apparition, their hands joined

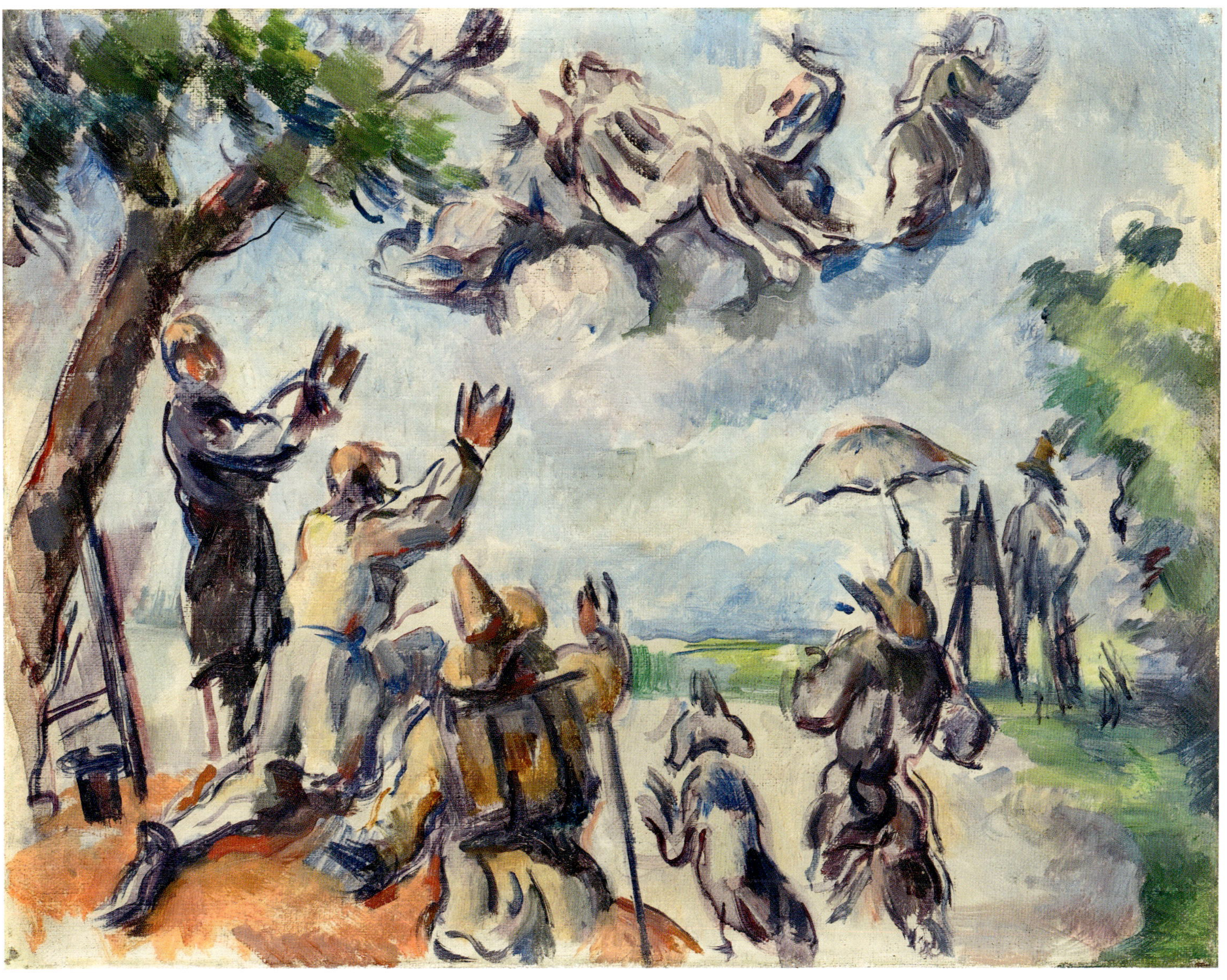

Cat. 25
Apotheosis of Delacroix
1890–94
Oil on canvas
27 × 35 cm
Musée d'Orsay, Paris
(in deposit at Musée Granet, Aix-en-Provence)
R 746

in prayer, the earthly worshippers of the master form a semicircle in the foreground. From left to right we can identify the figures of: Victor Chocquet in a black frock coat with his top hat placed on the ground; an (unidentified) man in a painter's smock; Cézanne himself, seen from behind with a stick, wearing a pointed straw hat, laden with his artist's equipment and accompanied by his dog Black; Monet, in a straw hat, also seen from behind; and Pissarro shown at his easel at the back right of the picture, also in a straw hat.

This project's origins in the 1860s and the return to it in the 1890s closely follow the historical trajectory—punctuated by periods of quiet and sudden revivals of interest—of Delacroix's posthumous reputation. The painter's death in 1863 produced a series of events that aroused a great deal of publicity and, in February 1864, his studio sale was a resounding success. People fought over his drawings, engravings, sketches, and

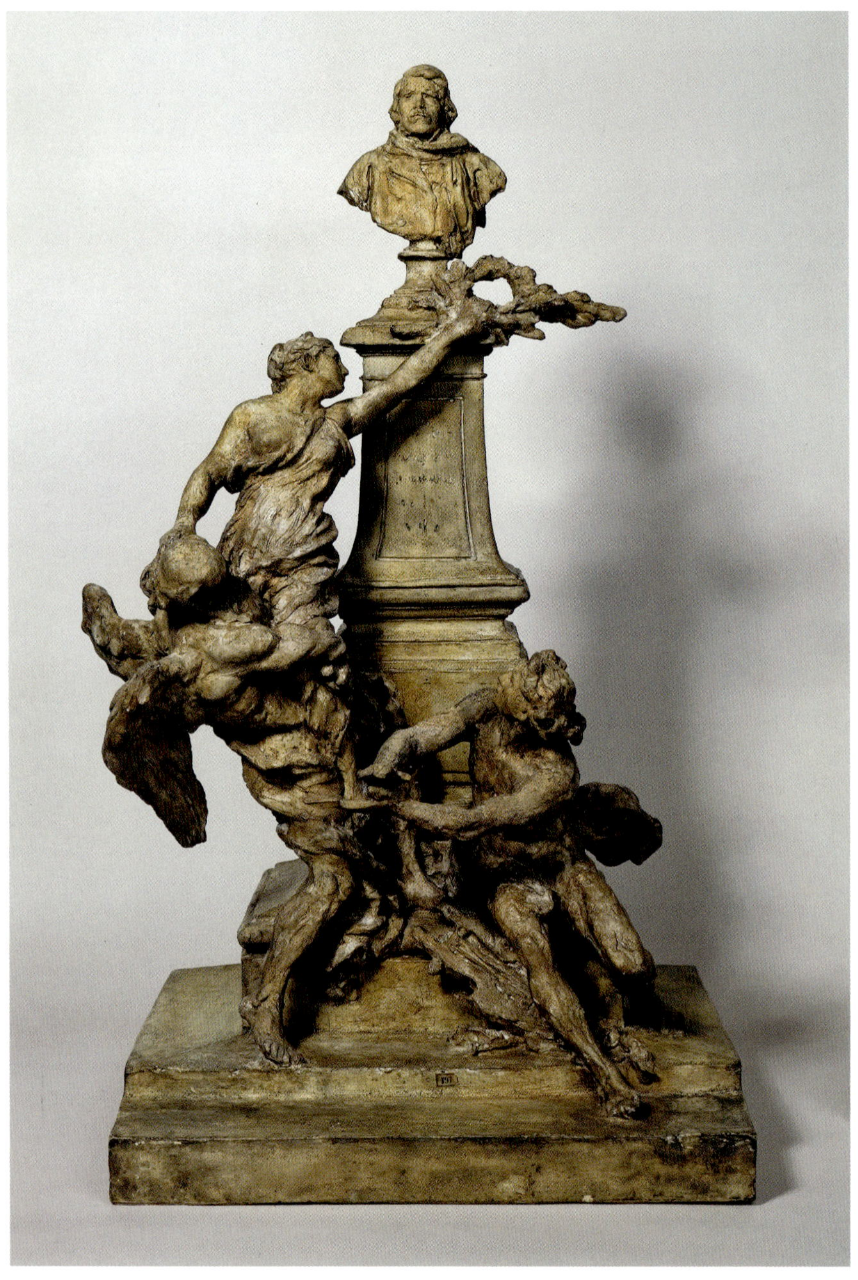

Fig. 27
Jules Dalou
Maquette for the *Monument à Eugène Delacroix*
1885–90
Plaster with patina
91 × 62 × 46 cm
Petit Palais, Musée des Beaux-Arts de la Ville de Paris, Paris

paintings, which achieved unexpectedly high prices. In August the same year, a retrospective exhibition mounted by the French National Fine Arts Society brought together more than 300 works by Delacroix in the rooms of the Galerie Martinet on the boulevard des Italiens. In addition to this exhibition, Delacroix's major decorative works in churches and public buildings transformed Paris into a vast homage to the dead painter. Critics went into raptures about the quality of the great artist's work and his prodigious productivity. Théophile Silvestre stated that Delacroix "had finally been consecrated as the foremost painter of his period,"[2] while D'Arpentigny declared that the exhibition was a "homage to this immortal genius."[3] According to Paul de Saint-Victor, "France has lost the most extraordinary and most powerful of its painters; one of those men whose *oeuvre* epitomizes the aspirations and spirit of the century."[4] And Gautier announced that "Delacroix lives again in glory... everything has been devotedly brought together."[5] In 1864, Henri Fantin-Latour painted his *Homage to Delacroix* in which the painter's self-portrait dominates his assembled disciples, including Whistler, Baudelaire, and Manet. A year later, the first biography of Delacroix was published by his sole heir, Achille Piron. It incorporates numerous extracts from the painter's journal and from his correspondence and his writings on art. A first volume of correspondence, published by Philippe Burty, appeared in 1878, followed by a second revised and enlarged edition in 1880. Artists, art critics, and collectors came together to call for a monument to be erected to celebrate the memory of the great man: the words used were eternal "glory" and "apotheosis."

It was in 1884–1885, when the monument in memory of Delacroix was being planned, that interest in the painter experienced a renewed vigor. Initiated by Auguste Vacquerie, brother of Victor Hugo's son-in-law, and a friend and admirer of Delacroix, the monument was commissioned from sculptor Jules Dalou (fig. 27). The Senate granted a piece of ground in the allée des Platanes in the Luxembourg Gardens. The funding needed was provided by a second retrospective of Delacroix's work at the École des Beaux-Arts from March 6 to April 15, 1885. Even more than the 1864 exhibition, this contributed to idealizing the painter's image, an image that had been considerably idealized already. The variety of works exhibited—paintings, drawings, engravings, as well as manuscripts, letters, and extracts from Delacroix's journal—brought back to life the entire personality of the painter, who was both a man of wit and an artist of genius. The painter Paul Guigou underlined the importance of this new exhibition, describing it as an "apotheosis awarded."[6] Cézanne was present in Paris for the whole of the exhibition and one can imagine him to have been a particularly assiduous visitor[7]. It was perhaps then that he embarked on his free copy of Delacroix's *Wrathful Medea* (Musée du Louvre). A new crayon drawing based on the painter's self-portrait (1837, Musée du Louvre) also appears to date from around 1885 (CH 619).

For his monument to Delacroix in the Luxembourg Gardens, Dalou decided upon an allegorical apotheosis with its particular blend of the real and the supernatural. This piece, which was to be erected in the center of a white marble basin, was a combination of robust and idealized allegorical personifications in bronze (Time, Fame, and Apollo, god of the arts), in striking contrast with the poignant realism of the bust of Delacroix that rises above them. The painter appears fragile, his face heavily lined, wrapped up snugly in his cape and muffler. The inaugural ceremony, held on October 5, 1890, brought together politicians, artists, art critics, and friends of the painter in a respectful semicircle around the statue. The word "apotheosis" features repeatedly in the official speeches given on this occasion. Referring to the monument's allegorical figures, Léon Bourgeois, the Minister for Education and the Arts, declared that "the spirit of the arts saluted this apotheosis."[8] Similarly, Albert Wolff, art critic from *Le Figaro*, stated that "Monsieur Dalou's composition is the apotheosis of Delacroix."[9] Dalou's monument appeared on the front page of the major newspapers of the time, such as *L'Illustration* and *Le Monde illustré*. The publication in 1893 of the first edition of Delacroix's *Journal*, under the supervision of René Piot and Paul Flat, would extend the artist's memory still further in the minds of the public.

It was against this background of a collective feeling of adulation that Cézanne returned to his painting *Apotheosis*. We know that he reread the Baudelaire obituary that appeared in 1863 in *L'Opinion nationale*, and perhaps too Delacroix's recently published *Journal*. Biographers of the time, notably Joachim Gasquet, whom Cézanne first met in 1896 in Aix, take up this theme of unquestioned admiration for the great Romantic artist, ranking him alongside Veronese, Titian, Tintoretto, and Rubens, whom Delacroix revered. For Cézanne, Delacroix, like the Venetian painters and like Rubens, was first and foremost an incomparable master of color. "It is still the finest palette in France, and no one... more than he has displayed both the charm and the pathos, the vibration of color."[10] He banished grey, a tone that does not exist in the sun-soaked Provence of southern France; he created surfaces gleaming with silken colors; he was the inventor of colored shadow and pointed the way to nature[11]. In nature "as Delacroix has it", he says repeating Gasquet, "we have a dictionary in which we can find every word. Let us now go outside and study the beauty of nature..."[12]

However, the shadow of a doubt creeps almost silently into this apparently laudatory discourse. Although still known for "the finest palette in France" and as the great apostle of nature, Delacroix would be linked, in spite of everything, to a bygone tradition of art, that of a bituminous and bookish Romanticism. Cézanne reveals this in a small, short oil stain of a phrase among his flattering comments. Delacroix—he announces—"may be Romanticism. But he is too steeped in Shakespeare and Dante, he has read Dante too much."[13] Cézanne was aware of this from the earliest years of his time in Paris. Was this perhaps the reason why his copy of *The Barque of Dante* dragged on unfinished, as he bemoans to his friend Numa Coste?[14] Was it perhaps because of his own fear of "becoming steeped" in literature himself? The ambivalent nature of his judgment is echoed in the opinions formulated by the painter Claude Lantier, the main protagonist of the novel *L'Œuvre* (1886) by his friend Zola, and for whom the young Cézanne is believed to have served partly as a model. Indeed, when it comes to Delacroix, whom he refers to as "the great lion of Romanticism," Lantier vacillates. On the one hand, the master is prized for the unrivalled splendor of his color and his love of nature, but on the other hand is seen as representing an outmoded style that still clung to a bituminous palette showing little concern for the real outdoors. His influence may indeed have been harmful: "For heaven's sake. It's black again," exclaims the disappointed Lantier on looking at his painting of a country scene: "I've got this blasted Delacroix stuck in my head... Oh! we're all drenched in the sauce of Romanticism. We paddled about in it too much in our youth and we're daubed in it up to the chin. We're in need of some remarkable detergent."[15] He goes on to say: "But what I feel is that the great Romantic décor of Delacroix is cracking and collapsing... You see, perhaps we need the sun, we need the open air, a clear, young way of painting, living beings just as they behave in true light..." And Lantier concludes: "We now need something else."[16]

In the sketch in paint at the Musée Granet, there is a visual restatement of this dual view that adores yet denigrates the Romanticism of the past. Cézanne and his Impressionist friends worked out in the open in the sun-soaked south of France, radiant with pure color. The Assumption scene in which Delacroix, cradled by angels in the "bluish" sky of Provence, poses as Christ in the style of his *Entombment* for Saint-Denis-du-Saint-Sacrement, which was copied by Cézanne, displays a traditional, even Academy-based iconography that sits ill with the naturalism of the countryside and the tastes of the adoring artists. The inordinate grandiloquence of their reverent gestures and their puppet-like forms borders on caricature. The presence of the dog Black barking at the celestial apparition even introduces a sacrilegious note. Could these hands joined in prayer in fact be goodbye gestures to the great Romantic departing in glory? The small sketch bears some striking analogies with those paintings by Cézanne where the manifest inspiration of Delacroix is tinged with ironic touches. It is true of *The Feast (The Orgy)* (fig. 36), a development of the Saint-Sulpice paintings transformed into a decadent, lascivious banquet, and of *The Eternal Feminine* (cat. 44), an epiphanic and allegorical image analogous to the *Apotheosis*, which uses the composition of *The Death of Sardanapalus* but inverts its terms—a prostitute replaces the Assyrian king—in the satirical spirit and bombastic style of caricature.

If any doubts exist about Cézanne's position, his *Apotheosis of Delacroix* carries within it revealing signs. Already the target of an ambivalent attitude when Cézanne was young, by the end of the century, the example set by this master of Romanticism had become outmoded. Delacroix may have been a much-revered master, but he was no longer imitated. Unfinished, the *Apotheosis* was in the end a failure.

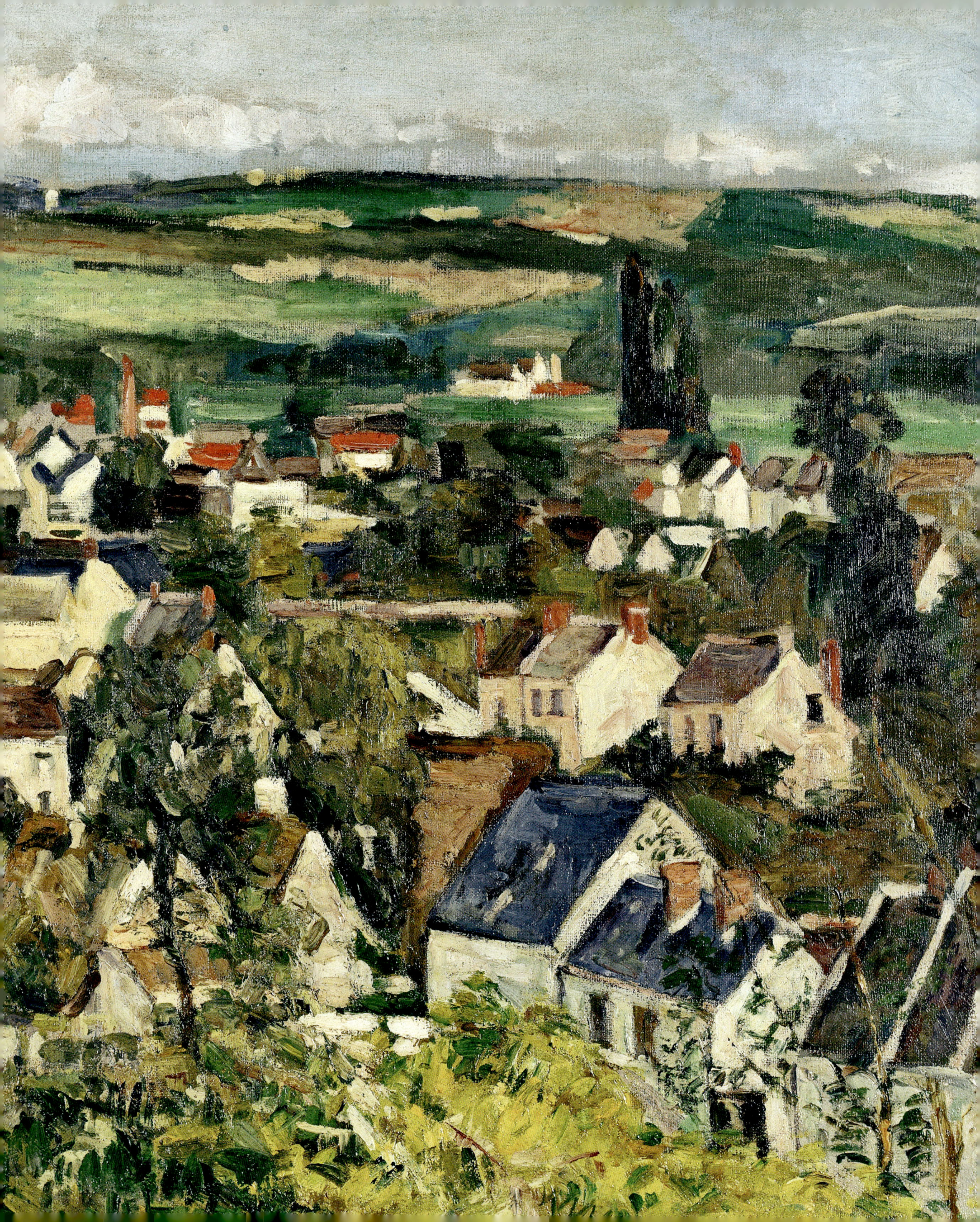

PARIS OUTSIDE THE WALLS

When Zola urged his friend Cézanne to join him in Paris, he certainly praised the museums, but he went on: "On Sundays, we will go out and visit a few places around Paris; the sites are charming and, if you feel like it, you will sketch the trees under which we have dined on a scrap of canvas."[1] In fact, from summer 1861, Zola dragged Cézanne off to Marcoussis. This means that "Paris" was more than just what lay inside the walls, especially as the surrounding countryside was becoming accessible with the arrival of the railroads. As early as 1866, at Guillemet's instigation, a small colony of artists and writers, mostly from Aix, spent the whole summer of 1866 at Bennecourt, on the right bank of the Seine, opposite Bonnières (cat. 29). Cézanne was among them.

Having returned to Provence for a few months in the fall of that year, Cézanne learned a lesson from his stay: "You see, all the pictures painted indoors in the studio will never be worth as much as those painted in the open air. When you paint outdoor scenes, the contrast between figures and landscape is amazing."[2] But it was not until after the Franco-Prussian war in 1870 that he really started working in the Paris region. Cézanne realized that what he had done from provocation and violence was leading him to a dead end. He would henceforth have to confront nature, whose existence had been revealed to him by Pissarro and Guillaumin. Nature would have several different faces depending on where he was living (Auvers, Pontoise, Melun, Médan...) and the subjects he chose. Later, during the 1890s, the pursuit of nature would lead him to the Île-de-France and other parts, mainly along the banks of the Marne and at Fontainebleau. In the meantime, Provence—l'Estaque, Gardanne, Bellevue, le Jas de Bouffan—would also crop up in his works.

There is no doubt that the friendship between Cézanne, Pissarro, and Guillaumin was a determining factor in this venture over the ten years from 1872 to 1882, which mark the first part of Cézanne's "Parisian" works and during which he made two long stays at Auvers or Pontoise.

During his first stay, from the middle of 1872 to the beginning of 1874, Cézanne lived in Auvers, in a house not far from that of Doctor Gachet, at 66, rue Rémy, and often walked the three kilometers to Pontoise to work with Pissarro. His second visit, from May to October 1881, involved mainly Pontoise and the district of Valhermeil. Between these two definite periods, Cézanne's trips to Pontoise (numbering four, apparently) were relatively short. Though we know he returned to Auvers after 1874, it appears that he did not stay there; his time in Auvers really only applies to the year 1873. At any rate, Cézanne did not make a return trip to the banks of the Oise after 1882.

In the meantime he spent a whole year in Melun, where he painted the forest in the snow. However, I have not been able to discover the reason for Cézanne's choice of this town. Some of the subjects have been identified very recently, such as that of the painting *Village Square* (R 495), which is now recognized as a view of the church of Saint-Aspais in Melun, but others have been known for longer, such as *The Bridge at Maincy* (cat. 70). Of course, he stayed as many as six times in Médan with his friend Zola, sometimes for periods of several weeks.

D. C.

Auvers-sur-Oise, Panoramic View
(detail)
See cat. 33 p. 73

James H. Rubin

ARMAND GUILLAUMIN AND PAUL CĒZANNE IN ÎLE-DE-FRANCE

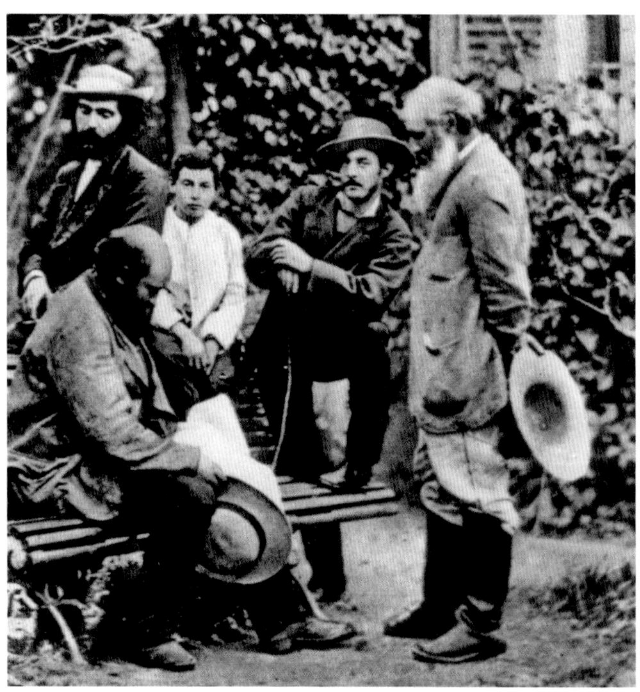

Fig. 28
Anonymous
Paul Cézanne, Camille Pissarro, Armand Guillaumin, and an unidentified painter
Photograph
c. 1873
Musée d'Orsay, service de documentation, Paris

The close personal and artistic friendship between Armand Guillaumin and Paul Cézanne has always been overshadowed by Cézanne's relationship with Camille Pissarro.[1] There is evidence, however, that Cézanne was just as close to Guillaumin as to Pissarro, whom he met around the same time as Pissarro, probably at a studio or a café in the mid-1860s.[2] Indeed, it might make sense to regard both friendships not only as pairs—Cézanne/Pissarro and Cézanne/Guillaumin—but also to consider a triadic relationship. Two simple documents support this point of view. First, in a photograph of about 1873 (fig. 28), Guillaumin, Cézanne, and Pissarro appear together with a fourth painter.[3] Thanks to Cézanne's etching of Guillaumin, made at about the same time (cat. 39) and in which Guillaumin wears the same hat, and a *Self-Portrait* by Guillaumin formerly in the Gachet collection (Musée d'Orsay), Guillaumin is identifiable as the figure standing above the others.[4] Second, when Pissarro made a will on January 3, 1875, he named his "friends," Cézanne and Guillaumin (along with Ludovic Piette) as his executors.[5] With the emergence of Pissarro's reputation and the relative submergence of Guillaumin's, it could naturally be assumed that the former was of prime importance to Cézanne during the 1870s, when the three were together most often. I suggest here that Guillaumin was equally important.

It is widely understood that in the late 1860s and early 1870s Cézanne was seeking a way to distinguish himself from other artists, including his early Impressionist cohorts, in order to impose his own personal "temperament," which, with his boyhood friend Émile Zola, he believed was the key to authentic art. For the most part, his strategies were negative and reactive, sometimes violently so. He refused any intercourse with academic concepts or techniques, and he disdained the elegance and worldly Parisian art of Manet, whom Zola had begun defending and was the idol of the new generation to which Cézanne belonged. When Cézanne looked to other artists, they were from the past, like the recently deceased Eugène Delacroix, or Venetian old masters, such as Tintoretto or Veronese, the latter admired by Delacroix. Or there was his friendship with the provincial painter Adolphe Monticelli, with whom Cézanne shared Provençal origins. Many of Cézanne's early works have narrative themes rather than reflecting the naturalist vision of his companions, and even when he did produce landscapes or still lifes, his heavy-handed technique, which Cézanne called his *style couillard* [ballsy style], seemed calculated to disrupt normative viewing even more than the styles of his comrades. The only contemporary to whom Cézanne might be compared at this time would have been Gustave Courbet, whose provincial origins and reputation for challenging convention must have lent support to Cézanne's provocations.

To these links and strategies, there is one positive exception. It is still generally acknowledged that Cézanne's association with Pissarro cured the former of his so-called early artistic maladies. Yet at the same time as Pissarro was painting with Cézanne, Guillaumin was present, too. One path explored by the two of them, although not ignored by Pissarro, was the representation of industrial landscapes of the sort for which Guillaumin would become better known.[6] Another player in this inter-artistic conversation was Doctor Paul Gachet, a collector and amateur artist, whose printing press at Auvers-sur-Oise was a site for experimentation and collaboration. It was there, for example, that Cézanne made his first etching, *Barges on the Seine* (cat. 26), which was based on a painting by Guillaumin in Gachet's possession (fig. 29). Gachet encouraged subjects from modernity and was an important supporter of all three artists. One of Guillaumin's most important industrial scenes, *Sunset with Factories at Ivry* (c. 1869, Musée d'Orsay) belonged to him when it was exhibited at the first Impressionist exhibition of 1874.

Moreover, Guillaumin owned paintings that Cézanne had given him. For example, a painting by Guillaumin of his own studio shows a *Portrait of Madame Cézanne* (c. 1872, whereabouts unknown, R. 180) leaning against other pictures.[7] Similarly, *The Rue des Saules in Montmartre* (cat. 27) was certainly a gift from Cézanne to Guillaumin, its first owner.

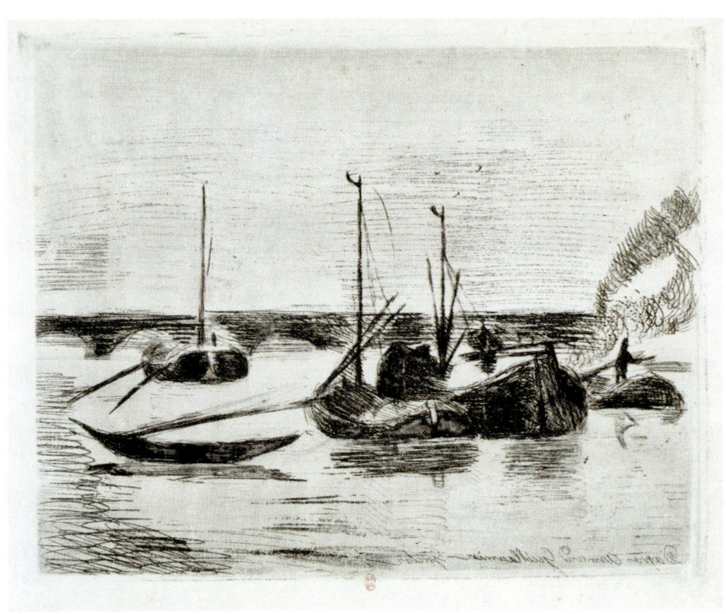

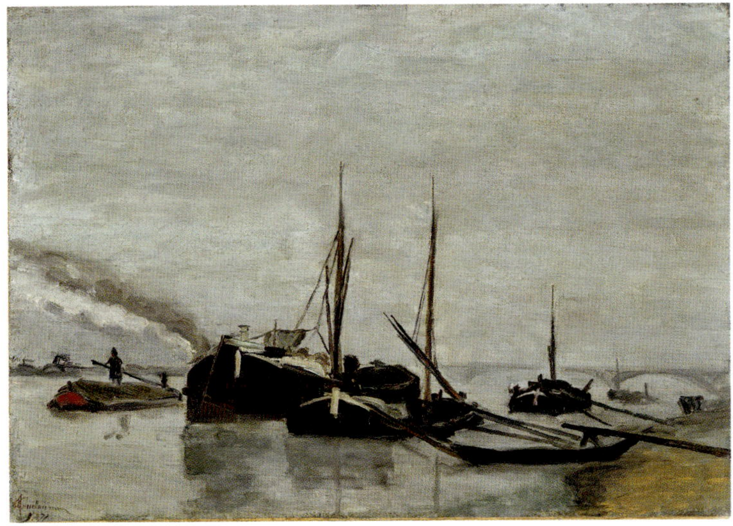

Fig. 29
Armand Guillaumin (1841–1927)
Barges on the Seine
c. 1869
Oil on canvas
Musée d'Orsay, Paris

Cat. 26
Barges on the Seine at Bercy
After Guillaumin
Etching, only known copy
21.5 × 26.5 cm
Bibliothèque nationale de France, Département des Estampes et de la Photographie, Paris
Cherpin 1

This painting, often dated prior to 1870, seems more likely to fall within the same period of Cézanne's relationship with Guillaumin, since its theme reflects the interest in urban settings toward which Guillaumin's practice pointed, and because of its stylistic relationship to village scenes Cézanne painted in 1872–73 while staying with Doctor Gachet at Auvers.

An even more direct link between Cézanne and Guillaumin is through the other important painting Guillaumin exhibited at the first Impressionist exhibition, *The Seine: Rainy Weather* (fig. 30), for it appears in the background of Cézanne's *Self-Portrait* (fig. 31). The *Self-Portrait* was painted in Guillaumin's studio at 13, quai d'Anjou on the Île Saint-Louis, and although it is usually dated c. 1875, it could have been done at any time between 1873 and 1875. One could hardly ask for a more explicit example of solidarity with a colleague than a portrayal of oneself in the other's studio, with a seminal work of that colleague in the background. It is worth comparing it to Pissarro's *Portrait of Paul Cézanne*. Whereas Pissarro's background of caricatures refers to politics and to Courbet, while including one of his own landscapes, Cézanne's *Self-Portrait*, by contrast, concentrated singularly on the dialogue with Guillaumin.

Cézanne was searching for a tenable artistic position, and the relationship with Guillaumin offered him a too often overlooked category of experimentation. One immediate result, most likely concurrent with or earlier than the *Self-Portrait*, was Cézanne's *The Wine Market at Jussieu* (cat. 28). The relationship of this picture to Guillaumin stems from its location in Guillaumin's territory. In the latter's *The Seine: Rainy Weather*, the viewer looks from the Quai Henri IV across to the left bank of the river to witness the loading of wine barrels onto horse-drawn carts heading for the nearby warehouses represented by Cézanne. Although there are not many other pictures that fall into the same category as *The Wine Market* at this time, the industrial subject is nonetheless a category worth exploring for its

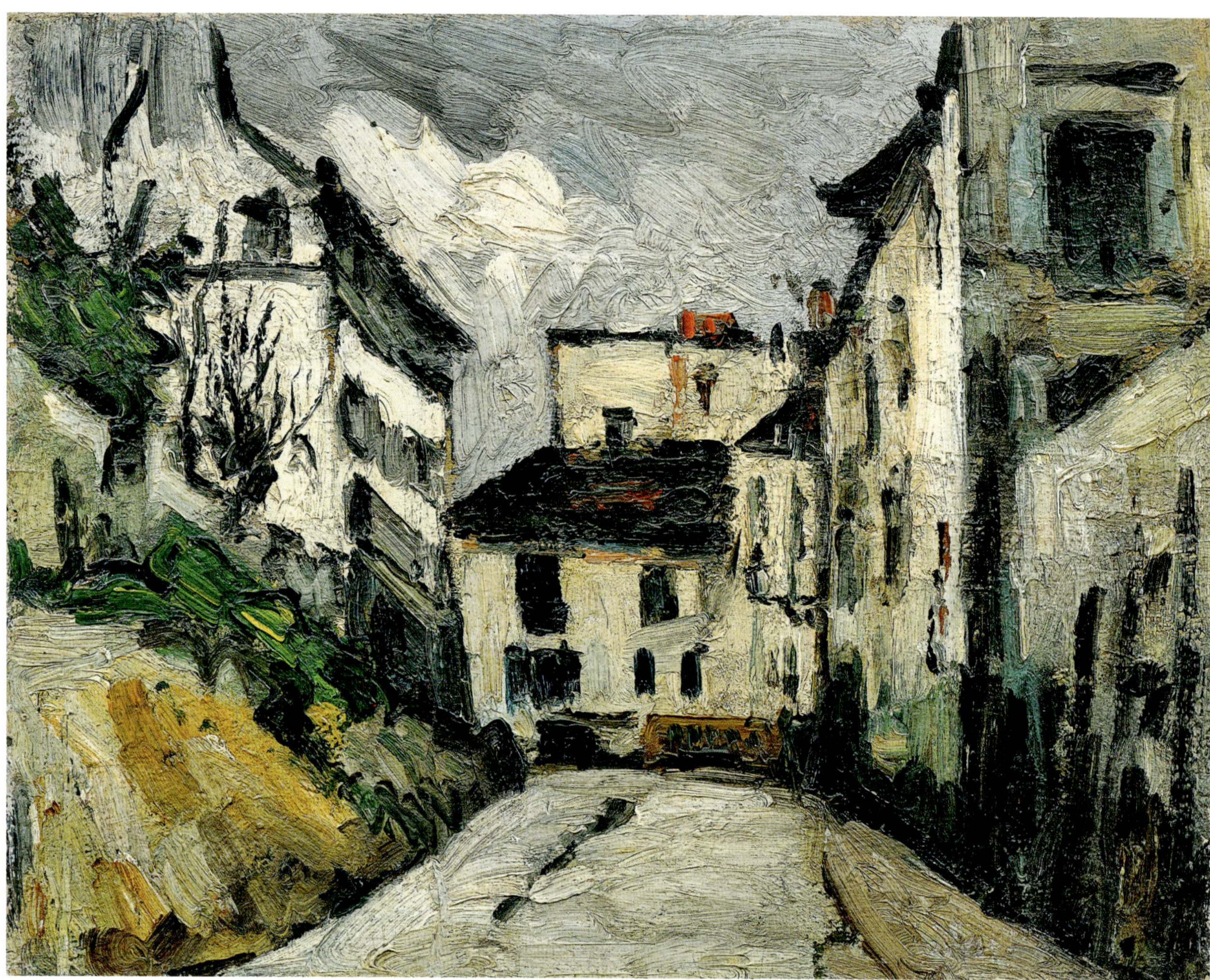

Cat. 27
The Rue des Saules in Montmartre
c. 1873–74
Oil on canvas
31.5 x 39.5 cm
Private collection
R 131

place in contemporary critical discourse, its roots in Cézanne's previous work, and its consequences for Cézanne's development.

Industrial scenes and related modern subjects were heralded in the *Salons* of Jules-Antoine Castagnary beginning in 1863 and by Zola in his *Salon of 1868*.[8] During a stay with Zola on the banks of the Seine at Bennecourt, sometime between 1866 and 1869, Cézanne painted the *Ferry at Bonnières* (cat. 29), the town across the river.[9] Stylistically this picture seems closer to Pissarro than to Guillaumin. Thematically as well, Cézanne's subtle juxtaposition of gasworks chimney and church steeple, while the railroad tracks that ran along the embankment are hidden, resembles Pissarro's early pictures of factories more than Guillaumin's.[10] It seems likely that companionship with Zola was the first impetus for such works by Cézanne, for one of the earliest was a watercolor of *Factories and a Train at L'Estaque* (Musée Granet, Aix-en-Provence) he made for Madame Zola's workbox in 1869. In that year, while in Aix-en-Provence, Cézanne began seriously producing industrial landscapes, as witnessed by his *Factories near the Mont de Cengle* (Private Collection) and especially, the large *Railroad Cut* (c. 1869–70, Bayerische Staatsgemäldesammlungen, Munich). The latter, preceded by drawings and an oil sketch, was a major effort, possibly meant for public view.

It is known through correspondence and other testimony that just as Cézanne worked side by side with Pissarro, he did so as well with Guillaumin. Surely the latter accompanied Cézanne around Auvers and Pontoise, to the north of Paris. But in addition, Cézanne and Guillaumin worked together without Pissarro in the newly expanding suburbs southwest of Paris, for example in the park of Issy-les-Moulineaux, the Vallée de Chevreuse, and near Arcueil. Doctor Gachet accompanied them on at least one occasion, as can be seen by comparing an etching of *Les Hautes-Bruyères near Arcueil* (1873, Bibliothèque nationale de France, département des Estampes et de la Photographie, Paris), signed with Gachet's pseudonym, Louis Van Ryssel.[11]

Guillaumin's parents lived in Levallois-Perret, and it is known that Cézanne's father, on a visit to Paris, dined at their house.[12] The relationship must have been close at the time, for it was at the same time as Cézanne had been visiting Guillaumin in the latter's studio. Juxtapositions between landscapes by Pissarro and Cézanne during the 1870s are relatively common and gave rise in a recent exhibition to substantial analysis of their stylistic connections.[13] Those between Cézanne and Guillaumin are harder to find, given that fewer of Guillaumin's works are on public view. John Rewald published a few comparisons including Cézanne's *Houseboats on a River* (The White House, Washington) and Guillaumin's painting of the same houseboats (whereabouts unknown).[14] Other juxtapositions are less obvious but entirely plausible.[15] Unknown to Rewald at the time, however, was a drawing by Cézanne that closely matches, without being identical to, Guillaumin's *Aqueduct at Arceuil, Sceaux Railroad Line*, dated 1874. The drawing belonged to Dr. Gachet.[16] The proximity of the two views demonstrates that Guillaumin and Cézanne worked together at the same site, or at least that Cézanne visited Guillaumin there. It is closer than any other comparison found so far, but it supports the idea that others are valid and exist.

Of course, Cézanne's copies of Guillaumin's works present even firmer evidence for their relationship than juxtapositions. Surely the most important instance of such copying is Cézanne's *The Seine at Bercy* (cat. 31). In this case, however, Cézanne's picture is a copy only of the scene and its motifs. For he transformed Guillaumin's style through what Théodore Reff called the "constructive stroke," a methodical system of parallel diagonal brushstrokes that Cézanne began developing in the second half of the 1870s.[17] Reff showed decisively that Cézanne's method emerged first in figure paintings of imaginative subjects, such as *The Eternal Feminine* (cat. 44). Based on Cézanne's copy of the Guillaumin and at least two other copies done in an equally rigorous "constructive" style—one after an engraving of a Rococo vase (The National Gallery of Art, Washington D.C.), the other from a photograph of the Fontainebleau Forest (The Museum of Modern Art, New York)—it seems clear that Cézanne's

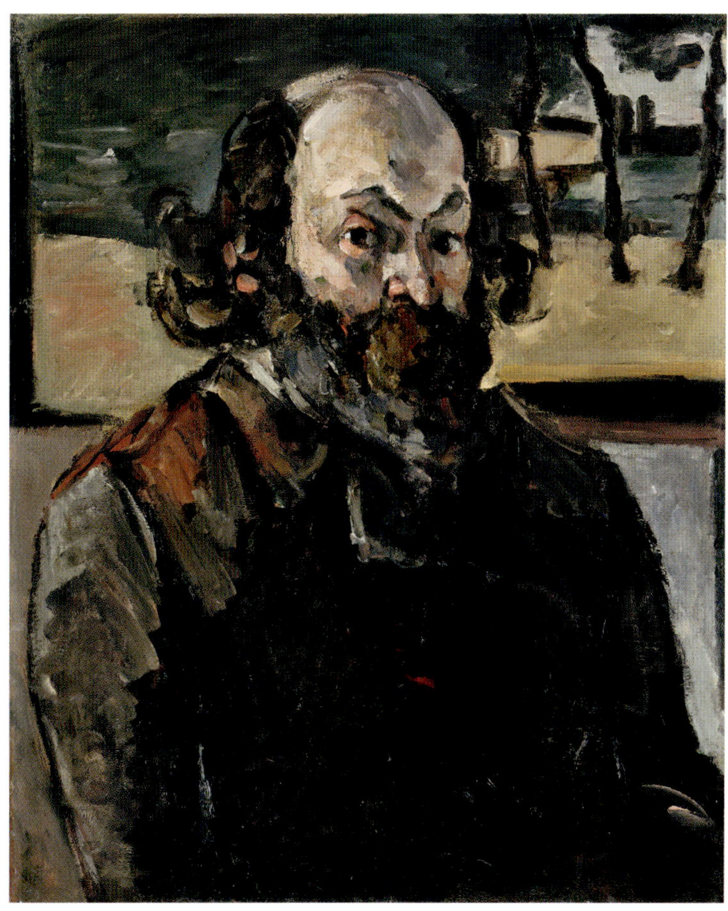

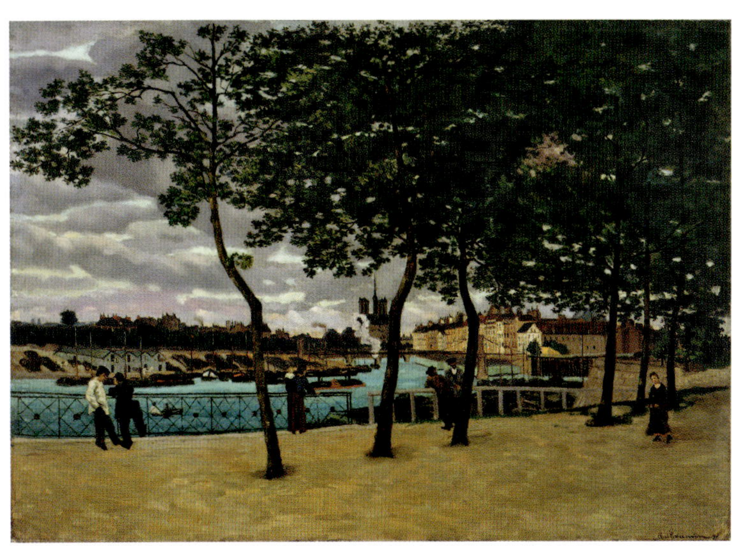

Fig. 30
Armand Guillaumin (1841–1927)
The Seine: Rainy Weather
1873–74
Oil on canvas
The Museum of Fine Arts, Houston

Fig. 31
Self-Portrait
c. 1873–75
Oil on canvas
64 x 53 cm
Musée d'Orsay, Paris
R 182

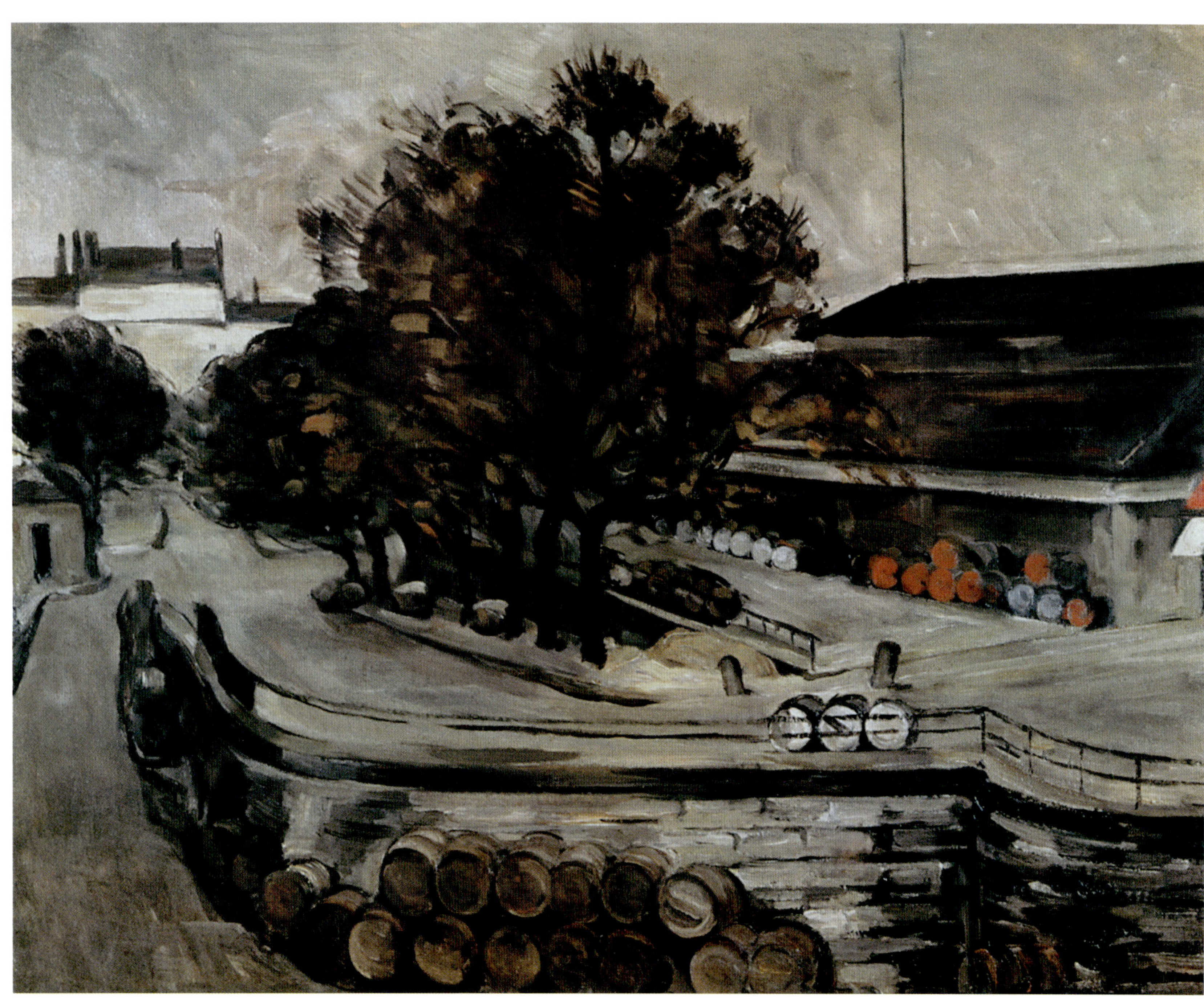

Cat. 28
The Wine Market at Jussieu
1872
Oil on canvas
73 x 92 cm
Portland Art Museum, Oregon, Museum Purchase
R 179

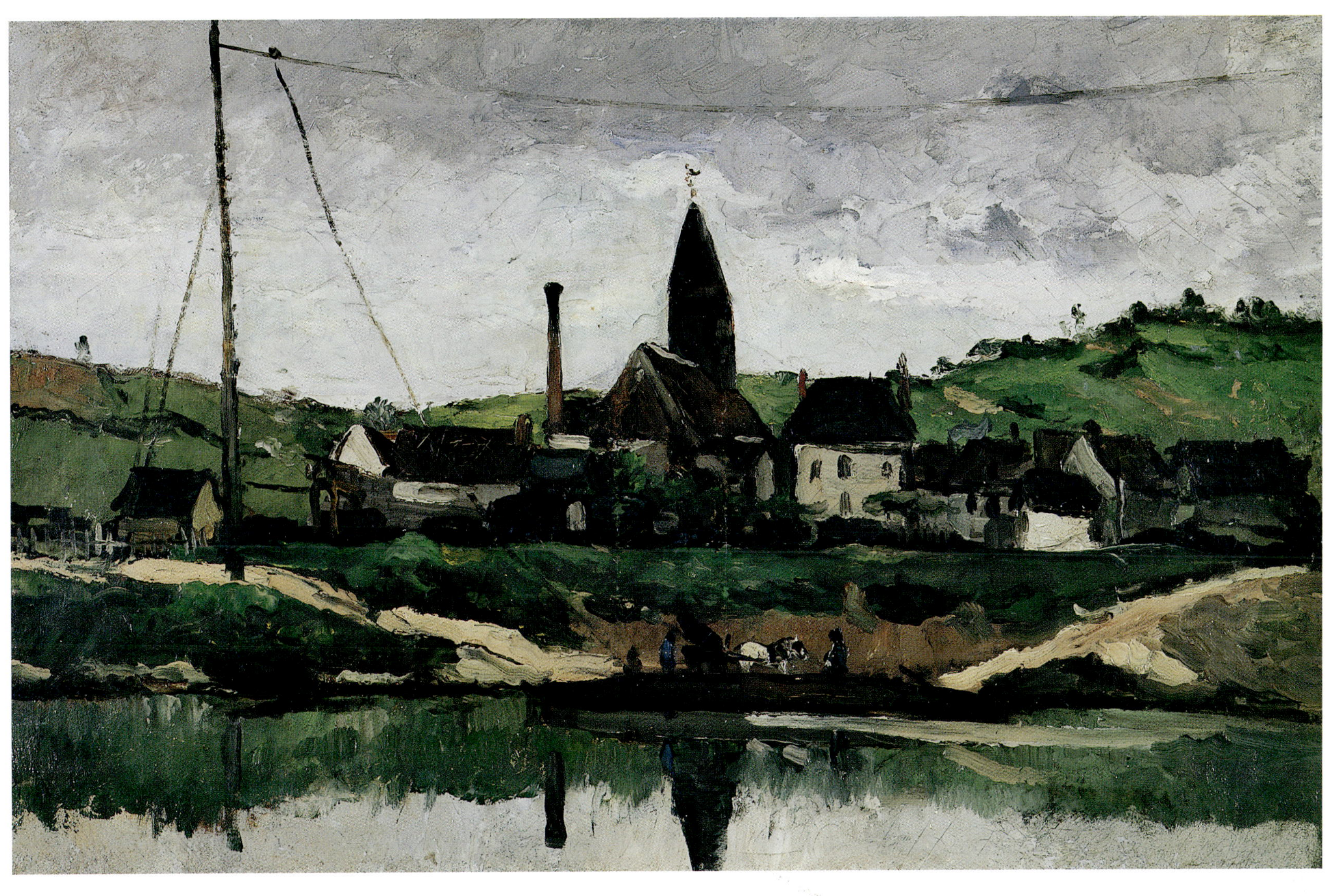

Cat. 29
The Ferry at Bonnières
Summer 1866
Oil on canvas
38.5 × 60 cm
Musée Faure, Aix-les-Bains
R 96

purpose was to limit his imagination to the production of this new system.[18] Unlike his copy of Pissarro's *Louveciennes* (fig. 34), in which Cézanne seems to have been attempting a genuine copy in order to acquire Pissarro's technique, in this case the differences were willful rather than simply the unconscious propensities of a different hand.[19]

Since Cézanne so far as is known did not own the painting by Guillaumin, he must certainly have used it with his friend's knowledge and consent. Guillaumin's original is far less scattered and irregular in its technique than the landscapes he may have painted with Cézanne in the south Paris suburbs (fig. 34). It shows Guillaumin's temporary mellowing after 1875 toward the more mainstream styles more or less shared by Monet, Pissarro, and Sisley rather than that of Cézanne. Cézanne's painting implies therefore a parting of ways with Guillaumin. Had Cézanne followed Guillaumin's industrial direction more consistently, he might have distinguished his work more completely from the primarily suburban and pleasurable landscapes that have come to characterize mainstream Impressionism, but which, as in Guillaumin's case, led nowhere commercially. Not that commercial success mattered for Cézanne, but nor, it seems, did hewing to one particular theme or trend. What mattered to him were visibility and a manner that conveyed the distinctness and originality of his temperament.

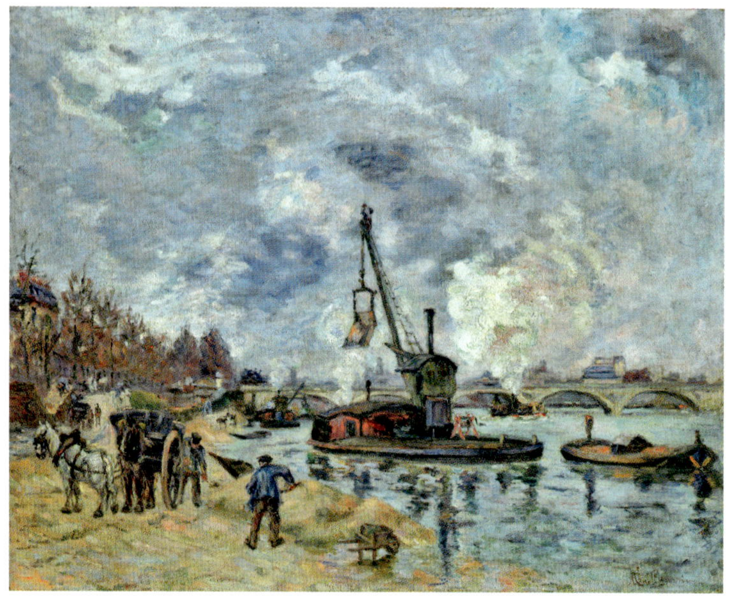

That Cézanne and Guillaumin were still seeing each other as late as 1881 is documented by an etching of an *Impressionist Picnic* made by Georges Manzana-Pissarro dated to the summer of that year. Gauguin had joined the group by that time and was present as well.[20] At the end of his article on Cézanne and Guillaumin, Rewald told the story of how Pissarro vehemently rejected the suggestion that Guillaumin had influenced Cézanne. Such vehemence might be suspect. Although history has agreed with Pissarro up to now, it may be time to revise that point of view.

Whereas once Cézanne may have admired the modern values associated with productivity, rationality, and industry manifested in Guillaumin's images of modern subject matter, his copy of *The Seine at Bercy* transposed those values into the pictorial from the thematic realm. As such, one could be modern without the necessity of subject matter drawn from modern surroundings, or one could altogether transcend the question of subject matter by projecting modern values through technique. In the late 1860s, Zola had referred to the Impressionists more than once as "workers," and he admired Pissarro in particular as an "honest man."[21] Cézanne's new technique conveyed labor, rigor, and consistency. There could be no better lesson or embodiment of Cézanne's effort, then, than his workaday and yet highly personal transformation of the Guillaumin. From the viewpoint of the history of modernism, one could say that there is no better example of Cézanne's conversion of representations of modern motifs into a modern form of representation.[22] Even if not by stylistic or technical example, it was a conversion in which Guillaumin played a significant conceptual and dialogical role.

Cat. 30
Armand Guillaumin (1841–1927)
Quai de Bercy in Paris
c. 1876–78
Oil on canvas
60 × 80 cm
Kunsthalle, Hamburg

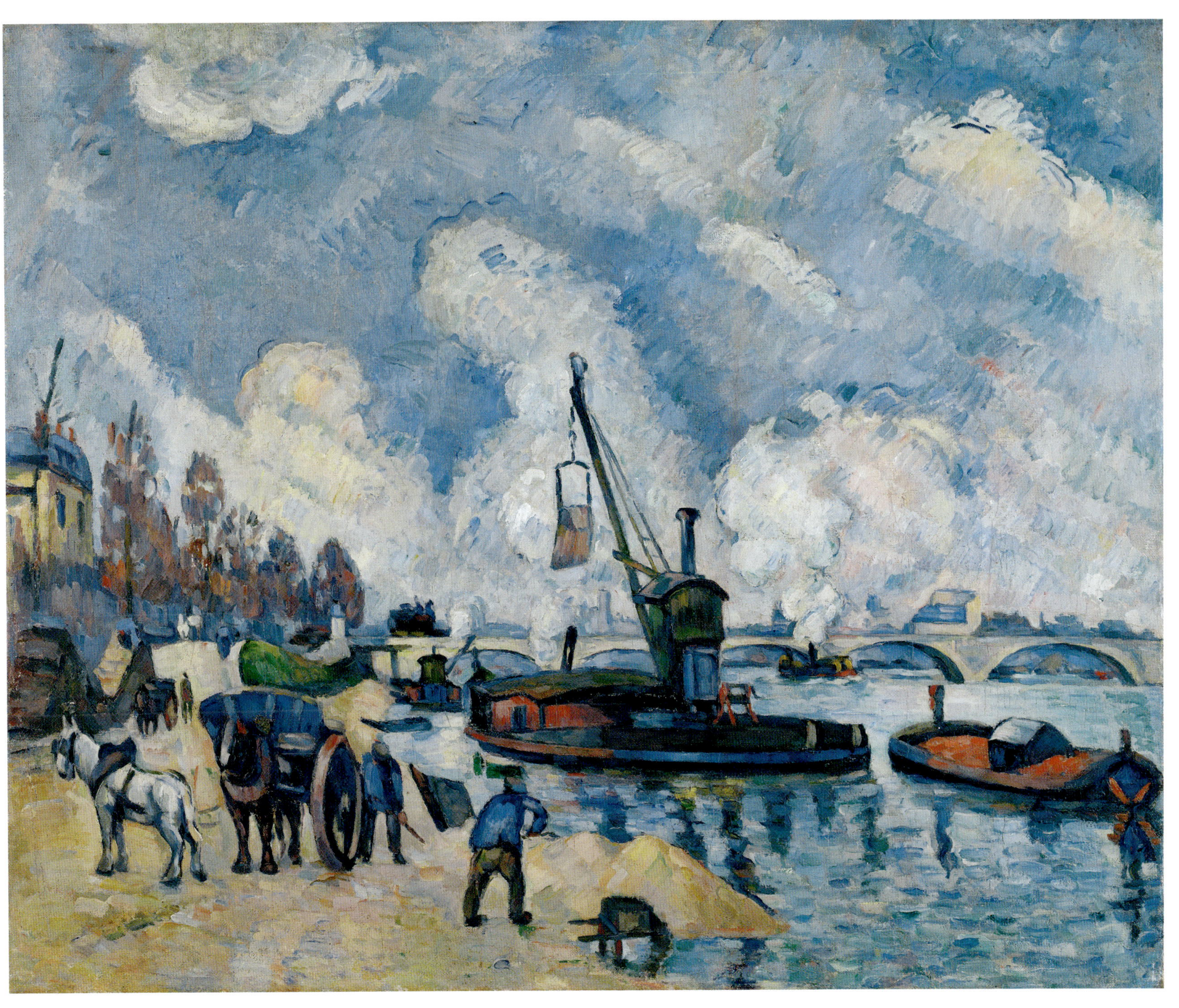

Cat. 31
The Seine at Bercy
Copy after Guillaumin
c. 1876–78
Oil on canvas
59 x 72 cm
Kunsthalle, Hamburg
R 293

Joachim Pissarro

CÉZANNE AND PISSARRO THE AESTHETICS OF RESISTANCE AND RESISTANCE TO ANY AESTHETICS

To T. J. Clark

Born around ten years apart (Pissarro in 1830, Cézanne in 1839), on two different continents (Cézanne was born in Aix-en-Provence, Pissarro on the Isle of St Thomas in the Danish West Indies), and raised in two different religions (Catholicism in the case of Cézanne and Judaism in the case of Pissarro), the chances of a meeting between Cézanne and Pissarro (cat. 32) might have seemed very slight. However, what these two outsiders had in common in both their physiological characteristics and their backgrounds was a striking dissimilarity to the artists of Paris.

Cézanne, as we know, spoke French with a heavy Provençal accent. This left an impression on Lucien Pissarro (Camille's older son) as a child and several decades later, in a letter addressed to his brother, Ludovic Rodo, he felt obliged to transcribe the strong southern inflection of Cézanne's voice, so pronounced were the lilting intonations of his southern accent.[1] In Pissarro's case, a large number of literary portraits draw attention to his strong physical features, the "mosaic-like" appearance of his face and the long beard that gave him a certain patriarchal dignity and charisma.

The encounter between Cézanne and Pissarro took place at the Académie Suisse. The two men shared a great deal more than a common passion: they shared the same vision of the world and an attachment to the same principles of life, and to the same values—artistic, certainly, but also ethical and political. A strong friendship, both professional and personal, was forged between them immediately. It lasted around twenty-five years, with particularly intense periods in Auvers and Pontoise (cat. 33, 34), and still constitutes one of the major driving forces in the history of Impressionism. To the end of their lives, Pissarro (who died in 1903) and Cézanne (who died in 1906) continued to refer to their collaboration as a major event.

It was indeed their radical "otherness" that brought Cézanne and Pissarro together. They did not belong to the Parisian system within which they had come to study and learn, but, far from seeing this distance from it as an obstacle, they turned it into the linchpin of their artistic alliance or, better still, their own identity. From the start, their approach to the Paris fine arts system was therefore marked by what Mikhaïl Bakhtine called an "exotopic" perspective: It was the very fact that they did not belong to the established art world that gave such force to Cézanne and to Pissarro, and it was this new and pitiless perspective on the world of art that formed their artistic training. It was from this that the strong personality of each artist was born. And it was through their mutual co-optation that Pissarro and Cézanne were to discover the comfort of not finding themselves alone against the world. This objective otherness—this radical non-belonging of Pissarro and Cézanne to the Paris art world of the 1860s—was coupled

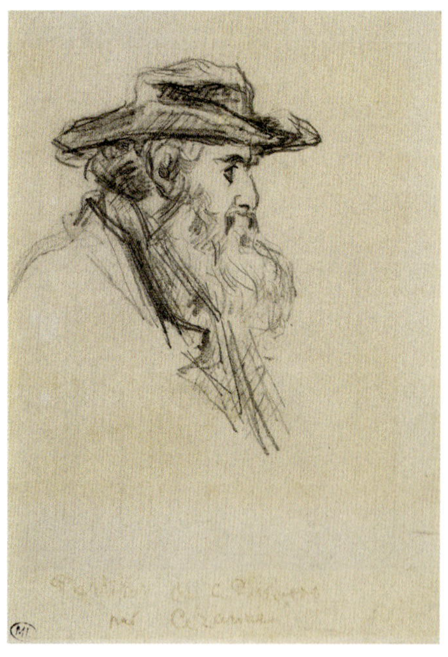

Cat. 32
Portrait of Pissarro
c. 1873
Graphite on laid paper
13.3 × 10.3 cm
Musée d'Orsay, Paris (kept at the Musée du Louvre, Département des Arts Graphiques), gift of John Rewald, 1975
CH 298

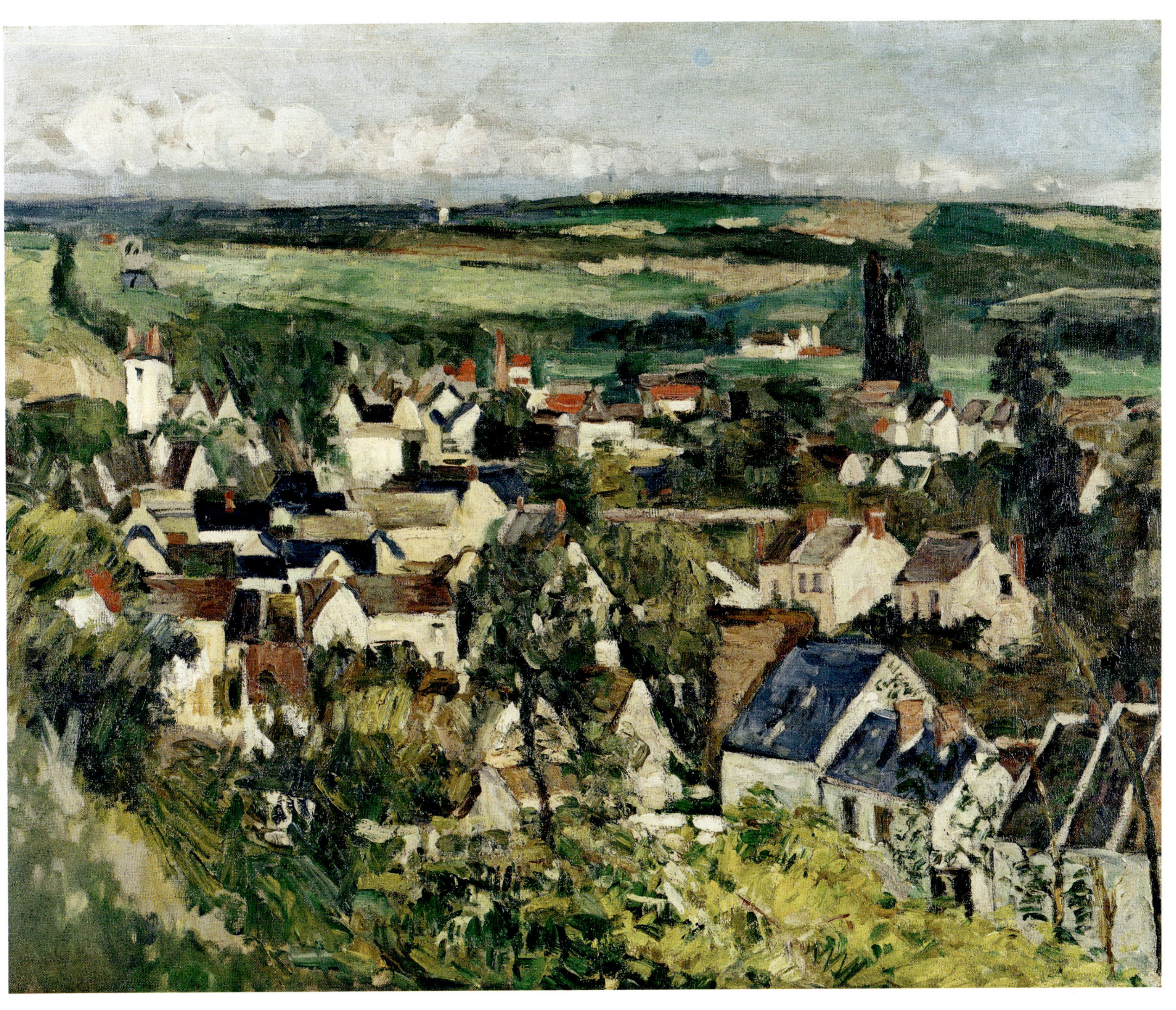

Cat. 33
Auvers-sur-Oise, Panoramic View
1873–74
Oil on canvas
65.2 × 81.3 cm
The Art Institute of Chicago, Chicago
R 221

with a subjective otherness: and it is here perhaps that the encounter between Pissarro and Cézanne becomes so significant and so striking for each of them.

In terms of objective otherness, both artists became objects of rejection (or non-inclusion) by a system that did not recognize them as its own. Cézanne and Pissarro were making their mark and their presence within the world of art indicated originality, in every sense of the word.

In terms of subjective otherness, both artists were the subjects of this exclusion. And it was they, in their turn, who peremptorily refused to be part of a world that chose to exclude them. Cézanne and Pissarro no more recognized themselves in the values of a system that rejected them than the system itself recognized them.

A revolutionary commando group battling against the system

Cézanne and Pissarro were very similar in many ways.[2] While they were keen to be recognized, this was always and steadfastly in the face of and against the system: Their friendship was born of a kindred resistance; they came together and supported one another in an unfailing refusal to compromise within a system of values that defined them negatively.

They were not alone in this open conflict with the system. Francisco Oller (to whom far too little attention has been given in the history of Impressionism) shared with Pissarro the fact that he was born in the tropics, in Puerto Rico in fact, and he too had come to Paris to learn his trade as a painter. Two other artists, Guillaumin and Guillemet, joined Oller, Cézanne and Pissarro in forming a group of five inseparable friends who constituted an anti-Salon "strike force."

This battle was, of course, necessarily based in Paris, as can be seen in a letter sent by Guillemet to Oller who had decided to return to Puerto Rico: "What on earth do you think you can do in Puerto Rico? What could Pissarro do in St. Thomas? And what could I do in China? We are painting on a volcano; the painting Revolution is going to sound its knell: The Louvre will burn, the museums, the ancient ones will disappear and, as Proudhon said, new art can only emerge from the cinders of the old civilization... Let us go into battle and strike down the infamous... build, paint with a full brush and dance on the belly of the terrified bourgeois. We too shall have our day. Joking aside, we have just had lunch. Keep working old friend, keep at it, apply the paint, use the right strokes, we will eventually prevail with our way of seeing. Pissarro sends you every good wish and we, all of us, with Cézanne, hope to see you soon."[3]

In addition to the militant tone and the revolutionary-style rhetoric of this writing, Guillemet drafts this letter of attack in the name of "all of us." But of those who represent this collective voice, amplified and defended by Guillemet, only two names are mentioned: those of Pissarro and Cézanne.

Rejection by the Salon[4]

An anthology could be made from the writings of these five famous figures: All share a similar explosive dose of polemical opposition toward the fine arts system embodied by the Academy under the aegis of the Institut de France and its most visible product: the Salons.

On March 15, 1865, Cézanne entered the fray: "On Saturday, we [Cézanne and Oller] will go to the shack on the Champs-Elysées [the Salon] and take our canvases, which will make the Institut blush with rage and despair."[5]

Fortuné Marion, a childhood friend of Cézanne, also echoes these sentiments in April 1866[6]: "Cézanne expects not to be accepted at the exhibition and the painters he knows are preparing an ovation for him."[7] Or again: "We have no choice but to exhibit our work ourselves and mount a competition fatal to all these half-blind old idiots [from the Salon]."[8] Bazille states loud and clear his refusal to present his work to the Salon jury: "I shall send nothing more to the jury. It is all too ridiculous... to be at the mercy of these whims of administration... And as for what I'm saying, there are a dozen talented people who think like me. We have therefore decided each year to rent a large studio where we will exhibit as many of our works as we wish. We shall invite the painters we like... With such people and Monet, who is stronger than all of them, we are bound to succeed. You'll see, people will talk about us."[9]

One of the most choice pieces of radical "anti-Salon" writing is found in a letter sent by Cézanne to the Superintendent of Fine Arts, the Comte de Nieuwerkerke: "I shall merely say that I cannot accept the unwarrantable judgment of colleagues whom I have not tasked with appraising me... I wish to appeal to the public and to be exhibited all the same. I believe that there is nothing outrageous about my wish and, if you were to question all the painters who find themselves in my position, they would all reply that they renounce the Jury and that they wish to participate in one way or another in an exhibition that must of necessity be open to all serious workers."[10]

In fact, Cézanne's virulence against the Salons soon turned him into an "anti-establishment" figurehead—a hero, to some extent. This position won him the unfailing admiration of this small group of artists led by Pissarro, who, more than anyone, recognized in the young Cézanne a force of opposition to the system that fully supported his own resistance.

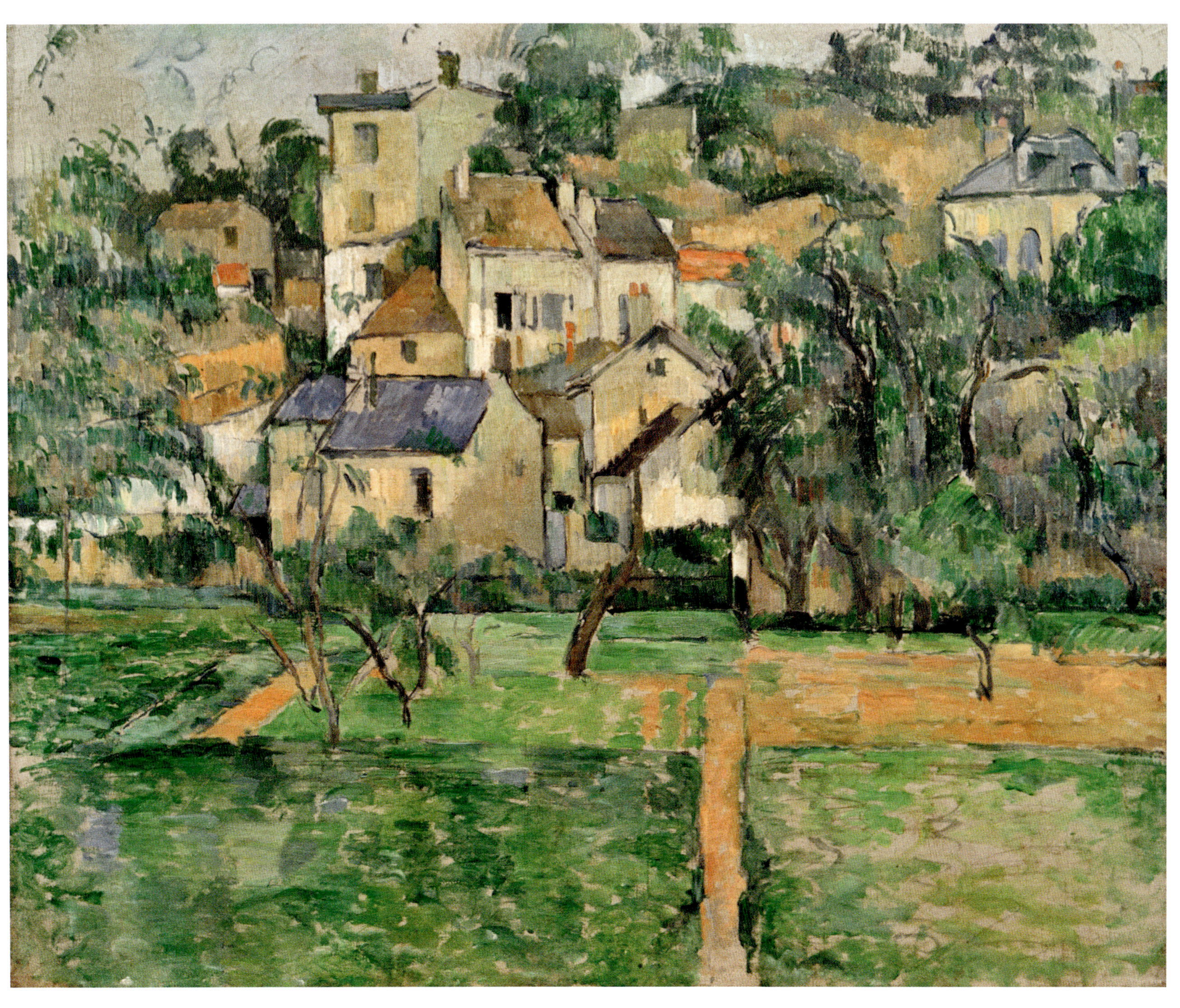

Cat. 34
The Hermitage at Pontoise
1881
Oil on canvas
46.5 × 56 cm
Von der Heydt-Museum, Wuppertal
R 484

The practical example set by Cézanne and the moral and political example set by Courbet would lead Pissarro to an anarchic commitment that determined his ideological position throughout his life. While Cézanne may never have openly declared himself a follower of anarchism, there can be no doubt that for Pissarro the example he set and the words he uttered presented a real and practical anchorage for the major arguments of the anarchist ideology: the rejection of any authoritarian system; the rejection of any judicial hierarchy presiding over the granting of honors and rewards (the jury); the rejection of traditional inherited educational systems; and a profound belief in the virtues of the individual, restored to what he was after a long campaign of institutional cleansing[11].

The Impressionist movement would, to a very large extent, take its inspiration from these principles.

A new truth in painting

The term "serious worker" constitutes the mainspring of the ideological system constructed by Cézanne and Pissarro. The provenance of this goes back to Émile Zola,[12] who made this concept key to the new criteria of true artistic success—based on each artist being in contact with the aesthetic substance (or "feeling"). Within this new system, a new concept of truth emerged: It was no longer a matter of veracity (i.e. of concordance between the image and what it represented); what mattered was the intimate truth of the artist as he himself expressed it—or according his "*petite sensation*" [small feeling].

With this turning point in the 1860s, sincerity made its entrance on to the stage of the avant-garde and, for a very long time, ousted the ideal of veracity inherited from the Renaissance. These were two concepts of truth that were poles apart. The truth of the artistic ideal, which renders the artist's work entirely transparent and reveals the beauty of the object depicted in its pure ideal nature—this was the concept of truth that Cézanne and Pissarro abhorred. They, by contrast, highlighted the need for the artist to draw from within himself, to render visible the work of the senses through the very labor of spreading the paint on the canvas, to render his feelings visible.

Cézanne, however, goes further than anyone. He moves from an aesthetics of resistance—based, as we have seen, on a rejection of the system—to a new aesthetics which, in a contradictory way, appears to reject any aesthetic model. It was on this specific point that the artistic paths of Pissarro and Cézanne diverged during the 1860s.

The "inaesthetic"—a term that has recently become much valued among the postmodern critics of today—appeared to gain ground and powerfully stimulate the young Cézanne. More than any other artist of his generation, he appeared only to be satisfied when he had created some monster that broke all taboos, when he had brought down all the principles of the aesthetics of Western painting.

Much later, in the 1880s, Pissarro would be tempted by caricature, but during the 1860s we might imagine that he would have experienced difficulty in accepting works as brutal and as hard as *The Murder* (fig. 48) or *The Abduction* (fig. 35). Cézanne is committing "venericide"! The murder victim is none other than Venus herself—beauty, in its traditional sense. Dirty work... but somebody had to do it and Pissarro could admire Cézanne for pulling it off!

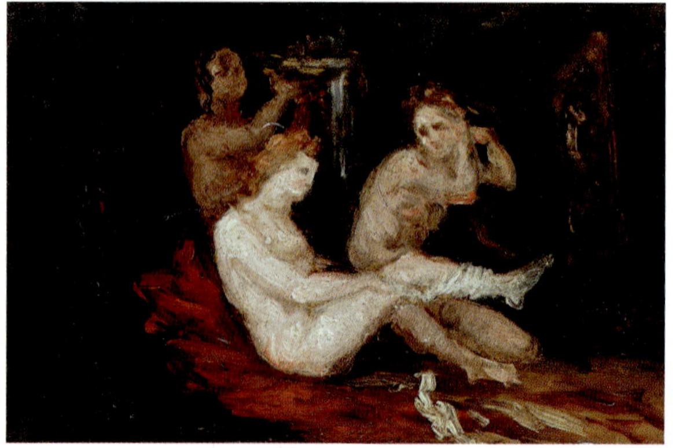

Fig. 32
Women Dressing
c. 1867
Oil on canvas
22.5 × 33 cm
Private collection
R 123

Women Dressing

A small painting by Cézanne purchased in 1885 by Pissarro may well reflect this admiration (fig. 32). The subject, perhaps mythologically inspired, is a group of nude women. Two are dressing while the third stands behind them, holding a large bowl of grapes above their heads. Devoid of all narrative content or feeling, this painting turns in on itself.

In this work by Cézanne, Pissarro perceived how, even in his early years, his friend had been adept at creating an interlacing of mad subtleties, between his feelings and the touches of pigment applied to the surface of the painting. René Char speaks of attaining the right tone in poetry through "the stunning compression of metaphor." In the same way, in this small painting, the artist's achievement in depicting, in a few zigzags of capillary fineness, the folds of the translucent stocking the woman in the foreground is putting on must certainly have made a strong impression on Pissarro.

Bachelard referred to scientists as the "workers in search of proof." Today, I am tempted to transpose this term and apply it to Cézanne and Pissarro as two "workers in search of feeling." These two determined artists in a sense wove their feelings together, very often finding themselves working with the same motif, working at their painting, rather like some musicians work at the piano, with two pairs of hands.

The reciprocal input made by each painter

What Cézanne gave to Pissarro was, I believe, reciprocated by Pissarro to Cézanne. Pissarro was able to see in these early works, these works of sordid beauty, of quite raw sensuality, of bare paint applied directly to the surface with nervous tension, works of an astonishing fineness, of a subtle and poetic harmony, and, not least, a certain tenderness.

Moreover, Pissarro helped Cézanne to understand (not intellectually, but in his flesh and bones) that it was not necessary to depict a murder or a rape in order to produce a work with a very strong impact. A period of intense exchange between the two artists began around *Louveciennes* (fig. 33), this impressive canvas that Cézanne borrowed for two weeks in order to produce his own *Louveciennes* (fig. 34)—a work that has everything yet nothing to do with Pissarro's painting.[13]

The day when Cézanne decided to leave Paris and go to live in Pontoise to be close to Pissarro was the start of a new chapter in the painter's work and life. Undermining the foundations of the institutional art of Paris was no longer his central task. For the first time, he could allow himself the luxury of listening to his own feelings. And in this Pissarro had shown him the way.

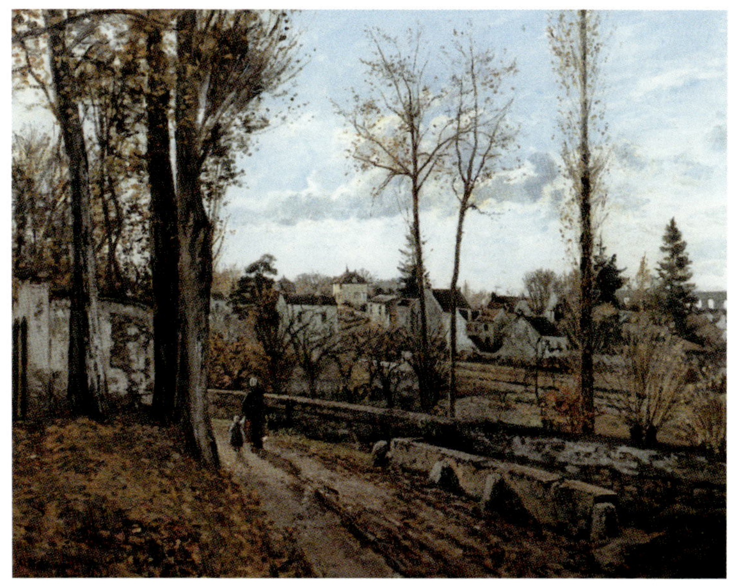

Fig. 33
Camille Pissarro (1830–1903)
Louveciennes
1871
Oil on canvas
Private collection

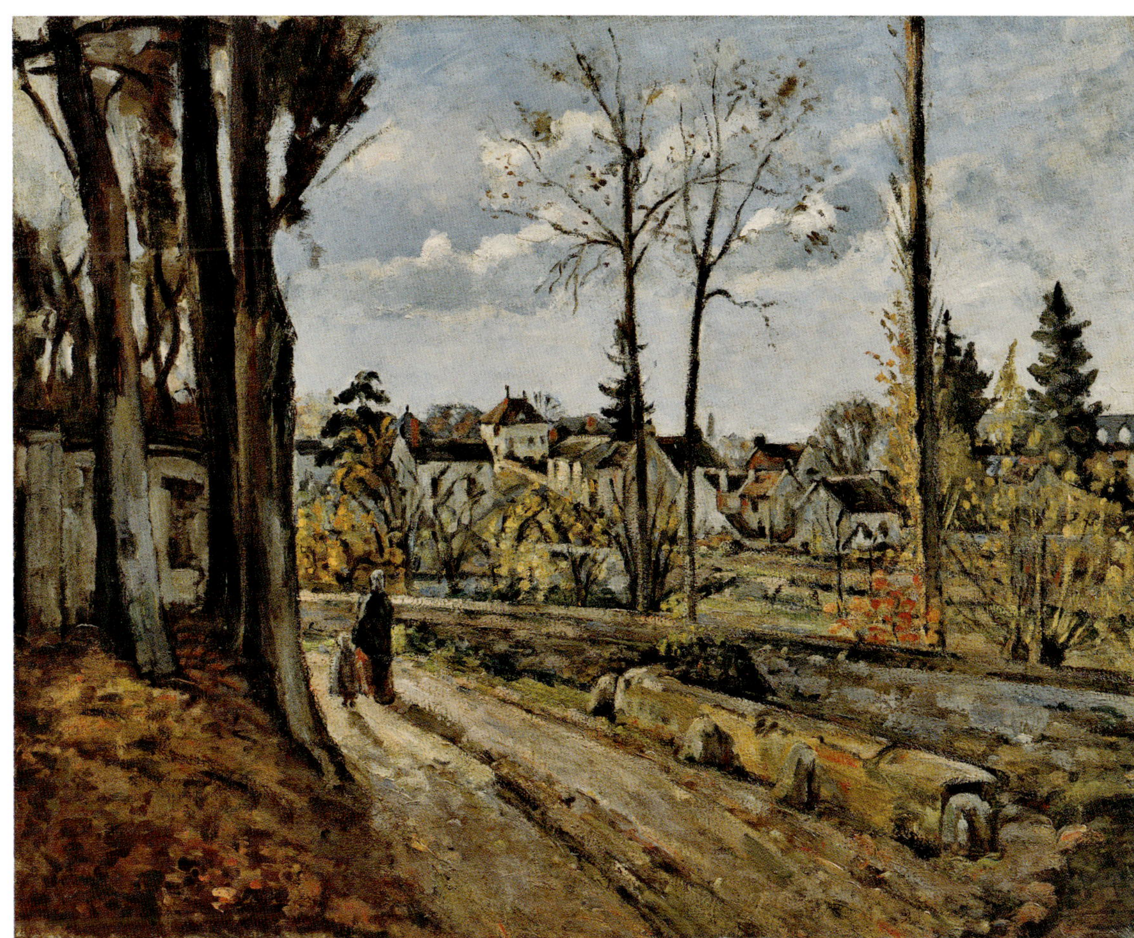

Fig. 34
Louveciennes
After Pissarro
c. 1872
Oil on canvas
73 × 92 cm
Private collection
R 184

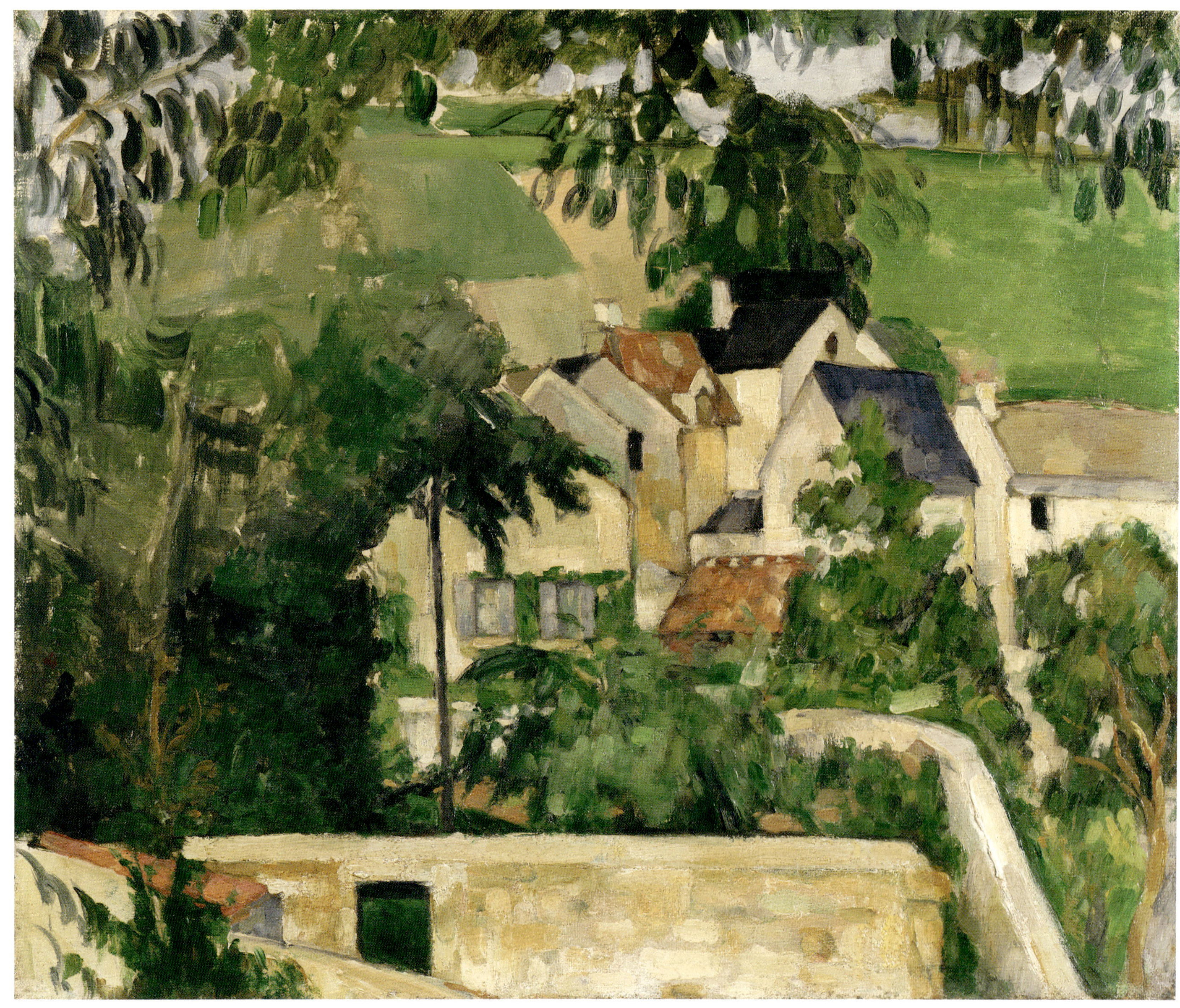

Cat. 35
Quartier du Four, Auvers-sur-Oise
(Landscape, Auvers)
c. 1873
Oil on canvas
46.3 × 52.2 cm
Philadelphia Museum of Art, Philadelphia,
The Samuel S. White 3rd and Vera White
Collection, 1967
R 198

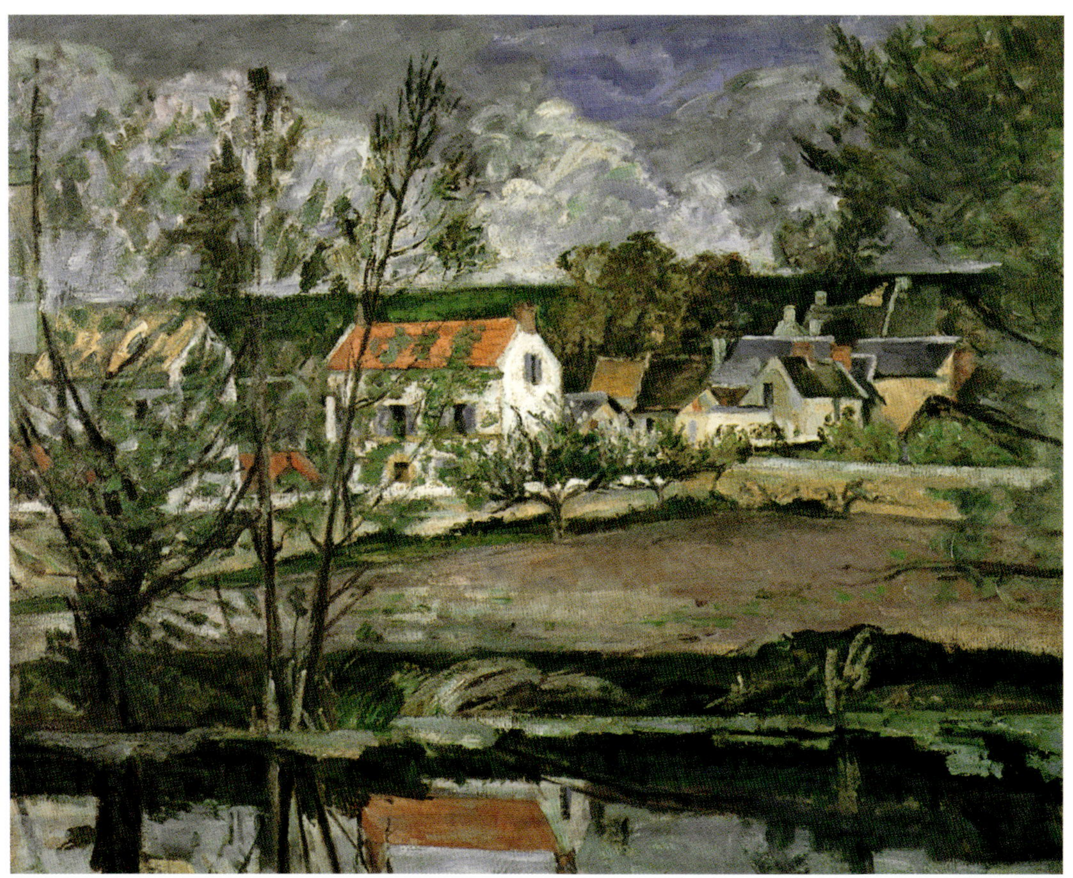

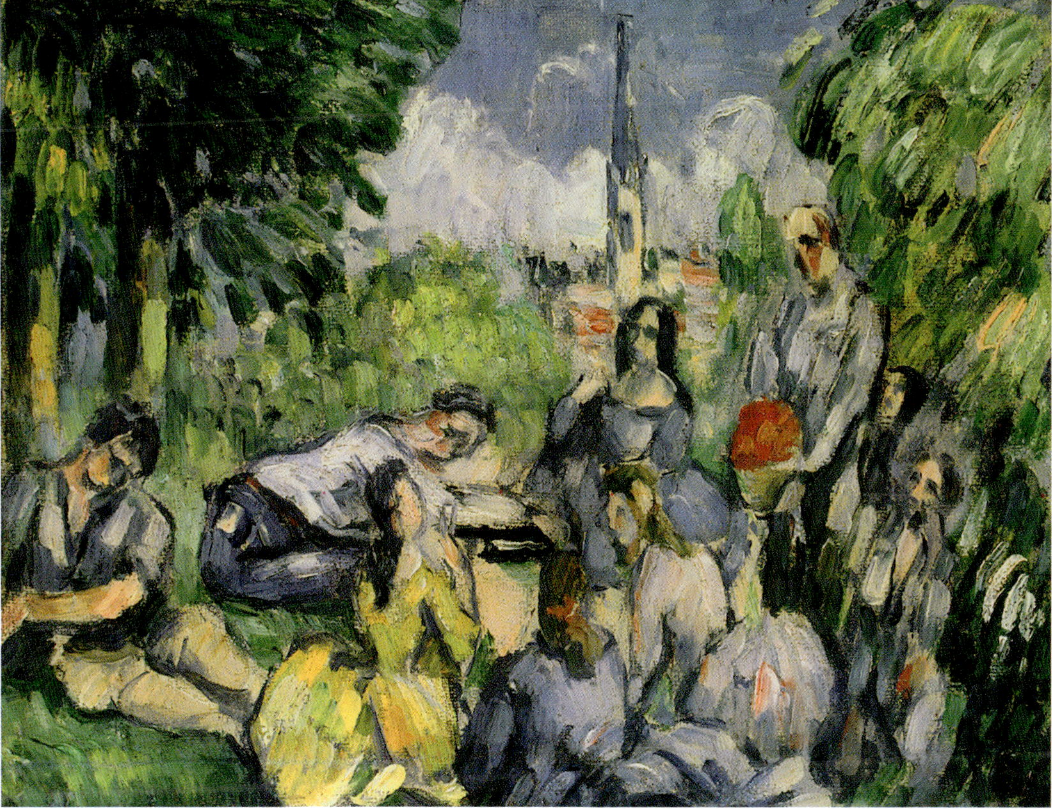

Cat. 36
Landscape by the Oise
(House on the banks of the Oise)
1873–74
Oil on canvas
73.5 × 93 cm
Palais Princier, Monaco
R 224

Cat. 37
Luncheon on the Grass
1876–77
Oil on canvas
21 × 27 cm
Musée de l'Orangerie, Paris,
collection of Jean Walter
and Paul Guillaume
R 287

Cézanne's engravings

Maryline Assante di Panzillo

Doctor Paul Gachet, who signed his works with the pseudonym Van Ryssel, was passionate about engraving and willingly made his etching materials available to his friends. Pissarro had already produced a few prints for the Société des Aquafortistes between 1863 and 1867 and he took advantage of this opportunity to take up the art of etching again. After that he continued to work in this medium and left a substantial body of engravings. Gachet initiated Cézanne and Guillaumin into the mysteries of biting and gave them a varnished copper plate and an etching needle. Pissarro undoubtedly encouraged the novices. When the weather was favorable, the three artists went out to work *sur le motif* together. In the evenings and on rainy days, they worked on their engraving at the doctor's house, practicing by reproducing a subject that one of them had painted, or producing portraits of themselves (cat. 38). For instance, Gachet engraved a view of L'Estaque after a (lost) drawing by Cézanne. The few plates created by Cézanne and Guillaumin—only Guillaumin's were published in *Paris à l'eau forte* through the intervention of Gachet—date from 1873 and bear witness to the artistic friendship between the four men.

For his first attempt, which is clumsy in its technique, Cézanne took his inspiration from a painting by Guillaumin, *Barges on the Seine at Bercy* (fig. 29), which belonged to Gachet. The inversion of the subject and inscription confirm that Cézanne drew directly onto the copper plate, as if he had had a sketch book in his hand. He drew the first lines with a fine point then he accentuated the shadows with big, thick strokes, which caused the varnish to crack, creating what engravers call *crevés*. The subtlety of Guillaumin's half-tones was lost: Cézanne went for the essentials, simplifying forms and using bold, aggressive outlines. In the painting, the bridge fades into the distance. Here, by contrast, the heavy black lines of the bridge project the line of the horizon toward the foreground.

The *Portrait of the Painter A. Guillaumin with the Hanged Man* (cat. 39) is drawn more delicately and in humorous vein. This friendly gesture is embellished with a hanged man, a reference to *The House of the Hanged Man* (cat. 74). Maybe this is the distinctive mark chosen by Cézanne at the suggestion of Gachet, who adopted a duck as his own emblem, while Pissarro chose a small flower and Guillaumin a cat.

According to Paul Gachet Jr., the *View of a Garden in Bicêtre* (cat. 40) is a souvenir of a walk in the Bièvre valley with Guillaumin and Van Ryssel. The artists are said to have drawn side by side. The wall running across Cézanne's plate is continued in an engraving by Van Ryssel, *A Street in Bicêtre*. Cézanne has made progress; his lines are shorter and thoughtfully broken up, although a few *crevés* can still be detected.

Farm Entrance, Rue Rémy in Auvers (cat. 41), which reproduces in reverse a painting given to Pissarro (R 196), is probably the last etching of the series and is technically the least flawed. Cézanne skillfully uses the contrast between the dark zones and the white of the paper to give rhythm to the composition, indicating that he was beginning to understand the precise details of the art of engraving.

The model for the *Head of a Young Girl* (cat. 42) has been identified as Elmyre Roger, the daughter of one of Gachet's neighbors. The plate is dated and signed on the front, which suggests that a tracing was used. Though his first etchings were done quickly, this portrait is clearly more carefully worked

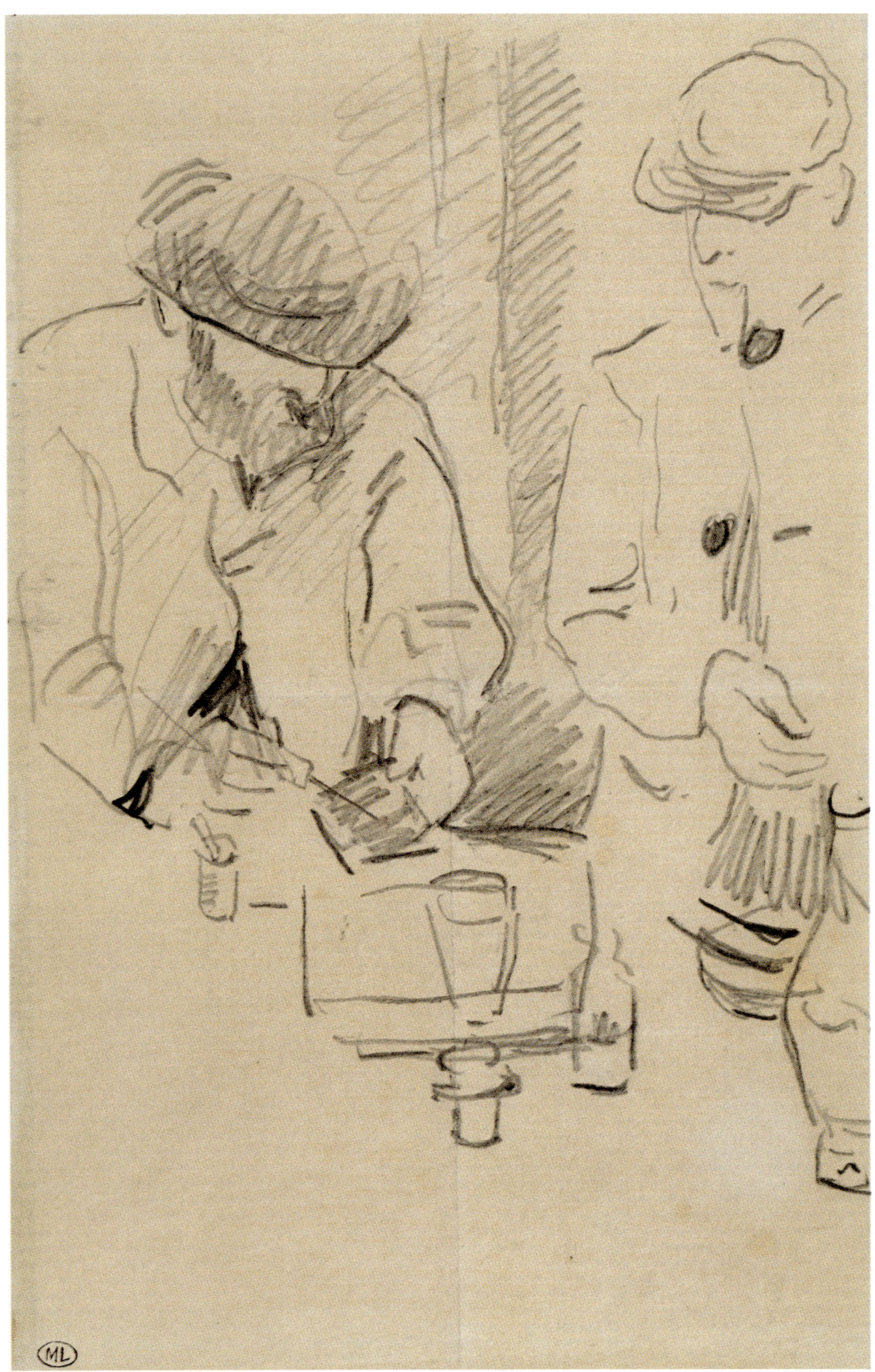

Cat. 38
Attributed to Paul Cézanne,
Camille Pissarro, or Armand Guillaumin
Cézanne engraving at Doctor Gachet's house
1872–73
Pencil drawing
20.5 × 13 cm
Musée d'Orsay, Paris (kept at the Musée du Louvre, Département des Arts Graphiques),
gift of Paul Gachet,
the son of Dr. Gachet, 1951
CH 292

out. In the same way as he returned to his canvases, gradually adding superimposed flat areas of paint that give rise to the form, Cézanne built up the face by increasing the hatching. The oblique strokes are reinforced by crossed incisions which shade the forehead and the eyes are hollowed out with the etching needle, becoming two holes full of ink staring intently at the spectator. On the left, a big shadow created on a second occasion using the roulette, adds depth and drama to the composition.

Cézanne's five plates exist in only one state, except for the *Head of a Young Girl,* whose plate was later beveled with a view to publication. In other words, he never reworked his plates after they were first created and he gave up etching for good when he left Auvers in 1874. According to the peremptory judgment of Loys Delteil[1], "his sketches drawn on copper would go quite unnoticed by interested people with inquiring minds, were they not from the hand of a master painter of his stature." It is hard to deny that these engravings are technically flawed. It is understandable that Cézanne was disappointed with the result and abandoned such a demanding "profession," especially as the slow pace of the work did not suit his nature. However, there is an impressive, almost violent, energy emanating from these clumsy attempts. Looking at them more closely, you get a sense of all that the painter might have got out of etching and you find yourself imagining... Cézanne and engraving: the story of a missed opportunity?

Cat. 39
Portrait of the Painter A. Guillaumin with the Hanged Man
1873
Etching
15.6 × 11.8 cm
Musée Granet, Aix-en-Provence, Communauté du Pays d'Aix
Cherpin 2

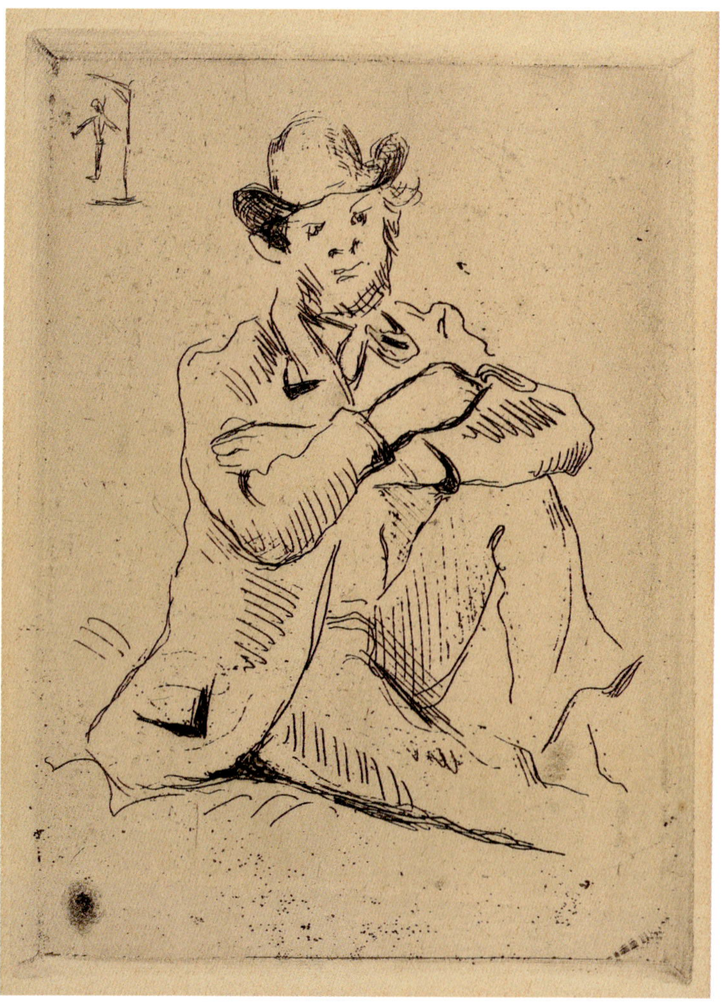

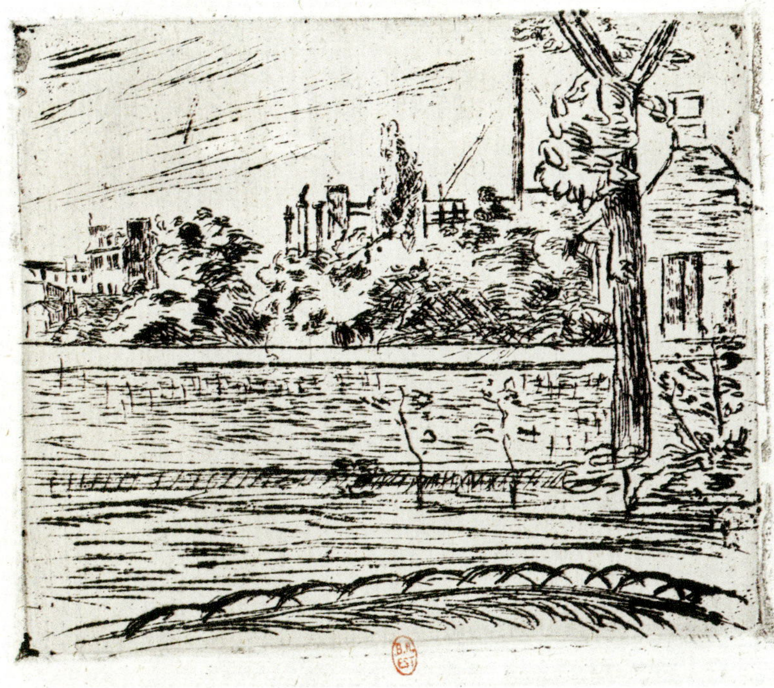

Cat. 40
View of a Garden in Bicêtre
1873
Etching, only known copy
Bibliothèque nationale de France,
département des Estampes
et de la Photographie, Paris
Cherpin 3

Cat. 41
Farm Entrance, Rue Rémy in Auvers
1873
Etching
13.4 × 11.1 cm
Musée Granet, Aix-en-Provence,
Communauté du Pays d'Aix
Cherpin 5

Cat. 42
Head of a Young Girl
1873
Etching and roulette work, second copy
12.3 × 9.8 cm
Musée Granet, Aix-en-Provence,
Communauté du Pays d'Aix
Cherpin 4

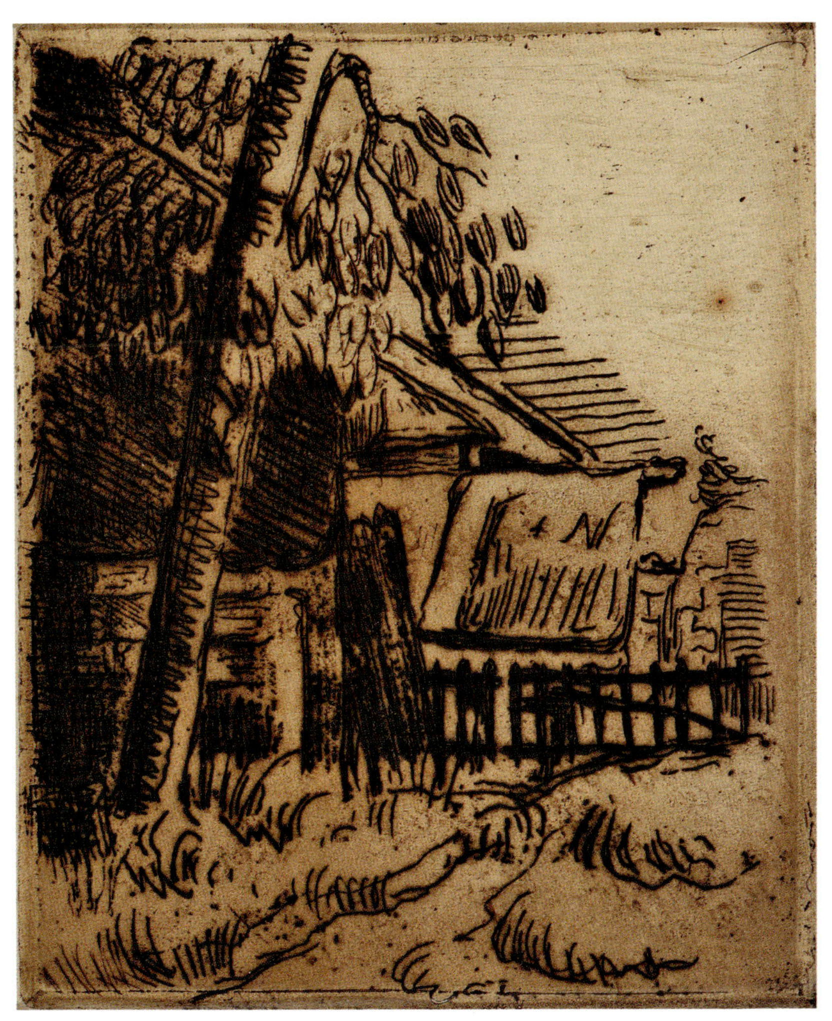

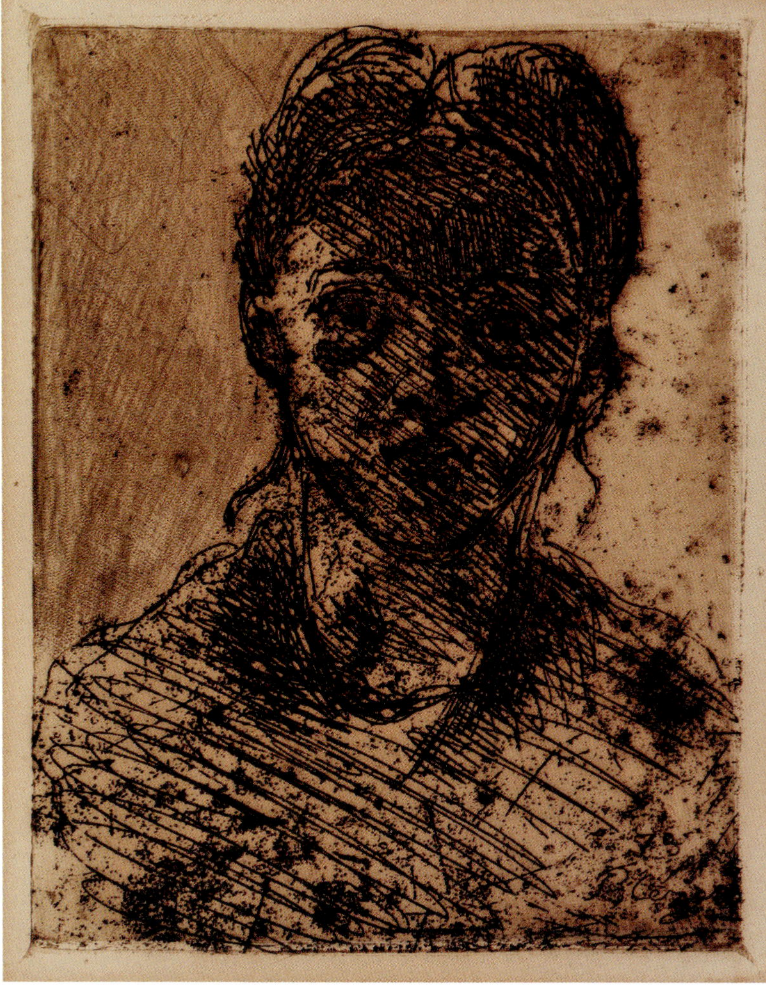

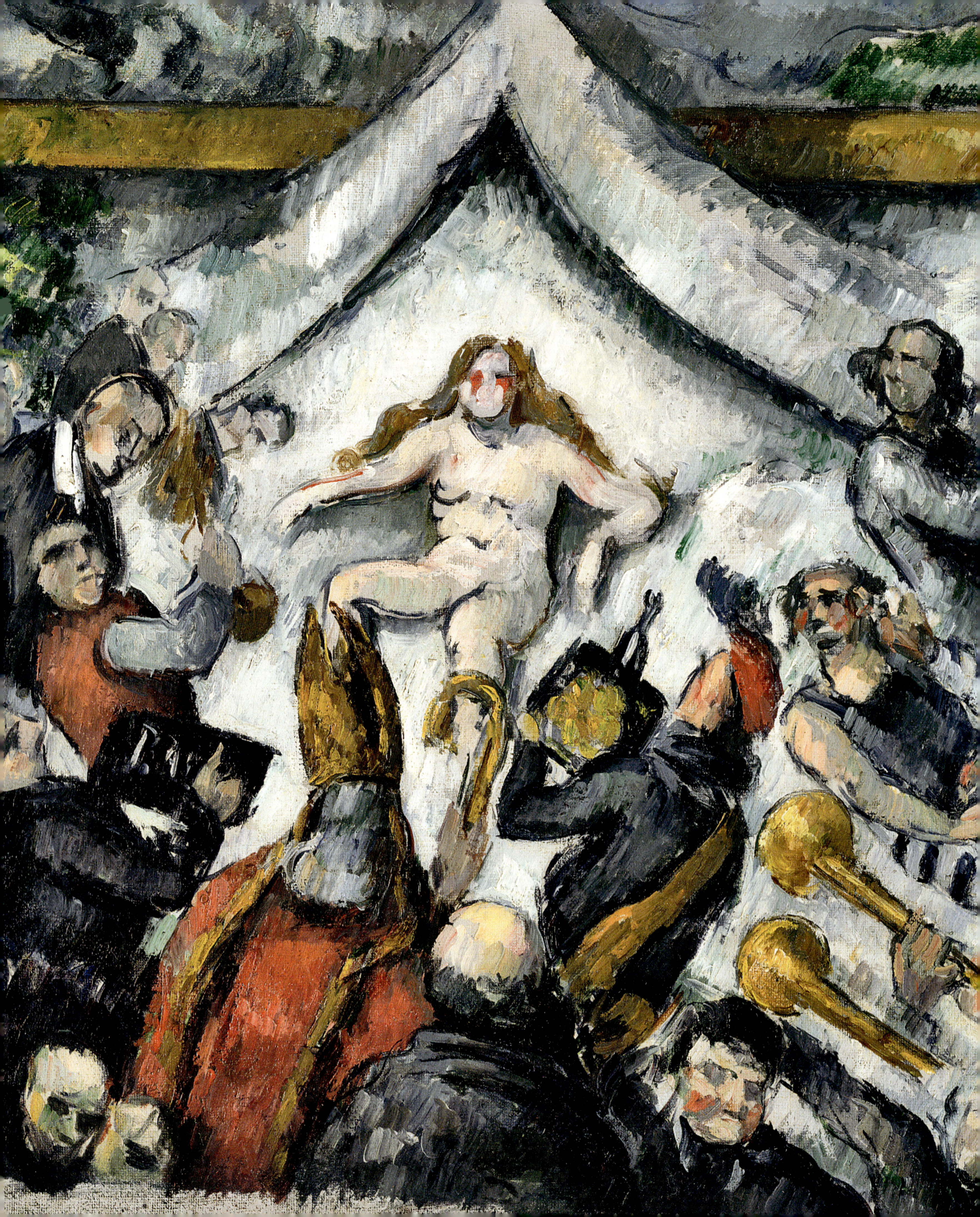

THE TEMPTATION OF PARIS

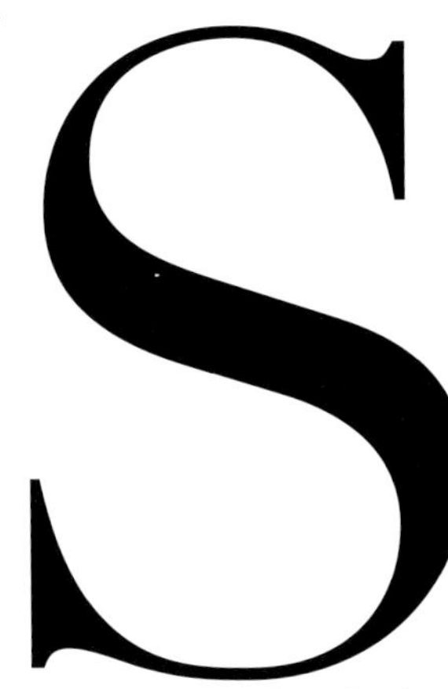till in Aix, Cézanne is twenty years old and in love. Her name is Justine. "We would go to Paris together, where I would become an artist and we could be together. I was thinking this way we would be happy, I was dreaming of paintings, a studio on the fourth floor, you and me."[1] This was Cézanne's dream of Paris: an illusion, if not a temptation! Already settled in the capital, Zola stepped up his invitations to join him there, the only possible place "to be an artist."[2] The letters written to Cézanne during those years verged on harassment: in Paris, there is the Louvre, the Musée du Luxembourg, the Académie Suisse, and the surrounding countryside. Faced with Paul's reservations, and those of Louis Auguste Cézanne, who had no desire to let his son abandon law for the bohemian life, Zola might even sense he was playing the role of tempter: "I would be a bad influence on you, if I were to cause you unhappiness by extolling the virtues of art and daydreaming. I cannot believe this however; the devil cannot be hiding behind our friendship, dragging us both to our ruin..."[3]

Zola was especially effusive about models: "You draw them by day, and caress them by night (the word caress is rather weak). They are equally for the daytime and for the nighttime poses; I am assured that they are very accommodating, particularly for the night hours..."[4]

Once he had "gone up" to Paris, Cézanne was confronted with his own demons, those of the city as much as those of academic painting: He painted three versions of *The Temptation of St. Anthony* between 1870 and 1877 (cat. 43, fig. 40, 41), probably after a lecture by Flaubert or, just as likely, following his visits to the Louvre. Women held the same fascination for the painter as a sumptuous banquet. So we then find him appropriating a theme that has come to symbolize modernity, in his unrestrained reworking of the *Olympia* painting. The painting was then not afraid of being provocative.

According to Vollard, Cézanne was preoccupied by a large canvas featuring female bathers when he was painting his portrait in 1896.[5] The provocative aspect was now strictly artistic rather than erotic, given Cézanne's determination to be the early master of a new art that would give rise to both Picasso's *Les Demoiselles d'Avignon* and Matisse's *La Joie de vivre*, from as early as 1906–1907.

The essays in this section are primarily concerned with Cézanne's fascination for the female nude and his desire for Paris, while at the same time focusing on some favored themes, such as murder or Zola's *Nana*.

D. C.

The Eternal Feminine
(detail)
See cat. 44 p. 91

Denis Coutagne

THE EXPOSED WOMAN

No sooner had Cézanne arrived in Paris in 1861 than he paid a visit to the hallowed halls of the Salon, where academic nudes were on display: "A pretty girl on purple cushions spreads splendor and freshness from her breasts."[1] While it is unclear which painting Cézanne was referring to here, we do know that he saw a monumental canvas by Cabanel, *Nymph Abducted by a Faun*, the subject of which inspired his own painting *The Abduction,* dated 1867 (fig. 35). Reference may have been made to Niccolo dell'Abbate's *The Abduction of Proserpine* for such a canvas (Sainte-Victoire replacing Mount Etna as the sacrificial altar where the woman was to be placed) but the subject is no less essentially Cézannian: What should we make of this already cadaverous body that he had to snatch from the waters of the Styx? Could it have been that the painter had succumbed to the temptation of Paris, as expressed in the woman, only to walk toward a still distant and inaccessible mountain, Sainte-Victoire? But then could this desired and possessed woman be none other than painting itself, like a dead weight that had to be carried to the top of the mountain in order to be revived? And once up there, like a new Moses, perhaps he saw the Ten Commandments and came back down in triumph? Indeed it was an ambition that the elderly painter, back in Provence, would express in the form of a question to Vollard: "I am working obstinately; I am beginning to see the promised land. Shall I be like the great leader of the Hebrews or shall I be able to enter it?"[2]

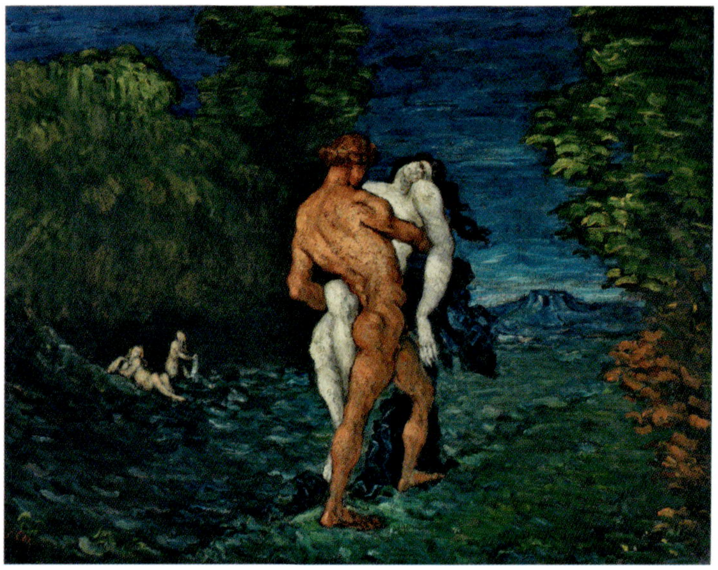

Paris, then, as a temptation? More than those of women and painting?

There would be many paintings arising from the violent eroticism inside the young painter, starting with a small canvas *Lot and His Two Daughters*. Cézanne threw himself impetuously into some extremely carnal paintings: *The Feast (The Orgy)* (fig. 36), *The Courtesans* (R 144, but see also R 122, 123, 124), *Afternoon in Naples* (fig. 37, R 289, 290), the three versions of *The Temptation of Saint Anthony* (R 167, 240, 300), *The Eternal Feminine* (R 299), *A Modern Olympia* (cat. 48, fig. 44), *Leda and the Swan* (cat. 50, fig. 45, 46).

Did he need, then, to experience these Parisian temptations, sometimes succumbing to them, in order to become the painter of *Large Bathers?* After all we know from Vollard that he sketched some versions of this painting in Paris. Finding an answer involves looking at certain paintings that have been deliberately selected to explain this challenge, the theatre of which could only have been Paris.

Fig. 35
The Abduction
1867
Oil on canvas
90.5 × 117 cm
Fitzwilliam Museum, Cambridge
R 121

Luncheon on the Grass

One of Cézanne's pictures more than any other, painted in 1870–71, may throw light on what this Paris temptation was all about: *Luncheon on the Grass* (fig. 38). Undeniably, the artist was reappropriating a classical theme for the new generation of painters. In 1862–1863, Monet had

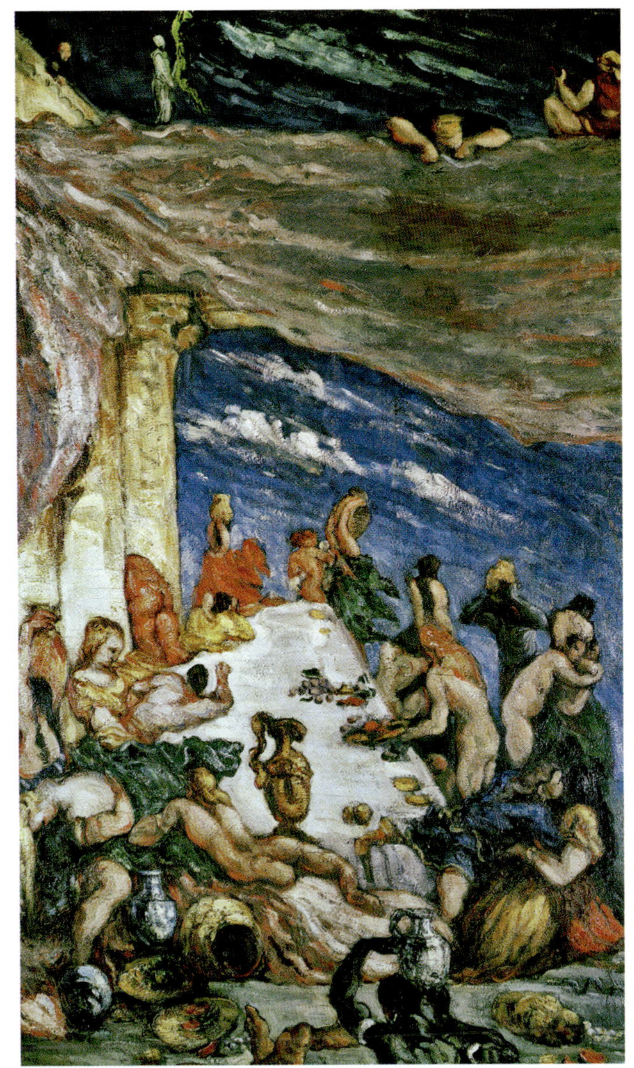

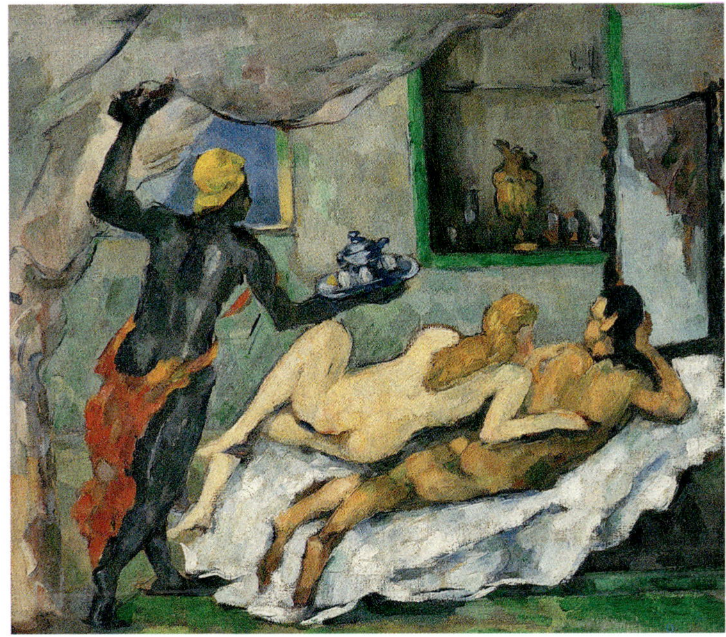

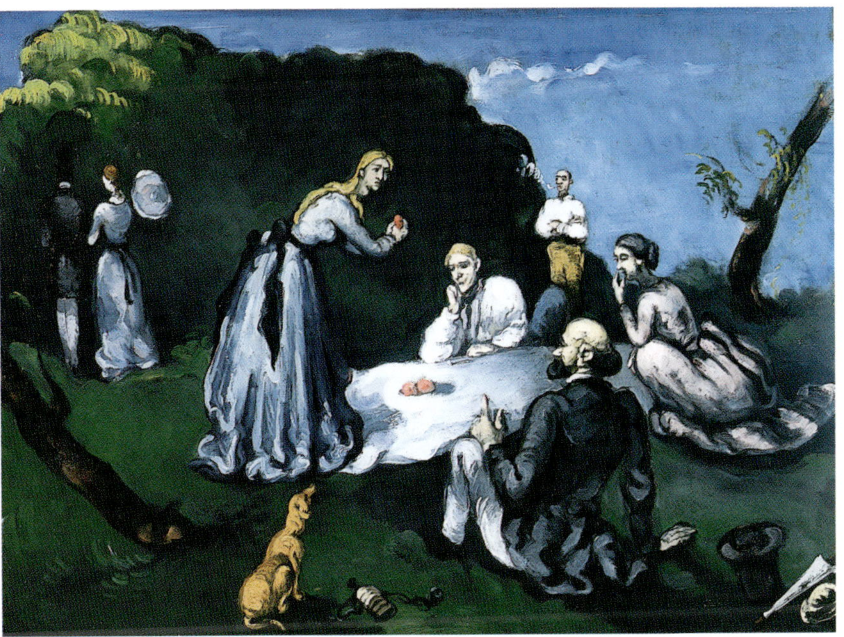

Fig. 36
The Feast (The Orgy)
c. 1867 (perhaps later)
Oil on canvas
130 × 81 cm
Private collection
R 128

Fig. 37
Afternoon in Naples (with a Black servant)
1876–77
Oil on canvas
37 × 45 cm
National Gallery of Australia, Canberra
R 291

Fig. 38
Luncheon on the Grass
c. 1870
Oil on canvas
60 × 81 cm
Private collection
R 164

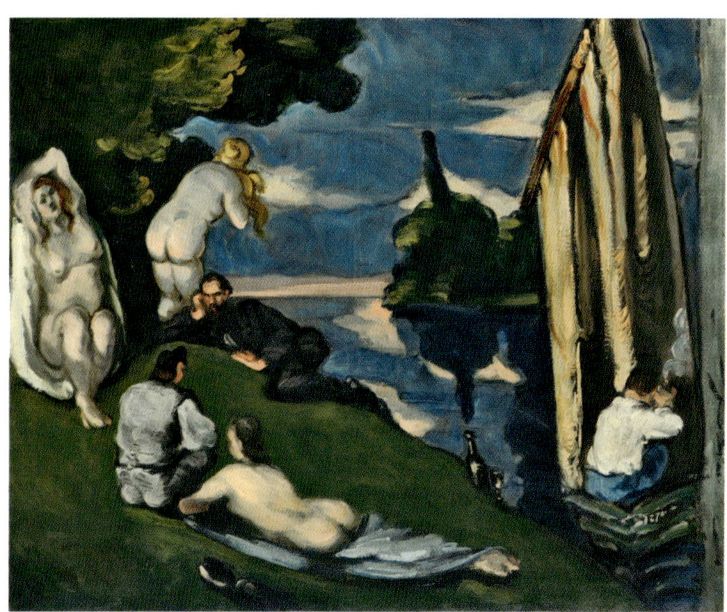

planned a huge canvas on the theme of a trip to the country and Manet had distinguished himself as a master at the Salon des Refusés in 1863 by exhibiting his *Luncheon on the Grass*. And Cézanne had been able to see in the Louvre *The Pastoral Concert* by Giorgione (deriving its composition from a drawing) and Watteau's *The Embarkation for Cythera*.

Here, Cézanne inserts himself in the picture in the figure in the foreground wearing a frock coat, giving the painter the unexpected—and quintessentially Parisian—look of a dandy. Facing him, a young man with very pale skin has been identified as the painter's doppelganger: "I see you in my life as the same pale young man of whom Musset speaks," Zola had written in the preface to his work *Mon Salon*, in 1866, dedicated to Cézanne. The writer is said to be represented in the pipe-smoking figure standing in the distance, a character that would reappear in the painting *Pastorale* (fig. 39)[3].

Two women are represented in *Luncheon on the Grass* of 1870. One of them is standing, a slender figure with loose, straw-colored hair who leans toward the man seated in the foreground, looking coldly at him. The other woman seems more reserved: She is seated, her brown hair tied back in a chignon on her neck, and holding back a word or a smile with her hand placed in front of her mouth. This shows Cézanne caught between two female figures. The woman, who is standing and holding an apple, is definitely an evocation of Eve, the temptress. In the middle ground the man and woman dressed in very elegant Parisian style, are moving away toward the shrubbery, suggesting a second stage in this temptation; we are not told the third.[4]

The Temptations of Saint Anthony

Around 1870–1877 Cézanne painted three versions of *The Temptation of Saint Anthony* (cat. 43, fig. 40, 41). He was doubtless inspired by the literary memory of Flaubert's texts[5] as much as the writer's imagination was fed by his memory of Brueghel's painting on this theme (exhibited in the Balbi Palace in Genoa). Of course Cézanne did not in any way attempt to paint all of St. Anthony's temptations, like Flaubert, who explored the more arcane ones (particularly because the main temptation is intellectual rather than sensual, in a way a temptation of God); instead the painter

Fig. 39
Pastorale
1870
Oil on canvas
65 × 81 cm
Musée d'Orsay, Paris
R 166

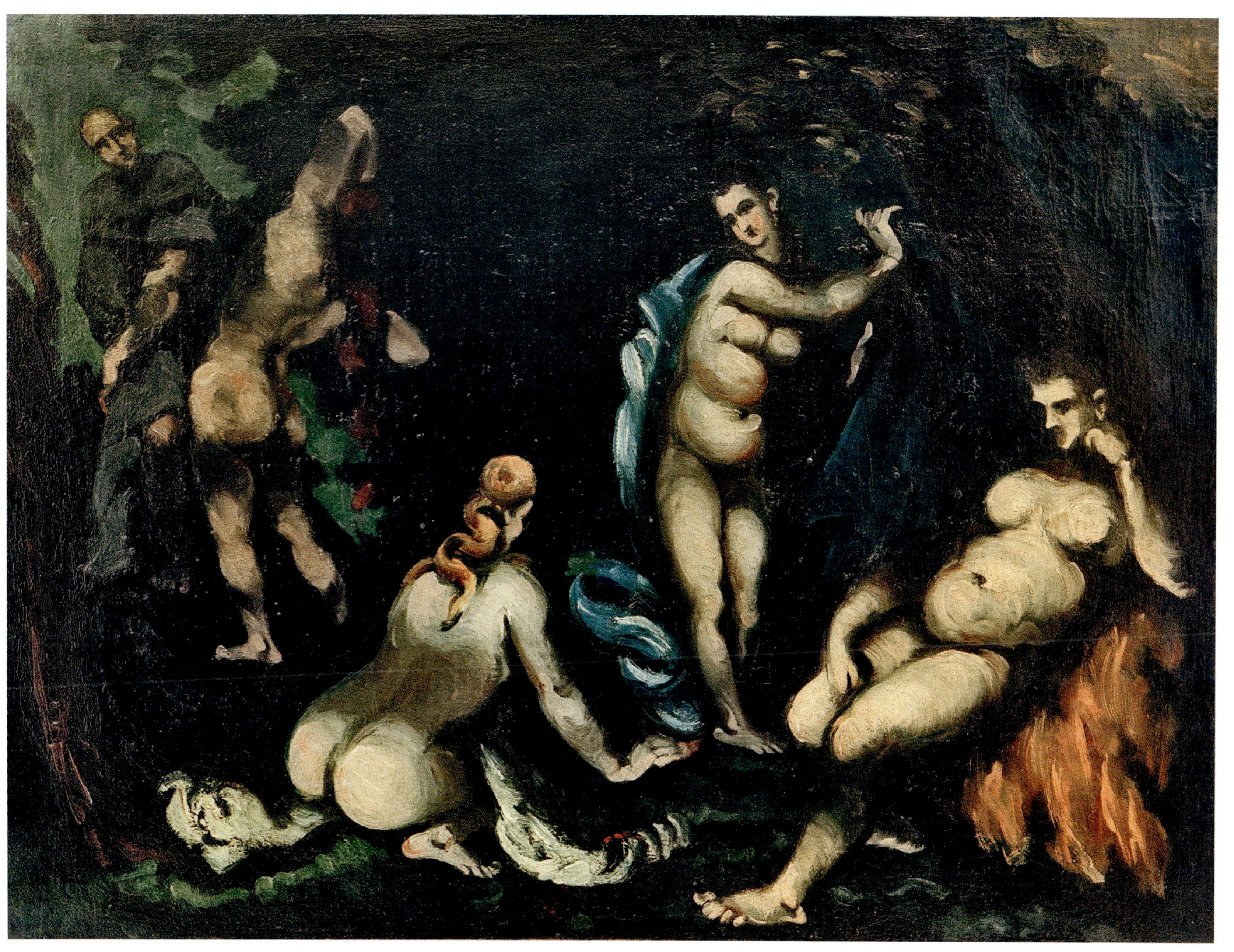

Cat. 43
The Temptation of Saint Anthony
1870
Oil on canvas
Fondation Collection E. G. Bührle, Zürich
R 167

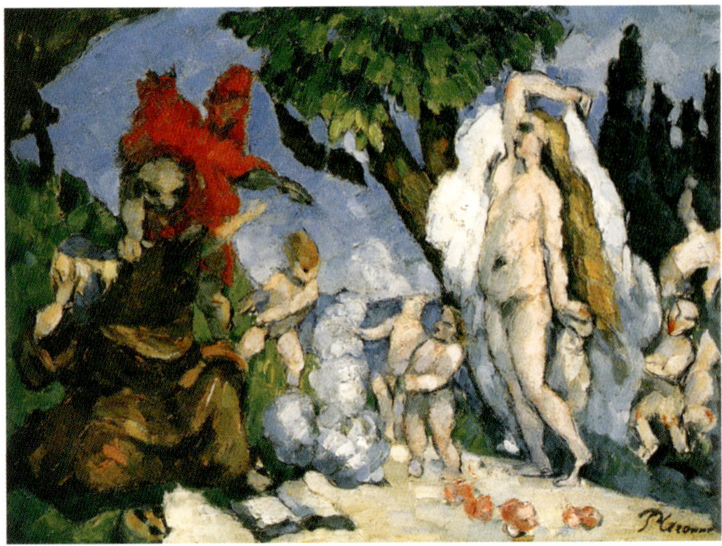

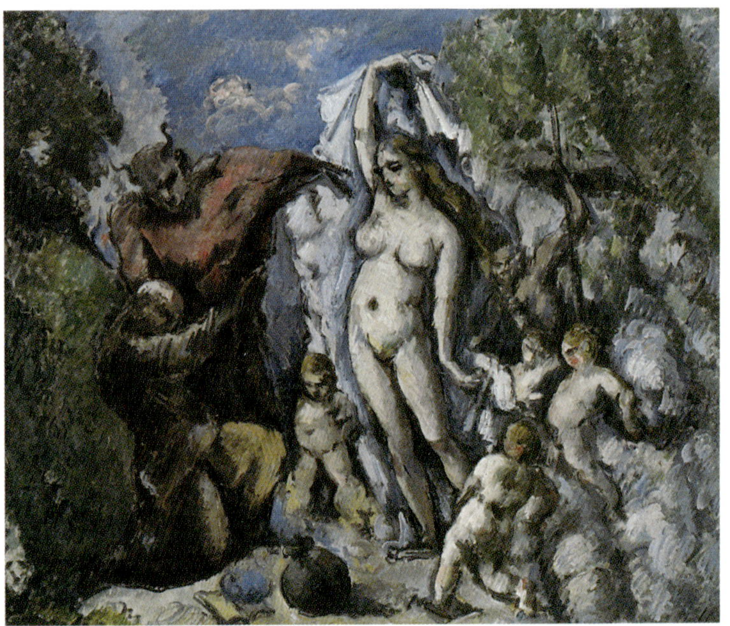

Fig. 40
The Temptation of Saint Anthony
c. 1874
Oil on canvas
25 × 33 cm
Private collection
R 240

Fig. 41
The Temptation of Saint Anthony
c. 1877
Oil on canvas
47 × 56 cm
Musée d'Orsay, Paris
R 300

latched on to one episode—the temptation of the flesh, symbolized in the Queen of Sheba. It goes without saying that this temptation, in the guise of a woman whose beauty symbolizes nature and the world, is at the same time that of a tempting God whose immediate presence gives clear meaning to everything. Here Cézanne dispenses with all demonic representations, deformed and imaginary animals, and earthly splendors that accompany the female apparition, in this case a nude without jewelry. In the two other versions (fig. 40 and 41) the devil is like a horned Satan far removed from the chimeras that traditionally haunt the saint as much as painters like Brueghel, Téniers, or Bosch. In painting this classical theme (not treated by other Impressionist painters) Cézanne scales it down in an attempt to go beyond the sensual dimension of desire and talk about the nature of the relationship between the painter and his model.

The first version of *The Temptation of Saint Anthony* (cat. 43)[6] makes explicit reference to Delacroix's *Death of Sardanapalus*.[7] The monk in top left replaces the sybarite, who on the point of committing suicide wants to take his concubines, slaves, and even horses with him amid the confusion of treasures, jewels, and jugs that the threatening fire will soon devour. The temptress in front of the monk is like the woman whose throat is about to be cut by the slave in the Romantic painter's work: In Delacroix, the most radical way of yielding to temptation is murder and destruction, which Cézanne apparently wants to apply to himself; what other explanation can there be for the rising flames on the point of burning alive one of the figures on the right in the picture? The composition of the last two versions of *The Temptation of Saint Anthony* (fig. 40 and 41) focus on the Woman, a carnal vision in front of diamond-shaped hangings that cannot help but evoke female genitalia. In her glorious nudity, the woman tries to arouse the desire of the monk, who is more than ever reaching out toward her to repel her. His hand wants to establish distance and to touch at the same time. The monk, in any case, turns his face away so as not to see her, as if "seeing" were a graver offence than touching.

The temptation of Paris was actually something quite different from a "consummation"[8]: in this case, the woman is seen as triumphing at the Salon in its Venus-like forms, whose perfected appearance was worshipped by "post-Ingres" academicism but challenged by Cézanne.

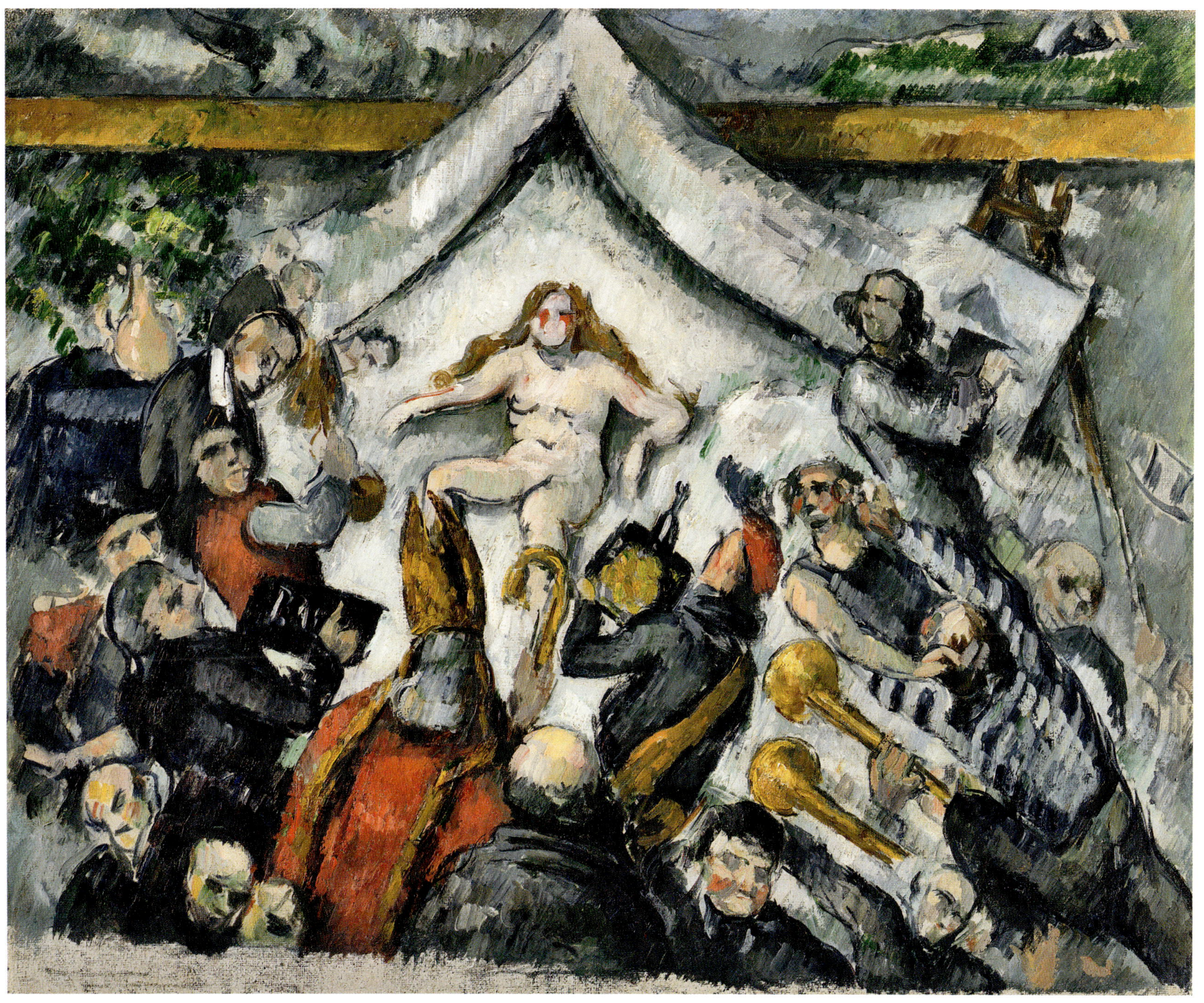

Cat. 44
The Eternal Feminine
1877
Oil on canvas
43 × 53 cm
The J. Paul Getty Museum, Los Angeles
R 299

The Eternal Feminine[9]

Even more astonishing than any *Temptation of Saint Anthony* or *Modern Olympia* was a work produced by Cézanne in 1877 (according to Rewald). A nude woman[10] lounges under a canopy—a far cry from all the canonical notions of beauty represented by the Venuses—displaying her worn-out body to 17 male onlookers, representatives of the Parisian society of which Cézanne was now a part (cat. 44). So there can be no doubt that the painter from Provence was inspired by the paintings he had seen in the Louvre, and drawings executed in a studio, especially at the Académie Suisse.

The composition of Cézanne's painting, if not simple, is at least immediately identifiable: The canopy above the woman forms the sharp tip of a triangle, and the drapery is developed in a similar way to the one forming a halo around Saint Anthony's temptress (fig. 40, 41). This mandorla, or full-body halo, is in the shape of a diamond, like the clouds which create a burst of light around the half-clothed woman representing Liberty in Delacroix's work, which Cézanne could see in the Louvre.[11] The scene is set in a studio, suggested by the horizontal wooden strips like a picture frame at the top of the composition. The woman is flooded with light, as if in the theatre, a woman without shadow in a way.

This picture is also redolent of Courbet's *The Artist's Studio*, in which an artist at his easel is painting a landscape before a motley crew. A woman, the regular model who was probably the artist's mistress (the child in the foreground could be his son), stands behind the painter, who seems unaware of her presence. As for the figures in the audience, not one of them is interested in either the painter or the model.

More provocatively, Cézanne isolates the woman in the middle of the canvas, exposing her as much as she makes her presence decisively felt. Courbet used a drape to hide some of her delicate parts. Cézanne reveals the model in the coarsest way possible, in the style of Manet. But to be frank, why should any of this woman with faded flesh and flabby limbs be hidden? Cézanne quite consciously refrains from any representation of a Venus-like woman. Yet he was able to create a Venus of poignant youthful grace, as shown in the drawing he executed after Raphael.[12] Deliberately

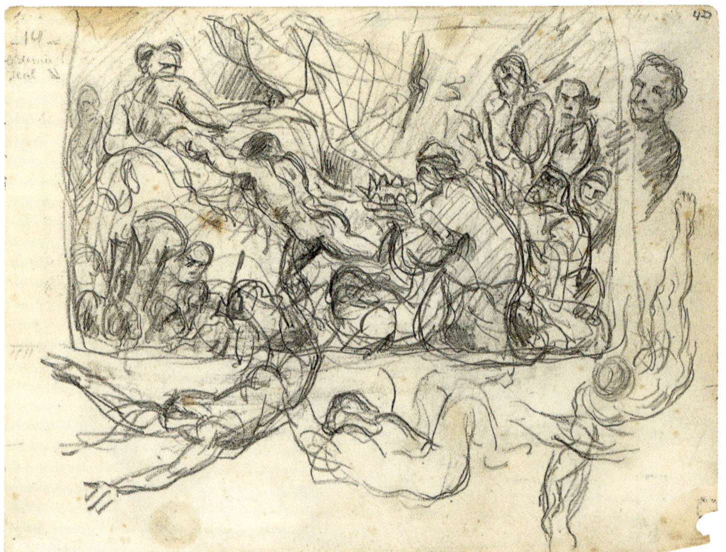

Fig. 42
Study for The Eternal Feminine
1870–75
pencil and black pastel on paper
17 × 23 cm
Kunstmuseum Basel,
Kupferstichkabinett, Basel
CH 258

Cat. 45
Preparation for the Banquet
1888–90
Oil on canvas
45 × 53 cm
Osaka, The National Museum of Art
R 640

Cat. 46
Still Life
1888–90
Oil on canvas
27.5 × 51 cm
Pola Museum of Art, Kanagawa
R 642

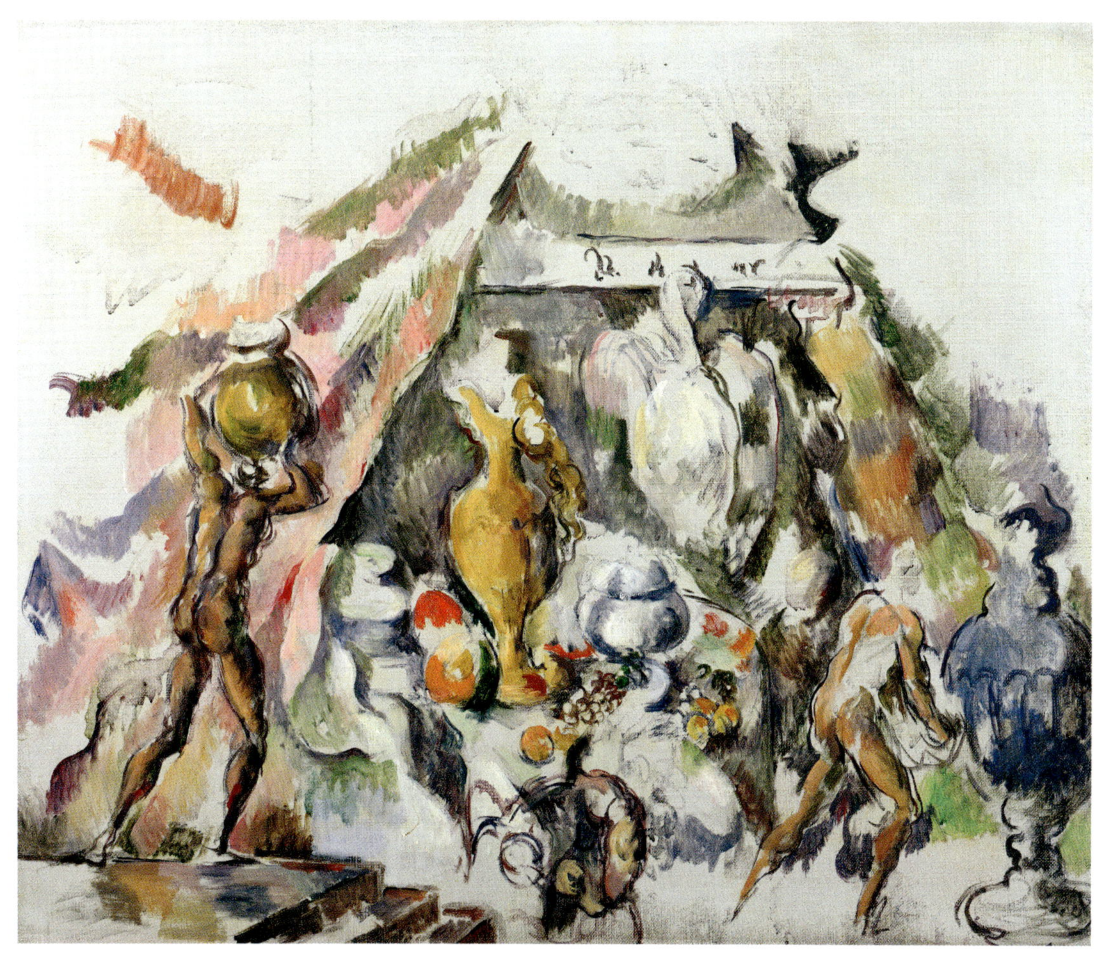

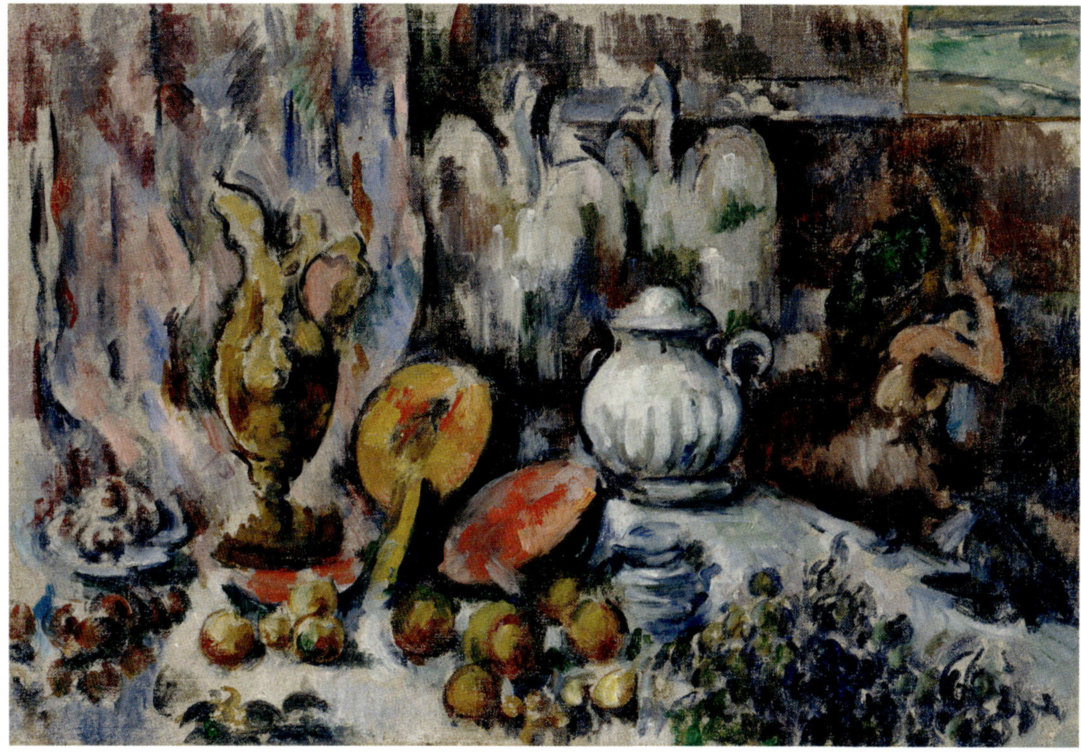

ugly, the woman in *The Eternal Feminine* flaunts her distortions and the twisted forms that would be introduced by painters like Picasso, Bacon, and de Kooning.

Like Courbet, Cézanne arranges the men in the studio into two groups: On the left the references are essentially social; a soldier, a financier, a banker, and a bishop. The male figures on the right side represent the world of the arts: a painter, a musician, a conductor, and entertainers. A man in a red beret brings fruit and wine. Occasionally the men are indicated by no more than a hand gesture: holding a trumpet at right, and brandishing a baton even further to the right. A hat floats in the air as if by magic, apparently blown off the bald head of the man in the near foreground, who reminds us of Cézanne himself. Another painter is sketching on a canvas.

In the months leading up to the creation of *The Eternal Feminine*, Cézanne was working quietly on landscapes at Pontoise, painting gentle still lifes in his studio in rue de l'Ouest, and working on the Quai de Bercy theme with Guillaumin. So how should we interpret such a painting, one that can certainly be approximated to the *Temptations of Saint Anthony* (cat. 43, fig. 40, 41) and *Afternoon in Naples* (see fig. 37)? There is no erotic excess here: The consummation is only supposed to be visual.

Paradoxically any temptation has gone: We are far removed from the drawing of the same title *Study for The Eternal Feminine*[13] (fig. 42). The figure in this case, the object of all desire, does not leave her onlookers indifferent. The model is not centered in the composition, but placed top left. The admirers are practically throwing themselves on the bed of their idol, like the women in Delacroix's Sardanapalus harem throwing themselves at the impassive despot.

Another, similar theme received the Cézanne treatment: the painting known as *The Feast (The Orgy)* (see fig. 36) also known as *The Banquet of Nebuchadnezzar*. Critics and art historians have had an easy time demonstrating the extent to which the painter proved faithful to Flaubert's text down to specific details (columns, witnesses leaning forward from the center of the clouds at the top, etc.), or how much Cézanne devoured the painting of Veronese (*The Wedding Feast at Cana*), Delacroix (*The Death of Sardanapalus* or *The Entry of the Crusaders into Constantinople*), and Rubens (see the series on Marie de Médicis in the Louvre). There is nothing but debauchery, wealth, confusion, and intertwinings. Cézanne the poet was inspiring Cézanne the painter. After all, he had composed a fiery poem in honor of Zola in 1858, called *Songe d'Annibal* (*Annibalis somnium*,or *Dream of Hannibal*):

"On leaving a feast, the hero of Carthage,
In whom there was excessive use
Of rum and cognac, stumbled and staggered."[14]

Other references also spring to mind, especially Balzac in *The Wild Ass's Skin*.[15] Note the significance of jugs: One had already featured in the painting *Lot and His Daughters*; and we would find them repeated in the versions of *Afternoon in Naples* (voir fig. 37). They would reappear in later still lifes, at a time when Cézanne was looking for a new baroque form of expression in the paintings *Preparation for the Banquet* (cat. 45) and *Still Life* (cat. 46) of 1888–1890.

Toward the bathers' theme

Once this temptress was removed, Cézanne owed it to himself to look at her in a paradise regained, or hoped for. The woman would become a bather, that is, innocent in her nudity, as if restored to an earthly paradise (cat. 47). And right up to the end of his life, he would strive to compose a symphony of these bodies that could be looked at without further fear of punishment. Cézanne's female bathers would not be identified with simple representations of nymphs in some glade or other, or by scenes of cheerful bathing in the style of Renoir. It is not formal, but pictorial beauty they seek. Do they remind us of the Pharaoh's daughter and her friends who discover the baby Moses? Their meaning cannot be ascribed to any mythology: They have simply become "Cézanne's bathers". The painting bought by Matisse, which he donated to the Musée du Petit Palais in 1936, has become a kind of icon, such was his respect for it:

"Allow me to tell you that this picture is of prime importance in the work of Cézanne, because it is a very dense, complete realization of a composition that he carefully considered in several canvases, which though now in important collections, are only the studies that culminated in this work.

"In the 37 years I have owned this canvas, I have come to know it quite well, though not entirely I hope; it has sustained me morally in the critical moments of my venture as an artist; I have drawn from it my faith and perseverance. For this reason, allow me to request that it be positioned so that it may be seen to its best advantage. For this it needs both light and adequate space. It is rich in color and surface, and if seen at a distance it is possible to appreciate the sweep of its lines and the exceptional sobriety of its relationships.

"I know that I do not have to tell you this, but nevertheless, I think it is my duty to do so; please accept these remarks as the excusable testimony of my admiration for this work, which has grown ever greater since I have owned it."[16]

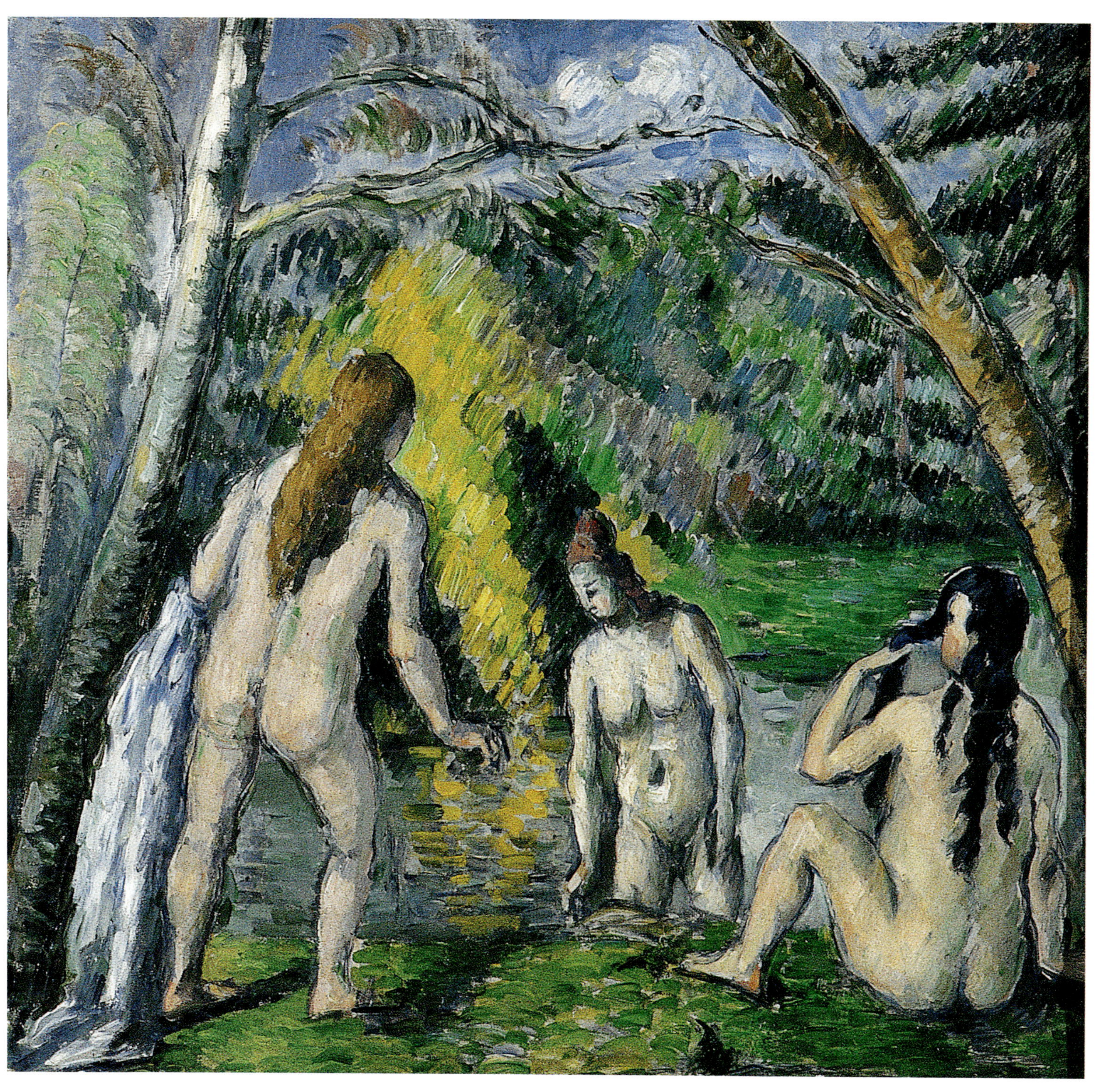

Cat. 47
Three Bathers
1876–77
Oil on canvas
55 × 52 cm
Petit Palais, Musée des Beaux-Arts
de la Ville de Paris, Paris
R 360

Olympia

Marie-Paule Vial

It was at Auvers-sur-Oise, at the home of Dr. Paul Gachet, in 1873 or early 1874, that Cézanne is believed to have painted this small work whose title makes explicit reference to the work of his older colleague, Édouard Manet. Dr. Gachet, an amateur painter and a collector of art[1], was also a loyal sponsor to the young band of artists living in Auvers and the surrounding area. His home was an open house to them and no doubt conversations there revolved around their shared passion for painting and its future. Dr. Gachet's son reports that during one of these discussions, in which his father was praising Manet's *Olympia* (fig. 43), a rather irritated Cézanne set himself a challenge to do better. He then immediately began painting this piece, which remained no more than a sketch as, according to this account, Dr. Gachet prevented Cézanne from taking it further for fear that, in his desire for perfection, the artist might destroy the balance he had so rapidly achieved.

The story is an appealing one and, given Cézanne's reputation for irritability, and indeed, easily losing his temper, it is quite believable. The pictorial treatment of the work, the light touches that elevate the creamy substance of the paint, the canvas left visible in certain places, and the obviously rapid execution are all aspects that lend credence to this story. However, it is important to be cautious about taking too literally this recollection of an evening in Auvers, which is more hagiographic than it is historical.

This memorable evening was not the first time that Cézanne had found himself faced with Manet's work. As all those who studied this painting have pointed out, this *Modern Olympia* (cat. 48) was preceded by a version dated 1870 (fig. 44), also entitled *The Pasha*, and by two drawings. Cézanne would return to this subject again in a watercolor in 1875 (cat. 49). This shows that the genesis of *A Modern Olympia*, which involved a series of variations on a theme, is more complex, and the time that elapsed between these variations reveals the ambivalence of his relationship with Manet. Manet was unquestionably the admired master, but here the choice of the term "modern" to describe Cézanne's Olympia relegates his predecessor's painting to an outmoded past and this *Modern Olympia* can therefore be seen as an attempt by Cézanne to bring the painting up to date.

In Cézanne's interpretation only a few elements, and of course the theme, remain. The amply rounded form of the body, with its sheen of pink and blue, placed on a white cloud being pulled back by the black servant girl has nothing in common with the frozen beauty of Manet's model. Among the amusing little variations that have led to this piece being described as an artistic joke is the small, black dog, its ears pricked, and quivering with curiosity, which here replaces the black cat. In terms of both composition and decoration, Cézanne appears to take pleasure in calling upon elements of baroque rhetoric and in making use of a pale palette and the rapid style of execution associated with popular 18th century sketches. Through this system of overlapping references, the artist, who is shown in the foreground contemplating this scene in which a sense of unreality prevails, pays a certain humorous tribute to his predecessor, engaging with him in a form of dialogue, and also with other masters of the past such as Titian, Veronese, Rubens, Watteau, and Delacroix, whom he revered.

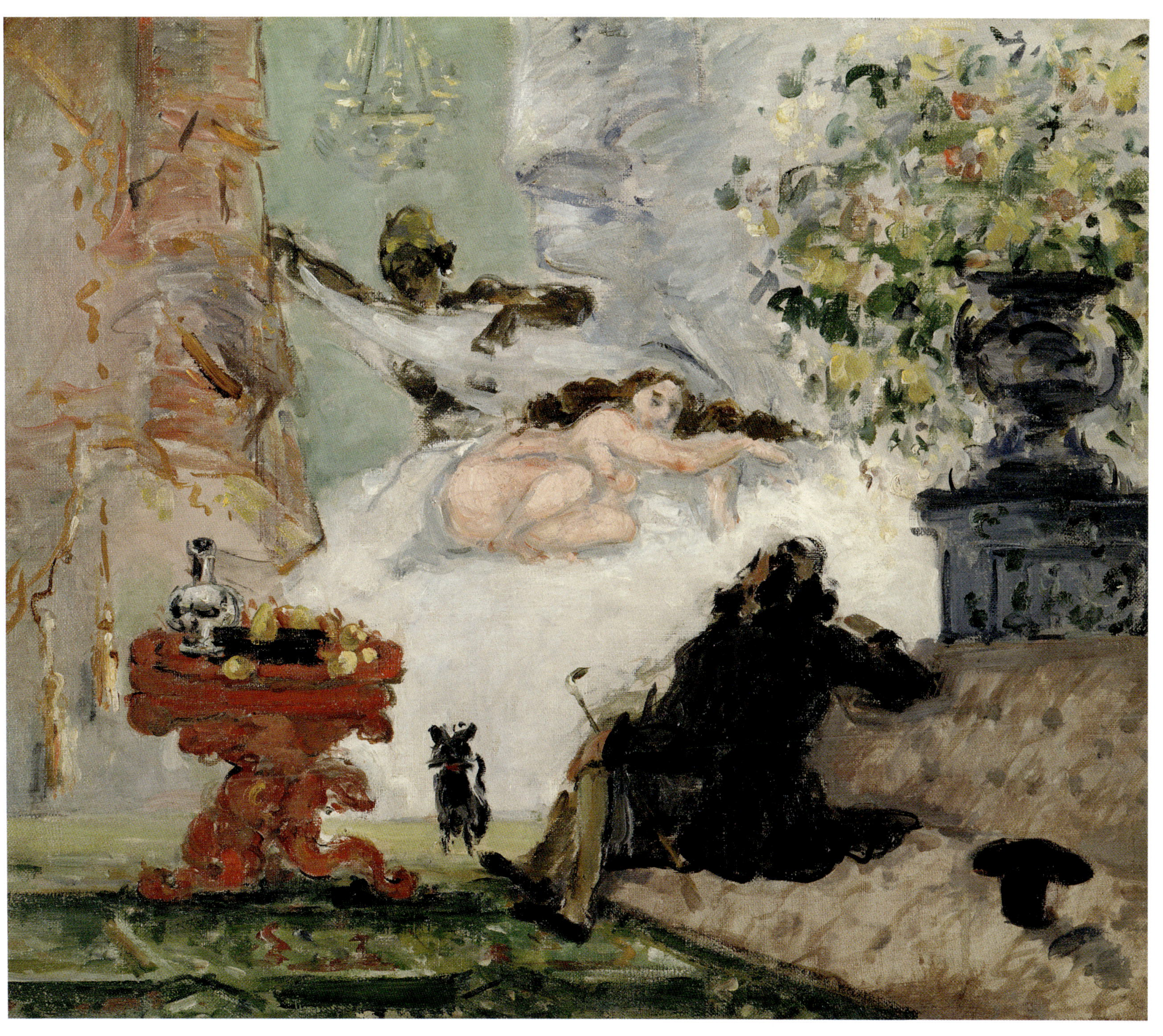

Cat. 48
A Modern Olympia
1873–74
Oil on canvas
46 × 55 cm
Musée d'Orsay, Paris, gift of Paul Gachet, son of Dr. Gachet, 1951
R 225

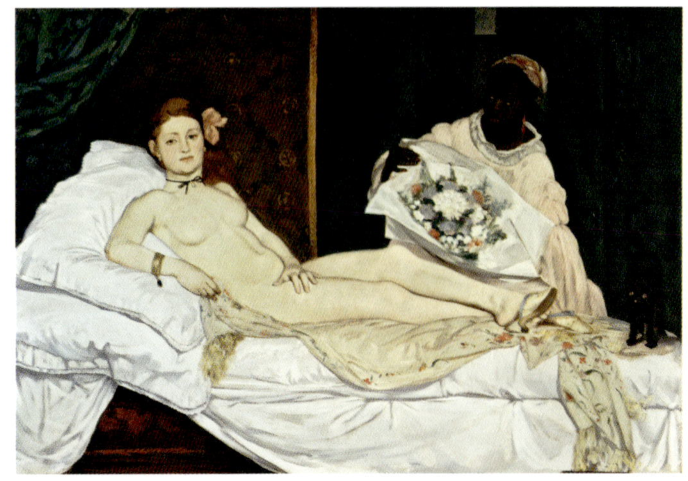

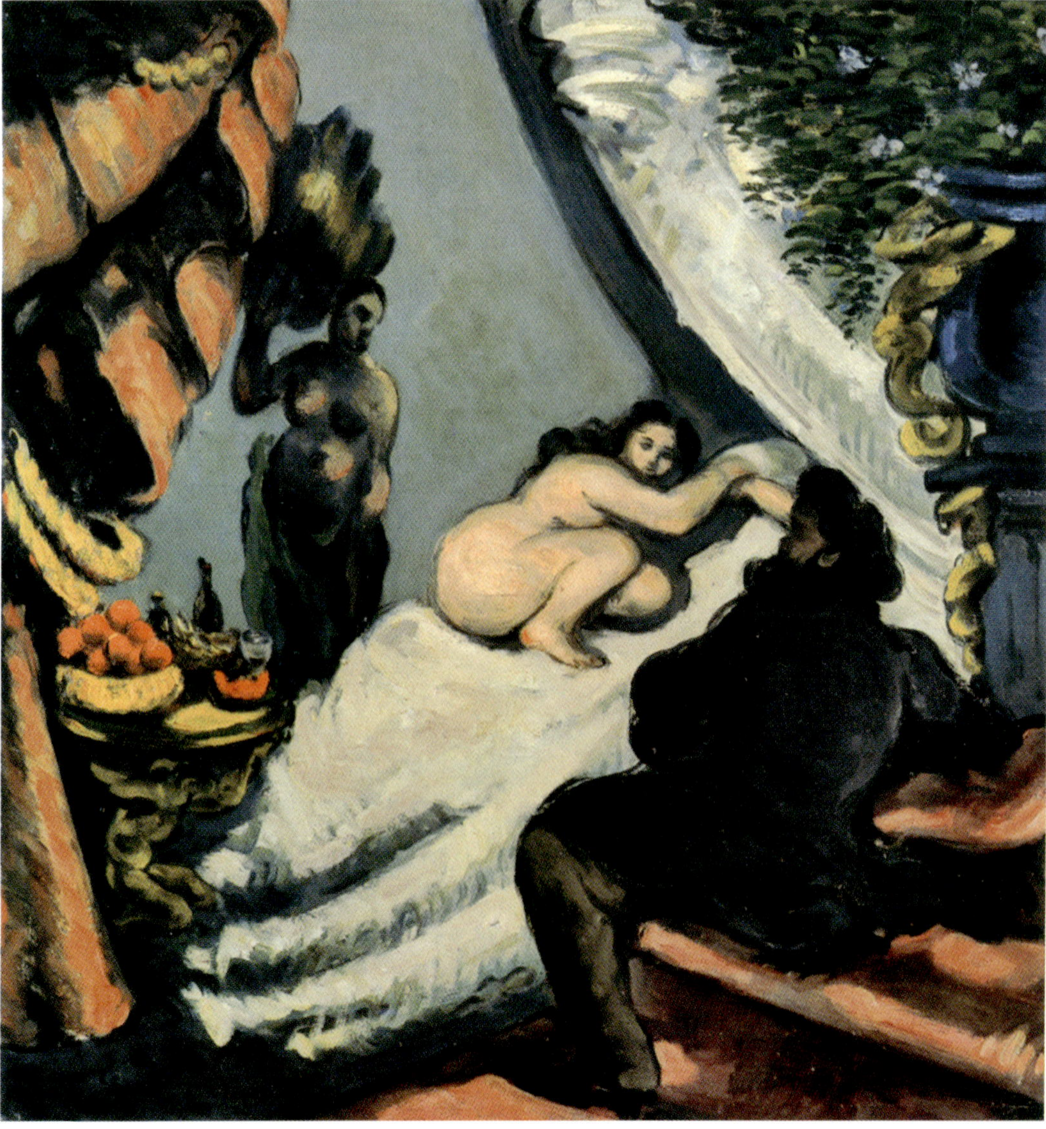

Fig. 43
Édouard Manet (1832–1883)
Olympia
1863
Oil on canvas
Musée d'Orsay, Paris

Fig. 44
A Modern Olympia
c. 1870
Oil on canvas
56 × 55 cm
Private collection
R 171

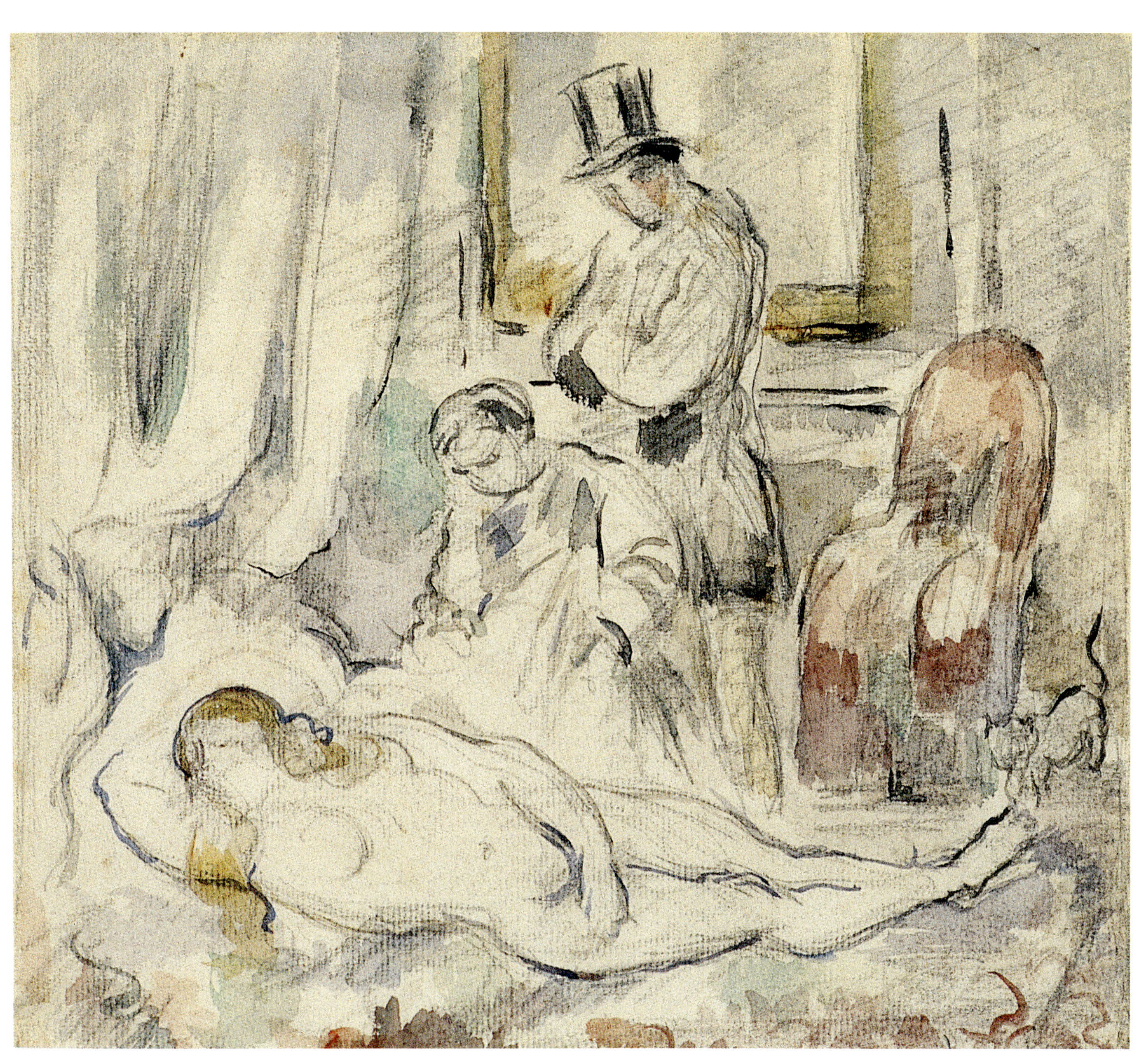

Cat. 49
Olympia
c. 1877
Watercolor
24.1 × 27 cm
Philadelphia Museum of Art, Philadelphia,
The Louis E. Stern Collection,
1963
RWC 135

When Cézanne read Zola's "Nana"

Denis Coutagne

Wuppertal Museum's *Female Nude* (fig. 1) belongs to the Cézannist tradition of the *Olympias*, and has the subtitle *(Leda II ?)*. As Cézanne had already painted *Leda and the Swan* (fig. 45) we can make a connection between these two works, which we believe were separated by an approximately ten-year gap. Moreover *Leda and the Swan* makes explicit reference to the preparatory drawings held in the Philadelphia collection: *Study for Leda* (fig. 46), 1880, and *Studies for Leda and the Swan* (fig. 4), 1880. The first drawing anticipates the pose of the woman when Cézanne later painted her on her sofa. All of our attention is taken by the champagne glass she is holding in her right hand. The second, less accomplished, drawing employs the same pose, but this time, a swan's head appears beside the right hand, which no longer carries the champagne glass. Both Adrien Chappuis and Théodore Reff suspected that these graphic compositions were reproducing an iconography that they believed had its source in a then unknown engraving. Jean-Claude Lebenstzejn[1] came across the answer to these queries in the Musée de la Contrefaçon, Rue de la Faisanderie in Paris: "...an image suddenly leapt out: it was the label on a champagne bottle, and the name of his friend Zola's novel."[2]

The novel *Nana* by Zola was published in serial form in 1879 and then in a separate volume in 1880. It had caused a scandal, but its success prompted illustrators to get hold of the book, and thus an illustrated edition appeared, packed with plates by André Gil, Nielsen Bellenger, and Clairin among others. Nana was depicted, practically nude sometimes, and often looking at herself in a mirror or drinking champagne in the company of gentlemen.

It seems obvious that Cézanne copied this label, perhaps after sharing a bottle of this first-rate champagne with his friend in Médan in 1880 (fig. 47).

In the Wuppertal painting (fig. 50) the swan is replaced by a still life. The swan has undergone a transformation, but its silhouette—that matches the shape of the tablecloth—can still be clearly discerned; it remains a hollow form, incomplete. Faced with this painting, Walter Feilchenfeldt suggests looking at *Still Life* (R 664), which depicts two pears arranged in similar fashion.[3]

Exhibited for the first time by Cassirer in 1909, *Female Nude* was entitled *Study for Zola's Nana* on the basis of a note made by Cézanne's son on a photograph of the work.[4] This shows at any rate that the reference to Zola and the Nana character was already being made in describing the painting during Vollard's time.

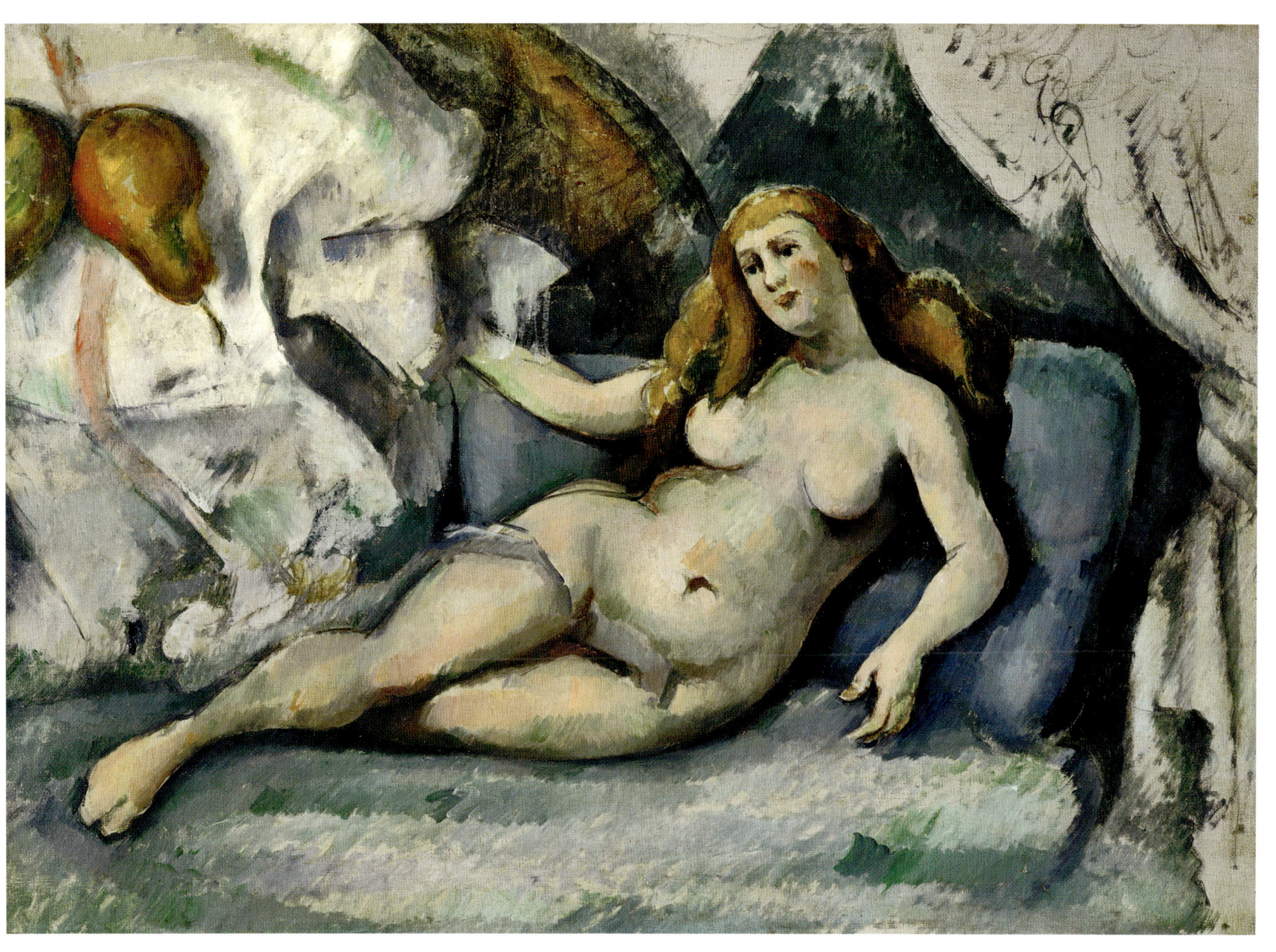

Cat. 50
Female Nude (Leda II ?)
1886–1890? (Rewald: 1885–87)
Oil on canvas
44 × 62 cm
Von der Heydt-Museum, Wuppertal
R 590

Fig. 45
Leda and the Swan
c. 1880
Oil on canvas
58.5 × 73.5 cm
Barnes Foundation, Merion
R 447

Fig. 46
Study for Leda
1880? (Chappuis: 1876–1879)
Pencil
Notebook I, p. 6, recto
11.6 × 18.2 cm
Philadelphia Museum of Art, Philadelphia, gift of Mr. and Mrs. Walter H. Annenberg, 1987
CH 483
See also cat. 3, the drawing originating from the same notebook

Fig. 47
Champagne Nana
1880
Champagne label
8 × 11.5 cm
Paris, Archives of the Institut national de la propriété industrielle (National Institute of Industrial Property)

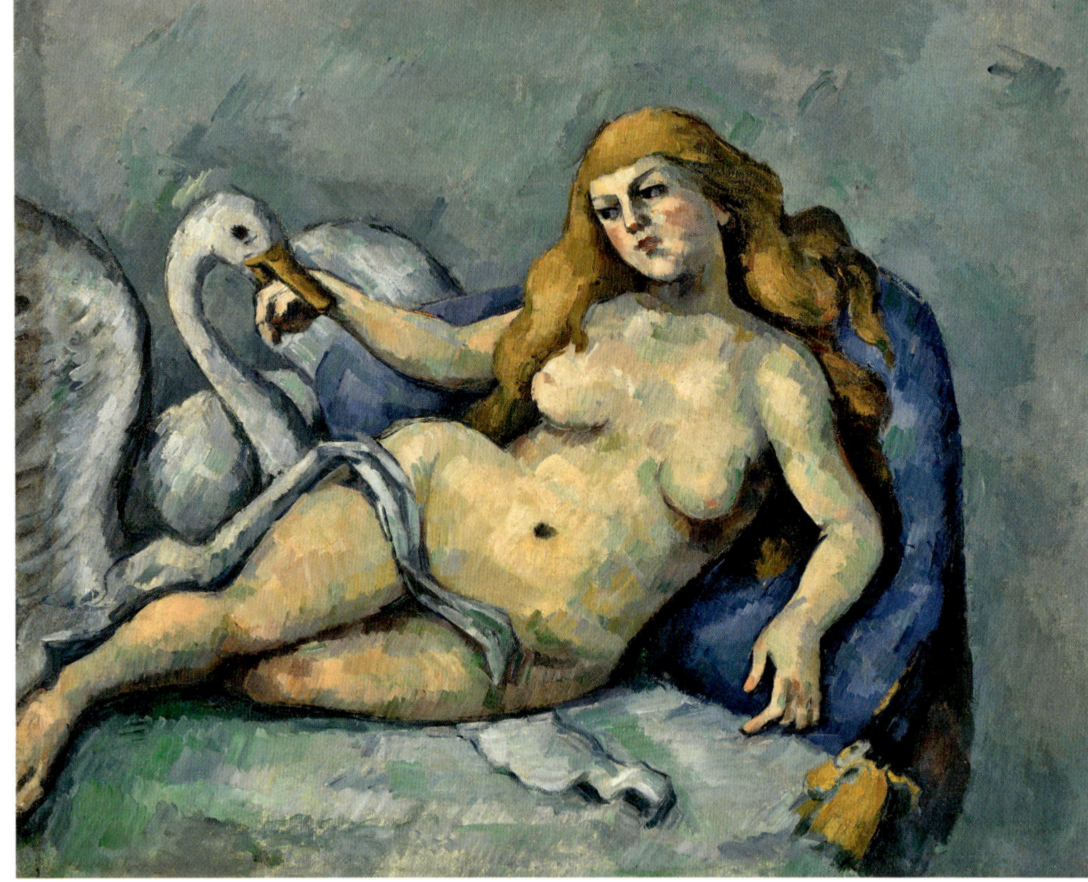

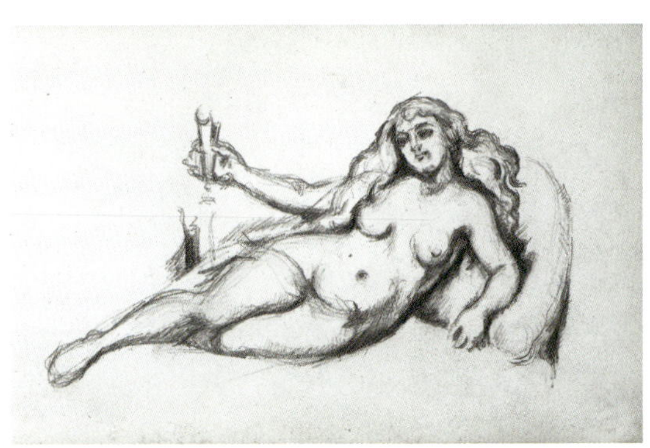

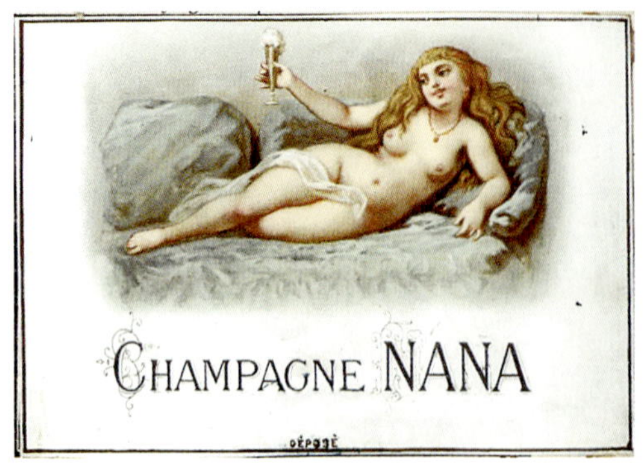

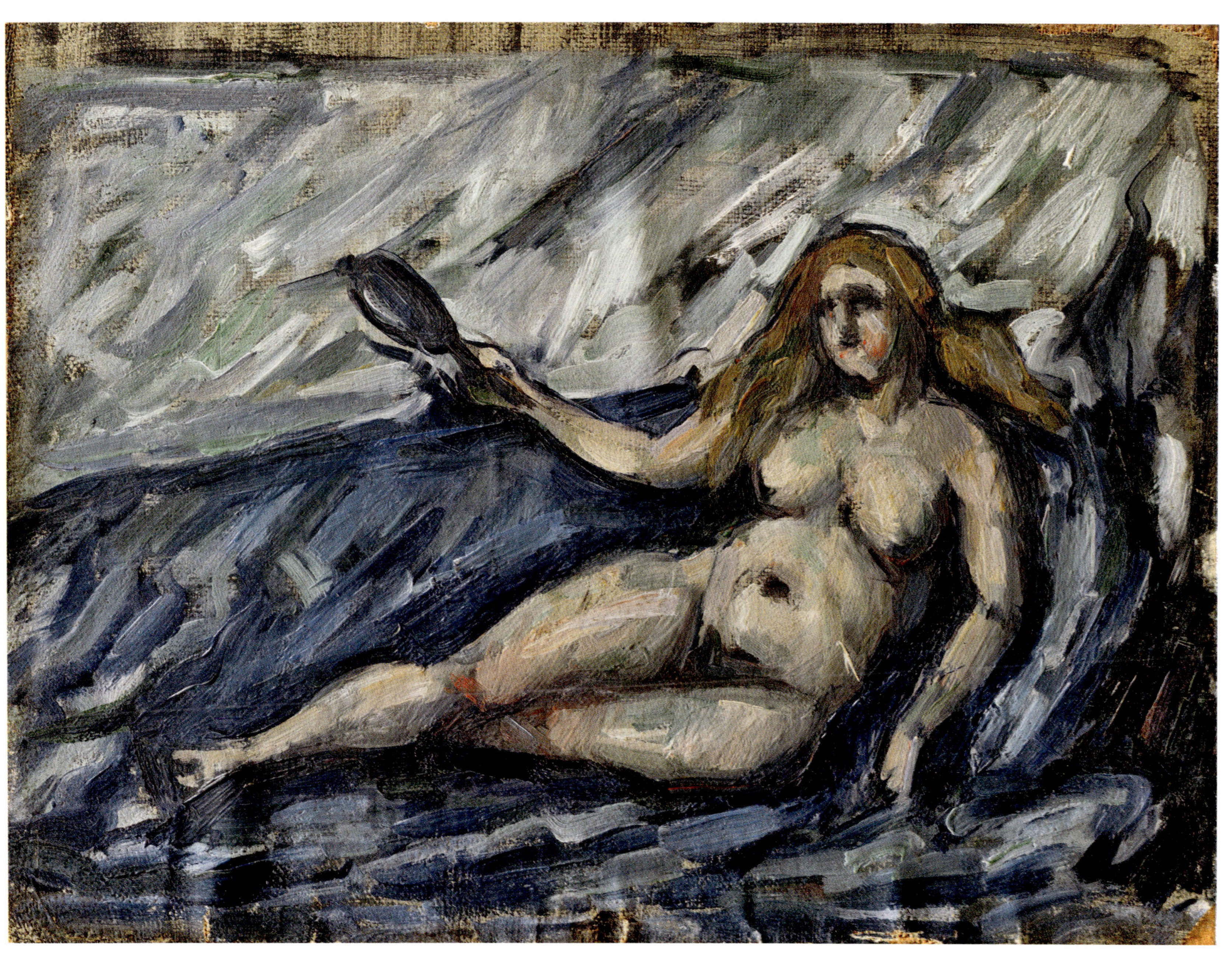

Cat. 51
Woman with a mirror
1866–67
Oil on canvas
17 × 22 cm
Paris, musée d'Orsay
(in deposit at Musée Granet, Aix-en-Provence)
R 127

Cézanne: Painting Murder

André Dombrowski

Murder was perhaps Cézanne's ultimate early subject.[1] He repeated the theme with disturbing frequency, from the more finished canvases like *The Murder* (fig. 48) and *The Strangled Woman* (fig. 49) to many a work on paper. The theme of violence persisted in Cézanne's work even into the period of the so-called "constructive stroke," as in paintings like *The Battle of Love* (cat. 52), even if the scene was now considerably brighter and seemingly more Arcadian, the violence dispersed onto several struggling couples. In the later 1860s and early 1870s, the subject even developed its own distinct iconography: a male perpetrator towers over a female victim who is lying on her back, either strangling or stabbing her, while a female accomplice either watches or actively aids the killing. As a subject, this particular vision of murder offered three interlocked agents: an active aggressor, a passive victim, and an observing bystander, presenting the viewer with three points of identification with radically different ethical implications.

The paintings seem deliberately to work against any traditional narrative, anything that would help explain their violence. Their surroundings are vague, like some bleak Parisian suburb at night or an anonymous boudoir. Profoundly dislocated, and without bearings, the viewer thus has to confront what seems to be an almost instinctual, animal violence, including sexual transgression and ultimately death. It is a strange version of modernity that murder should be Cézanne's haystacks or cathedral façade, an unavoidable, and thus generic, element of modern life. Depictions of sexualized violence were thus central to Cézanne's early artistic formation because of their particular relevance to his imagined Parisian and Aix-en-Provence audiences, which were made up largely of his inner circle of friends and colleagues, including painters like Manet and Pissarro, but of course also novelists, poets, and scientists like Zola, Alexis, Roux, Valabrègue, Baille, and Marion.

Because paintings like *The Murder* offered a subject distant from the topics of landscape and bourgeois leisure scenes favored by Manet and the early Impressionists, Cézanne was able to open a window onto a version of modern life that his fellow practitioners carefully edited out of view. The theme of murder allowed Cézanne to cast into relief the paradoxical decorum with which the Impressionists often approached their time—no matter how avant-garde and adventuresome their painting. Yet Cézanne's work was as much in tune with modernity as theirs, at times even deliberately venturing close in form to the popular illustrations of the spectacular murders that littered the period's illustrated press, such as the infamous Troppmann affair of 1869–70, which involved the killing of the Kinck family in Pantin, northeast of Paris (fig. 50).[2] Cézanne mined such imagery in order to access the commodified image-form of the visceral and emotive it provided, and the spectacle of crime and violence at the heart, not the margins, of modern bourgeois culture.

He even conceived a pictorial style—often referred to as his *manière couillarde* (ballsy

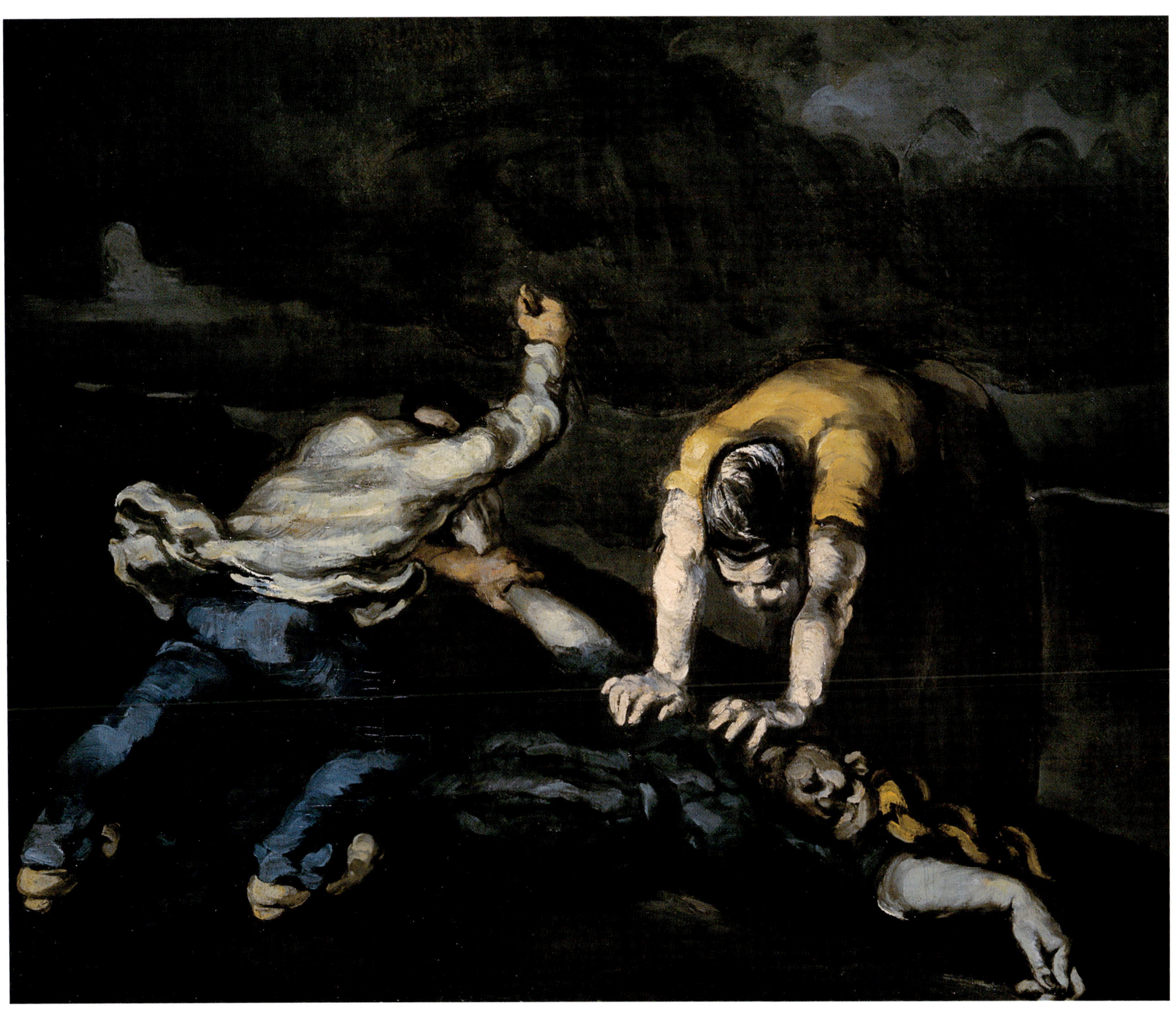

Fig. 48
The Murder
c. 1867–68
Oil on canvas
64 × 81 cm
Walker Art Gallery,
National Museums, Liverpool
R 165

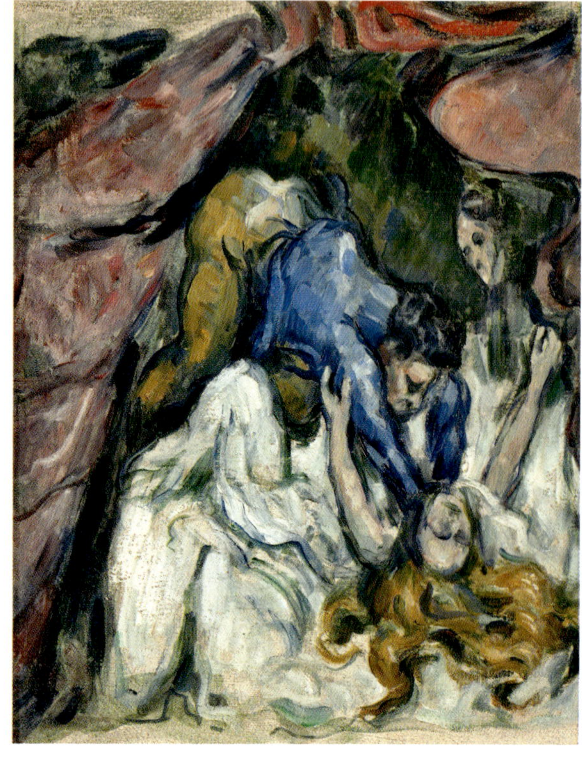

Fig. 49
The Strangled Woman
c. 1875–76
Oil on canvas
31 × 25 cm
Musée d'Orsay, Paris
R 247

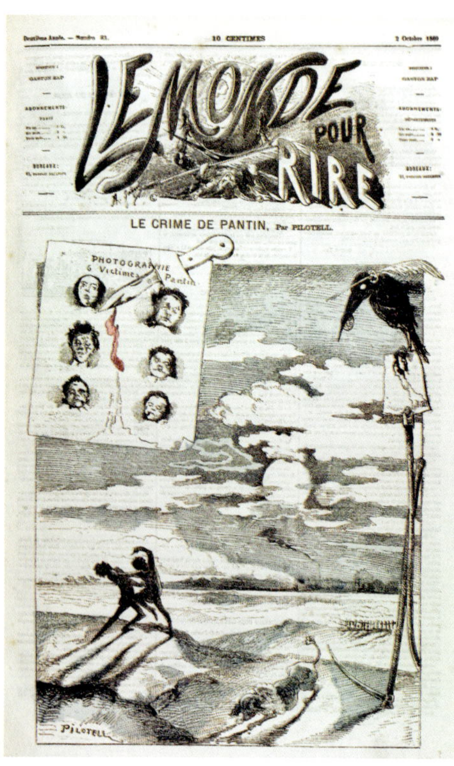

LE MONDE POUR RIRE

10 CENTIMES

LE CRIME DE PANTIN, Par PILOTELL.

Fig. 50
Georges Pilotell
"Le Crime de Pantin"
Le Monde pour rire,
no. 83 (October 2, 1869)

technique)[3]—perfectly geared to his early themes of ethical violation in murder: paint layered and thick, at times even applied with a palette knife, meant to highlight a pictorial universe as unconcerned with the rules of art as the world he depicted was with the rule of law. The transgression of norms thus became programmatic on every front in Cézanne's first decade—including both content and form—as he sought to emerge as a modern painter in late Second Empire Paris. These multiple violations of course chime with his virulent institutional critique of the Parisian academic establishment that is the subject of other essays in this catalog.

Another advantage of depicting murder was the theme's parallels with Zola's literary universe, to the crimes of *Thérèse Raquin* for instance. Violence was the ideal way for Zola to express his profound interest in the somatic and neurological basis of all human action and thought, for it showed bodies as concatenations of instinct, impulse, and lust, lacking any measure of rational thought. Cézanne's scenes of murder seem to illustrate not just Zola's novels, as has frequently been suggested, but also the theoretical and scientific literature that was at the heart of Zola's literary conceits, including books like Charles Letourneau's 1868 *Physiologie des passions*.[4] Henri Joly even proposed in 1869 that instinctual reaction is the most beautiful behavior of all, because it is the only one in which aim and outcome are coterminous, resulting in the most perfected of expressions.[5]

Cézanne's murderous world was therefore also a deeply modern world, in touch, via Zola, with the latest psycho-physiological characterizations of the body/mind dualism, a world that favored the immediacy of full somatic contact over the inherent distance imposed by Impressionism's elevation of the eye. Cézanne's murder scenes are thus manifestoes of a new form of modern life painting, freed from the well-mannered constraints of even the most radical formal experimentation, forging an aesthetic of complete transgression that his colleagues gestured toward, but—or so he seemed to want to prove—dared not inhabit.

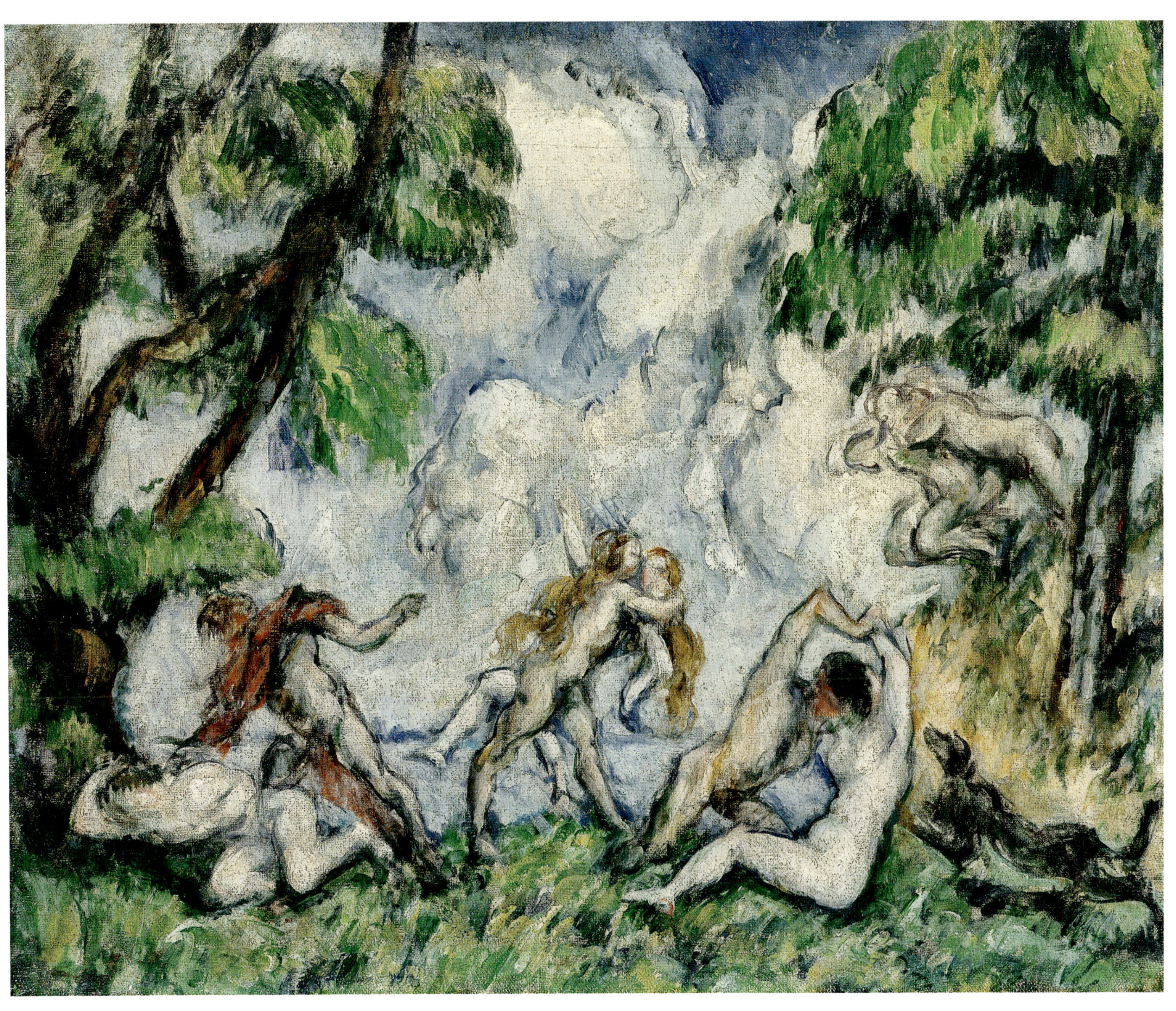

Cat. 52
The Battle of Love
c. 1880
Oil on canvas
37.8 × 46.4 cm
National Gallery of Art, Washington,
gift of the W. Averell Harriman Foundation
in memory of Marie N. Harriman
R 456

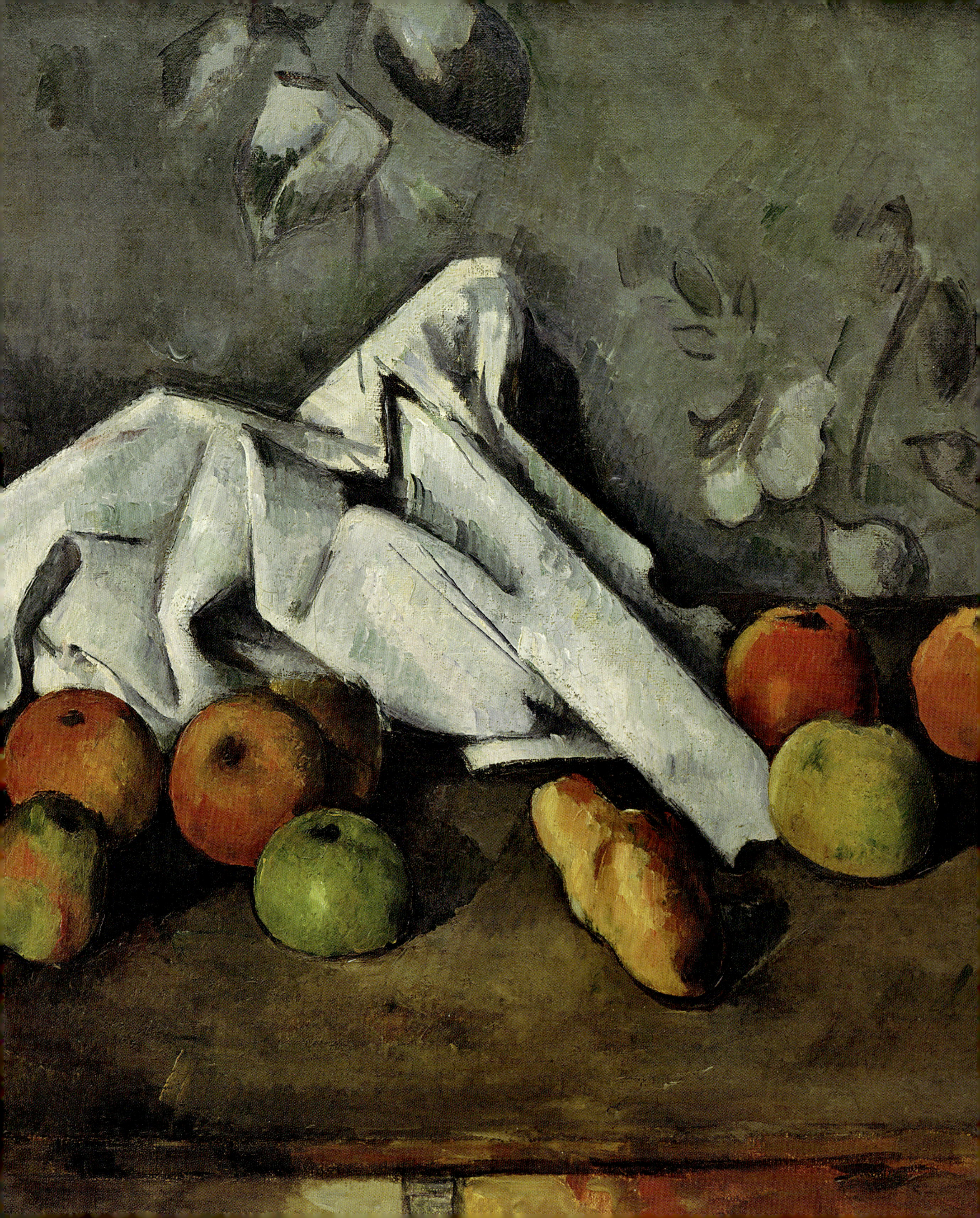

THE VOICES OF THE THINGS

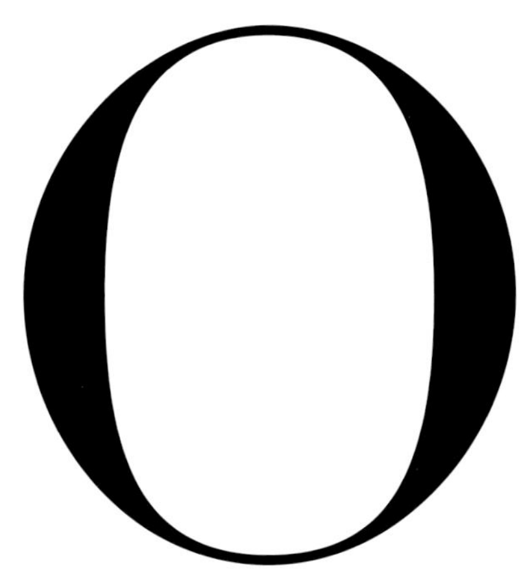

Once again Cézanne is confusing. How can we reconcile still lifes painted on an almost black background, portraying very ordinary objects on a wooden chest with still lifes that are joyful, not to say orgiastic, referring to some feast or erotic scene, translated into fluid materials by a lively hand? One minute, he favors poor subjects, next he uses objects that, if not exactly rich, are certainly rare and unexpected. The still lifes are sometimes arranged in a random manner on a white napkin, the linen looking like the sheet of an unmade bed on which the apples are scattered between glasses and bottles. Sometimes he chooses a perfectly ironed tablecloth allowing the folds to impose a strongly marked rhythm in an intelligently constructed composition (cat. 54). More soberly Cézanne contents himself with kitchen utensils and fruits (apples) placed on the wooden lid of his traveling chest. On just one occasion, the still life consists of beautiful objects (a crystal champagne glass, a tasteful carafe, a porcelain plate) arranged on a paneled chest of drawers used as a sideboard (R 337). But in this case the painter was a guest in the house of his friend and patron Victor Chocquet, for whom he had just painted two pictures at L'Estaque. Still lifes indicating a profession or a middle-class interior are rare. This makes the exceptions all the more remarkable and interesting, as in the *Portrait of Gustave Geffroy* (fig. 61) in his library, in front of his desk; however, the objects on the desk (inkwell, papers, the little Rodin statuette, an artificial rose) and the books belong to a world that was familiar to Cézanne, who remained a great reader throughout his life.

Another exception is the *Still life with Phillip Solari's Medallion* (cat. 6), a work of dull, lackluster tonalities, composed of objects and documents belonging to the sculptor and friend of Cézanne. Though the living quarters of a bohemian painter are evoked in the painting *The Studio Stove* (fig. 51), no trace of the artist's materials can be seen in Cézanne's painting, unless you consider a picture painted in Provence of a plaster cupid (R 786), and the little anatomical model standing between stretchers and painted canvases to be evidence of his world of pictures.

So there is no doubt that while in the French capital, far from depicting the "belly of Paris" as evidence of the exuberance of the fruits of the earth, Cézanne committed himself to meditating on the city in a minimalist style, reducing it to a few isolated objects placed in front of a papered wall that forms a geometric screen, signifying the entirely pictorial nature of the compositions. During the years 1877–1882 in the rue de l'Ouest, Cézanne devoted himself to a series of paintings (26, apparently) with a background of wallpaper, which heralded the arrival of Cubism.

Thadée Natanson stigmatized Cézanne as a "painter of apples,"[1] and in 1891, Huysmans observed these "rough, unpolished apples, built up by using the back of a trowel and rolling the thumb, a coarse treatment of vermillion, yellow, green, and blue."[2] D. C.

Milk Can and Apples
(detail)
See cat. 71 p. 170

"[The ideal for art and artist should be] the individual, put forth by the individual, reconstituted and conjoined, by means of the brush or the knife (*ciseau*), to the explosive truth of his native harmony."

Charles Baudelaire,
Curiosités esthétiques, Salon de 1846[1]

Benedict Leca

THE WORLD IS AN APPLE: CĒZANNE'S PARISIAN STILL LIFES AND PORTRAITS

To the memory of Philip Conisbee who taught me much about collegiality and Cézanne's art

I want to retain from Baudelaire's maxim the notion of reconstitution as not only reasoned design but also deliberate self-fashioning, a dual meaning that parallels Cézanne's self-construction as it relates to his own quest to render his "native harmony." From such a perspective the sensory Cézanne of art-historical mythology emerges as his own opposite: a manipulator of things and of his image for whom still life was the ready medium. What better way—if we recall Cezanne's avowal—to "astonish Paris [than] with an apple[?]."[2]

Parisians would see that so transcendent was his skill that he might simultaneously reconstitute himself and outrage others with the humblest of still-life motifs.

By this time, still life was also more than just silent arrangement. Like the once peaceable landscape, still life—for long the lowliest genre in the hierarchy propounded by the Academy—had gained a certain oppositional weight, marking any public practitioner as independent and ambitious. But it is still life's discursive prefiguration as a painterly exercise—and for this reason ostensibly the most directly revealing of the artist—that made it particularly resonant for Cézanne. With its basis in objecthood and human manipulation, still life broached most directly the relation of material "embodiedness" and abstract conception. In this way, Cézanne's disposition of still-life objects was bodily intervention as well as abstract thinking, making his painting of still lifes the materialization of his thoughts. Through still life Cézanne could "reconstitute" his thoughts and himself; hence it was that he knew immediately to adapt still life to his would-be matchless practice. Affirming his mastery across registers of meaning and boundaries of genre, Cézanne routinely transmuted portraits to still life and still lifes into landscapes, as he made perceptual leaps unavailable to more conventional artists. What follows therefore is an attempt to trace certain of Cézanne's formal and perceptual patterns, tracking how a still life might render a self-portrait; how portraits and landscapes, and still-life forms of all kinds might doubly re-inscribe the presence of the artist, through the physicality of his paint as well as through the discernible clarity of his "logic." For it can be said that in Cézanne's hands still lifes weren't still at all, but in fact alive with living objects, part of a dynamic conceptual and pictorial process: how else to account for a "sugar pot with [a] soul?"[3]

We can begin with Cézanne's first major painterly affirmation in Paris during the mid-1860s: the compound pairing of Cincinnati's *Still Life with Bread and Eggs* (cat. 53), his most elaborate painting to date, and the portrait of the Provençal poet Antony Valabrègue (fig. 60), pictures which the artist vowed "...would turn the Institute red faced with anger and desperation," and which were both rejected by the 1866 Salon jury.[4] Internal to both pictures and shared between them through formal and tactile correspondences is a play on the varied registers of our cognition: physical, intellectual, and indeed, imaginative. Our "seeing" a Cézanne oil, for example, might reside in our visual apprehension of his touch, i.e. a touch of paint—usage that was commonplace for Cézanne and which located

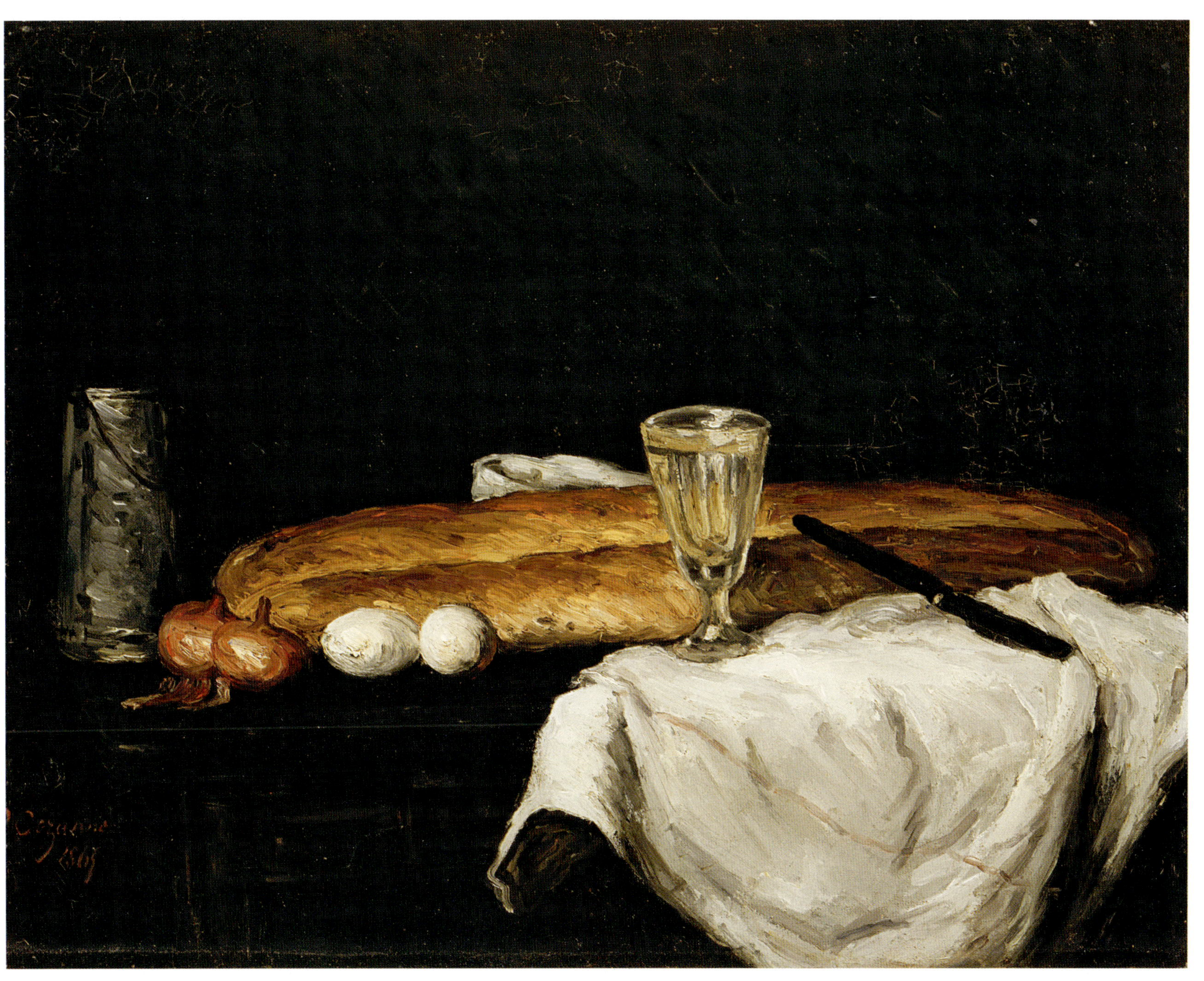

Cat. 53
Still Life with Bread and Eggs
1865
Oil on canvas
59 × 76 cm
Cincinnati Art Museum, Cincinnati,
gift of Mary E. Johnston
R 82

perception in a sensory, embodied application and appreciation of paint.[5] We might also apprehend intellectually Cézanne's formal design, itself the product of some deliberation, or recognize his learned formal adaptations of color, object selection, and mood taken from the earlier Spanish and French still-life masters (Ribera, Zurbarán, and Chardin). Cézanne, in fact, might be said to have been cloaking himself in these intellectualist references to moderate the self-conscious tactility of his facture. For these hallowed predecessors—visibly mobilized here in a Spanish-inflected treatment of the humble kitchen of Chardin, the painter of "honest" people of a deeply French heritage—enabled Cézanne to affirm a material and conceptual daring couched in the virility of muscular Provençal painting, then routinely described as rough, sculpted, or troweled.[6] In doing so, he was gesturing to tradition while locating his and his region's rough-hewn vernacular alongside the more progressive elements of the Parisian avant-garde, notably the preceding anti-academicism of Gustave Courbet.

Thus the initial impression of the *Bread and Eggs* still life is of a haptic apprehension of writhing strokes of buttery paint that strongly materialize objects as they refer directly to their embodied application by an artist displaced by us as viewers. Here especially it is in the disposition of forms, notably the recessive darkness under the table top at left, which invites us to occupy that space at waist level, next to the seat foreclosed by the draped tablecloth at right. Such a play of negative and positive space based around tactile and visual effects would of course become Cézanne's stock in trade, although more immediate here was the implication of a viewer participating in a highly constructed vignette reprising the authentic gestures of artisanal painting. We viewers are at the table partaking of this primeval meal, sustenance for the humble gastronome. The knife that projects into our space at right thus takes on a metaphoric value. It suggests a weapon-like tool, such as a sculptor's chisel, an implement couched for Cézanne in Courbet's masculinity, if not a degree of physical violence. We can recall that Claude Lantier, the fictional artist largely based on Cézanne from Émile Zola's novel *L'Oeuvre*, routinely slashed or scraped canvases with a palette knife in dissatisfaction.[7] In either case, the artist in possession of the knife figures as a life-giver/destroyer, or part of a register of symbolic meaning akin to the vanitas tradition in still life. Thus authorized, and in the context of Cézanne's young ambitions in Paris and the more sexualized broodings of his early work, testicular onions and eggs form the base of the two hyper-sexualized breads that bisect the canvas and structure the scene (see fig. 52). It is no accident in this light that the phallic breads are extended prosthetically by the knife.

The portrait of Valabrègue (fig. 60) literalizes this force in the monumental person of the Provençal poet. Here a sculpted, velvety background serves as a support for the sitter's head and hands, rendered in heavy touches of paint that have been obsessively layered in an additive build-up of *matière* that literalizes them as statuary—or indeed still life. Like its companion *Bread and Eggs*, Valabrègue's portrait is painted almost entirely of black, white, and gray, except for colored accents such as the luminous fists which, along with part of the gray of the sitter's pants and waistcoat, form a still-life arrangement at lower center that leads the eye upward to the picture's culminating node of emphasis: the poet's illuminated head. Cézanne clearly perceived his "constructedness" as enabling more than just physical presence, since fundamental to his practice was not just the recording of sensation, but the valorization of the craftsman's handiwork as "equal and rival of the mind." (Paul Valéry) The topographic treatment of Valabrègue's head is consonant with the relief-like mass of the hands, creating a correspondence of head to hand that establishes Cézanne's handiwork in painting as equal to the intellectual substance of the poet.

Such correspondences, couched in the peculiar modularity of a still life and its manipulable elements, at the very least corroborate period sources: Gasquet mentions that Cézanne processed his perception of things through still life; according to Émile Bernard, "any platter, fruit, or glass, any object near [Cézanne] was the subject of his commentary or reflection."[8] We can also turn directly to the peculiar imbrication of still-life painting in Cézanne's world view and personal relationships—with Zola for example—to note how the reasoned procedure of still-life painting reappears in the dialogue between writer and painter as a governing metaphor, and indeed how actual still lifes were exchanged between them in a symbolic gift economy. Cézanne painted his famous *Still Life with Black Clock* as a reciprocal gift to Zola (cat. 54), who had dedicated his first pamphlet of art writings (*Mon Salon*) to Cézanne in a prefatory letter rife with oracular allusions of writer and painter decrypting and reconstituting an atomized world of things.[9] According to Zola, he and Cézanne "had examined and rejected all systems, deciding after this rude labor" on individualism as the ruling virtue. Further along, both artists searched for the imprint "of men in all things," as they lauded those "...masters [who] are creators, who each created a world of all parts."[10] Certainly the *Black Clock* was conceived as just such a cosmographic still life. The tripartite sections of the tablecloth appear as a sort of geologic construct that bespeaks a fundamental geometry. The picture is rigorously partitioned and inclusive iconographically, a tableau that evokes both a conflation of space and time (clock and mirror at upper right), and the iconography of the counterbalancing forces of flora (lemon and budded vase), fauna (conch shell), and the human world (cup and ink well). The Austrian poet Rainer Maria Rilke, upon seeing the *Black Clock* in 1907, for example, tellingly perceived Cézanne's fractured spaces as being contained by the picture "as a basket contains fruit and leaves."[11]

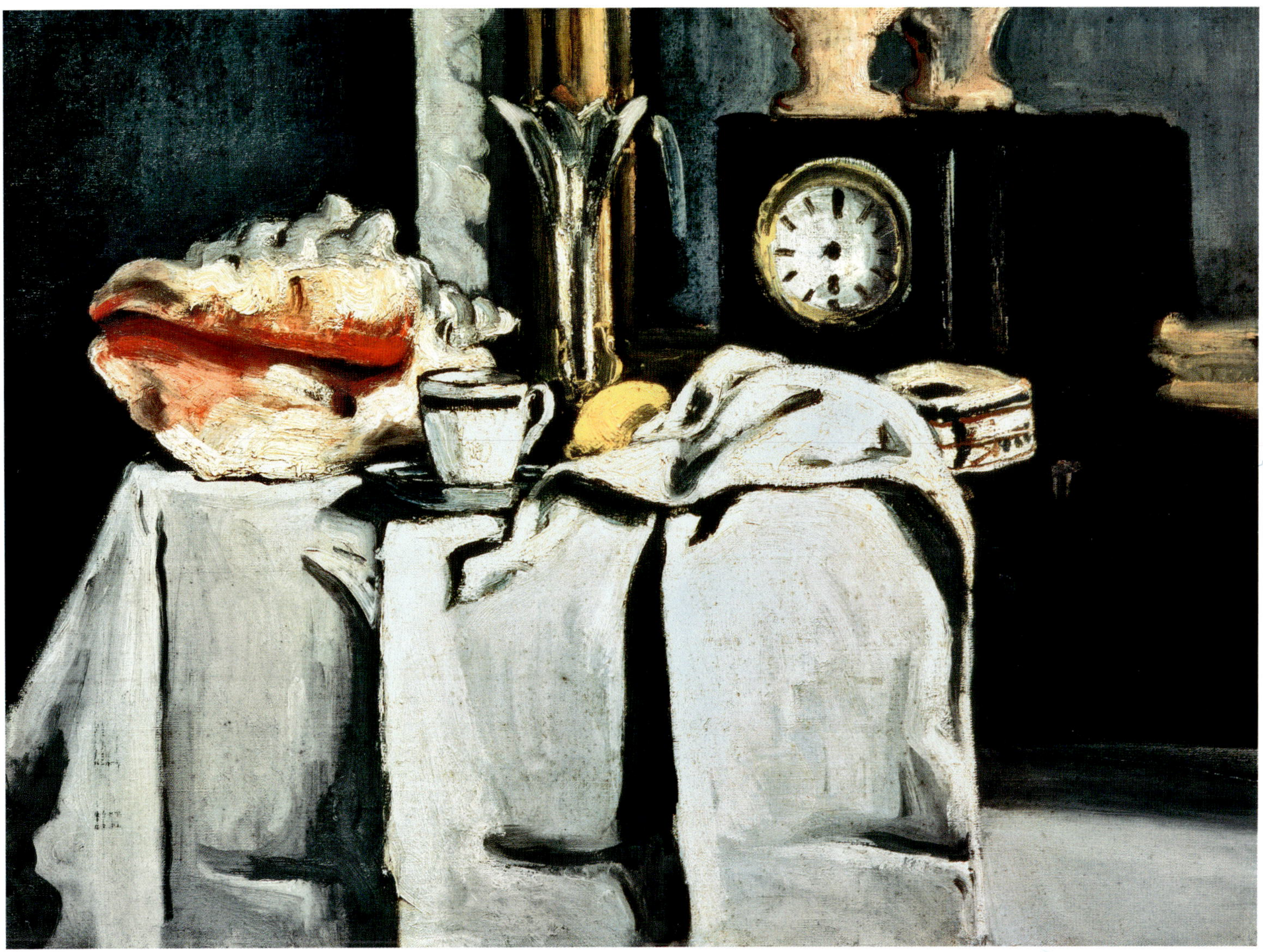

Cat. 54
Still Life with Black Clock
1869–70
Oil on canvas
55.7 x 74.3 cm
Private collection
R 136

In fact Cézanne and Zola insistently returned to still life during the mid-1860s, as evidenced in another work that figures in this interchange: Cézanne's 1865 view into the hard luck interior of his early Parisian studio, a still life entitled *The Studio Stove* (fig. 51) first owned by Zola and kept until his death.[12] In an abbreviated view onto what is presumably a corner of Cézanne's studio, a vertical interior is scaled to complement our viewing of a scene that invites one into a meagerly furnished space dominated by a sooty stove and cauldron. The picture presents the bohemian artist's anti-establishment hovel, making the contrast of sensibilities between stove and black clock easy to recast as persons. The still life with stove is a self-portrait of Cézanne, of the humble realities of his world, especially in Paris, while the *Black Clock* is his deferential portrayal of Zola's—and indeed Manet's—urbane erudition. Here the reversed canvas at the middle of Cézanne's studio beckons as the structuring motif across multiple registers of meaning, including indeed the early mythology surrounding

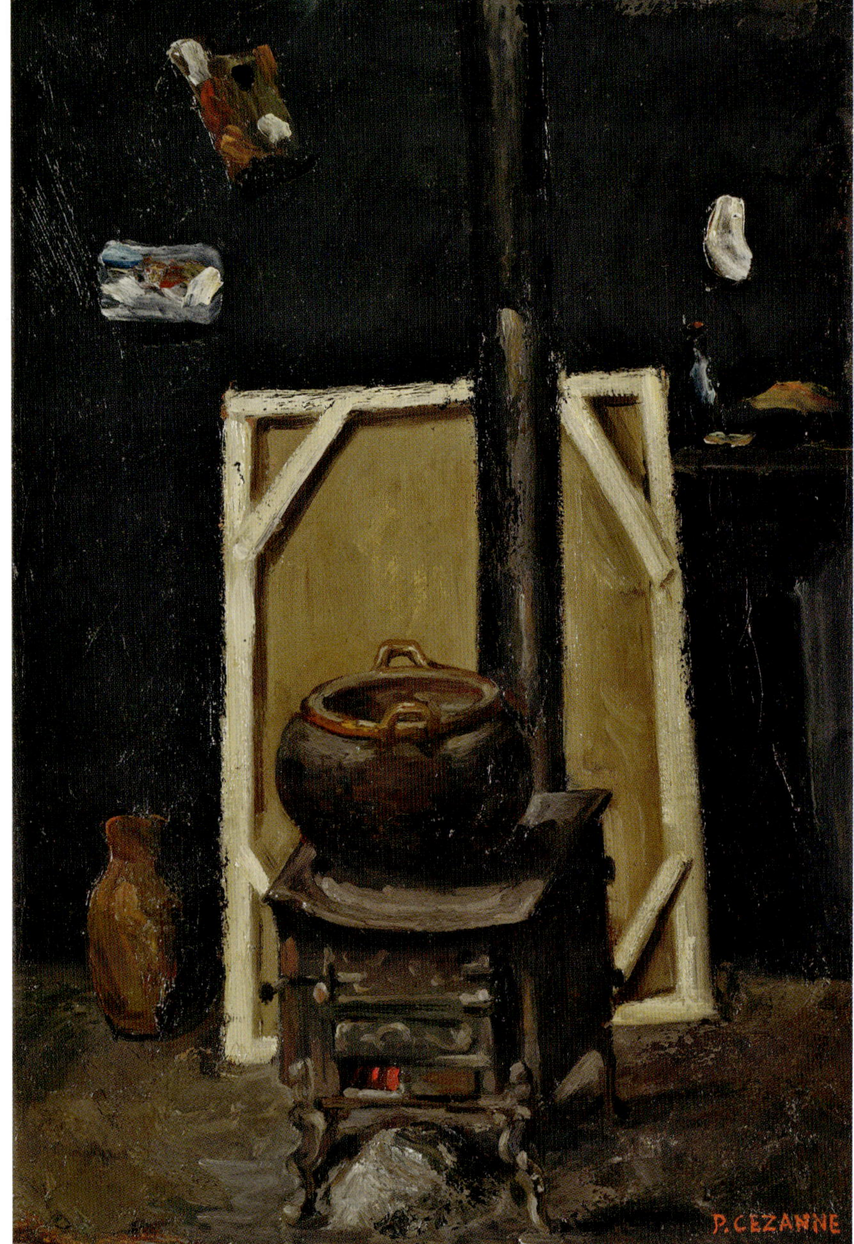

Fig. 51
The Studio Stove
c. 1865
Oil on canvas
42 x 30 cm
National Gallery, London
R 90

Zola himself: notably his eclectically curated cabinet, or work space, which, by the 1860s, had evolved, as per Manet's famous portrait, into an aesthete's parlor (fig. 11). The *Studio Stove* figures in Zola's posthumous inventory of his cabinet, allowing us to imagine it as part of the latter's more or less fluid arrangement of evocative objects or images, in which Cézanne's painting of a recess in his studio, stacked chockablock with canvases and a stove, would have surpassed laws of space and time to provide Zola with a view into the rustic lineage of his own "studio."[13] Late in life Zola affirmed that his imagined alternative career would have been to decorate houses and "to combine assortments of fabric and arrangements of things."[14] Meanwhile we know from the aggregate of contemporary commentary, notably Gasquet, and also from the contents of Cézanne's last studio, that Cézanne himself sought to enhance inspiration through an evolving still-life-like collage of prints, reproductions, images of all kinds, and even possibly bolts of wallpaper he affixed to his studio wall.[15]

In this sense Cézanne's "forgettings" of convention were but fantasy avowals that confirmed the opposite: that he could never forget, especially with still life. Any still life painting would necessarily be composed of manipulable objects presumably recombined a priori by the artist as a prologue to the creation of a picture. In other words, still life tested Cézanne's sensory mode of painting because unlike the physical reactions elicited outdoors by a swaying branch or shifting natural atmospheres—i.e. sources outside human intervention—the abstract design of a still-life arrangement would precede a painter's sensory reaction in depicting it. All the more significant, then, that Cézanne's art was early on taken by some as the paragon of intuitive reaction, free of "regulative conception" or theoretical motivation.[16] As we know, Cézanne's demonstrative paint handling, irregular drawing, and spatial dissonances were the subject of many early interpretations that ranged the gamut: from an intuitive painting of sensations, as per the artist's own rhetoric, to an art beholden to abstract logic.[17] At the very least, then, Cézanne succeeded in communicating the ideal of unmediated sensory painting while he was mobilizing a historiography of forms and intellectualizing his work. To wit, what Cézanne adapted from Chardin was not just an eye for the haunting materiality of the kitchen maid's world, but Chardin's subtlety in creating plastic effects of rotundity or "sphericness."[18] Looking globally at Chardin still lifes—for example the early masterpiece pair bought by the Louvre in 1852 that Cézanne might have seen there a decade later (fig. 52 and 53)[19]—the repeated formal conceit is the convex disposition of elements projecting outward, which, furthered by visual tropes such as the window sill, creates a spatial interaction between real and depicted elements. Cézanne would have affirmed this very adaptation when, according to Gasquet, he claimed that among Chardin's original discoveries was his recognition of the "atmosphere of things," where they remain ever alive "[and] interpenetrate one another."[20]

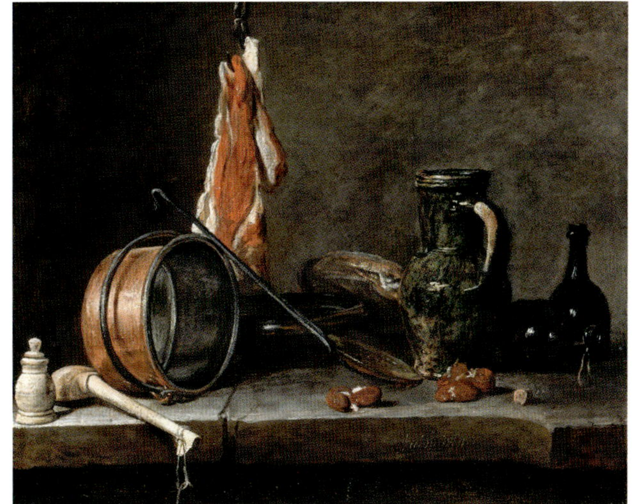

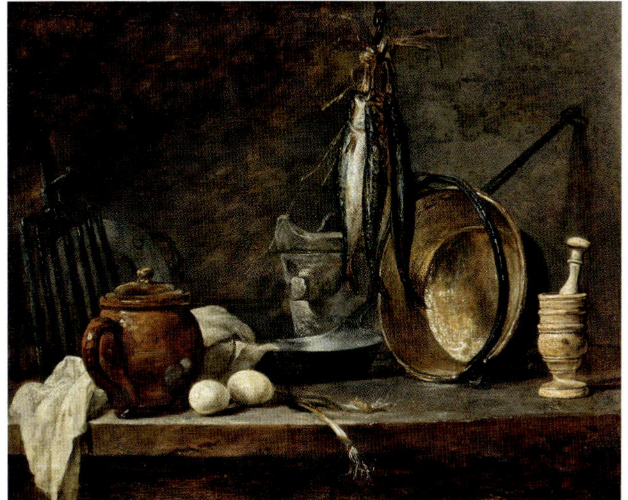

Cézanne's achievement, if we follow the early critique of his boyhood friend Marius Roux, was that after having absorbed his Old Master lessons as one of the viable artists Aix "had provided Paris," he "went his own way."[21] And indeed, whereas Chardin traded in a comparatively contained anthropomorphism of object relations, Cézanne eventually redrew the physical and perceptual relations between people and things. Drawing is here the operative term for a working artist who we know sketched obsessively and synthesized objects and formal problems through still life. Among the more striking of Cézanne's surviving sketch sheets is one preserved in Cincinnati (fig. 54), where the artist, reduced to his portrait head in graphite, is positioned next to the analogous bulb of an apple, with both head and apple defined as solids through a play of restrained pencil work which wrests form from the all-enveloping reserve of the sheet. The drawing is a sort of pictogram reduction of the play of voids and solids that is a hallmark of Cézanne's art, as it forces us to contemplate the contingence of mass, rendered here as penciled contours encircling thin air. Indeed, the effect turns on both Cézanne's peculiar ability to create positive projections from the paper ground as well as his delimiting lines, which fool the eye as by investing marks with tremulous energy.[22]

Not only could Cézanne's slightest drawn marks yield the solid mass of an apple, they also stood in for a physicality of touch made all the more emphatic in the representation of graspable fruit. Meanwhile the apple denoted a symbolic orb, with its meanings reciprocally interchanged with the artist's head, the source of this palindromic design, if this last term is the word.[23] This duplication of spherical effects on a single sheet during a sketching episode begs the question: What was the ratio of design to chance when Cézanne produced such a still-life sketch, especially when both genre and medium could be located in a priori design—as rendering or explanation—as well as in reactive, sensory art making? Cézanne is of course ambiguous: Tapping his forehead and affirming that painting "was all in there," he preached sensory contingence.[24]

Fig. 52
Jean-Baptiste Siméon Chardin (1699–1779)
Fast Day Meal
1731
Oil on copper
Musée du Louvre, Paris

Fig. 53
Jean-Baptiste Siméon Chardin (1699–1779)
Meat Day Meal
1731
Oil on copper
Musée du Louvre, Paris

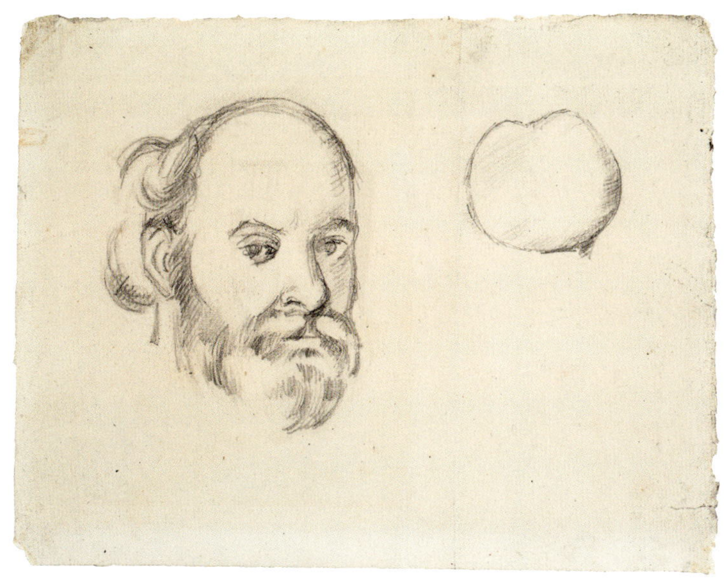

Fig. 54
Self-Portrait and Apple
1880–84
Drawing
17.1 x 17.4 cm
Cincinnati Art Museum, Cincinnati
CH 406

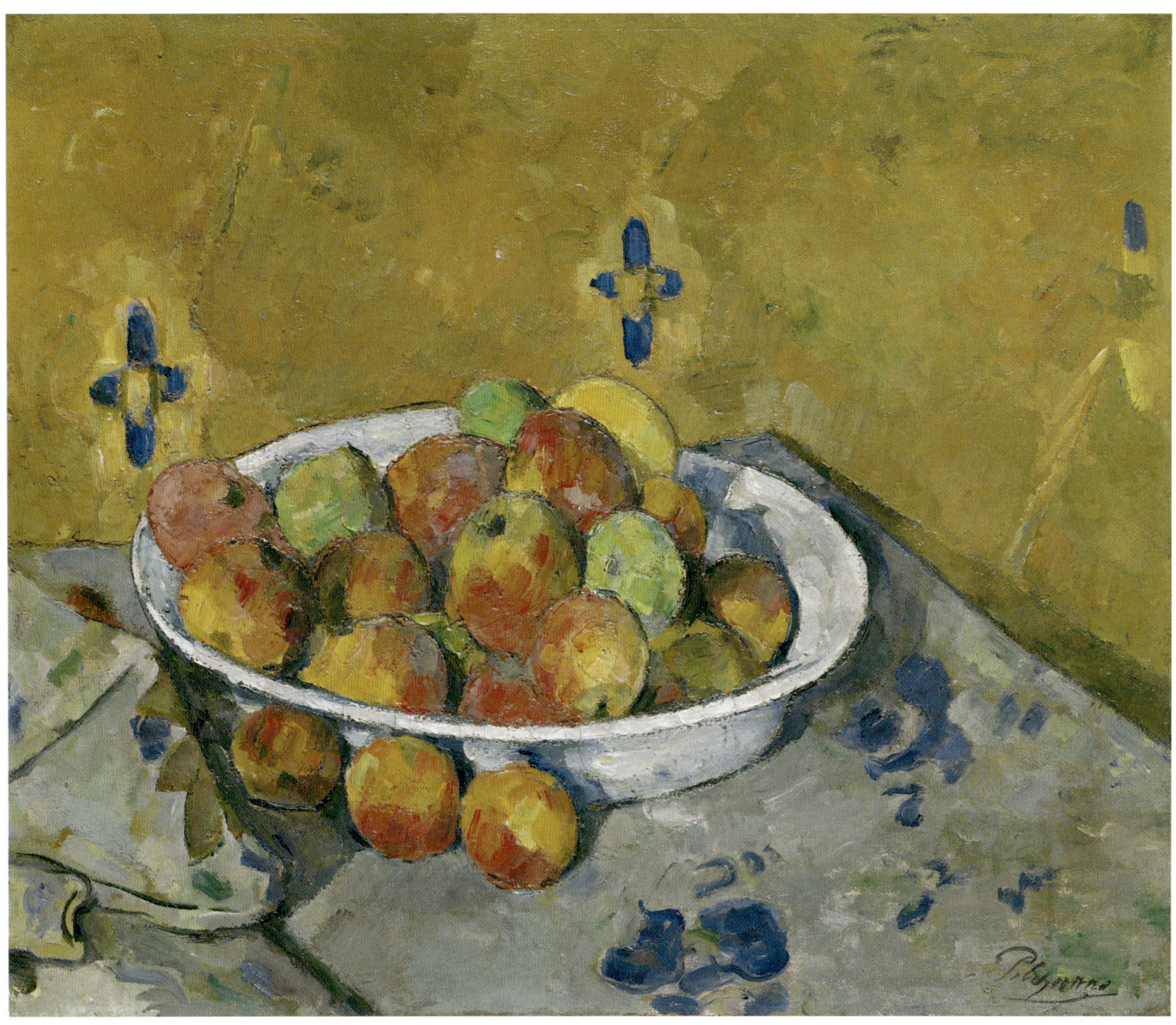

Cat. 55
The Plate of Apples
c. 1877
Oil on canvas
45.8 x 54.7 cm
The Art Institute of Chicago, Chicago
R 328

Cat. 56
Madame Cézanne Sewing
c. 1877
Oil on canvas
59.5 × 49.5 cm
Nationalmuseum, Stockholm, bequest in 1970 by
Grace and Philip Sandblom
R 323

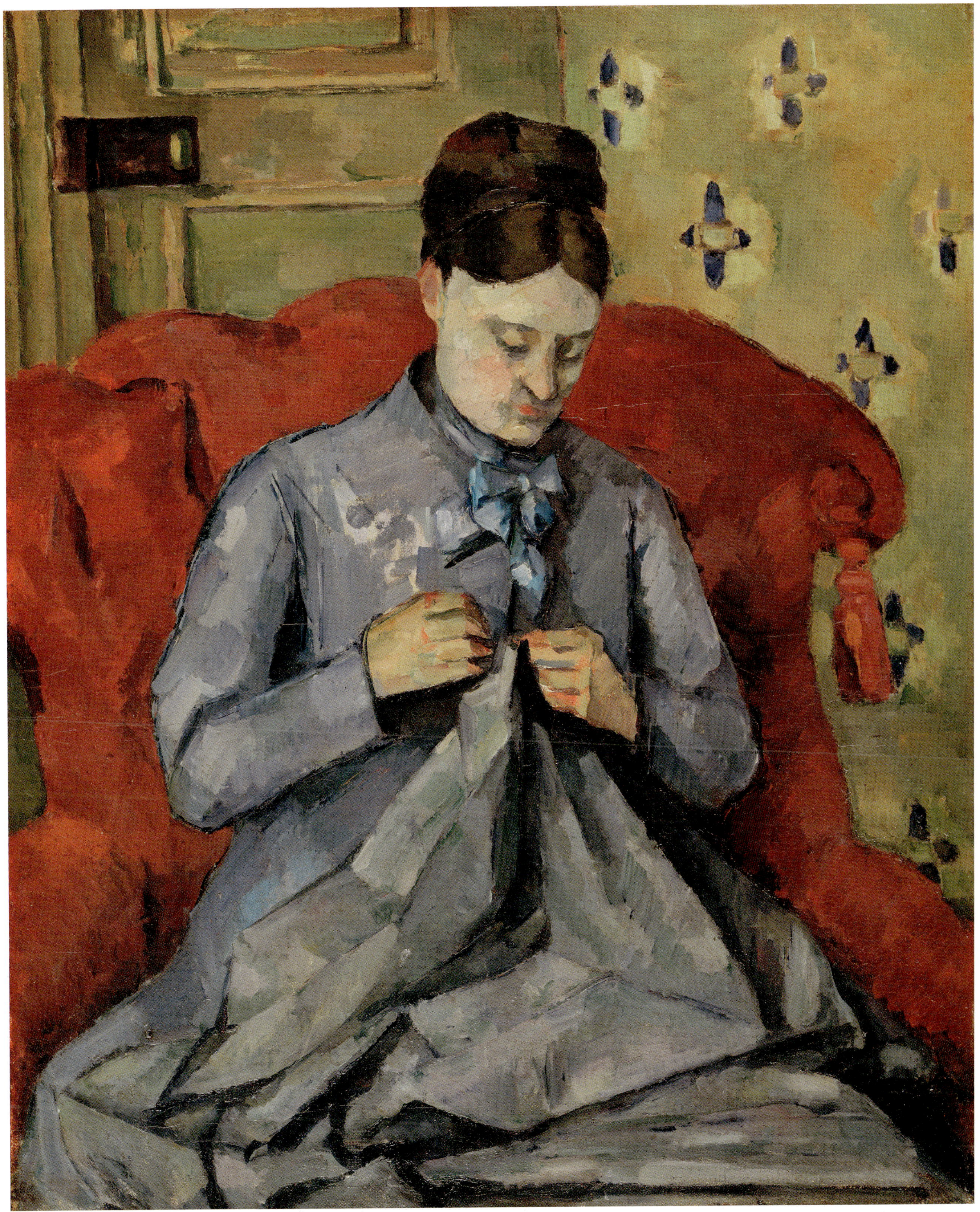

But it is Cézanne's interactivity that signifies here, for the mirroring of head to apple parallels a sort of reflexive self-imaging of both artist and viewer induced by the viewing of the work and its constituent marks. If Cézanne defines himself through the experiential body of phenomenology, one aim is to communicate his experience to us as viewers so that we may replicate the artist's somatic creative moment, something we do when we consider his draftsmanly gesture and palpable hatching. The artist's head is the intellectual node that engendered the spherical apple, a causality materialized in the pencil strokes, which extend diagonally from left to right and are disposed laterally across the sheet from head to apple. Our apprehension of this relation depends on our apprehension of Cézanne's gesture with his pencil, through which we ourselves re-enact his self-construction through touch. Indeed, "as Cézanne's painting set an example of a certain level of concentrated seeing and personalized touching, it made that mode of sensory understanding possible for other."[25]

Cézanne's work exemplifies 20th century notions of artistic creation as producing reciprocal subjectivities of artist and audience, which almost requires us to account for his transmutation of plastic effects into embodied ones, whereby his touch in a painterly space linked not only to his body, but also to ours. Cézanne "depict[ed] matter as it takes form," a visible process of becoming that he likewise applied to space itself.[26] Materialized in paint, the atmosphere in Cézanne's paintings often assumes the mass of solid things, interrelating with people or objects in evocative spatial constructions that thematize self-reference as a bodily, situated experience. For to remain true to his "native harmony" in the metropolis, the Provençal rebel artist would necessarily want to signal an intuitive unrestraint to trump bourgeois smugness, a posture often communicated via a dissonant space in which all of a painting's elements—and the atmosphere—might seditiously be "discussing among themselves."[27]

Among the most significant of Cézanne's still lifes are some that he created when he occupied an apartment at 67, rue de l'Ouest in Paris in 1876–77, sharing it intermittently with his partner, Hortense Fiquet, and their young son, Paul, and which, according to the Parisian cadastre, comprised "an entrance area, kitchen, living room, and secondary room with a fireplace or a stove."[28] The still lifes from this period are characterized by a pictorial space defined by a common ochre wallpaper decorated with blue cruciform motifs, a decoration that plausibly belonged to this address, but which is significant for us here as the impetus for our painter to undertake what might be described as the "nuanc[ing of] the atmosphere of things," a turn of phrase imputed to Cézanne by Gasquet in their discussion of none other than Chardin.[29] In purely formal terms, the pictures' spatial ambivalences and unconventional object relationships announced Cézanne's peculiar radicalness. These are nonetheless pictures that aim to signal beyond themselves: as evidence of Cézanne's deep engagement with the problems posed by the representation and perception of things; or indeed as visible grapplings with his most deep-seated existential concerns.

In assessing select paintings from the seven still lifes and portraits that make up the group "with decorative wallpaper," one is witness first to the artist's experimentation with a variety of purviews, which determine the prominence of the wallpaper and in turn the place of the viewing subject in relation to the spaces defined. In the Metropolitan Museum's *Still Life with Jar, Cup, and Apples* (cat. 58), we look upon a table full of fruit and pottery believably of our space as real objects, in an illusion that is at first blush abetted by the wallpaper behind. But it is an illusion ultimately problematized by plastic effects of paint that create a surface topography that is incongruous with the depicted objects and the spatial parameters of normative experience. The concave interior of the tea cup at the center of the painting, for example, is given to us in the form of an embossed lateral oval that rises up from the painting surface; at center, the apples appear as spheres with mass but are in fact formed via thinner, recessed paint layers. To the right of the cup, the line that delimits the wallpaper from the back edge of the table is incised into viscous paint, creating a raised accumulation of ochre pigment (wallpaper), which projects out over the table, making it appear as if the wallpaper precedes the table in space. Elsewhere, Cézanne accumulates paint around the cruciform motif, which is strategically placed next to solid three-dimensional objects, so that the flat wall decoration sits adjacent to the bulging contours of a pot. Meanwhile, the lower half of the painting remains ambiguous. The dissipated motifs suggest a watery realm that oscillates as both a lateral surface and vertical wall beneath the table with overhanging cloth.

Perhaps the most suggestive composition from the group in terms of compositional arrangement, spatial construction, and effect is *The Plate of Apples* at Chicago (cat. 55), a picture in which we are proffered a platter of apples tilted forward within an interior scene where the conventional spatial clues have been minimized, making us hover over the apples, which seem on occasion to morph into a craggy landform in a desert landscape punctuated by two starry blue apparitions overhead. It is an irresolution whereby the canvas "breathes" between regimes of space and genre, "becoming" dynamically at once a close-up still life and a distant, atmospheric landscape.[30] Cézanne of course understood the effect of a tight, proximate purview, which more readily aligns the canvas to our own physical viewing close to, or indeed within the depicted scene, rather than outside the painting as spectators. This is a moment of experience before the artwork that has been much theorized; indeed, one that has also been shown to be specifically scaled physiologically and otherwise adaptable to greater metaphoric meaning.[31] Elaine Scarry has shown how as humans we see and imagine flowers as always proffered to us in "the

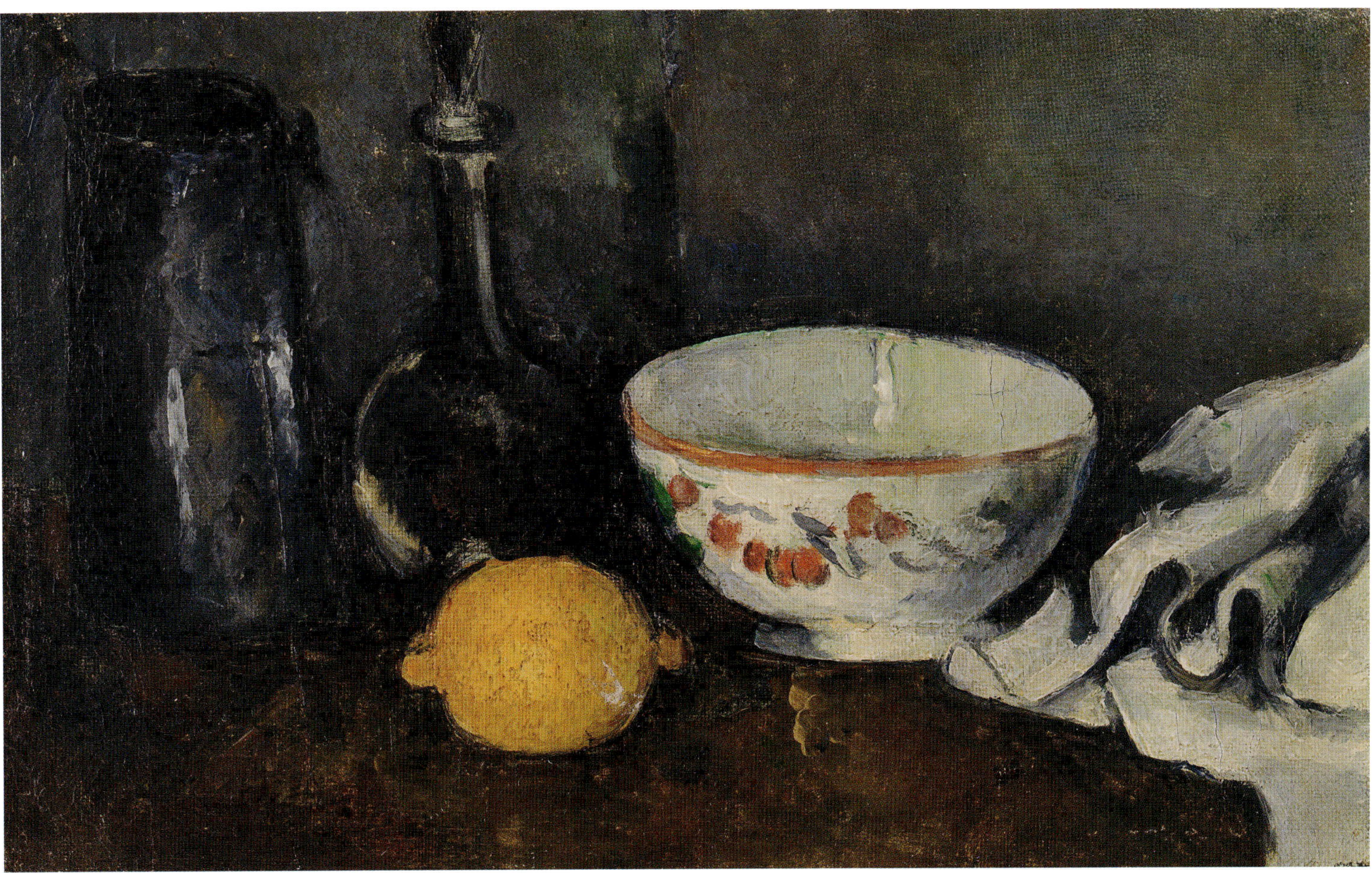

small bowl of space in front of one's eyes," which in turn directly impacts the structures of our imaginings about flowers.[32] As Cézanne clearly invites us to perceive, the apples are here the locus of a picture surface that has itself become a metaphor for consciousness: Cézanne's consciousness that he has shared with us in instantiating our own.

Cézanne could use apples in an analogous sense because the apple—like the flower—was self-contained, symbolically charged, and possessing a natural geometry that made it serviceable as just such a portal to a sensory, imaginative realm far beyond itself. One might be tempted here to venture into a psychoanalytic interpretation, which would find a dislocated Cézanne shuttling back and forth from Aix to Paris, living precariously with a hidden wife-to-be and child, unmoored psychologically and thus creating spaces of disorientation. But for all of the corroborating evidence of Cézanne's maladjustment, it is still his art that we should ultimately turn to—just as he did. We can here revisit Meyer Schapiro's seminal article on the meaning of apples, and consider the life-generating potential of the apple that was evidently for Cézanne the module of living nature itself, just as it had been for Manet.[33] "A painter," the latter once said, "can express all that he wants with fruit or flowers." It is with this in mind that we might conclude by only touching on the possible meanings of Cézanne's masterpiece *Portrait of Mme Cézanne in a Red Armchair* (cat. 75), where the basketlike lower body of the sitter contains a potted "flower" that rises up from the earthy clasped hands, with a stalk of blue ribbon leaves sustaining a blossoming, illumined face. Such a generative faculty would be ascribed to the artist himself, with the striations of Mrs. Cézanne's dress now a stand-in for "the weave of the canvas . . . in the process of starting to appear."[34] It is, however, the apple that concerns us here. That is, the enormous red orb that encapsulates the sitter; the literalization of what Barnett Newman felt were Cézanne's "super apples," or a solar orb of a piece with its atom the apple, and here conflated with the artist's mate, Hortense Fiquet, as a classical Demeter emblematic of fecundity, itself a metaphor for his own creativity.

Cat. 57
Still Life in Blue with Lemon
c. 1873–77
Oil on canvas
18.4 × 29.8 cm
Cincinnati Art Museum, Cincinnati, bequest of Mary E. Johnston
R 428

Realizing Nature through Painting

Jean Colrat

Cézanne always maintained that painting was not a matter of producing a canvas but of "realizing" nature. Left to its own devices, nature seemed to him to remain below the threshold of its own reality, a threshold it could only cross through the gateway of painting. According to Cézanne, nature's failing, its deficiency, was its torn garments, its way of always spreading itself out. Painting, on the other hand, could and must keep the subject to a unifying dynamic at the completion of which nature could finally and genuinely be revealed. He called this "clasping the errant hands"[1] of nature, a gesture that meant moving the hands apart and then bringing them together very slowly, clasping them very tight, their fingers intertwined.

The still life known as *Straw-covered Vase, Sugar Bowl, and Apples* (fig. 55) is almost a manifesto for this unusual way of conceiving the relationship between painting and nature, or the contribution that painting makes to nature. The elements of the subject are crowded together on the table top, which is steeply angled. This rejection of the use of perspective has the effect of keeping the fruit and the objects within the pictorial surface of the table top, which they never extend beyond. The diamond shape of the table is more than an interior frame to the canvas; it acts as an intermediary between the table as object and the picture. It draws the elements of the subject from their horizontal dispersal to their vertical unity, in order to realize them. The aim is certainly to shift nature toward painting. Nature is here controlled through painting, the diamond restraining it and achieving the desired "clasping of hands."

By imposing this control on nature, the powerlessness of its desire is overcome and it is this that produces the restrained violence of Cézanne's painting. It is a force at work according to different dynamic schemes. Easiest to identify is the subject's aspiration toward unity at the summit point of a triangle and it is this that gives Cézanne's Sainte-Victoire its exemplary function as a subject. *Straw-covered Vase, Sugar Bowl, and Apples* demonstrates that this tendency could also be created by the rhythm of the diamond shape, where this form has the power to take possession of the subject and convey it toward unity by imposing on it a dynamic of concentration toward its center, at the intersection of its axes, highlighted here by the straw latticework of the vase. The pictorial interest of this wickerwork effect, often used by Cézanne around 1880, lies in the diamond-shaped pattern of the straw. The sides of the diamond act as forces of compression, which seize hold of the subject, bringing it all together in separate pieces. They create pressure toward the center, which appears to rise up toward the viewer, like a pyramid seen from above. Before nature and before painting, for Cézanne, it was this that had to be seen and be made to be seen: "In order for progress to be achieved, there is but nature, and the eye becomes educated on contact with it. It is all focused on a single point through looking and working. What I mean is, that in an orange, an apple, a bowl, a head, there is a summit, a peak..."[2]

In *The Eternal Feminine* (cat. 44), this dynamic center coincides with the woman's navel. This canvas plays repeatedly on the restraining force of the diamond form, through the white canopy that enfolds the nude, the canvas of the painter on the right, and the piece of still life on the black table top, that anticipates the angled nature of *Straw-covered Vase*. This major work demonstrates that it is often through painting from the imagination that Cézanne pushes further his pursuit, both dynamic and formal, of the realization of nature, before putting this into practice when painting from the subject. This was the case with the still lifes executed in the studio in rue de l'Ouest in Montparnasse around 1880 (cat. 58, 59), during or shortly after the execution of *The Eternal Feminine*. The wallpaper that allows us to link these still lifes provided the possibility of a subject very close to becoming a theme. It provided diamond shapes in abundance. The most remarkable thing about the six pictures in this "series" is that Cézanne never paints the geometry of the walls in the same way, sometimes representing the whole of the structure, sometimes showing only the central crosses in a diamond-shaped halo. But the diamond always indicates this plane of support of the visible that the canvas seeks to be, consequently belonging neither to the wall nor to an element in the foreground. In reality, it does more than indicate this plane; it is not replacing the canvas but acting for it. The variation in the representation of the wallpaper responds to the nature and arrangement of the elements of the still life; careful study will reveal that Cézanne is playing here with these diamond forms in order to merge foreground and background into an imaginary plane, where the diversity of the subject realizes its desire for unity while losing nothing of its distinction, thanks to the pictorial motif that Cézanne's depiction of the visible discovers and creates for it.[3]

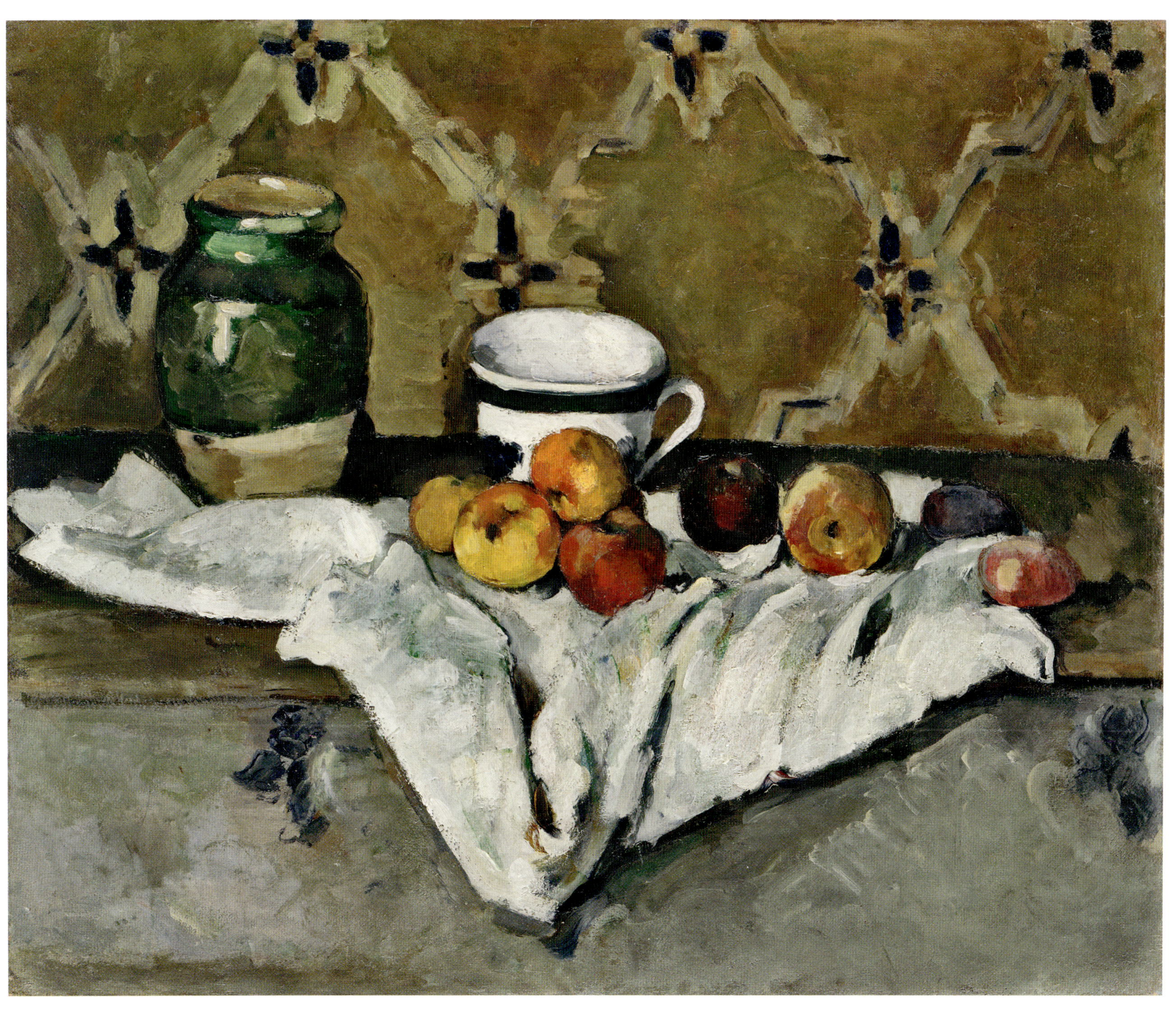

Cat. 58
Still Life with Jar, Cup and Apples
c. 1877
60.6 × 73.7 cm
The Metropolitan Museum of Art, New York
R 322

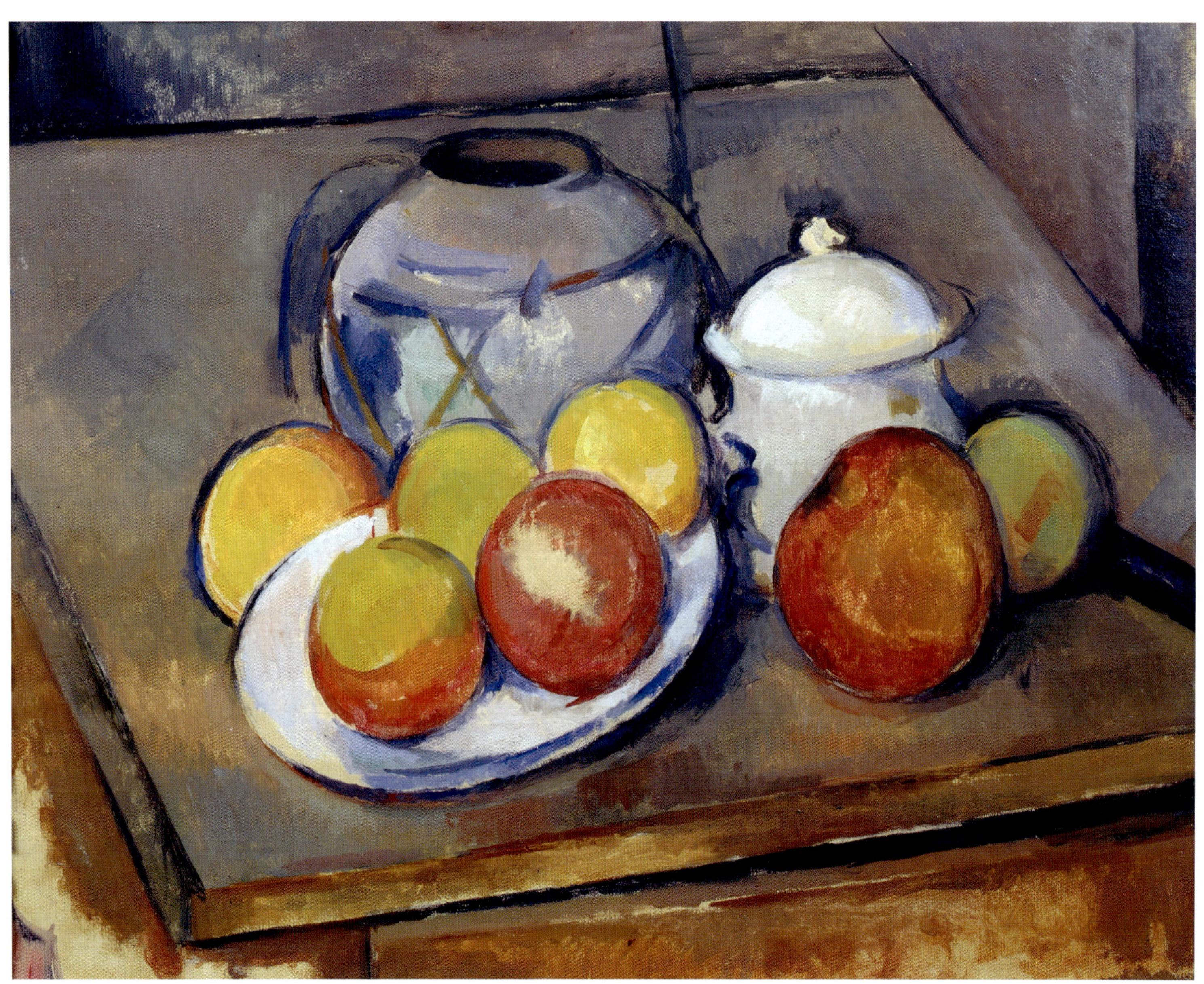

Fig. 55
Straw-covered Vase, Sugar Bowl, and Apples
1890–93
Oil on canvas
35 × 45 cm
Musée de l'Orangerie, Paris
R 733

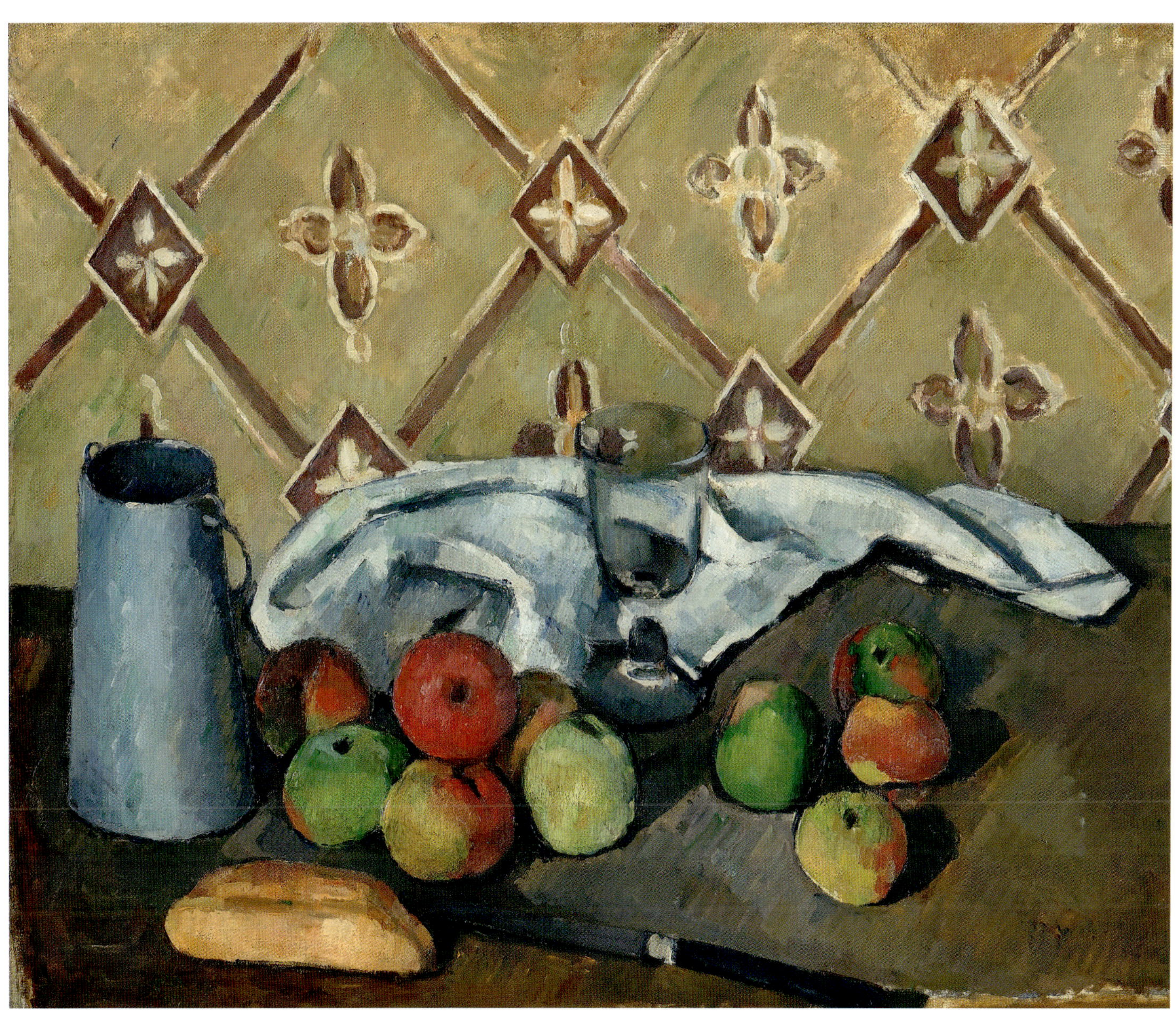

Cat. 59
Apples, Napkin, and Milk Can
1880–81
Oil on canvas
60 × 73 cm
Musée de l'Orangerie, Paris, collection Jean Walter and Paul Guillaume
R 479

The Boy in the Red Vest Experimenting with Figures

Laure-Caroline Semmer

Between 1888 and 1890, Cézanne produced four oils on canvas and two watercolors featuring the model Michelangelo Di Rosa, identified by John Rewald,[1] and in doing so, demonstrated his widely diverse treatment of the human figure. Accustomed to painting his close friends and family who agreed to the uncomfortable sittings,[2] the inheritance he received from his father in 1888 allowed him to buy in the services of a professional model whose youth suited the iconography the painter was developing around that time. At the end of the 1880s, mainly in Paris, Cézanne painted several canvases showing teenagers: firstly in rue du Val-de-Grâce, where his son remembers posing for *Harlequin* (R 620) and for *Mardi Gras*[3] along with his friend Louis Guillaume; then at quai d'Anjou, where the young Italian model posed for his various portraits. These four versions, all different in both their iconographic treatment and their approach to modeling, show the great attraction for Cézanne in being able to work with a professional model. One might add that this diversity was perceived initially as something incongruous, a further reason to emphasize the experimental side of Cézanne's aesthetic.[4]

After the exhibition at the Vollard gallery in 1895, where three versions were exhibited in rotation, Thadée Natanson talked of his difficulty in understanding this group of pictures, as the painter subjects the young boy to such a range of treatments in them.[5] In the versions held in the Museum of Modern Art (fig. 56) and the Barnes Foundation (fig. 57), the only changes relate to the tighter framing and the angle from which the model is painted. In the work held in the Foundation Bürhle (fig. 58), the young Italian boy's childlike expression is replaced by a more melancholic pose that is supported by the general composition of the canvas: Done in a very Ingresque style, the extreme lengthening of the arms, and body especially, creates a remarkable visual coherence. But above all the Washington version (fig. 59)—the most interesting according to Thadée Natanson and Meyer Schapiro[6]—is the one that shows the stylization peculiar to the early stage of his mature works. In this canvas all the elements complement each other, producing a visually unified whole: The model's face, less and less delineated, becomes a motif and his pants merge into the drapes in the background. Closer to the variations around the *Harlequin* than to the painter's usual portraits, it is indicative of the distance that Cézanne maintains to the physical reality of his model: He gradually erases his identity in favor of a lengthening of forms and a concentrated play on color variations. What is more, the use of red is not neutral, as it is indicative of the search for balance specific to Cézanne's art: In Washington's *The Boy in the Red Vest* the color creates a visual foundation while in the more "traditional" version in the Barnes Foundation the color red forms a break. Marking a further stage in the painter's research with working drawings and effective modeling, this series of variations on the subject of the *Boy in the Red Vest* reveals the beginnings of a type of treatment found in the large compositions at the end of the painter's career. Far from being improvised, these works were laboriously reworked, showing that Cézanne constantly adapted to his subject and to the canvas size in order to produce a well-balanced, constructed work. This was demonstrated by André Lhote in relation to the exhibition of *Boy in the Red Vest* in Théâtre Pigalle in 1930. Attempting to re-establish the truth about the patient, constructed work of the artist, he writes: "If I am once more tackling the infinite problem of patience in art, it is because I was surprised to hear young painters talking of 'inspired' canvases when looking at *The Young Man in the Red Vest* and *Big Trees* in the Vollard collection. The unfinished look and light brushwork of these canvases led them to believe that the old master had suddenly begun to improvise, in a burst of fleeting emotion and eccentric harmonies of line and color. They were in fact attributing to the methodical old man an approach that is taken mostly only by present-day artists, and the only famous example could be Van Gogh."[7] These versions using the Italian model paved the way for *The Card Players* and show that the artist was following the same approach in both Paris and Provence.

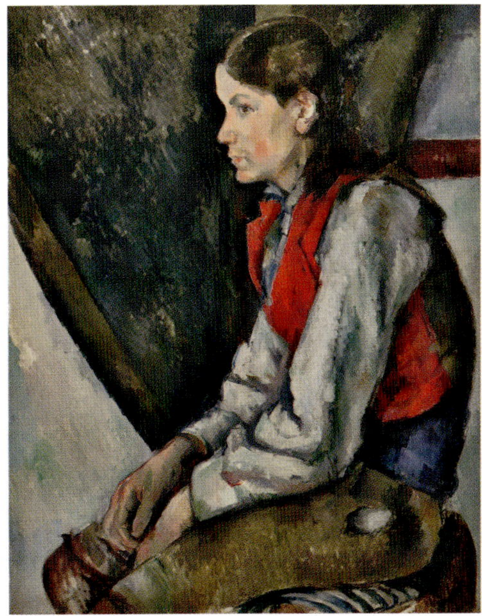

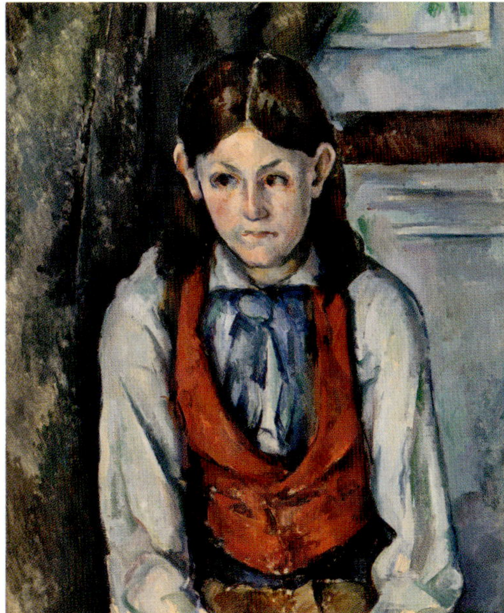

Fig. 56
The Boy in the Red Vest
1888–1890
Oil on canvas
81 × 65 cm
Museum of Modern Art, New York, fractional gift of David and Peggy Rockfeller
R 657

Fig. 57
The Boy in the Red Vest
1888–1890
Oil on canvas
65.4 × 54.6 cm
The Barnes Foundation, Merion
R 656

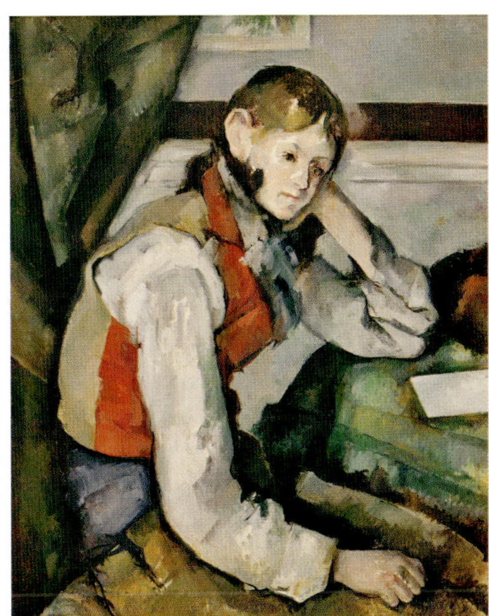

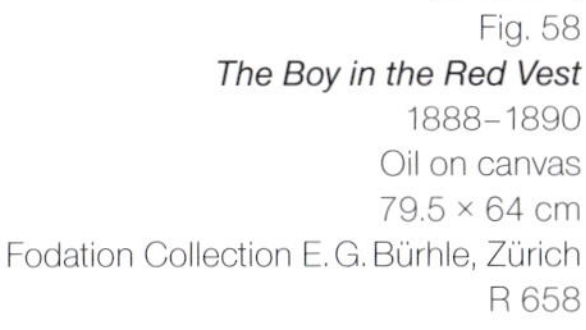

Fig. 58
The Boy in the Red Vest
1888–1890
Oil on canvas
79.5 × 64 cm
Fodation Collection E. G. Bürhle, Zürich
R 658

Fig. 59
The Boy in the Red Vest
1888–1890
92 × 73 cm
National Gallery of Art (Paul Mellon collection), Washington
R 659

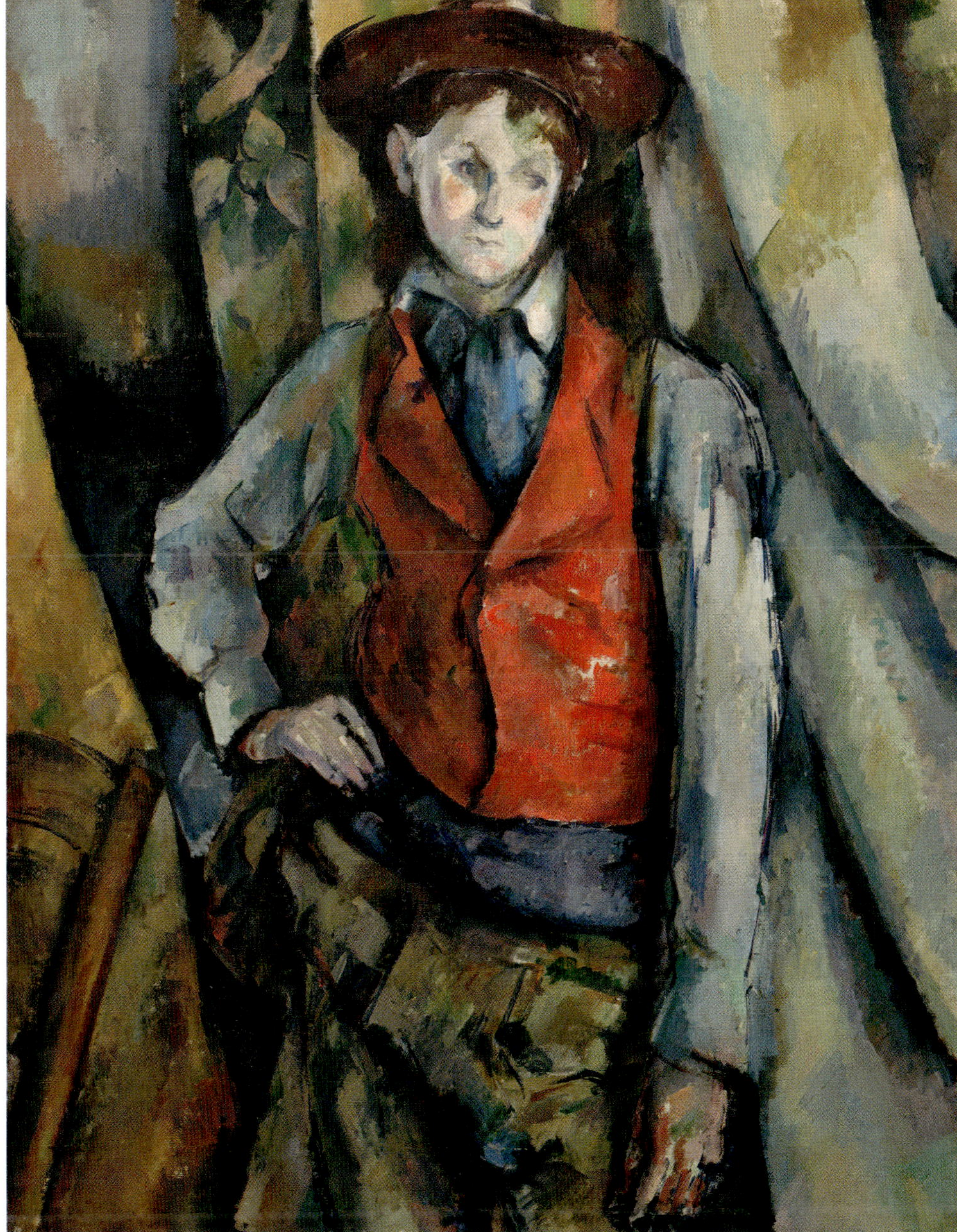

Paul Cézanne: the large format portraits

Walter Feilchenfeldt

Cézanne painted four large portraits of men in Paris. The subjects were his friend Anthony Valabrègue[1] (fig. 60), an art historian and poet; Gustave Geffroy[2] (fig. 61), an art critic and man of letters; Ambroise Vollard[3] (cat. 72), Cézanne's art dealer; and a man whose identity still remains unknown[4] (fig. 62).
Added to these is a large unfinished painting that does not appear in the 1996 *catalogue raisonné* and which was perhaps created by Cézanne[5].
When, together with the publisher Harry N. Abrams, John Rewald was planning his *catalogue raisonné*, it was agreed to abandon the idea of color illustrations. However, just before it went to print—John Rewald having died in the meantime—I was asked to include a few of these in this catalog. I decided to reproduce only large-format pieces, 40 F and over—and, in so doing, to choose works which, because of their size, had been of great importance to Cézanne. The result of this selection can be read, or rather seen, in the catalog published in 1996[6].
In the late 19th century, it was the artists themselves who, after reflecting for a while, chose both the format of the canvas and the subject. Large paintings acted as statements of his style. While these large-format portraits depicted close friends of the artist, this was less because he found them particularly interesting and more because they were prepared to pose for him and comply with his demands. We know the patience Vollard must have shown as he refers to no fewer than one hundred and fifteen sessions[7].
Having kept this portrait throughout his life, Vollard bequeathed it to the Petit Palais. Valabrègue, on the other hand, was never in possession of his portrait. Vollard and Bernheim-Jeune owned their portraits prior to their purchase by Auguste Pellerin. We do not know the identity of the person who appears in the fourth work entitled *Seated Man*. It is thought that Odilon Redon was the first owner. But who is the man depicted? He closely resembles Cézanne's friend, the composer Emmanuel Chabrier (fig. 63). Moreover, Chabrier would no doubt have been prepared to act as a model for his friend. However, assuming that Cézanne produced this portrait in Aix-en-Provence—and not in Paris—during the last years of his life, according to Françoise Cachin, it cannot possibly be Chabrier[8].
Recently, another 40 F large format painting

Fig. 60
Portrait of Antony Valabrègue
Spring 1866
Oil on canvas
116 × 98 cm
National Gallery of Art, Washington
R 94

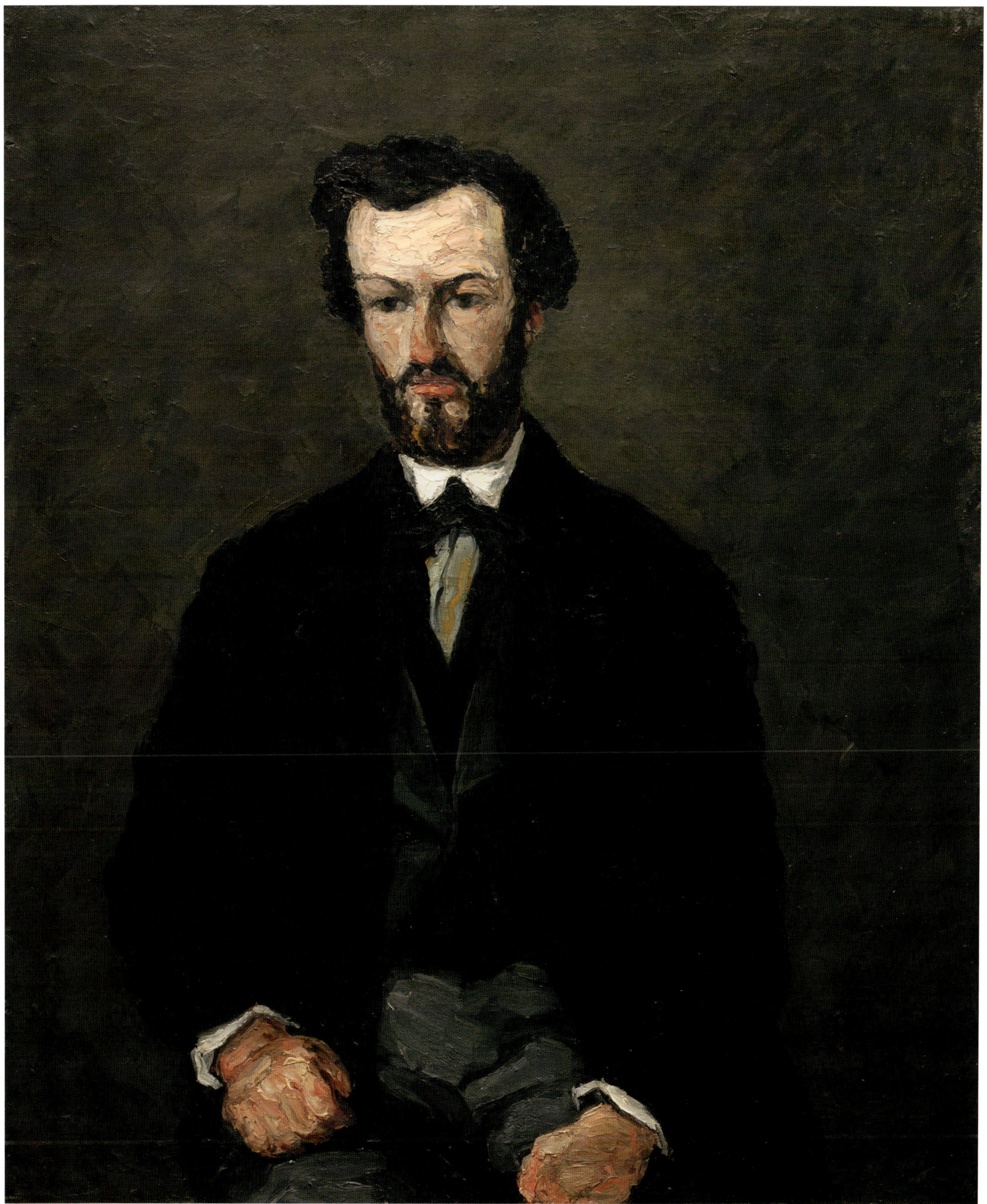

was presented to me for appraisal. This was a preliminary sketch of a portrait that was barely started and appears to have been abandoned and put aside by the artist. It later appeared as part of Vollard's estate and was purchased after the war by Étienne Bignou, whose daughter presented it to me, suggesting that the man depicted could be Auguste Pellerin. It is entirely possible that this great collector of Cézanne's work would have wished to be painted by the artist he so revered. It is also possible that the two men may have quarreled during the very first session, thus bringing the project to an end. And we can well imagine that this large canvas had originally remained in Cézanne's studio. What we do know is that it was later found in Vollard's warehouse. On March 21, 1944, Lucien Vollard sold the painting to the art dealer Étienne Bignou. At the time it was described as "Cézanne: sketch of a portrait of a man—paint (very sketchy)." (fig. 64).

As this piece is perhaps a first sketch done by Cézanne, at auction in 2005 it fetched the sum of 90,000 euros, a price that reflects who the artist possibly was, but this could not be guaranteed. The period when experts proclaimed "the" truth *ex cathedra* is long gone[9].

The four large portraits of men discussed here are matched by four portraits of women, also large-format, three of which depict Cézanne's wife, Hortense Fiquet. Before she met the artist she was already working as a model and was therefore accustomed to posing. However, as these works show, her physical abilities were placed under great strain. It cannot have been pleasant to pose for hours at a time for this demanding artist who, for want of models, preferred to copy sculptures—such as those of Puget and Houdon—or the fleshy bodies shown in paintings by Rubens and Delacroix. Cézanne experts constantly question how important his choice of subject was to the artist. John Rewald, Pavel Machotka, Denis Coutagne, and others have persistently identified and photographed his landscapes in the greatest of detail. Moreover, the objects used for his still lifes are kept at Cézanne's studio in Aix-en-Provence and arranged for comparison with these pictures. However, it is important to remember that Cézanne was not so much interested in the subject itself as in its translation into art, into the pictorial form, regardless of whether it was a portrait, a landscape, a still life, a true-life scene (harlequins and card players) or an imaginary one (bathers).

Fig. 61
Portrait of Gustave Geffroy
1895–96
Oil on canvas
116 × 89 cm
Musée d'Orsay, Paris
donation of Mme Renée Lecomte, 1969
R 791

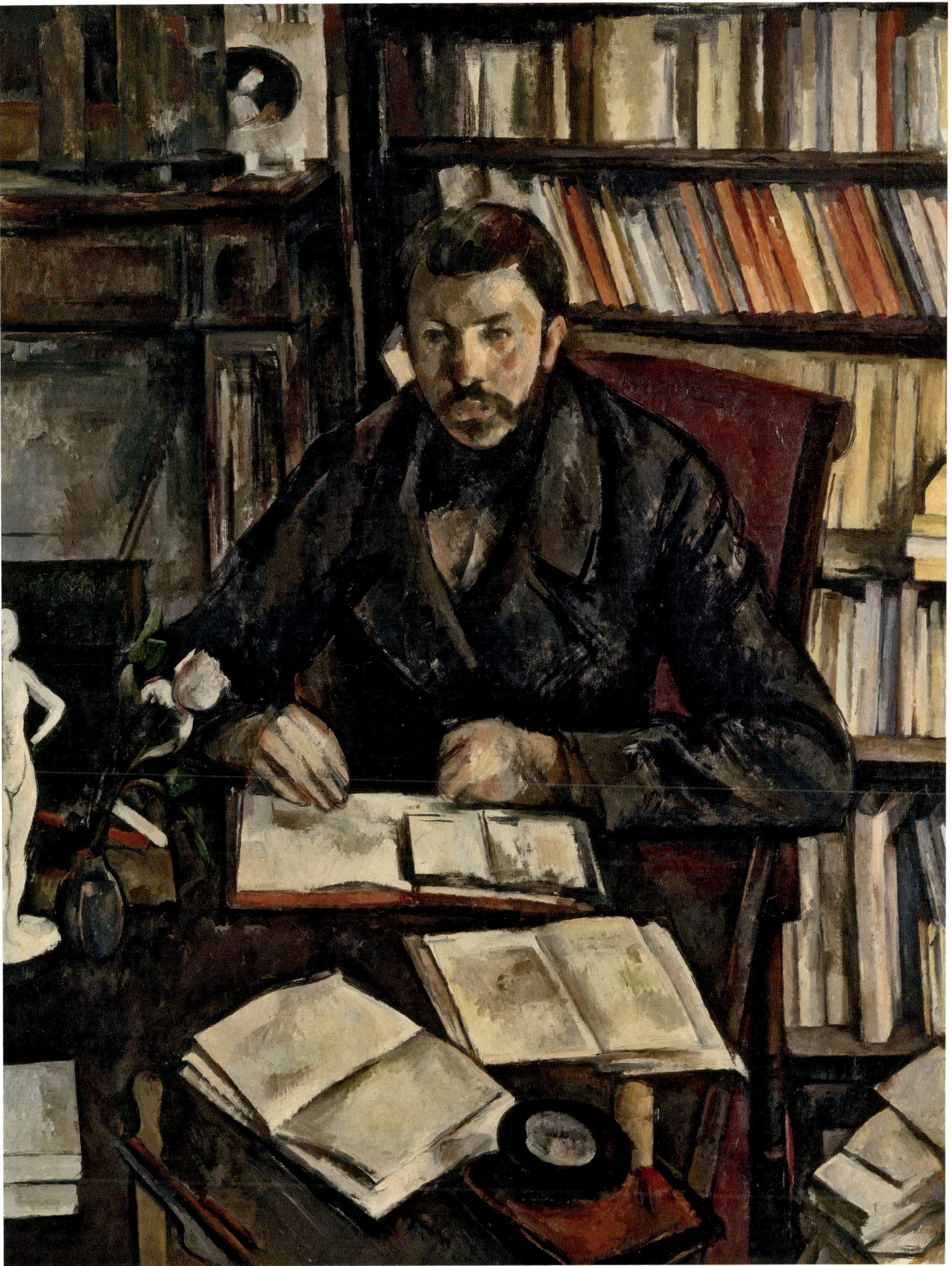

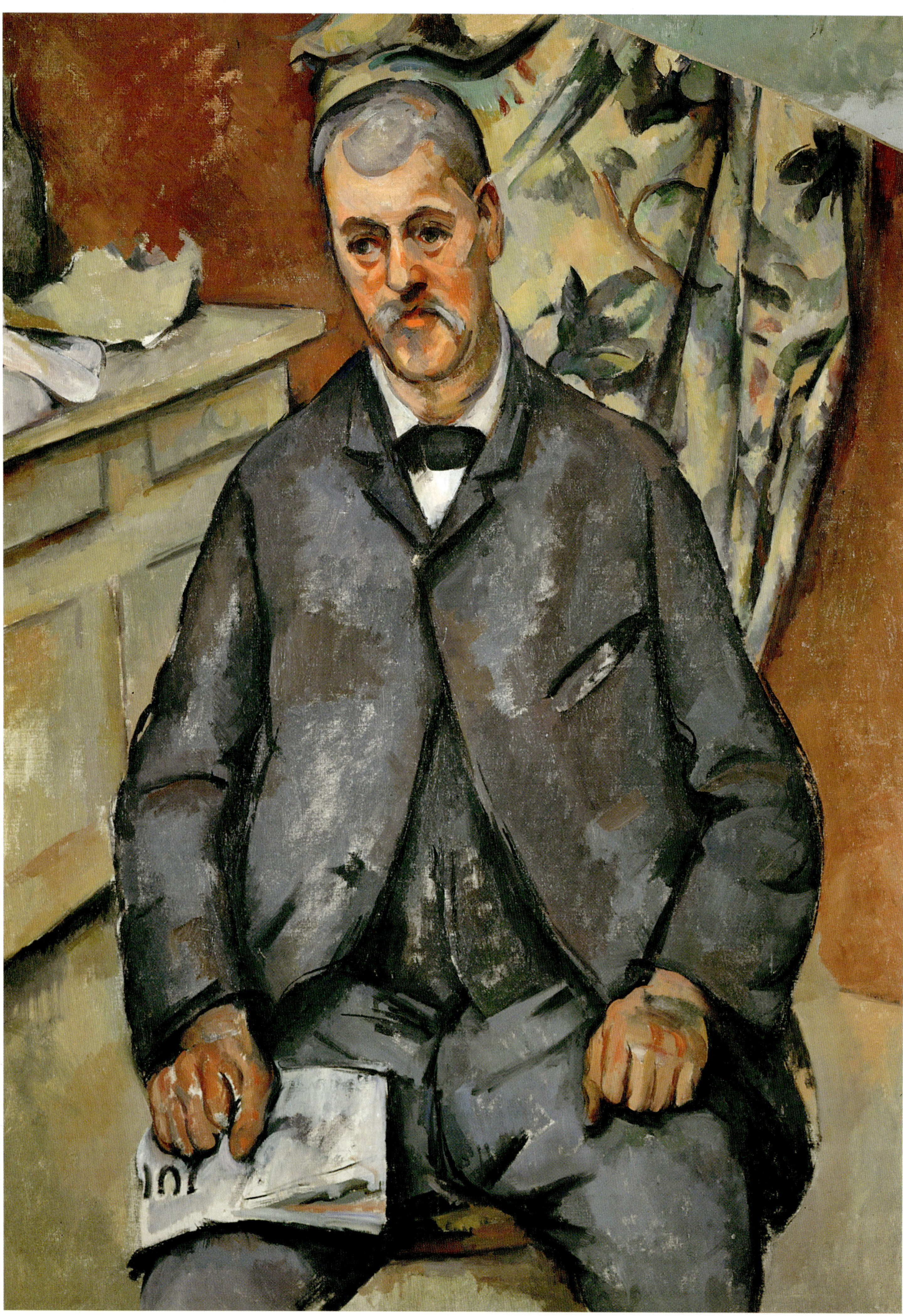

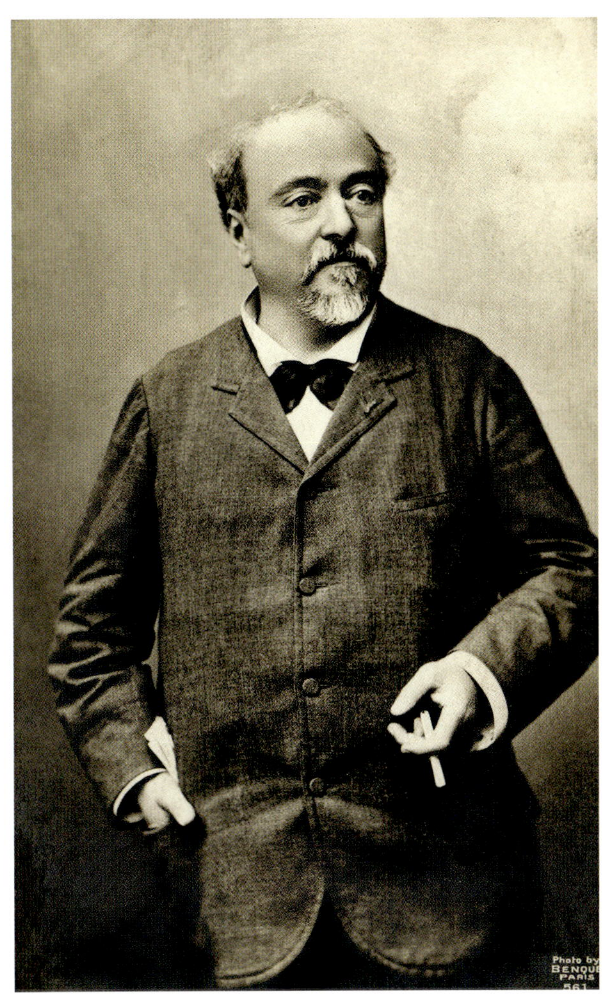

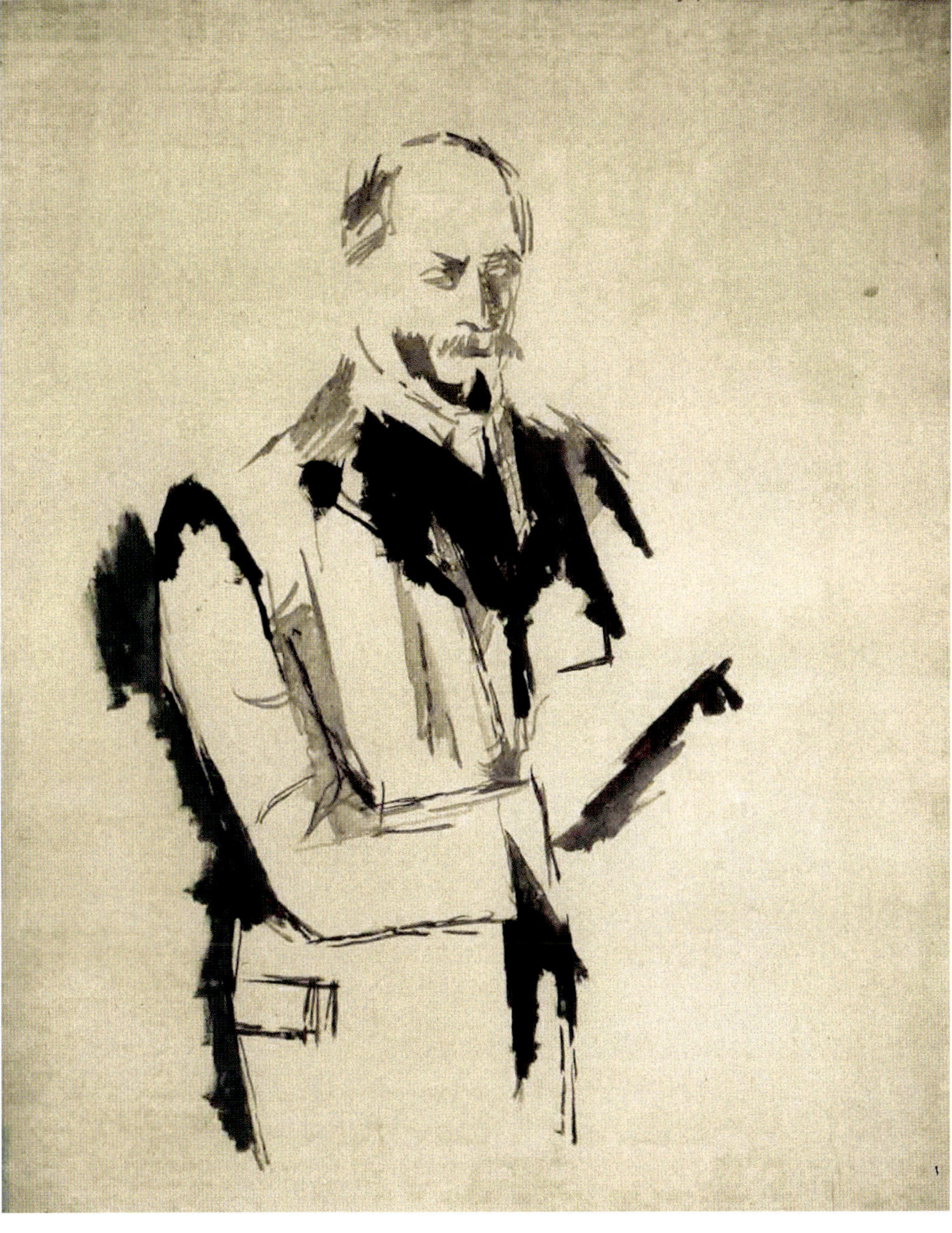

Fig. 62
Seated Man
1898–1900
Oil on canvas
Nationalgalerie, Oslo
R 789

Fig. 63
Anonymous
Emmanuel Chabrier
Photograph by Benque

Fig. 64
Paul Cézanne ?
Portrait presumed to be that of Auguste Pellerin
100 × 82 cm
Private collection

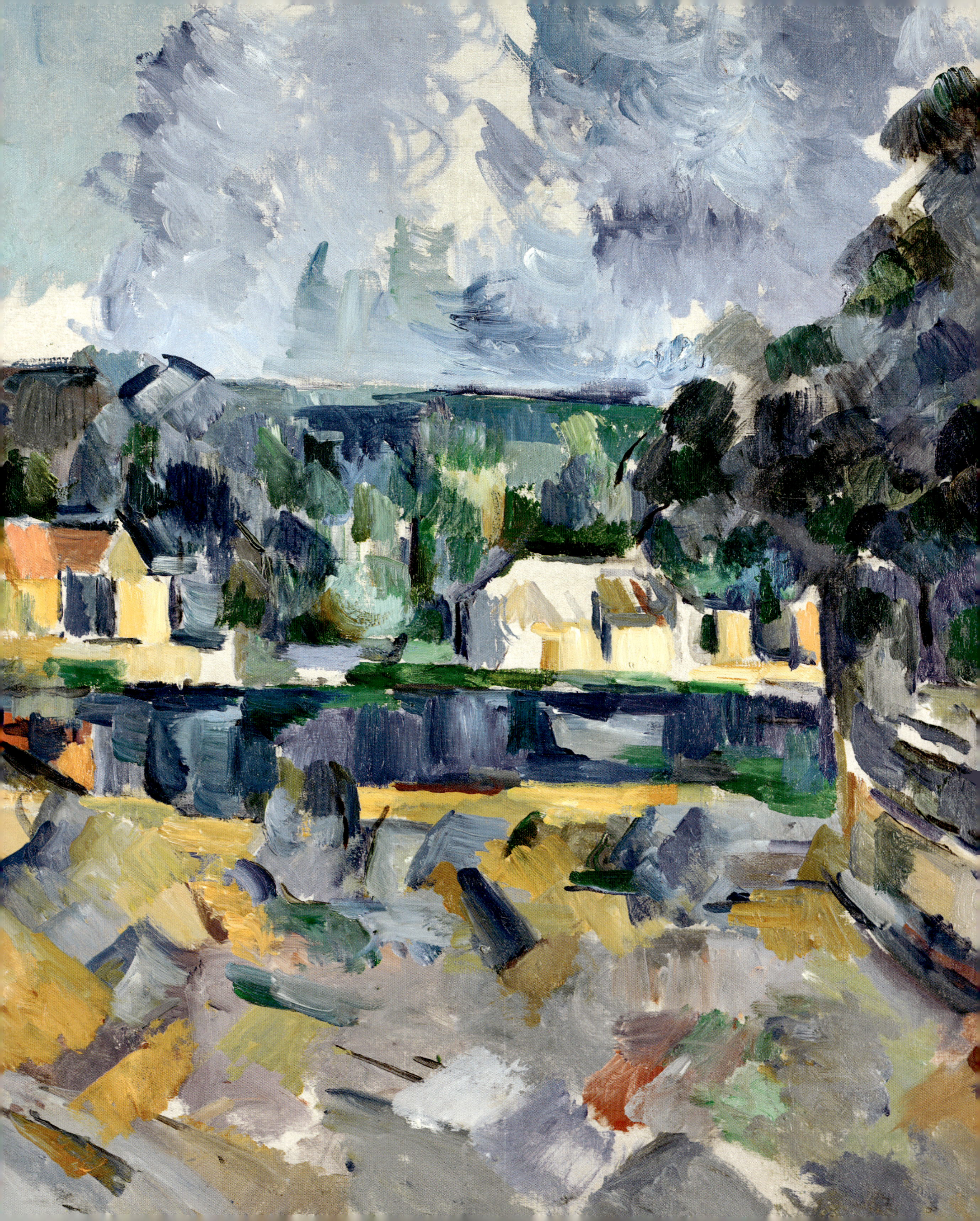

PATHS OF SILENCE

In 1888 Cézanne returned to Paris and Île-de-France after a long spell of around six years in Provence. He was no longer the ambitious and troubled young man of the 1860s, nor the painter of the 1870s discovering nature as he worked *sur le motif* and looking for supporters. At L'Estaque, Gardanne, Bellevue, and Jas de Bouffan he had been able to establish himself as an artist by going beyond Impressionism. There were no more family worries to disrupt his life. His friends, Zola for one, were far away. It was just Cézanne now. The fact remains that, at a time in his life when he could have settled for good in his home territory in the South (with no financial problems, and access to houses, studios, and friends), he often gravitated back to Paris, sometimes for extended periods, while the other trips he made—to Switzerland in 1890 and Savoy and Annecy in 1896—were undertaken out of necessity.

Until 1899 Cézanne came to stay in the Paris area with increasing frequency, even though he no longer felt any compulsion to work with friends like Pissarro or Guillaumin. He did take a trip to visit Monet in 1894 at Giverny, but he had no intention of deriving inspiration from his work. He did not return to Auvers or Pontoise, and stayed well away from his old haunt Issy-les-Moulineaux. He was to be found in Chantilly for a large part of 1888, and was seen at Montgeroult to the west of Paris. He was mainly to be found on the banks of the Marne, near Maisons-Alfort or Saint-Maur-des-Fossés, or around Melun and Fontainebleau, especially at Marlotte.

Did he need solitude and silence? A haven far from the capital where his name was beginning to circulate and his works were becoming sought after? While he was in Provence during these years, he worked near Château-Noir and Bibémus. So the canvases were more sharply contrasting: playing with sun-drenched trees and rocks of the Midi, and the more verdant colors of northern riverbanks and rivers. It meant that a secret dialogue was established between the Provence sunlight and the cloudier skies of Paris, between the steep contours of the Midi and the gentler banks and landscapes of Île-de-France.

A pictorial walk in the footsteps of Cézanne is provided here, in the hope of identifying the strictly Parisian imprint left by these stays in Île-de-France, as well as giving some thought to certain linking themes like water. Some locations, such as Marlotte, assume greater significance. D. C.

Banks of the Marne, I
(On the island of Machefer at Saint-Maur-des-Fossés)
(detail)
See cat. 63 p. 144

Denis Coutagne and Raymond Hurtu

LANDSCAPES OF THE YEARS 1888–05

Between 1888 and 1905, Cézanne made the journey to Paris eight times. In the same period he also went on a trip to Franche-Comté and Switzerland (1890), as well as to Vichy and then Talloires, near Annecy (1896). When the time spent in Île-de-France is added up, it comes to almost ninety-six months, or eight years. This would seem to indicate that Cézanne had deeply rooted reasons for going to northern France, at a time in his life when his friendships with Pissarro, Guillaumin, and Renoir, let alone Zola, had cooled. Death robbed him of some friends, like Chocquet (April 7, 1891) and Tanguy (February 6, 1894). Caillebotte died in February 1894, leaving a bequest to the State of sixty-five paintings, five of which were by Cézanne.[1] Admittedly, he did meet new people like Geffroy in 1894, and Vollard in 1896, but more than ever before Cézanne trod a solitary path in increasingly profound silence, mainly in Chantilly, Fontainebleau, Melun, Giverny, Marlotte, Mennecy, Montgeroult, and Marines in Île-de-France, or Hattenville in Normandy.

Chantilly

When Cézanne stayed in the Paris region after 1888, he initially made Chantilly his summer base, and he painted here the forest avenue leading to the château. The three known pictures on this theme (fig. 103, 104, 105) are redolent of the avenue of chestnut trees at Jas de Bouffan that opened out through a foliage tunnel onto a house—a country house or farm. But the pictorial climate was changing: The artist was now forced to deal with trees with thick foliage that were impenetrable by light. A barrier precluded venturing onto the road leading to the château, which emerged within a highly geometric triangle formation. A profound silence ensued. The work in Paris took on a different kind of gravity from the experimentation carried out within the family home.

Chantilly would be the sole geographic reference to a landscape north of Paris in Cézanne's entire body of work; and the reasons for his stay there are unknown.

Fontainebleau and Melun

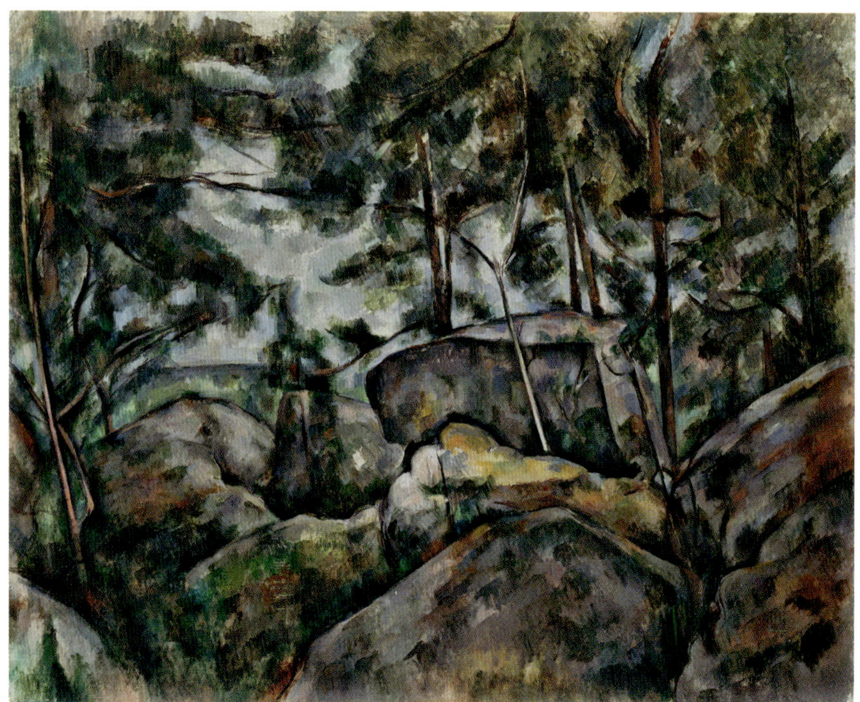

Cat. 60
Rocks in the Forest
c. 1893
Oil on canvas
75 × 92 cm
The Metropolitan Museum of Art, New York
R 775

In searching for landscapes near to the town, Cézanne was to go back in the familiar direction of Fontainebleau and Melun, where he lived for a whole year from 1879 to 1880. It may be that he had already been there, well before these already distant years, if we accept that a painting dating from 1865–1868 represented the Forest of Fontainebleau. In any case, after 1890 he did go to the forest locations loved by the Barbizon painters, following in the footsteps of Corot and Daubigny. It is more difficult, however, to identify the rocks, the erosion of which conveys centuries or even thousands of years of existence; it was as if Cézanne then wanted to give painting foundations as solid as these centuries-old rocks.

A nobleman, Denys Cochin,[2] was out riding one day in what can reasonably be assumed to be the Forest of Fontainebleau. He was accompanied by his son Augustin, who pointed out to his father a painter who was working alone at a bend in the road, exclaiming "Cézanne!". His father, having expressed surprise at his son recognizing an artist he had never met, received the reply: "But Papa, it's because he is painting a Cézanne!".

The banks of the Marne

If there was one memorable spot in these Paris years, it was the banks of the Marne—near Maisons-Alfort and Créteil to be more precise. The year was 1894, and maybe a bit earlier or later. At any rate written documentation places the artist in Alfort in 1894.[3]

Our attention is drawn to a first series of canvases, as much for the subjects he chose as for the brushwork he used.

The painter found quiet riverbanks: just the murmur of the wind, birds singing, lapping water, and the occasional sound of oars or a boat with people sporting straw boaters, accompanied by a play of light between the verdant foliage—willows, birches, and beech trees forming lush, delicate vegetation, sometimes gently swaying or still, that Zola made a point of describing when he took his characters to a little restaurant on Île Fanac near Joinville.[4]

Some fifteen pictures can be identified as having been painted by the side of the Marne, enough to determine just how much the man and the artist loved these riverbanks.

Our concern, then, is to understand why Cézanne chose this place. He was probably able to reach Maisons-Alfort by boat and Saint-Maur-des-Fossés by train from Gare de la Bastille, quite close to his lodgings. More than likely he also hoped to find tranquillity and a degree of freshness outside the town, in the same way he had sought peace on the shores of Lake Annecy in 1896. River water had always held an attraction for him since his dips in the Arc with Zola, and his Impressionist studies on the banks of the Oise near Pontoise, or the Seine by Melun.[5] In Provence he began work on *The Card Players* (R 706–710, 713, 714), and he took advantage of new territories beside the Bibémus plateau (fig. 111, 112, 115) and not long after Château-Noir, looking toward Sainte-Victoire (fig. 114). In Île-de-France he had recently stayed near Marlotte and painted the rocks in the forest in the style of those at Bibémus (cat. 60). The rocks beside Barbizon or Melun however still rooted him too much in the tradition of the "Fontainebleau" painters like Corot, Daubigny, Diaz de la Peña, Rousseau, or even Courbet, whom he had tried to emulate at one time. So it is understandable that for a time he set up his easel alongside the Marne, even at the risk of running into some students of Gérôme, like Gueldry.[6]

At the very most he might have recalled two friends with whom he had worked in these parts: Pissarro had lived not far from Maisons-Alfort, in Saint-Maur-des-Fossés, a hamlet nestling in a meander of the Marne, from 1863 to 1866[7]; Guillaumin had created a canvas representing the Seine-Marne confluence at Ivry, and produced two versions of the bridge at Charenton in 1878 and 1885. But the memories of times spent with these close friends, now far away, were resurfacing after ten, twenty, and even thirty years!

The Burnt Mill at Charentonneau

Raymond Hurtu[8] has identified two pictures that represent the site of the "burnt mill" at Charentonneau. In the *catalogue raisonné* of Cézanne's works, the first is called *The Aqueduct and the Lock* (cat. 61), dated 1895–1898. The second, dated around 1890, is entitled *Villa on the Banks of a River* (fig. 65). An old postcard (fig. 66) justifies the fresh identification of a hitherto unknown Cézannian motif in these paintings;[9] this is reinforced by one of the first published works on Cézanne in 1923, in which Georges Rivière—who staunchly defended the painter after 1877—kept the title *The Burnt Bridge* for the first painting (cat. 61), based on information passed on to him by his son-in-law, Cézanne's son, who had additionally noted down "Alfort 1889" for the second picture.[10]

In Cézanne's work, there is barely a trace of the mill and even the one at the Maincy bridge can only be discerned by the initiated eye; the mill on the Couleuvre at Pontoise can hardly be made out at all (fig. 67). The artist preserved a world that was fading and disappearing. By its very symbolism, the mill signifies the passing of time as it turns the wheel. Henceforth time would be suspended like the footbridge with supports that disappear into the abstract foliage. The painting is holding its breath: The still intact gallery rests on arches that could well be Roman, reflected in the water that has become the mirror of the painting, beside the lost mill's still-standing pilasters. More than ever, Cézanne is examining painting between tradition and modernity, representation and abstraction, and ruins and construction. Van Gogh, who had painted water mills in Holland, grew fond of the windmills in Paris. Cézanne was a man of forests, rocks, and rivers.

Around the Bridge at Créteil

The Marne near Créteil was to hold greater attraction for the painter than the location beside its confluence with the Seine. Does the geography follow the chronology? It is difficult to answer such a question, as Cézanne's works during the years 1890–1894 were very similar in terms of style. At any rate, the painter moved southward. He found his "spot" on an island, later connected to the town by a causeway, which became a road: Île Jambon, which could be reached on foot in a few minutes from the station at Saint-Maur. Turning toward Créteil, the artist discovered the bridge then known as Pont de Créteil, which he painted in 1894 (fig. 68).

The bridge crosses the Marne in three arches, only two of which can be seen in Cézanne's picture. It is a suspension bridge that was destroyed in 1870 and rebuilt in iron between 1872 and 1874 using industrial engineering. To the right of the composition the bank comprises the Île Brise-Pain,[11] owned by the chapter of Notre Dame, giving the name "Arm of the Chapter" to a part of the Marne extending to the island's interior.

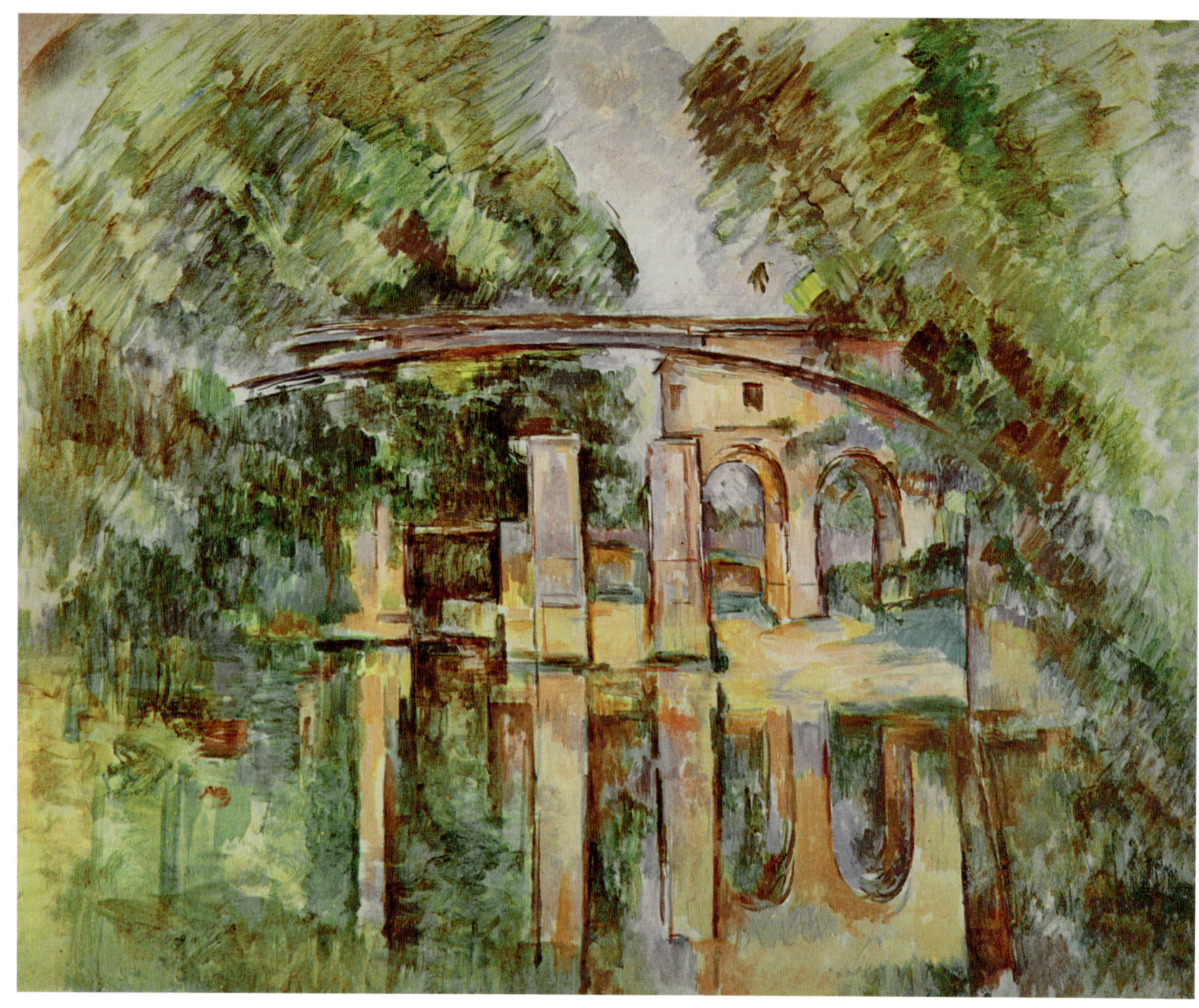

Cat. 61
The Burnt Mill at Charentonneau I
(The Aqueduct and the Lock)
c. 1894
Oil on canvas
74 x 93.3 cm
Private collection
R 765

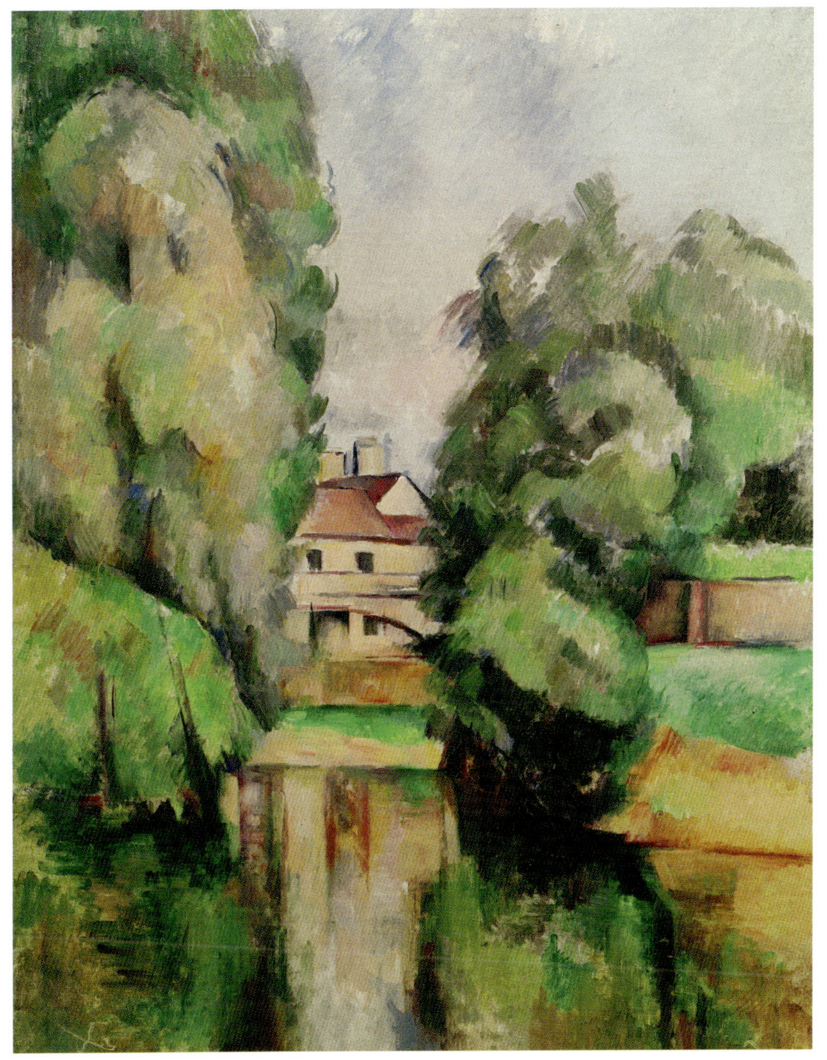

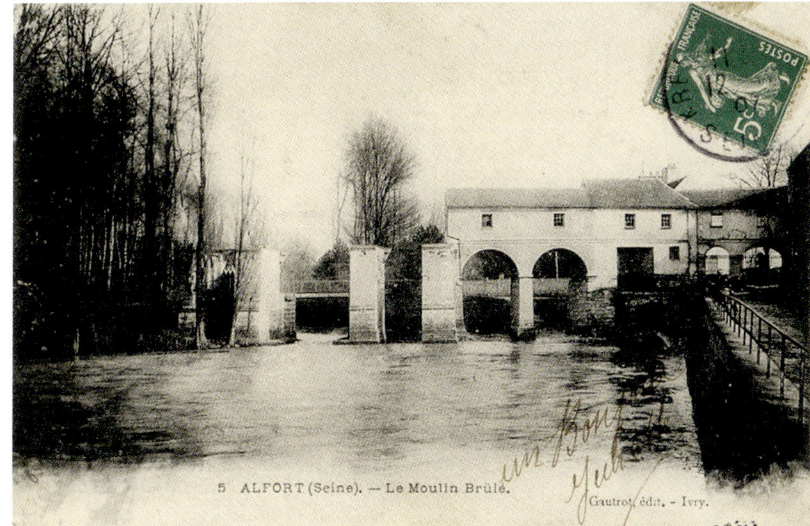

Fig. 65
The Burnt Mill at Charentonneau II (Villa on the Banks of a River)
c. 1890
Oil on canvas 81 × 65 cm
The Tel Aviv Museum of Art, Jerusalem, from the collection of Miriam and Edmond de Rothschild
R 727

Fig. 66
Alfort (Seine), The Burnt Mill
c. 1900
Postcard
Private collection

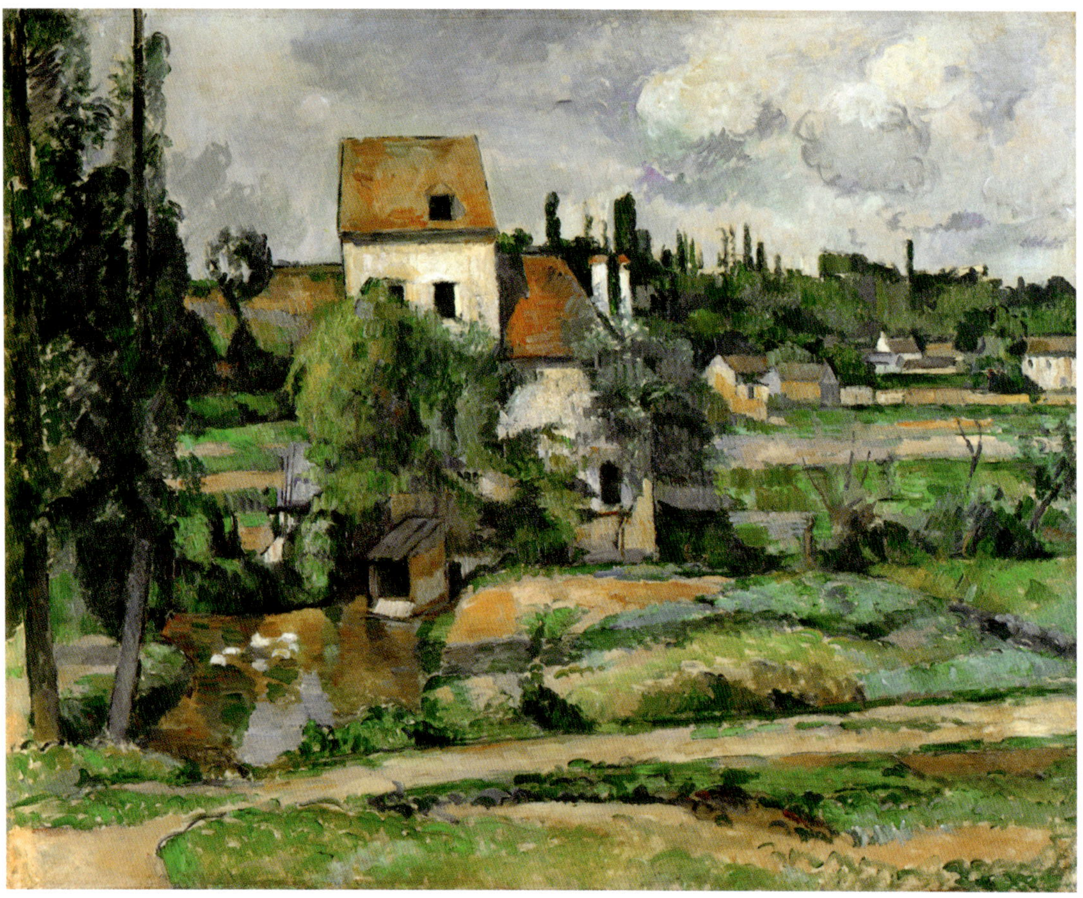

Doing a 180-degree turn from looking at the bridge at Créteil, Cézanne spotted, still from Île Jambon, a house that was probably used for water sports, situated at the southern end of Île Machefer. He was inspired by this subject on three occasions (cat. 62, fig. 69, R 624) within a very short timescale that must correspond to the one for his completion of *The Bridge at Créteil*[12]. Turning then slightly to his left, the painter's viewpoint produced the picture *Banks of the Marne* (R 628): Further investigation allows us to identify it as a group of houses near a towpath on the Créteil side, opposite Saint-Maur-des-Fossés.

Returning to Île Machefer and locating himself alongside the house identified for nautical use, Cézanne discovered another small arm of the Marne (between Saint-Maur and Île Machefer), now transformed into a road, bordered by an embankment dotted with flowers. A small, traditionally constructed wooden bridge gave access to the island that was hidden by a mass of foliage. A detailed postcard makes it possible to identify one of Cézanne's extremely abstract paintings featuring this bridge, recorded by Rewald as *Bridge over a Pond* (fig. 70). We suggest that from now on the following, more specific, title should be used: *Bridge over an Arm of the Marne linking Saint-Maur to Île Machefer.*

A few other pictures then spring to mind, including *Riverside Landscape* (R 722), *Trees and Houses by a River* (R 723), *On a Riverbank* (R 724), *Reflections in Water* (R 726), and *Water and Foliage* (R 728). We might also add to this group *The Brook* (fig. 71) because a distinctly un-Provençal willow can be seen at right in the composition.

This all suggests that these paintings reflect landscapes that have changed very little, accessible even nowadays to anyone walking along the Bras-du-Chapitre, especially well preserved a few yards from the bridge at Créteil.

So we are suddenly surprised to find that within a quite specific and relatively restricted area, Cézanne painted what should be regarded as a series. He probably found a space where he could breathe in this corner of France, very near to Paris but far from the social, and even artistic, bustle of the city. Even in Auvers his territory was limited to the area around Doctor Gachet's house.

Fig. 67
The Mill on the Couleuvre at Pontoise
1881
Oil on canvas
72.5 x 90 cm
Staatliche Museen zu Berlin, Alte Nationalgalerie, Berlin
R 483

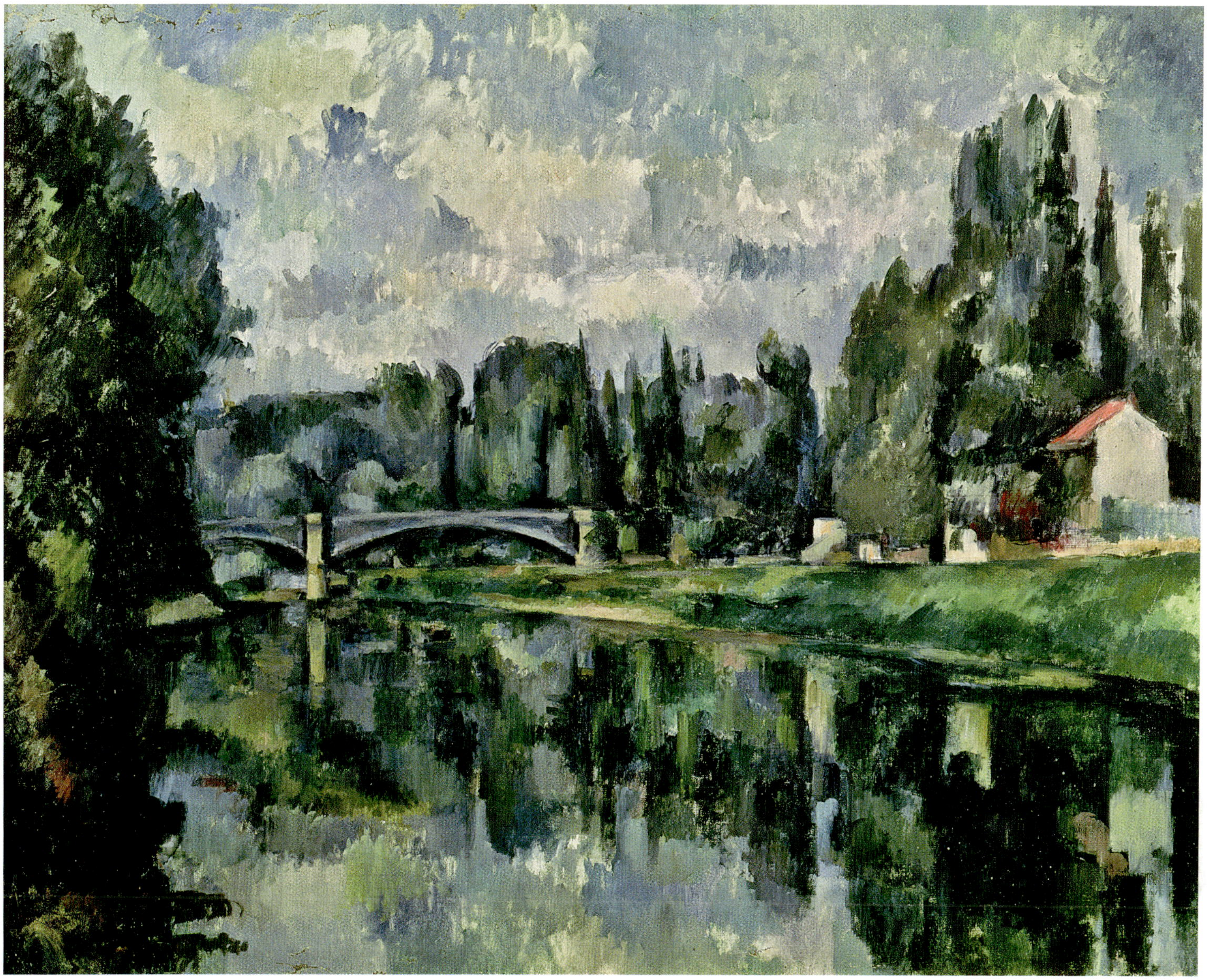

Fig. 68
The Bridge on the Marne at Créteil
c. 1894
Oil on canvas
71 x 90 cm
Pushkin Museum, Moscow
R 729

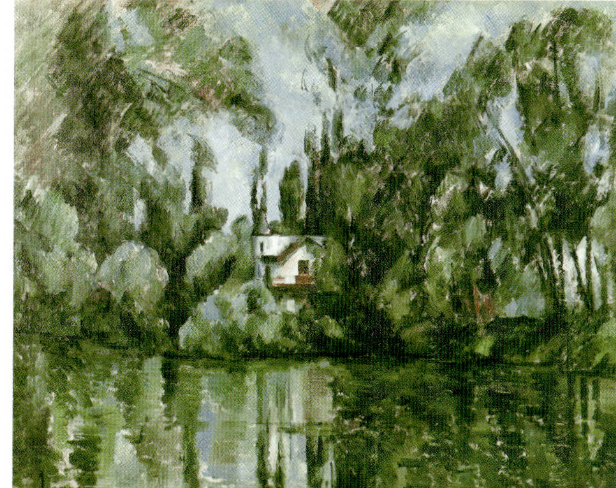

Fig. 69
House on the Banks of the Marne
(On the island of Machefer
at Saint-Maur-des-Fossés)
c. ?1894 (Rewald: 1888–1890)
Oil on canvas
73 × 91 cm
White House Collection, Washington
R 622

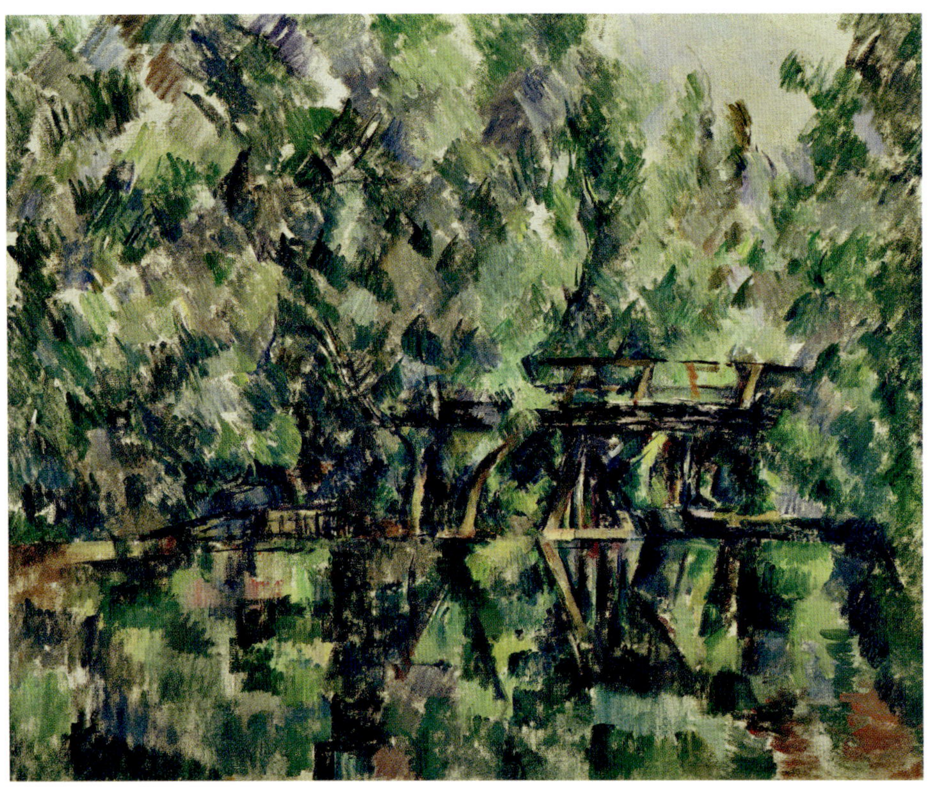

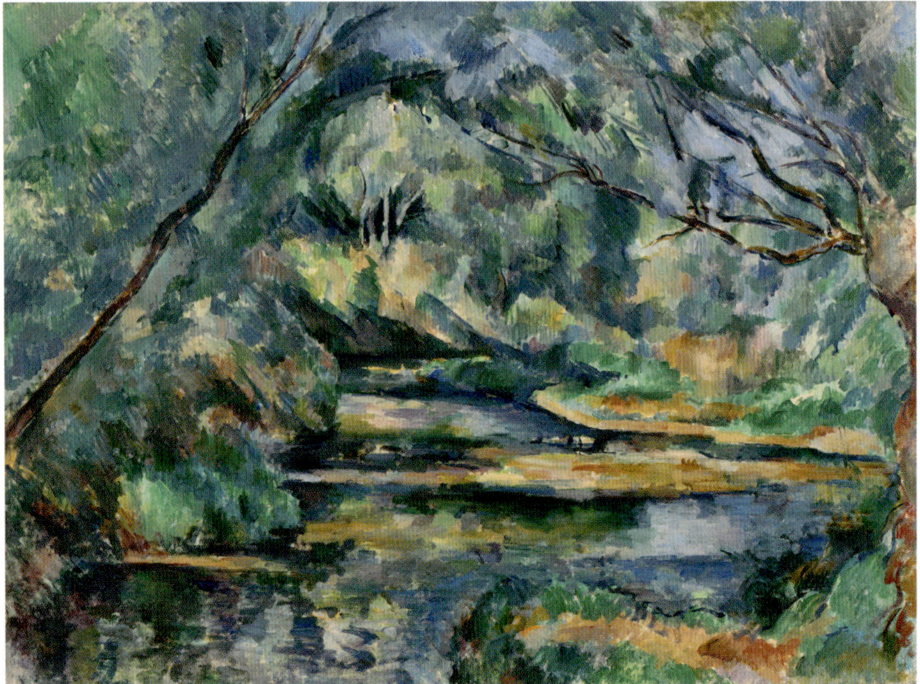

Fig. 70
Bridge over an Arm of the Marne linking Saint-Maur to the Île Machefer (The bridge over the pond)
c. ?1894 (Rewald: 1896–1898)
Oil on canvas
64 × 79 cm
Pushkin Museum, Moscow
R 725

Fig. 71
The Brook
1895–1900
Oil on canvas
60 × 81 cm
The Cleveland Museum of Art, Cleveland, bequest of Leonard C. Hanna, Jr.
R 766

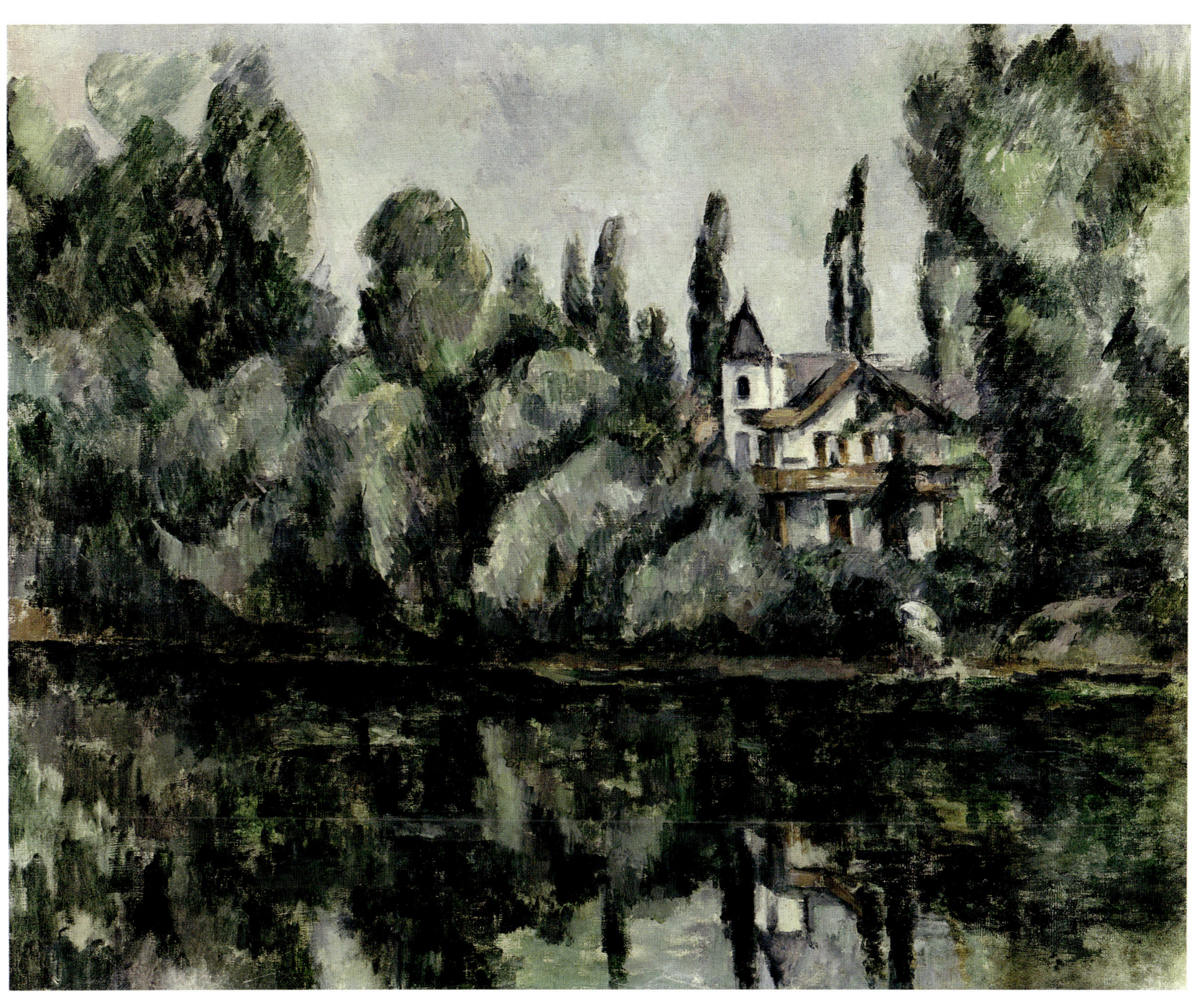

Cat. 62
Banks of the Marne, I
(On the island of Machefer
at Saint-Maur-des-Fossés)
c. ?1894 (Rewald: 1888–1890)
Oil on canvas
65 × 81 cm
Hermitage Museum, St. Petersburg
R 623

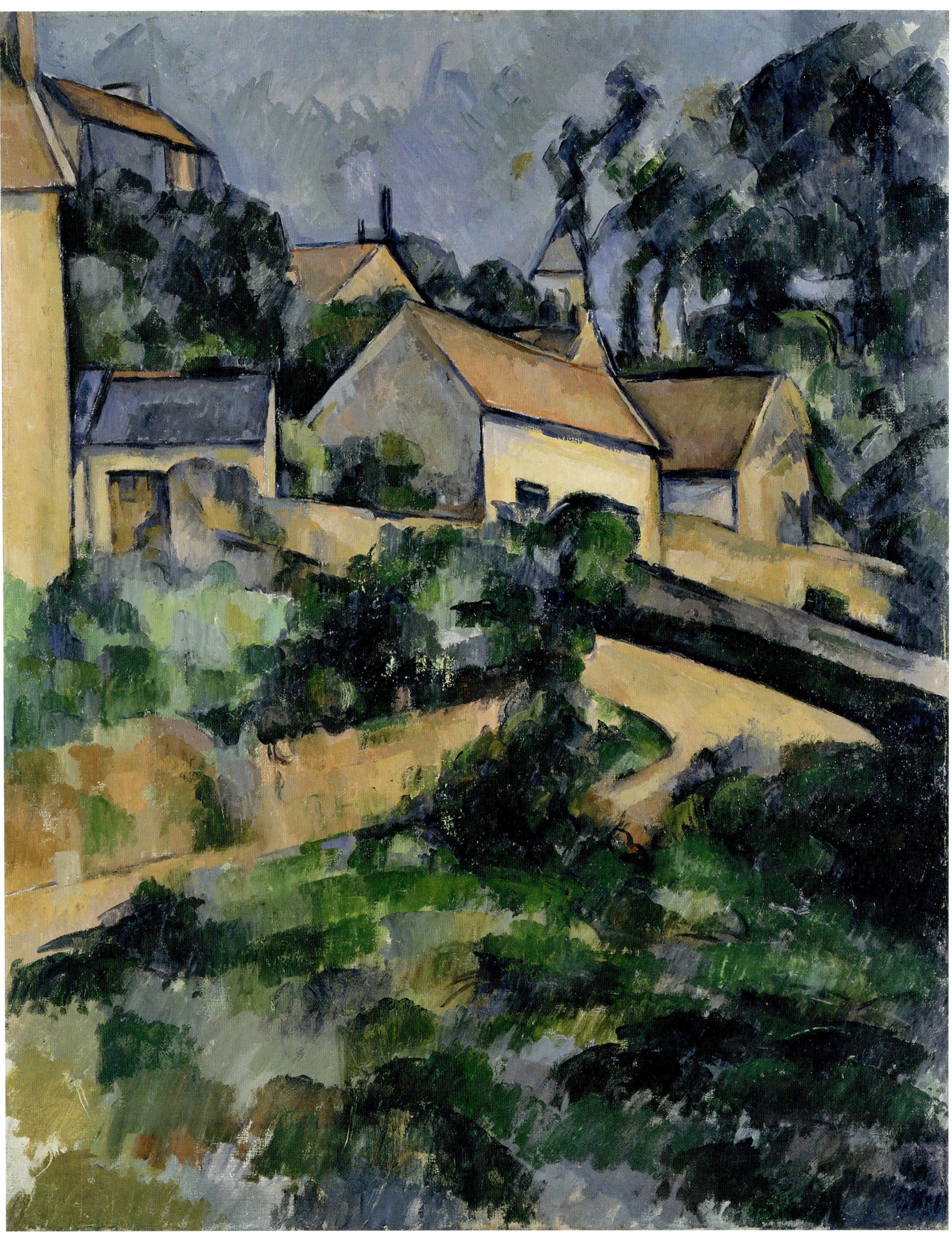

Montgeroult

Two paintings with locations that have been definitely identified allow us to place Cézanne in Montgeroult in 1898, *Turning Road at Montgeroult* (fig. 72) and *Farm at Montgeroult* (fig. 73), as confirmed in correspondence with a young artist, Le Bail.[13] The latter finds Cézanne using a color palette of highly contrasting ochers that he would always go back to in Provence; in this case, however, the greens are verging on densely dark. The first painting has an equally surprising composition: The village is squeezed tightly into the top of the canvas; the bell tower seems imprisoned by the roofs and walls that form a barricade; while the foreground purports to be wild, painted with forceful brushstrokes. Cézanne seems to be returning to the violence of his youth, in contrast to the gentle approach in the canvases painted on the banks of the Marne.

A year later, he went back to Marlotte and set up his easel facing a smooth expanse of water formed by the Loing river in front of the church at Montigny: There "all is order and beauty" (though without Baudelaire's luxury and sensuality) in the dialogue between a tree, a church, and the water. A blue-tinted response in Île-de-France to what he had painted in Provence in greenish-ocher and red around the Gardanne bell tower[14] (*Church at Montigny-sur-Loing*, 1898, fig. 113).

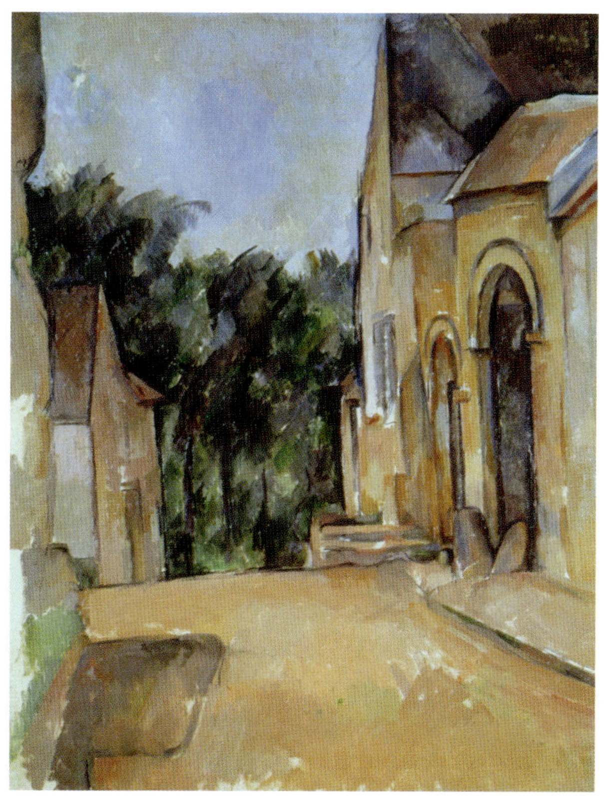

The last two summers near Fontainebleau

The two paintings *Riverbanks* (cat. 63) and *The Turning Road* (cat. 64) are dated 1904. The first one conveys an almost aggressive force through the violently contrasting colors (combining pure reds and ochers with dark Prussian blue and ultramarine), the powerfully sweeping brushwork on the canvas, and the formal construction emphasized by the horizontal band, identifiable as an arm of the river. The only thing that attenuates this violent impression is the abstract scattering of gray touches that open up this painting.

In close chronological proximity, the *Turning Road* canvas is, in its perhaps unintentional incompleteness, characteristic of the way of working of the artist who brings full harmony to a work at whatever moment he leaves it. Here the canvas exudes peaceful serenity. The strokes have a gentle manner, and the muted colors are based on a palette of violet, orangey-gray, and grayish-green that is also found on a Provence canvas—*The Montagne Sainte-Victoire* (R 901). In this play on associations, the first painting should thus be seen in the light of *Bend in the Road, Spring Morning at Saint-Antonin* (R 930).

Naturally our aim would be to identify the locations. *Riverbanks* takes us back to the banks of the Seine near Melun. *The Turning Road* could be a representation of Mennecy village, between Fontainebleau and Paris (still conditional, even though an old postcard leads us to identify it as such): A letter was written by Cézanne in 1897 from Hôtel de la Belle-Étoile in this village. It is entirely possible that he could have returned there at a later stage when the sky was so striking.

One watercolor remains as a legacy of Fontainebleau, a place we know Cézanne returned to in 1904 and 1905. The painter preserved a visual memory of a monument, in this case a very famous château. But the pictorial work appears light and transparent, relying on strong elements (tree trunks and plants) to provide line, color, and value. The lesson would not be forgotten in Provence: two months before he died, Cézanne wrote: "I began a watercolor in the style of those I did at Fontainebleau."[15]

Fig. 72
Turning Road at Montgeroult
1898
Oil on canvas
56.6 × 45 cm
The Museum of Modern Art, New York
R 828

Fig. 73
Farm at Montgeroult
1898
Oil on canvas
64 × 52 cm
The Museum of Fine Art, Houston
R 833

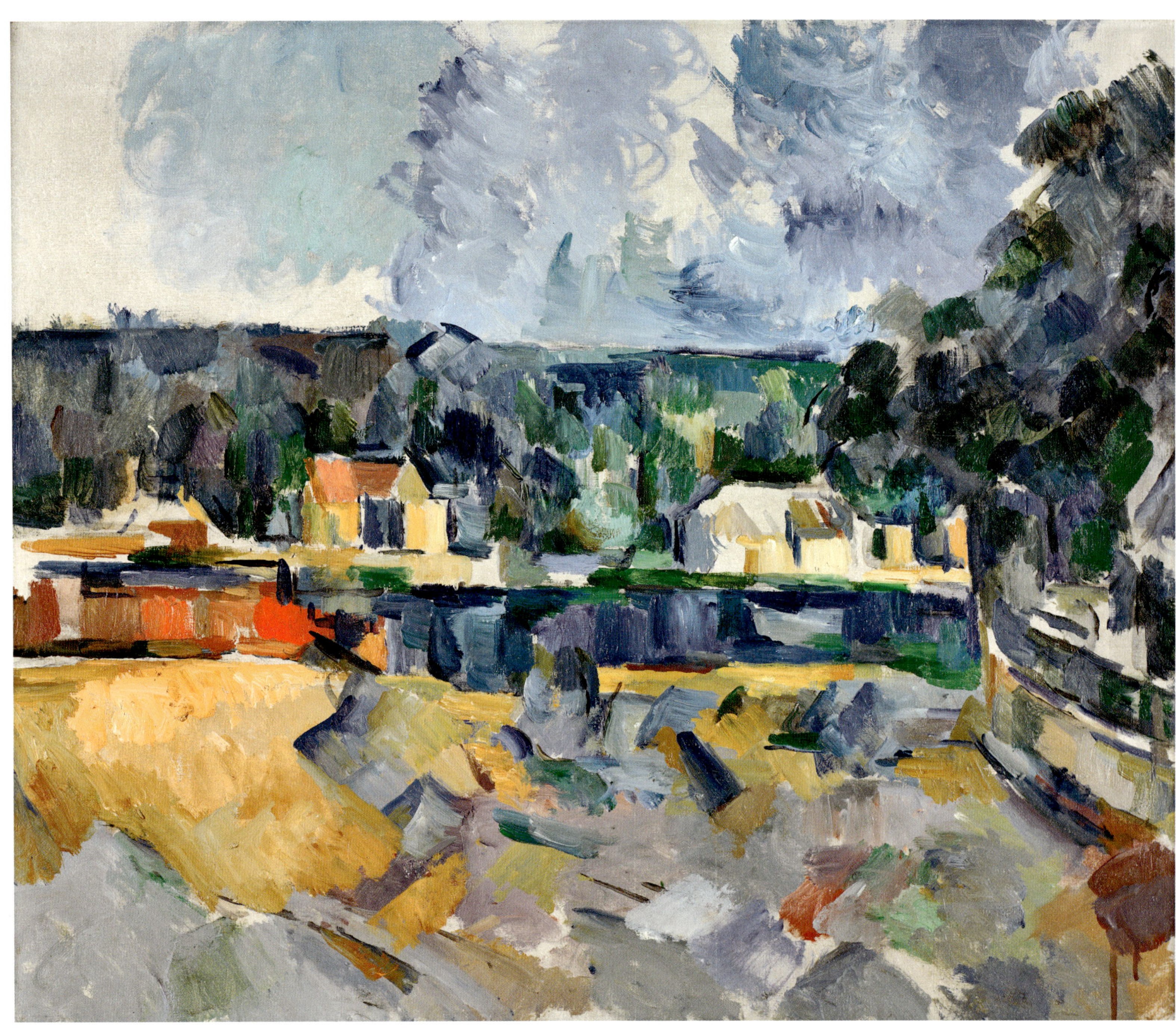

Cat. 63
Riverbanks
1904–5
Oil on canvas
60.9 x 73.6 cm
Museum of Art, Rhode Island School of Design, Providence
R 920

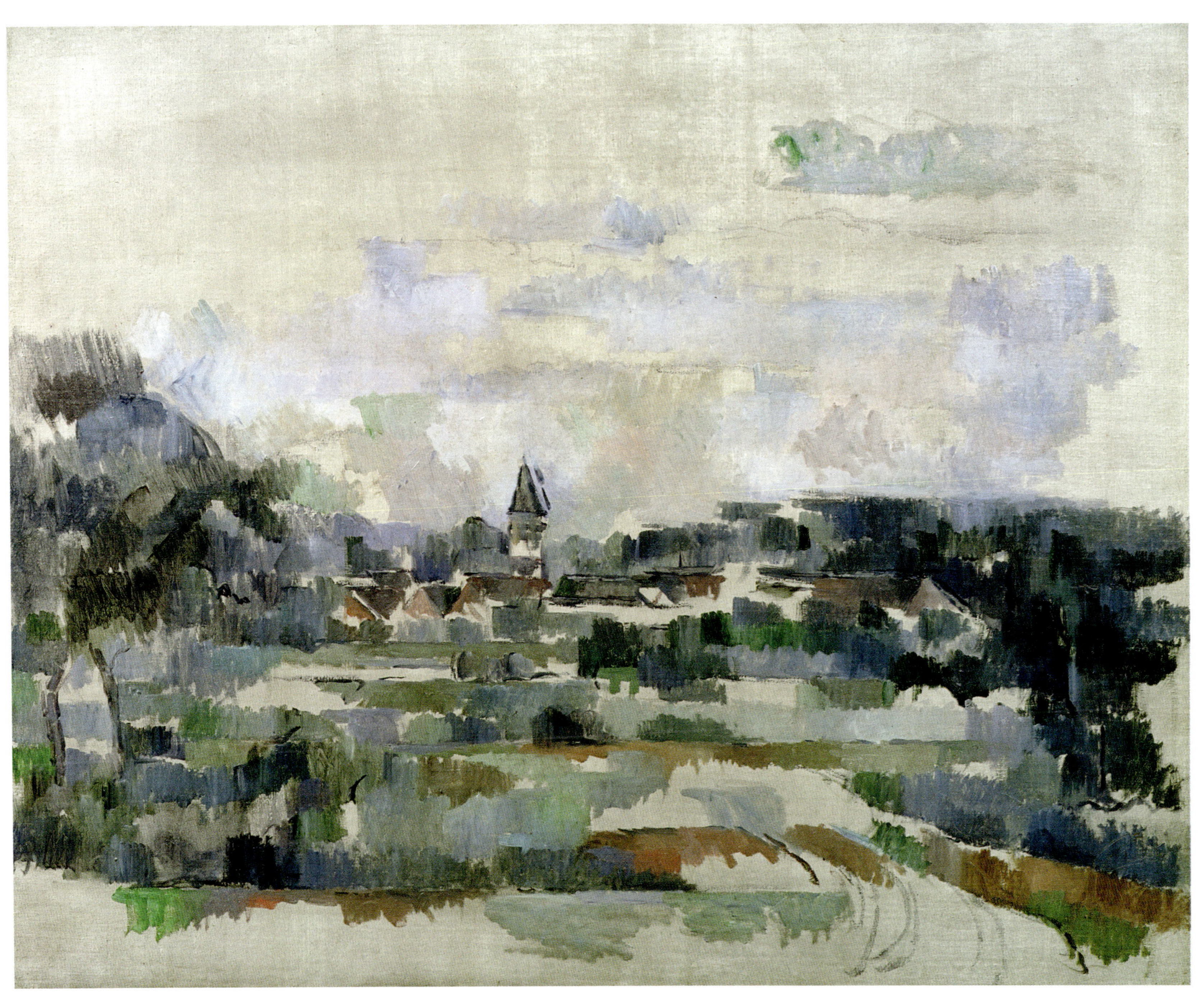

Cat. 64
The Turning Road
1904
Oil on canvas
73 × 92 cm
The Samuel Courtauld Trust,
The Courtauld Gallery, London
R 921

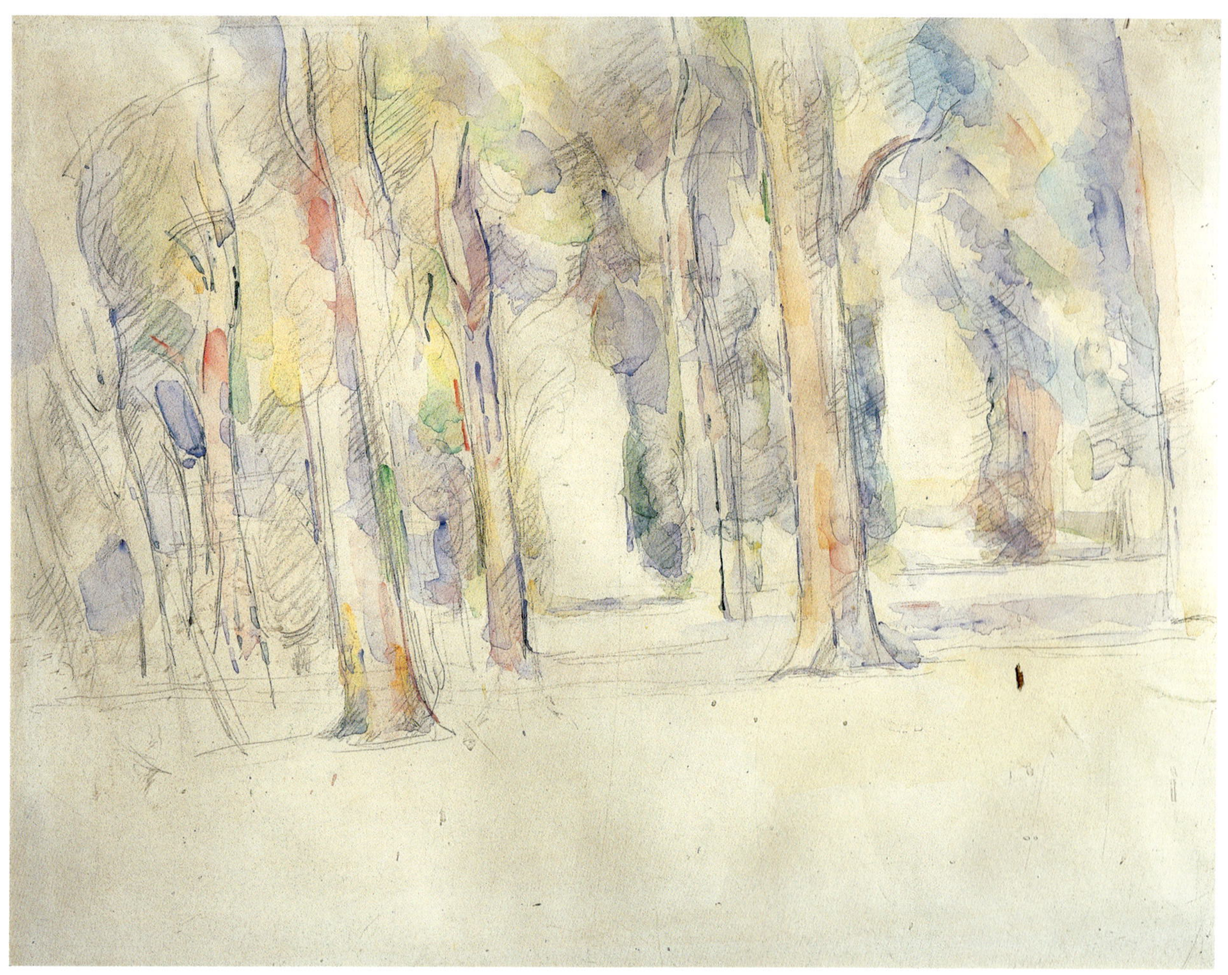

Cat. 65
Woodland with Large Trunks (Fontainebleau?)
1892–94
Watercolor, recto
42 x 57 cm
Private collection
RWC 451

Cat. 65 bis
Edge of the Forest (Fontainebleau?)
1892–94
Watercolor, verso
42 x 57 cm
Private collection
RWC 453
Not on view

Paving the way to abstraction?

Some have been inclined to see Cézanne as the forerunner of abstraction, supporting their interpretation with the artist's own words: "Now at the old age of about seventy, the coloring effects that create light give rise in my work to abstractions which stop me from covering the canvas, and pursuing the delimitation of objects when the points of contact are fine, delicate."[16]

We do not believe that Cézanne ever suspected that his pictorial process was a stage in a Hegelian history of art that would end in abstraction in the style of Malevich's *Suprematist Composition: White on White*, or Kandinsky's expression of the soul through color, or the formal expression of a painting reduced to its lines and primary colors, Mondrian-style. Cézanne remained viscerally attached to nature, as if it were an uncompromising mistress. After all, did he not put all his energy into "pursuing the realization of that side of nature which falls within our vision and gives us the picture"?[17] According to him, Provence provided him with pre-

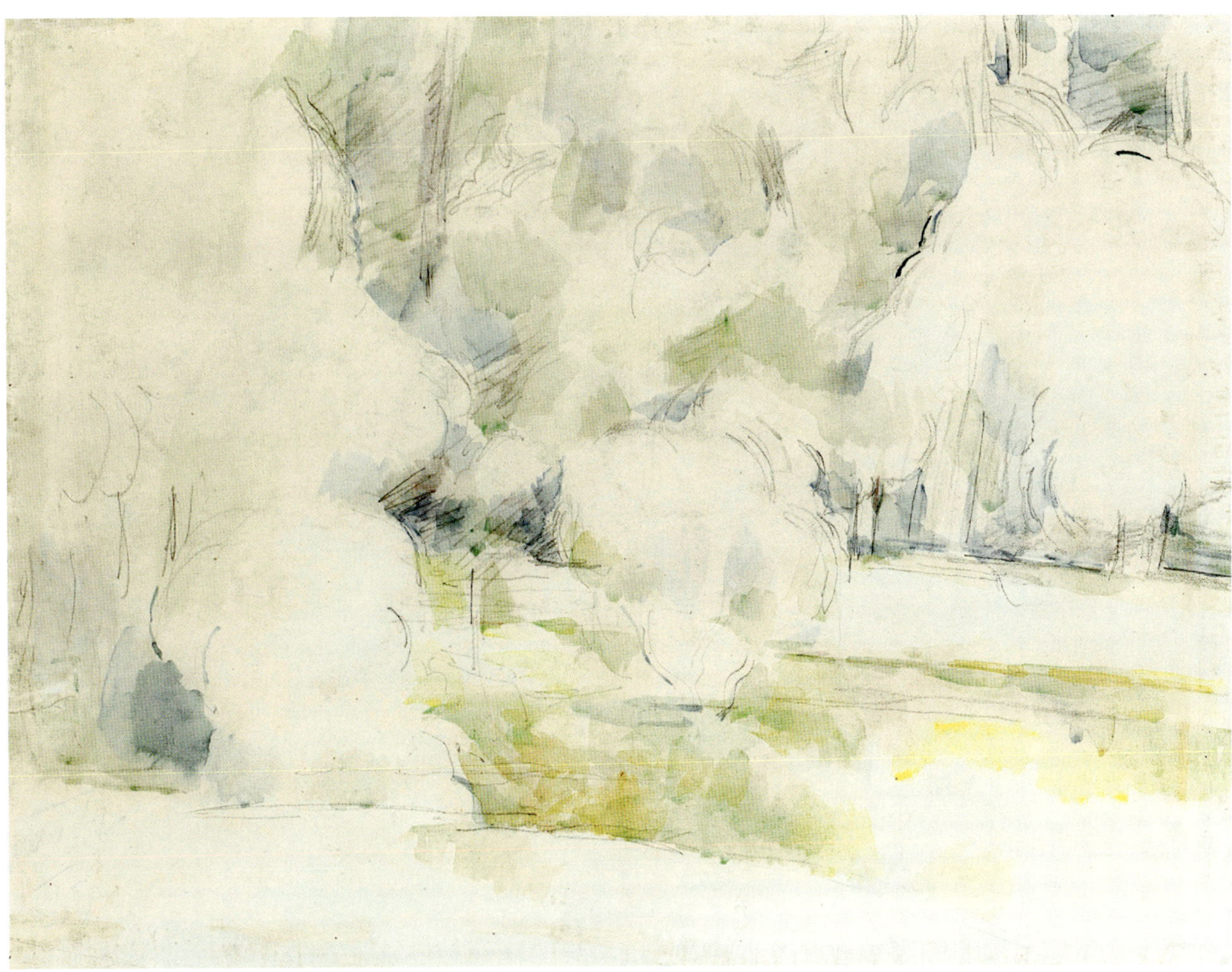

formed landscapes that would allow him to "invigorate Poussin directly from nature"[18] without having to go to Rome. He needed Île-de-France, then, as a form of nature at the limits of abstraction: More than ever, the banks of a river, clearings, a forest, distant villages on a plain dominated in a more secretive, intuitive, and mysterious exploration. Of course once back in Provence, the painter would not forget the lesson: "I began a watercolor in the manner of the ones I did at Fontainebleau, and it seems more harmonious to me; the whole must give the greatest possible balance."[19]

Let us consider a double watercolor: On the recto, it bears the title *Woodland with Large Trunks (Fontainebleau?)* (cat. 65), and the title on the verso is *Edge of the Forest (Fontainebleau?)* (cat. 65 bis). The first relies on tree trunks as if they were columns with space circulating freely between them, given color by the foliage and leaves. The second version is barely drawn and colored: Everything becomes indistinct, trees as well as plants, even down to the place represented, expressed with a question mark. It is now but a breath of nature. The painter is trying to capture a sunny glimpse of existence rather than an actual presence: "Nature loves to hide," as Heraclitus said at the dawn of Western thought. Closer to Cézanne, Hölderlin stated that "The gods have turned away."[20] The painter is standing at the water's edge, or at the edge of the forest. He is at the frontier of the invisible, charged with capturing nature on the point of vanishing. And, following the example of the German writer who asked the question of the modern age, "Why are there poets in these difficult times?", the painter wrote: "Have I made some progress so late and so painfully? Is Art in fact a tomb that demands pure souls that will belong entirely to it?"[21] The poet's sole mission was to wander "from land to land through the sacred night."[22] Cézanne would look at the mountain here, and sit down at the edge of the water or the forest there.

"I make slow progress... I have sworn to myself that I will die painting."[23]

Admittedly, some of the rocks in the Forest of Fontainebleau might conjure up images of Bibémus, but for certain there was no Sainte-Victoire mountain in the Paris region. Similarly, the Marne did not flow in Provence.

Giverny

Joseph Rischel

On January 17, 1956, the New York book and print dealer Carl Zigrosser wrote to John Rewald to help clarify the history of a Cézanne painting belonging to his friend Alice Newton Osborn (widow of Frank), who would will the picture to the Philadelphia Museum of Art at her death in 1966.

"She has a painting which she and her husband bought in 1920 from Mme C. Baudy proprietor of the Hotel Baudy at Giverny, Eure. She also has the hotel register of the Maison Baudy where under the date of Sept. 7, 1894, Cézanne is registered... Now the very painting is reproduced and listed in Venturi as 'Paysage d'Hiver' [Winter Landscape] No. 440 from the Pellerin Collection. Also in Rivière Cézanne Floury, pages 65 and 120; ditto, Floury 1930, pages 69 and 130 with the same provenance and attribution... But what about the provenance from the Pellerin Coll.? Could it be true, or is there a mistake somewhere?"[1]

Rewald is quick to reply on January 20, explaining that Mrs. Osborn's painting must be the same as No. 440 in Venturi, who listed it in fact without any owner (but with the Rivière reference which does mention Pellerin), noting that Venturi knew the Pellerin Collection well and is the one to be trusted. At that point Rewald knew, from Gustave Geffroy's biography, about Monet's report[2] of Cézanne's three-week visit to stay with him at Giverny that winter of 1894 but had not yet made the Baudy connection; he clarified in an interview with Madame Suzanne Bruno[3] that this painting, with two others, indeed was in the possession of her grandmother, as he relates to his old friend and colleague in Aix, Leo Marchutz, March 15, 1974.

"Through speaking at Giverny to the daughter of the innkeeper where Cézanne had been resident in 1894, and who had passed on to me the page of their account book[4], I learnt that Cézanne had left behind him a portrait of himself that Monet had then come to reclaim, and then that in the 20th century some Americans had discovered in the attic of the inn two unfinished canvases attributed to Cézanne. I have now been able to describe these two."[5]

Which he does, as published in his posthumous Rewald's catalog, numbers 774, 777, and 778.

The Giverny visit also provides a rare insight into the character and temperament of Cézanne, softening somewhat the by now rather rigid view of him as a completely antisocial and uncommunicative person. He was, to judge from the hotel register, in close company for three weeks with a large group of people, nearly all Americans, most of them with very little French, without conflict. A charming description by the American artist, Matilda Lewis, also staying at the hotel, notes[6] both his rustic ways (scraping the soup bowl with his spoon) which are quickly compensated for by his old-fashioned good manners, with a particular diffidence and gallantry to women which she found very pleasing. Geffroy described a party organized by Monet when a number of people came out from Paris—Mary Cassatt, Octave Mirbeau, and Rodin, where the shy and awkward Cézanne was genuinely sociable, and delighted when Rodin honored him with a handshake. However, Cézanne's touchiness and fear of even those most sympathetic to him was soon evident. At a special artists' gathering, which included Renoir and Sisley, when Monet greeted him with, "At last we are here all together and happy to seize the occasion to tell you how fond we are of you and how much we admire your art," [7] the dismayed Cézanne answered, "You, too, are making fun of me," and left the room, soon to depart from Giverny, abandoning at the Hotel Baudy the paintings which had occupied him during those three weeks. Despite some early confusion (via Geffroy's report) that Monet had gathered up the works left behind and sent them to Cézanne in Aix, it is now fairly clear that Monet (on instruction from Cézanne?) did visit the hotel with Vollard (?) to take possession of the self-portrait. The two landscapes did not reappear until the twenties with the Osborn purchase in 1920, as documented here. Another well-heeled American painter, Waldo Pierce "sometime between 1925 and 30" bought another landscape from the Hotel Baudy[8]. Cézanne was never to see Monet again following his abrupt departure from Giverny that winter, abandoning his works in progress. He does with some good grace, albeit some six months later, write Monet from Aix: "So, here I am back in the South of France—perhaps I should never have left, in order to devote myself to the chimeric pursuit of art..."

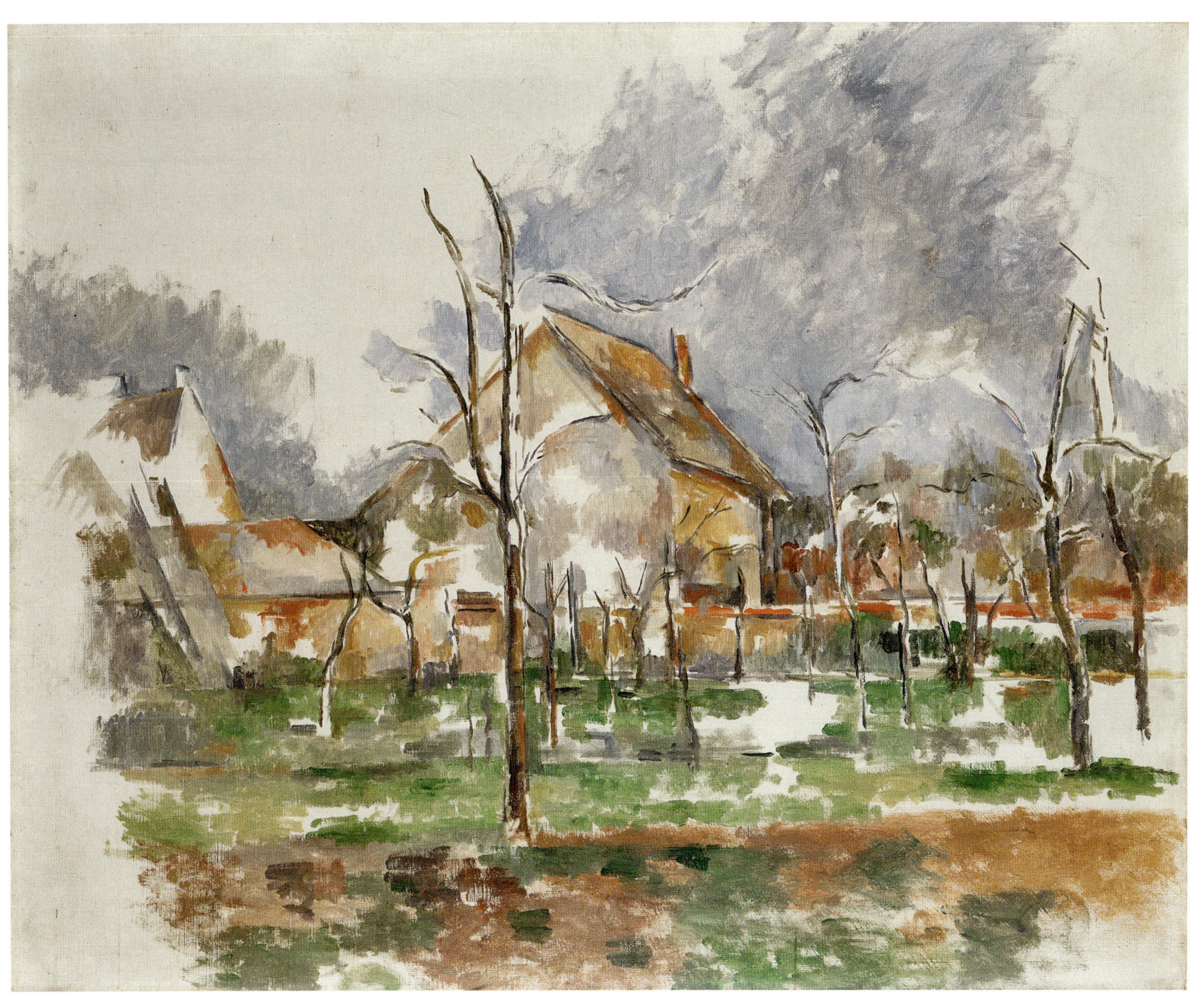

Cat. 66
Winter Landscape (Giverny)
1894
Oil on canvas
65 × 81 cm
Philadephia Museum of Art, Philadelphia,
gift of Frank and Alice Osborn, 1966
R 777

Cat. 67
Portrait of Alfred Hauge
August 1899
Oil on canvas
71.8 × 60.3 cm
Norton Gallery and School of Art,
West Palm Beach,
gift of R.H. Norton, 48.5
R 835

A Forgotten Visitor

Jean Colrat

Cézanne was not the prickly and unsociable character he is often described as, but it is true that the number of contemporaries who talk of meeting him is rather limited, and rarer still are those who are able to describe their visit to one of his many successive studios. Though Michael Doran's work[1] may have been thought to be exhaustive, we are now able to add a forgotten visitor who met Cézanne in one of the studios he occupied at Marlotte in Fontainebleau Forest. The account is not exactly unknown but it would appear that, thus far, studies on Cézanne have neglected to include the *Memoirs* of the Hungarian painter Jozsef Rippl-Rónai. For many years, these memoirs were difficult to access: Published in 1911 in Budapest, where they were not published again until 1957, they are now only accessible in English and German translation in the form of extracts. Jozsef Rippl-Rónai came to Paris in 1887, working first in the studio of his celebrated compatriot Muncàksy, then, around 1890, gaining access to a more innovatory environment through Pitcairn Knowles, Maillol, and Vuillard[2]. After explaining how the presentation of his canvas entitled *My Grandmother* at the Champ-de-Mars Salon of 1894 brought him into contact with Gauguin, Denis, and Toulouse-Lautrec and led to him being accepted by the Nabis, Rippl-Rónai goes on to describe his visit to Cézanne: "I spoke to Cézanne only once, when I visited him at his studio. This studio was known for containing no paintings by Cézanne; they had all been sold at his first exhibition organized by Vollard—at the time a penniless art dealer who was just starting out. I was told that his paintings had fetched around 30,000 francs and that he had divided this amount between his wife, his son, and himself, before asking them to leave, while he continued to work at Marlotte in the company of a very young Swedish writer. I saw only an old image of a beautiful Italian-looking woman and a chromolithograph nailed on the wall, crooked and without a frame. (It is interesting, almost incomprehensible, yet characteristic of Cézanne that he should have enjoyed these chromos.) He spoke little, particularly when I asked him about other artists. It is perhaps worth mentioning the distinction that this unquestionably great artist made with regard to three outstanding painters of the time. He described Puvis de Chavannes as "a very great artist"; Renoir he called only "a man of talent"; and when I wanted to know his opinion of Gauguin, he said with disdain "I do not know this gentleman", although he knew him perfectly well. Gauguin, on the contrary, greatly admired Cézanne's work."[3] Rippl-Rónai then describes his earlier visit to Gauguin: "My meeting with him was for me of the same importance as that with Cézanne at Marlotte, near Fontainebleau, although the circumstances with Gauguin were less simple and more bohemian." A letter to his brother, as yet undated, in which Rippl-Rónai gives an account of his visit to Marlotte, provides a few further details: "The names of these artists are not unknown to you—P. Cézanne is probably the only one you don't know, unless you may have seen his self-portrait in *La Revue blanche*? He is an elderly man, the oldest modern French Impressionist and one of the greatest masters. An example for us. Last summer I had a half-hour conversation with him—very interesting. He is an old man, simple and very modest. He complains about not being able to paint well enough and not having achieved his goals thus far."[4]
The account is not rich in information but it does confirm the fact that Cézanne had a studio at Marlotte. Local recollection claimed this to be the case although there was nothing to show that he had really settled there during the numerous times he stayed in the Fontainebleau area between 1879 and 1905. According to the locals, he lived in a small house where, on the second floor, one can still see the large window of a studio. It is also said that a later owner had murals of female nudes erased from the walls and found an accounts book which included the names of Cézanne and his wife.[5] In addition to providing this information, Rippl-Rónai's account is primarily interesting for the questions it raises, the first being the date of the visit, which according to the letter is simply during the summer. Biographies of Rippl-Rónai place it in 1895, as the Hungarian painter attributes the emptiness of Cézanne's studio to the fact that he had sent his canvases for the "first exhibition organized by Vollard," in November 1895. This deduction seems legitimate, as Vollard writes that he was informed that Cézanne was probably in the Fontainebleau area when he tried, during the summer of 1895, to meet up with him and propose the exhibition.[6] He was unaware that Cézanne had been in Aix since

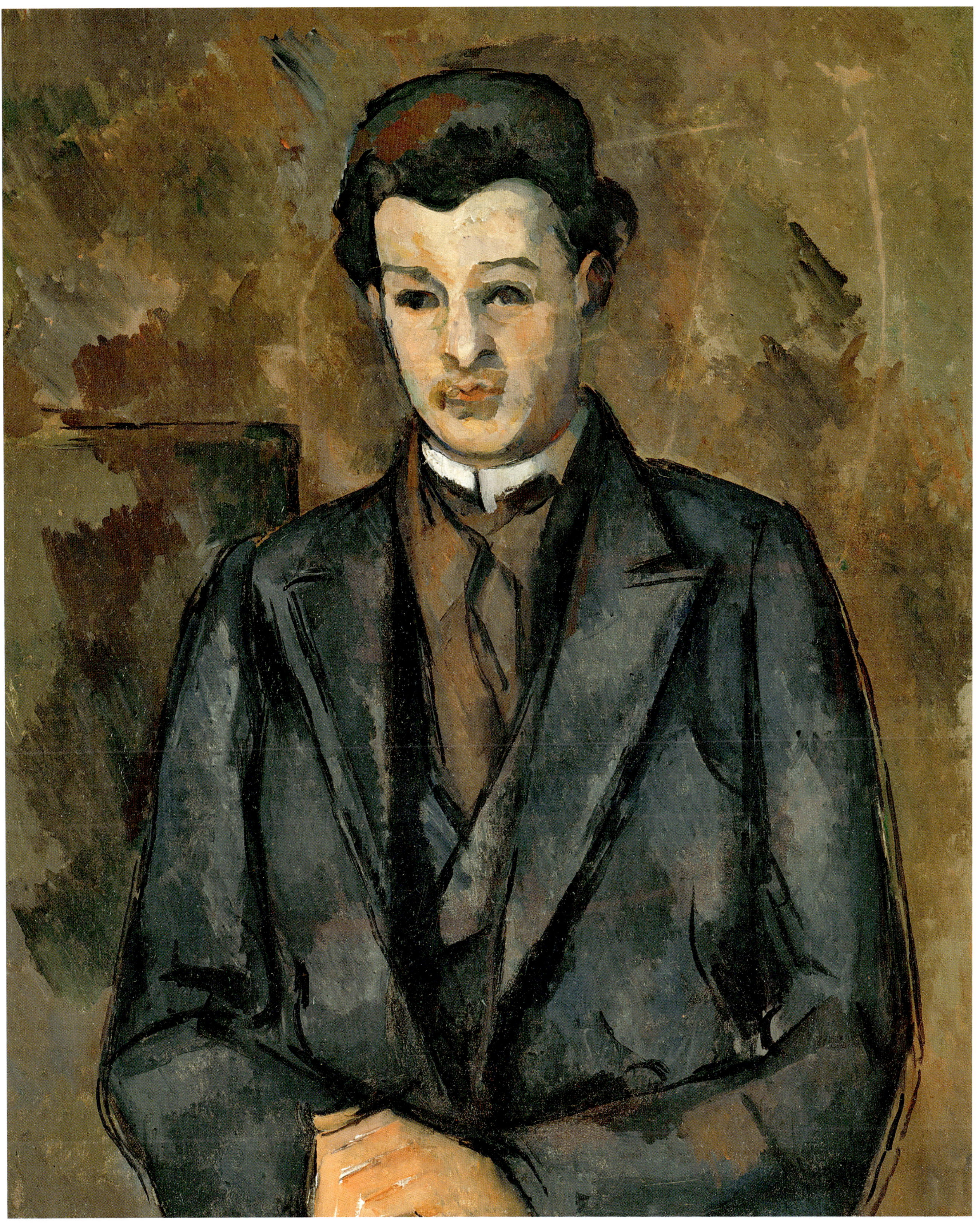

mid-June, after hastily leaving Paris and abandoning the portrait of Geffroy on which he had been working since April. Cézanne did not return to Paris before September 1896, except perhaps for a few brief visits.[7] However, Rippl-Rónai had left the city then. He returned the following year, whereas Cézanne spent the summer in Aix. The only time that Cézanne and Rippl-Rónai were present in Paris simultaneously was during the summer of 1899. This is confirmed if we look again at the fragment of the letter from Rippl-Rónai to his brother. This was in fact a loose page from a letter dated February 20, 1900. "Last summer" is therefore the summer of 1899, and we can understand better how Rippl-Rónai was able to meet Cézanne at that time, as Cézanne's son and also Vollard—with whom Rippl-Rónai was working—knew the exact whereabouts of the artist. Furthermore, another witness confirms Cézanne's presence in Marlotte during the summer of 1899. This was the young Norwegian painter Alfred Hauge, whose portrait Cézanne painted at that time. Hauge was 23 and was most probably the "very young Swedish writer" whom Rippl-Rónai saw in the studio. He was mistaken about the nationality but he saw him posing, as the phrase "he continued to work in the company [of this young man]" suggests.

An article by Tone Skedsmo published in a Norwegian magazine establishes that Hauge's portrait is the one now kept at the Norton Gallery in West Palm Beach[8] (cat. 67). The author supports this identification through Hauge's correspondence with a number of Norwegian friends, including Munch, during the summer of 1899. In these letters, Hauge gives a precise idea of the circumstances of Cézanne's stay in Marlotte. On July 7, 1899, he announces this news to Munch: "Cézanne, the great French painter, is living here at the Hôtel Mallet. He is 63 and is inordinately nice. If there is a painter in the world whom I should like to meet, it is him, and lo and behold I've met him in an unexpected way." On August 26, 1899, still writing from Marlotte but to a different correspondent, Hauge describes this meeting in detail: "As you'll have heard, I am with Cézanne. It was strange to meet this man for whom I have felt so much enthusiasm in recent years. It was June 1. An old man introduced himself to me at dinner; he asked me if I was a painter; it appears he could tell that I was; he took the liberty of introducing himself; he was a painter too; his name was Cézanne. Oh! But that's the same name as the famous Cézanne who's dead, I said. He then told me that there wasn't another painter called Cézanne and that he wasn't dead—I had always believed that Cézanne was dead. From then on, we ate together at a little table in the garden. He painted a small but quite extraordinary portrait of me, but one day, seized by a sudden fit of anger or madness, he took a knife and ripped it into several pieces. However, his son intends to "remount" it and give it to me without his father knowing. At present, Cézanne is 62 *[sic]* but he seems older, bald, with a small amount of white hair at the nape of his neck, a white mustache and a small white goatee beard on his chin. I'm sure he doesn't have many years left to live; he is diabetic, suffers a great deal at certain times and is completely antisocial." Above these lines Hauge has drawn a small sketch of the "old man" which shows us how Cézanne was at Marlotte. He then adds: "He is half separated from his wife who, nevertheless, out of decorum, comes every Sunday from Paris with their son to visit him, but leaves again on Monday; I'll say no more because he is often nasty to her."[9] According to Tone Skedsmo, other letters from Hauge show that Cézanne admired his drawings, that they painted watercolors together and that he exchanged a drawing of his for a watercolor by Cézanne, who gave him a still life[10]. On the subject of Monet, Cézanne told Hauge that "work is beneath the man," and he believed that Gauguin copied him.

What then can we learn from Rippl-Rónai's account and from the fragments of correspondence by Hauge? Firstly, we need to be aware of the errors and approximations associated with the ten years that separate the Hungarian artist's visit from his account of it in his *Memoirs*. Rippl-Rónai is mistaken about the reason why the studio was empty, because four years had passed since the first Vollard exhibition and, if indeed it was a question of money being shared between Cézanne, his wife and his son, this was done well before this exhibition,[11] which raised less than 30,000 francs. But Rippl-Rónai does confirm the existence of the Marlotte studio, and that it was dedicated exclusively to work, since Cézanne resided at the Hôtel Mallet. This was probably the last studio Cézanne had in the Paris region, as he moved once and for all to Aix-en-Provence in the fall of 1899. He did return for a few weeks in 1904 and even went to work in Fontainebleau, but there is no evidence to suggest that he took a studio. These accounts also allow us to assert that although Cézanne often lived in Fontainebleau Forest, this was not simply in pursuit of subjects. He was able to work there at length on the portrait of Hauge, as he had done a few months earlier with Vollard in his Paris studio, and indeed on still lifes, since he gave one to Hauge. Cézanne clearly wished to concentrate on his work, fleeing the society that was imposed on him rather being chosen by him and, more than this, fleeing his own home. The Sunday visits may have been an opportunity for his son to take his canvases away to Paris, as the episode of Hauge's lacerated portrait suggests. This would also explain the empty studio encountered by Rippl-Rónai. Furthermore, Cézanne no doubt needed the solitude at Marlotte as, although only in his sixties, Rippl-Rónai regards him as an "old man" and Hauge comments, correctly, that he did not have long to live.

However, Cézanne's inability to achieve "his goals," as he puts it, has nothing to do with this extreme fatigue. It is a constant theme, according to reports of visits to the studio, although here we can see that Cézanne goes as far as to decide that he is "not able to paint well enough." When Rippl-Rónai questions him about Gauguin, Renoir, and Puvis de Chavannes—who at the time were the Hungarian painter's major references, the ferocious rejection of Gauguin and the reserved judgment on Renoir do not surprise either. The disparagement of Monet reported by Hauge also has its antecedents, even though here it is more abrupt. The same is not

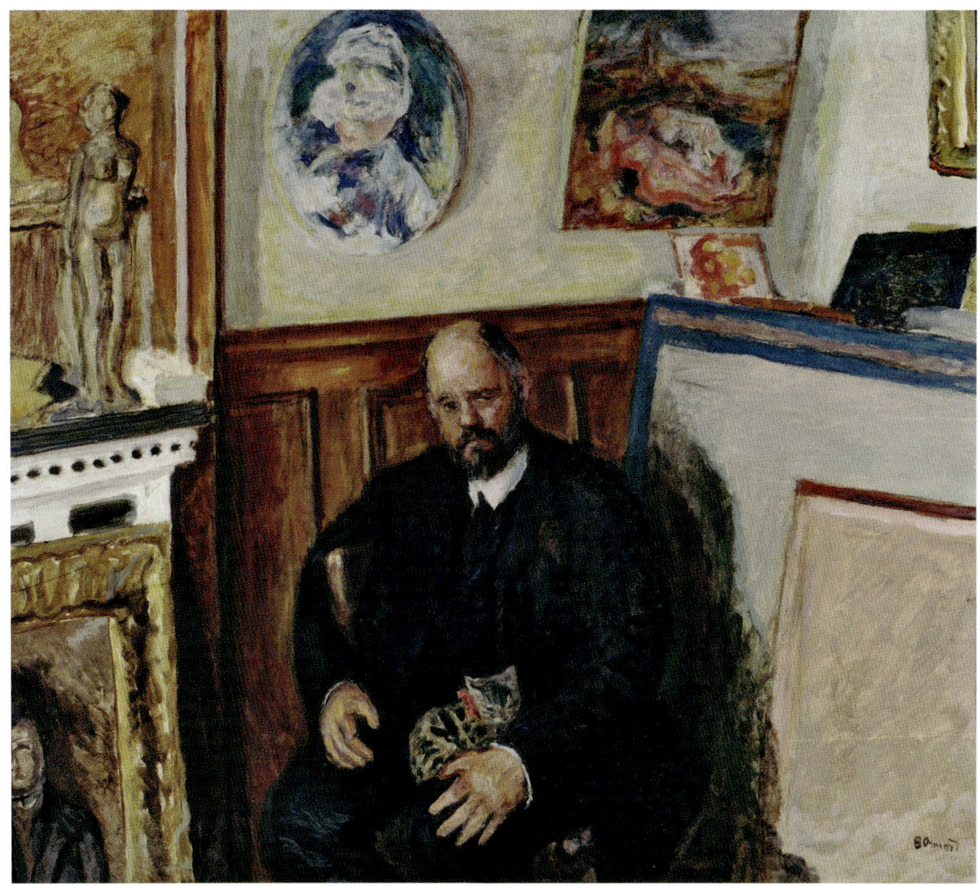

Cat. 68
Pierre Bonnard (1867–1947)
Portrait of Ambroise Vollard with a Cat
Around 1924
Oil on canvas
94.6 x 111 cm
Petit Palais, Musée des Beaux-Arts de la Ville de Paris, Paris
At bottom on the left is the *Portrait d'Alfred Hauge*

true of Puvis de Chavannes, who had died a year earlier. There is no question of taking this as some passing remark: Cézanne was uncompromising when it came to judging painters and paintings. It is difficult to imagine an affinity between the painter of Sainte-Victoire and the artist recognized at the time as the master of mural painting. According to Gasquet, Cézanne "loathed" Chavannes and spoke of "bad literature" when referring to the decoration of the Sorbonne[12]. Vollard, reporting an account by Renoir, states that Cézanne, on the subject of *Pauvre pêcheur*, commented that "It's a passable imitation." He adds that when Chavannes visited Cézanne's exhibition, he left shrugging his shoulders[13]. Thus began a rivalry and recently there have been attempts to resurrect this by playing Chavannes off against Cézanne in order to arrive at a different modernity for the 20th century, a modernity that is non-modernist, that is to say not like Cézanne.[14] However, it is important to remember that the celebrated formula by which Cézanne defined art as "a harmony parallel to nature,"[15] which some believed represented the modernist postulate of the autonomy of the pictorial surface, is in fact borrowed from Chavannes. We should also note that Émile Bernard and Maurice Denis never mention the hostility between the two masters and were able to link them together with their highest admiration. One has only to hear Cézanne say that Chavannes was a "very great artist" to wonder about this tardy admiration—at a time when he himself was returning, with his *Bathers*, to the large formats he had abandoned thirty years earlier and for which he had the Les Lauves studio built after leaving the one at Marlotte.

In the end, the Cézanne that Rippl-Rónai describes is far removed from the painter in Fontainebleau Forest that he was, perhaps twenty-five years earlier, when he began to work there regularly. The pursuit of subjects and of painting outdoors was no longer the main reason for Cézanne staying there and the extreme fatigue from which he suffered did not, in any case, allow him to go out a great deal. He speaks plainly of the great distance between him and those who had exhibited with him under the Impressionist banner and who were still his friends. Cézanne worked there because there were fewer disturbances and these were controllable, which gave him the opportunity to work in isolation in a studio where it occurred to him that the silence of Chavannes' painted walls were evidence of a "very great artist." Did the female nudes erased from the walls of the Marlotte studio, during these years devoted to three versions of the *Bathers*, indicate the dream of great decorative art, inspired by painting *sur le motif* in the open air? Perhaps he sometimes thought back to this project of his early years in Paris—as incongruous as it was underrated—when, around 1870, Pissarro went to ask the director of the Opéra to commission Cézanne to decorate the building that Garnier was just completing.[16]

Jean Arrouye

WATER THE MIRROR OF PAINTING

The works by Cézanne in which water plays a role can be divided up into various categories. The first comprises paintings that could be based on personal memories, such as *The Fishing Party* (1873, R 245 and 1875, R 246). Cézanne quickly abandoned this source of inspiration but oddly enough, *Boy Resting* (cat. 69), probably a portrait of his son Paul painted around 1890, seems to revive this practice. As with the many portraits of Mme Cézanne, however, the representation of a family member was mainly due to the readiness of the model to oblige. Cézanne used the figure to study pictorial issues, in this case its integration into the landscape and matching the brushwork to the nature of the person being painted.

Other paintings were prompted by a story, sometimes taken from mythology or the Bible, such as *The Abduction* (fig. 35), in which nymphs lounge on the riverbanks as Hades seizes his prey; *Pastorale* (fig. 39), which could be a humorous expansion on Manet's *Luncheon on the Grass; Bathers and Fisherman with a Line* (c. 1872, R 231), where the fisherman's rod pointed at voluptuous female nude bathers transforms him into an ithyphallic satyr, and the various *Bathshebas* (cat. 24, fig. 24, R 592, 593). *The Brook* (1872–1875, R 241) is a rare example of the water flowing vertically from the horizon to the foreground and dividing the picture into two equal sections: One shows two figures apparently talking, and the other consists entirely of a regular arrangement of shrubs. It is as if two subjects are being set against each other, one of which dissolves in uncertainty as we will never know what it is that interests the figures, and the other involving the act of painting itself, as the leaves depicted are no more than a series of brushstrokes. In these works, we see Cézanne sowing his wild oats, playing around with thematic or dramatic corruptions of familiar subjects, as in the two versions of *A Modern Olympia* (cat. 48, fig. 44). He would gradually give up this ironic practice to devote himself to serious pictorial problems

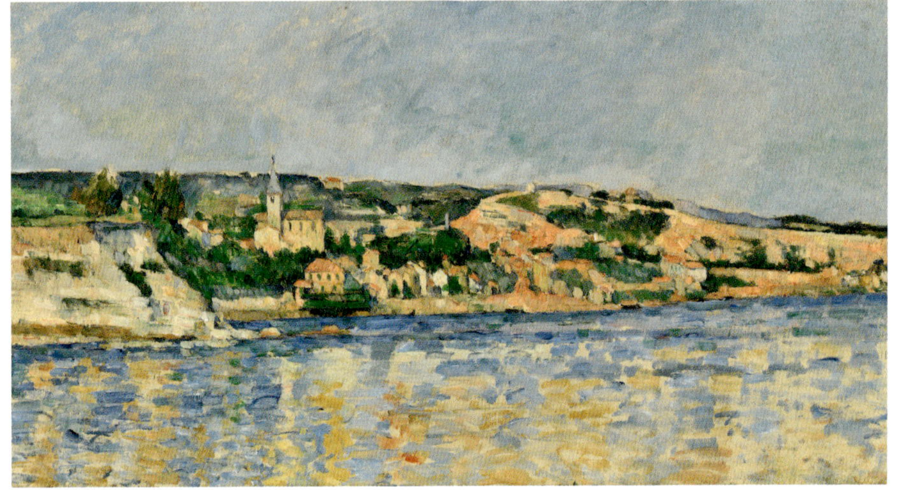

Fig. 74
Village at the Water's Edge
c. 1876
Oil on canvas
43 × 80 cm
The Barnes Foundation, Merion
R 280

The representation of the sea in numerous views of the Gulf of Marseille from L'Estaque is a good example of this. Cézanne uses it as an opportunity for active reflection, pursued over the years, on the possibility of reconciling two contradictory demands: simultaneously a return to the "motif" which recalls the characteristics that originally kindled the artist's desire to paint, presupposing a recourse to perspective; and the composition of a work that achieves a legitimizing harmony through its organization of structure, form, and color that is played out on the surface of the canvas. So it is then a question of deciding in a canvas where, how and to what extent the illusion of depth can be restricted in favor of relationships of line, color, shape, and volume that gradually form this harmony. In the paintings where the sea takes up considerable space, the area devoted to it becomes a key locus of this challenge.

When seen in the distance, at the end of a long sweep over cultivated and developed landscape, and when it only takes up a limited section of

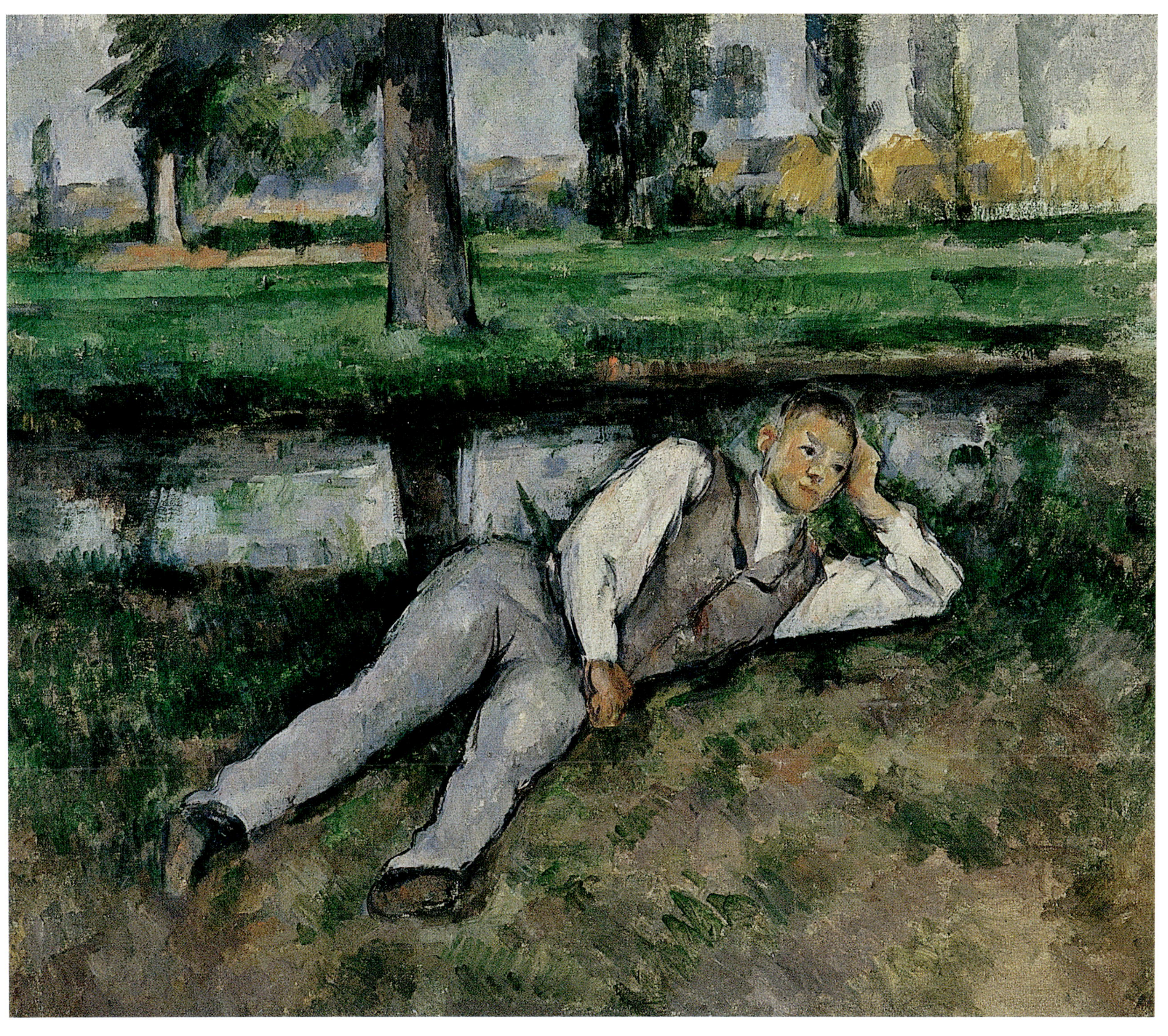

Cat. 69
Boy Resting
c. 1890
Oil on canvas
54 × 65.3 cm
The Armand Hammer Collection, Los Angeles,
gift of the Armand Hammer Foundation,
Hammer Museum
R 682

the picture, between groups of trees and a rise in the ground, as in *L'Estaque* (c. 1882, R 491), the sea becomes integrated into the overall perspective. It does not work in this way, however, in *Village at the Water's Edge* (fig. 74), where it extends across the entire width of the canvas, and about a third of its height. Rather improbably, Cézanne makes it reflect the houses of the village and the rocky coastline in broad ochre strokes that are superimposed. The length of the reflections indicates the distance, but at the same time the vertical layering of the strokes weakens our perception of it. Light ochre is blended into the blue of the sky, painted in edgy diagonal strokes, with the result that earth, sea, and sky are all echoed chromatically. The harmony of the painting resides in these symmetries, which are also the means of creating a relative flattening of the landscape. In *Saint-Henri and the Bay of L'Estaque* (1877–1879, R 281), the sea and sky are similarly modulated in blue, purple, and green, without any aerial perspective effect, and although this links their two surfaces, they are distinguished by the direction of their brushwork: diagonal for the sky and horizontal for the sea, the expanse of the latter kept in perspective by the line of the shore that delimits it to the left. But when it occupies the same size of surface as the land, its shoreline crossing the picture at an angle, in *Gulf of Marseille, seen from L'Estaque* (fig. 93) or in *The Sea at L'Estaque*, where Cézanne also shrewdly depicts the horizon line as being held by two branches of the trees growing in the foreground,

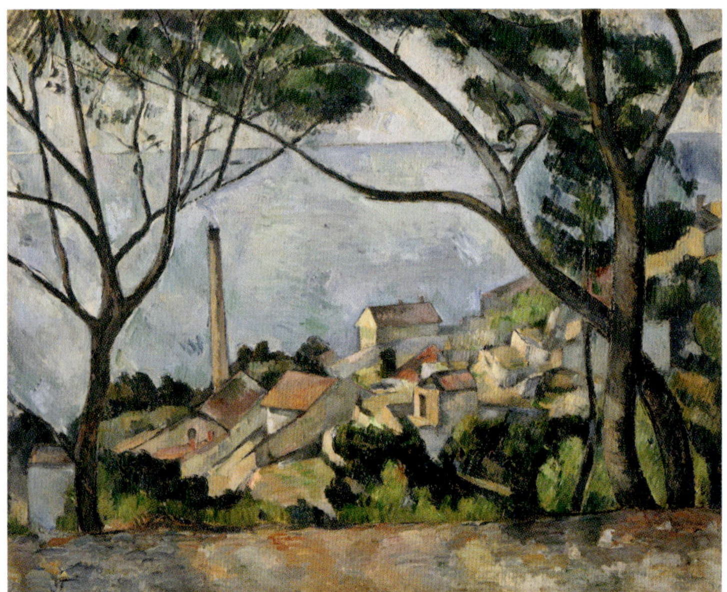

Fig. 75
The Sea at L'Estaque Behind the Trees
1878–1879
Oil on canvas
73 × 92 cm
Musée National Picasso, Paris
R 395

the sea with its completely modulated surface is aligned to the pictorial plane. In the first of these works, this favors the color relations between the L'Estaque bank in the foreground and the Marseille bank in the distance and in the second, makes the brushwork on the blue surface of the sea echo the modulation of the complementary color on the land in the foreground.

More boldly in the two paintings entitled *The Gulf of Marseille, seen from L'Estaque* (c. 1885, R 625 and R 626), Cézanne—granting a slightly larger expanse to the sea than to the land in the foreground—achieves harmony between the intense blue of the sea and the dominant orange of the earth across most of the canvas; the sea in its apparent vertical nature (due to the same value of blue in the immediate foreground and in the distance) looks as if it is pulling at the land which rises up toward it with all its chimneys. In this way Cézanne presents us with something that accorded with Maurice Denis' declaration five years later that: "... a painting... is basically a flat surface covered in colors that are assembled in a particular order."[1] In Cézanne's case we would have to say "forms and colors" and clarify that this flatness can be used to reduce the effect of perspective as much as to emphasize other plastic effects, as in *Red Roofs, L'Estaque* or *View of L'Estaque and the Château d'If*, both 1883–1885 (R 517 and R 531), where the relative flatness of the sea highlights the rhythmic articulation of the rooftops, for Cézanne was not guided by a systematic mindset but by one of experimentation.

He would paint in this spirit for over thirty years—particularly in a great number of pictures of male and female bathers. This experimentation is about the representation of the human body and the possibility of adapting its appearance or proportions for the purposes of inserting figures into a landscape, and organizing groups and the composition of works, all part of the same problem for someone who saw painting as "the art of establishing relationships."[2] Some lone bathers—such as *Bather with Arms Outstretched*, from 1877–1878 (fig. 86), or *The Bather* (1885, R 555)—are at the seaside; all the others, both male and female, frolic on the banks of a river or a body of water shaded by trees, more often than not pines. However this river or body of water is not always depicted, or sometimes—in *Three Women Bathing* (cat. 47)—it is reduced to a cursory line of blue paint on the green background of the meadow where the bathers are standing; thus, an analogous chromatic relationship is established in the lower part of the painting, but in inverse proportion to the green of the foliage in the sky background of the top section, as the painter is less interested in the water than in the pictorial issues already mentioned.

Occasionally, however, the presence of water plays a determining role in the design of the works, or their success. This applies to the last of the three paintings entitled *Five Bathers* (1876–1877, R 254; 1879–1880, R 448; 1880–1882, R 449) in which each bather can be seen successively from left to right as follows: a bather sitting facing us, leaning against a tree trunk; another standing with his back to us; a third in three-quarter view in the river, up to his thighs in the water and looking at the first two bathers; a fourth in profile, standing and also facing toward the first two (these four bathers look as if they are engaged in conversation); and the last bather in profile in the river, up to his waist in the water, bending forward but facing to the right. A rhythm emerges as the standing figures, which take up three quarters of the painting height, alternate with those seated or bathing, most of which only come up to half the height. In addition, Cézanne establishes plastic relationships between the people and the trees in the background: The first painting is characterized by the marked contrast between the rendering of the tree foliage with broad constructive strokes and the painting method used for the rest of the canvas ("painting means contrasting," as Cézanne also said[3]); in the second, the painter makes an original link between the standing figures and the mass of foliage bathed in light above them, endowing the figure in profile with an extravagant halo; in the third, he establishes a very subtle color harmony between the green-shadowed bathers' bodies and the green and ochre foliage, a harmony supported by the surface of the water where these colors become intimately combined.

Subsequently, between 1890 and 1904, Cézanne went on to paint a dozen bather compositions, most of which feature, from left to right: a bather seated, another one standing facing us, and then a second standing figure, only in profile and facing left. These works contain five, six, or seven figures that continue to build formal relationships with the trees, but Cézanne adds a further complication to his other plastic challenge: providing a lateral rhythm across the painting by introducing people on the opposite bank or swimming, interspersed between the tall figures. In the course of these variations, the possibility of identifying the narrative of a conversation gradually disappears, especially when the second standing figure stops looking at those next to him, and is also represented from the back: The concern for pictorial qualities overrides the narrative pretext. The boldest and most complex of these attempts to organize a classically inspired frieze is *Bathers* (fig. 76), which brings together ten people. To counter the dilution of attention that this number entails, Cézanne positions his bathers almost symmetrically, the figure seated to the left and the one getting ready to dive on the right becoming almost like structural buttresses for the rest of the group; he also replaces the dark foliage with a chain of luminous clouds which draw the eye across the canvas, while also puffing out their curves to match the arrangement of the bathers. In all of these paintings, the rhythmic scansion for the whole group derives above all else from the bathers in the water and the others on the opposite side of the river, who are smaller in size than the standing figures in the foreground.

In painting female bathers, Cézanne began by engaging in this same experimentation with scansion across the picture: In the successful outcome *Bathers* (1875–1876, R 256), not only does he harmoniously alternate the female bathers, he also blends them intimately with the landscape and the broad, luminous river running through it. Soon though, he began exploring other issues, including matching the angle of the trunks of two trees and the bending of their branches, reaching out to each other, to the poses of three bathers—like reincarnations of the Three Graces of Antiquity, two of which are seen from the back, one standing and the other seated, and facing toward the third figure that is about to step out of the water. In 1876–1877 he painted three versions of these *Three Bathers* (R 358, 359 and 360); the one believed to be the final version would later be acquired by Matisse (cat. 47), captivated by the blaze of color of the autumnal shrubs, their reflection rekindled in detail on the water between the two female bathers on the left who have become red-haired in order to blend in better with their surroundings.

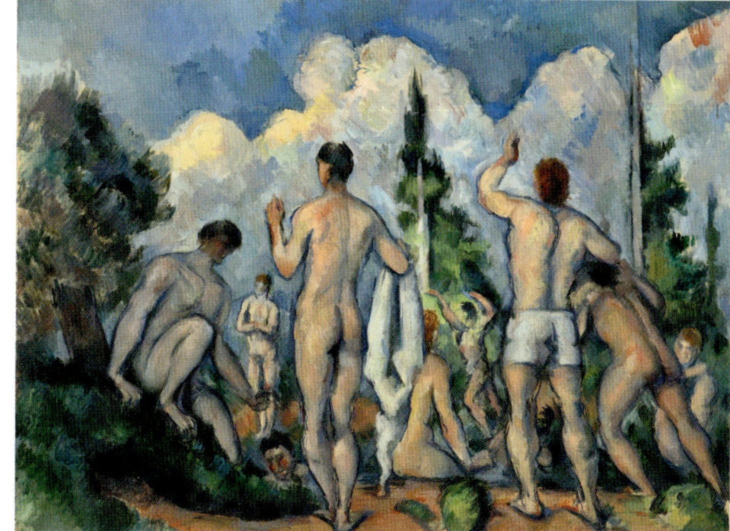

Fig. 76
Bathers
c. 1890
Oil on canvas
60 × 81 cm
Musée d'Orsay, Paris
R 665

After realizing this project, Cézanne then set himself another challenge, doubling the problem of harmonizing the figures with the location by arranging two groups of female bathers at either side of horizontal format canvases, which also involved harmonizing the groups themselves. This would be achieved by the river itself, its visible blue section in *Bathers* (fig. 77) like a hyphen linking the two groups of blue-shaded female bodies. The water ceases to be just a complement to the bathers or the excuse for their presence, becoming an essential compositional element in terms of balancing the parts as well as the colors. The painting is intended as the allegory of this role. Above the river—in the gap between the foliage of the two trees at the side, to which the bathers are plastically matched as in previous works—a pink cloud that is apparently condensation caused by steam rising from the river assumes the form of a female body; her presence establishes a triangulation of figures, the eminently classical way of subsuming their positional differences within an overall harmony. So this canvas seems to suggest that from now on, water would play a decisive role in the "realization" of female bather paintings.

It was only ten years later that canvases like the *Bathers* from 1899–1904 (fig. 78) and 1902–1906 (R 867) seemed to put this theory into

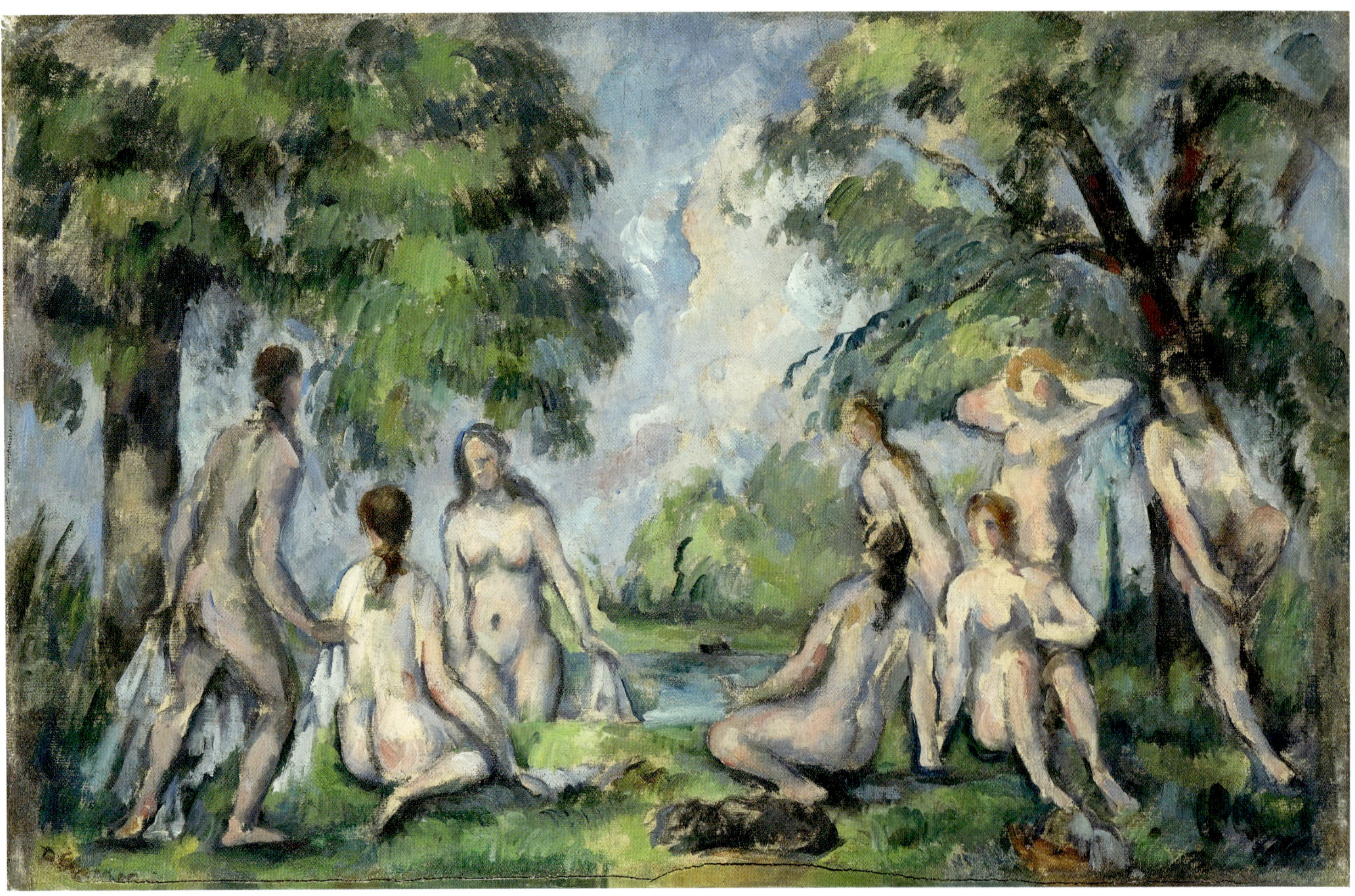

practice, by applying the blue color of the water to the entire works, mingling it with the green of the trees, which continued to carry out their function of framing and positioning the figures. However the overall impression produced by these paintings is one of freshness and fluidity (in drawing the eye from one area of similar tones to the next) which by analogy seem like the qualities of the water itself, into which female bathers dip in the middle of every work.

In his last venture, however, *The Large Bathers* of 1906 (R 857), Cézanne abandons this lyrical hymn to a dominant color and bases the unity of his work on the complementary nature of the blue color of water and sky and the orange of the earth and tree trunks, which structure the painting and increasingly determine the bathers' poses. Yet it is the water, its presence highlighted by the bathers' gestures, that unifies the close and distant areas and the two different bather groups; through its carefully measured range and tone, and visual weight, it provides balance in a painting which as a whole pretends to be organized symmetrically, while it rejects this all too simple rule in the overall detail. So in this case water is responsible for its plastic realization.

Fig. 77
The Bathers
1896
Oil on canvas
24 x 44 cm
Musée Granet, Aix-en-Provence,
Communauté du Pays d'Aix

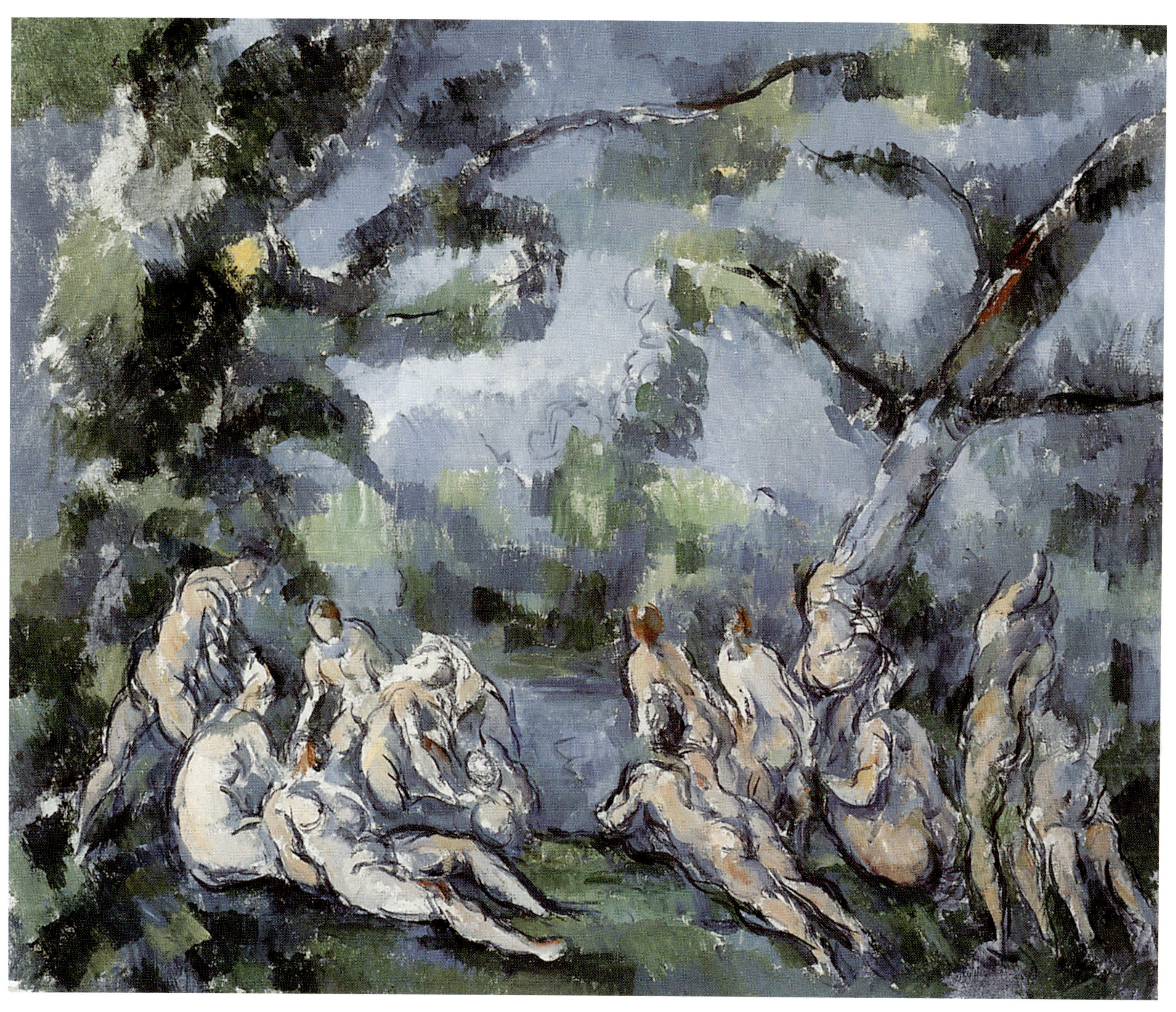

Fig. 78
The Bathers
1899–1904
Oil on canvas
51.3 x 61.7 cm
The Art Institute of Chicago, Chicago,
The Amy McCormick
Memorial Collection
R 859

Of the paintings devoted to the pool at Jas de Bouffan, few focus especially on water. In *Jas de Bouffan, the Pool* (c. 1876, R 278) a section of the pool occupies a quarter of the picture's height and all of its width, reflecting the lower part of the landscape that extends beyond it; red and yellow flowers grow at its edge, and flowerpots also feature—yet none of this appears in the reflections he painted. Cézanne is pruning it, as the area of still water is being used to anchor his landscape, and he wants to set up a contrast between the relative emptiness of the latter and the profusion of plants in the former. This treatment of the water shows the liberties the painter could take with his subject in order to compose a painting the way he wanted. In *The Pool at the Jas de Bouffan in Winter* (fig. 79) the liberties taken with reality are even greater. The picture is divided into two by a tree and its reflection in the pool, which again occupies the entire width of the bottom of the painting, but is slightly higher: Cézanne has simplified the tree's branches, and to its right in the pond he shows the reflection of a building that is too far away for it to be seen in this way. He did this because he had a strong desire to contrast the two sections of his painting separated by the tree: The left space is filled with numerous buildings and is structured by the articulation of their simplified geometric forms; on the right, the land is not built up, and alternating bands of grassy and cultivated ground create a rhythmic organization of the space. In this way Cézanne compares two methods of organizing landscape—one analytical and, we are tempted to say, early Cubist; the other schematic and abstract in form. The contradictions between them are accentuated in the pool; the mirror of the water increases the stakes of this poietic reflection.

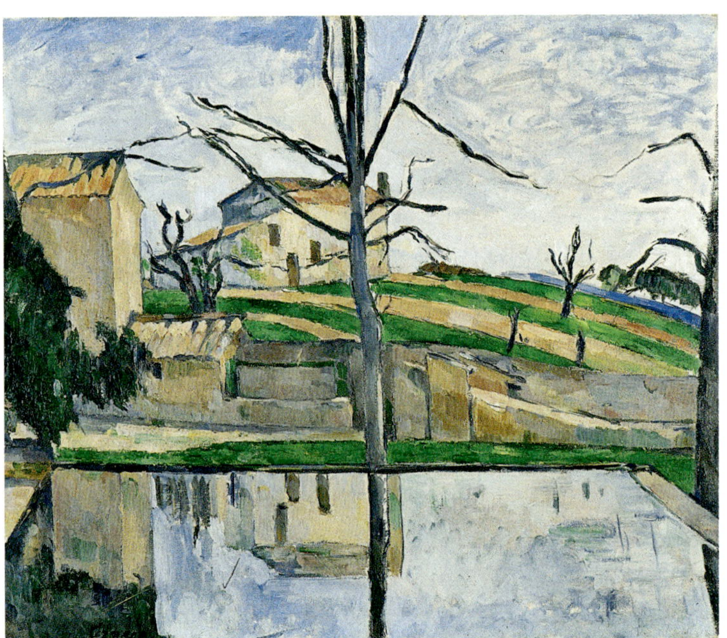

Fig. 79
The Pool at the Jas de Bouffan in Winter
c. 1878
Oil on canvas
52.5 x 56 cm
Private collection
R 350

The Brook (1872–1875) seems to have been an early picture that allowed Cézanne to reflect, brush in hand, on what his painting might become. *Maincy Bridge* (cat. 70) is probably another speculative work. Above the level of the bridge, from left to right, Cézanne renders the undergrowth in three different ways, following a rhythmic scansion that highlights the dynamic of the tree trunks, using short diagonal strokes as if scribbling down sensations, and scumbling, an effective technique for registering the light effects. By way of counterpoint to these various attempts simultaneously to convey both the appearance of and a sensitivity toward what is being painted, Cézanne used large brushstrokes to paint the water, showing its expanse and at the same time giving the suggestion of depth.

As soon as the painter's chosen viewpoint involves the picture having a large expanse of water, we find him speculating in this way about methods of painting and the kind of effects he could produce: certainly in *The Lake of Annecy* (1896, R 805), where he devotes half of the canvas to a representation of water, but also in *The Bridge over the Marne at Créteil* (fig. 68), where he subtly brings out the analogous relationships and chromatic dissimilarities of the sky and water reflecting it; or in *Bridge over a Pond* (fig. 70), in which he expresses through large multi-angled patches of tight diagonal strokes, in myriad greens mixed with hints of ochre, merging plant and aquatic life in places, as well as spatial and water depth, into a remarkable painting that anticipates the simplifications and radical deconstructions of his late works.

Yet none of the canvases painted by Cézanne on riverbanks around Paris make water the main object of observation. He did not favor—like his contemporaries Monet, Boudin, Bonnard, Lebarque, and so many others—lateral compositions that allowed him a view of a large expanse of the river. For the great majority of his paintings, it is a house, a hamlet, or a bridge that makes him decide where to set up his easel; as a rule he did so on the opposite bank, with the result that the water invariably occupies the foreground of his pictures, its presence sometimes reduced to no more than a narrow band. Nor does Cézanne attempt to provide a narrative of human activity in the manner of these other painters: no carts on the bridges he chooses to represent, no navigation on his rivers (once only, in *The Banks of the Marne* around 1888 (R 628), featuring a fisherman in a small boat) and no one walking along their banks. He paints what might be called pure landscapes, because his reasons for doing so are purely pictorial. So of the natural elements in widely differing forms, among which the painter chose to represent a construction of geometrically simple shapes, in order to highlight this diversity, the flatness and power of reflection of one of these elements is to some extent reminiscent of the flatness of the canvas and the arduous business of making the image of a transformed world appear in it: and that is water. As a result it is understandable that when water becomes a pictorial object, it often gives rise to a statement, and sometimes clarification, of the pictorial issues that fascinated Cézanne.

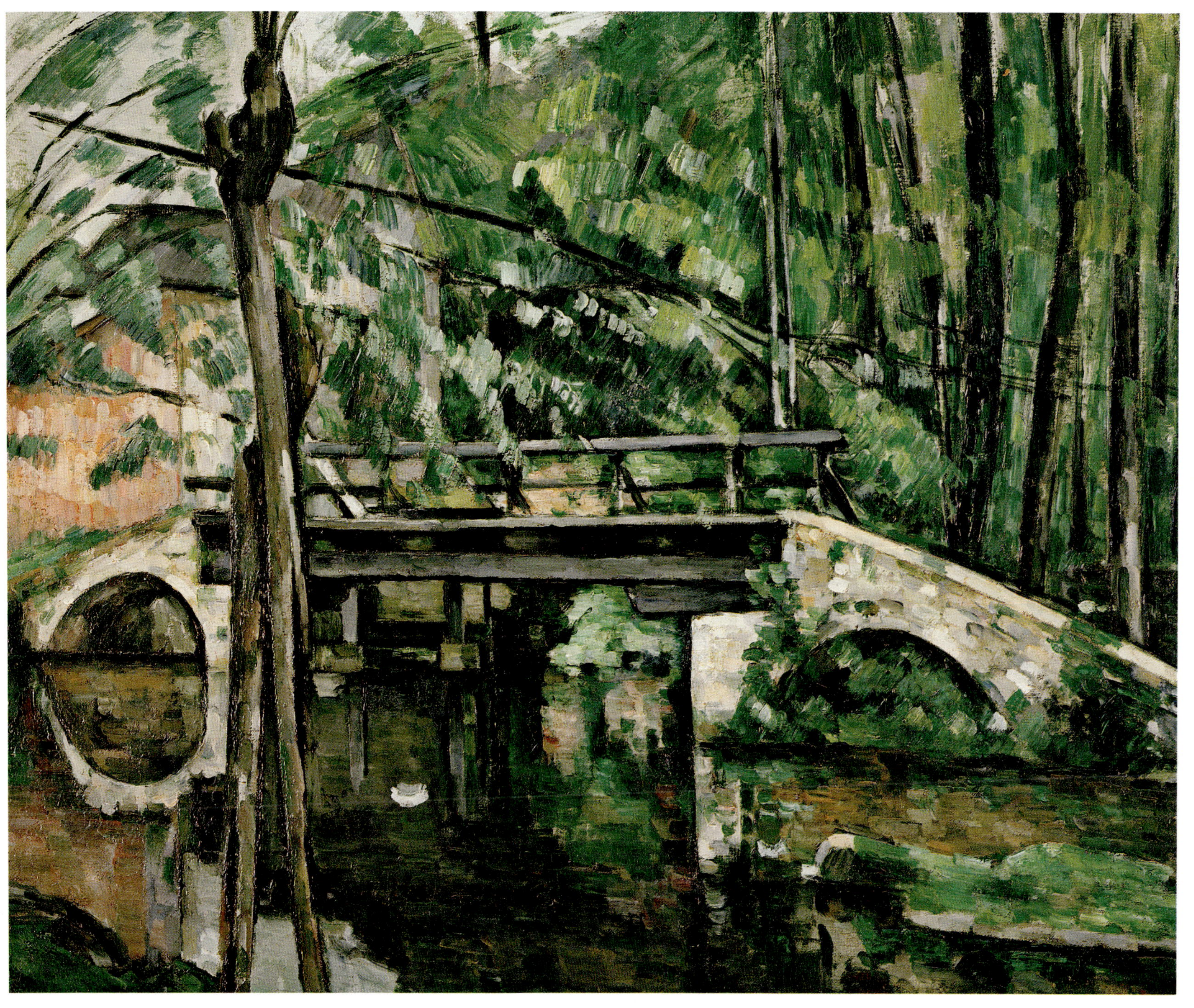

Cat. 70
Maincy Bridge
1879–80
Oil on canvas
58.5 × 72.5 cm
Musée d'Orsay, Paris,
acquired trough an anonymous Canadian
donation, 1955
R 436

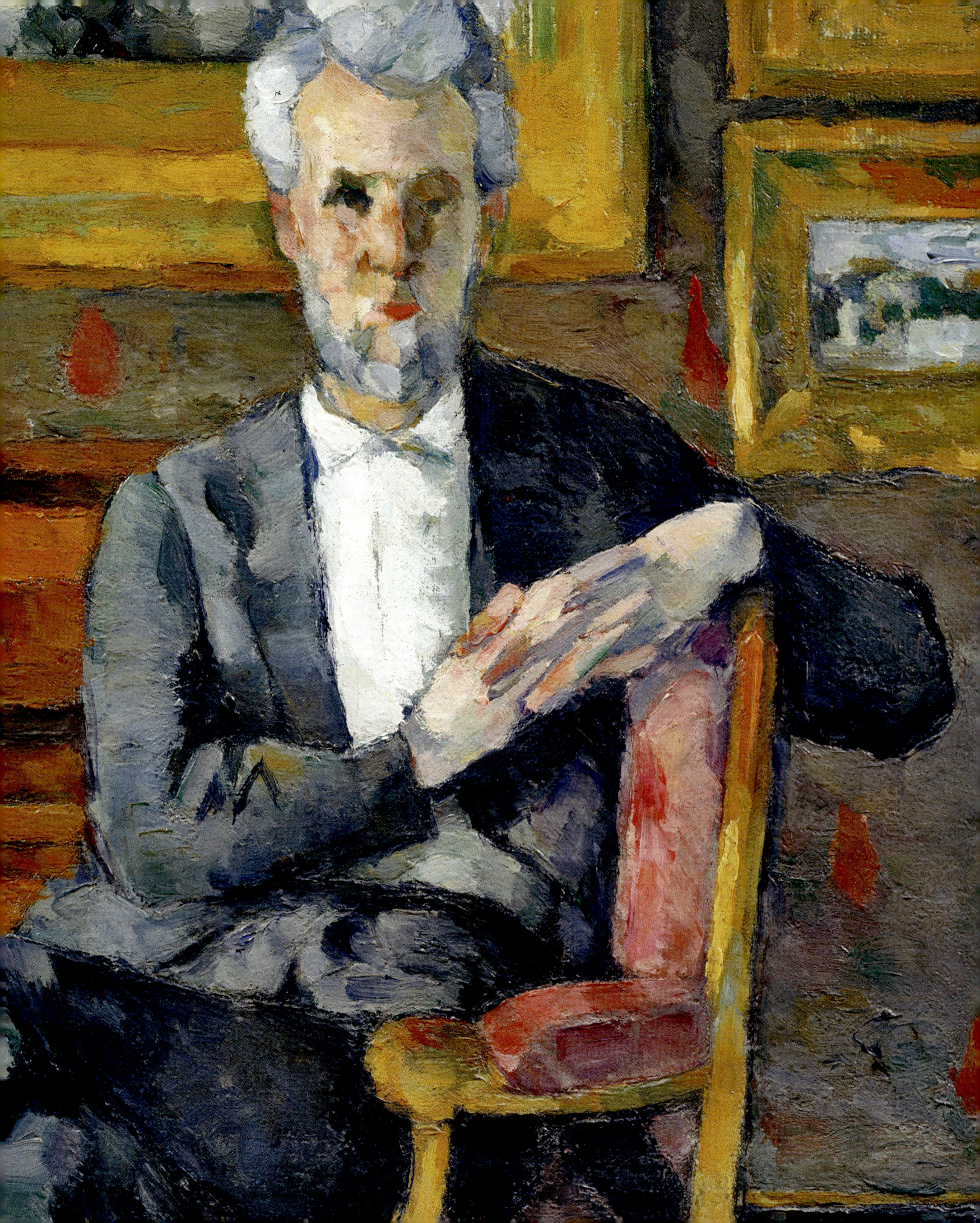

CĒZANNE'S FAME

"If only painting's sun of Austerlitz was shining for me", sighed Cézanne in a letter dated September 25, 1903. It shows that the elderly painter was occasionally worried about his fame. The man, who in his youth had fruitlessly provoked the Salon jury, knew that he was appreciated by painters, as well as by some collectors and dealers, though the only one he wanted to keep was Vollard. Paris, the city he was able to "astonish with an apple," was then to be the ultimate location of this growing fame. Without question as far as he was concerned, one museum alone was worthy of him at that time, and that was the Louvre, where he found "admirable works that have conveyed the ages to us,"[1] along with the Musée du Luxembourg, acting as antechamber to the Louvre for modern painters.[2] Did they not come all the way from Paris to visit the artist in Aix-en-Provence, where he had built himself a studio in 1902?

In fact recognition for Cézanne was to come essentially from painters (even Picasso referred to him as "father to us all"), especially those who were his contemporaries and collected his works, like Monet, Degas, and Pissarro; from critics and writers, beginning with Gustave Geffroy, Émile Bernard, and Maurice Denis; and from collectors and dealers, two names of whom immediately stand out—Victor Chocquet and Ambroise Vollard, the latter taking over from *père* Tanguy. As early as the late 19th century, Cézannes could be found in Germany, the United States, and Italy.

The aim of the following essays is to give an account of this growing spotlight on Cézanne during his lifetime, in Paris and beyond.

The 1907 Salon was to firmly establish Cézanne's importance in the eyes of the entire cultural and artistic intelligentsia. The final word goes to the poet Rilke, who abandoned a trip to Venice that October so that he could see the painter's canvases every day: "I leave you... for today; perhaps all this gives you some idea of the old man to whom the same words apply that he used to describe Pissarro: 'humble and colossal.' Today is the anniversary of his death..."[3]

D. C.

Portrait of Victor Chocquet Seated
(detail)
Voir cat. 73 p. 179

Jayne S. Warman

CĒZANNE, PAINTER OF PAINTERS

Ambroise Vollard was once asked whom he considered the greatest authority on Paul Cézanne. He replied without hesitation, "the painters."[1] That unequivocal statement was certainly confirmed by the generations of artists who recognized Cézanne's unique qualities as a painter and who shared an appreciation of his genius—many also acquired his work. Artists like Gustave Caillebotte, Paul Gauguin, Camille Pissarro, Edgar Degas, Paul Signac, Claude Monet, Henri Matisse, and Pablo Picasso formed impressive art collections that prominently featured Cézanne's paintings; others like Pierre Bonnard, Maurice Denis, Ker-Xavier Roussel, Max Liebermann, Georges Braque, Henry Moore, Jacques Lipschitz, and Jasper Johns acquired only one or two canvases by Cézanne but counted them among their most prized possessions.[2] To these artists Cézanne was "a holy painter [Gauguin],""the greatest of us all [Monet]," my one and only master [Picasso]," "a sort of god of painting [Matisse]," and "a point of reference [in his work] [Johns]." While the public and critics vilified Cézanne during his life, it was the artists who first understood his emancipating influence and new form of expression that would give inspiration and direction to their own work. This so-called "Cézanne effect" manifested itself throughout the 20th century and continues to this day with artists most often leading the discussion. Cézanne's powerful influence on painters has been mined in a number of groundbreaking exhibitions in the last decade[3] and is, therefore, not examined here.

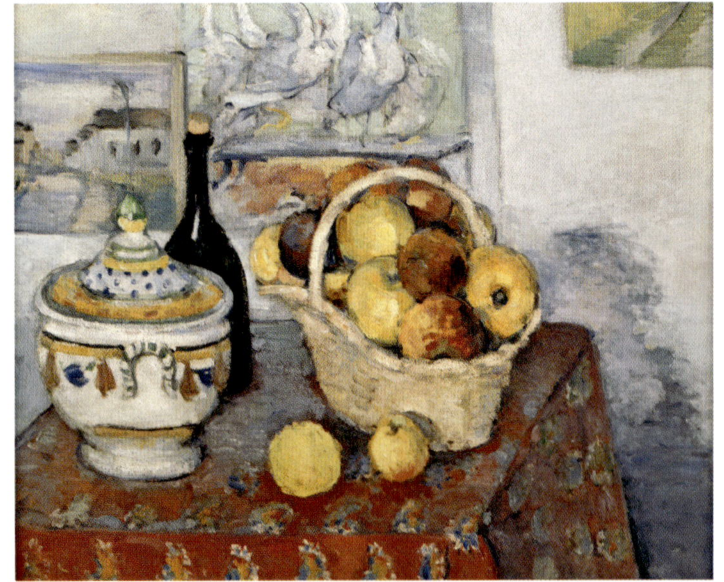

Fig. 80
Still Life with Soup Tureen
1877
Oil on canvas
65 x 83 cm
Musée d'Orsay, Paris
R 302

It is natural that among the earliest collectors of Cézanne's art would be the artist's contemporaries. Pissarro may have been the first; he received most of his canvases as gifts from Cézanne when the two painters worked together in Auvers and Pontoise in the 1870s and early 1880s (fig. 80). Monet is said to have acquired his first painting in the early 1870s from the dealer père Martin as partial payment for one of his own canvases—he eventually assembled an extraordinary group of fourteen oils and one watercolor. Gauguin, who was a resolute follower of the artist and determined to find the secret to Cézanne's art, bought at least six paintings before 1884; he studied them very closely. Caillebotte, the recognized financial backer of the Impressionist exhibitions (and to a large extent his colleagues as well), added five Cézannes to his celebrated collection between 1877 and 1883. Both Armand Guillaumin and Auguste Renoir were presented with canvases directly by Cézanne; the latter was occasionally the beneficiary of a painting that the artist left with him, unfinished and forgotten.

Cézanne was notoriously reclusive, "a person at once unknown and famous, having rare contact with the public."[4] He often retreated to his native Aix-en-Provence where he could paint undisturbed, "living in savage isolation, reappearing, then disappearing suddenly from the sight of his intimate friends."[5] His canvases, however, could be found at the little

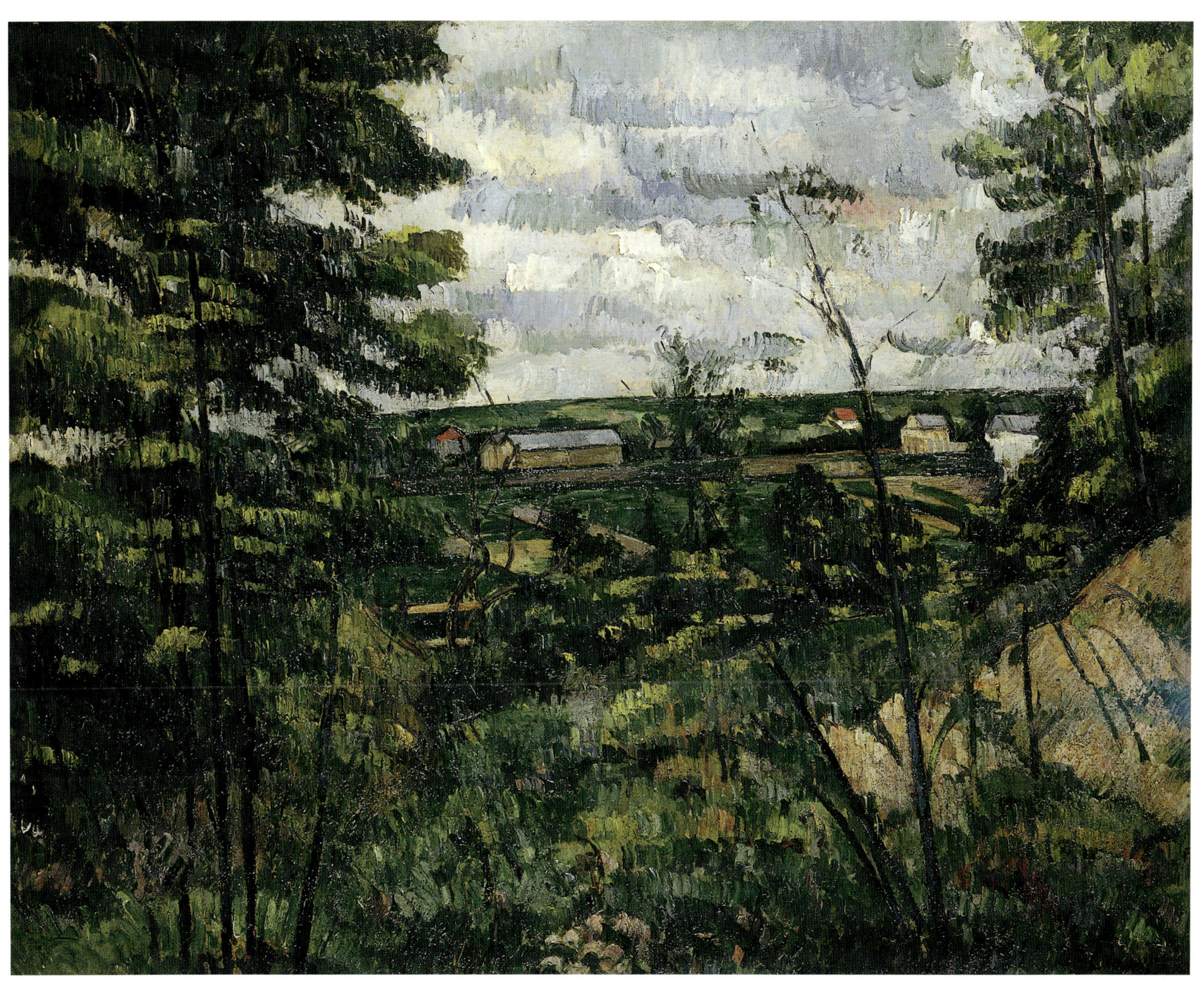

Fig. 81
The Valley of the Oise
c. 1880
Oil on canvas
72 x 91 cm
Private collection
R 434

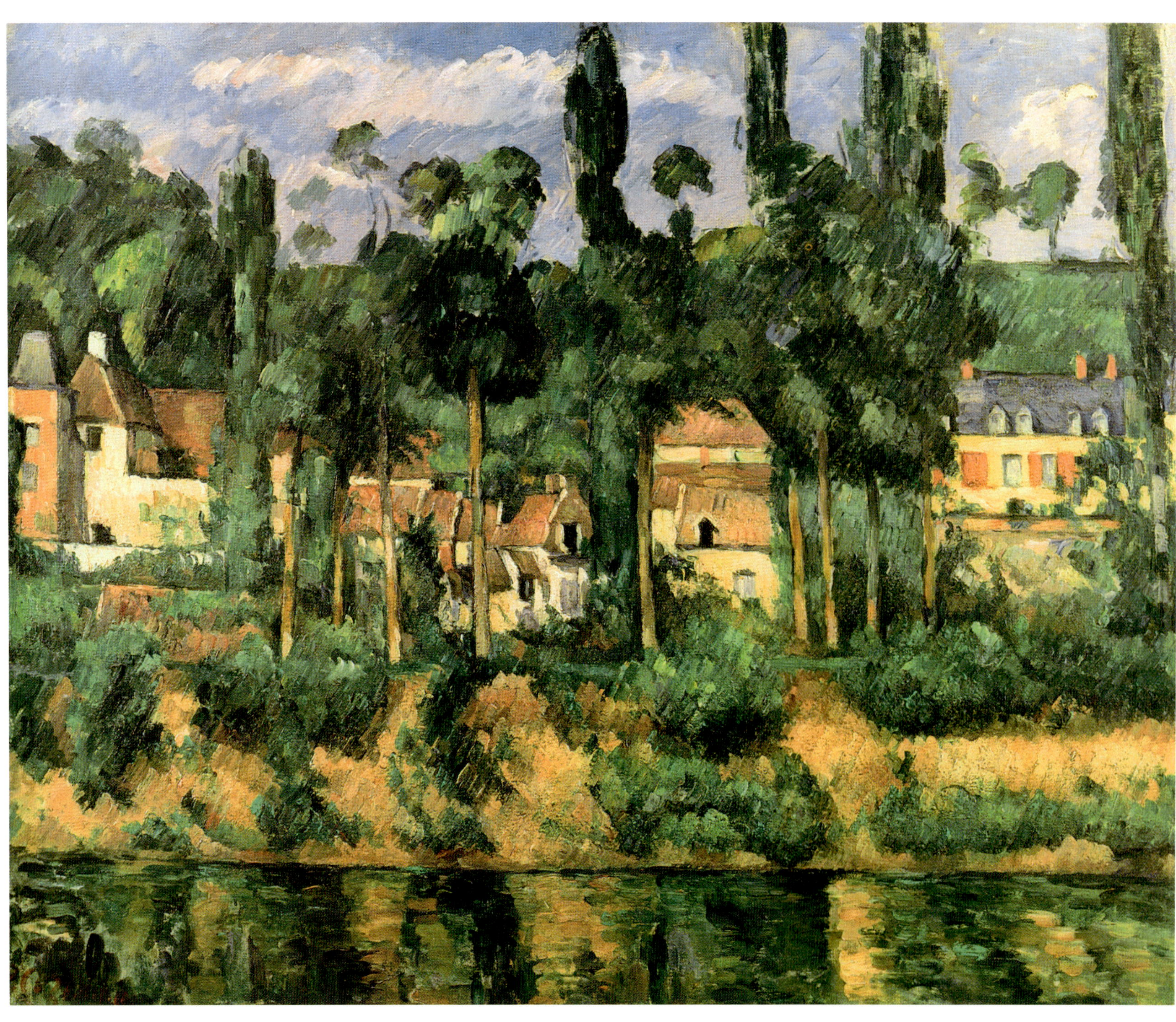

Fig. 82
The Château of Médan
c. 1880
Oil on canvas
59 x 72 cm
City Art Gallery, Glasgow
R 437

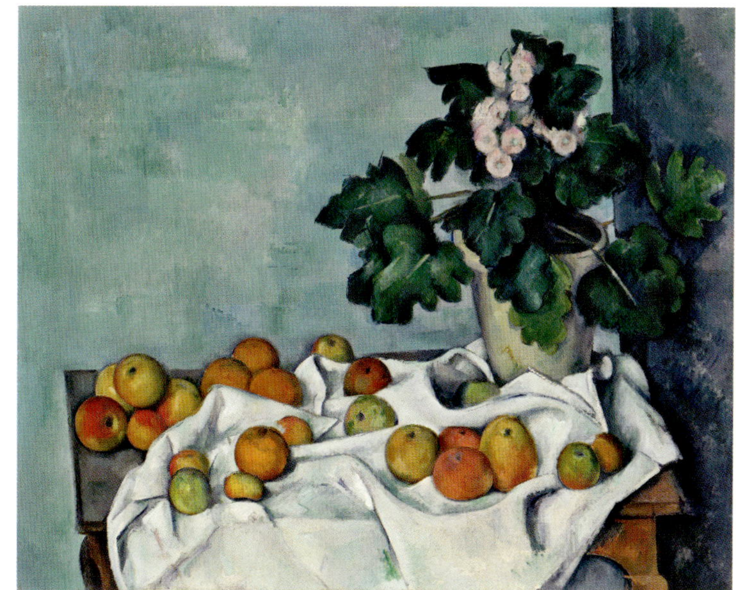

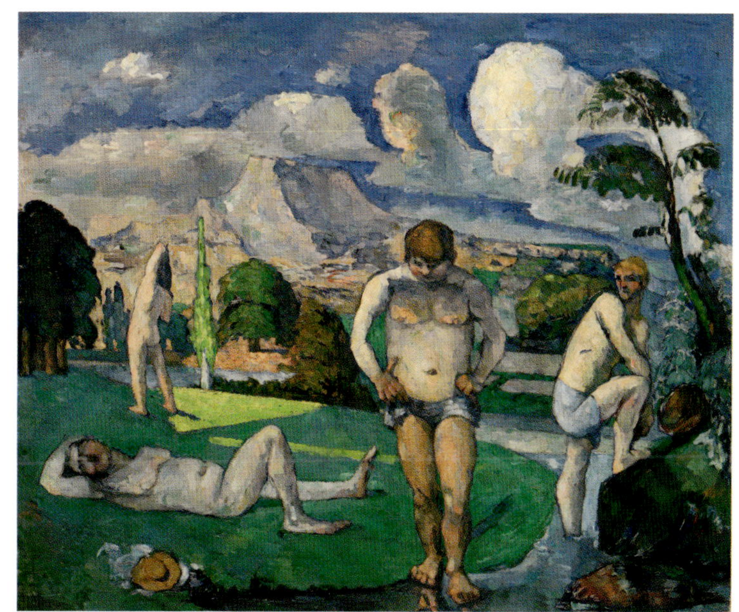

shop of the color merchant Julien Tanguy on the rue Clauzel in the Montmartre area of Paris. The artist left paintings with him in exchange for canvases and supplies. It was at Tanguy's that the young Neo-Impressionist painter Paul Signac bought a landscape of the Oise Valley (fig. 81) and a still life; the landscape was the pride of his collection. The Belgian artist Eugène Boch bought a large portrait of Achille Emperaire (fig. 92) which had been rejected at the Salon of 1870 following the suggestion of Émile Bernard, another admirer of Cézanne. Gauguin also acquired at least four paintings from Tanguy (fig. 82), including an immense painting of a reclining woman also rejected at the 1870 Salon. Pissarro bought four studies in 1884 and Paul-César Helleu a still life, which he later presented to Claude Monet (fig. 83). Émile Schuffenecker, a friend of Gauguin's, probably acquired several canvases there as well. For nearly a quarter of a century Tanguy's shop was the principal showplace for artists and collectors of the new art—but that situation was about to change.

1894 turned out to be a pivotal year for Cézanne. On February 9, père Tanguy died of stomach cancer and the contents of his shop were sold at auction. Gustave Caillebotte's death on February 21 set off a heated controversy surrounding his bequest of sixty-five paintings to the French State; three of the five Cézannes in the estate were withdrawn by the executors, *Bathers at Rest* (fig. 84) being the most important of that group. A month later on March 25, Gustave Geffroy published a laudatory article on Cézanne in *Le Journal*,[6] and the critic Thadée Natanson declared the artist to be "the only theoretician, almost without disciples. [His work] advances the idea of an absolute overthrow of the art of painting."[7]

These events caught the attention of Ambroise Vollard (cat. 72), an enterprising young dealer who would effectively change the course of Cézanne's reputation as an artist. He saw Cézanne's paintings at Tanguy's for the first time in 1892 and described the experience as a "kick in the stomach." With Tanguy's death, the door was open for him to fulfill his ambition to exhibit the works of this obscure and elusive artist. (Almost as if to prove a point, Vollard bought four of the six Cézannes from the

Fig. 83
Still Life with Apples and a Pot of Primroses
c. 1890
Oil on canvas
72 x 92.7 cm
The Metropolitan Museum of Art, New York
R 680

Fig. 84
Bathers at Rest, III
Oil on canvas
c. 1876–77
79 x 97 cm
The Barnes Foundation, Merion
R 261

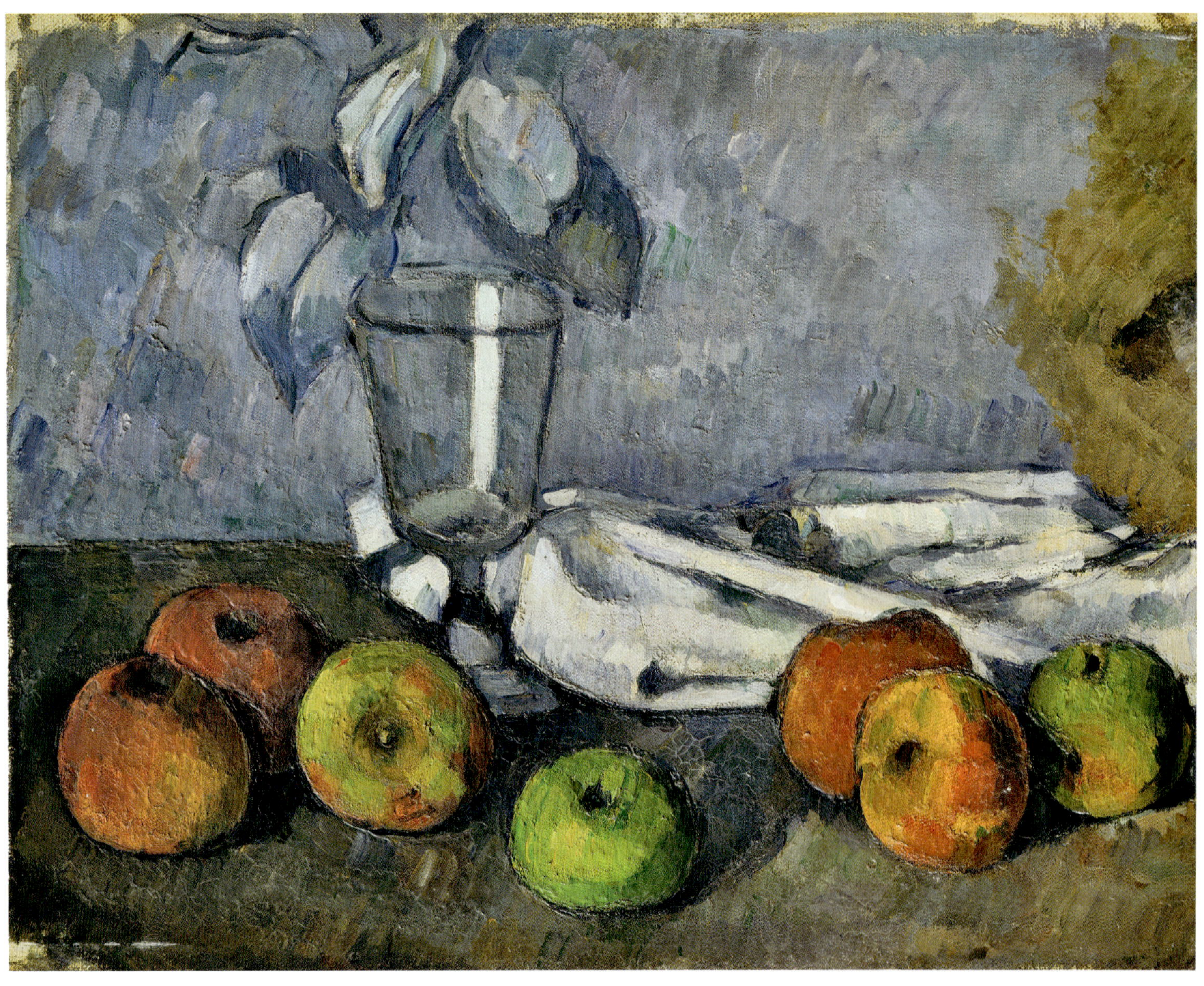

Tanguy sale and sold them within a year at a handsome profit). In addition, the wrangle over the Caillebotte bequest made him more determined than ever, he later recalled, to organize an exhibition of Cézanne's work. Renoir, Pissarro, Monet and Guillaumin, Cézanne's most ardent supporters, encouraged Vollard to do so. In November 1895 the 56-year-old painter's career was set in motion when the young dealer exhibited over 100 canvases on a rotating basis in his gallery. Almost overnight Cézanne became the talk of Paris. Thadée Natanson wrote a glowing review of the exhibition: "Cézanne can lay claim to more than the title of precursor... [H]is contemporaries, old like himself, respectfully bow down before his oeuvre."[8]

Fig. 85
Glass and Apples
1879–80
Oil on canvas
31.5 x 40 cm
Kunstmuseum Basel, Basel
R 424

The reaction of Cézanne's colleagues to the exhibition was unexpected—they were astonished at what they saw, "still lifes of irreproachable perfection... landscapes, nudes, and heads that are unfinished but yet

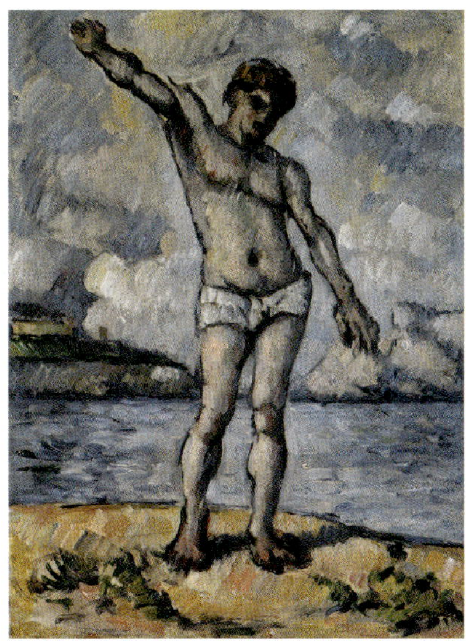

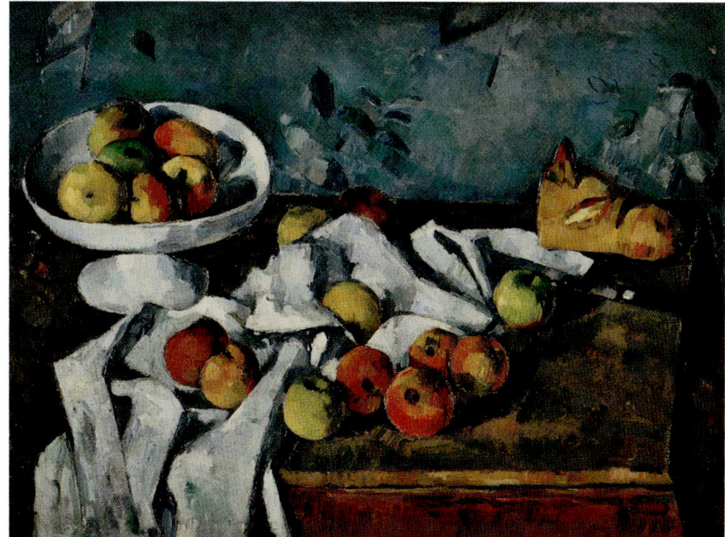

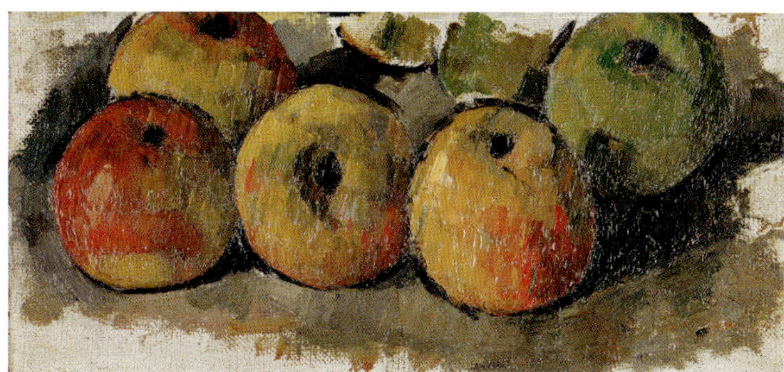

Fig. 86
Bather with Arms Outstretched
1877–78
Oil on canvas
33 x 24 cm
R 369
Private collection

Fig. 87
Fruit Dish, Apples, and Loaf of Bread
1879–80
Oil on canvas
55 x 74.5 cm
Sammlung Oskar Reinhart
"Am Römerholz"
R 420

Fig. 88
Five Apples
1877–78
Oil on canvas
12.7 x 25.5 cm
Private collection
R 334

grandiose, and so *painted*, so supple."[9] They had never seen such a large and comprehensive assemblage of the artist's work—"My enthusiasm," wrote Pissarro, "was nothing compared to Renoir's. Degas himself is seduced by the charm of this refined savage. Monet, all of us... Are we mistaken? I don't think so."[10] Renoir and Degas drew straws for a watercolor in the exhibition. At that point Degas began to add Cézanne's work (fig. 85 and 86) in quick succession to his already large art collection. Mary Cassatt, who was not known as a champion of the artist, bought two still lifes (fig. 87) from Vollard (and later claimed that it was she who first saw merit in Cézanne's painting). Pissarro bought three small paintings, Renoir two, Monet three, Maxime Maufra, a follower of Gauguin, three studies (fig. 88), and Victor Vignon a large still life painted around 1877. Egisto Fabbri, an American expatriate living in Florence and Paris, was an amateur painter and collector who attended the exhibition and bought three canvases

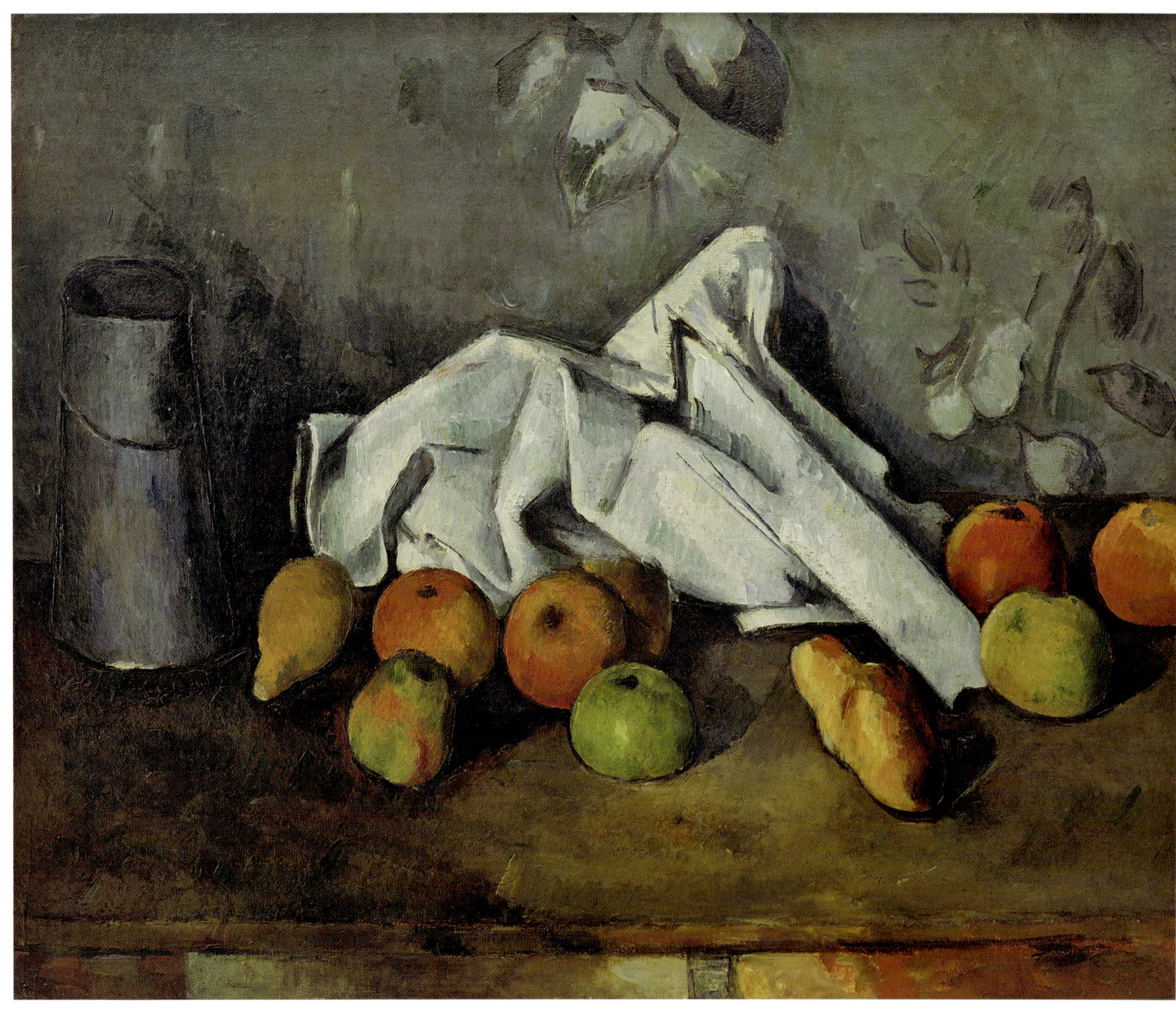

Cat. 71
Milk Can and Apples
1879–80
Oil on canvas
50.2 × 61 cm
The Museum of Modern Art, New York,
The William S. Paley Collection, 1990
R 426

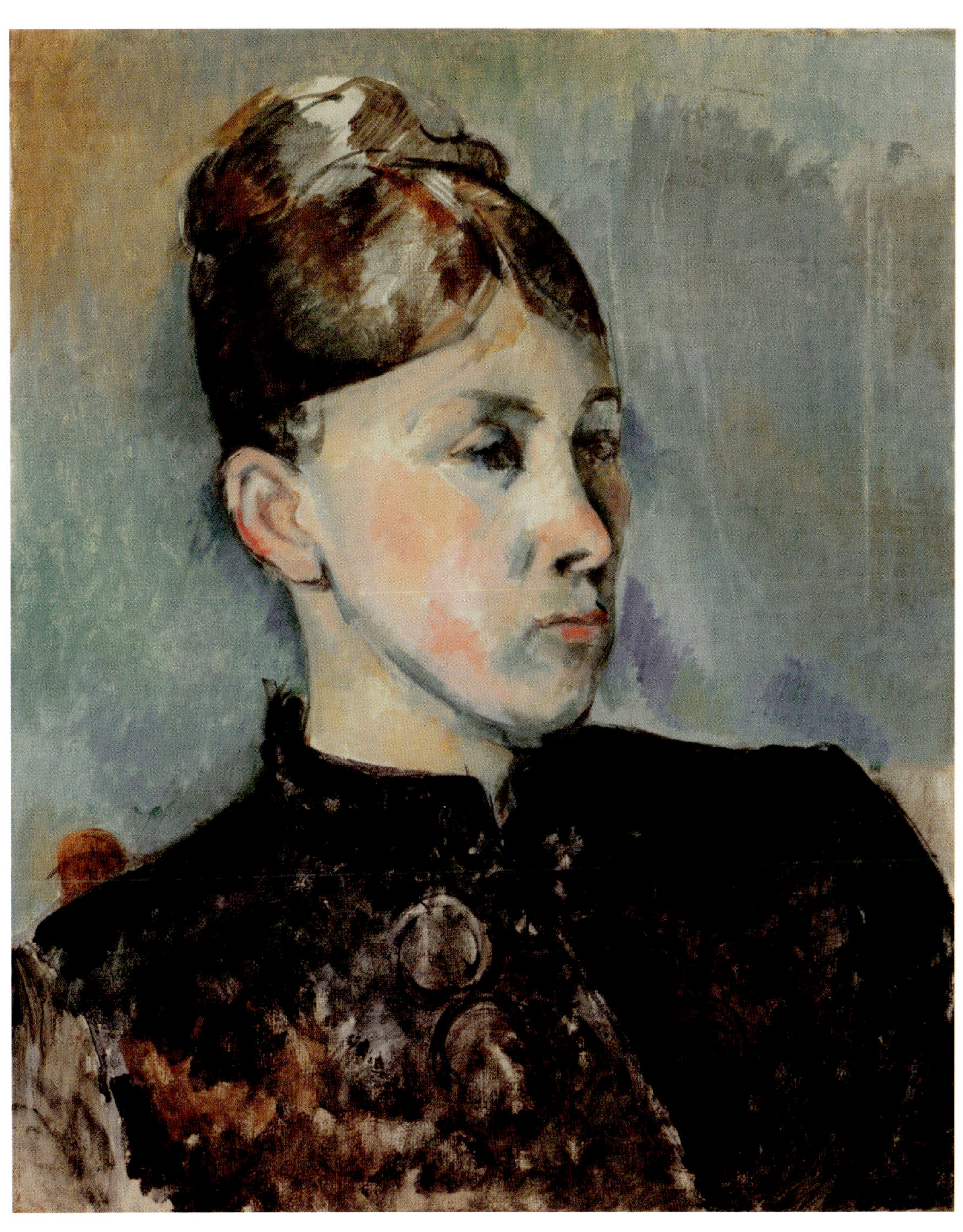

Fig. 89
Portrait of Madame Cézanne
1886–87
Oil on canvas
46 x 38 cm
Philadelphia Museum of Art, Philadelphia
R 576

there. He possessed, he said, sixteen Cézannes when he wrote to the artist in May 1899, adding that he valued them for their "aristocratic and austere beauty—for me they represent what is most noble in modern art."[11] (cat. 71) Bonnard and Redon, who were among the artists Vollard represented, also acquired paintings by Cézanne, probably by exchange. Since the dealer was a very poor bookkeeper, these transactions are not recorded in his archive.

As his reputation grew, Cézanne received the adulation of a new and younger generation of painters. In 1904 Émile Bernard published a landmark article praising Cézanne as "the only master on whom future art can graft its development."[12] Three years later he published his correspondence with the artist that was read by, among many others, George Braque and Pablo Picasso. Maurice Denis' celebrated *Homage to Cézanne* (fig. 95) was first exhibited in Paris in 1901 and represents a group of young painters and writers standing in Vollard's gallery admiring the Cézanne still life that once belonged to Gauguin (fig. 94). In a letter to the aging artist, Denis wrote: "Perhaps this will give you some idea of the position as a painter which you occupy in our time, of the admiration you evoke and of the enlightened enthusiasm of a group of young people to which I belong and who can rightly call themselves your pupils, as they owe to you everything which they know about painting."[13] One of these artists was Henri Matisse, who saw Cézanne's paintings, probably for the first time, at the 1895 retrospective. It was not until 1899, however, that he became haunted by *Three Bathers* (cat. 47) and bought the canvas from Vollard at great financial sacrifice. He later proclaimed: "it has sustained me morally in the critical moments in my venture as an artist."[14] Matisse would become an important link between Cézanne and a new wave of impressionable American painters who had come to Paris to study art (fig. 89).

By the end of the first decade of the 20th century, Cézanne's artistic legacy was keenly felt in the French capital. "Hitherto Cézanne had been important only to a few; he was about to become important for everybody. At the Autumn Salon of 1905 people laughed themselves into hysterics before his pictures, in 1906 they were respectful and in 1907 they were reverent—Cézanne had become the man of the moment."[15] The Galerie Bernheim-Jeune exhibited almost eighty watercolors taken from the artist's last studio, the first large-scale exhibition devoted exclusively to this genre previously unknown to the public and artists as well. Cézanne's "memorial" exhibition in autumn 1907 comprised fifty-six paintings and seven watercolors that attracted new artists and reinforced the admiration of those who knew of his work. Weber was later to recall: "Almost everywhere in Montmartre and Montparnasse... one could find groups of young painters in heated discussion on Cézanne's art. So great was the anticipation of the event, that students postponed their trips to Spain, Italy, or other parts of the continent."[16] "Cézanne was regarded and revered as the father and liberator, the Bach of art, to be emulated and worshipped. He was the beacon light in the stormy years of the historic transition and development."[17]

At about the same time the American expatriates, Gertrude Stein and her brother Leo, had assembled an important collection of avant-garde art in their rue de Fleurus apartment. The walls were filled with paintings by Renoir, Cézanne, Matisse, Picasso (The Big Four, as Leo Stein called them), Gauguin, Van Gogh, Toulouse-Lautrec and others. Writers, artists, critics, intellectuals, and collectors gathered at their Saturday night soirées—the discussion was animated and insightful. "This salon was sort of an international clearing house of ideas and matters of art for the young and aspiring artists from all over the world."[18] Cézanne was, of course, the topic of much discussion and his paintings in the Steins' collection a source of inspiration. The American painters Morgan Russell and Andrew Dasburg asked to borrow the Steins' little still life with apples (see fig. 88) and executed paintings that were modeled on Cézanne's picture. Dasburg later wrote to his wife: "To me the original is infinitive. It will rest in my mind as a standard of what I want to attain in painting."[19]

Little by little Cézanne's reach moved beyond the French capital as he became known to artists and collectors from America, Russia, Germany, Italy, Switzerland, Japan, and elsewhere. The "Cézanne effect" had taken hold. Although the 20th century produced few artists who could afford to collect Cézanne's increasingly high-priced paintings, it did produce painters who professed to be guided by his example—the numbers were legion. Those artists who did buy, such as Henry Moore, Picasso (fig. 90), Braque, and Jasper Johns, counted their Cézannes as their most important acquisitions. Braque and Moore hung their Cézannes in their bedrooms; Picasso bought his three paintings and one watercolor rather late in his career but he made it clear: "You know very well that I looked at [Cézanne's] pictures... I spent years studying them.[20] Since 1989 Jasper Johns has owned the small *Bather* (see fig. 86) that once belonged to Degas.[21] *The Bather* hangs over the fireplace in his living room not far from his collection of about a dozen of Cézanne's drawings and watercolors that are displayed in a bookcase. Johns is the last living artist to have a collection of works by Cézanne.

More than a century has passed since Paul Cézanne's death. Art has taken on many new forms and seems increasingly far removed from the issues that concerned him. Yet, many contemporary painters still draw inspiration from Cézanne's genius, which gives them the ability to cultivate their own perceptions and inventions. Cézanne taught them to rely on themselves, a very simple formula indeed. "If Cézanne is right, I am right."[22]

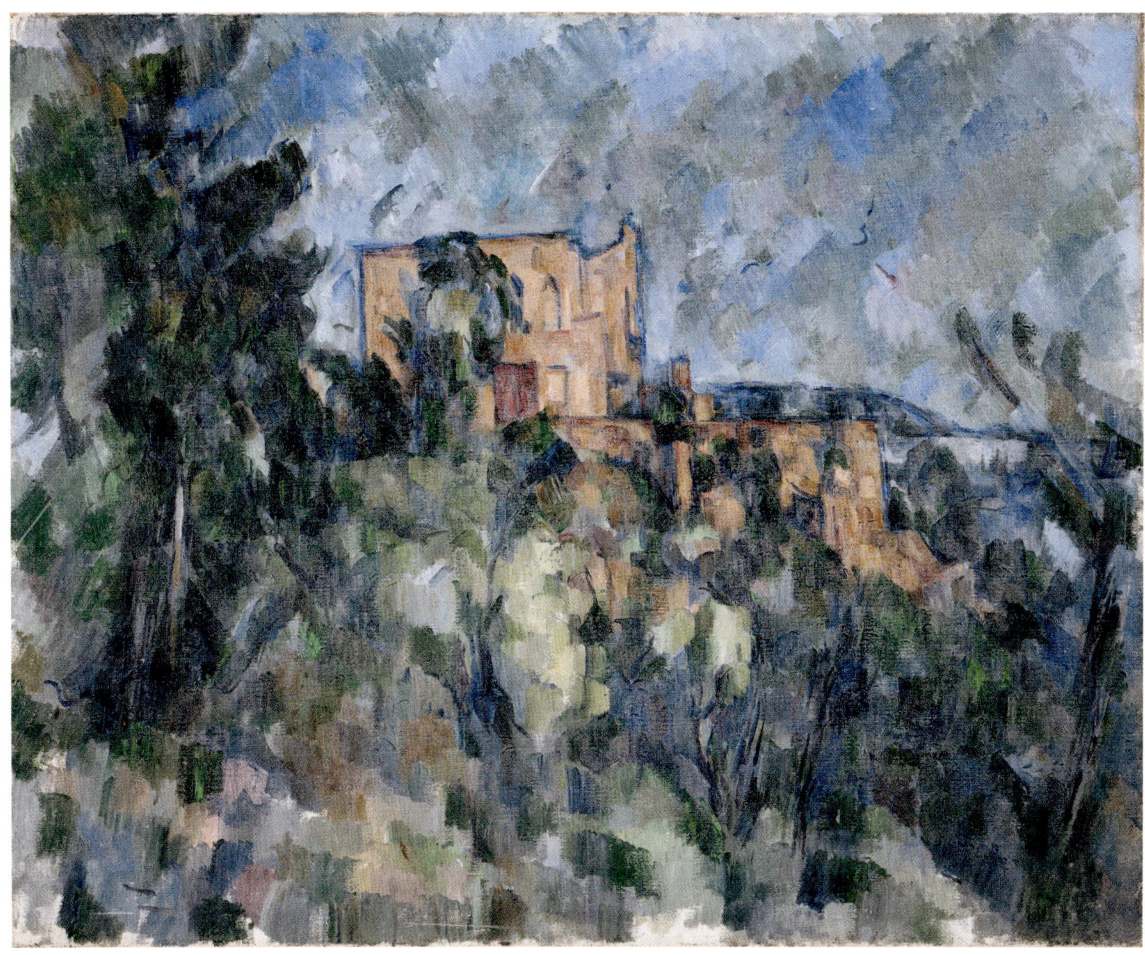

Cézanne lived to paint and expressed this view time and time again—it is what meant the most to him, he said. In his letters toward the end of his life he revealed that he struggled constantly to recreate what he perceived in nature and to translate those sensations into a new pictorial language. "He bound his life into his art, his art into his life,"[23] said Braque. Picasso explained Cézanne's struggle a bit differently: "It's not what the artist does that counts, but what he is... What forces our attention is Cézanne's anxiety—that's Cézanne's lesson."[24]

Fig. 90
Château Noir
1903–04
Oil on canvas
73 x 92 cm
Musée Picasso, Paris
R 941

See the list of the works of Cézanne having belonged to artists pp. 207–209.

Maryline Assante di Panzillo

SALONS, DEALERS, AND COLLECTORS

When Cézanne was a determined young man setting out from Provence to conquer Paris, the Salon—the only place where an artist could gain official recognition—was the focus of his dreams of success. Each year was marked by failure and each failure increased his contempt for the champions of academic art who prevailed in the matter of official acceptance. Alongside the young generation of independent artists led by Manet, Cézanne took part in all the battles that would overcome the jury system twenty years later. The paintings he sent to the Salon, each one causing a scandal and disgusting the juries, delighted his friends and eventually won him a certain notoriety. This provocation reached its height with the Salon of 1870, when the *Portrait of Achille Emperaire* (fig. 92) and *Recumbent Female Nude* (R 140), nicknamed *The Cesspool-Emptier's Wife,* gained him the honor of a caricature in Stock's album (fig. 91).

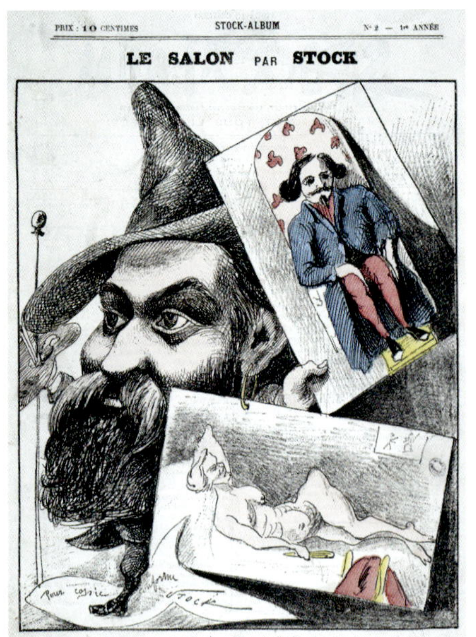

Fig. 91
Stock
Caricature of Cézanne: *The Salon*
1870

The period of provocation came to an end when Cézanne returned to Paris at the end of the Franco-Prussian War. After suffering another refusal at the 1872 Salon, he began a period of experimentation during which, according to his friend Émile Zola, "he would no longer allow anyone to enter his studio."[1] He then joined Pissarro and Guillaumin between Auvers and Pontoise to explore with them a new way of painting directly from the subject. At Pissarro's instigation, Cézanne took part in the Impressionist exhibition of 1874, where Count Doria bought *The House of the Hanged Man* (cat. 74), and shortly afterwards he made the acquaintance of Victor Chocquet, who became the only real collector of his work until Chocquet's death in 1891. Without completely losing contact with his Impressionist friends, Cézanne gradually distanced himself from them. Père Tanguy, a dealer in artists' materials who had opened a little shop in lower Montmartre, took canvases from him in exchange for supplies. For almost twenty years, the modest shop in the rue Clauzel became the only place in Paris where the occasional avant-garde critic and young artists such as Signac and Maurice Denis could discover a few works by a "strange" man from Provence, who was shrouded in mystery. It was still a question of old canvases, because Cézanne was never satisfied with his work and preferred his recent creations to stay in his studios away from prying eyes.

Let us summarize, with the help of Gustave Geffroy. At the beginning of the 1890s, where could you see works by this "ghostly Cézanne"? "There was a portrait at Émile Zola's house, two trees at Théodore Duret's, four apples at the home of Paul Alexis—or perhaps a canvas had been seen the previous week at M. Tanguy's shop... But you had to hurry to find it, because where Cézanne's paintings were concerned, there were always art-lovers ready to pounce on these rare trophies. There was also talk of extensive collections... To see them, you would have had to gain access to the houses of M. Chocquet in Paris, M. Murer in Rouen, or Dr. Gachet in Auvers, near Pontoise".[2]

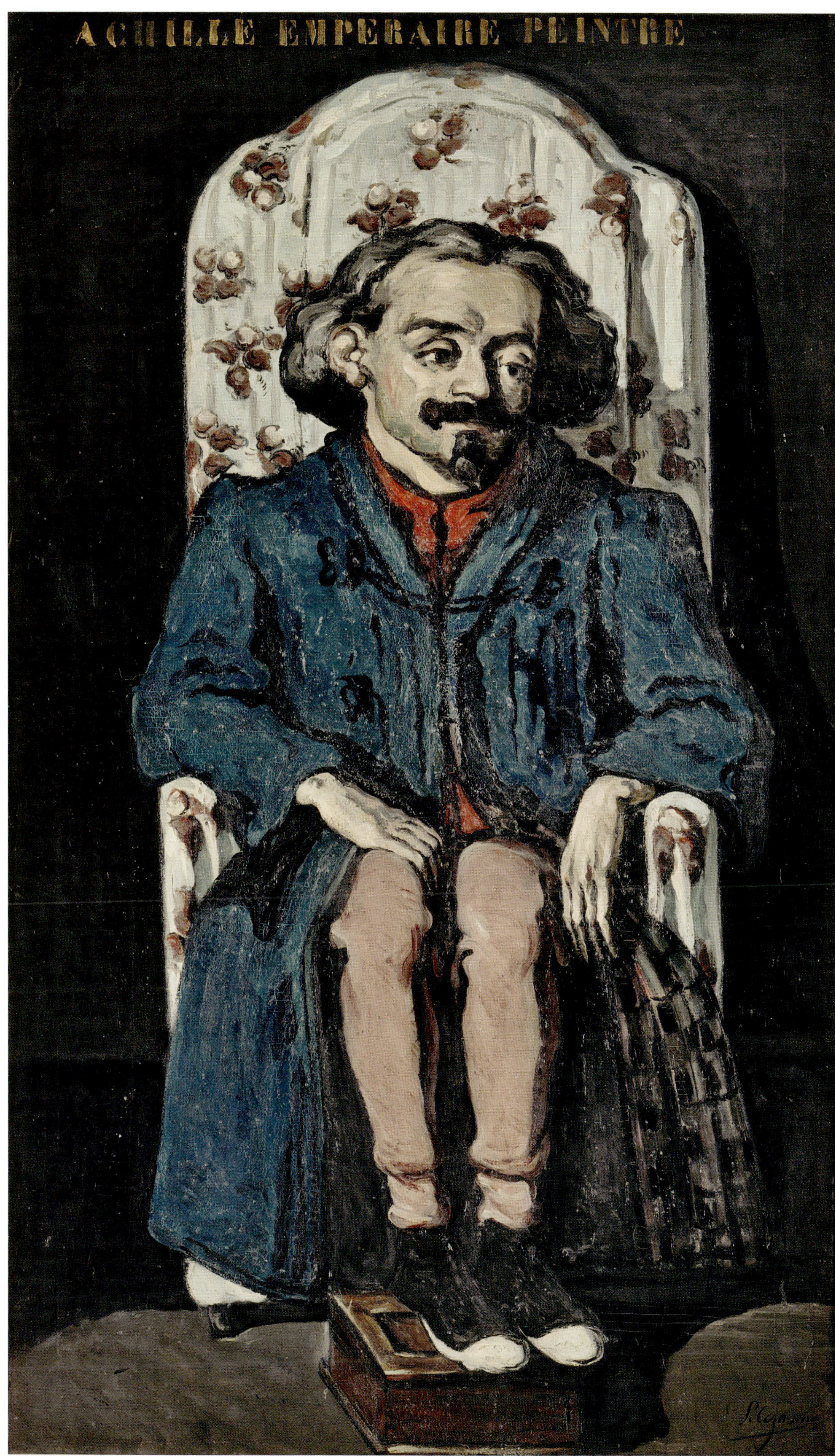

Fig. 92
Portrait of the Painter Achille Emperaire
1867–68
Oil on canvas
200 × 122 cm
Musée d'Orsay, Paris
R 139

Everything changed in 1894, when Geffroy published his first article on Cézanne in *Le Journal*. Père Tanguy had just died and the painter was searching for a new dealer. Ambroise Vollard, a impecunious young man with few connections but endowed with a certain natural flair, was on the lookout for new talents who would launch him on the art market. He bought his first Cézannes at the sale organized in aid of Tanguy's widow and sold them in less than a year at a substantial profit. Encouraged by this early success, and no doubt comforted by favorable comment from Geffroy and advice from Renoir, Vollard took control of the future sales of Cézanne, the only painter of the Impressionist generation as yet undiscovered by the major gallery owners of the Rue Laffitte, such as Durand-Ruel and Berheim-Jeune.

The Caillebotte affair began in the same year. Gustave Caillebotte, who passed away on February 27, 1894, left his collection of some sixty Impressionist pictures to the state, on condition that they should go to the Musée du Luxembourg and later be transferred to the Louvre. The administration of the Académie des Beaux-Arts was very embarrassed by this unwanted bequest. After a lengthy period of confusion, on February 9, 1897, 28 masterpieces by Degas, Manet, Renoir, Pissarro, Sisley, and two landscapes by Cézanne—*Farmyard at Auvers* (R 389) and *Gulf of Marseille, seen from L'Estaque* (fig. 93)—went to the Musée du Luxembourg. On learning that he had finally been accepted by the museum, Cézanne is said to have shouted: "Now I can say f*** Bouguereau."[3] The paintings not selected remained the property of Martial Caillebotte, the brother of the deceased. Among them were three paintings by Cézanne.

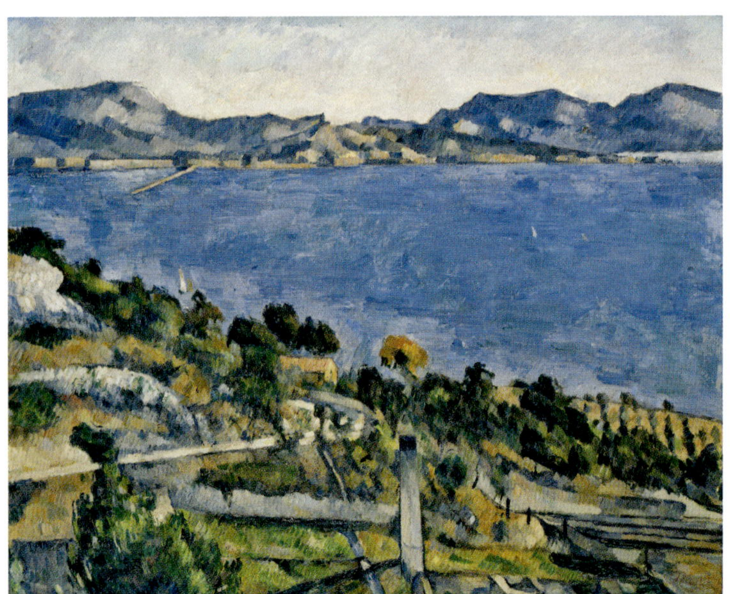

Fig. 93
Gulf of Marseille, seen from L'Estaque
1878–79
Oil on canvas
58 × 72 cm
Musée d'Orsay, Paris
R 390

Cat. 72
Portrait of M. Ambroise Vollard
1899
Oil on canvas
101 × 81 cm
Petit Palais, Musée des Beaux-Arts
de la Ville de Paris, Paris
R 811

Vollard reported that the refusal of the administration of the Académie des Beaux-Arts to accept the Caillebotte bequest in its entirely, and especially the "refusal"[4] of Cézanne's *Bathers Resting* (fig. 84), had considerably increased his long-standing desire to organize a general exhibition of Cézanne's works in Paris.[5]

He did not yet know Cézanne when he organized the artist's first solo exhibition in November 1895 at his little shop in the Rue Laffitte. Through Paul Cézanne Jr. he obtained around a hundred paintings, watercolors, and drawings representing a relatively complete overview of the artist's work. Of course, the *Bathers Resting*, lent by Martial Caillebotte, and *Leda and the Swan* (fig. 45), which were on show in the window, caused such a scandal that the dealer had to withdraw them. But he was a canny businessman and well aware that scandals boost sales. Moreover, this first Cézanne retrospective was more favorably received than Vollard's *Souvenirs* would suggest.

Apart from art critics, artists and people with inquiring minds, the exhibition attracted the first buyers who had not known Cézanne personally, such as the Count of Camondo, who bought watercolors, or Ex-King Milan of Serbia, who went by the name of the Count of Takova. Vollard reports selling *Leda and the Swan to* Auguste Pellerin (1852–1929) during the exhibition but this sale was probably made later. Through a series of bulk purchases this great industrialist, nicknamed "the margarine king," built up an enormous and eclectic collection, ranging from Corot and Henner to Matisse, via the Impressionists and the Nabis. He is said to have forsaken Manet in favor of Cézanne and he eventually acquired 90 of the artist's paintings, notably 22 youthful works, in which he was the first collector to take an interest.

The name Fabbri also appears in Vollard's account books. Egisto Paolo Fabbri (1866–1933), a painter and architect but above all a collector of modern art, lived in Lautrec's studio in Paris. Fabbri wrote to Cézanne on May 28, 1899: "I have the good fortune to own six of your works. I am familiar with their austere, aristocratic beauty. For me they represent all that is most noble in modern art."[6] His collection eventually contained 32 Cézannes, including *The Studio Stove* (fig. 51) and *Portrait of Mme Cézanne in a Red Armchair* (cat. 75). He was one of a small group of connoisseurs of American origin living in Florence who began showing interest in Cézanne at the end of the 19th century.

Cézanne did not go to Paris to see his exhibition. Vollard, always a clever strategist, turned this to his advantage, maintaining an air of mystery around the painter in order to arouse the collectors' desire. What is the truth about Cézanne's supposed isolation? Contrary to the well-established legend, the artist did not close his door to those who made their way to his house. He even seems to have been grateful for the tributes he received, whether from art-lovers or other artists.

In 1896, once the exhibition was over, Vollard visited Cézanne in Aix and the artist and his new dealer appear to have been on the same wavelength. The juicy account that Vollard gave of the painting of his portrait (cat. 72) by Cézanne in 1899 is still famous today. During the "115" sittings—after which Cézanne abandoned the unfinished portrait in order to "return to Aix," "not dissatisfied with the shirt front"[7]—the artist and his

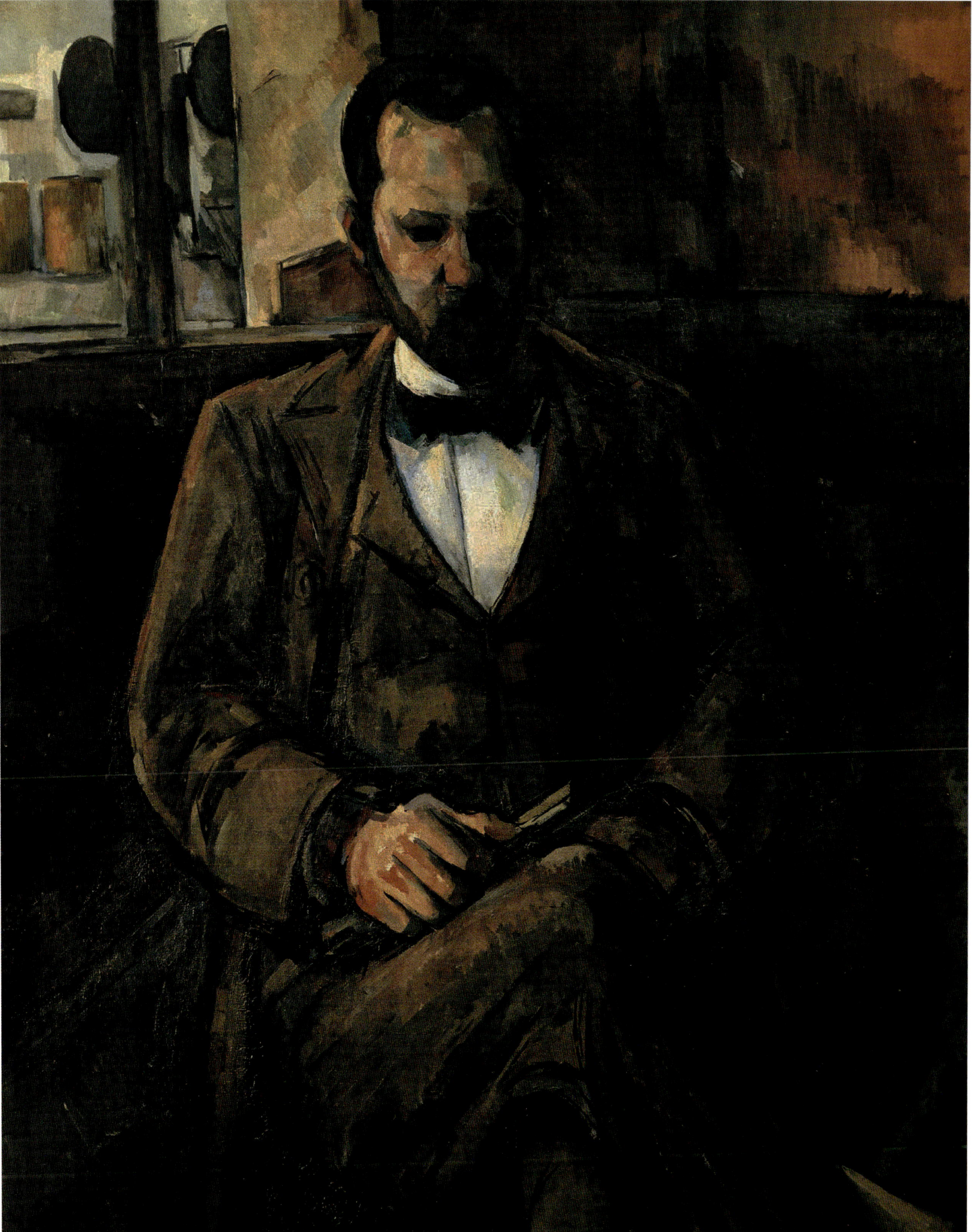

model got to know each other better, even though the latter was not allowed to say a single word while posing. Cézanne showed unfailing trust in Vollard over the years, even when new dealers such as the Berheim-Jeunes came knocking at his door. According to John Rewald's *catalogue raisonné*, 678 paintings by Cézanne, not including watercolors and drawings, passed through Vollard's hands.

The turn of the century marked the true beginning of Cézanne's fame. On October 25, 1897, Hugo van Tschudi, director of the Nationalgalerie in Berlin, acquired *The Mill on the Couleuvre at Pontoise* (fig. 67) through a patron. The arrival of a Cézanne in a German Museum caused considerable comment. Coming shortly after the Caillebotte affair, this was another opportunity for journalists to expose the negligence of French curators, who would not allow avant-garde artists onto their gallery walls. In fact Cézanne was recognized abroad before being accepted in France. His work very soon attracted the attention of dealers like Bruno and Paul Cassirer—who devoted an exhibition to him in their Berlin gallery in 1900—and Count Kessler, whose Weimar apartment, decorated by Van de Velde, contained three Cézannes, alongside paintings by Seurat, Gauguin, and Maurice Denis. Among the foreign collectors, mention should also be made of a strange, wealthy Dutchman, Cornelis Hoogendijk (1866–1911), who bought whole batches of Van Goghs and Cézannes from Vollard between August 1897 and December 1899.

In 1898, the Galerie Vollard arranged a new exhibition of 60 paintings by Cézanne. It was followed by a third exhibition of 40 paintings in 1899 and a fourth, consisting of 36 canvases, in 1901.

The early collectors of Cézanne's work passed away and, when their collections were sold after their deaths, prices rocketed. In May 1899, the collection of Count Doria was dispersed: Monet bought *Melting Snow at Fontainebleau* (R 413) for 6,750 francs. It was the highest price ever achieved by a work by Cézanne. Two months later, the Chocquet collection was put up for auction at the red-draped rooms of the Galerie Georges Petit. Camille Pissarro wrote to his son Lucien: "There are 33 first-class Cézannes, Monets, Renoirs and just one thing of mine. The Cézannes are selling for very high prices; they are already being quoted at 4,000 to 5,000 francs."[8] As Duret remarked, this sale established Cézanne as having marketable value. Though the *Portrait of Victor Chocquet Seated* (cat. 73) only made 450 francs, Durand-Ruel bought *Mardi-Gras* (R 618) for 4,400 francs and *Maincy Bridge* (cat. 70) for 2,200 francs; and on the advice of Monet, who assured him that the painting was "worthy of the Louvre," the Count of Camondo carried off *The House of the Hanged Man*, valued at 6,200 francs.

The Impressionist painters were admitted to the Centennial of the Exposition Universelle in Paris, opened on April 14, 1900. Cézanne was one of those selected, thanks to the support of Roger Marx. The time of provocation had long since passed and Cézanne carefully selected the three paintings to be shown: a landscape of the banks of the Oise, *The Pool at Jas de Bouffan* (R 278) and *Still Life with Fruit Dish* (fig. 94) later reproduced by Maurice Denis in his *Homage to Cézanne* (fig. 95).

At the urgent insistence of this great admirer, Cézanne agreed to participate in the Salon des Artistes Indépendants in the fall of 1899. He exhibited again with the Independents, alongside the younger generation of Neo-Impressionists in 1901 and allowed his hand to be forced one last time: "I have received a letter from Maurice Denis, who regards my refusal to take part in the Exposition des Indépendants as desertion... I seem to find it hard to detach myself from young people who have shown me such kindness, and I don't think that exhibiting will in any way compromise the course of my studies,"[9] he wrote to Vollard.

Cézanne's hesitations in respect of the independents are easier to explain if you know that he had not given up hope of being accepted for the Salon, or rather its last incarnation, the Salon des Artistes Français. In spring 1902, he was working on a bouquet of flowers for the Salon, but the painting was not ready in April. Cézanne was never admitted to the Salon des Artistes Français, just as he was never awarded the Légion d'honneur, despite various interventions on his behalf.

Real recognition came from the Salon d'Automne, the second of which (October 15–November 15, 1904) was held at the Grand Palais. An entire room was devoted to Cézanne. Thirty-one paintings and two drawings illustrated all the stages of his creative development, from 1873–1874 to 1899. Cézanne did not travel to Paris to be present at his triumph, but he must certainly have read the many reviews devoted to him. On November 11, 1894, Paul Cézanne Jr. wrote to Vollard: "My father is delighted with the success of the Salon d'Automne and he must be very grateful to you for the care you have taken over his exhibition."[10]

Ten pictures by Cézanne appeared in the catalog of the Salon d'Automne of 1905. The artist passed away during the fourth Salon, where a further ten canvases by him were exhibited.

Why did Cézanne, who had so hoped for this recognition in Paris, not come to the capital to visit "his" exhibition in 1904? Why this apparent indifference which has aroused so much comment? The answer can be contained in three words: Cézanne was working. After so many attempts, he had "made some progress" and glimpsed "the promised land."[11]. Convinced that only his work would enable him to fulfill himself, to become "Cézanne", a "Cézanne" worthy to be hung in museums, he refused to allow himself to waste the time remaining to him. This resolve did not arise from either indifference or contempt, but only from an overriding need. Let us leave the last word to him: "My age and my health will never allow me to make the dream of art that I have pursued all my life come true. But I will always be grateful to the intelligent, art-loving public, who have intuitively understood—through my hesitations—what I wanted to do in order to renew my art."[12]

Cat. 73
Portrait of Victor Chocquet Seated
1877
Oil on canvas
45.7 × 38.1 cm
Columbus Museum of Art, Columbus
R 296

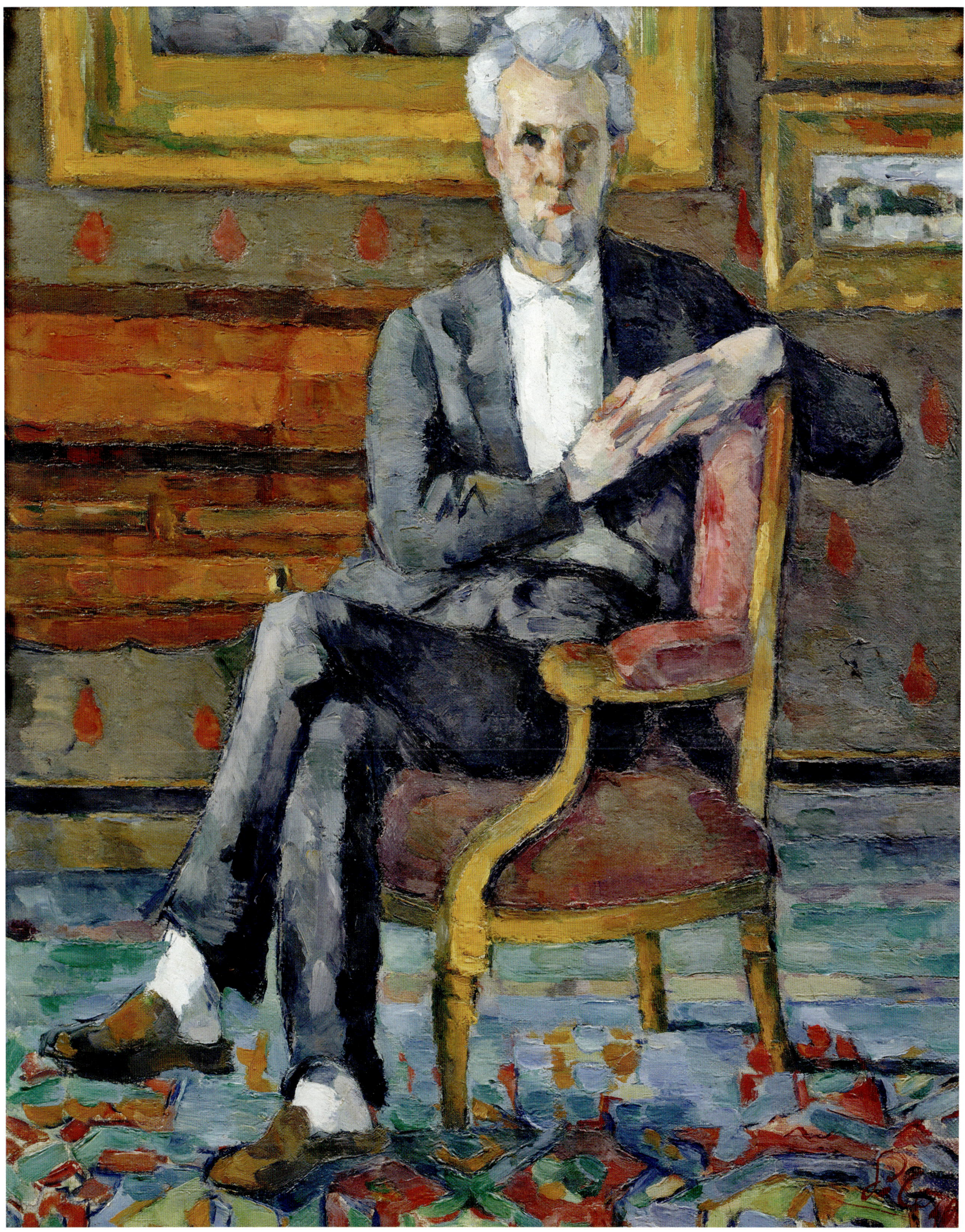

"The approval of others is a stimulant which it is sometimes best to distrust."[1]

Isabelle Cahn

CĒZANNE'S ATTITUDE TO CRITICISM

Cézanne was 35 years old at the time of his first exhibition and 43 when, for the only time in his life, he was admitted to the Salon, the major center of artistic recognition. As a result of this situation he remained isolated from the world of criticism for a long time. Even more than Courbet or Manet, he was notably excluded from official events and his participation in the Salon of 1882 went almost unnoticed. Two factors worked in favor of his admission that year: the reorganization of the official event[2] and the support of his friend, the painter Antoine Guillemet, whose pupil he claimed to be in the exhibition catalogue. By this time, Cézanne had lost some of his provocative energy, and the Impressionists, the first group of artists with which he was associated, were no longer considered scandalous. His unusual presence at the Salon had been preceded by at least eleven fruitless attempts[3], and was followed by a final failure in 1884. As a result, all the work of his youth and early maturity escaped judgment by the public and the press. It remained unknown, even despised, until its greatness was revealed a century later on the occasion of an exhibition[4]. Paradoxically, the paintings he produced after 1884 during his years of isolation were more immediately recognized, thanks to the initiative of Ambroise Vollard.

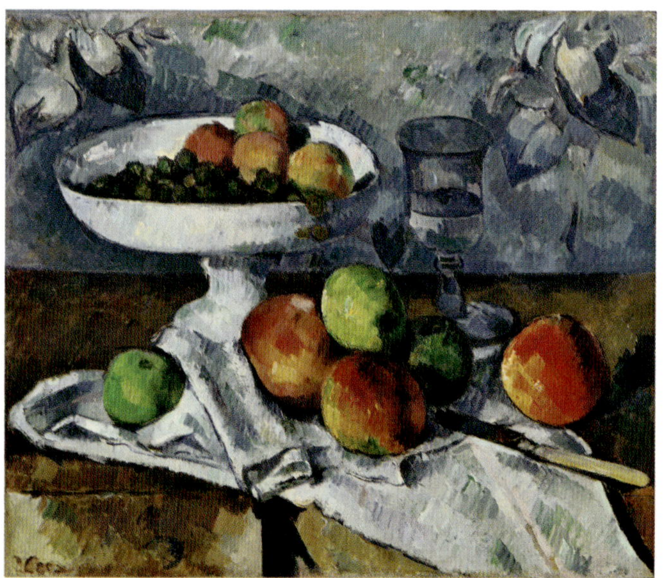

Fig. 94
Still Life with Fruits and Dish
1879–80
Oil on canvas
46 × 55 cm
The Museum of Modern Art, New York
R 418

"I take risks"

For almost twenty years, Cézanne remained the *bête noire* of the Salon jury, whose task it was to defend official morals and aesthetics. They persistently rejected his rough-hewn paintings with their frank depiction of human passions: scenes of love or violence that were considered licentious[5]. What most disgusted them about Cézanne's anti-bourgeois painting was his refusal to idealize reality. "Realist painting today ... is ... further than ever from achieving success in the eyes of the official world," noted one of Cézanne's friends when his canvases were refused in 1868, adding, "and it will certainly be a long time before Cézanne will be able to display officially sponsored works. His name is already too well known and he is linked to too many revolutionary artistic ideas for the jury members who are painters to weaken for a single moment. I admire the persistence and composure with which Paul writes to me: 'Oh, well! That way we'll get back at them even more persistently in the afterlife.'"[6]

Although conscious of his rejection, Cézanne remained no less determined to pursue his unusual path. In response to Stock's caricature[7] mocking his submission to the Salon of 1870 (fig. 91), he asserted that the rejection of his canvas guaranteed his creative freedom: "Yes, dear Monsieur Stock, I paint things as I see and feel them—and I have very strong feelings; they [Courbet, Manet, Monet] feel and see as I do, but they do not take risks... They are salon painters. I take risks, Monsieur Stock, I take risks... I have the courage of my convictions... and he who

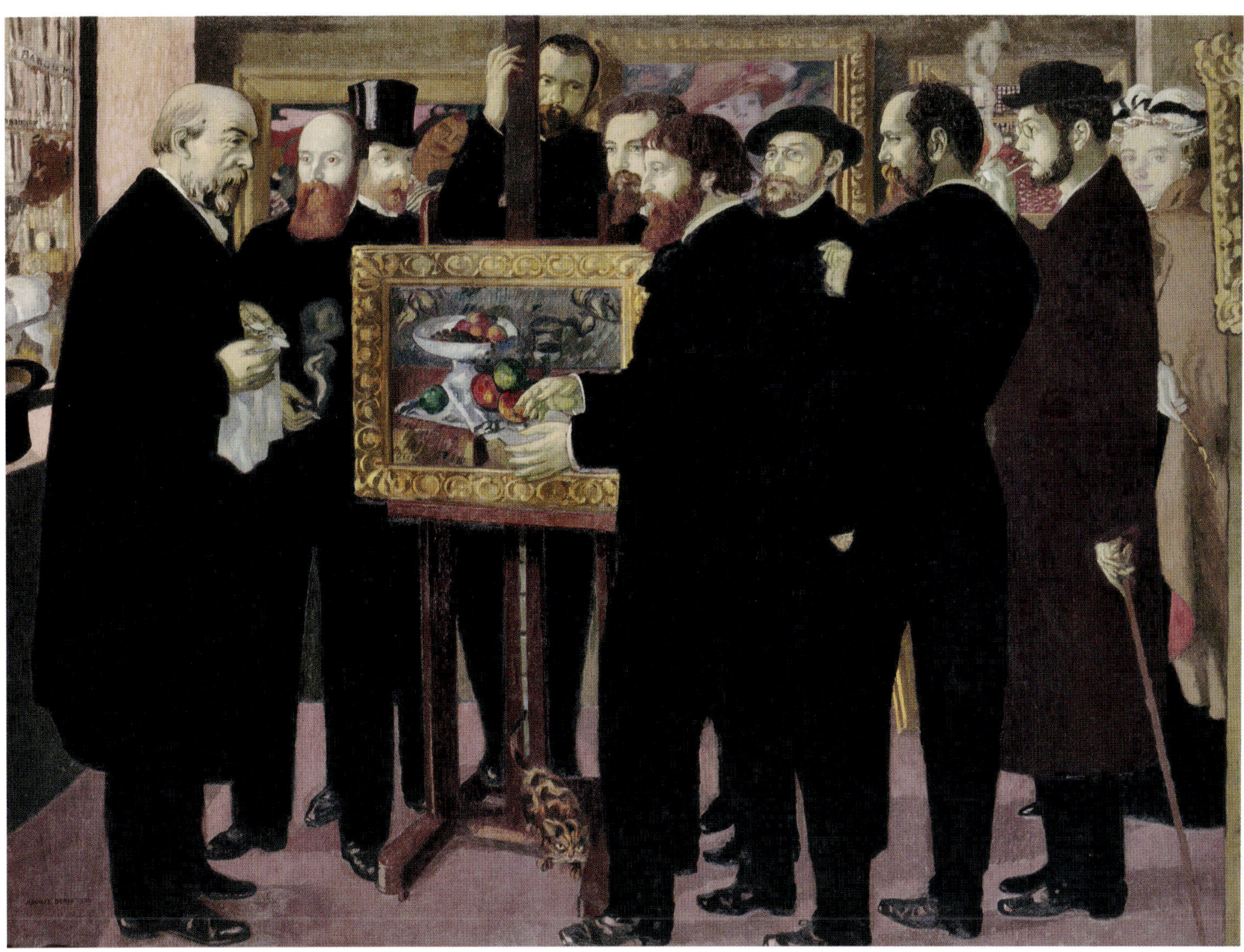

laughs last laughs longest."[8] In 1872, the painting jury was particularly strict, excluding a good number of already well-known artists from the Salon. Along with Manet, Fantin-Latour, Renoir, Pissarro (by proxy) and about forty other artists, Cézanne signed a petition demanding that a Salon des Refusés should be organized, similar to the one held in 1863. However, the time for dissent was past and it became a private initiative. The independent artists formed a limited company to exhibit and sell their works freely. Zola, who saw the new painting as an opportunity to link his name to an aesthetic movement, lent them his support.

Fig. 95
Maurice Denis (1870–1943)
Homage to Cézanne
1900
Oil on canvas
Musée d'Orsay, Paris,
gift of André Gide, 1928

Inappropriately mystifying

In the conditions of freedom[9] offered by the first Impressionist exhibition, Cézanne's entry failed to win over either the public or the critics. His two landscapes of Auvers-sur-Oise, one of which was the peaceful *House of the Hanged Man* (cat. 74), left them bewildered at best, but his challenge to Manet in the form of *A Modern Olympia* (cat. 48) caused an outcry. Castagnary[10] warned the painter against what he considered to be a dangerous deviation from the naturalist program. In his turn, the journalist from *La Presse*[11] mused: "It makes you wonder whether this is either inappropriately mystifying for the public or the result of insanity, for which we could only pity him." The terms "demonic vision" and "hallucination" appeared frequently in the critics' descriptions of the prostitute and her client; "... this little 'artificial paradise' has shocked even the bravest, it must be said, and M. Cézanne now appears to be nothing more than some kind of madman, painting while suffering from *delirium tremens*,"

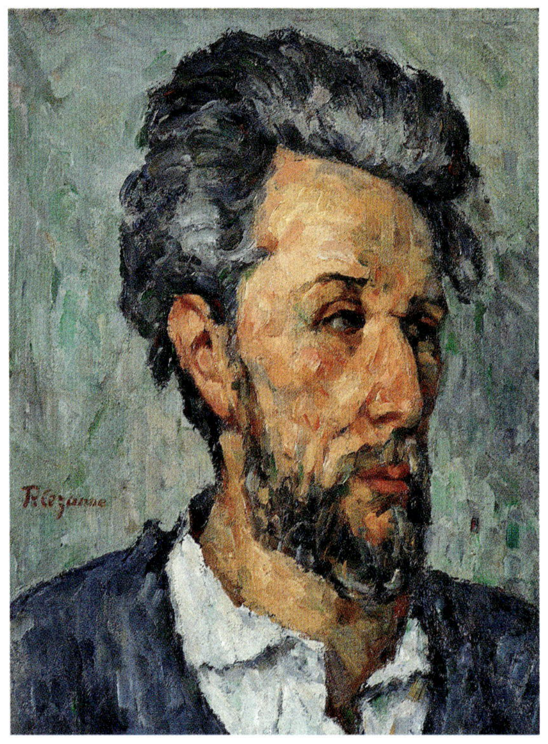

concluded the columnist of L'Artiste.[12] Far from lending his fervent support, Zola contented himself with lukewarm encouragement[13]. Despite these official attacks, Cézanne's artistic beliefs remained unshakable. In fact, these criticisms strengthened his awareness of his own artistic value. He intended to paint only for himself and a small number of art-lovers. "I still have to work," he confided to his mother after the 1874 exhibition closed, "not to achieve the end result that stupid people admire.... I have to try to complete paintings simply for the pleasure of making them truer and cleverer. And, believe me, there always comes a time when one makes a name for oneself and wins admirers who are much more ardent and firmly convinced than those who are only flattered by hollow appearances."[14]

It is difficult to assess the confusion and pride in the artist's reactions to criticism. The articles that appeared on the occasion of his participation in the third Impressionist exhibition in 1877 had a major effect on his relations with the group and his contacts generally. Only two of the works he submitted[15], *The Bathers* (R 259) and *Portrait of a Man* (fig. 96), attracted comment in the press. The columnists, whose comments were often reprinted in different papers, drew particular attention to their strident colors, "a cacophony of shrill, clashing, acid tones."[16] The brownish yellow of Chocquet's skin appeared to them alarmingly grotesque[17]. Louis Leroy advised sensitive souls and pregnant women not even to look at it[18]. *The Bathers* also provoked criticism[19]. These canvases "... make you laugh", noted Roger Ballu, "and yet they are lamentable. They show a profound ignorance of drawing, composition, and color."[20] Few voices were raised to counter these attacks[21]. Cézanne was upset by this and, although he had been subjected to criticism for over fifteen years, he decided to isolate himself from the group in order to work in solitude and silence, and give up "making his reputation through friendships and coteries."[22] Zola distanced himself once and for all from Cézanne, and added weight to the notion of an incomplete artist engaged in a perpetual search[23]. Ignored for many years by the official art world[24] and the public, Cézanne acquired something of a mythical status until he was rediscovered in 1895 by Ambroise Vollard (cat. 72). "An enigmatic painter, solitary and nomadic, so magnificently instinctive, who seems an almost legendary figure to the people of our time—because we have never seen him. He wanders through the French countryside. He prowls, watches, scents, carrying his sensitivity with him ..."[25]

Late recognition

The first Cézanne exhibition, arranged at the Galerie de la Rue Laffitte in November 1895, came almost too late. The event did not succeed in bringing the artist back into public view. Though it would be going too far to say that he did not care much about this late recognition, he viewed it from a distance and did not even go to see his exhibition. The discovery of his painting by a new generation of artists and critics had a considerable influence on aesthetic developments at the turn of the 20th century. The young critics involved in his defense aroused the curiosity of their

Fig. 96
Portrait of Victor Chocquet
1876–77
Oil on canvas
46 × 36 cm
Private collection
R 292

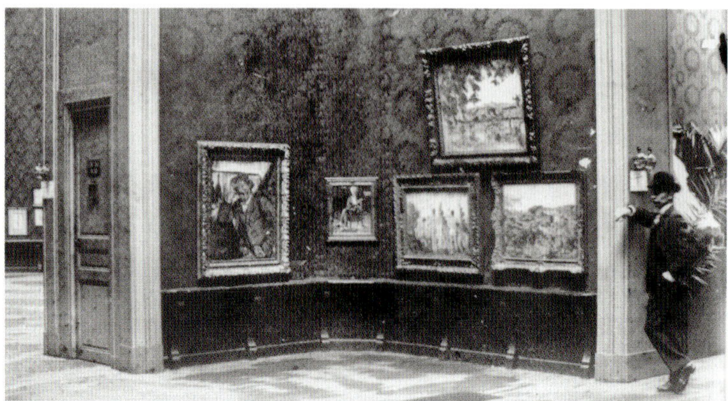

Fig. 97
The Cézanne room at the Salon d'Automne
1904
Photograph
Musée d'Orsay, Paris, Ambroise Vollard archives

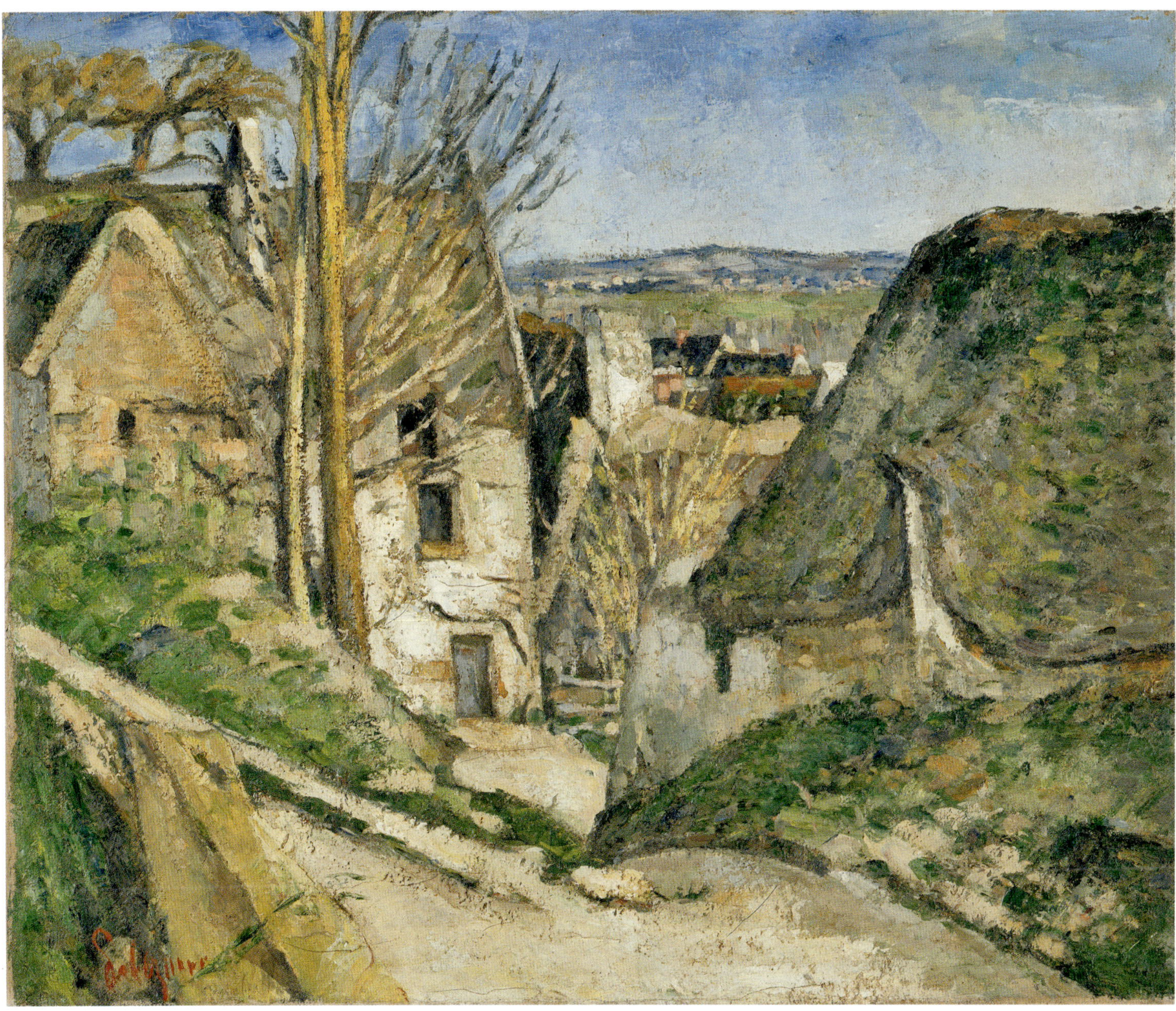

contemporaries, who nevertheless remained divided between admiration and rejection[26]. But the subtle analyses of Thadée Natanson[27], André Mellerio[28], and Gustave Geffroy swayed opinion in favor of the modernity of Cézanne's painting. As Manet had done with Zola, Duret, and Astruc, and Degas with Duranty, Cézanne thanked Geffroy by painting his portrait (fig. 61). The columnist of the *Journal*, a friend and defender of Monet, had devoted a major article to Cézanne[29] at the time of the Caillebotte bequest[30]: In it he had prophesied: "... all that is obscure and legendary in the story of Cézanne's life will fade away and we will be left with a body of work that is severe yet charming, intelligent but nevertheless simple."[31] The friendship between these two men constituted an exception to Cézanne's lack of response to the critics. However their voices became ever louder, allowing the painter to achieve international recognition at the end of his life (fig. 97). But the violence of the negative criticism of his work during the early part of his career had affected the painter's interest in the matter: "It is a great success," noted Georges Lecomte in 1899, "and Cézanne, caring nothing for all the glorious fanfares, continues to enjoy painting in the places he loves."[32]

Cat. 74
The House of the Hanged Man, Auvers-sur-Oise
c. 1873
Oil on canvas
55 x 66 cm
Musée d'Orsay, Paris,
bequest of Count Isaac de Camondo, 1911
R 202

Bruno Ely

AND PARIS CAME TO CĒZANNE

Towards the end of his life Cézanne replied to Joachim Gasquet's question "Which country would you prefer to live in?"—in a questionnaire entitled *Mes Confidences*[1]—by choosing "Provence and Paris." Indeed the artist lived either in the Midi—confined to three locations, Aix-en-Provence, L'Estaque, and Gardanne—or the capital until the day he died. Nevertheless we have to acknowledge two distinct time frames in considering the sometimes lengthy periods he spent in Paris and Île-de-France. In the first of these, Cézanne was an active participant in artistic life, fighting alongside his Impressionist friends to establish a new painting, a new form of art, from 1861 to the 1880s.[2] The second period up to his death (his last stay has been confirmed as 1905) found the artist increasingly in the self-imposed isolation he needed for his creativity, even in Paris. In November 1889, then, he broke his rules in writing to Octave Maus, who asked him to take part in the 7th annual exhibition of the Les XX group at the Palais des Beaux-Arts in Brussels: "...dreading all too justified criticisms, I had resolved to work in silence, until the time came when I would feel capable of defending the result of my attempts theoretically. In view of the pleasure of finding myself in such good company, I have no hesitation in modifying my resolution."[3]

This letter fragment reveals the two most striking facts about the last twenty-five years of Cézanne's life: his desire to withdraw from the public arena in order to confront painting alone, like Jacob wrestling with the angel; and simultaneously, after a very slow start, a sudden rush of recognition for the painter as one of the most important of his generation—better still, as *the* painter of his generation.

This choice made by Cézanne and the situation in which he found himself at the end of his life had such an effect that he was virtually reduced to a sort of distant legend: "... and as for him as a person, he seemed completely inaccessible, lost in the distant sparkle of the southern sun in Aix."[4] For the young generation of painters, all they knew about the Aix Master came from *père* Tanguy, whose gallery they visited "as they would a museum, to see some studies by the unknown artist who lived in Aix."[5] For others, he might as well have already departed this life: "Cézanne was nowhere to be seen. Many of those who recognized his name as some vague precursor and a 'strange fellow' thought he was dead."[6] The critic André Mellerio, who was among those portrayed by Maurice Denis in his picture *Homage to Cézanne* (fig. 95) wrote in 1896: "Although still alive, people talk about him as a man who has disappeared."[7]

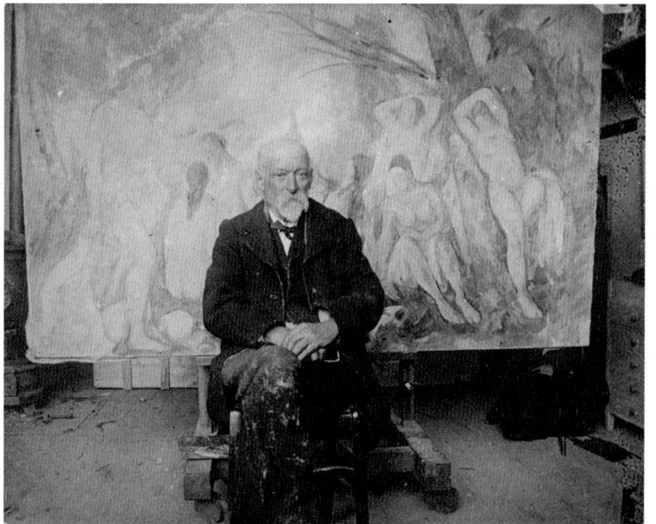

Fig. 98
Paul Cézanne at Les Lauves in front of *The Large Bathers* (Barnes Foundation)
1905
Photograph
Musée d'Orsay, Paris, gift of Société des amis du musée d'Orsay, 1994

While Cézanne had not "died" or "disappeared", his reputation as an irascible and antisocial character continued to grow. Yet many accounts confirm that Cézanne was at times happy to come out of the silence imposed by this desire for solitude, and one of his young fans, Léo Larguier, revealed how he could be even-tempered, and not afraid of being approached. In fact, the curiosity and enthusiastic interest shown by some young artists in his work would cause him, occasionally and temporarily, to take fresh heart and feel less alone. "You have no idea how stimulating it is to find yourself surrounded by young people who refuse to bury you right away," he confided to his childhood friend Henri Gasquet, referring to the latter's son Joachim.[8] He began to think that these young people were more capable of understanding his research: "I believe the young painters to be far more intelligent than the others, the old ones who can only see in me a terrible rival."[9] In a letter fragment to an unknown young artist, Cézanne went even further: "Perhaps I arrived too soon. I was the painter of your generation more than my own."[10] This desire to come and see Cézanne on his home ground, the place where he is deemed to have produced his main body of original work (which is of course unfair to Paris and the Île-de-France) went hand in hand with the growing interest in (and infatuation with) the Midi, its relaxed lifestyle, light, and motifs. This trend, which began in the mid-1800s, went on gathering momentum, reaching its high point in the next century.

The first painters to visit Cézanne in the Midi were his contemporaries, Renoir and Monet. Renoir was the most frequent visitor, as he came to work with Cézanne *sur le motif* on a regular basis from 1882 to 1895. Thus Paris came to Cézanne, the city having not totally abandoned the hermit of Provence. His Impressionist friends were later followed by his young admirers, who would be significant in the Aix painter's final years. These late visitors—painters, dealers, and literary figures—were motivated by different reasons, often depending on their circumstances and expectations. Of the painters, some came to see Cézanne to reinforce their theories about art, as in the case of Émile Bernard and Maurice Denis. After 1900 these painter-theoreticians had the profound sense of coming on a pilgrimage to absorb the words of a Messiah of painting, remembering a past passion of someone who could now serve as justification for their own artistic style. Then there were those who were there purely by chance, young artists like the painter Charles Camoin or the poet Léo Larguier, who was doing his military service in Aix. They were irresistibly drawn to Cézanne despite the awe he inspired, and could not resist paying him a visit. Ambroise Vollard and his fellow Parisians, Josse and Gaston Bernheim-Jeune, went to see Cézanne on several occasions, with differing levels of success: The artist was determined to stay faithful to his original dealer, Vollard, who had organized his first, very belated, solo exhibition in 1895. Literary figures, writers, art critics, journalists, novelists, and poets also flocked around Cézanne in Aix, some from Paris and others from elsewhere in Provence who would later continue their careers in Paris.

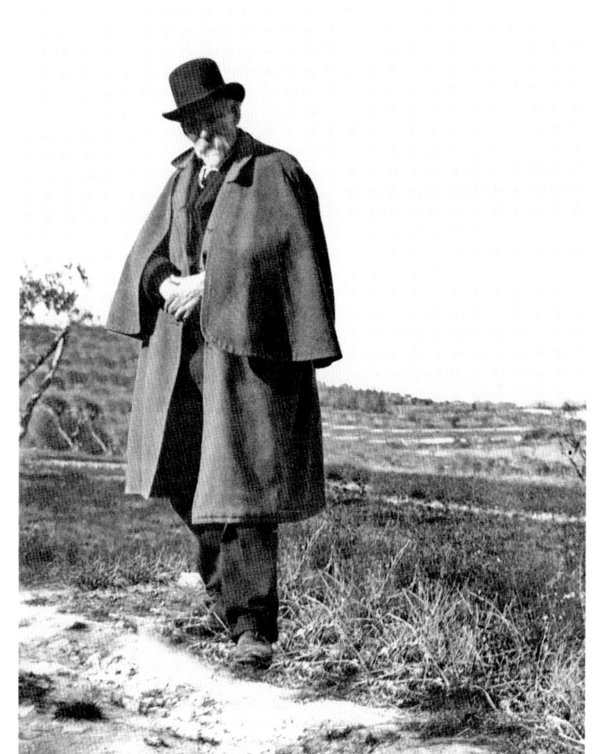

Fig. 99
Émile Bernard
Paul Cézanne on the Hill of Les Lauves
1905
Photograph
Musée d'Orsay, Paris

These profound connections between the capital and the provinces, these epistolary and literary exchanges, and influences of Cézanne in Paris (more often than is generally imagined) allow us to put Cézanne's self-imposed isolation at the end of his life into perspective. The accounts, articles, and books written by those who had the opportunity, the desire, and sometimes the courage to go to visit the Master of Aix combine to present this contrasting, multifaceted image of him, and highlight how extraordinary it was to have the experience of meeting him. By keeping abreast of the changes in taste and customs of society, which was attracted by the South, Cézanne played a powerful role through his distant influence—but becoming increasingly confident, and close to artists and intellectuals, he also brought the avant-garde world of Paris to the Midi. And if Van Gogh, along with Gauguin, failed to make the short trip from Arles to Aix in 1888, it was probably because he knew that Cézanne had a very definite opinion about him—"the painting of a madman"[11]—and because he accused his friend of "robbing him of the slightest feeling."[12] And if Braque, Derain, Dufy and the others were too late to follow in Cézanne's footsteps, L'Estaque and Cézanne's landscapes became a sort of Mecca for painting; Paris moved to the Midi, and stayed for a long time.

Pavel Machotka

FROM THE LANDSCAPES OF NORTHERN FRANCE TO THE BEGINNINGS OF CUBISM

There is general consensus that the late works of Cézanne, more than those of any other painter, stimulated the development of abstraction[1] at the beginning of the last century. Rubin, for example, noted that in 1907 Braque was inspired to develop a Cubist way of seeing landscape by the landscapes Cézanne had painted around 1900.[2] But while one can trace this evolution in art history clearly and attribute it to the need for young painters to push beyond the discoveries of their predecessor—thus seeing it as something inevitable[3]—to explain the evolution of a painter's style we have to look elsewhere. Can we attribute Cézanne's tendency toward abstraction to the inevitable push of art history, or can we instead pinpoint specific moments when it appeared and explain them by a logic inherent to the work itself?

The hypothesis of an inexorable movement is not without foundation. It has been attributed to artists such as Titian and Rembrandt, whose late period style—while losing neither its assurance nor its expressive power, quite the opposite in fact—is more fluid, less precise and more abstract. To explain it one points to the artists' ever more profound experience and the growing assurance in their means of expression, which allow them to move progressively toward an increasingly unadorned style, using notations that verge on the stenographic.[4] But if with some artists this deepening of their knowledge leads to a "simplification" of their style, it is by no means an inevitable development; with Cézanne, on the contrary, his styles became more complex with age.

According to another hypothesis, as the painter ages he becomes increasingly detached from the outside world[5] and progressively empties his forms of references to material things—this is the very definition of abstraction. But this hypothesis lays itself open to the same objection, that is to say, that the process is not inevitable—and besides, it would seem to describe Mondrian far better than Cézanne. For Cézanne, in his late works, displayed a passionate attachment to the real world, most powerfully in his ten oil studies of the same subject—Mountain Sainte-Victoire—which were based both on the intensity of his vision[6] and his constant development of means of representation.

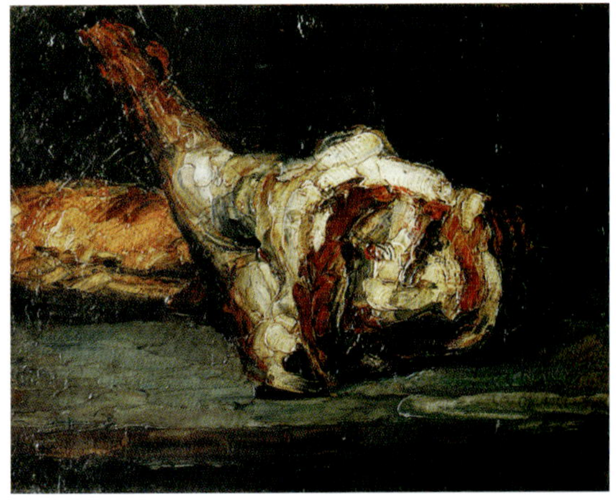

Fig. 100
Bread and Leg of Lamb
c. 1865
Oil on canvas
27 x 35.5 cm
Kunsthaus Zürich, Zurich
R 80

Cat. 75
Portrait of Mme Cézanne in a Red Armchair
c. 1877
Oil on canvas
72.4 × 55.9 cm
Museum of Fine Arts, Boston, bequest of Robert Treat Paine II
R 324

While Cézanne's late works contradict the theory of progressive detachment from reality, they do not entirely rule out the combined effects of confidence and experience; but those would instead explain his greater rigor, his refusal to be satisfied with what he already knew. In any case, no general theory can claim to account for the development of a body of work that does not follow a linear curve from one year to the next but responds, at least in part, to the demands of the chosen subject, whether it be a portrait, a still life, or a landscape.

Cézanne's work is, however, clearly punctuated by paintings in which the surface is "divided" into separate, abstract touches, which will later become the color patches of his mature style. All of these pictures are landscapes from the North, painted between 1888 and 1894. To note

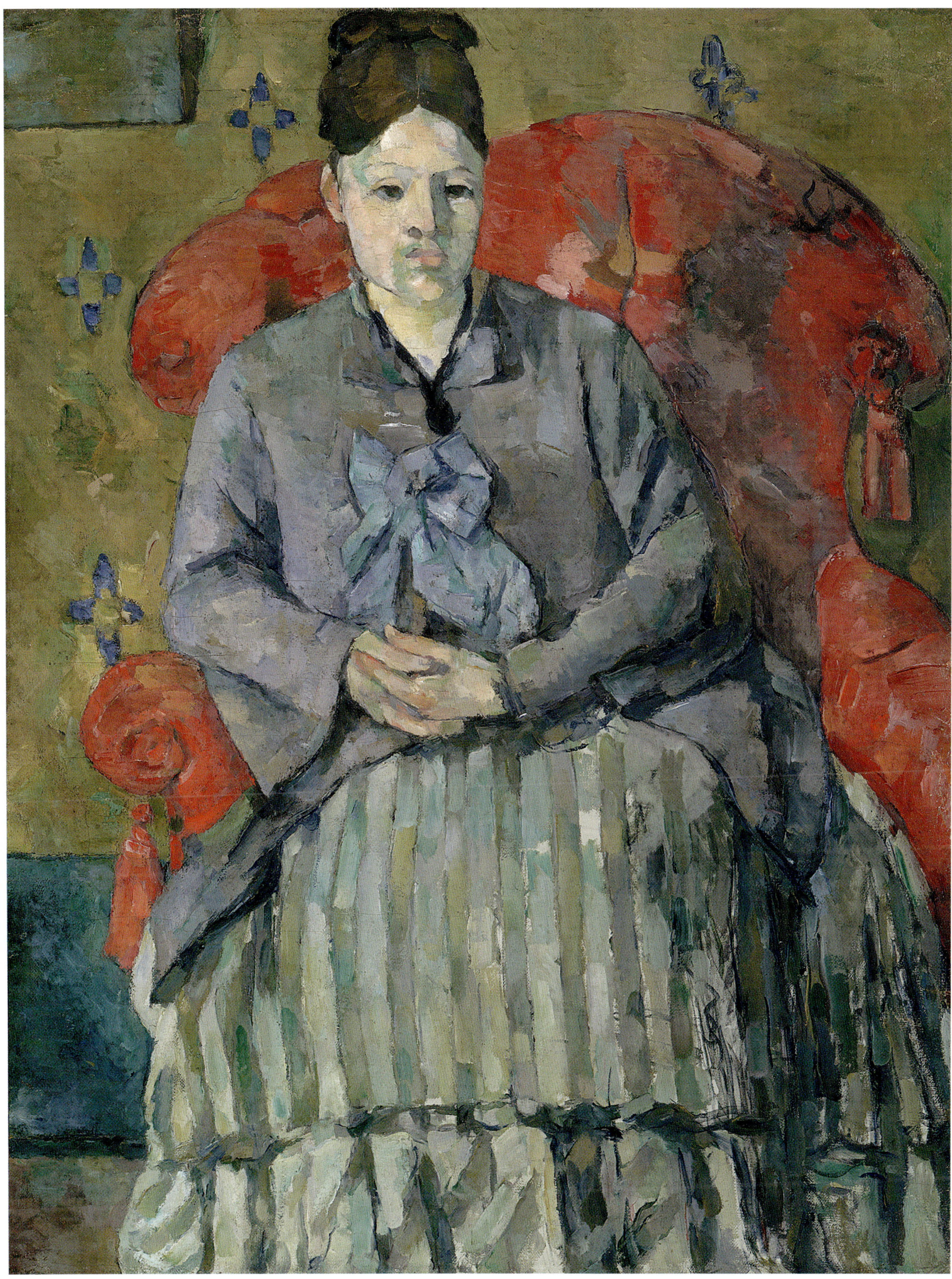

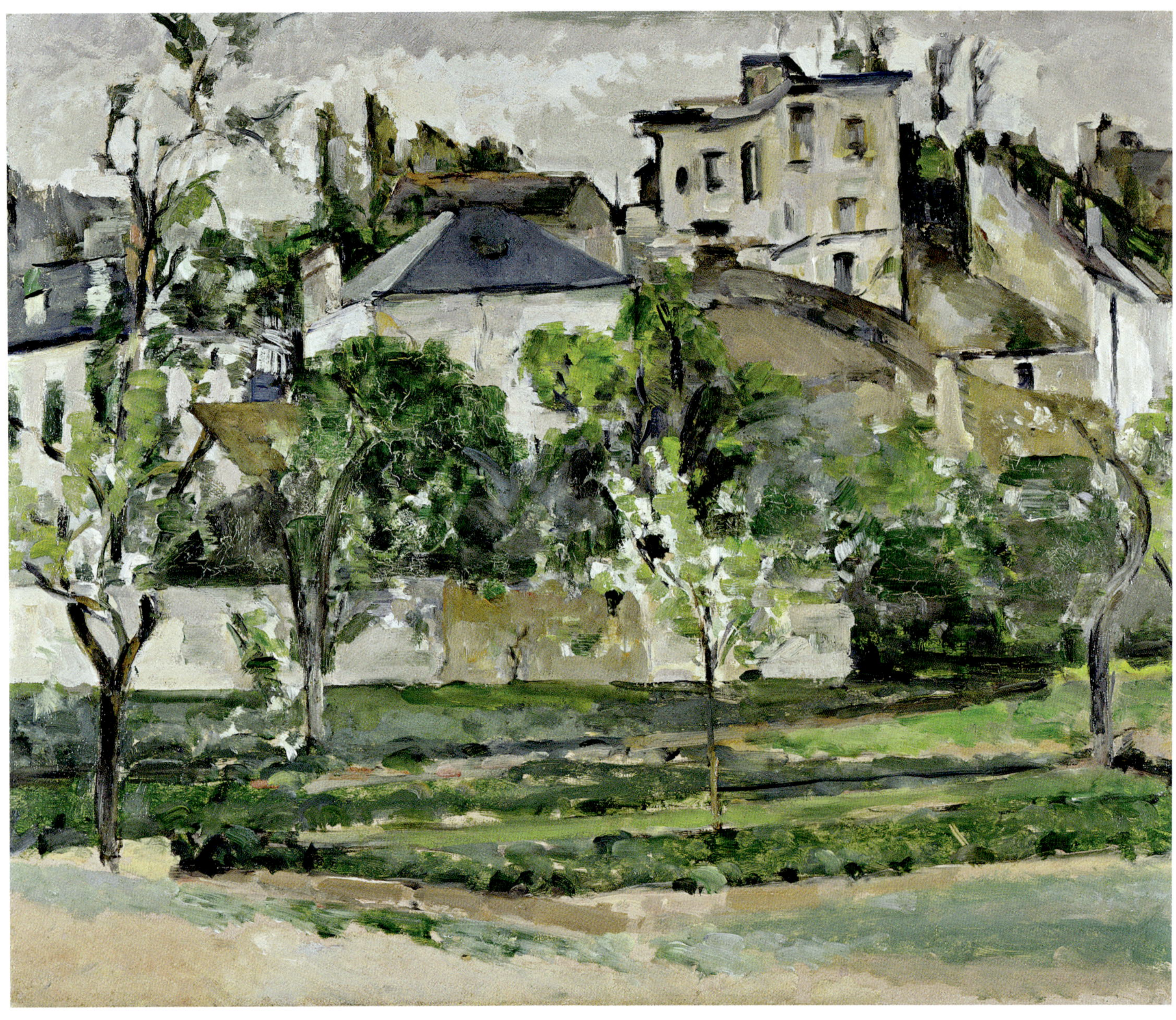

Fig. 101
Pissarro's Vegetable Garden at Pontoise
1877
Oil on canvas
50 × 61 cm
Private collection
R 311

Fig. 102
L'Étang des Sœurs at Osny
1877
Oil on canvas
60 × 73.5 cm
The Courtauld Gallery, London
R 307

this is to allow us to propose another, more specific, theory: that this new brushwork reveals a detached attitude on the part of the painter, encouraging an approach that is more analytical than sensual; this detachment is supported and encouraged either by work done in series or by a psychological distance from certain sites.

I should make clear that Braque and the young Cubists were inspired only by the abstractions that I am describing here. All work by a painter searching for a consistent touch is in a sense abstract, but the young artists were not interested in the abstractions of Cézanne's complete *oeuvre*. To give some examples: In the spirited, youthful *Landscape* (R 43) the subject is executed in sinuous movements of a loaded brush; on the other hand, in a still life (*Bread and Leg of Lamb,* fig. 100), all the objects and surfaces

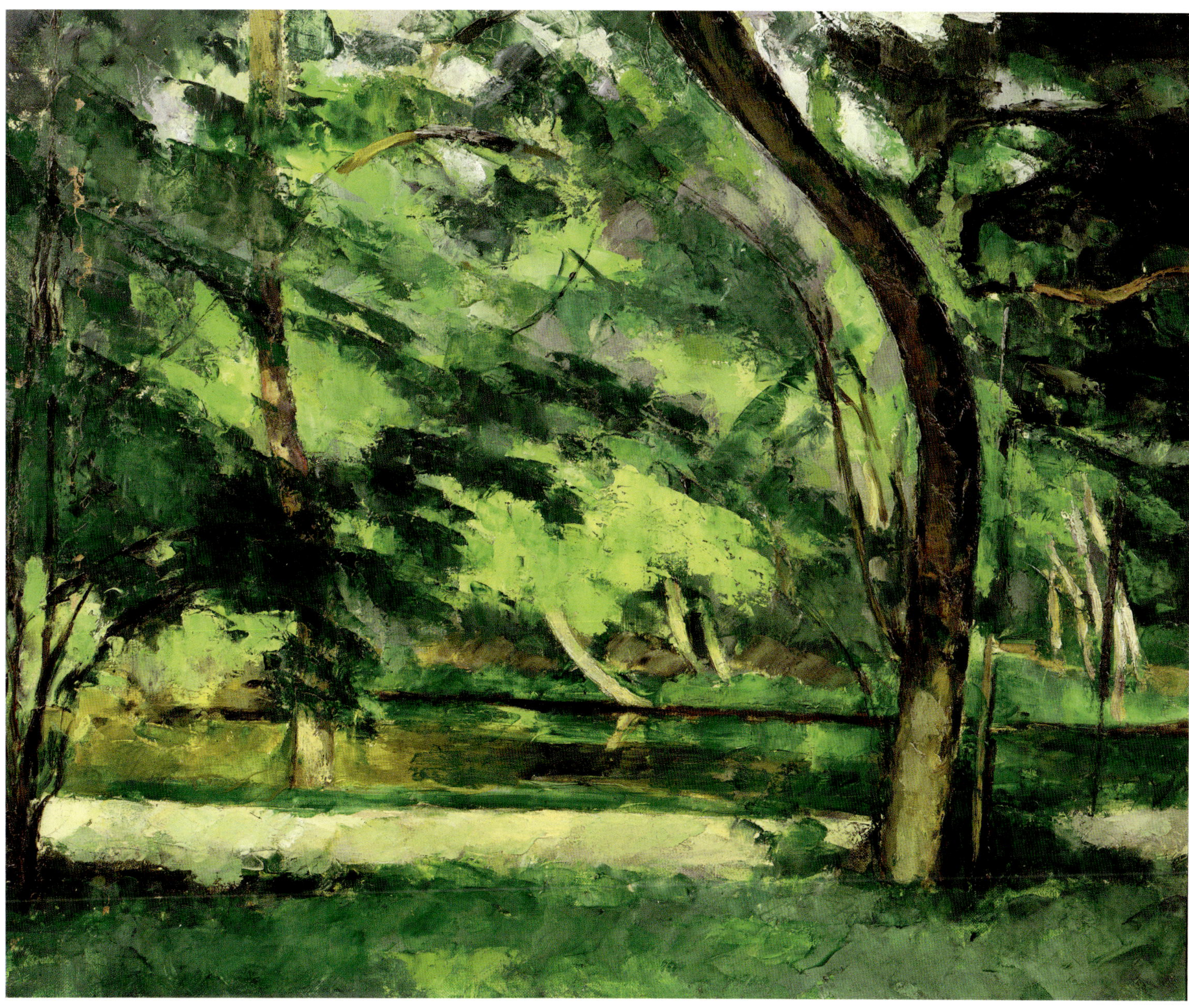

are rendered in short but firm applications of the palette knife. Blocks of color depict the face, hands, and clothing of *Mme Cézanne in a Red Armchair* (cat. 75) in 1877, the year of intense explorations of ways of unifying the surface of the painting; similarly they represent the buildings, fields, and trees in *Pissarro's Vegetable Garden at Pontoise* (fig. 101). Later still, from 1880 to 1885, the parallel touch, very disciplined and abstract, is applied with equal success to landscapes, still lifes, bathers, and portraits. The origin of these abstract styles can only be explained by the artist's constant search for consistency in his paintings.

Admittedly, however, there is one work that anticipates the "patch" style of his late period by twenty years—used only in *L'Étang des Sœurs at Osny* (fig. 102), it remains unexplained, perhaps even inexplicable. The color is applied with the knife, which Cézanne holds on its edge in order to take hold of the color and spread it downward, as Courbet had done before him, though less systematically. In Cézanne's case the painting becomes an integrated unit of patches that represent not only the branches and foliage of the trees, but the space between them as well. However, this work is unique: It relates neither to the series that leads to the parallel touch nor to subsequent styles. Its level of abstraction is a sublime aberration, but it has no progeny; one can neither explain it nor place it within a coherent logical sequence.

On the other hand, a series of three pictures painted in 1888 at Chantilly forms the real beginning of the late style. The series illustrates the stimulation of an analytical attitude by repetitive treatment of the same

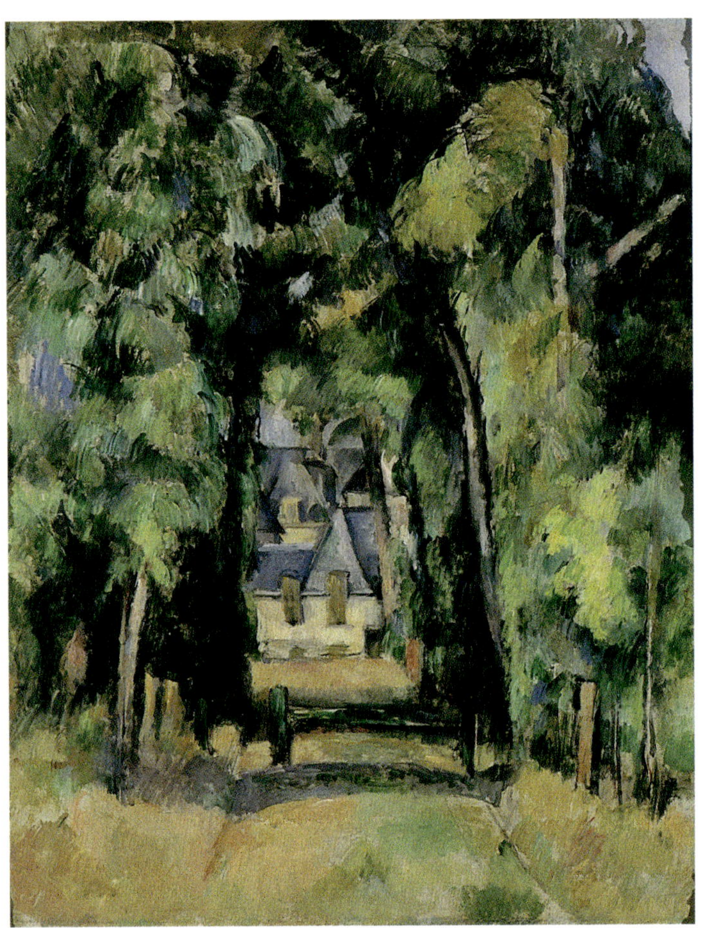

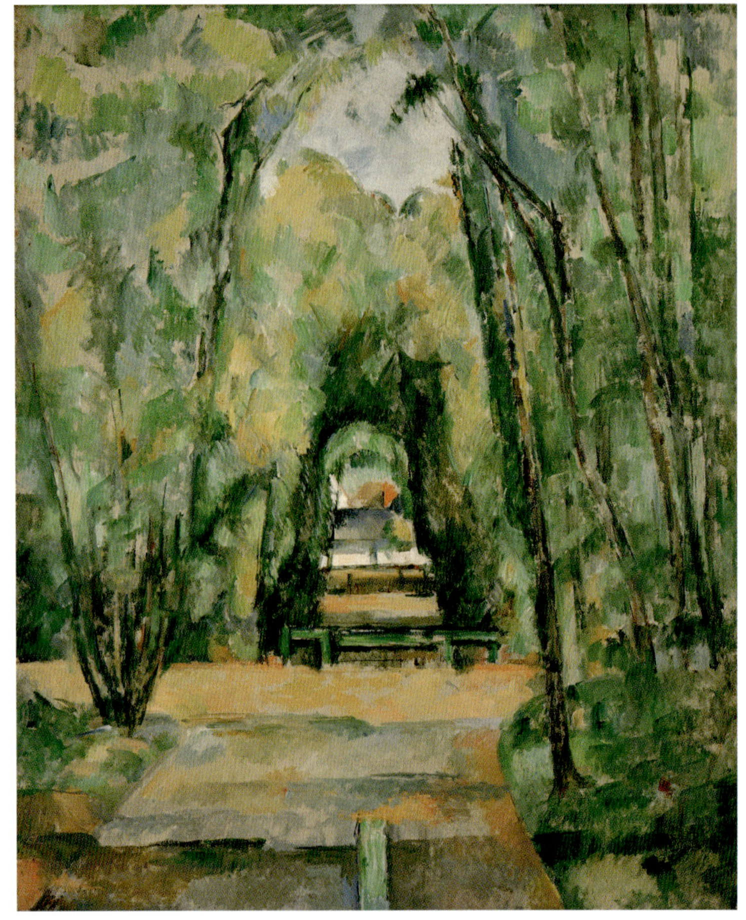

Fig. 103
The Avenue at Chantilly
1888
Oil on canvas
82 × 66 cm
Toledo Museum of Arts, Toledo, gift of Mr. and Mrs. William E. Levis
R 616

Fig. 104
The Avenue at Chantilly
1888
Oil on canvas
81 × 65 cm
The National Gallery, London
R 615

Fig. 105
The Avenue at Chantilly
1888
Oil on canvas
80.7 × 64.8 cm
The National Gallery, London
R 614

subject, and it culminates in a painting that has the brushstrokes grouped in patches which perform the same role as in Cézanne's late styles. In these three canvases Cézanne represents one of the bridle paths running through the forest belonging to the château at Chantilly; their common feature is not the château itself, but the painter's position in the centre of the path. I present them here in the order in which I believe they were painted, following a progression which begins with the style typical of 1888 and ends with an abstract and original conception. The first version of *The Avenue at Chantilly* (fig. 103) would be the one with the most recognizable subject: the roof of a château whose shape extends the diagonals established by the path. It is a well-executed composition in which spatial depth is both measured and limited, and the strokes depicting the leaves are grouped in such a way as to suggest the chestnut trees (which are still there).[7] In the next canvas (fig. 104), however, the groupings are no longer suggested by the leaves: Their independent form allows Cézanne to represent not only the foliage but also the path's progression toward the deepest point of the work, which is another, less distinct, château roof. In the final version of *The Avenue at Chantilly* (fig. 105), the touches become suddenly highly independent—the groups are detached one from another and align themselves more or less along two diagonals. This does not stop them from suggesting all of the visible objects.

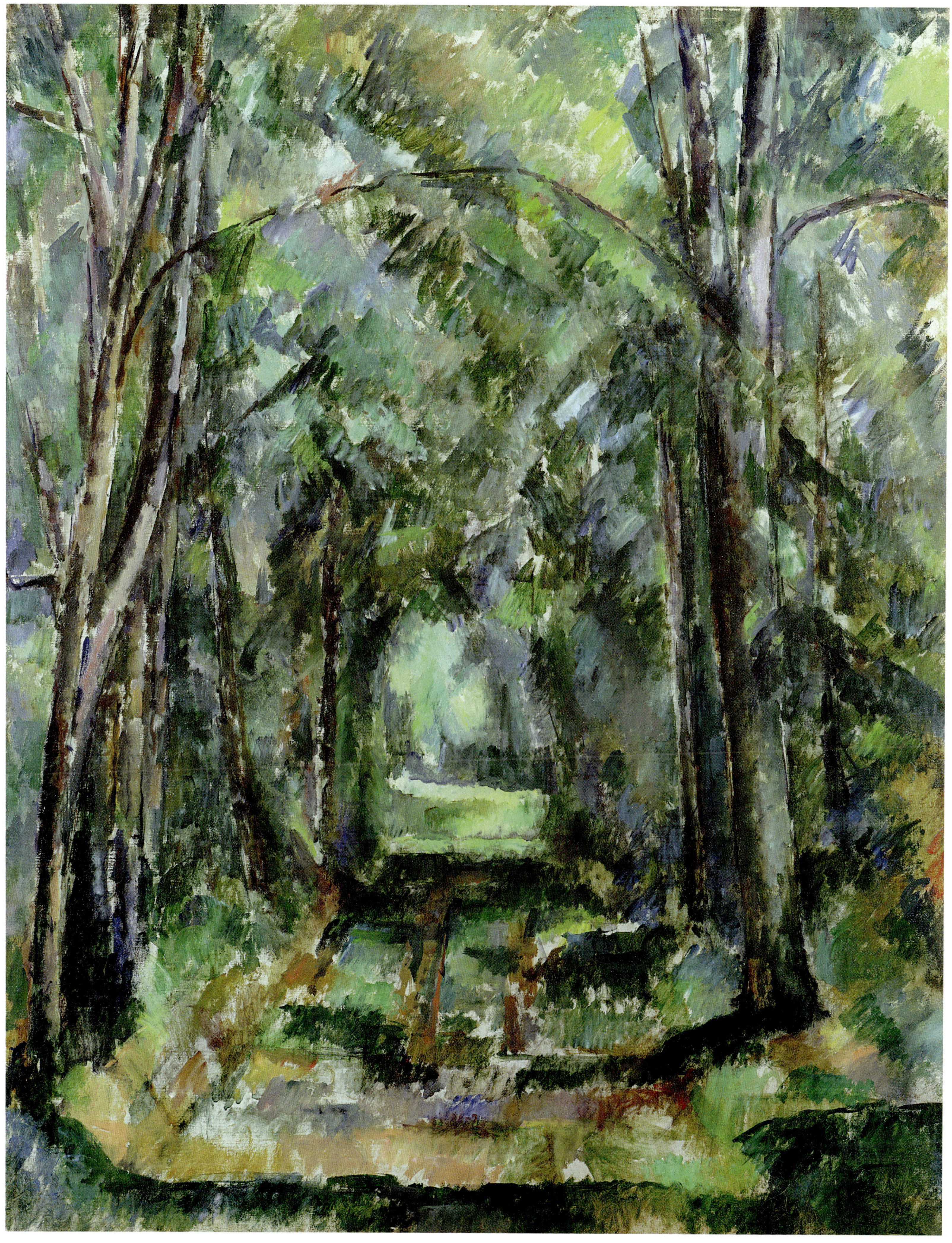

Cézanne no longer needs a concrete subject; the construction of space is what constitutes the real subject of the painting. In this canvas the painter has reached an unprecedented level of abstraction (apart from in the one-off *Étang des Sœurs*), one that is rarely seen in the Provençal landscapes of the time, or even of the years that immediately follow. Admittedly, the Chantilly style can be seen in *House with the Red Roof* (fig. 106), dated by Rewald as from the next year, 1889, but this painting is closer to the first, and least abstract, of the Chantilly series, rather than the other two.

Even this style, the one of *House with the Red Roof*, remains exceptional in the Provençal works of these years. Around 1889 we can follow Cézanne to Bellevue near Aix, which becomes the site for affirmative, even happy, paintings like *The House at Bellevue* (fig. 107) and *The Pigeon Loft at Bellevue* (fig. 108). The complex space of the first of these, with its dynamic verticals and the interlacing of the middle ground with the background, leaves a profound impression, as do the light, the warmth, and

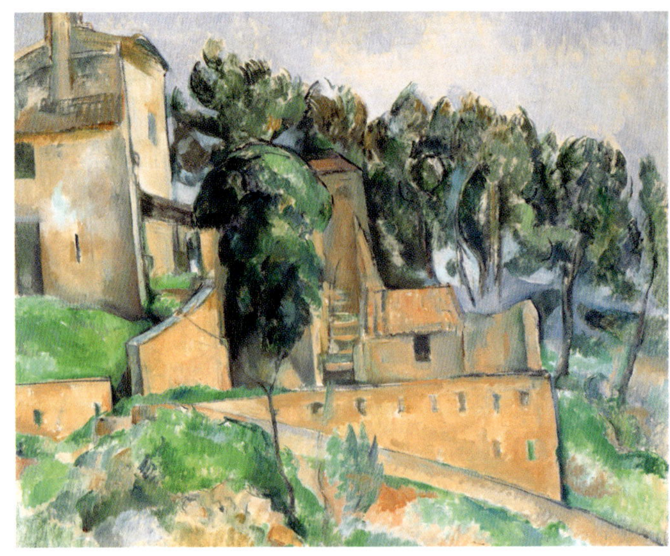

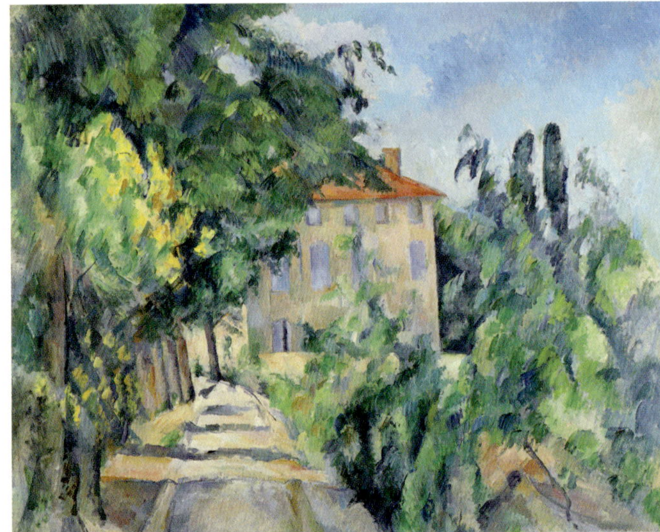

Fig. 106
House with the Red Roof
1887–1990
Oil on canvas
73 x 92 cm
Private collection
R 603

Fig. 107
The House at Bellevue
c. 1890
Oil on canvas
66 x 81 cm
Musée d'Art et d'Histoire, Geneva
R 691

the simple composition of the second. Yet in *The House* the touch itself is conservative, barely visible, while in *The Pigeon Loft*, it is altogether conventional compared to the level reached by Cézanne elsewhere, although it does subtly support the composition (note the counterpoint of the diagonals representing the sky and the roof of the pigeon tower). I suspect that it was the painter's strong attachment to this site that discouraged the impartial and detached study of the subject that we witnessed in the last Chantilly painting.

These comparisons are what leads me to believe that there were two major factors that encouraged the development of the abstractions in Cézanne's work that the Cubists held dear: work in series, at this point evident only in Chantilly; and his mental detachment from the site, noticeable by contrast, for now, with his strong emotional investment in the Midi locations. As far as work in series is concerned, we may assume that in achieving successive representations of a subject a painter comes to know it better and better; this in turn suggests that as the desire to represent it becomes satisfied, a search for an original way to paint it replaces it by degrees. Later in Cézanne's development we will see a striking illustration of this evolution in the Midi: in the series already mentioned comprising ten paintings of Mountain Sainte-Victoire (seen from Les Lauves) which, in Gowing's view,[8] begins with a quite realistic representation—despite the aging painter's mastery of all his styles—and moves progressively toward abstraction.

As for the second factor previously alluded to—the affective relationship between the painter and his site—it became apparent when we compared the landscapes of northern France with contemporary ones done in the South. This is not a mere impression: The painter himself, in a letter confessing his resignation to the disappointments in his life, reassures himself by saying that there are still "treasures to be taken" from the land of his birth[9], meaning *le Midi* of course. Admittedly, between about 1889 and 1892 a comparison of styles can only remain inexact, as the dating is sometimes uncertain; nevertheless it is clear that during this period the

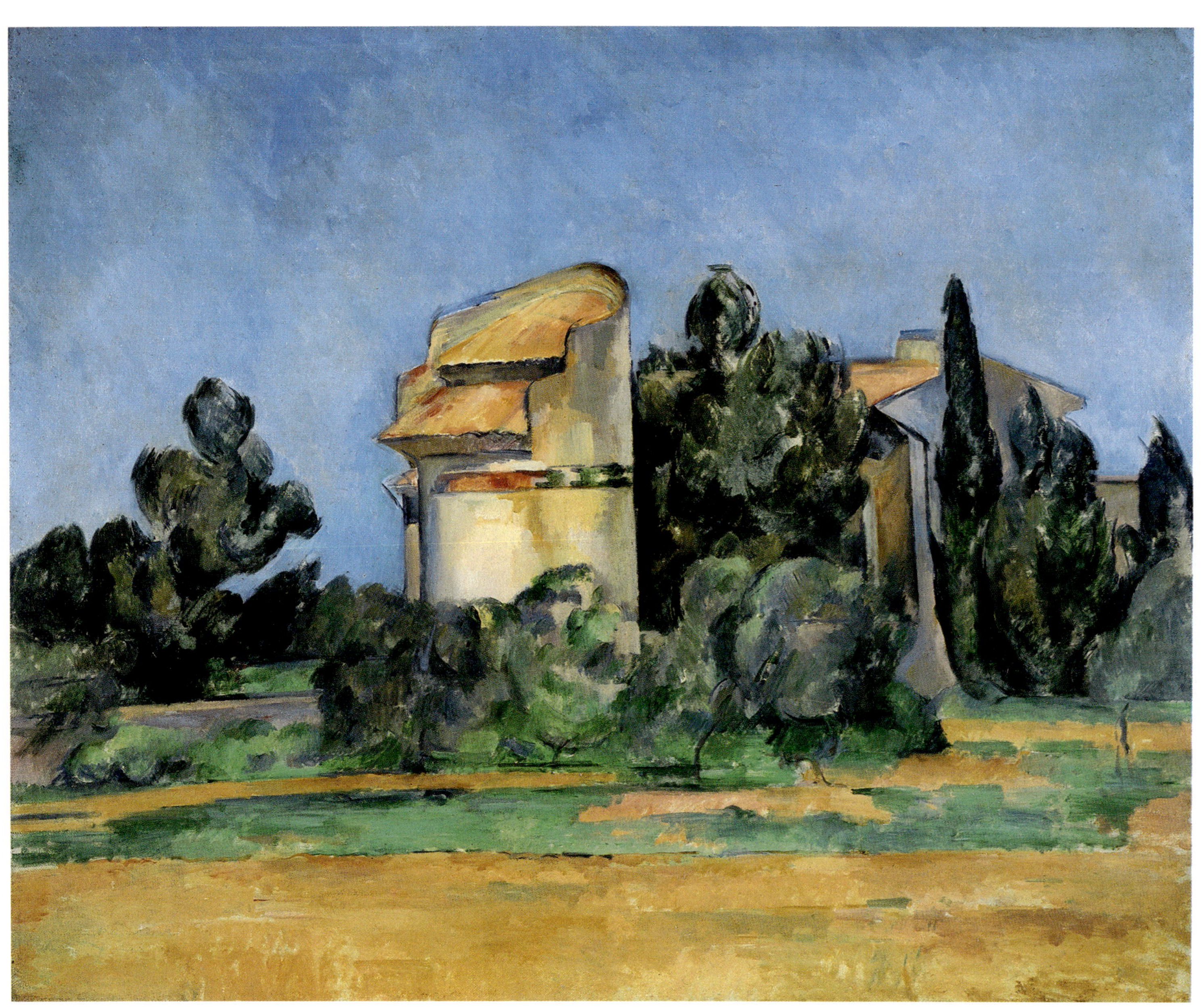

Fig. 108
Pigeon Loft at Bellevue
1889–1890
Oil on canvas
64 × 80 cm
The Cleveland Museum of Art, Cleveland
R 692

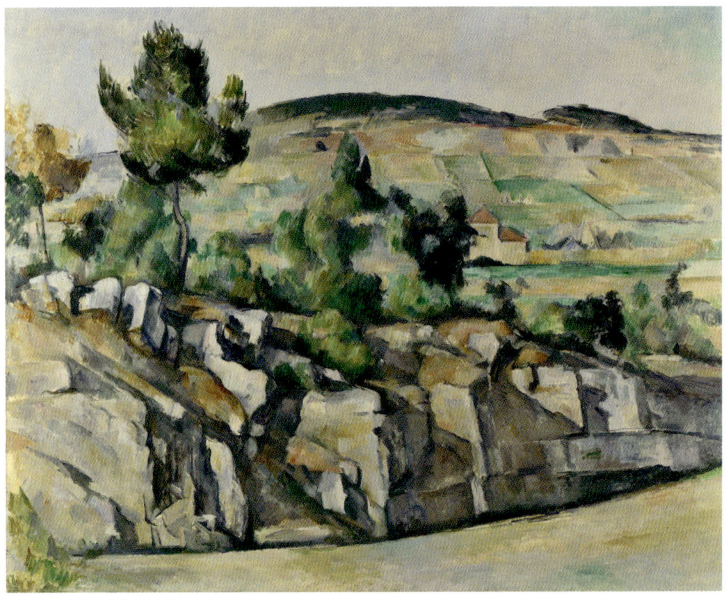

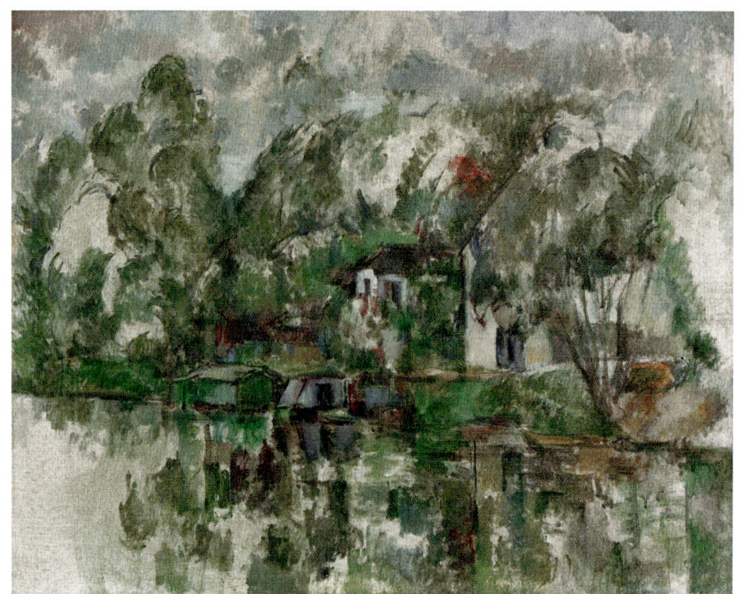

Fig. 109
The Road in Provence
1890–1892
Oil on canvas
65 × 81 cm
The National Gallery, London
R 718

Fig. 110
At the Water's Edge
c. 1890
Oil on canvas
73 × 92.5 cm
National Gallery of Art, Washington, gift of the W. Averell Harriman Foundation in memory of Marie N. Harriman
R 724

Fig. 111
Bibémus
1894–1895
Oil on canvas
71 × 90 cm
Guggenheim, New York
R 794

Fig. 112
The Bibémus Quarry
c. 1895
Oil on canvas
65 × 81 cm
Museum Folkwang, Essen
R 797

most abstract Chantilly style will not be found in the Midi.[10] Quite the opposite, in fact, as there we find representations that are quite realistic (for instance, in other landscapes of the area around Bellevue, R 716 and 717, and in an Aix landscape, *The Road in Provence* (fig. 109), dated between 1890 and 1895), while abstract patches of color are already frequent in the northern works. Thus in *At the Water's Edge* (fig. 110), the strokes are grouped together and rhythmical, and the groups are distinct from each other; in another fluvial painting, *The Reflections in the Water* (R 726), the touch, now even more abstract, does not even draw its inspiration from the form of the foliage; admittedly we are only dealing with a rough sketch, but that only confirms the difference in treatment: The canvas is conceived from the outset in abstract touches.

It is from a painting done in 1894 that the conclusions of this comparison become much clearer and the painter's detached approach more evident. *Giverny* (cat. 66), dated from Cézanne's visit to Monet's house, was the first picture, as far as we know, that he painted using vertical strokes aligned in horizontal groups. While in *The Reflections in the Water* the groups of brushstrokes are counterbalanced to the right and to the left to create a dynamic equilibrium, in *Giverny* they remain almost immobile; making no reference to the texture of the objects, they are replicated across the full breadth of the hill that forms the background and are barely clear in their reference elsewhere in the picture. It is true that the view is *contre-jour*, the light that of a drab November day, and the landscape itself flat; all this suggests a restrained treatment. These flat patches reveal the painter's response to the character of the site, which would not occur to him in Provence at the time, and which would prove useful there only much later.

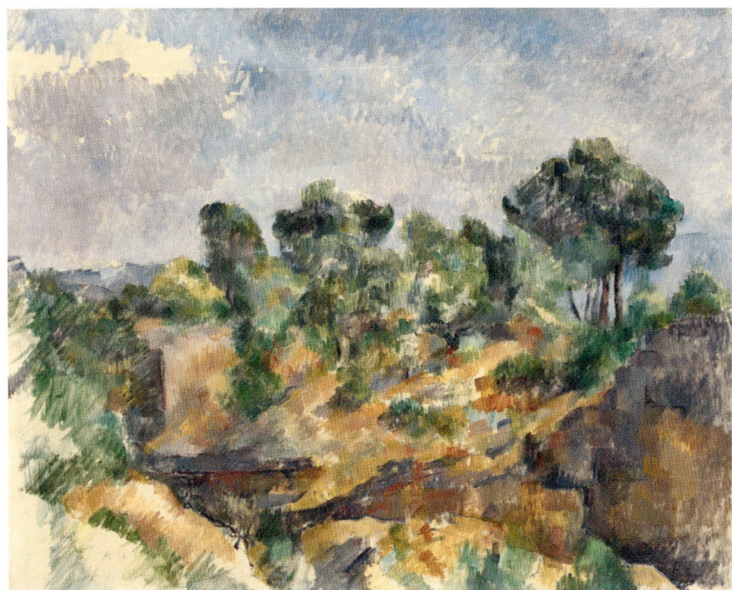

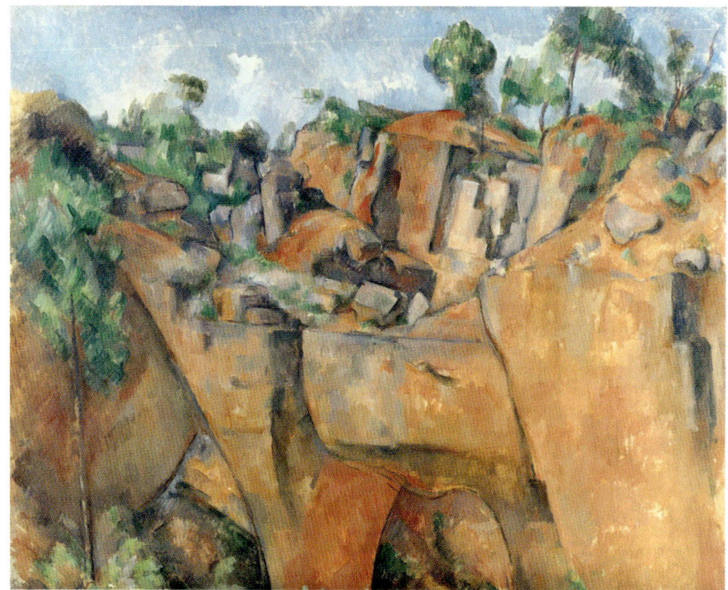

His manner of representing the landscape of Provence during these years—even up to 1898—is best illustrated by the paintings he did in the Bibémus quarry. There, the paintings rarely reach a comparable level of abstraction. In *Bibémus* (fig. 111), for instance, we see groupings of short, parallel strokes, but they are much more faithful to the structure of the landscape than the landscapes from the North: The green patches form easily recognizable bushes, and the red-orange patches that stand out from them are in fact spots of colored earth typical of the region. One could say that it is these contrasts between natural patches of color that interested Cézanne and that explain the considerable density of the picture. If, elsewhere in the quarry, it is not color contrasts that attract him, it may be the strange rock formations: In *The Bibémus Quarry* (fig. 112), he gives a very faithful rendering of the elephantine shape of the rocks (Erle Loran's photo is proof of this[11]), and he supports it by simple, flat brushwork that does not interfere with the grand contours. Admittedly, Cézanne changes the angle of the small rocks on top, making them lean to the right to balance the lower part, but even this adjustment, daring as it is, is painted in a realistic manner. It is as if the location had control over Cézanne, as if the painter were far more deeply attached to it than to the sites in northern France.

I use the words "as if" because we have no indication of what he was feeling or thinking when faced with these specific sites. There can be no question about the difference in the level of abstraction in the landscapes of the North and those of the South; equally incontrovertible is his lesser attachment to the former. But what is more difficult to determine is how the attitude translated into painting. Was it the psychological detachment that favored the analytical approach, or the reverse, that is, his attachment to the South that prevented it? It is well nigh impossible to decide; the crucial matter, as far as the origin of the color patches is concerned, is to locate it in its time and place.

In any case, we cannot separate the response to a specific site from the general attitude toward a region by examining a single painting. The painting *Giverny* could equally well be an example of Cézanne's response to a dull landscape (the site's middle ground is devoid of relief, the month—November—is one with bleak weather, and the tonality of the canvas obviously indicates low light) or an instance of a more general attitude toward the North (its climate, accents, city life). The same dilemma applies to most of the sites in northern France (though not all), which are flatter than those of the Midi, with less saturated colors and less intense light; it goes without saying that in these cases the form of the site itself—in structure and colors—would have influenced Cézanne. Occasionally, however, it is possible to differentiate the two factors; thus patches almost identical to those in *Giverny*—vertical strokes grouped in horizontal blocks—represent a northern site that is vivid in colors and high in relief, and painted in bright sunlight: *The Church of Montigny-sur-Loing* (fig. 113). It is almost as if a "Nordic" way of doing things were prevailing over the structure of the vegetation.

As I said earlier, in about 1898 or 1900 the levels of abstraction in the North and South become nearly equal. Adopting color patches as a governing conception for all landscape, whatever its geographical location, Cézanne finds that the conception has an exceptional capability to organize the elements of his vision.[12] If he is ever faced with the need to adjust his style, his decision will be dictated sometimes by the structure of the site, at other times by his emotional response to it. In *Mount Sainte-*

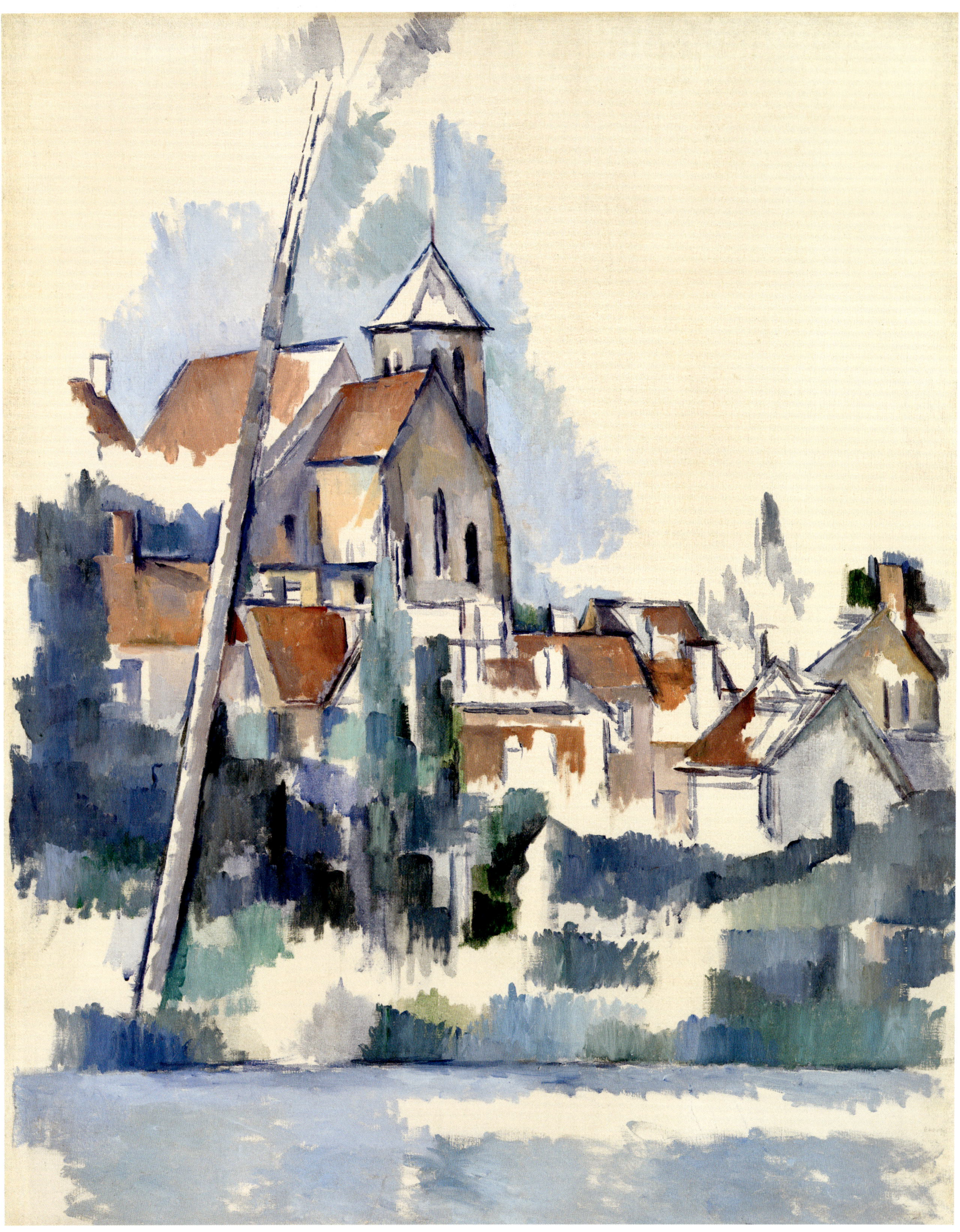

Victoire seen from Bibémus Quarry, painted around 1897 (fig. 114), both factors came into play: Cézanne saw a site with a complex structure—with the diagonals interlaced at the center of the painting and reflected on the mountain's surface, for example—yet also resplendent in the afternoon sun, incandescent in its colors, harmonious in the contrast between the violet-gray of the mountain and the orange ochre of the rocks. A site, then, that was both complex and joyous. Here the subject dominates and Cézanne's brushwork seems best left without abstraction. But in *The Bibémus Quarry* (fig. 115), with its simple, geometric composition, he adopts a more distant attitude: Naturally, he respects the grand forms of the site—we know this from the photos taken by Erle Loran—but all the major movements and all the dynamic thrusts become those of his brushstrokes, which are abstract, staccato, and rhythmical. The site does not force itself on the painter; it yields to the rhythms of Cézanne's brush.

It has been said that the history of painting is a succession of misunderstandings.[13] If Georges Braque and the later Cubists searched for a new style in the late works of Cézanne, they found it only too easily. They did not see its flexibility, for they did not inquire into the various purposes that it served; they did not study the differences in the landscape styles of Bibémus, nor did they compare the styles of landscapes to those of the portraits and still lifes.[14] This is not a reproach, but a simple observation. Their aesthetic ends were not those of Cézanne: Their brush analyzed and dominated the subject in much the same way throughout. While for Cézanne the aim of the stylistic abstractions was to render his visual and emotional experience of landscapes (of those in the North first of all), for the Cubists abstractions were rather a way of defining painting itself.

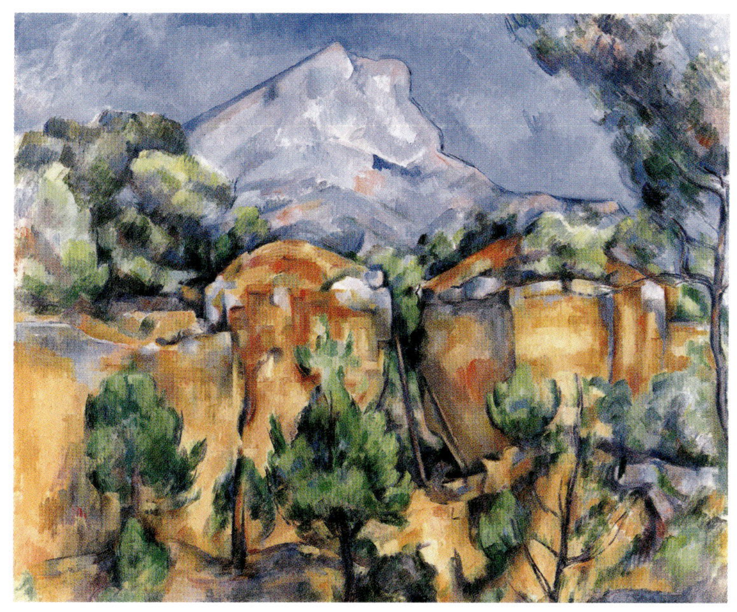

Fig. 114
Mount Sainte-Victoire seen from Bibémus Quarry
c. 1897
Oil on canvas
65 × 81 cm
Baltimore Museum of Art, Baltimore
R 837

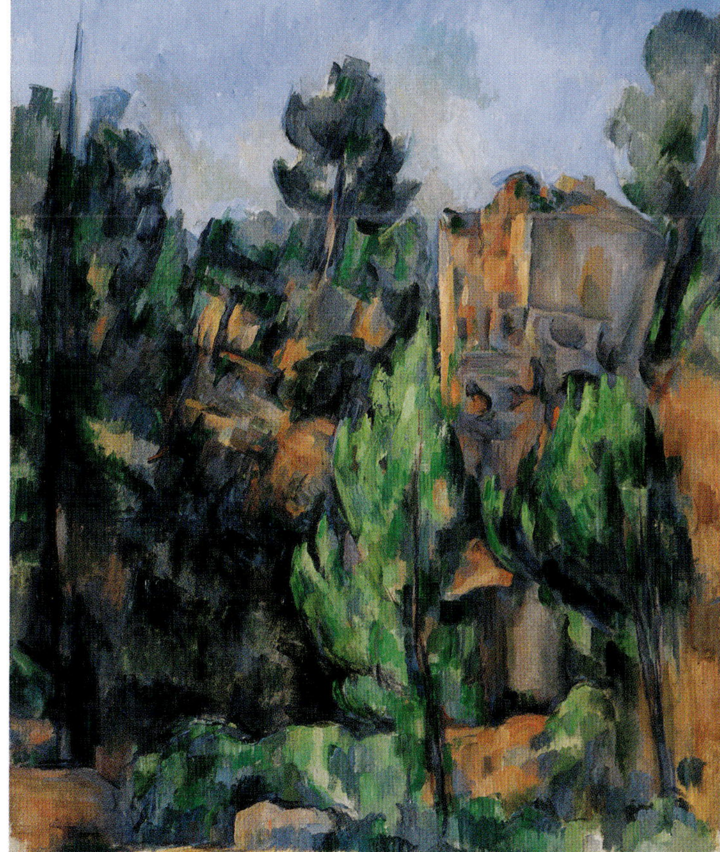

Fig. 115
The Bibémus Quarry
c. 1898
Oil on canvas
65 × 54 cm
Private collection
R 838

Fig. 113
The Church of Montigny-sur-Loing
1898
Oil on canvas
93 × 74 cm
The Barnes Foundation, Merion
R 832

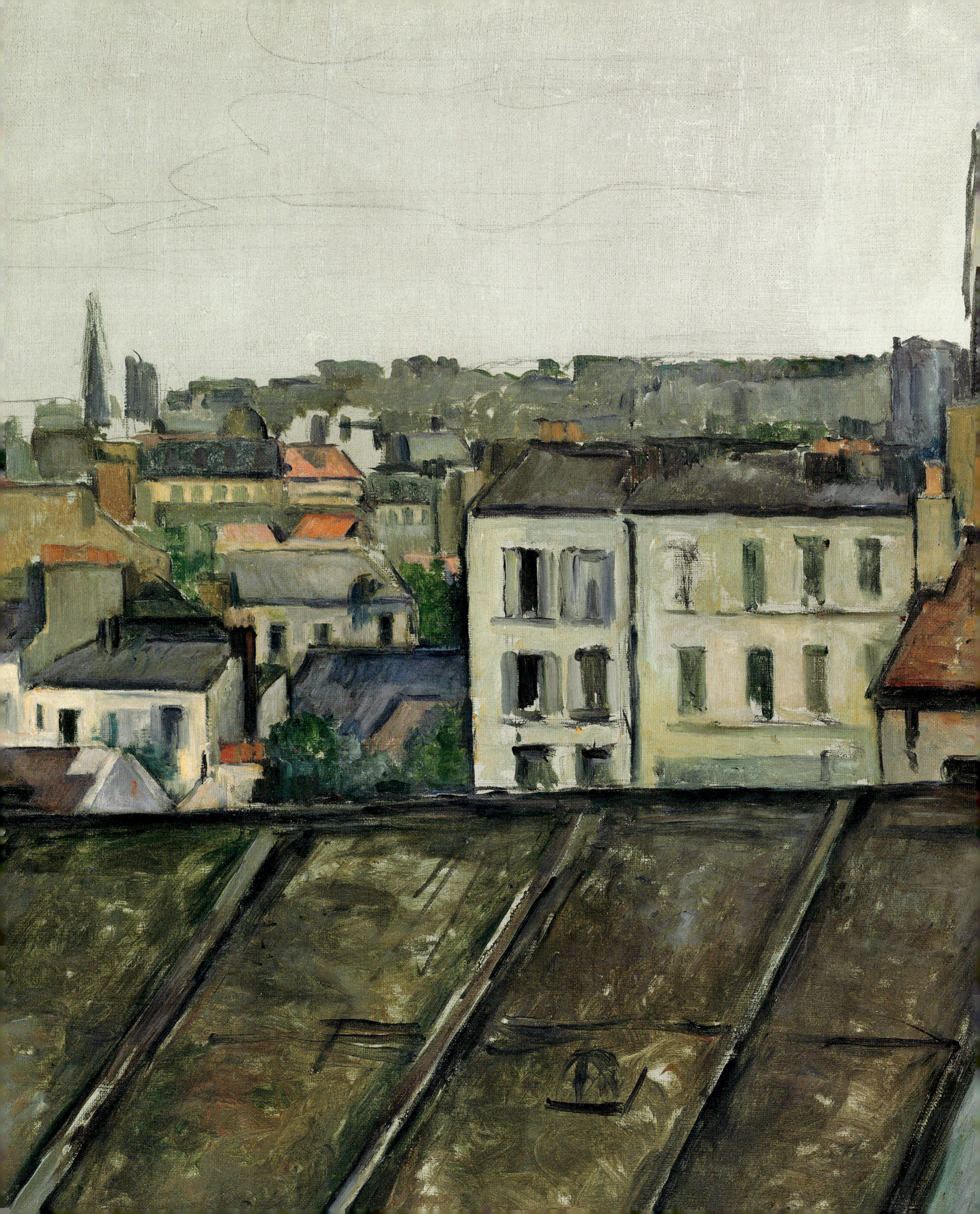

Notes

The Challenge of Paris for Cézanne

pp. 15–21

1. Baille, later to become a student of France's elite École Polytechnique, was one of the trio of friends (Cézanne, Zola, and Baille) from Aix, known as the three inseparables, who had studied together at Aix's Collège Bourbon.

2. Henri Murger, *Scènes de la vie de bohème*, 1850.

3. Letter to Huot, July 1861, in Rewald 1978.

4. Zola to Baille, probably August 1861, in Rewald 1978.

5. Letter to Baille, probably in August 1861, in Rewald 1978.

6. In Cézanne's own words. We owe this information to Thadée Natanson (Natanson 1895, pp 496–500, and exhibition catalog. Paris—London—Philadelphia 1995–1996, p. 35).

7. This should not be seen as entirely accurate. We are also unaware of why he chose to rent particular properties, unless for their proximity to certain places (close to Gare Montparnasse, Île Saint-Louis, and Gare Saint-Lazare).

8. Although the properties he chose were, if not exactly opulent, at least well appointed.

9. John Rewald states that Cézanne bought a house in Marlotte in 1892. There is nothing to support this claim: Marlotte, like Barbizon, would become home to many painters and writers including George Sand, Zola, and Renoir. Cézanne was definitely there in 1899. In his novel *Le Sabot rouge* (1860), Henri Murger describes Marlotte and Mère Antony's inn, but this lodging disappeared just before Cézanne first stayed in the village.

10. It is only in Auvers and Melun that we know Cézanne stayed for definite periods of time; around a year and a half in Auvers (between 1872 and 1874) and almost a year in Melun (between April 1878 and April 1879).

11. This number can only be approximate as it is so difficult to decide whether a particular painting of apples or bathers was painted in the North or in the South. Also, of the precisely 954 paintings listed, it must be remembered that around a hundred were produced in his youth, a proportionally high number, painted at Jas de Bouffan or L'Estaque. Furthermore, there can be no doubt that some paintings that were started in Paris were completed in Provence (for example, one of the versions of the *Large Bathers*).

12. Cézanne to Roger Marx, January 23, 1905, in Rewald 1978.

13. This painting is believed to have been destroyed during the Second World War. Only a black and white photograph survives. A copy was made around 1899 (private collection) giving an idea of the colors of the lost original.

14. Views of Paris, from Van Gogh's room in rue Lepic, spring 1887 (oil on cardboard, 54 x 38 cm, private collection, and oil on canvases, 46 x 38 cm, Amsterdam, Rijksmuseum Vincent Van Gogh).

15. Zola's novel was adapted for the stage by William Busnach and Oscar Gastineau.

16. *Le Charivari*, April 23, 1879.

17. Letter of October 9, 1907, in Rilke 1991, p. 42.

18. Cézanne to Zola, Melun, September 27, 1879, in Rewald 1978.

The Rooftops of Paris
(detail)
See cat. 2 p. 18

Paul Cézanne—the man

pp. 23–31

1. Cézanne family archives.

2. De Beucken 1955, p. 82.

3. Barr 1937, pp. 37–58.

4. Zola 1928, p. 199.

5. Letter to Pissarro dated March 15, 1865, in Rewald 1937.

6. A short story, *La Rivière*, and *Bohèmes en villégiature*, Paris, Plon, Nourrit et Cie, 1889. See Rodolphe Walter, " Cézanne à Bennecourt," *Gazette des beaux arts*, 1962.

7. Letter to Zola dated June 30, 1866, in Rewald 1937, and Rewald 1996, no. 98, p. 96.

8. However, in his portrait of Cézanne, Jean de Beucken (1955, p. 187), who had lengthy discussions with Cézanne's son Paul when preparing his book, suggests that this may be one of the portraits of Uncle Dominique.

9. Letter of November 1895, in Bailly-Herzberg 1980-1991, IV p. 121.

10. Coquiot 1919, p. 61.

11. Rivière 1933, p. 2.

12. Rewald 1937, p. 289.

13. Venturi 1939, I, p. 118.

14. Rose Cézanne was the younger sister of Paul; she married a lawyer, Maxime Conil, in 1881. She purchased the Montbriand property in 1884.

15. Rivière 1933, p. 19.

16. Bernard 1978.

17. *Ibid.*

18. Bourges, *Le Gaulois*, December 5, 1885.

19. Mirbeau, "Rengaines", *L'Écho de Paris*, June 23, 1891.

20. Coquiot 1919, p. 117.

21. Larguier 1925.

22. Borély, in *Vers et Proses*, 1911, XXVII, pp. 109–113.

23. Bernard 1891, and Bernard 1925.

24. Rivière et Schnerb, "L'atelier de Cézanne," *La Grande Revue*, December 25, 1907, pp. 811–817.

25. Bernard 1978, pp. 92–95.

Astonish Paris with an apple

p. 33

1. Comment reported by Gustave Geffroy, in *Claude Monet, his life, times and works*, Paris, 1922, reprinted in Doran 1978, p. 4.

2. Letter from Zola to Baille, July 1860 (in Rewald 1978): "A charming expression found in a letter from Cézanne: 'I am nurturing illusions'."

3. Zola to Cézanne, January 20, 1862, in Rewald 1978.

4. Zola 1866.

Brothers in Art: Cézanne and Zola

pp. 34–43

1. Cézanne to Zola, December 7, 1878, in Rewald 1978, p. 39.

2. Zola to Cézanne, March 25, 1860, in Zola 1978–1995, I (1978), p. 141.

3. *Ibid.*

4. Zola to Jean-Baptistin Baille, April 22, 1861, in Zola 1978–1995, I (1978), p. 284.

5. A portrait of his parents and the *Spanish Guitar Player.*

6. Zola to Jean-Baptistin Baille, Paris, June 10, 1861, in Zola 1978–1995, I (1978), p. 294.

7. "M. Manet," *L'Événement*, May 7, 1866. See Mitterand 1966–1970, XII (1969), pp. 801–806, and Mitterand 2002–2010, II (2002), pp. 636–641.

8. For *Le Grog au vin*, see Venturi 1936, p. 91, and Mack 1938, p. 122. *Ivresse* is now lost. According to Venturi, these two pictures were painted in 1863.

9. To Francis Magnard, *Le Figaro*, c. April 8, 1867, in Zola 1978–1995, I (1978), p. 490.

10. Mitterand 1966–1970, XII, pp. 857–891, and Mitterand 2002–2010, III, pp. 639–670.

11. In Rewald 1978, p. 123

12. Zola to Numa Coste, Paris, July 26, 1866, in Zola 1978–1995, I (1978), p. 453.

13. Zola to Antony Valabrègue, December 10, 1866, in Zola 1978–1995, I (1978), p. 464.

14. Zola to Cézanne, July 4, 1871, in Zola 1978–1995, II (1980), p. 294.

15. An article published by Zola in *Le Corsaire*, December 22, 1872, in which he took the Duc de Broglie (the leader of the conservative coalition) to task, led to the newspaper being withdrawn.

16. Apart from a letter from the end of 1885, recently rediscovered by Philippe Cezanne, the painter's great grandson.

17. Vollard 1937.

18. Cézanne to Zola, July 29, 1878, in Rewald 1978, pp. 169–170. There are 19 letters from Cézanne to Zola for the year 1878.

19. *Ibid.*, February 1880, p. 189. Eight letters to Zola in 1880 and eight in 1881.

20. *Ibid.*, December 19, 1878, p. 177.

21. Literary supplement of *Le Figaro*, April 20, 1879, and *La Revue bleue*, April 25, 1879, reprinted in *Le Roman expérimental*, Paris, Charpentier, 1880.

22. "Le Naturalisme au Salon," *Le Voltaire*, June 18–22, 1880, in Mitterand 1966–1970, XII, p. 1018.

23. Cézanne to Zola, August 5, 1881, in Rewald 1978, p. 203.

24. *Ibid.*, p. 215.

25. *Ibid.*, p. 218.

26. *Ibid.*, p. 221.

27. *Ibid.*, p. 222

28. *Ibid.*, p. 223

29. See above, note 7.

30. In Rewald 1978, p. 225.

31. Even today. See Sollers 2003; Fauconnier 2006; Marcelin Pleynet 2010. "For thirty years now, wrote Zola in 1896, I have 'swallowed my toad' every morning before starting work, on opening the seven or eight newspapers that wait for me on my table.": "The Toad", *Le Figaro*, February 28, 1896 (*Nouvelle campagne*, Paris, Charpentier-Fasquelle, 1897), in Mitterand 1966–1970, XIV (1970).

32. Gasquet 1921.

33. Bernard 1978.

34. Gasquet 1921, p. 110.

35. I am indebted to Alain Pagès for the following information. The first preserved letter from Cézanne to Zola appeared in *Le Gaulois* on June 17, 1894: It was a letter written in his youth, dated June 14, 1858 (Zola had been in Paris for five months), found and sent by the newspaper correspondent at Draguignan, Joseph Gubert. The latter could only have obtained it from Cézanne, who was a friend of his. It is risky to attempt any explanation for this publication, other than to note that Cézanne had no hesitation in showing third parties the proof of his earlier friendship.

Cézanne's early years in Paris

pp. 44–53

1. On the Académie Suisse, see Henry Herbert, "Physionomie d'un atelier libre a Paris," *Revue illustré du cercle des Beaux-Arts Genève,* Oct. 1, 1879, E.R., "Les Arts. L'atelier Suisse," *Paris Midi*, Jan. 2, 1925, and Daniel Wildenstein, *Claude Monet: biographie et catalogue raisonné*, Lausanne, Paris, La Bibliothèque des arts, 1974, vol. 1, pp. 8–9.

2. Elisabeth Maréchaux Laurentin, *Paul Huet, peintre de la nature, 1803–1869,* Paris, Bibliothèque de l'Image, 2009, p. 5.

3. Pierre Andrieu, *Galerie Bruyas,* Paris, 1876, p. 362; cited in Lee Johnson, *The Paintings of Eugène Delacroix,* I, Oxford, Oxford University Press, p. 75.

4. Bruce Laughton, *Honoré Daumier*, New Haven and London, Yale University Press, 1996, p. 6; Charles W. Millard, "La vie d'Auguste Préault" in *Auguste Préault, sculpteur romantique, 1809–1879,* exh. cat., Musée d'Orsay, Paris, 1997, pp. 12–13. Although Camille Corot's earliest biographer, Théophile Silvestre, places the artist there in the 1820s, he does not offer any substantiation and later scholars have questioned his assertion. On this, see Théophile Silvestre, *Histoire des artistes vivants, français et étrangers: Études d'après nature,* Paris, 1853, p.76 and Vincent Pomarède, "The Making of an Artist," *Corot 1821-34*, exh. cat., New York, The Metropolitan Museum of Art, 1996, p. 8 and p. 11, no. 26.

5. Georges Riat, *Les Maîtres de l'art moderne: Gustave Courbet, peintre*, Paris, 1906, p. 29; cited and reproduced in *Gustave Courbet*, exh. cat., The Metropolitan Museum of Art, New York, 2008, p. 353 and cat. no. 169. The drawing is in the collection of the J. Paul Getty Museum.

6.Martin L.H. Reymert *et al.*, *Ingres and Delacroix through Degas and Puvis de Chavannes, The Figure in French Art 1800–1870*, exh. cat., Shepherd Gallery, New York, 1975, p. 336.

7. Rewald 1973, p. 49.

8. Pissarro 2005b, I, p. 108. Joachim Pissarro notes, in *Camille Pissarro*, New York, Harry N. Abrams, 1993, p. 153 (ills.; private collection), that Pissarro's drawing of a nude model of c. 1855 was probably executed at the Académie Suisse. Richard Bretell and Christopher Lloyd note, in *A Catalogue of the Drawings by Camille Pissarro in the Ashmoleon Museum, Oxford*, Oxford, The Clarendon Press, 1980, p. 104, cat. 36 (ills.), that Pissarro's early study of a male nude, now in the collection of the Ashmoleon Museum, could also have been made at the Académie Suisse. I am grateful to Joachim Pissarro and his research assistant, Cate Alsop, for discussing Pissarro's early drawings with me and directing me to this material.

9. In a letter of Feb. 20, 1860 to his former teacher Eugène Boudin, Monet noted that "at the Academy, there are only landscapists. They begin to perceive that it's a good thing." G. Geffroy, *Claude Monet, sa vie, son temps, son oeuvre,* Paris, 1922, vol. 1, ch. IV; cited by Rewald 1973, p. 48.

10. *Francisco Oller, un Realista del Impressionismo*, exh. cat., El Museo de Arte de Ponce, Ponce, PR, 1983, p. 32.

11. Letter to Lucien Pissarro, Osny, December 21, 1884, in Bailly-Herzberg 1980-1991, no. 211; Pissarro 2005b, I, p. 108.

12. Letter to Lucien Pissarro, Paris, December 4, 1895, in Bailly-Herzberg 1980–1991, IV, no. 1181; Pissarro 2005b, I, p. 113.

13. Gowing 1988, p.12

14. Rewald 1973, p.62. Rewald notes that this story was recounted to him by Henri Matisse, who had heard it from Monet.

15. Chappuis 1973, nos. 201–204.

16. Vollard 1914, pl. 4.

17. Solari's plaster was a fragment of an uncompleted allegory, the "War of Independence" (Gasquet 1921, p. 31). In the catalogue of the Salon of 1868, the sculptor's name was misspelled as *Salari* ; cf. Paris, *Salon de 1868*, p. 497, no. 3843; cited in Honour 1989, IV, part 2, p. 209 and p. 275, n. 55.

18. See e.g. Chappuis 1973, no. 57. Bruno Ely (Ely 1984, p. 182–83), has also suggested that a painting in the collection of the Musée Granet in Aix by Joseph de Lestang-Parade, *Le Camoens meurt à l'hopital de Lisbonne*, may have been a source for Cézanne's motif.

19. Émile Zola, "Mon Salon," in Zola 1959, pp. 143–44. Cited in Honour 1989, p. 209 and p. 275, n. 58.

20. Honour 1989, p. 209.

21. Letter to Camille Pissarro, Paris, March 15, 1865, in Rewald 1978.

22. Letter to M. de Nieuwerkerke, Paris, April 19, 1866, in Rewald 1978.

23. Alfred Barr, "Cézanne d'après les lettres de Marion à Morstatt," *Gazette des Beaux-Arts*, January 1937.

24. On this see Tinterow and Loyrette 1994–95, p. 317.

25. Register of student authorizations, LL 10, card no. 2097, Archives du Louvre, Paris; cited by Isabelle Cahn in exh. cat. Paris—London—Philadelphia 1995–96, p. 532. On Cézanne's copies in this period see especially Theodore Reff, "Copyists in the Louvre, 1850–1870", *The Art Bulletin*, 46, no. 4, December 1964, pp. 552–59.

26. Reff, *id.*, p. 555.

27. Register of copyists of the French and Flemish schools, 1851–71, LL22, card no. 3246, Archives du Louvre, Paris; cited by Isabelle Cahn in exh. cat. Paris—London—Philadelphia 1995–96, p. 532.

28. For example, Mary Louise Krumrine has suggested that Cézanne's image may have been shaped in part by a sepulchral scene in Zola's *L'Oeuvre* (1886); see Lawrence Gowing, "Parisian Writers and the Early Work of Paul Cézanne," in Gowing 1988-1989.

29. For a copy of the Titian painting that Rewald accepted as Cézanne's, see Rewald 1996, cat. no. 143.

30. Chappuis 1973, p. 167.

31. Marius Roux, *Mémorial d'Aix*, December 3, 1865.

32. On the Ribera, see Musée National du Louvre, *Catalogue des peintures*, Paris, cat. no. 1722, and my discussion of Ribera's influence in Lewis 1989, pp. 124–129 and p. 248, nos. 28–30. For an excellent recent study of the motif in Ribera's art, see *Ribera, La Piedad,* exh. cat., Madrid, Museo Thyssen-Bornemisza, 2003.

33. Gowing 1988, p. 15.

Bathsheba

pp. 54–57

1. Although she appears not to have known Cézanne's copy, my discussion of the broader Rembrandt phenomenon as it narrowly applies to Cézanne is indebted to McQueen's *The Rise of the Cult of Rembrandt, Reinventing an Old Master in Nineteenth-Century France*, Amsterdam, Amsterdam University Press, 2003. The massive literature on the Raphael/Rembrandt dialectic in 19th century France, cited extensively by McQueen, is discussed pp. 94–106. As noted below, I am also indebted to an number of the essays collected in *Rembrandt's "Bathsheba Reading King David's Letter,"* ed. Ann Jensen Adams, Cambridge, Cambridge University Press, 1998, to Eric Jan Sluijter's *Rembrandt and the Female Nude*, Amsterdam, Amsterdam University Press, 2006, and to Guillaume Faroult et. al, *La Collection La Caze, chefs-d'oeuvre des peintures des XVIIIe et XVIIIe siècles*, exh. cat., Musée du Louvre, Paris, 2007. Finally, I would like to thank the owners of the Cézanne painting, who graciously allowed me and my colleagues to see the painting in their home and also shared with us Rewald's related letter.

2. McQueen, *op. cit.*, p. 47 *et passim.*

3. On this, see McQueen, *op. cit.*, pp. 23–25.

4. In his treatise of 1876 on the Netherlandish schools, for example, the painter Eugène Fromentin struggled to reconcile the unforgiving naturalism of Rembrandt's female figures with the painter's mythic standing, and finally declared that the painter had depicted only deformed women. Eugène Fromentin, *Les Maîtres d'autrefois, Belgique-Hollande*, Paris, Le Livre de Poche, 1965 ed., p. 410; cited by McQueen, *op. cit.,* p. 92.

5. "Rembrandt n'a jamais connu la beauté et l'élégance du nu. Qui voit de lui, par exemple, une Bethzabée ou une Suzanne au bain, ne voit qu'une nudité grossière et informe; cela est incontestable." Paillot de Montabert, *Traité complet de la peinture*, vol. 3, Paris, 1828, p. 188; cited by McQueen, p. 92. For a discussion of the reception of the La Caze Bathsheba, see Gary Schwartz, "'Though Deficient in Beauty': A Documentary History and Interpretation of Rembrandt's 1654 Painting of Bathsheba,"*Rembrandt's "Bathsheba,"* 1998 pp. 177–203. Hix's caricature after Rembrandt's Bathsheba appeared in "La galerie La Caze, au Louvre,"

La Vie Parisienne, April 26, 1870, and is reproduced in McQueen, *op. cit.*, p. 93, fig. 8.

6. The fullest discussion of the narrative and visual traditions surrounding the subject is Eric Van Sluijter's "Rembrandt's Bathsheba and the Conventions of a Seductive Theme," in *Rembrandt's "Bathsheba,"* 1998, pp. 48–99. The author discusses the motif of the letter, pp. 56–59 *et passim*.

7. Sluijter argues convincingly that Rembrandt cut down his original canvas to bring the nude closer to the viewer and to focus on her face and body—in *Rembrandt and the Female Nude*, 2006, pp. 352–54.

8. Sluijter, 2006, *op. cit.*, pp. 356–57.

9. Sluijter's beautiful word picture and description of Rembrandt's efforts within his canvas to "do everything in his power to create the epitome of beauty and to confront the viewer with a sense of intensely tangible corporeality" (2006, *op. cit.*, pp. 352–58) can be neither adequately framed nor summarized in this brief format.

10. The words are Sluijter's (1998, *op. cit.*, p. 85).

11. The literature on Courbet's admiration for the Dutch painter is considerable. To cite two specific examples, Courbet's painting, of which there is an almost identical version in the collection of Oskar Weinhart, Winterthur, Switzerland, has been likened to Rembrandt's *Bathsheba* by Linda Nochlin in "Gustave Courbet's *Toilette de la mariée,"* reprinted in Linda Nochlin, *Courbet,* London, Thames and Hudson, 2007, p.80. Additionally, in his discussion of Courbet's unfinished study of a bather of c. 1866–68 (private collection), Laurence des Cars notes that it "bears the mark of Rembrandt's *Bathsheba*, a picture Courbet loved and had studied." See *Gustave Courbet*, exh. cat., New York, The Metropolitan Museum of Art, 2008, p. 377.

12. As discussed by Cachin in *Manet 1832–1883*, exh. cat., The Metropolitan Museum of Art, New York, 1983, cat. 19, pp. 83–86, Antonin Proust recounted that Manet's composition in its original, larger format, depicted *The Finding of Moses*. Among other sources, Theodore Reff, for example, has suggested that Manet could have also drawn from reproductions of a lost painting by Rubens on the biblical theme of *Susannah and the Elders*. Theodore Reff, "Manet and Blanc's 'Histoire des peintres,'"*Burlington Magazine* CXII, January 1975, p. 457.

13. Rewald 1996, I, cat. 173, p. 138; Venturi 1936, cat. 125 (notes on Cézanne's copy after Delacroix's *The Barque of Dante*).

14. Hollis Clayson, *Paris in Despair, Art and Everyday Life under Siege*, Paris and London, The University of Chicago Press, 2002, pp. 199–207. Of special interest is Clayson's discussion of Courbet's pivotal role in governance of the Louvre and its collection during this period. On the loss of some registers for copyists in this period, see Theodore Reff, "Copyists in the Louvre, 1850–1870", *The Art Bulletin*, vol. 46, no. 4, December 1964, pp. 552–59. See also *la Collection La Caze,* 2007, pp. 163–65.

15. Tamar Garb, "Paul Cézanne's 'The Eternal Feminine' and the Erotics of Vision" in *Bodies of Modernity, Figure and Flesh in Fin-de-Siècle* France, London, Thames and Hudson, 1998, pp. 191, 215.

16. I discussed this at length in Lewis 2000, pp. 151–66.

Cézanne and Delacroix—the story of a failed tribute

pp. 58–61

1. Rivière and Venturi suggest a date around 1870; Lichtenstein, Ratcliffe and Reff opt for around 1890; see Rewald 1996, I, p. 458.

2. Théophile Silvestre, *Eugène Delacroix. Documents nouveaux*, Paris, Michel Lévy, 1864, preface, p. 7.

3. D'Arpentigny, Société nationale des beaux-arts, 26, bd des Italiens, *Exposition des œuvres d'Eugène Delacroix*, Paris [1864], p. 6.

4. Paul de Saint-Victor, "Exposition des œuvres d'Eugène Delacroix," *La Presse*, September 26, 1863.

5. Théophile Gautier, "Exposition du boulevard des Italiens," *Le Moniteur universel*, November 17, 1864.

6. Paul Guigou, "Eugène Delacroix," *La Revue moderniste*, April 4, 1885, p. 2.

7. We know that Cézanne regularly travelled between Provence and Paris, even after moving permanently to Aix in around 1886. For several months a year, he lived in Paris, where he had a studio.

8. Léon Bourgeois, quoted in "Chronique," *L'Artiste*, 1890, p. 307.

9. Albert Wolff, "Courrier de Paris," *Le Figaro*, October 4, 1890.

10. Gasquet 1921, p. 109.

11. *Ibid.*, pp. 86–87. It is said that Cézanne responded to Gasquet's protestations about an "often gray" Provence by saying "Never. Silvery, perhaps ... blue, bluish ... never gray."

12. Gasquet 1921, p. 102. "Nature is simply a dictionary": Cézanne may also have read these lines in Baudelaire's obituary, "L'œuvre et la vie de Delacroix" [The Life and Work of Delacroix], in *Baudelaire. Œuvres complètes*, Paris, Gallimard, "Bibliothèque de La Pléiade," 1951, p. 1121.

13. Gasquet 1921, p. 109

14. A letter of February 27, 1864: "For months I have not touched my [illegible word] after Delacroix. I will go back to it though before leaving for Aix...", in Rewald 1995, p. 111. Andersen (2004, pp. 157–58) also suggests Cézanne's ambivalence toward Delacroix, arising out of Romanticism: "Cézanne's feelings about Delacroix were most likely discomforting. Signs of uneasiness surfaced very early, at the age of twenty-four, two years after he resolved to become a painter."

15. Zola 1874, p. 103.

16. *Ibid*, p. 101.

Paris outside the walls

p. 63

1. Zola to Cézanne, March 3, 1861, in Rewald 1978.

2. Cézanne to Zola, around October 19, 1866, in Rewald 1978.

Armand Guillaumin and Paul Cézanne in Île-de-France

pp. 64–71

1. The only previous essay dedicated to the relationship between Cézanne and Guillaumin is John Rewald, "Cézanne and Guillaumin," (1975), republished in Rewald 1985, pp. 102–119).

2. Although it makes sense that Cézanne knew Guillaumin prior to their friendship at Auvers-sur-Oise, the concrete evidence is slight. An early landscape by Cézanne (R 59, whereabouts unknown) purports to show Guillaumin reclining under a tree, but the figure is far too generalized for the identification to be secure. The painting was in the Gachet collection, but was said to have been painted before their encounter and brought by Cézanne with him to Gachet in Auvers. Another painting, *Head of a Man* (R 113, c. 1866–67, The Jewett Art Center, Wellesley College, Wellesley, Massachusetts) might be a portrait of Guillaumin. However, its authorship by Cézanne has been questioned.

3. Photograph taken near Auvers-sur-Oise, c. 1873 (Musée d'Orsay, Paris).

4. Guillaumin was quite thin at the time. The Guillaumin *Self-Portrait* is presumed to be from c. 1875. In earlier self-portraits dated around 1872 (Gray 1972, pp. 196–97), he has a two pointed beard, the remains of which can be seen in the photograph but which has filled out and become shorter in the etching and the later self-portrait. I believe a drawing representing Guillaumin in a Cézanne sketchbook owned by the Museum Boymans van Beuningen, Rotterdam, dates from c. 1874–75 or later, not 1872, as dated by Rewald (R 295), in which the drawing is reproduced. I suspect the fourth painter in the photograph could be another Cézanne friend, Fortuné Marion, unless it turns out to be Ludovic Piette. In the etching, the figure of a hanged man to the upper left stands in as Cézanne's signature. On the one hand, it alludes to the *House of the Hanged Man* (1872, Musée d'Orsay, Paris), which Cézanne exhibited at the first Impressionist exhibition; on the other, it suggests solidarity with Guillaumin as an artist, like Cézanne himself, condemned to public scorn. Each of the four artists experimenting with etching had chosen a motif as his signature. Guillaumin chose a cat, Pissarro a flower, and Dr. Gachet a duck.

5. "Testament de C. Pissarro, Montfoucault, 3 janvier 1875," in Bailly-Herzberg 1980–1991, no. 39, p. 97.

6. The theme of industrial and other "modern" landscapes in Impressionism is treated at length in Rubin 2008.

7. Guillaumin, *Pissarro's Friend Martinez in Guillaumin's Studio* (private collection). See John Rewald 1996, no. 180, in which the Guillaumin is reproduced. Paintings by Cézanne are henceforth referred to by their "R" number where the owner is unknown.

8. Castagnary 1892, I., p. 102. (On Castagnary, see Rubin 2008 pp. 121–122.) Émile Zola, "Les Actualistes," *L'Événement illustré*, May, 24, 1868, *Mon Salon* (1868), in Mitterand 1966-1970, XIV (1969), p. 871.

9. The painting's style seems later than 1866. Isabelle Cahn, "Chronology," in Paris—London—Philadelphia 1995–1996, p. 536, suggests Cézanne may have returned to Bennecourt in 1869.

10. Examples by Pissarro are *La Petite Fabrique*, 1865, Musée d'Art Moderne de Strasbourg, and *Landscape with Factory*, 1867, The Denver Art Museum, Colorado.

11. A related etching by Guillaumin exists, as well (*Chemin creux aux Hautes-Bruyères*, 1873, Bibliothèque nationale de France, département des Estampes et de la Photographie, Paris).

12. Gray 1972, p. 15.

13. Pissarro 2005a.

14. The Guillaumin is reproduced under Rewald, no. 266, which is where Rewald published the comparison.

15. See Rewald 1985, pp. 110–115, figs. 58–63.

16. Paris—New York—Amsterdam 1999, p. 249.

17. Reff 1962, pp. 214–227.

18. Rewald discusses these three and a fourth copy (after a lithograph of a tiger by Antoine Barye, R 298, in the entry for the *Rococo Vase*, R 265).

19. See Pissarro 2005a, pp. 106–107.

20. The print is reproduced in Rewald 1985, p. 116. Fig. 64. Guillaumin, to the left, has the same hat and a similar slightly forked beard.

21. " ... travailleurs cachés," "travailleurs sérieux," and "jeunes travailleurs" ("Le Jury," *L'Événement*, April 27, 1866, *Mon Salon* (1866), in Mitterand 1966–1970, XIV (1969), pp. 790–792.) "Un beau tableau de cet artiste [Pissarro] est un acte d'honnête homme." (*Ibid.*, p. 868.)

22. As a coda to this paper I note that there is no evidence that Guillaumin simultaneously embarked on a parallel path of stylistic reform to Cézanne's. Yet he would respond somewhat in the early 1880s, when he began echoing Cézanne's approach lightly from time to time. In this he contrasts with Paul Gauguin, with whom Guillaumin became closely associated, and who in many cases imitated Cézanne overtly. A comparison between certain paintings by Guillaumin and works by Van Gogh from the 1880s might suggest, however, that Guillaumin transmitted some of Cézanne's principles to the younger man. I make this point in "Van Gogh and Cézanne: Overlooked Affinities," in *Perspectives on the Collection of the Stedelijk Museum*, Amsterdam, forthcoming Fall, 2011. Van Gogh knew relatively little of Cézanne's actual pictures but was aware of his growing reputation. Although I do not see Van Gogh imitating Cézanne's brushwork, I do suspect that Van Gogh adopted certain of his elder's underlying technical principles of rigor, pattern, and consistency.

Cézanne and Pissarro
The aesthetics of resistance and resistance to any aesthetics

pp. 72–79

1. Pissarro Archives, Ashmolean Museum, Oxford, "Correspondence between Lucien Pissarro and Ludovic Rodo Pissarro".

2. Both artists had to rely on parental assistance to pursue their careers.

3. Guillemet to Oller, September 12, 1866, in *Francisco Oller, un realista del impressionismo*, exh. cat., Puerto Rico, Museo de Arte de Ponce, 1983, p. 227.

4. On this subject, see Lewis 1989.

5. Rewald 1978, pp. 112-113.

6. Marion to Heinrich Morstatt, in Barr 1937.

7. See Barr 1937, p. 45.

8. Barr 1937; Rewald 1978, p. 139.

9. Bazille to his family: see Poulain, *Bazille et ses amis*, Paris, La renaissance du livre, 1932, pp. 78–79, and Rewald 1986c, p. 126.

10. Cézanne to M. de Nieuwerkerke, April 19, 1866, in Rewald 1978, pp. 114–115.

11. A lot has been said about Cézanne's conservative attitudes in the final years of his life. We know that he faithfully attended church. It is suspected, though without any great justification, that he was anti-Dreyfusard. Overall, little note is taken of the fact that Cézanne had become a figurehead among the small, marginal group of the Paris avant-garde which, at the time, was laying the foundations of the Impressionist movement.

12. See Zola 1991, p. 97.

13. Tim Clark, lecture at the Museum of Modern Art, New York, 2006.

Cézanne's engravings

pp. 80–83

1. Delteil 1925–1927, vol. II.

The Temptation of Paris

p. 85

1. Cézanne to Zola, June 20, 1860, in Rewald 1978.

2. Zola to Cézanne, July 1, 1860, in Rewald 1978.

3. Zola to Cézanne, June 25, 1860, in Rewald 1978.

4. *Ibid.*

5. "He began this canvas in 1895, and worked on it until the end of 1905" wrote Vollard in 1914 in his biography on Cézanne, referring to a painting of nudes. Critics think that two of the *Large Bathers* could correspond to R 855 and R 856.

The exposed woman

pp. 86–95

1. Letter to Huot, June 4, 1861, in Rewald 1978.

2. Letter dated January 9, 1903, *ibid.*

3. The pipe smoker would not appear again until included in the subject of card players; this allowed some critics to maintain that the two opposing protagonists in the different versions were Zola and Cézanne.

4. For a highly pertinent analysis of this painting, see Mary Louis Krumrine in *Cézanne. Les années de jeunesse (1859–1872)*, (exh. cat. London—Paris—Washington 1988–1989).

5. While the definitive version of Flaubert's *The Temptation of Saint Anthony* appeared in 1874 (the author had been impressed by a Brueghel painting on this theme as early as 1845), some versions were published back in 1856 in *L'Artiste*; see also Reff 1962b.

6. See article by Mary Louise Krumrine "Les écrivains parisiens et l'œuvre de jeunesse de Cézanne", in exh. cat. London–Paris–Washington 1988-1989, p. 31 *ff.*

7. The theme goes back to Byron's play which is also entitled *Sardanapalus.*

8. Ending a love affair in 1885, Cézanne coarsely declared "The brothel in the town, or elsewhere, but nothing more. I pay, it is a dirty word, but I need peace."

9. This is the title commonly ascribed to this painting, currently dated 1877. Coquiot called it *The Triumph of Woman*, Sterling, *The Apotheosis of Woman*. Rivière described it as *The Golden Calf*. Max Dellis suggested calling it *La Belle Impéri,* as this was Cézanne's illustration for one of Balzac's *Cent Contes drolatiques [A Hundred Drole Stories], La Belle Impéria mariée [The Fair Imperia married]* (see note on the painting *The Eternal Feminine*, in *Arts et Livres de Provence*, quarterly review, No. 81, 1972, pp. 7–10).

10. See Reff 1962a, pp. 214–227.

11. See Colrat 2005.

12. c. 1866–1869, 0.24 x 0.17 cm, CH 85.

13. CH 25, Basel, Kunstmuseum Basel.

14. Cézanne to Zola, November 23, 1858, in Rewald 1937. See Theodore Reff's analysis of this painting in Reff 1963, pp. 28–31.

15. See no. 15 by Henri Loyrette, in exh. cat. Paris–London–Philadelphia 1995-1996.

16. Letter from Matisse to Escholier, Nice, November 16, 1936, in exh. cat. Paris–London–Philadelphia 1995-1996.

Olympia

pp. 96–99

1. Dr Gachet was the first person to own this painting, which was shown at the first Impressionist exhibition in 1874.

When Cézanne read Zola's *Nana*

pp. 100–103

1. Lebenstzejn, "A forgotten Cézanne source" in Lebensztejn 2006. Text published in the *Cahiers du musée national d'Art moderne*, No. 68.

2. Lebensztejn 2006, p. 50. "... on May 24, 1880 the champagne vintner Louis Rameau registered the design of the Champagne Nana brand with the office of the commercial court; according to his own description the design featured 'a fair-haired woman lying on a sofa, holding a champagne flute in her right hand, the foam spilling out of the glass, together with the following designation *Champagne Nana*'" (*ibid.*, pp. 52–53).

3. See *Finished Unfinished* catalog, Zurich, Hatje Cantz Publishers, p. 246-248.

4. Vollard, Archives, photo 418.

Cézanne: Painting Murder

pp. 104–107

1. Paris 2010, p. 326.

2. Simon 1991, pp. 120–35, 185–86.

3. Lebensztejn 1988, pp. 1031–47.

4. Letourneau 1868.

5. Joly 1869, p. 10.

The voices of the thing

p. 109

1. *La Revue blanche*, December 1, 1895.

2. Huysmans, "Paul Cézanne," *La Plume*, September 1, 1891.

The World is an Apple: Cézanne's Parisian Still Lifes and Portraits

pp. 110–119

1. Charles Baudelaire, *Curiosités esthétiques*, Paris, Michel Lévy Frères, 1868, repr. in *Œuvres complètes*, II, Paris, Gallimard, 1976, p. 456.

2. Cezanne's words are recorded Geoffroy 1924, II, p. 68.

3. See Cézanne comments as recorded by Joachim Gasquet in Doran 2005, p. 157. See also on this point Sidlauskas 2009, p. 94 and passim.

4. Rewald 1996, I, 88–89, no. 82 and 92–94, no. 94. Cézanne to Pissarro (March 15, 1865) in Rewald 1978, p. 144.

5. I would refer the reader to Richard Shiff's influential writings on Cézanne's touch and physicality.

6. See Leca 2006, p. 55.

7. Zola 1886, p. 199 *et passim*.

8. Joachim Gasquet and Émile Bernard in Doran 2005, pp. 106–162 and 165 respectively.

9. Rewald 1996, I, p. 115, no. 136.

10. Zola 1991, pp. 90–91.

11. Rainer Maria Rilke to Clara Rilke (October 24, 1907) in Rilke 2002, p. 78.

12. Rewald 1996, I, p. 91, no. 90.

13. Adhémar 1960, pp. 285–297 and no. 127 bis.

14. Cited in Adhémar 1960, p. 285.

15. Reff 1960, pp. 303–04. See also John Rewald's discussion (Rewald 1996, I, p. 218) of Gowing's assertion that Cézanne pinned bolts of decorative wallpaper on the wall to create some of his paintings.

16. Shiff 2001, pp. 44–5.

17. *Ibid.*, p. 44.

18. See Reff 1997, pp. 11–28 and Bois 1998, p. 35.

19. The two paintings dated 1731 are: *Fast-Day Meal* and *Meat-Day Meal*. See Pierre Rosenberg, *Chardin 1699-1779*, Paris, Réunion des Musées Nationaux, 1979, p.163–66, nos. 37 and 38.

20. Joachim Gasquet in Doran 2005, p. 157.

21. Marius Roux, "La Confession de Claude par Émile Zola," *Mémorial d'Aix* (December 3, 1865), cited by Isabelle Cahn in her chronology in Cachin 1996, p. 533.

22. Shiff 2009, p. 448.

23. For the iconographic meaning of the apple see Schapiro 1968, pp. 34–53.

24. As told by Jourdain in Doran 2005, p. 84.

25. Shiff 1994, p. 4.

26. Maurice Merleau-Ponty, "Le doute de Cézanne," in Merleau-Ponty 2004, p. 277.

27. See the citation by Baudelaire at the beginning of the essay; and Cézanne's affirmation as recounted by Joachim Gasquet in Doran 2005, p. 157.

28. Cited by Rewald 1996, I, p. 217.

29. This is recounted by Joachim Gasquet. See Doran 2005, p. 157. For a discussion of the wallpaper, Cézanne's use of it, and the facts of his living conditions see Rewald 1996, I, pp. 217–18.

30. See Yves Alain Bois's stimulating discussion on just these issues of breathing and becoming in Bois 1998, p. 39; and also Merleau-Ponty 2004, pp. 277, 279 *et passim*.

31. See Jacques Lacan on Holbein in *Les quatre concepts fondamentaux de la psychanalyse* (Paris, 1973).

32. Elaine Scarry, "Imagining Flowers : Perceptual Mimesis (Particularly Delphinium)," *Representations*, 57, winter 1997, pp. 90–115.

33. Schapiro 1968, pp. 34–53.

34. Foucault 2009, p. 42.

Realizing Nature through Painting

pp. 120–123

1. Gasquet 1921 (1988, p. 130).

2. Cézanne to Émile Bernard, July 25, 1904, in Rewald 1978.

3. For further details, please see my thesis: Colrat 2005, chap. 4.

The Boy in the Red Vest

pp. 124–125

1. R 659. We probably have Ambroise Vollard to thank for Rewald's discovery of this model's identity, as Vollard makes the following note in his archive relating to painting R 656: "face of child blue tie, red vest, shirt sleeves undone, background tones gray, blue, and brown. Half-length portrait of young Italian boy" (Ambroise Vollard collection, No. 3373, Musée d'Orsay).

2. Gustave Geffroy, Ambroise Vollard and others provide ample evidence of Cézanne's slow work pace that sometimes involved around a hundred sittings in uncomfortable conditions. See notably Vollard 1996, p.14: "And after 150 sittings, Cézanne said to me in a satisfied manner, 'I am not displeased with the shirt' ..."

3. R 618.

4. During the artist's lifetime, and especially among critics close to the Impressionist circle, Cézanne was often seen as an experimenter whose painting was not completely finished. For example, see Thadée Natanson (1895, p. 497): "Yet again he was being criticized for not being *complete*"; and J.-K. Huysmans in response to Pissarro, who had reproached him for not mentioning Cézanne in his study *L'Art moderne* : "In my humble opinion, the

Cézannes typify the Impressionists who didn't make the grade. You know that after so many years of struggle it is no longer a question of more or less manifest or visible intentions, but of works that are real contributions, that are not monsters, odd cases for a Dupuytren museum of painting," quoted in Rewald, 1986a, p. 142.

5. Natanson 1895, pp. 497–500: "A tall boy, an Italian-style model, is slouched in an armchair, leaning against drapes, or in another picture, he completely relaxes his lanky body."

6. Natanson 1895, and Schapiro 1962, p. 92. Meyer Schapiro mentions the model's academic pose, which reminds him of the Italian Renaissance masters. Gustave Geffroy (1892–1903, VI, p. 218) shared this opinion, writing: "... it could bear comparison with the most beautiful figures in painting."

7. Lhote 1950, p. 131.

Paul Cézanne: the large format portraits

pp. 126–131

1. R 94, 50 (116 x 98 cm).

2. R 791, 50 (116 x 89 cm).

3. R 811, 40 (100 x 82 cm).

4. R 789, 40 F (102.5 x 75.5 cm).

5. Sold at the Philippe Rouillac auction, Cheverny, June 5, 2005, no. 58, Paul Cézanne, portrait presumed to be that of Auguste Pellerin.

6. Rewald 1996, I, pp. 16–17 (formats and subjects), and 21–63 (colour illustrations).

7. Rewald 1996, p. 488.

8. Paris—London—Philadelphia 1995–1996, no. 187, p. 444.

9. Letter of May 26, 2005 from Walter Feilchenfeldt to Philippe Rouillac: "Neither I nor anyone else can guarantee to you that the painting is authentic. If I were to publish a new edition of Cézanne's catalog raisonné, I would include your painting, discussing all the points I have just mentioned. I repeat that—in my opinion—I can imagine that this sketch is by the hand of Cézanne. I cannot guarantee it."

Landscapes of the years 1888–1905

pp. 134–147

1. See essay by Jayne Warman, p. 167 in this book.

2. Denys Cochin (1851–1922), a French politician, began to collect Cézanne's paintings in the early 20th century, and had dealings with Vollard. The story told here is recounted by Vollard in *Cézanne* (1914).

3. Cézanne to Geffroy, Alfort, March 26, 1894, in Rewald 1937.

4. The first *guinguette* in Île Fanac in Joinville-le-Pont, Restaurant Jullien, described in Zola's *Au Bonheur des Dames.*

5. See essay by Jean Arrouye, p. 154 in this book.

6. Ferdinand Gueldry (1858–1945).

7. Pissarro lived in rue Hyacinthe (now rue du Capitaine-Charton), opposite Chennevières-sur-Marne. Several of his paintings recall this stay: *Ferry at Varenne-Saint-Hilaire*, 1864; *Landscape at La Varenne-Saint-Hilaire*, 1864; *Banks of the Marne in Winter*, 1866.

8. The Cézanne sites identified in this chapter are all due to the insights of Raymond Hurtu, painter and retired professor of Fine Arts, who readily shared his discoveries and entrusted us with his postcards. His passion for Cézanne is matched only by his discretion. We should also note the other things he was able to identify in Melun. In painting R 495 (*Village Square*) his expert eye recognized Saint-Aspais church, seen from Cézanne's apartment in Place de la Préfecture. In fact a bombing raid in 1944 had destroyed the church spire. Painting R 414 (*Small Town in Île-de-France*) again features the Seine at Melun, seen from Le Mée-sur-Seine.

9. In 1902 Victor Marec, a painter and pupil of Gérôme, composed a painting called *The Burnt Mill of Château Gaillard at Maisons* (30.5 x 46.5 cm, Sceaux, Musée de l'Île-de-France). The framing is practically the same as the one chosen by Cézanne. He too plays with the reflections on the water.

10. Vollard Archives, ph. No. 488.

11. The name of this is a distortion of the original term *brise-train*, a reference to shipments of timber that were floated down the river, crashing into the island.

12. We also think it wise to date these three paintings around 1894, and not 1888 as John Rewald did.

13. "Please give the person who comes to your house the glass and canvas remaining in your studio," Cézanne wrote to Louis Le Bail in 1898 from Marines, a village very close to Montgeroult.

14. See the essay by Jean Colrat, p. 153 in this book.

15. Letter to his son, August 14, 1906, in Rewald 1937.

16. Cézanne to Émile Bernard, October 23, 1905, in Rewald 1937, p. 314.

17. *Ibid.*

18. Often formulated as "faire du Poussin sur nature" (doing Poussin directly from nature), this is one of the phrases commonly attributed to Cézanne. The oldest expression "Viviez Cézanne sur nature" (you should experience Cézanne directly from nature) seems to have been made by Camoin in reply to an investigation begun by Charles Morice in 1901 *(Mercure de France).* It is then found in Émile Bernard in a letter to his mother dated February 5, 1904. It is picked up again by Joachim Gasquet as "Poussin *sur nature*" (see Doran 1978, p. 122).

19. Letter to his son, August 14, 1906, in Rewald 1937.

20. Hölderlin, Elegy *Brot und Wein*, in *Œuvres*, Gallimard, 1967, p. 813.

21. Cézanne to Ambroise Vollard, January 9, 1903, in Rewald 1937.

22. Hölderlin, Elegy *Brot und Wein*, *op. cit.*, p. 815.

23. Letter to his son, September 21, 1906, in Rewald 1937.

Giverny

pp. 148–149

1. Archives of American Art: Zigrosser Papers. The dates of Cézanne's visit to Giverny taken from the Osborn registry, now at Philadelphia, are difficult to read. The actual date was November 1894.

2. See Geffroy 1922, pp. 196–199.

3. Madame Bruno was actually the granddaughter of the founders of the Hotel Baudy in 1887, Angelina and Lucien, who turned the running of it over to their daughter Clarisse in 1896 (the "C" of the Osborn contact), the mother of Madame Bruno.
The Osborn/Philadelphia registry which covers from June 1887 until July 1899 is an important witness to the number of artists who joined the Giverny Colony, the majority of them Americans. It is completely published by William Gerdts: *Monet's Giverny: An Impressionist Colony*, New York, 1993, p. 222–227.

4. This document is still with the family and confirms. See Bourguignon 2007, p. 21.

5. Archives of the National Gallery of Art: John Rewald.

6. Letter to her family, published in Rewald 1986b, pp. 186 and 188.

7. Rewald 1986b, p. 188.

8. *Giverny* (R 778). See Rewald 1996, II, p. 471.

A Forgotten Visitor

pp.150–153

1. Doran 1978.

2. Szineyei-Merse 1998.

3. I have translated this text from partial publications in English and German and would like to express my warm thanks to Katalin Kovacsk, lecturer at the University of Szeged, for checking the Hungarian text and her very considerate help.

4. Document MNG Adattàr 20408 / 1979 /8b. I should like to express my extreme gratitude to Judit Boros, head of the archives at the Hungarian National Gallery for having so generously provided me with this document and its translation, and for her research which made it possible to date it.

5. I should like to thank Madame Roesch-Lalance for confirming this information. See Roesch-Lalance 1986.

6. Vollard 2003, p. 62.

7. An 1896 letter from Coste to Zola (Rewald 1978, p. 236) indicates that Cézanne sometimes had to make brief visits to his wife in Paris. But we know that Cézanne would sometimes invent these absences to escape from his acquaintances in Aix.

8. Skedsmo 1991.

9. Letter to Thorvald Erichsen, August 26, 1899. I owe this translation of Hauge's Norwegian letters to the generous offices of Professor Jean-Marie Maillefer (Paris IV University-Sorbonne). I should like to express my thanks to him for this and for the many related pieces of

information that he has been kind enough to provide.

10. There is further evidence of this sharing of work in a painting by Hauge kept at the Oslo National Museum which shows, near Marlotte, the church of Montigny-sur-Loing and the surrounding houses at night. The viewpoint in this piece painted from the subject is roughly the same as that chosen by Cézanne for the same subject. If the two painters did not actually work together, Hauge must at least have seen Cézanne's painting, which it seems likely was executed during this summer of 1899. Hauge died in Madrid in 1901 and all trace of the works by Cézanne that he received appears to be lost.

11. This division is more likely to have been associated with the inheritance left by Cézanne's father, who died in 1886. Paul Alexis mentions the three-way division in a letter to Zola dated February 1891.

12. Gasquet 1988, p. 75.

13. Vollard 2003, p. 79.

14. Lemoine 2002.

15. Letter to Gasquet, September 26, 1897, in Rewald 1978.

16. "Many years before the period of which we speak, Camille Pissarro presented himself one day at the home of Halanzier, director of the Opéra. After three hours of waiting he was finally received and tried to persuade the astounded civil servant (who, moreover, was in no way involved in questions of this order) to commission Paul Cézanne to execute the pictorial decoration of the building that Garnier was completing": *Cézanne* 1914, p. 14.

Water, the mirror of painting

pp. 154–161

1. Maurice Denis, "Définition du néo-traditionalisme", *Art et critique*, August 30, 1880.

2. Conversations XXXVIII with Cézanne, as told by Léo Larguier (Larguier 1925).

3. *Ibid.*, Conversations XXXIII.

Cezanne's fame

p. 163

1. Cézanne to Émile Bernard, December 23, 1904, in Rewald 1978.

2. Hence the Caillebotte bequest, numbering around sixty Impressionist paintings, was presented with two Cézannes in 1897 for the Musée du Luxembourg as part of a national collection.

3. Letter dated October 23, 1907, in Rilke 1991, p. 74. Original title: Briefe über Cézanne, Frankfurt am Main, Insel Verlag, 1952.

Cézanne, painter of painters

pp. 164–173

1. "Vollard Speaks," *The Art Digest* (November 1936), p. 7.

2. By contrast, Cézanne, who was so often critical of his contemporaries, acquired only one work, a floral watercolor by the one artist for which he had a lifelong obsession—Eugène Delacroix—and that work was a gift from Vollard (Eugène Delacroix, *Bouquet of Flowers*, c. 1849, Paris, Musée du Louvre). On Delacroix and Cézanne, see N. Kallmyer's essay in this volume.

3. For example, *Cézanne and Pissarro*, New York—Los Angeles—Paris 2005–06, *Cézanne a Firenze*, Florence 2007, *Cézanne and Giacometti*, Copenhagen 2008, *Homage to Cézanne*, Yokohama—Sapporo 2008–09, *Cézanne and American Modernism*, Montclair—Baltimore—Phoenix (2009–10), *Cézanne and Beyond*, Philadelphia 2009, *Picasso/Cézanne*, Aix-en-Provence 2009.

4. Gustave Geffroy, "Paul Cézanne," *Le Journal*, March 25, 1894. Reprinted in Geffroy 1892-1903, III (1894), p. 249.

5. *Ibid.*

6. Geffroy, *ibid.*, pp. 249–60.

7. Thadée Natanson, "Exposition Théodore Duret," *La Revue Blanche*, April 1894.

8. Natanson, "Paul Cézanne," *La Revue blanche*, Dec. 1, 1895, p. 500.

9. Camille Pissarro to his son, Lucien, Paris, Nov. 21, 1895 in Bailly-Herzberg 1980–1991, IV, p. 119.

10. *Ibid.*

11. Egisto Fabbri to Paul Cézanne, Paris, May 28, 1899, in Rewald 1978, p. 269.

12. Émile Bernard, "Paul Cézanne," *L'Occident*, July 1904, p. 30.

13. Maurice Denis to Paul Cézanne, Paris, June 13, 1901, in Rewald 1978, pp. 275–76.

14. Matisse to Raymond Escholier, Nice, Nov. 10, 1936, in Dominique Fourcade (dir.), *Henri Matisse, écrits et propos sur l'art*, Paris, Hermann, 1972, p. 134.

15. Stein 1947, p. 174.

16. Max Weber, "Rousseau and the Cézanne Memorial Exhibition, 1907," untitled transcript; cited in Bratis 2009, "Chronologie," p. 24.

17. Weber cited in *The Reminiscences of Max Weber*, interviews with Carol S. Gruber, 1958, Oral History Research Office, New York, Columbia University, p. 67.

18. Weber, cited in Brenda Wineapple, *Sister Brother: Gertrude and Leo Stein*, Lincoln, Nebraska, 2008, p. 243.

19. Dasburg, quoted in Van Deren Coke, *Andrew Dasburg*, Albuquerque, 1979, p. 16.

20. Picasso, quoted in Brassaï, *Conversations avec Picasso*, Paris, Gallimard, 1964, p. 113.

21. In the late 19th century, critics identified Cézanne as the painter of apples, but his bather compositions and single figure nudes seemed to have exerted a special significance on his artist contemporaries and 20th century followers. Caillebotte, Pissarro, Renoir, Degas, Boch, Fabbri, Monet, Signac, Roussel, Denis, Bonnard, Matisse, Picasso, Jacques Lipschitz, Moore, and Johns each possessed one or more of these works. On this subject, see Christian Geelhaar in *The Bathers*, [exhib. cat.], Basel, 1989, pp. 275–303.

22. Matisse to Ramond Escholier, Nice, November 10, 1936, in Fourcade, *op. cit.*, p. 134.

23. Georges Braque, in André Verdet, "Avec Georges Braque," *XX siècle*, Feb. 1962, supplement.

24. Pablo Picasso, transcription by Christian Zervos of an interview of Picasso, *Cahiers d'Art*, X, 1935, in M.-L. Bernadac and A. Michael (ed.), *Picasso. Propos sur l'art*, Paris, Gallimard, 1998, pp. 35–36.

Salons, dealers, and collectors

pp. 174–179

1. Letter from Zola to Duret, May 30, 1870, Zola 1978–1995, II, p. 219.

2. Gustave Geffroy, article published in *La Vie Artistique*, 1900.

3. Vollard 1938, p. 61.

4. In reality, the word "refusal" is inadequate in respect of the Cézannes. Martial Caillebotte and Renoir chose not to submit them for examination by the administration. Perhaps they practiced self-censorship in order to avoid risking the rejection of the entire bequest. See Berhaut and Vaisse 1983, Vaisse 1995, and Distel 1994.

5. *Ibid.*

6. Fabbri to Cézanne, May 28, 1899, in Rewald 1978.

7. Vollard 1938, p. 97.

8. Letter of June 1, 1899, in Bailly-Herzberg 1980–1991, vol. V (1991), no. 1639, p. 28.

9. Letter of March 17, 1902 in Rewald 1978.

10. Letter of November 11, 1904, quoted in Cahn 1995, p. 564.

11. Letter to Ambroise Vollard, January 9, 1903, in Rewald 1978.

12. Letter to Roger Marx, January 21, 1905, in Rewald 1978.

Cézanne's attitude to criticism

pp. 180–183

1. Cézanne to Louis Aurenche, January 25, 1904, in Rewald 1978, p. 298.

2. In 1881, the state handed over the organization of the Salon to the Société des Artistes Français.

3. The jury refused his works in 1866, 1867, 1868, 1869, 1870, 1872, 1876, 1878, 1879, 1880, 1881.

4. London—Paris—Washington 1988–1989.

5. "I have also been told about two rejected paintings submitted by M. Sésame *[sic]* (nothing to do with the *Arabian Nights*), the same person who caused general hilarity at the Salon des Refusés in 1863—again!—with a canvas representing two pig's trotters arranged in a cross. This time, M. Sésame *[sic]* has sent two compositions to the Exhibition, which, even if not equally bizarre, were at least equally worthy of

exclusion from the Salon. These compositions are entitled *The Wine Grog;* one represents a naked man being served with a wine grog by a woman in formal dress, the other a naked woman and a man dressed as a Neapolitan beggar. Here the grog has been spilt": Alexandre Mortier in the French-language Frankfurt daily *L'Europe politique, scientifique, commerciale, industrielle et littéraire*, quoted by F. Magnard in *Le Figaro*, April 8, 1867.

6. Fortuné Marion to Heinrich Morstatt, April 27, 1868, quoted in Barr 1937, no. 30, p. 48.

7. "*The Salon* by Stock", *Album Stock*, March 20, 1870.

8. Cézanne, in Rewald 1978 p. 135, note 3.

9. "Of all known juries, none has ever, even in their dreams, envisaged the possibility of accepting any painting submitted to the Salon by this artist, who carried his own canvases on his back like Christ carrying his cross. Until now, too strong a predilection for yellow has compromised Cézanne's future. However, the jury was wrong, as is the nature of juries": Prouvaire 1874.

10. "... if there are subjects that that can put up with an impressionistic state or be happy to exist as rough sketches , there are others, and many more of them, that require clarity of expression ... As for the others who, failing to reflect and to learn, might have considered taking impressionism to extremes, the example of M. Cézanne *(A modern Olympia)* may show them the fate that now awaits them." Castagnary 1874.

11. Cardon 1874.

12. Montifaud 1874, p. 310.

13. "Among the follies that have struck me, I would draw particular attention to a remarkable landscape by M. Cézanne, a compatriot of ours from Aix, which shows great originality. M. Paul Cézanne, who has been struggling for a long time, has the character of a truly great painter". Zola 1874a.

14. Cézanne to his mother, September 26, 1874, in Rewald 1978, p. 148.

15. Cézanne exhibited sixteen paintings, including three watercolors.

16. "Exposition des Impressionnistes," *La Petite République française*, April 10, 1877.

17. "I would also like to mention the head of a man who looks like a Billoir [the name of a murderer of that time] made of chocolate." Vassy 1877.

18. "This strange-looking head, the color of the cuff of a top boot, might make such a vivid impression and give her offspring yellow fever even before it is born into the world". Leroy 1877.

19. "... they look to me like school dunces who have never done well in class, are useless at spelling, grammar, history, geometry, drawing, or anything else, and enjoy relentlessly teasing the swots, the grinds, and the hardworking". Bertall 1877.

20. Ballu 1874, p. 147, repeated in *Beaux-Arts illustrés*, April 23, 1877, p. 392.

21. Georges Rivière, an adherent of the Impressionist cause and editor of the short-lived journal *L'Impressionniste*, described Cézanne as the "Greek of the belle époque", saying that "his canvases have the calm and the heroic of the paintings and terra cotta pots of antiquity, and the ignorant people who laugh at the *Bathers*, for example, remind me of the barbarians criticizing the Parthenon." Rivière 1877, pp. 1–3. Zola declared that Cézanne was "the greatest colorist of the group", but added more ambiguously: "the strong, realist canvases of this painter may also shock the bourgeois, but all the same they suggest that he has the elements of a very great artist. One day when M. Cézanne is in full control of himself, he will produce works of the very highest quality." Zola 1877.

22. Bernard 1891.

23. "M. Paul Cézanne, a naturally great painter still struggling to find his technique, is closer to Courbet and Delacroix." Zola 1880.

24. Count Doria lent *The House of the Hanged Man* to the centennial exhibition of French art at the 1889 Exposition Universelle, and it occasioned no comment in the press.

25. Lecomte 1899, pp. 81–87.

26. "The exhibition of these masterpieces, or these monstrosities, if you prefer, aroused the deepest emotion among all the enlightened and eclectic art lovers who ... wandered past the gallery windows of the Rue Laffitte every day." Vollard 1914, p. 78.

27. Natanson 1895, pp. 496–500.

28. Mellerio 1896, pp. 13–14.

29. Geffroy 1894, reprinted in *La Vie parisienne* on November 16, 1895 on the occasion of the exhibition at Vollard's.

30. The state accepted two paintings by Cézanne, *Farmyard in Auvers* (R 389) and *The Gulf of Marseilles seen from l'Estaque* (R 390), for the Musée du Luxembourg—museum of living artists—after having refused three.

31. Geffroy 1895, reprinted in *La Vie artistique*, 6th series, Paris, 1900 p. 214.

32. Lecomte 1899, pp. 85–86.

And Paris came to Cézanne

pp. 184–185

1. Uncovered in 1973 by Adrien Chappuis (Chappuis 1973, I, pp. 49–52).

2. In a symbolic gesture, Cézanne refused to exhibit with his Impressionist friends in 1879, 1880, and 1881, preferring to save himself for the Salon, where he was rejected.

3. Cézanne to O. Maus, November 27 and December 21, 1889, in Rewald 1978, pp. 229, 230–231.

4. Bernard 1925, p. 6.

5. Bernard 1926, I, p. 128.

6. Francis Jourdain, "À propos d'un peintre difficile: Cézanne", *Arts de France*, No. 5, 1946, p. 7.

7. Mellerio 1896b, p. 26.

8. Cézanne to Henri Gasquet, Paris, December 23, 1898, in Rewald 1978, pp. 266–267.

9. Cézanne to his son, October 15, 1906, in Rewald 1978, p. 332.

10. Fragment of a letter to an unknown artist, undated, in Rewald 1978, p. 256.

11. Bernard, *Mercure de France*, December 16, 1908, p. 607, quoted in Vollard 1937, p. 35, and Vollard 1938, p. 49.

12. Vollard 1938, p. 49.

From the landscapes of northern France to the beginnings of Cubism

pp. 186–197

1. The author is very grateful to Joëlle Naïm for her assistance in preparing this article.

2. For example, Rubin compares Braque's painting *Terrace of the Hotel Mistral* with *The Cistern in the Park at Château Noir* by Cézanne. See "Cézannisme and the beginnings of Cubism", in Rubin 1977.

3. Martindale 1990.

4. Gombrich 1972, pp. 195–96.

5. Simonton 1997.

6. *Joachim Gasquet's Cézanne* 1991, p. 121.

7. See the photo of the site in Machotka 1996, p. 130.

8. Gowing 1992.

9. Letter to Victor Chocquet, May 11, 1886, in Rewald 1978, pp. 226–27.

10. *The Large Pine Tree and Red Earth*, R 761, dated approximately between 1890 and 1895, could be an exception if the first of these dates were probable, but it is not definite.

11. Loran 1985, p. 70.

12. Even in some of his late portraits, for instance *Vallier the Gardener* (R 950, R 953) and *The Seated Man* (R 952). However these are studies of complex relationships between a figure and its landscape, rather than recognizable portraits.

13. Gowing 1992, p. 7.

14. Many analyses of these styles are found in Machotka, 2008.

Works of Cézanne having belonged to artists

List compiled by Jayne S. Warman

Following is a list of paintings and watercolors by Cézanne owned by artists.
The provenance, date of acquisition and price is included if known.

Eugène Boch (1855–1941)
Portrait of the painter Achille Emperaire, 1867–68 (R139)
Provenance: Tanguy (late Dec. 1891, Fr 800)
See fig. 92

Madame Cézanne Leaning on her Elbow, 1873–74 (R217)
See fig. 6

Bather, Seen from Behind, 1877–78 (R368)
Provenance: possibly from Vollard (Feb. 1897)

Pierre Bonnard (1867–1947)
Bather with Arms Outstretched, c. 1876 (R252)
Provenance: Vollard (stockbook no. 3809A) possibly in an exchange after April 1899

Georges Braque (1882–1963)
Bouquet of Peonies in a Green Pot, c. 1898 (R875)
Provenance: Vollard (stockbook no. 7158C) (after 1918)

An unidentified watercolor

Gustave Caillebotte (1848–1894)
Couples Resting by a Pond, 1876–77 (R244)

Bathers at Rest, III, 1876–77 (R261)
See fig. 84

The Rococo Vase, 1875–77 (R265)

The Farmyard, c. 1879 (R389)

The Gulf of Marseille seen from L'Estaque, 1878–79 (R390)
See fig. 93

Caillebotte acquired his five Cézannes between 1877 and November 1883, although it is not known when exactly they entered his collection. He probably bought two works from Tanguy (R244, R389) and two canvases directly from Cézanne (R265, R390), as the latter two are signed. The large bather composition (R261) was bought from Ernest Cabaner's estate in 1881 for 300 francs. Only two of the five Cézannes in the original Caillebotte bequest of 1894 were admitted to the Musée du Luxembourg (R389, R390); the rest were withdrawn.

Mary Cassatt (1844-1926)
Apples and Linen, 1879–80 (R339)
Provenance: Vollard (April 16, 1896, Fr 200); Cassatt to Vollard (stockbook no. 3576B) (Nov. 19, 1904, Fr 500)

Fruit Dish, Apples, and Loaf of Bread, 1879–80 (R420)
Provenance: Vollard (April 28, 1896, Fr 100); Cassatt to Vollard (Nov. 16, 1906, Fr 8000).
See fig. 87

Arthur B. Davies (1863-1928)
Study, c. 1890, watercolor (RWC361)

Study of Trees, c. 1890, watercolor (RWC397a)

Pine Trees, 1890–95, watercolor (RWC399)

The Well in the Park of Château Noir, 1895-98, watercolor (RWC428)

Drawings and lithographs

The American artist collected at least seven drawings and watercolors of landscapes and nudes.

Edgar Degas (1834–1917)
Portrait of Victor Chocquet (bust), c. 1877 (R297)
Provenance: Vollard (May 6, 1896, Fr 150)
See fig. 5

Apples, c. 1878 (R346)
Provenance: Vollard (Nov. 29, 1895, Fr 200)

Bather with Arms Outstretched, 1877–78 (R369)
Provenance: Vollard (Nov. 20, 1895, Fr 200)
See fig. 86

Venus and Cupid, c. 1878 (R374)
Provenance: Vollard (June 25, 1897, Fr 150)

Portrait of the Artist, 1879–80 (R416)
Provenance: Vollard, Fr 150

Glass and Apples, 1879–80 (R424)
Provenance: Vollard (Jan. 6, 1896, Fr 400)
See fig. 85

Two Fruits, c. 1885 (R557)
Provenance: Vollard (March 19, 1896. Fr 200)

Three Pears, 1888–90, watercolor (RWC298)
Provenance: Vollard (Nov. 29, 1895, Fr 100)

See Richard Kendell, "Degas and Cézanne: Savagery and Refinement," in *The Private Collection of Edgar Degas*, exh. cat., New York, 1997, p. 196–219.

Maurice Denis (1870–1943)
Still Life, 1888–90 (R642)
See cat. 46

Bathers, 1899–1900 (R862)
Provenance: probably from Vollard

André Derain (1880–1954)
The Tour de César, c. 1862 (R24)
Provenance: possibly from Cézanne *fils*

Egisto Fabbri (1866–1933)
The Studio Stove, 1865 (R90)
See fig. 51

Satyrs and Nymphs, c. 1867 (R124)

Luncheon on the Grass, 1876–77 (R287)
See cat. 37

Madame Cézanne in a Red Armchair, c. 1877 (R324)
See cat. 75

Portrait of Louis Guillaume, 1879–80 (R421)

Milk Can and Apples, 1879–80 (R426)
See cat. 71

The Valhermeil District near Pontoise, 1881 (R489)

Banks of the Marne, II, 1888–90 (R624)

Boy in a Red Vest, 1888–90 (R659)
See fig. 59

Seated Man, 1898–1900 (R789)
See fig. 62

Portrait of the Artist in a Beret, 1898–1900 (R834)

Fabbri was not only a major collector of Cézanne's paintings (and one of the earliest), but a painter as well. In all, he accumulated at least 34 canvases in his lifetime, many of which were bought or traded at Vollard's. In addition to the paintings listed above, Fabbri owned R62, 64, 314, 341, 345, 394, 410, 423, 425, 429, 438, 448, 449, 458, 496, 501, 506, 551, 554, 569, 571(?), 715, 717, and 724 (fig. 110). On Fabbri's collection, see *Cézanne and Florence*, exh. cat., Milan, 2007.

Othon Friesz (1879–1949)
Road in the Forest, c. 1890, watercolor (RWC 266)

Lucian Freud (1922–2011)
Afternoon in Naples (with a White servant), 1876–77 (R290)

Paul Gauguin (1848–1903)
Female Nude, before 1870 (R140)
Provenance: Tanguy (by 1884); with Gauguin until 1891; to Tanguy; now lost
The Harvest, c. 1877 (R301)

Provenance: probably from Tanguy (before 1884); he copied the motif on a fan and a ceramic

Mountains in Provence (near L'Estaque), c. 1879 (R391)
Provenance: Tanguy (Summer 1883 with R409, Fr. 120 the pair); he has it relined

The Path, c. 1879 (R409)
Provenance: Tanguy (Summer 1883 with R391, Fr. 120 the pair); he has it relined

Still Life with Fruit Dish, 1879–80 (R418)
Provenance: Tanguy or Cézanne (by 1884); sold by Chaudet to Vollard (May 23, 1896)
See fig. 94

The Château of Médan, c. 1880 (R437)
Provenance: Tanguy or Cézanne (by 1884)
See fig. 82

It is possible that Gauguin acquired two paintings directly from the artist (R418, R437), as they are both signed. Gauguin claimed to have had 12 Cézannes in a January 1900 letter to Vollard (Malingue, CLXXIII).

Armand Guillaumin (1841–1927)
The Rue des Saules in Montmartre, 1867–68 (R131)
Provenance: Gift from the artist
See cat. 27

Portrait of Madame Cézanne, c. 1872 (R180)

Paul-César Helleu (1859–1927)
Turn in the Road, c. 1881 (R490)
Provenance: Tanguy to Théodore Duret; Duret sale, March 19, 1894; Helleu to Vollard

Still Life with Apples and a Pot of Primroses, c. 1890 (R680)
Provenance: Tanguy; Helleu gift to Monet (March 1894)
See fig. 83

Jasper Johns (1930–)
Female Nude lying down, 1875–77 (R242)

Bather with Arms Outstretched, 1877–78 (R369)
See fig. 86
About a dozen small watercolors and drawings

Johns owns more works by Cézanne than any other artist in his collection.

André Lhote (1885–1962)
Study of a Tree, 1885–90, watercolor (RWC267)

Mercury, after Pigalle, drawing (Ch. 973)

Max Liebermann (1847–1935)
The Fishermen (Fantastic Scene), c. 1875 (R237)
Provenance: P. Cassirer (stockbook no. 1071) (Jan. 26, 1909, DM 13,200)

Meadow and Farm of the Jas de Bouffan, c. 1885 (R523)
Provenance: P. Cassirer (stockbook no. 20168) (March 22, 1916, DM 36,000)

Liebermann was an early admirer of the French Impressionists and assembled one of Berlin's most important collections of these artists.

Jacques Lipschitz (1891–1973)
Bathers, c. 1900 (R863)

Maximilien Luce (1858–1941)
Two Women with a White Dog, c. 1872 (R236)

Henri Matisse (1869–1954)
Three Female Bathers, 1876–77 (R360)
Provenance: Vollard (stockbook no. 4121A, Dec. 7. 1899, Fr 1200)
See cat. 47

Portrait of Madame Cézanne, 1886–87 (R576)
Matisse to Rosenberg (by 1922)
See fig. 89

Portrait of Madame Cézanne, 1888–90 (R581)
Provenance: Paul Rosenberg (Nov. 1916)

Fruit and Leaves, c. 1890 (R647)
Provenance: Bernheim-Jeune (April 25, 1911)

Rocks near the Caves above Château Noir, c. 1904 (R909)
Provenance: Galerie Barbazanges (Jan 5, 1917?)

The Pool of the Jas de Bouffan, 1888–92, watercolor (RWC256)
Trees and Rocks, c. 1890, watercolor (RWC316)

Forest, c. 1890 (RWC323); verso, *Trees and Shrubs*, 1890–95, watercolor (RWC416)

Tree, c. 1860 (RWC334); verso, *Trees and Rocks*, c. 1895, watercolor (RWC415)

House and Trees, c. 1890, watercolor (RWC340)

Provençal Landscape, 1900–04, watercolor (RWC541)
Provenance: Vollard (Dec. 15, 1908, Fr 2,000, the six watercolors)

Maxime Maufra (1861–1918)
Five Apples, 1877–78 (R334)
See fig. 88

Two unidentified paintings

Maufra bought three painted studies by Cézanne from Vollard on April 29, 1896, including *Five Apples*. He sold the still life to Galerie Bernheim-Jeune in November 1907. A month later it entered the collection of the American expatriates Leo and Gertrude Stein.

Claude Monet (1840–1926)
Portrait of a Man (Uncle Dominique?), c. 1866 (R110)

The Negro Scipio, c. 1867 (R120)
Provenance: Vollard (one of three paintings purchased from the 1895 exhibition, Fr 400)
See cat. 16

Picnic by the River, 1873–74 (R245)
Provenance: père Martin (1870s in an exchange)

The Beach, 1877–78 (R382)
Provenance: Tanguy; Tanguy sale, June 2, 1894; Vollard; Bauchy; Vollard(?) to Monet (? Dec. 1898, Fr 2,000)

Melting Snow, 1879–80 (R413)
Provenance: Victor Chocquet to Count Armand Doria (c. 1889); Doria sale (May 4–5, 1899, Fr 6,750) to Monet

L'Estaque, 1879–83 (R443)
Provenance: Vollard (March 1896, Fr 600)

Bend in the Road, c. 1881 (R490)
Provenance: Vollard (May 7, 1907, Fr 5500)

Boy in a Red Vest, 1888–90 (R657)
Provenance: Vollard (one of three paintings purchased from the 1895 exhibition)
See fig. 56

Bathers, 1890–92 (R666)
Provenance: Vollard (March 29, 1906, Fr 2500)

Still Life with Apples and a Pot of Primroses, c. 1890 (R680)
Provenance: Gift from Helleu (March, 1894)
See fig. 83

Still Life with Ginger Pot, 1890–93 (R735)
Provenance: Vollard (Dec. 1, 1898, Fr 500)

Still Life with Milk Jug and Fruit, c. 1900 (R849)
Provenance: Vollard (possibly Feb. 1902, Fr 3500)

Vase in a Garden, 1900–04 (R891)
Provenance: Vollard (possibly Dec. 1906, Fr 8,000)

Château Noir, 1903–04 (R940)
Provenance: Vollard (Oct. 26, 1906, Fr 8000)

Boy in a Red Vest, 1889–90, watercolor (RWC376)

Henry Moore (1898–1986)
Three Female Bathers, c. 1875 (R361)

"It's the only picture I ever wanted to own. It's the joy of my life." In 1978 he modeled a small bronze sculpture after the painting in an edition of seven, plus one.

Pablo Picasso (1881–1973)
Five Female Bathers, 1877–78 (R365)
Provenance: Marlborough Galleries, London (via Louise Leiris) (November 1957)

The Sea at L'Estaque behind the Trees, 1878–79 (R395)
Provenance: Max Pellequier, Paris (c. 1952 in an exchange)
See fig. 75

Château Noir, 1900–04 (R941)
Provenance: Vollard (probably Feb. 1934, Fr 80,000)
See fig. 90

The Cathedral in Aix seen from the Lauves Studio, 1902–04, watercolor (RWC580)
Provenance: Vollard (by 1916)

See Hélène Seckel-Klein, "Paul Cézanne" in *Picasso collectionneur*, exh. cat., Paris, 1998, p. 72–78

Camille Pissarro (1830–1903)
Standing Female Bather Drying her Hair, c. 1869 (R114)
Provenance: Vollard (Dec. 12, 1895, Fr 200)

Women Dressing, c. 1867 (R123)
See fig. 32

Fisherman with a Line, 1868–70 (R162)
Provenance: Vollard (Nov. 19, 1895 with R385 and 250 in an exchange)

The Wine Market at Jussieu, 1872 (R179)
See cat. 28

Entrance to a Farm, rue Rémy, Auvers-sur-Oise, 1873 (R196)

Bend in the Forest Road, c. 1873 (R197)

Bathers, 1875–77 (R250)
Provenance: Vollard (Nov. 19, 1895 with R162 and 385 in an exchange)

Still Life with Soup Tureen, 1877 (R302)
See fig. 80

L'Étang des soeurs at Osny, near Pontoise, 1877 (R307)
Note: Georges Manzana Pissarro to Vollard (March 8, 1907, Fr. 2,000)
See fig. 102

Young Peasant Girl, c. 1877 (R309)
Pissarro's Vegetable Garden at Pontoise, 1877 (R311)
See fig. 101

Two Vases of Flowers, c. 1877 (R313)

Legendary Scene or *Sancho in the Water*, c. 1878 (R371)

Portrait of the Artist, c. 1877 (R385)
Provenance: Vollard (Nov. 19, 1895 with R162 and 250 in an exchange)
See cat. 1
Portrait of the Artist, after Renoir, 1881–82 (R446)

The Battle of Love, I, 1879–80 (R455)
The Hermitage at Pontoise, 1881 (R484)
See cat. 34

Citiscape around Paris, c. 1881 (R494)

Portrait of Jules Peyron, c. 1885 (R577)

Pool at the Jas de Bouffan, c. 1870, watercolor (RWC20)

Landscape in the Vicinity of Auvers-sur-Oise, 1872–73, watercolor (RWC 38)

Most of Pissarro's Cézannes were gifts from the artist, yet he felt compelled to buy several works from Tanguy in 1884 and from Vollard's 1895 exhibition. [See J. Pissarro's essay in this volume]

Hans Purrmann (1880–1966)
Entrance to the Garden, II, 1878–80, watercolor (RWC84)

House in Provence, 1890–94, watercolor (RWC389)

Odilon Redon (1840–1916)
Seated Man, 1898–1900 (R789)
See fig. 62

It is not known where Redon acquired this painting. He sold or consigned it to Vollard around 1900, valued at only 200 francs (stockbook no. 3868A). Fabbri later acquired it from Vollard in an exchange.

Auguste Renoir (1841–1919)
Thatched Cottages at Auvers-sur-Oise, 1872–73 (R188)

The Battle of Love, II, c. 1880 (R456)
Provenance: Vollard
See cat. 52

Houses in the Verdure, c. 1881 (R485)

Bend in Road at La Roche-Guyon, 1885 (R539)

"red rocks, lilac hill" (unidentified)
Provenance: Vollard (Nov. 15, 1896, Fr 2000 in an exchange)

Carafe and Bowl, 1878–80, watercolor (RWC107)
Bathers, c. 1888, watercolor (RWC132)

An unidentified bather composition

Henri Rouart (1833–1912)
Woman Looking in a Mirror, 1866–67 (R127)
See cat. 51

Woman Suckling her Baby c. 1872 (R216)

Two and a Half Apples, 1878–79 (R330)

Bunch of Grapes and Peach on a Plate, 1877–79 (R342)

Five Bathers, 1877–78 (R364)

Ker Xavier Roussel (1867–1944)
Bathers, c. 1900 (R865)
Provenance: probably from Vollard

Émile Schuffenecker (1851–1934)
Amédée Schuffenecker, Émile's brother (1854–1936)
Pool at the Jas de Bouffan in Winter, c. 1878 (R350)
Provenance: Tanguy; Schuffenecker to Vollard (no. 4403B) (June 1, 1906, Fr 3500)
See fig. 79

Madame Cézanne in a Red Armchair, 1883–85 (R536)
Provenance: Tanguy or père Thomas (by 1894); Amédée to Vollard (June 13, 1906, Fr 3000)

Large Pine and Red Earth, c. 1885 (R537)
Provenance: père Thomas (Fr120); "finished" by Émile; Amédée to Vollard and Bernheim-Jeune (May/June, 1907, Fr 5000)

Harlequin, 1888–90 (R620)
Provenance: Vollard (no. 3369A) (Oct. 5, 1899, possibly in an exchange)

Paul Signac (1863–1935)
Standing Bather, c. 1876 (R262)
Provenance: Bernheim-Jeune (March 1909)

Possibly *Three Pears*, 1878–79 (R345)
Provenance: Tanguy (by 1892) to Signac; Vollard (1898) to Fabbri (before 1899)

The Oise Valley (The Plains of Saint-Ouen l'Aumône), c. 1880 (R434)
Provenance: Tanguy (around 1884)
See fig. 81

See Marina Ferretti-Boquillon, "Signac as a Collector," *Signac 1863–1935*, exh. cat., New York, 2001, p. 51–66.

Félix Vallotton (1865–1925)
The Barge, c. 1878 (R372)

Trees among Rocks, c. 1890, watercolor (RWC336)

Victor Vignon (1847–1909)
Fruit Dish and Plate of Biscuits, c. 1877 (R325)
Provenance: Tanguy to Vignon; Vollard (June 26, 1898, Fr 500); Rosenberg (Dec. 16, 1898, Fr 1800)

Edouard Vuillard (1868–1940)
Apples, 1877–79 (R340)
Provenance: probably from Vollard (before c. 1902–04)

Mountains in Provence (near L'Estaque), c. 1879 (R391)
Provenance: See Gauguin; Vuillard to Vollard (stockbook no. 3460A; April 22, 1899, Fr 800)

Apples appears in a photograph of Madame Vuillard dated c. 1902–04 sitting in her living room (see Guy Cogeval, *Edouard Vuillard*, exh. cat., Washington, D.C.–Montreal, 2003, p. 262).

Timeline

Maryline Assante di Panzillo
Denis Coutagne

While not exhaustive, this chronology gives an overview of Cézanne's various movements between Paris (and its region) and Provence, as well as the main events that precipitated his journeys. In order to understand the alternating pattern of Cézanne's stays, the dates of the painter's arrival in Paris are indicated in bold black, while the dates when he went to Provence are in bold gray.

January 19, 1839: Birth of Paul Cézanne in Aix-en-Provence.
His father, Louis Auguste Cézanne, is a hat dealer and in 1848 he opens the Cézanne & Cabassol Bank.
Paul studies at Collège Bourbon in Aix-en-Provence. His best friend is Émile Zola.

April 1861: Paris

Cézanne's first stay in Paris, where he meets up with Émile Zola.
He works on studies from life at the independent studio, Académie Suisse, without a teacher, and there he meets Emperaire, Guillemet, Oller, Pissarro, and Guillaumin.

September 1861: Aix-en-Provence

Cézanne works in his father's bank, but finds it excruciatingly tedious.

November 1862: Paris

Cézanne goes back to stay with Zola; he meets Bazille and Renoir, sharing his time between the Académie Suisse and the Louvre, where he copies Delacroix's *The Barque of Dante*.
May 15, 1863: Opening of the Salon des Refusés, where Manet's *Luncheon on the Grass* causes a scandal. It is very likely that Cézanne took part (but no reference has ever been made to any work he showed there).
August 13, 1863: Death of Delacroix.

July 1864: Aix-en-Provence

March 1865: Paris

Cézanne's submission to the Salon—comprising canvases "which would make the Institute blush with rage and despair"—is rejected.

Autumn 1865: Aix-en-Provence

February 1866: Paris

April 1866: His submission to the Salon is rejected (*Portrait of Valabrègue*, and *Still Life with Bread and Eggs*).
Pays a visit to Manet, who has also been rejected by the Salon.
April–May 1866: Zola publishes a series of articles in defense of the rejected artists in the journal *L'Événement*.
May–August 1866: Stays in Bennecourt (on Guillemet's recommendation), where Zola spends the early summer, opposite Bonnières: *The Ferry at Bonnières* (cat. 28).
Cézanne claims to have painted some 4–5-meter canvases, now lost.

September 1866: Aix-en-Provence

February 1867: Paris

April 1, 1867: Opening of the Great Exhibition.
Two of Cézanne's paintings are rejected by the Salon: *Le Grog au vin* and *Ivresse*, as were the canvases by Guillemet, Sisley, Bazille, and Renoir.

June 1867: Aix-en-Provence

January 1868: Paris

Cézanne is registered as a copyist in the Louvre.
His submission to the Salon is rejected.

May 1868: Aix-en-Provence

Mid-December 1868: Paris

Meets his future companion, Hortense Fiquet, a young girl of 18 from Franche-Comté.

April 1869: Aix-en-Provence

Summer 1869: Île-de-France

Probably stayed in Bennecourt and Gloton with Zola, who rented Maison Pernelle on the banks of the Seine.

September 1869: Provence

Cézanne is in L'Estaque with Hortense Fiquet. From there, he travels to Aix on a regular basis.

March 1870: Paris

Cézanne's submissions to the Salon, *Portrait of Achille Emperaire* (fig. 92) and *Reclining Nude*, are rejected, earning him a caricature in the *Album Stock* (fig. 93). Cézanne takes this latest failure badly, and withdraws from society.
May 31, 1870: Zola marries Alexandrine Meley, with Cézanne as his witness.
July 19, 1870: France declares war on Prussia.

September 1870: Provence (Aix-en-Provence, L'Estaque)

September 2, 1870: French defeat at Sedan.
September 4, 1870: Proclamation of the Third Republic.
November 28, 1870: Death of Bazille, killed at the front.
Siege of Paris. Pissarro and Monet flee to live in London.
May 1871: Treaty of Frankfurt, Commune crushed.
Courbet is arrested, imprisoned at Versailles, and then transferred to Sainte-Pélagie prison. Once freed, he goes back to his birthplace in Franche-Comté and from there, into exile in Switzerland, where he dies in 1877.

July 1871: Paris

Manet is in Paris, Renoir has returned there, and Monet goes back to Argenteuil.
Pissarro returns to Louveciennes where he finds his house vandalized.
Summer/Fall 1871: Back in Paris, Cézanne moves in with Philippe Solari.
December 1871: Cézanne moves to rue Jussieu, near the Halle aux Vins (Wine Market).
January 4, 1872: Birth of his son Paul.
April 1872: Dr. Gachet, a friend of Pissarro and Cézanne, buys a house in Auvers, in rue Rémy. Cézanne's submission to the Salon is rejected. He signs a petition demanding a new Salon des Refusés, but does not take part in the rejected artists' exhibition the following year.
August 1872: Cézanne meets up with Pissarro near Pontoise, before settling in Auvers, not far from Dr. Gachet.
Painting *en plein air* with Pissarro and Guillaumin: start of his period widely referred to as "Impressionist ."
Early 1874: Returns to Paris.
April 15–May 15, 1874: First Impressionist exhibition in Nadar's studio: Cézanne shows three pictures, *House of the Hanged Man* (cat. 74), *Modern Olympia* (cat. 46), and *Landscape at Auvers*, which are mocked by the critics (Leroy's article in *Le Charivari*).
Count Doria buys *House of the Hanged Man*.

End of May 1874: Aix-en-Provence

September 1874: Paris

Père Tanguy becomes his first dealer.
1875: During this year in Paris, Cézanne travels to Pontoise in summer. He meets Victor Chocquet, who goes on to be his main collector and his friend.

December 1875: Aix-en-Provence

February 1876: Paris

Cézanne and Chocquet pay Monet a visit in Argenteuil.

April 1876: Provence (Aix-en Provence, L'Estaque)

Cézanne does not take part in the Second Impressionist Exhibition. His submission to the Salon is rejected.

End of August 1876: Paris

Cézanne paints the *Portrait of Victor Chocquet* (fig. 97).
April 2–30, 1877: Cézanne exhibits 16 works at the Third Impressionist Exhibition. During this stay in Paris, he often works in the park at Issy-les-Moulineaux, near Guillaumin, in Pontoise at Pissarro's home, and in Auvers.
He paints still lifes and portraits against the wallpaper background in his Paris apartment.

March 1878: Provence

Cézanne stays mainly in L'Estaque during this period.

March 1879: Paris

April 1879–April 1880: Moves to Melun; in spite of the cold, Cézanne spends the winter there. He paints landscapes (*Maincy Bridge*; cat. 70).
End of the period known as "Impressionist." Cézanne enters into a more "constructive" phase: "*faire du Poussin sur nature*" (creating Poussin through nature) Back in Melun, he lives at 32, rue de l'Ouest, in Paris' 14th arrondissement.
June 1879: Cézanne stays at Zola's new house in Médan for the first time.
April 1880: Cézanne paints *Rooftops of Paris* (cat. 2).
June 1880: Zola publishes a series of articles in *Le Voltaire:* "Naturalism in the Salon".
August 1880: Cézanne stays with Zola in Médan, where he meets Huysmans.

February 1881: Aix-en-Provence
Cézanne attends his sister's wedding.

May 1881: Paris
Cézanne spends most of his time in Pontoise. He stays with Zola in Médan for a week before leaving for the South.

Autumn 1881: Provence (Aix-en Provence, L'Estaque)
Renoir visits him in L'Estaque.

March 1882: Paris
May 1882: One of Cézanne's works (the still unidentified *Portrait of M.L.A.*) is accepted by the Salon thanks to Guillemet.
In summer he goes to Pontoise, and possibly stays in Choquet's house in Normandy, in Hattenville. He spends several months in Médan in September before heading for Aix.

October 1882: Provence
Cézanne stays in Aix-en-Provence, mainly in L'Estaque.

June–July 1885: Paris and Île-de-France
Cézanne stays briefly with Renoir at La Roche-Guyon, and at Zola's house in Médan, where he seeks solace because he has fallen in love with a woman whose identity remains unknown. This passion finds expression in an attack of pain.

August 1885: Aix-en-Provence
Moves to Gardanne. This stay extends through the whole academic year 1885–1886.
March 1886: Publication of Zola's novel *L'Œuvre*. Cézanne thanks him for sending the book. The two men would never write to, or see, each other again.
April 28, 1886: Marriage of Cézanne and Hortense Fiquet.
October 23, 1886: The artist's father, Louis Auguste Cézanne, dies.

Summer 1888: Paris and Île-de-France
Summer 1888: Stays in Chantilly (Hôtel Delacourt).
December 1888: Paris.
June 1889: Stays at Choquet's house in Hattenville then returns to Paris.
July 1889: *House of the Hanged Man* is shown at the Great Exhibition.
Monet launches an appeal to purchase Manet's *Olympia* and offer it to the Louvre.
June–November 1890: Cézanne accompanies his wife and son to Le Doubs and Switzerland, but does not enjoy the journey. He begins to suffer from diabetes.

November 1890: Aix-en-Provence
Cézanne returns to Aix and his wife moves to Paris. Renoir visits him in Provence.
April 7, 1891: Death of Victor Chocquet. Cézanne does not attend the funeral.

September 1891: Paris
Fall 1891: Cézanne moves to 69, rue d'Orléans.
1892: Cézanne lives for a time in Avon, and rents a studio in Fontainebleau.
September 1892: Stays in Bourron-Marlotte. It is conceivable, though not certain, that this stay extended into 1893.
February 6, 1894: Death of *père* Tanguy. When the old paint merchant's pictures are sold, Ambroise Vollard buys his first four Cézannes.
February 21, 1894: Death of Gustave Caillebotte who leaves his collection of Impressionist paintings to the State, five of which are by Cézanne. Beginning of the "Caillebotte controversy."
March 1894: Cézanne is in Alfort (Maisons-Alfort).
March 25, 1894: Gustave Geffroy publishes the first article devoted entirely to Cézanne.
September 1894: In Melun.
End of September 1894: Barbizon.
November 7–30, 1894: In Giverny. On November 28 Monet organizes a reception in his honor in Giverny, attended by Mary Cassatt, Clemenceau, Rodin, and Geffroy.
January 5, 1895: Captain Dreyfus discharged from the army.

February 1895: Provence
Cézanne paints in the Aix countryside with Renoir.

April 1895: Paris
Cézanne works on the *Portrait of Gustave Geffroy* (fig. 62) in Paris. He goes to see Monet's "Cathedrals" exhibition at the Durand-Ruel gallery.

End of June 1895: Provence
November 1895: Ambroise Vollard organizes Cézanne's first solo exhibition at his gallery in rue Lafitte. Cézanne does not travel up for the event.
Early 1896: Vollard pays a visit to Cézanne in Aix-en-Provence.
June–July 1896: Trip to Vichy and Lake Annecy with Hortense.
August 1896: Brief stay in Aix.

End of August 1896: Paris

October 1896: Aix-en-Provence

December 1896: Paris
February 1897: Two of Cézanne's landscapes feature among the paintings of the Caillebotte bequest accepted by the Musée du Luxembourg.
May 1897: He works in Mennecy near Corbeil (sets out for Aix on May 31).

June 1897: Aix-en-Provence
Cézanne stays at his sick mother's bed-side; she dies on October 25, 1897 in Aix.
January13, 1898: Publication of "J'accuse" by Zola in *L'Aurore*.

January 1898: Paris
May 9–June 10, 1898: New exhibition in Vollard gallery.
Summer 1898: Cézanne lives in Fontainebleau, working in Marlotte and Montigny-sur-Loing.
Part of the summer 1898: He paints landscapes in Marines and Montgeroult.
First half of 1899: Cézanne spends several months in Paris, and completes Vollard's portrait (cat. 73).
August 1899: Cézanne travels to Marlotte where he paints Alfred Hauge's portrait (cat. 67).

September 1899: Aix-en-Provence
Cézanne returns to Aix for the sale of Jas de Bouffan.
December 1899: New Cézanne exhibition at Vollard's.
April 1901: *Homage to Cézanne* by Maurice Denis (fig. 95) is exhibited at the Salon of the Société Nationale des Beaux-Arts.
November 1901: Work begins on the construction of the Lauves studio (he moves into it in April 1902).
September 29, 1902: Death of Zola. This affects Cézanne badly.
February–March 1904: Émile Bernard pays a visit to Cézanne. He photographs him in the Lauves studio in front of the *Large Bathers*.

Summer 1904: Fontainebleau
Cézanne stays in Fontainebleau with his son.

September 1904: Aix-en-Provence
October 1904: Second Salon d'Automne in the Grand Palais: an entire room is devoted to Cézanne.

Summer 1905: Last stay in Fontainebleau.

Fall 1905: Aix-en-Provence
End of January 1906: Cézanne receives a visit from Maurice Denis and Ker Xavier Roussel.
April 1906: Osthaus pays a visit to the Lauves studio.
Night of October 22–23, 1906: Death of Cézanne in Aix-en-Provence.
October 1907: Salon d'Automne: Major Cézanne retrospective.

Known addresses for Cézanne in Paris and Île-de-France

It is possible that Cézanne kept an address in Paris while he was away (on a trip to Provence for instance). Our list gives the dates when the tenancy began and ended. We do not mention all the places Cézanne stayed, such as Médan (at Zola's house), Chantilly, Giverny, Mennecy (in the hotel).

April–September 1861: 39, rue d'Enfer, Paris 9th arrondissement
November 1862 – July 1864: Cul-de-sac Saint-Dominique (now rue Royer-Collard), Paris 5th
End of 1863: 7, rue des Feuillantines, Paris 5th
March 1865–May 1868: 22, rue Beautreillis, Paris 4th
March–summer 1870: 53, rue Notre-Dame-des-Champs, Paris 7th
July 1871: 55, rue de Chevreuse, Paris 6th, at Solari's house
December 1871: 45, rue Jussieu, Paris 5th
August 1872: Hôtel du Grand Cerf, Saint-Ouen-l'Aumône, then 66, rue Saint-Rémy, Auvers-sur-Oise
Early 1874: 120, rue de Vaugirard, Paris 6th
End of August 1876–March 1879: 67, rue de l'Ouest, Paris 14th
April 1879–end of March 1880: 2, place de la Préfecture, Melun
April 1880: 32, rue de l'Ouest, Paris 14th
May–October 1881: 31, quai de Ponthuis, Pontoise
March–October 1882: 32, rue de l'Ouest, Paris 14th
December 1888 – summer 1890: 15, quai d'Anjou, Paris 4th
September 1891: 69, rue d'Orléans, Paris 14th
1892: Studio in Fontainebleau
Late summer 1894–end of June 1895: 2, rue des Lions-Saint-Paul, Paris 4th (studio in rue Bonaparte until January 15, 1896)
End August 1896–October 1896: 58, rue des Dames, Paris 17th
January 1897: moves to 73, rue Saint-Lazare, Paris 9th
January 1898–1899 (end of June?) : studio in Villa des Arts, 15, rue Hégésippe-Moreau, Paris 18th
Early summer 1898: 11, rue Saint-Louis, Fontainebleau
End of October 1899: 31, rue Ballu, Paris 9th
Summer 1905: 8, rue de la Coudre, Fontainebleau

Bibliography

Adriani 1980: Götz Adriani (1980), *Paul Cézanne. Der Liebeskampf*, Munich, R. Piper.

Adhémar 1960: Jean Adhémar (November 1960), "Le Cabinet de travail de Zola," *Gazette des beaux-arts*, special issue 6, vol. 56, no. 1102.

Andersen 1967: Wayne V. Andersen (June 1967), "Cézanne, Tanguy, Choquet," *The Art Bulletin*, vol. 49.

Andersen 2003: Wayne V. Anderson (2003), *The Youth of Cézanne and Zola. Notoriety at its Source, Art and Literature in Paris*, Geneva, Fabriart.

Andersen 2004: Wayne V. Anderson (2004), *Cézanne and the Eternal Feminine*, Cambridge (Massachusetts), Cambridge University Press.

Armstrong 2004: Carol Armstrong (2004), in exh. cat. Los Angeles 2004–2005.

Arrouye 1995: Jean Arrouye (1995), *Cézanne. Paris-Provence*, Paris, Textuel.

Assante 2011: Maryline Assante di Panzillo (2011), *Cézanne et l'argent–Salons, marchands et collectionneurs*, Paris, RMN–GP.

Athanassoglou-Kallmyer 1990: Nina Maria Athanassoglou-Kallmyer (September 1990), "An Artistic and Political Manifesto for Cézanne," *The Art Bulletin* 72, no. 3, pp. 482–492.

Bailly-Herzberg 1980–1991: Janine Bailly-Herzberg (ed. 1980–1991), *Correspondance de Camille Pissarro*, Paris, Presses universitaires de France et Valhermeil.

Ballu 1877: Roger Ballu (April 23, 1877), "L'exposition des peintres impressionnistes," *La Chronique des arts and de la curiosité*, April 14, 1874, p. 147, reprinted in *Beaux-Arts illustrés*.

Barr 1937: Alfred Barr (January 1937), "Cézanne d'après les lettres de Marion à Morstatt, 1865-1868," *Gazette des beaux-arts*, XVII, no. 883, pp. 37–58.

Barr 1938: "Cézanne in the letters of Marion to Morstatt 1865–1868," trans. M. Scolari and A. Barr Jr (February, April, and May 1938), *Magazine of Art*.

Becker 1990: Colette Becker (1990), "Cézanne et Zola. Réalité et fiction Romanesque," *Quarante-Huit/Quatorze* (Musée d'Orsay publication), no. 2, pp. 78–89.

Berhaut, Vaisse 1985: Marie Berhaut and Pierre Vaisse (1985), "Le legs Caillebotte. Vérités et contre-vérités," *Bulletin de la Société d'histoire de l'art français*, Year 1983, Paris, pp. 209–237.

Bernard 1891: Émile Bernard (1891), "Paul Cézanne," *Les Hommes d'aujourd'hui*, no. 387.

Bernard 1925: Émile Bernard (1925), *Sur Paul Cézanne*, Paris, Michel.

Bernard 1926: Émile Bernard (1926), *Lettres de Vincent Van Gogh, Paul Gauguin, Paul Cézanne…. à Émile Bernard*, Tonnerre, La rénovation esthétique, I.

Bertall 1877: Bertall (April 9, 1877), "L'exposition des impressionnistes," *Paris-Journal*.

Beucken 1955: Jean de Beucken (1955), *Un portrait de Cézanne*, Paris, Gallimard.

Bizardel 1974: Yvon Bizardel (August 1974), "Théodore Durand. An early friend of the Impressionnists," *Apollo*.

Bodelsen 1968: Merete Bodelsen (June 1968), "Early impressionist sales 1874–94 in the light of some unpublished minutes," *Burlington Magazine*, pp. 330–349.

Bois 1998: Yve-Alain Bois (Spring 1998), "Cézanne: Words and Deeds," *October*, 84.

Bourguignon 2007: Katherine M. Bourguignon (ed. 2007), *Impressionism in Giverny: A Colony of Artists 1885–1915*, Giverny, Musée d'Art Américain.

Brady 1968: Patrick Brady (1968), *"L'œuvre" d'Émile Zola. Roman sur les arts*, Geneva, Droz.

Bratis 2009: Adrianne O. Bratis (ed. 2009), *Cézanne and Beyond*, exh. cat. Philadelphia 2009.

Cahn 1995: Isabelle Cahn (1995), "Chronology," in exh. cat. Paris—London—Philadelphia 1995–1996, Paris, Réunion des Musées Nationaux.

Cahn 1997: Isabelle Cahn (1997), "L'exposition Cézanne chez Vollard en 1895," in *Cézanne aujourd'hui. Actes du colloque organisé par le musée d'Orsay* (ed. by Fr. Cachin, H. Loyrandte, S. Guéguan), 29–30 November 1995, Paris, Réunion des Musées Nationaux, pp. 135–144.

Cardon 1874: Émile Cardon (April 29, 1874), "Avant le Salon. L'exposition des Révoltés," *La Presse*.

Castagnary 1874: Jules Antoine Castagnary (April 29, 1874), "L'Exposition du boulevard des Capucines," *Le Siècle*.

Castagnary 1892: Jules Antoine Castagnary (1892), "Salon de 1863," *Salons (1857–1879)*, edited by Eugène Spuller, Paris, I.

Cézanne 1914: Octave Mirbeau, Théodore Durand, Léon Werth et al. (1914), *Cézanne*, Paris, Bernheim-Jeune.

Chappuis 1973: Adrien Chappuis (1973), *The Drawings of Paul Cézanne. A Catalogue Raisonné*, Greenwich, Connecticut, New York Graphic Society, I, p. 49–52, and London, Thames & Hudson.

Cherpin 1972: Jean Cherpin (ed. 1972), *Cézanne. L'œuvre gravé*, exh. cat. Aix-en-Provence 1972, preface by Michel Melot, Marseille, Arts et livres en Provence.

Clark 2001: T. J. Clark (2001), "Phenomenality and Materiality in Cézanne," in Tom Cohen et al., *Material Events: Paul de Man and the Afterlife of Theory*, Minneapolis, University of Minnesota Press, pp. 93–113.

Clayson 1991: Hollis Clayson (1991), *Painted Love: Prostitution in French Art of the Impressionist Era*, New Haven, Yale University Press.

Colrat 2005: Jean Colrat (2005), "'Joindre les mains errantes de la nature.' La reprise picturale du visible par Cézanne," edited by Claude Massu, Université d'Aix-Marseille. Awaiting publication by Presses Universitaires de Paris-Sorbonne.

Coquiot 1919: Gustave Coquiot (1919), *Paul Cézanne*, Paris, Libraire Paul Ollendorf.

Corand 2003: Noël Corand (2003), *L'Art en effervescence. 100 ans de Salon d'automne 1903–2003*, Paris, Castadiva.

Coutagne 2006: Denis Coutagne (2006), *Cézanne en vérités*, Arles, Actes Sud.

D'Souza 2008: Aruna D'Souza (2008), *Cézanne's Bathers. Biography and the Erotics of Paint*, University Park (Pennsylvania), Pennsylvania State University Press.

Daix 1967: Pierre Daix (1967), introduction to *L'Œuvre*, in Mitterand 1966–1970, vol. V, pp. 425–433.

Delteil 1925–1927: Loys Delteil (1925–1927), *Manuel de l'amateur d'estampes des* XIX*e and* XX*e siècles*, Paris, Dorbon-Aîné, vol. II.

Distel 1989: Anne Distel (1989), *Les Collectionneurs des impressionnistes*, Lausanne, La Bibliothèque des arts.

Distel 1994: Anne Distel (1994), "Gustave Caillebotte, peintre mécène and collectionneur," in exh. cat. Paris—Chicago 1994–1995, Paris, Réunion des Musées Nationaux, pp. 21–30.

Dombrowski 2006: André Dombrowski (September 2006), "The Emperor's Last Clothes: Cézanne, Fashion, and 'l'année terrible'," *The Burlington Magazine*, 148, no. 1242, pp. 586–594.

Dombrowski 2011: André Dombrowski (2011), "Cézanne, Manet, and the Portraits of Zola", in Temma Balducci, et al., *Interior Portraiture and Masculine Identity in France, 1789–1914*, Farnham, Ashgate, pp. 101–119.

Doran 1978: Paul Michael Doran (ed. 1978 and 2005), *Conversations avec Cézanne: Émile Bernard, Joachim Gasquand, Maurice Denis, etc.*, scholarly edition by P. M. Doran, Paris, Macula; 2005 (8th reissue).

Doran 2001: Paul Michael Doran (ed. 2001), *Conversations with Cézanne*, Berkeley, University of California Press.

Doran 2005: see Doran 1978.

Eisler 1983: Colin Eisler (1983), "Rembrandt and Bathsheba," in

Essays in Northern European Art Presented to Egbert Haverkamp Begemann on His Sixtieth Birthday, edited by Anne-Marie Logan, Doornspijk, pp. 84–88.

Ely 1984: Bruno Ely (1984), *Cézanne au Musée d'Aix*, Aix-en-Provence, Musée Granet.

Fauconnier 2006: Bernard Fauconnier (2006), *Cézanne*, Paris, Gallimard.

Feilchenfeldt 1995: Walter Feilchenfeldt (1995), "Les collectionneurs de Cézanne de Zola à Annenberg," in. exh. cat. Paris–London–Philadelphia 1995-1996, Paris, Réunion des Musées Nationaux, pp. 570-579.

Foucault 2009: Michel Foucault (2009), *Manet and the Object of Painting*, London, Tate Publishing.

Freudenberg 2001: Inken Freudenberg (2001), *Der Zweifler Cézanne*, Heidelberg, Kehrer.

Gachet 1952: Paul Gachet (1952), *Cézanne à Auvers, Cézanne graveur*, Paris, Les Beaux-Arts.

Gantheret 2005: François Gantheret (2005), *Petite route du Tholonet*, Paris, Gallimard.

Gasquet 1921: Joachim Gasquet (1921, 1926, and 1988), *Cézanne*, Paris, Bernheim-Jeune, 1st edition; 1926; Paris, Cynara, 1988.

Gasquet 1926: see Gasquet 1921.

Gasquet 1988: see Gasquet 1921.

Gasquet 1991: *Joachim Gasquet's Cézanne. A Memoir with Conversations*, New York, Thames and Hudson.

Geffroy 1892–1903: Gustave Geffroy (1892–1903), *La Vie artistique*, Paris, Dentu, 8 volumes.

Geffroy 1895: Gustave Geffroy (November 16, 1895), "Paul Cézanne," *Le Journal*, March 25, 1894, reprinted in *La Vie parisienne*.

Geffroy 1900: Gustave Geffroy (1900), "Paul Cézanne," *Le Journal*, November 16, 1895, reprinted in *La Vie artistique*, 6th series, Paris, p. 214.

Geffroy 1922: Gustave Geffroy (1922 and 1924), *Claude Monet, sa vie, son œuvre*, Paris, G. Crès (1st ed.), 2 vols.; 1924 (3rd ed.).

Geffroy 1924: see Geffroy 1922.

Gerdt 1993: William H. Gerdt (1993), *Monet's Giverny: An Impressionist Colony*, New York, Abbeville Press Publishers.

Gombrich 1972: Ernst Hans Gombrich (1972), *Art and Illusion*, Princeton (New Jersey), Princeton University Press.

Gowing 1988: Lawrence Gowing (1988), *Paul Cézanne: The Basel Sketchbooks*, exh. cat. New York 1988, New York, Little, Brown and Company.

Gowing 1988: Lawrence Gowing (1988), "Parisian Writers and the Early Work of Paul Cézanne," in exh. cat. London–Paris–Washington, 1988-1989.

Gowing 1992: Lawrence Gowing (1992), *Cézanne. La logique des sensations organisées*, Paris, Macula.

Gray 1972: Christopher Gray(1972), *Armand Guillaumin*, Geneva, Alice Darling Gray.

Groom 2007: Gloria Groom (2007), "Vollard et les collectionneurs allemands," in exh. cat. New York–Chicago–Paris, 2006-2007, Paris, Réunion des Musées Nationaux, pp. 246-257.

Harrison 1997: Charles Harrison (September 1997), "Cézanne: Fantasy and Imagination," *Modernism/Modernity*, 4, no. 3, pp. 1-18.

Honour 1989: Hugh Honour (1989), *The Image of the Black in Western Art*, New York, Morrow.

Jensen 2007: Robert Jensen (2007), "Vollard et Cézanne: anatomie d'une relation," in exh. cat. New York–Chicago–Paris 2006-2007, Paris, Réunion des Musées Nationaux, pp. 39-57.

Joly 1869: Henri Joly (1869), *L'Instinct, ses rapports avec la vie et avec l'intelligence, essai de psychologie comparée*, Paris, E. Thorin.

Joyeux-Prunel 2009: Béatrice Joyeux-Prunel (2009), *Nul n'est prophète en son pays. L'internationalisation de la peinture des avant-gardes parisiennes 1855–1914*, Paris, Nicolas Chaudun.

Kitschen 1995: Friederike Kitschen (1995), *Cézanne. Stilleben*, Ostfildern-Ruit, Hatje Cantz.

Kostenevich 2007: Albert Kostenevich (2007), "Vollard et les collectionneurs russes," in exh. cat. New York–Chicago–Paris 2006-2007, Paris, Réunion des Musées Nationaux, p. 258-271.

Krumrine 1988: Mary Louise Krumrine (1988), "Parisian Writers and the Early Works of Cézanne," in George Mauner, et al., *Paris. Center of Artistic Enlightenment. Papers in Art History from the Pennsylvania State University*, 4, University Park (Pennsylvania), Pennsylvania State University Press, pp. 188-221.

Larguier 1925: Léo Larguier (1925), *Le Dimanche avec Paul Cézanne (souvenirs)*, Paris, L'Édition.

Lebensztejn 1988: Jean-Claude Lebensztejn (December 1988), "Les couilles de Cézanne," *Critique*, no. 499.

Lebensztejn 2006: Jean-Claude Lebensztejn (2006), *Études cézanniennes*, Paris, Flammarion.

Leca 2006: Benedict Leca (2006), "Sites of Forgetting: Cézanne and the Provençal Landscape Tradition," in *Cézanne in Provence*, edited by Philip Conisbee and Denis Coutagne, New Haven, Yale University Press.

Lecomte 1899: Georges Lecomte (December 9, 1899), "Paul Cézanne," *Revue de l'art*, no. 6.

Leduc-Adine and Mitterand 2004: Jean-Pierre Leduc-Adine and Henri Mitterand (eds. 2004), *Lire/Dé-lire Zola*, Paris, Nouveau Monde Éditions.

Lemaire 2004: Gérard-Georges Lemaire (2004), *Histoire du salon de peinture*, Paris, Klincksieck.

Lemoine 2002: Serge Lemoine (ed. 2002), *De Puvis de Chavannes à Matisse et Picasso. Vers l'art moderne*, Paris, Flammarion.

Leroy 1877: Louis Leroy (April 11, 1877), "L'École des impressionnistes," *Le Charivari*.

Letourneau 1868: Charles Letourneau (1868), *Physiologie des passions*, Paris, Germer Baillière.

Lewis 1989: Mary Tompkins Lewis (1989), *Cézanne's Early Imagery*, Berkeley, University of California Press.

Lewis 2000: Mary Tompkins Lewis (2000), *Cézanne,* London, Phaidon.

Leymarie and Melot 1971: Jean Leymarie and Michel Melot (1971), *Les Gravures des impressionnistes Manet, Pissarro, Renoir, Cézanne, Sisley*, Paris, Arts and métiers graphiques.

Lhote 1950: André Lhote (1950), "L'exposition Cézanne au théâtre Pigalle" (NRF, no. 197, February 1930), in *La peinture, le cœur et l'esprit, suivi de Parlons peinture*, Paris, Denoël.

Lobstein 2003: Dominique Lobstein (2003), *Dictionnaire des indépendants 1884–1914*, Dijon, L'Échelle de Jacob.

Loran 1985: Erle Loran (1985), *Cézanne's Composition*, Berkeley, University of California Press.

Loyrette and Tinterow 1994–1995: Henri Loyrette and Gary Tinterow (eds. 1994–1995), *Origins of Impressionism*, exh. cat. Paris–New York, 1994–1995.

Machotka 1996: Pavel Machotka (1996), *Cézanne. Landscape into Art*, New Haven and London, Yale University Press.

Machotka 2008: Pavel Machotka (2008), *Cézanne. La sensation à l'œuvre*, Marseille, Éditions Crès.

Mack 1935: Gertsle Mack (1935), *Paul Cézanne. A Biography*, New York, A.A. Knopf, p. 122; (reissued 1990, Paragon).

Martindale 1990: Colin Martindale (1990), *The Clockwork Muse. The Predictability of Artistic Change*, New York, Basic Books.

Mellerio 1896a: André Mellerio (January–February 1896), "L'art moderne," *La Revue artistique*.

Mellerio 1896b: André Mellerio (1896), *Le Mouvement idéaliste en peinture*.

Melot 1994: Michel Melot (1994), *L'Estampe impressionniste*, Paris, Flammarion.

Merleau-Ponty 2004: Maurice Merleau-Ponty (2004), "Cézanne's Doubt," in *Merleau-Ponty Basic Writings*, edited by Thomas Baldwin, London and New York, Routledge.

Mitterand 1960–1967: *Émile Zola. Les Rougon-Macquart*, annotated edition by Henri Mitterand (1960–1967), preface by Armand Lanoux, Paris, Gallimard, 5 vols., 1st ed.

Mitterand 1966–1970: *Émile Zola. Œuvres complètes*, edited by Henri Mitterand (1966–1970), Paris, Cercle du livre précieux, 15 vols. See in vol. XII, "Salons et études de critique d'art," with a preface by Georges Besson, pp. 773–1071, 1018.

Mitterand 1999–2002: Henri Mitterand (1999–2002), *Zola*, Paris, Fayard, 3 vols.

Mitterand 2002–2010: *Émile Zola. Œuvres complètes*, chronological edition by Henri Mitterand (2002–2010), Paris, Nouveau Monde Éditions, 20 vols.

Mitterand 2009: Henri Mitterand (2009), *Zola, tel qu'en lui-même*, Paris, Presses universitaires de France.

Monnerand 1978: Sophie Monnerand (1978), *Cézanne, Zola. La fraternité du génie*, Paris, Denoël.

Montifaud 1874: Marc de Montifaud (May 1874), "Exposition du boulevard des Capucines," *L'Artiste*.

Morel 2007: Jean-Paul Morel (2007), *C'était Ambroise Vollard*, Paris, Fayard.

Natanson 1895: Thadée Natanson (December 1895), "Paul Cézanne," *La Revue blanche*, IX.

Niess 1968: Robert Niess (1968), *Zola, Cézanne and Manet*, Ann Arbor, The University of Michigan Press.

Pagès 2012: Alain Pagès (2012), "Les sanglots de Cézanne," Seminar at Université de Rouen, awaiting publication by Publications des universités de Rouen et du Havre.

Patin 1988: Sylvie Patin (1988), "The collectors of Cézanne's early works," in exh. cat. London—Paris—Washington 1988-1989, Paris, Réunion des Musées Nationaux, pp. 54-65.

Perruchot 1955: Henri Perruchot (June 15, 1955), "Le Père Tanguy," *L'Œil*.

Perruchot 1956: Henri Perruchot (1956), *La Vie de Cézanne*, Paris, Gallimard.

Pissarro 2005a: Joachim Pissarro (ed. 2005), *Cézanne and Pissarro: Pioneering Modern Painting, 1865-1885*, exh. cat. New York—Los Angeles—Paris 2005-2006, New York, Museum of Modern Art.

Pissarro 2005b: Joachim Pissarro (2005), *Pissarro, critical catalogue of paintings*, Paris, Wildenstein Institute.

Platzman 2001: Steven Platzman (2001), *Cézanne: The Self-Portraits*, Berkeley, University of California Press.

Pleynet 2010: Marcelin Pleynet (2010), *Cézanne*, Paris, Gallimard.

Prouvaire 1874: Jean Prouvaire (April 20, 1874), "L'Exposition du boulevard des Capucines", *Le Rappel*.

Reff 1960: Theodore Reff (November 1960), "Reproductions and Books in Cézanne's Studio," *Gazette des beaux-arts*, special issue 6, vol. 56, no. 1102.

Reff 1962a: Theodore Reff (autumn 1962), "Cézanne's Constructive Stroke," *The Art Quarterly*, vol. 25, no. 3, pp. 214-227.

Reff 1962b: Theodore Reff (June 1962), "Cézanne, Flaubert, St. Anthony, and the Queen of Sheba," *The Art Bulletin*, 44, no. 2, pp. 113-125.

Reff 1962c: Theodore Reff (March 1962), "Cézanne's Bather with Outstretched Arms," *Gazette des beaux-arts*, 59, no. 1118, pp. 173-190.

Reff 1963: Theodore Reff (June 1963), "Cézanne's Dream of Hannibal," *The Art Bulletin*, 45, no. 2, pp. 148-152.

Reff 1997: Theodore Reff (1997), "Cézanne and Chardin," in *Cézanne aujourd'hui. Actes du colloque organisé par le musée d'Orsay* (edited by Fr. Cachin, H. Loyrette, S. Guéguan), 29-30 November 1995, Paris, Réunion des Musées Nationaux.

Rewald 1937: *Paul Cézanne. Correspondance*, compiled, annotated and with preface by John Rewald (1937 [1st ed.], 1978, and 1995), Paris, Grasset, 1937 1st ed.; 1978; 1995.

Rewald 1938: John Rewald (May 1938), "Achille Emperaire, ami de Paul Cézanne (Petits maîtres du XIXe siècle)," *L'Amour de l'art*, 19, no. 4, pp. 151-158.

Rewald 1969: John Rewald (July-August 1969), "Chocquet and Cézanne," *Gazette des beaux-arts*, pp. 33-96.

Rewald 1973: John Rewald (1973), *The History of Impressionism*, New York, The Museum of Modern Art.

Rewald 1974: John Rewald (1974), *Cézanne Letters*, New York.

Rewald 1978: see Rewald 1937.

Rewald 1985: John Rewald (1985), *Studies in Impressionism*, New York, Harry N. Abrams.

Rewald 1986a: John Rewald (1986), *Cézanne*, trans. J. Bonniort, Paris, Flammarion.

Rewald 1986b: John Rewald (1986), *Cézanne. A biography*, New York, Harry N. Abrams.

Rewald 1986c: John Rewald (1986), *Histoire de l'impressionnisme* (1955), new revised edition with added material, Paris, Albin Michel.

Rewald 1995: see Rewald 1937.

Rewald 1996: John Rewald, in collaboration with Walter Feilchenfeldt and Jayne Warman (1996), *The Paintings of Paul Cézanne. A Catalogue Raisonné*, 2 vols., New York, Harry N. Abrams.

Rilke 1991: Rainer Maria Rilke (1991), *Lettres sur Cézanne* (1952), trans. Philippe Jaccottet, Paris, Seuil.

Rilke 2002: Rainer Maria Rilke (2002), *Letters on Cézanne*, edited by Clara Rilke, trans. Joel Agee, New York, North Point Press, 2002.

Rivière 1877: Georges Rivière (April 14, 1877), "L'exposition des impressionnistes," *L'Impressionniste*.

Rivière 1933: Georges Rivière (1933), *Cézanne*, Paris, H. Floury.

Roesch-Lalance 1986: Marie-Claude Roesch-Lalance (1986), *Bourron-Marlotte. Si les maisons racontaient...*, Bourron-Marlotte, Association des amis de Bourron-Marlotte.

Roquebert 2007: Anne Roquebert (2007), "Vollard et le monde des collectionneurs," in exh. cat. New York—Chicago—Paris 2006-2007, Paris, Réunion des Musées Nationaux, pp. 232-245.

Rubin 1977: William Rubin (ed. 1977), *Cézanne. The Late Work*, New York, The Museum of Modern Art.

Rubin 2008: James H. Rubin (2008), *Impressionism and the Modern Landscape: Productivity, Technology, and Urbanization from Manet to Van Gogh*, Berkeley, University of California Press.

Sanchez and Seydoux 2006: Pierre Sanchez and Xavier Seydoux (2006), *Les Catalogues des Salons*, vol. X, 1882-1884, Dijon, L'Échelle de Jacob.

Schapiro 1962: Meyer Schapiro (1962), *Cézanne*, New York, Harry N. Abrams.

Schapiro 1968: Meyer Schapiro (1968), "The Apples of Cézanne: An Essay on the Meaning of Still-Life", *Art News Annual*, 34.

Schapiro 1978: Meyer Schapiro (1978), "The Apples of Cézanne: An Essay on the Meaning of Still-Life (1968)", *Modern Art, 19th and 20th Centuries. Selected Essays*, New York, George Braziller, pp. 1-38.

Seckel-Klein 1998: Hélène Seckel-Klein (1998), *Picasso und seine Sammlung/Picasso collectionneur*, exh. cat. Munich 1998, Paris, Réunion des Musées Nationaux.

Shiff 1984: Richard Shiff (1984), *Cézanne and the End of Impressionism. A Study of the Theory, Technique, and Critical Evaluation of Modern Art*, Chicago, The University of Chicago Press.

Shiff 1994: Richard Shiff (1994), "An Impressionist Touch," in *Paul Cézanne*, New York, Rizzoli International Publications.

Shiff 1995: Richard Shiff (1995), *Cézanne et la fin de l'impressionnisme. Étude sur la théorie, la technique et l'évaluation critique de l'art moderne*, trans. J.-F. Allain, Paris, Flammarion.

Shiff 2001: Richard Shiff (2001), "Apples and Abstraction," in *Impressionist Still Life*, edited by Eliza E. Rathbone, et al., New York, The Phillips Collection/Harry N. Abrams.

Shiff 2009: Richard Shiff (winter 2009), "Distractions: Cézanne in a Sketchbook," *Master Drawings*, 27, pp. 447-451.

Sidlauskas 2009: Susan Sidlauskas (2009), *Cézanne's Other. The Portraits of Hortense*, Berkeley, University of California Press.

Simms 2008: Matthew Simms (2008), *Cézanne's Watercolors. Between Drawing and Painting*, New Haven, Yale University Press.

Simon 1991: Robert Simon (May 1991), "Cézanne and the Subject of Violence," *Art in America*, 79, no. 5.

Simonton 1997: Dean Keith Simonton (1997), *Genius and Creativity*, Greenwich (Connecticut), Ablex Pub.

Skedsmo 1991: Tone Skedsmo (1991), "Omkkring and portrett malt av Paul Cézanne," *Kunst ung Kultur*, Oslo.

Smith 1998: Paul Smith (October 1998), "Joachim Gasquet, Virgil and Cézanne's Landscape: 'My Beloved Golden Age'," *Apollo*, 147, no. 439, pp. 11-23.

Sollers 2003: Philippe Sollers (2003), "Le paradis de Cézanne," in *Éloge de l'infini*, Paris, Gallimard.

Stein 1947: Leo Stein (1947), *Appreciation: Painting, Poetry and Prose*, New York, Crown Publishers.

Szineyei-Merse 1998: Anna Szineyei-Merse (1998), "Rippl-Rónai en France. Ses relations avec les nabis," in exh. cat. *Rippl-Rónai. Le nabi hongrois*, Saint-Germain-en-Laye.

Vaisse 1995: Pierre Vaisse (1995), *La Troisième République et les peintres*, Paris, Flammarion.

Vassy 1877: Georges Vassy (April 6, 1877), "L'exposition des impressionnistes," *L'Événement*.

Venturi 1936: Lionello Venturi (1936), *Cézanne, son art, son œuvre*, Paris, Paul Rosenberg.

Venturi 1939: Lionello Venturi (1936), *Les archives de l'Impressionnisme*, Paris, Durand-Ruel, 2 volumes.

Vollard 1914: Ambroise Vollard (1914), *Paul Cézanne*, Paris, G. Crès.

Vollard 1937: Ambroise Vollard (1937 [1st ed.], 1984, and 2007), *Souvenirs d'un marchand de tableaux*, Paris, Albin Michel.

Vollard 1938: Ambroise Vollard (1938 [1st ed.)], 2003, and 2008), *En écoutant Cézanne, Degas, Renoir*, Paris, Grasset.

Vollard 1984: see Vollard 1937.

Vollard 1996: Ambroise Vollard (1996), *De Cézanne à Picasso. Mes portraits* (1938), Paris, Séguier.

Vollard 2003: see Vollard 1938.

Vollard 2007: see Vollard 1937.

Vollard 2008: see Vollard 1938.

Walter 1961: Rodolphe Walter (March 1, 1961), "Émile Zola et Paul Cézanne à Bennecourt, en 1866," *Bulletin de la société des amis du Mantois*.

Walter 1962: Rodolphe Walter (February 1962), "Cézanne à Bennecourt," *Gazette des beaux-arts*.

Zola 1866: Émile Zola (1866), *Mon Salon*, extended with dedication and appendix, Paris, Librairie centrale, imp. Gaittet, 18mo.

Zola 1874: Émile Zola (1874, 1886), *L'Œuvre*, Paris, Flammarion ; Charpentier.

Zola 1874a: Émile Zola (April 18, 1874), "Lettre de Paris," *Le Sémaphore de Marseille*.

Zola 1877: Émile Zola (April 19, 1877), "Notes parisiennes. Une exposition: les peintres impressionnistes," *Le Sémaphore de Marseille*.

Zola 1880: Émile Zola (June 18–22, 1880), "Le Naturalisme au Salon," *Le Voltaire*.

Zola. 1886: see Zola 1874.

Zola 1928: Émile Zola (1928), *Correspondance 1858–1871*, Paris, François Bernouard.

Zola 1959: Émile Zola (1959), *Salons*, F. W. J. Hemmings and Robert J. Niess (ed.), Geneva, Publications romanes et françaises.

Zola 1978–1995: *Émile Zola. Correspondance*, edited by B. H. Bakker, C. Becker, H. Mitterand, Montreal, Presses de l'université de Montréal, and Paris, Éditions du CNRS, 10 vol.

Zola 1991: Émile Zola (1991), *Écrits sur l'art*, edited with commentary by Jean-Pierre Leduc-Adine, Paris, Gallimard.

Zola 1983: Émile Zola (1983), *L'Œuvre*, preface by Bruno Foucart, annotated edition by Henri Mitterand, Paris, Gallimard.

Zola 2010: *Émile Zola. Lettres retrouvées*, Paris, Presses de l'université de Montréal and Éditions du CNRS.

EXHIBITION CATALOGUES

Aix-en-Provence 1972: *Cézanne. L'œuvre gravé*, exh. cat. (Aix-en-Provence, Pavillon de Vendôme, May 30–Aug 15, 1972), edited by Jean Cherpin, preface by Michel Melot, Marseille, Arts et livres de Provence.

Aix-en-Provence 2009: *Picasso Cézanne*, exh. cat. (Aix-en-Provence, Musée Granet, May–Sept 2009), Paris, Réunion des Musées Nationaux.

Basel 1989: *Paul Cézanne: The Bathers*, exh. cat. (Basel, Basel Museum of Fine Arts, September–December 1989), Basel, Öffentliche Kunstsammlung.

Basel 1999: *Manet, Zola, Cézanne: Das Porträt des modernen Literaten*, exh. cat. (Basel, Kunstmuseum Basel, February–June 1999), Katharina Schmidt (ed.) et al., Basel, Gerd Hatje.

Copenhagen 2008: *Cézanne and Giacometti : Paths of Doubt*, exh. cat. (Copenhagen, Louisiana Museum of Modern Art, February–June 2008), Ostfildern, Hatje Cantz.

Florence 2007: *Cézanne a Firenze: due collezionisti e la mostra dell'impressionismo del 1910*, exh. cat. (Florence, Palazzo Strossi, March 2–July 29, 2007), edited by Francesca Bardazzi, Milan, Electa.

London 2008: *The Courtauld Cézannes*, exh. cat. (London, The Courtauld Gallery, June–October 2008), edited by Stephanie Buck, et al., London.

London—Paris—Washington 1988: *Cézanne. Les années de jeunesse (1859–1872)*, exh. cat. (London Royal Academy of Arts, April–August 1988; Paris, Musée d'Orsay, September 1988–January 1989; Washington, National Gallery of Arts, January–April 1989), edited by Sylvie Patin and Isabelle Cahn, Paris, Réunion des Musées Nationaux.

Los Angeles 2004: *Cézanne in the Studio. Still Life in Watercolors*, exh. cat. (Los Angeles, The J. Paul Getty Museum, October 2004–January 2005).

Montclair—Baltimore—Phoenix 2009: *Cézanne and American Modernism*, exh. cat. (Montclair, New Jersey, Montclair Art Museum, Sept. 2009–Jan. 2010; Baltimore, Maryland, Baltimore Museum of Art, Feb.–May 2010; Phoenix, Arizona, Phoenix Art Museum, July–Sept. 2010), edited by Gail Stavitsky, Katherine Rothkopf, New Haven, Yale University Press.

New York 1988: *Paul Cézanne: The Basel Sketchbooks*, exh. cat. (New York, The Museum of Modern Art, March–June 1988), edited by Lawrence Gowing, New York.

New York 1997: *The private collection of Edgar Degas*, exh. cat. (New York, Metropolitan Museum of Art, October 1, 1997–January 11, 1998), New York.

New York—Chicago—Paris 2006–2007: *De Cézanne à Picasso. Chefs d'œuvre de la galerie Vollard*, exh. cat. (New York, The Metropolitan Museum of Art, Sept. 2006–Jan. 2007; Chicago, The Art Institute of Chicago, Feb.–May 2007; Paris, Musée d'Orsay, June-Sept. 2007), edited by Anne Roquebert, et al., Paris, Réunion des Musées Nationaux.

New York—Los Angeles—Paris 2005–2006

—Id. 2005–2006: *Cézanne and Pissarro: Pioneering Modern Painting, 1865–1885*, exh. cat. (New York, Museum of Modern Art, June–Sept. 2005; Los Angeles, Los Angeles County Museum of Art, Oct. 2005–Jan. 2006), edited by Joachim Pissarro and Jean-Patrice Marandel.

—Id. 2006: *Cézanne and Pissarro 1865–1885*, exh. cat. (Paris, Musée d'Orsay, Feb.–May 2006), edited by Sylvie Patin, Paris, Réunion des Musées Nationaux.

Paris 2010: *Crime & châtiment*, exh. cat. (Paris, Musée d'Orsay, March 16–June 27, 2010), by Robert Badinter, Laura Bossi, Jean Clair, et al., Paris, Musée d'Orsay-Gallimard.

Paris—Chicago 1994: *Gustave Caillebotte 1848–1894*, exh. cat. (Paris, Grand Palais, Sept. 1994–January 1995; Chicago, The Art Institute, Feb.–May 1995), edited by Anne Distel, et al., Paris, Réunion des Musées Nationaux.

Paris—London—Philadelphia 1995: *Cézanne*, exh. cat. (Paris, Grand Palais, Sept. 1995–Jan. 1996; London, Tate Gallery, Feb.–April 1996; Philadelphia, Philadelphia Museum of Art, May-Aug. 1996), edited by Françoise Cachin and Joseph J. Rishel, Paris, Réunion des Musées Nationaux.

Paris—New York 1994–1995: *Impressionnisme, les origines, 1859–1869/Origins of Impressionism*, exh. cat. (Paris, Grand Palais, 1994; New York, The Metropolitan Museum of Art, 1994–1995), edited by Henri Loyrette and Gary Tinterow.

Paris—New York—Amsterdam 1999: *Un ami de Cézanne et Van Gogh: le docteur Gachet*, exh. cat. (Paris, Grand Palais, Jan. 28–April 26, 1999; New York, Metropolitan Museum of Art, May 17–Aug. 15, 1999; Amsterdam, Van Gogh Museum, Sept. 24–Dec. 5, 1999), edited by Anne Distel, Michael Pakenham, Jean-Pierre Mohen, et. al., Paris, Réunion des Musées Nationaux.

Philadelphia 2009: *Cézanne and Beyond*, exh. cat. (Philadelphia, Philadelphia Museum of Art, February–May 2009), Philadelphia.

Washington—Aix-en-Provence 2006: *Cézanne en Provence*, exh. cat. (Washington, National Gallery of Art, January 29–May 7, 2006; Aix-en-Provence, Musée Granet, June 9–September 17, 2006), edited by Philip Conisbee and Denis Coutagne, Paris, Réunion des Musées Nationaux, 2006.

Yokohama—Sapporo 2008: *Homage to Cézanne. His Influence on the Development of Twentieth Century Painting*, exh. cat. (Yokohama Museum of Art, November 15, 2008–January 25, 2009; Sapporo, Hokkaido Museum of Modern Art, February 7–April 12, 2009), 2008.

List of exhibited works

Only the provenances before 1906 (death of Paul Cézanne) are given in this list.

Cat. 1
Self-Portrait
c. 1877
Oil on canvas
25.5 × 14.3 cm
Musée d'Orsay, Paris, work recovered after the Second World War and placed in the safekeeping of France's national museums, inv. MNR 228
R 385
Prov.: exhibition Vollard, 1895; former collection Camille Pissarro
Ill. p. 16

Cat. 2
The Rooftops of Paris
1881–82
Oil on canvas
59.7 × 73 cm
Private collection
R 503
Prov.: former collection Ambroise Vollard
Ill. p. 18

Cat. 3
St. Sulpice, view of Paris
1882
Pencil
Sketchbook I, p. 8, verso
11.6 × 18.2 cm
Philadelphia Museum of Art, Philadelphia, gift of Mr. and Mrs.Walter H. Annenberg, 1987, inv. 1987-53-7b
CH 806
Ill. p. 19

Cat. 4
Tree and bridge
1888–90
Watercolor and pencil
Private collection
RWC 325
Ill. p. 20

Cat. 5
Portrait de l'artiste au papier peint olivâtre [Self-Portrait]
1880–81
Oil on canvas
33.6 × 26 cm
The National Gallery, London. Bought by the Trustees of the Courtauld Fund, 1925, inv. NG 4135
R 482
Prov.: former collection Josse and Gaston Berheim-Jeune, bought to Paul Cézanne Jr. in 1902
Ill. p. 22

Cat. 6
Still Life with a Medallion of Solari
c. 1873
60 × 81 cm
Oil on canvas
Musée d'Orsay, Paris, gift of Paul Gachet, son of Dr. Gachet, 1951, inv. RF 1954-7
R 211
Prov.: former collection of Dr. Gachet
Ill. p. 25

Cat. 7
Page of Studies: Psyche Abandoned, after Pajou
c. 1876, c. 1883, and c. 1885
Pencil on laid paper
48.5 × 32 cm
Museum Boijmans Van Beuningen, Rotterdam, inv. F II 122
CH 363
Ill. p. 26

Cat. 8
Plaster Cupid
Drawing of the plaster copy of a sculpture of Cupid attributed to Puget, kept by Cézanne in his studio.
c. 1890
Pencil on paper, verso
(recto: *Sainte-Victoire with Pine Tree and Viaduct*)
48.2 × 31 cm
Museum Boijmans Van Beuningen, Rotterdam, inv. F II 27
CH 986
Ill. p. 27

Cat. 9
Hercules Resting, after Puget
1884–87
Pencil on laid paper
47.3 × 31.3 cm
Museum Boijmans Van Beuningen, Rotterdam, inv. F II 215
CH 999
Ill. p. 27

Cat. 10
Study of Legs, after Signorelli
1884–86
Graphite
19.4 × 11.8 cm
Musée Granet, Aix-en-Provence, Communauté du Pays d'Aix, inv. 984.13.1
CH 674
Ill. p. 27

Cat. 11
Bellone
After Peter Paul Rubens
c. 1885–95
Pencil, recto
20.9 × 12.2 cm
Kunstmuseum Basel, Kupferstichkabinett, Basel, inv. 1935.157
CH 1140
Ill. p. 27

Cat. 12
Portrait of Doctor Gachet in his Studio
c. 1873
Charcoal on paper that was originally gray with traces of fixative
32.5 × 21.5 cm
Musée d'Orsay, Paris (kept at the Musée du Louvre, Département des Arts Graphiques), gift of Paul Gachet, son of Dr. Gachet, 1951, inv. RF 29926 recto
CH 295
Ill. p. 28

Cat. 13
Madame Cézanne in a Yellow Chair
1888–90
Oil on canvas
81 × 65 cm
The Art Institute of Chicago, Chicago, Wilson L. Mead Fund, inv. 1948-54
R 653
Prov.: former collection Ambroise Vollard
Ill. p. 31

Cat. 14
Paul Alexis Reading at Zola's house
1869–70
Oil on canvas
52 × 56 cm
Private collection
R 150
Prov.: former collection Émile Zola
Ill. p. 37

Cat. 15
Paul Alexis Reading to Émile Zola
1869–70
Oil on canvas
130 × 160 cm
MASP, Museu de Arte de São Paulo Assis Chateaubriand, São Paulo
R 151
Prov.: former collection Émile Zola
Ill. p. 39

Cat. 16
The Negro Scipio
c. 1867
Oil on canvas
107 × 83 cm
MASP, Museu de Arte de São Paulo Assis Chateaubriand, São Paulo
R 120
Prov.: former collection Ambroise Vollard; former collection Claude Monet
Ill. p. 45

Cat. 17
Male Nude
c. 1865
Charcoal
24.9 × 29.8 cm
Kunstmuseum Basel, Kupferstichkabinett, Basel, inv. 1934.196 recto
CH 104
Ill. p. 47

Cat. 18
Male Nude seen in profile and right leg of the same model
1864–67
Charcoal on laid paper
20 × 25.7 cm
Private collection
CH 208
Ill. p. 48

Cat. 19
Naked Man seen in Profile
1867–70
Charcoal on laid paper
41.3 × 29.9 cm
Kunstmuseum Basel, Kupferstichkabinett, Basel, inv. 1935.170
CH 112
Ill. p. 48

Cat. 20
David, after Mercié
1877–80
Pencil on paper, recto
21.5 × 12.4 cm
Petit Palais, Musée des Beaux-Arts de la Ville de Paris, Paris, inv. PPD03288
CH 470
Ill. p. 50

Cat. 20 bis
Portrait of Paul Cézanne Jr.
1877–80
Pencil on paper, verso
21.5 × 12.4 cm
Petit Palais, Musée des Beaux-Arts de la Ville de Paris, Paris
CH 851
Ill. p. 50
Not on view

Cat. 21
Milo of Crotona
After Puget, with *Genre scene, Three Men Lighting a Wood Fire*
1879–80
Pencil on laid paper, verso
23.8 × 31 cm
Museum Boijmans Van Beuningen, Rotterdam, inv. F II 118
CH 207
Ill. p. 51

Cat. 22
Milo of Crotona
After Puget
1882–85
Pencil on paper
21.1 × 12.1 cm
Kunstmuseum Basel, Kupferstichkabinett, Basel, inv. 1935.151
CH 506
Ill. p. 51

Cat. 23
The Wedding Feast at Cana
After Paul Veronese
1866–71
Black crayon
17.7 × 22.8 cm
Kunstmuseum Basel, Kupferstichkabinett, Basel, inv. 1934.172
CH 168
Ill. p. 52

Cat. 24
Bathsheba, after Rembrandtt
1871–1874? (Rewald: c. 1870)
Oil on canvas
37 × 45.5 cm
Private collection
R 173
Ill. p. 55

Cat. 25
Apotheosis of Delacroix
1890–94
Oil on canvas
27 × 35 cm
Musée d'Orsay, Paris (in deposit at Musée Granet, Aix-en-Provence), inv. RF 1982-38
R 746
Prov.: former collection Ambroise Vollard; former collection Auguste Pellerin
Ill. p. 59

Cat. 26
Barges on the Seine at Bercy
After Guillaumin
Etching, only known copy
21.5 × 26.5 cm
Bibliothèque nationale de France, Département des Estampes et de la Photographie, Paris.
Gift of Paul Gachet, 1953, inv. Réserve AA3-Cézanne
Cherpin 1
Ill. p. 65

Cat. 27
The Rue des Saules in Montmartre
c. 1873–74
Oil on canvas
31.5 × 39.5 cm
Private collection
R 131
Prov.: former collection Armand Guillaumin
Ill. p. 66

Cat. 28
The Wine Market at Jussieu
1872
Oil on canvas
73 × 92 cm
Portland Art Museum, Oregon, Museum Purchase, inv. 1999.25
R 179
Prov.: former collection Camille Pissarro; former collection Auguste Pellerin
Ill. p. 68

Cat. 29
The Ferry at Bonnière
Summer 1866
Oil on canvas
38.5 × 60 cm
Musée Faure, Aix-les-Bains, inv. 1948.01.27
R 96
Prov.: former collection Émile Zola
Ill. p. 69

Cat. 30
Armand Guillaumin (1841–1927)
Quai de Bercy in Paris
c. 1876–78
Oil on canvas
60 × 80 cm
Kunsthalle, Hamburg, inv. HK-5321
Ill. p. 70

Cat. 31
The Seine at Bercy
D'après Guillaumin
Copy after Guillaumin
c. 1876–78
Oil on canvas
59 × 72 cm
Kunsthalle, Hamburg, inv. HK-2374
R 293
Prov.: former collection of Baron Denys Cochin
Ill. p. 71

Cat. 32
Portrait of Pissarro
c. 1873
Graphite on laid paper
13.3 × 10.3 cm
Musée d'Orsay, Paris (kept at the Musée du Louvre, Département des Arts graphiques), gift of John Rewald, 1975, inv. RF 35818
CH 298
Prov.: former collection Camille Pissarro
Ill. p. 72

Cat. 33
Auvers-sur-Oise, Panoramic View
1873–74
Oil on canvas
65.2 × 81.3 cm
The Art Institute of Chicago, Chicago, inv. 1933.422
R 221
Prov.: former collection Ambroise Vollard
Ill. p. 73

Cat. 34
The Hermitage at Pontoise
1881
Oil on canvas
46.5 × 56 cm
Von der Heydt-Museum, Wuppertal, inv. Nr. G 0276
R 484
Prov.: former collection Camille Pissarro; former collection Auguste Pellerin
Ill. p. 75

Cat. 35
Quartier du Four, Auvers-sur-Oise (Landscape, Auvers)
c. 1873
Oil on canvas
46.3 × 52.2 cm
Philadelphia Museum of Art, Philadelphia, The Samuel S. White 3rd and Vera White Collection, 1967, inv. 1967-30-16
R 198
Prov.: former collection Théodore Duret
Ill. p. 78

Cat. 36
Landscape by the Oise (House on the banks of the Oise)
1873–74
Oil on canvas
73.5 × 93 cm
Palais Princier, Monaco, inv. 50243
R 224
Prov.: former collection Édouard Béliard; former collection Ambroise Vollard; former collection Auguste Pellerin
Ill. p. 79

Cat. 37
Luncheon on the Grass
1876–77
Oil on canvas
21 × 27 cm
Musée de l'Orangerie, Paris, collection of Jean Walter and Paul Guillaume, inv. RF 1963-11
R 287
Prov.: former collection Egisto Fabbri
Ill. p. 79

Cat. 38
Attributed to Paul Cézanne, Camille Pissarro, or Armand Guillaumin
Cézanne engraving at Doctor Gachet's house
1872–73
Pencil drawing
20.5 × 13 cm
Musée d'Orsay, Paris (kept at the Musée du Louvre, Département des Arts graphiques), gift of Paul Gachet, the son of Dr. Gachet, 1951, inv. RF 29925 recto
CH 292
Ill. p. 81

Cat. 39
Portrait of the Painter A. Guillaumin with the Hanged Man
1873
Etching
15.6 × 11.8 cm
Musée Granet, Aix-en-Provence, Communauté du Pays d'Aix, inv. 983.1.23
Cherpin 2
Ill. p. 82

Cat. 40
View of a Garden in Bicêtre
1873
Etching, only known copy
Bibliothèque nationale de France, département des Estampes et de la Photographie, Paris. Gift of Paul Gachet, 1953, inv. Réserve AA3-Cézanne
Cherpin 3
Ill. p. 83

Cat. 41
Farm Entrance, Rue Rémy in Auvers
1873
Etching
13.4 × 11.1 cm
Musée Granet, Aix-en-Provence, Communauté du Pays d'Aix, inv. 951.9.1
Cherpin 5
Ill. p. 83

Cat. 42
Head of a Young Girl
1873
Etching and roulette work, second copy
12.3 × 9.8 cm
Musée Granet, Aix-en-Provence, Communauté du Pays d'Aix, inv. 951.8.1
Cherpin 4
Ill. p. 83

Cat. 43
The Temptation of Saint Anthony
1870
Oil on canvas
57 × 76 cm
Fondation Collection E. G. Bührle, Zurich,
inv. No. 15
R 167
Prov.: former collection Ambroise Vollard; former collection Auguste Pellerin
Ill. p. 89

Cat. 44
The Eternal Feminine
1877
Oil on canvas
43 × 53 cm
The J. Paul Getty Museum, Los Angeles, inv. 87. PA. 79
R 299
Prov.: former collection Ambroise Vollard; former collection Auguste Pellerin
Ill. p. 91

Cat. 45
Preparation for the Banquet
1888–90
Oil on canvas
45 × 53 cm
Osaka, The National Museum of Art
R 640
Prov.: former collection Ambroise Vollard
Ill. p. 93

Cat. 46
Still Life
1888–90
Oil on canvas
27.5 × 51 cm
Pola Museum of Art, Kanagawa
R 642
Prov.: former collection Maurice Denis
Ill. p. 93

Cat. 47
Three Bathers
1876–77
Oil on canvas
55 × 52 cm
Petit Palais, Musée des Beaux-Arts de la Ville de Paris, Paris, inv. PPP02099
R 360
Prov.: former collection Ambroise Vollard; former collection Henri Matisse
Ill. p. 95

Cat. 48
A Modern Olympia
1873–74
Oil on canvas
46 × 55 cm
Musée d'Orsay, Paris, gift of Paul Gachet, son of Dr. Gachet, 1951, inv. RF 1951-31
R 225
Ill. p. 97

Cat. 49
Olympia
c. 1877
Watercolor
24.1 × 27 cm
Philadelphia Museum of Art, Philadelphia, The Louis E. Stern Collection, 1963, inv. 1963-181-123
RWC 135
Prov.: former collection Ambroise Vollard
Ill. p. 99

Cat. 50
Female Nude (Leda II ?)
1886–1890? (Rewald: 1885–87)
Oil on canvas
44 × 62 cm
Von der Heydt-Museum, Wuppertal, inv. G1143
R 590
Prov.: former collection Ambroise Vollard
Ill. p. 101

Cat. 51
Woman with a mirror
1866–67
Oil on canvas
17 × 22 cm
Musée d'Orsay, Paris (in deposit at Musée Granet, Aix-en-Provence), inv. RF 1982-43
R 127
Prov.: former collection Henri Rouart
Ill. p. 103

Cat. 52
The Battle of Love
c. 1880
Oil on canvas
37.8 × 46.4 cm
National Gallery of Art, Washington, gift of the W. Averell Harriman Foundation in memory of Marie N. Harriman, inv. 1972.9.2
R 456
Prov.: former collection Ambroise Vollard; former collection Auguste Renoir
Ill. p. 107

Cat. 53
Still Life with Bread and Eggs
1865
Oil on canvas
59 × 76 cm
Cincinnati Art Museum, Cincinnati, gift of Mary E. Johnston, inv. 1955.73
R 82
Prov.: former collection Ambroise Vollard
Ill. p. 111

Cat. 54
Still Life with Black Clock
1869–70
Oil on canvas
55.7 × 74.3 cm
Private collection
R 136
Prov.: former collection Emile Zola
Ill. p. 113

Cat. 55
The Plate of Apple
c. 1877
Oil on canvas
45.8 × 54.7 cm
The Art Institute of Chicago, Chicago, gift of Kate L. Brewster, inv. 1949-512
R 328
Prov.: former collection Eugène Murer, Pontoise
Ill. p. 116

Cat. 56
Madame Cézanne Sewing
c. 1877
Oil on canvas
59.5 × 49.5 cm
Nationalmuseum, Stockholm, bequest in 1970 by Grace and Philip Sandblom, inv. NM 6348
R 323
Ill. p. 187

Cat. 57
Still Life in Blue with Lemon
c. 1873–77
Oil on canvas
18.4 × 29.8 cm
Cincinnati Art Museum, Cincinnati, bequest of Mary E. Johnston, inv. 1967.1425
R 428
Prov.: *Père* Tanguy Gallery; former collection Mogens Ballin, Copenhague
Ill. p. 119

Cat. 58
Still Life with Jar, Cup, and Apple
c. 1877
60.6 × 73.7 cm
The Metropolitan Museum of Art, New York, inv. 29.100. 66
R 322
Prov.: former collection Ambrollard; former collection Havemeyer
Ill. p. 121

Cat. 59
Apples, Napkin, and Milk Can
1880–81
Oil on canvas
60 × 73 cm
Musée de l'Orangerie, Paris, collection Jean Walter and Paul Guillaume, inv. RF 1960-10
R 479
Prov.: former collection Ambroise Vollard
Ill. p. 123

Cat. 60
Rocks in the Forest
c. 1893
Oil on canvas
75 × 92 cm
The Metropolitan Museum of Art, New York, inv. 29.100.194
R 775
Prov.: former collection Ambroise Vollard
Ill. p. 134

Cat. 61
The Burnt Mill at Charentonneau I (The Aqueduct and the Lock)
c. 1894
Oil on canvas
74 × 93.3 cm
Private collection
R 765
Prov.: former collection Ambroise Vollard
Ill. p. 136

Cat. 62
Banks of the Marne, I (On the island of Machefer at Saint-Maur-des-Fossés)
c. ?1894 (Rewald: 1888–1890)
Oil on canvas
65 × 81 cm
Hermitage Museum, St. Petersburg, inv. GE 6513
R 623
Prov.: Ambroise Vollard (?); former collection H.O. Havemeyer; Durand-Ruel; former collection Ivan Morosov
Ill. p. 141

Cat. 63
Riverbanks
1904–5
Oil on canvas
60.9 × 73.6 cm
Museum of Art, Rhode Island School of Design, Providence, Museum Special Reserve Fund 43.255, inv. 43-255
R 920
Ill. p. 144

Cat. 64
The Turning Road
1904
Oil on canvas
73 × 92 cm
The Samuel Courtauld Trust, The Courtauld Gallery, London, inv. P. 1978. P6. 61
R 921
Prov.: former collection Ambroise Vollard
Ill. p. 145

Cat. 65
Woodland with Large Trunks (Fontainebleau?)
1892–94
Watercolor, recto
42 × 57 cm
Private collection
RWC 451
Ill. p. 146

Cat. 65 bis
Edge of the Forest (Fontainebleau?)
1892–94
Watercolor, verso
42 × 57 cm
Private collection
RWC 453
Ill. p. 147
Not on view

Cat. 66
Winter Landscape (Giverny)
1894
Oil on canvas
65 × 81 cm
Philadephia Museum of Art, Philadelphia, gift of Frank and Alice Osborn, 1966, inv. 1966-68-3
R 777
Prov.: former collection Madame Baudy, Giverny
Ill. p. 149

Cat. 67
Portrait of Alfred Haug
August 1899
Oil on canvas
71.8 × 60.3 cm
Norton Gallery and School of Art, West Palm Beach, gift of R.H. Norton, inv. 48.5
R 835
Prov.: former collection Ambroise Vollard
Ill. p. 151

Cat. 68
Pierre Bonnard (1867–1947)
Portrait of Ambroise Vollard with a Cat
Around 1924
Oil on canvas
96.5 × 111 cm
Petit Palais, Musée des Beaux-Arts de la Ville de Paris, Paris, inv. PPP03052
Prov.: former collection Ambroise Vollard
Ill. p. 153

Cat. 69
Boy Resting
c. 1890
Oil on canvas
54 × 65.3 cm
The Armand Hammer Collection, Los Angeles, gift of the Armand Hammer Foundation, Hammer Museum, inv. AH. 90. 11
R 682
Prov.: former collection Ambroise Vollard
Ill. p. 155

Cat. 70
Maincy Bridge
1879–80
Oil on canvas
58.5 × 72.5 cm
Musée d'Orsay, Paris, acquired through an anonymous Canadian donation, 1955,
inv. RF 1955-20
R 436
Prov.: former collection Victor Chocquet; Durand-Ruel
Ill. p. 161

Cat. 71
Milk Can and Apples
1879–80
Oil on canvas
50.2 × 61 cm
The Museum of Modern Art, New York, The William S. Paley Collection, 1990, inv. SPC6. 1990
R 426
Prov.: Julien Tanguy; former collection Sarah Hallowell; Durand-Duel; former collection Egisto Fabbri
Ill. p. 170

Cat. 72
Portrait of M. Ambroise Vollard
1899
Oil on canvas
101 × 81 cm
Petit Palais, Musée des Beaux-Arts de la Ville de Paris, Paris, legs Vollard, inv. PPP 02100
R 811
Prov.: former collection Ambroise Vollard
Ill. p. 177

Cat. 73
Portrait of Victor Chocquet Seated
1877
Oil on canvas
45.7 × 38.1 cm
Columbus Museum of Art, Columbus: Howald Fund Purchase, inv. 1950. 024
R 296
Prov.: former collection Victor Chocquet; Durand-Ruel
Ill. p. 179

Cat. 74
The House of the Hanged Man, Auvers-sur-Oise
c. 1873
Oil on canvas
55 × 66 cm
Musée d'Orsay, Paris, bequest of Count Isaac de Camondo, 1911, 1911, inv. RF 1970
R 202
Prov.: former collection comte Doria; former collection Victor Chocquet; former collection Count Isaac de Camondo
Ill. p. 183

Cat. 75
Portrait of Mme. Cézanne in a Red Armchair
c. 1873
Oil on canvas
72.4 × 55.9 cm
Museum of Fine Arts, Boston, bequest of Robert Treat Paine II, inv. 44.776
R 324
Prov.: former collection Ambroise Vollard; former collection Egisto Fabbri
Ill. p. 117

List of artworks

Cézanne's works

Works of other painters

Photographs

List of names

Director of publishing
Henri Bovet

Head of publications
Marie-Dominique de Teneuille

Edited by
Sophie Zagradsky

Editorial assistant
Elsa Paris

Design
Caroline Chambeau

Layout
Frédéric Célestin

Translated, edited, and proofread by
Ann Drummond, Alayne Pullen, Rae Walter,
and David Price
in association with First Edition Translations Ltd,
Cambridge, UK

Image research
Consuelo Crulci
Élise Vanhaecke

RMN-Grand Palais photographic agency
Frédérique Kartouby

Production manager
Hugues Charreyron

Photo processing
Planète Couleurs, Paris

Printed in September 2011 by Ingoprint,
Barcelona, Spain

ISBN : 978-2-7118-5919-1
EC 40 5919

Photographic credits

© Aix-en-Provence, Musée Granet / Photo Jean Bernard: cat. 10, 39, 41, 42
© Aix-les-Bains, Musée Faure: cat. 29
© Artiste. com: fig. 17
© Bâle, Kunstmuseum Basel / Photo Martin P. Bülher: cat. 11, 17, 19, 22, 23, fig. 14, 19, 20, 42
© Cambridge, Fitzwilliam Museum: fig. 35
© Chicago, The Art Institute of Chicago: cat. 55, fig. 18
© Cleveland, The Cleveland Museum of Art: fig. 71
© Courtesy Wildenstein: fig. 34
© Étude Rouillac, commissaire-priseur: fig. 64
© Florence, Agence Scala: fig. 12, 58, 70, 82, 107 ; The Museum of Modern Art, New York / © Scala, Florence: cat. 71, fig. 56, 72 ; Philadelphia Museum of Art / Art resource / Scala, © Florence: cat. 3, 35, 66, fig. 46, 89, 94
© Hamilton, Picker Art Gallery, Colgate University: fig. 16
© Houston, Museum of Fine Arts: fig. 30
© Kanagawa, Pola Museum of Art: cat. 46
© Los Angeles, The J. Paul Getty Museum: cat. 44
© New York, Solomon R. Guggenheim Museum: fig. 11
© Paris, Akg-Images: cat. 14, 34, 43, 50, 53, fig. 28, 48, 110 ; Erich Lessing: cat. 67, fig. 2, 62, 65
© Paris, Bibliothèque nationale de France: cat. 26, 40
© Paris, Bridgeman Giraudon: The Barnes Foundation, Merion / Bridgeman Giraudon: fig. 45, 57, 74, 84, 113 ; Bibliothèque nationale de France, Paris / Archives Charmet / Bridgeman Giraudon: fig. 7 ; Christie's Images / Bridgeman Giraudon: cat. 36 ; Cincinnati Art Museum, Ohio / Bridgeman Giraudon: cat. 57, fig. 54, Cleveland Museum of Art, Ohio / Bridgeman Giraudon: fig. 108, private collection / Giraudon / Bridgeman Giraudon: cat. 54, 61, fig. 6, 32, 36, 69 ; Hamburger Kunsthalle, Hambourg / Bridgeman Giraudon: cat. 30 ; Hermitage, Saint Petersbourg / Bridgeman Giraudon: cat. 62 ; Kunsthaus, Zurich / Giraudon / Bridgeman Giraudon: fig. 100 ; Lefevre Fine Arts Ltd., Londres / Bridgeman Giraudon: cat. 45, fig. 105 ; Musée Granet, Aix-en-Provence / Giraudon / Bridgeman Giraudon: fig. 24 ; Musée de l'Orangerie / Giraudon / Bridgeman Giraudon: cat. 37, 59 ; Museu de Arte, Sao Paulo / Giraudon / Bridgeman Giraudon: cat. 15, 16 ; Museum of Fine Arts, Boston / Bridgeman Giraudon: cat. 75 ; Pushkin Museum, Moscou, Russie / Bridgeman Giraudon: fig. 68 ; Samuel Courtauld Trust, The Courtauld Gallery, Londres / Bridgeman Giraudon: cat. 64, fig. 102
© Paris, Institut national de la Propriété Industrielle: fig. 47
© Paris, Leemage: cat. 13, 33, 38, 49, 69, 73, fig. 96 ; AISA / Leemage: fig. 10, 78 ; Lylho / Leemage: cat. 47, fig. 25, 37, 79, 103, 106 ; Photo Josse / Leemage: fig. 55, 112, 114
Paris, Réunion des Musées Nationaux: fig. 8 ; Agence Bulloz: cat. 68, 72 ; Daniel Arnaudet: cat. 51 ; Martine Beck Coppola: fig. 21 ; René-Gabriel Ojéda: fig. 75, 90 ; Thierry Ollivier: fig. 22 ; Jean Schormans: fig. 23 ; RMN (Musée d'Orsay) / Jean-Gilles Berizzi: cat. 32 ; RMN (Musée d'Orsay) / Gérard Blot: cat. 12 ; RMN (Musée d'Orsay) / Thierry Le Mage: fig. 80, 93 ; RMN (Musée d'Orsay) / Hervé Lewandowski: cat. 1, 6, 25, 48, 70, 74, fig. 11, 31, 39, 41, 43, 52, 53, 61, 76, 77, 92, 95, 97 ; RMN (Musée d'Orsay) / René-Gabriel Ojéda: fig. 29, 98 ; BPK, Berlin, distr. RMN / Klaus Göken: fig. 67 ; BPK, Berlin, distr. RMN / Elke Watford: cat. 31 ; The Metropolitan Museum of Art, distr. RMN / Image of the MMA: cat. 60, fig. 15, 83 ; The Metropolitan Museum of Art, distr. RMN / Malcom Varon: cat. 58 ; Musée d'Orsay, distr. RMN / Patrice Schmidt: fig. 49 ; The National Gallery, Londres, distr. RMN / National Gallery Photographic Department: cat. 5, fig. 51, 104, 109
© Paris, Roger-Viollet: fig. 91 ; Patrick Pierrain / Petit Palais / Roger-Viollet: fig. 27 ; Petit-Palais / Roger-Viollet: cat. 20 et 20 bis
© Paris, Rue des Archives: fig. 99 ; FIA / Rue des Archives: fig. 4 ; Lebrecht / Rue des Archives: fig. 63
© Photo Dorothy Zeidman: fig. 85
© Photo J. Hyde: fig. 81
© Portland, Portland Art Museum: cat. 28
© Providence, Museum of Art, Rhode Island School of Design: cat. 63
© Richmond, Virginia Museum of Fine Arts: fig. 5
© Rotterdam, Museum Boymans-van Beuningen: cat. 7, 8, 9, 21
© Sotheby's, Inc.: fig. 44, 73, 101 ; ArtDigitalStudio / Sotheby's: fig. 9
© Stockholm, Nationalmuseum / Erik Cornelius: cat. 56
© Washington, National Gallery of Art: cat. 52, fig. 1, 59, 60 ; John Rewald Papers / Washington Gallery Archives: fig. 26
© Winthertur, collection Oskar Reinhart « Am Roemerholz »: fig. 87